Department for Economic and Social Information and Policy Analysis
Population Division

Population and Women

Proceedings of the United Nations
Expert Group Meeting on
Population and Women
Gaborone, Botswana, 22-26 June 1992

Convened as part of the substantive preparations
for the International Conference on Population
and Development, 1994

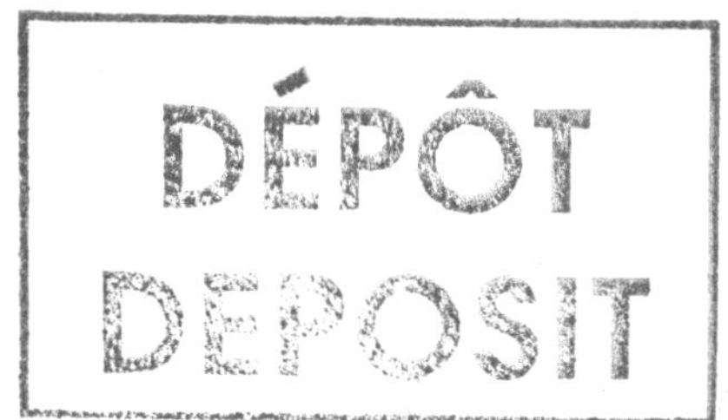

United Nations New York, 1996

NOTE

The designations employed and the presentation of the material in this publication do not imply the expression of any opinion whatsoever on the part of the Secretariat of the United Nations concerning the legal status of any country, territory, city or area or of its authorities, or concerning the delimitation of its frontiers or boundaries.

The designations "developed" and "developing" economies are intended for statistical convenience and do not necessarily express a judgement about the stage reached by a particular country or area in the development process.

The term "country" as used in the text of this publication also refers, as appropriate, to territories or areas.

The views expressed in signed papers are those of individual authors and do not imply the expression of any opinion on the part of the United Nations Secretariat.

Papers have been edited and consolidated in accordance with United Nations practice and requirements.

ST/ESA/SER.R/130

UNITED NATIONS PUBLICATION

Sales No. E.96.XIII.10

ISBN 92-1-151306-5

Manufactured in the United States of America

PREFACE

The Economic and Social Council, in its resolution 1991/93, decided to convene the International Conference on Population and Development in 1994, with population, sustained economic growth and sustainable development as the overall theme. Through its resolution 1992/37, the Council accepted the offer of the Government of Egypt to host the Conference and decided to hold it at Cairo from 5 to 13 September 1994.

At the request of the Council, the Secretary-General appointed the Executive Director of the United Nations Population Fund (UNFPA) to serve as the Secretary-General of the Conference and the Director of the Population Division of the Department of Economic and Social Development* of the United Nations Secretariat as Deputy Secretary-General.

Also, in its resolution 1991/93, the Council authorized the Secretary-General of the Conference to convene, as part of the preparations for the 1994 International Conference on Population and Development, six expert group meetings corresponding to the six groups of issues that it had identified as those requiring the greatest attention during the coming decade. One of those six expert group meetings was on population and women; it was convened at Gaborone, Botswana, from 22 to 26 June 1992. The Meeting was organized by the Population Division, in consultation with UNFPA.

Contained in this volume are the report and recommendations of the Meeting and the papers submitted to the Meeting. These materials not only made a valuable contribution to the 1994 Conference itself but will also serve as useful tools for future research on population and women, as well as contribute to the work of the United Nations in that area.

It is acknowledged with appreciation that the Government of Botswana, which hosted the Meeting, contributed significantly to both the substantive and the organizational aspects of the Meeting. Thanks are also due to the experts and other participants who prepared invited papers and contributed to the discussions.

*Now the Department for Economic and Social Information and Policy Analysis.

CONTENTS

Chapter *Page*

PART EIGHT. POPULATION, ENVIRONMENT AND DEVELOPMENT: ISSUES OF SPECIAL CONCERN FOR WOMEN

TABLES

No.

No. *Page*

FIGURES

BOXES

Explanatory notes

Symbols of United Nations documents are composed of capital letters combined with figures.

The following symbols have been used in the tables throughout this report:

Two dots (..) indicate that data are not available or are not separately reported.
An em dash (—) indicates that the amount is nil or negligible.
A hyphen (-) indicates that the item is not applicable.
A minus sign (-) before a number indicates a deficit or decrease, except as indicated.
A point (.) is used to indicate decimals.
A slash (/) indicates a crop year or financial year, e.g., 1994/95.
Use of a hyphen (-) between dates representing years (e.g., 1994-1995), signifies the full period involved, including the beginning and end years.

Details and percentage in tables do not necessarily add to totals because of rounding.

Reference to "dollars" ($) indicates United States dollars, unless otherwise stated.

The term "billion" signifies a thousand million.

The following abbreviations are used in the present report:

ASEAN	Association of South-east Asian Nations
ASFR	age-specific fertility rate
AIDS	acquired immunodeficiency syndrome
CAPMAS	Central Agency of Public Mobilisation and Statistics (Egypt)
CEDAW	Committee on the Elimination of Discrimination Against Women
CEDPA	Center for Development and Population Activities
CELADE	Centro Latinoamericano de Demografía (of ECLAC)
CPS	Contraceptive Prevalence Surveys
DAC	Development Assistance Committee (of OECD)
DHS	Demographic and Health Survey
DPT	diptheria-pertussis-tetanus
ECA	Economic Commission for Africa
ECLAC	Economic Commission for Latin America and the Caribbean
ESCAP	Economic and Social Commission for Asia and the Pacific
ESCWA	Economic and Social Commission for Western Asia
FAO	Food and Agriculture Organization of the United Nations
GNP	gross national product
GPA	Global Programme on AIDS
HIV	human immunodeficiency virus
HDI	human development index
IFAD	International Fund for Agricultural Development
ILO	International Labour Organization
IMR	infant mortality rate
INSTRAW	International Research and Training Institute for the Advancement of Women
IPPF	International Planned Parenthood Federation
IRO	Institute for Resource Development
ISIS	integrated set of information systems

IUCN	International Union for the Conservation of Natural Resources
IUD	intra-uterine device
IUSSP	International Union for the Scientific Study of Population
IWRAW	International Women's Rights Action Watch
KABP	knowledge, attitudes, beliefs and practices
KAP	knowledge, attitude and practice
MCH/FP	maternal and child health/family planning
NARAL	National Abortion Action League
NORAD	Norwegian Agency for International Development
OAV	Organization of African Unity
OECD	Organisation for Economic Co-operation and Development
ORS	oral rehydration salts
PAHO	Pan American Health Organization
PID	pelvic inflammatory disease
PPFA	Planned Parenthood Federation of America
PREALC	Programa Regional del Empleo para América Latina y el Caribe
SMAM	singulate mean age at marriage
STD	sexually transmitted disease
TFR	total fertility rate
UNDP	United Nations Development Programme
UNEP	United Nations Environment Programme
UNESCO	United Nations Educational, Scientific and Cultural Organization
UNFPA	United Nations Population Fund
UNICEF	United Nations Children's Fund
UNIFEM	United Nations Development Fund for Women
USAID	United States Agency for International Development
WCED	World Commission on Population and Development
WFS	World Fertility Survey
WHO	World Health Organization

Part One

REPORT AND RECOMMENDATIONS OF THE EXPERT GROUP MEETING

I. REPORT OF THE EXPERT GROUP MEETING

A. BACKGROUND OF THE MEETING

The Economic and Social Council, in its resolution 1991/93 of 26 July 1991, decided to convene the International Conference on Population and Development under the auspices of the United Nations and decided that the overall theme of the Conference would be population, sustained economic growth and sustainable development. The Council authorized the Secretary-General of the Conference to convene six expert group meetings as part of the preparatory work.

Pursuant to that resolution, the Secretary-General of the Conference convened the Expert Group Meeting on Population and Women at Gaborone, Botswana, from 22 to 26 June 1992. The Meeting was organized by the Population Division of the Department of Economic and Social Development[1] of the United Nations Secretariat in consultation with the United Nations Population Fund (UNFPA). The participants, representing different geographical regions, scientific disciplines and institutions, included 14 experts invited by the Secretary-General of the Conference in their personal capacity; representatives of four of the five regional commissions (Economic Commission for Africa (ECA), Economic Commission for Latin America and the Caribbean (ECLAC), Economic and Social Commission for Asia and the Pacific (ESCAP) and Economic and Social Commission for Western Asia (ESCWA)); representatives of United Nations offices and specialized agencies, including the United Nations Office at Vienna, the United Nations Children's Fund (UNICEF), the United Nations Development Programme (UNDP), the United Nations Development Programme for Women (UNIFEM), the United Nations Centre for Human Settlements (Habitat), the International Labour Organization (ILO), the Food and Agriculture Organization of the United Nations (FAO), the United Nations Educational, Scientific and Cultural Organization (UNESCO) and the World Health Organization (WHO). Also represented were the following non-governmental organizations: Center for Development and Population Activities (CEDPA); Institute for Resource Development (IRD); the International Planned Parenthood Federation (IPPF); and International Union for the Conservation of Nature/World Conservation Union (IUCN). Two additional non-governmental organizations were represented by experts who were also invited in their personal capacity—the International Union for the Scientific Study of Population (IUSSP) and the Population Council. There were also 19 observers.

As a basis for discussion, the experts had prepared papers on the main agenda items. The Population Division had prepared a background paper entitled "Population and women: a review of issues and trends". Discussion notes had been prepared by the Department of Economic and Social Development, ECA, ECLAC, ESCAP, ESCWA, the United Nations Office at Vienna, UNICEF, the ILO, FAO, WHO, CEDPA, IRD, IPPF, IUCN, the International Fund for Agricultural Development (IFAD), the United Nations Environment Programme (UNEP) and a member of the Australia International Development Assistance Bureau.

B. OPENING STATEMENTS

Opening statements were given by Dr. Nafis Sadik, Secretary-General of the Conference, by the Honourable Festus Mogae, Vice-President and Minister of Finance and Planning of the Government of Botswana; and by Mr. Shunichi Inoue, Deputy Secretary-General of the Conference and Director of the Population Division.

After welcoming remarks by Dr. Josephine Namboze, the United Nations Resident Coordinator in Botswana, *ad interim*, Dr. Sadik noted that Botswana provided an especially fitting venue for the meeting, citing the host country's history of attention to women's issues and concerns at the ministerial level. Botswana was also one of the few countries in which the educational attainment of women equalled or exceeded that of men. Mr. Mogae affirmed his Government's conviction that gender was an essential and critical factor in development, that women made major contributions to the wealth of countries; and that empowering women by enhancing their productive activities, income and education and, more generally, their right to make decisions in all spheres of their life would bring important benefits to society as a whole. Mr. Inoue also stressed the long-standing and increasing attention by the international community to women's roles and status as an important factor for understanding demographic change and as a vital feature of social and economic development.

Dr. Sadik's remarks introduced many of the themes that were discussed at the Meeting. She urged the participants, in considering population and development issues, to focus on practical actions that recognized women's rights and autonomy and that enhanced women's participation in the development process. She stressed particularly that women's reproductive rights were central to the realization of women's potential in economic production and community life. The ability to exercise free and informed choice with regard to the number and spacing of their children was the first step in enabling women to make choices in other areas. Dr. Sadik took note that in many societies, young women were trapped within a web of tradition that assigned a high value to their reproductive role, taking little note of any other role they could play; and that for too long, inequity between women and men had been tolerated and indeed excused because of so-called "customs" and "traditions". She stated further that there were practical steps that could be taken to promote equality between women and men. Among them were the removal of remaining legal barriers to women's full equality, policies to improve the education of girls; and programmes to provide reliable information about reproductive rights and reproductive health, high-quality family planning services and whatever health-care services were needed to combat disease and promote healthy childbirth. In discussing reproductive health, she pointed out the high rates of adolescent pregnancy in both developed and developing countries, noting in particular the elevated risks to life and health of early childbirth and the fact that all too frequently early motherhood foreclosed a girl's prospects for education, employment and self-realization. Men's involvement was, of course, essential if women's overall situation was to be improved and their effective role as agents of socio-economic development recognized. At the same time, it was also necessary to pursue initiatives that would put qualified women in positions of power and decision-making.

C. Summary of the papers and discussion

In addition to a more general exchange of views and evidence on women's roles and status in the course of development and on the interrelations between development and population programmes and women's status, the Meeting devoted particular attention to the following areas: women's health, especially reproductive health, and women's roles and status in relation to the health of children and other family members; adolescent fertility, marriage and reproductive health; a gender perspective on family planning needs and programmes; education of girls and women, and the relation of education to fertility and to child health and welfare; women's economic activity and its relation to fertility and to child health and welfare; and women's role as environmental managers and environmental issues in relation to women's health and reproductive and productive roles. The situations of both developed and developing countries were considered, although the main emphasis was on the latter group.

In drawing up recommendations, the Group sought to identify practical steps that would promote equality between women and men, that would help empower women and that would also have desirable economic and demographic effects. The Group also reviewed the state of knowledge on the topics mentioned above and made recommendations concerning needs for research and data collection.

Gender issues had been the focus of increasing international attention in a variety of contexts, including human rights and equity and women's integration into processes of social and economic development. There was currently an impressive array of international declarations and agreements concerning women's rights to equal status in many aspects of life. Those instruments included the Convention on the Elimination of All Forms of Discrimination against Women (1979) and agreements on equal pay for work of equal value (1953), equal political rights (1954), maternity protection (1955), equality in employment (1960), equality in education (1962) and equal marriage rights (1964). Other international agreements concerning women's roles and status and population included the World Population Plan of Action (1974) and the Recommendations for Further Implementation of the Plan (1984), the Nairobi Forward-looking

Strategies for the Advancement of Women (1985), the Safe Motherhood Initiative (1987) and the Amsterdam Declaration on a Better Life for Future Generations (1989). The Expert Group noted that although the international declarations and agreements provided sound guidelines, much remained to be done in terms of implementing them.

General issues of gender equality, population and development

Participants took note that the recommendations adopted at intergovernmental meetings often spoke of rights and responsibilities of families or couples, ignoring the practical reality of unequal authority and power in gender relations. One need identified at the Meeting was for more attention to be directed to men's roles in the family.

Paradoxically, although policy makers recognized that women's status remained inferior and their roles were restricted in many ways, women that acted on behalf of the family were seen as agents of change in all aspects of population policy, whether it be the adoption of family planning, the provision of health care for children or the acquisition of an independent economic livelihood. Yet women could not bring about the demographic transition alone. Men would have to play their part, and before that could be accomplished, much more must be understood about men's reproductive and familial roles and about the way in which the costs and benefits of children were distributed.

Population and development programmes made many assumptions—often implicit—about interrelations and changes within families which resulted in aggregate changes in fertility and mortality rates. Assumptions about the roles women and men played within the family and the intra-family distribution of resources were implicit in the linkage typically drawn between the rising costs of children and the declining demand for children:

(a) That improvements in women's individual livelihood outside the family provided them with greater individual economic mobility and thus less reliance upon children and other family members for future economic support;

(b) That fathers shared with mothers joint responsibility for their children's maintenance and upbringing; and

(c) That parents supported each of their children to the same extent.

These assumptions structured the collection and analysis of demographic data and the design of population policy, and some were not justified in certain settings. Researchers and policy makers thus needed to make a more careful and critical examination of particular social and cultural conditions if they were to design policies that would truly benefit women and those that depended upon them and would also have the expected demographic effects. That examination would also require gathering some types of information from men which were currently usually obtained only from women surveyed on fertility, family planning and child health.

On the basic question whether development tended to improve women's status, the Group saw no simple answer, because women had many roles and the various aspects of women's status did not change in unison or in response to the same forces. The Group agreed, however, that an improvement in women's status would advance development.

It was noted that in such areas as health and education, sooner or later, the economic gains did flow on to women. In other areas, however, such as legal rights, equal pay and treatment in the labour force and political decision-making power, where there was no necessary or clear relation between the status of women and the level of development, equality for women depended not upon the level of development or the economic resources available but upon the political will of Governments and upon the cultural setting in which women had to live. Equality was not attained in a zero-sum game in which gains for women could only result from losses to men. Instead, because equality for women promoted economic growth through more effective utilization of existing resources, by opting for equity (through equal legal rights and access to economic resources), poor countries could speed up the pace of development.

One recurrent theme of the discussions was the need for women to be represented in much greater numbers at all levels of planning, managing and executing population, health and development programmes—both for reasons of equity and as a precondition of success. Women's concerns could not be promoted effectively through a single ministry. The Expert Group took note that those needs were currently widely recognized in a variety of international agreements and in statements of goals and policies issued by many international groups. However, there remained a great divide between stated goals for involving women in programmes and current reality.

Another theme was the need to devise programmes that would help women living in poverty. Access to remunerative employment and effective control over the resources they needed to make a living would help poor women solve other problems, including poor access to health care for themselves and their children. Poor women also generally had higher fertility, including higher levels of both desired and unwanted fertility, than the rest of the population.

Gender analysis—a process of explicitly and systematically examining gender balance among those in decision-making roles, those involved in executing programmes and those who receive the benefits of programmes—was seen as a useful means of directing attention towards the extent to which development, health and other policies and programmes actually involved women and met their needs.

Health

The Expert Group agreed that the speed with which modern health services had been embraced by the populations of developing countries was worth noting, since it represented a break with traditions that were resistant to change in other ways. Equally notable, however, was the extent to which access to and use of health services was allocated according to status determined along the traditional lines of sex, age and familial role. In some societies, that meant that women and girls were often denied the benefits of modern health care. Despite their inferior position, women were commonly seen as the custodians of family health; yet, their poor education and limited authority undermined their ability to protect their own health and that of their family. Recommended policy responses to the situation included both actions directed to improving women's access to health care, and information and efforts to inform and involve other family members.

The Group took note that reproductive and sexual health implied much more than preventing maternal death. Health was defined in the WHO Constitution as a state of complete physical, mental and social well-being and not merely the absence of disease or infirmity. That definition implied that people had the ability to reproduce, that women could safely experience pregnancy and childbirth and that reproduction would be carried to a successful outcome, that is, infants would survive and grow up healthy. It implied further that people were able to regulate their fertility without risks to their health and that they were safe in having sex. It was agreed that the achievement of positive reproductive health would require policies and programmes that included but also looked beyond the prevention of maternal death. However, given the paucity of statistical information about many aspects of reproductive health, attention had tended to focus on maternal mortality as an index of reproductive health conditions more generally.

WHO had estimated that approximately 500,000 women died each year of causes related to pregnancy and childbirth, of which 99 per cent took place in developing countries. Most of those deaths were preventable. A major fraction of them—estimates ranged from about 100,000 to more than 200,000 deaths annually—were the consequence of unsafe abortion. Africa remained the major area where the risk of maternal death was highest, averaging an estimated 630 per 100,000 births; one in 20 African women could expect to die for pregnancy-related reasons, at prevailing levels of maternal mortality and fertility. Major contributors to maternal and infant mortality included poor nutritional status among pregnant women (WHO had estimated that 50 per cent of pregnant women worldwide suffered from nutritional anaemia) and the continuing lack of prenatal care and adequately trained birth attendants in many areas. Births at the extremes of the reproductive ages and closely spaced births also involved increased risks to mother and child. Since many of such high-risk births occurred to women that did not want any more children or would have preferred a delay, improved access to effective family planning methods could also reduce risks of maternal mortality. Better access to effective contraceptives could also greatly reduce unsafe abortion, although it would not by itself eliminate it.

Another aspect of sexual and reproductive health that received attention at the Meeting was the prevention and treatment of sexually transmitted diseases (STDs). The spread of such diseases was regarded as "one of the major disappointments in public health in the past two decades". STDs had important, and often hidden, health consequences for women. They were a major cause of infertility, for instance, and they increased the risk of life-threatening ectopic pregnancy. Some affected the developing foetus or were transmitted around the time of birth, often with devastating consequences for newborns. Those which produced genital ulcerations also heightened the risk of transmission of the human immunodeficiency virus (HIV), which caused acquired immunodeficiency syndrome (AIDS). The risk of transmission of STDs was generally much greater from man to woman than the reverse, and the health consequences of many of the diseases were also much more serious for women.

Although up to the time of the Meeting AIDS had been more common globally among men than women from the beginning of the AIDS epidemic, the disease had affected African men and women in roughly equal numbers; and WHO had estimated that by the year 2000 the number of AIDS cases would be equal in men and women worldwide. Infected women transmitted the infection to 30-40 per cent of their children.

Even though there had been a great deal of medical research into the diagnosis and treatment of STDs and the assessment of their prevalence in selected populations, the state of knowledge remained very poor with regard to the underlying behavioural risk patterns in different population groups, knowledge and beliefs among the general population concerning STDS and their treatment, how often sexual partners of those infected were, in practice, informed of their risk; and other social barriers to combating the spread of such diseases. The AIDS epidemic had given new urgency to those questions, and the results of social science research undertaken in response to the AIDS crisis were beginning to appear. The Expert Group had before it a paper summarizing results of a number of research projects carried out in sub-Saharan Africa under the auspices of the WHO Global Programme on AIDS (GPA).

Women were usually more at risk of STDs including AIDS, because of the behaviour of their male partners than through their own sexual activity. Societies with a strong double standard regarding sexual behaviour—such that men had numerous sexual partners before and after marriage while women's behaviour was strictly controlled and limited to marriage—were likely to place women at a particularly high risk, greater even than in societies where it was common for both men and women to be sexually active outside of marriage but where the number of different partners tended to be small.

A key factor to consider in programmes to combat the transmission of STD was whether women had the power to refuse sex or to insist that their partner use a condom. Cultural values concerning sexual abstinence, which predated modern concerns about disease transmission, differed among societies and by gender. Women's ability to negotiate with regard to sexual relations was likely to be tied to other aspects of their status, including their financial independence. Research into that aspect of women's autonomy was only beginning. Scattered research results pointed to marked differences between societies in women's degree of control over sexual relations, but in some cases had failed to confirm common preconceptions of women's lack of power in that regard.

The Expert Group agreed that combating reproductive health problems required more vigorous action than had so far been forthcoming from Governments and non-governmental organizations. Research was still needed to establish basic facts about sexual behaviour and risks and to improve the medical and pharmaceutical means available to combat risks. There was a pressing need for public education about reproductive and sexual health, including STDs and their prevention. In order to reach more of those at risk, educational channels beyond the formal health system, including schools and mass media, should be employed.

Family planning services were viewed as vital for improving reproductive and sexual health and the Group recommended that Governments, non-governmental organizations and the private sector should assure women and men as individuals confidential access to safe methods of fertility regulation within the framework of a health-care system that could provide adequate support services and information to users of contraception. The Group also recommended that women who wished to terminate their pregnancy should have ready access to reliable information, sympathetic counselling and safe abortion services. Governments and non-governmental organizations were urged actively to promote safer sex, including the use of condoms; and to provide preventive, diagnostic and curative treatment to inhibit the transmission of STDs. A potential was seen for family planning and other health programmes to become more actively involved in relevant screening, counselling, referral and treatment. That involvement would both increase physical access to services for those with STDs and would help break down social barriers to seeking treatment. Even for those with access to services, the risk of social stigmatization might discourage persons needing treatment from seeking it, and women were especially likely to be deterred. It was noted that providers of family planning and other specialized health services had sometimes resisted offering such services (and other types of service) out of concern about jeopardizing their core programmes. The representative of IPPF, the leading international non-governmental organization of family planning providers, strongly endorsed the need for family planning programmes to promote reproductive and sexual health more broadly, as did representatives of the United Nations Office at Vienna, UNFPA and WHO, among many others.

Reproductive health also implied the ability to bear children that were wanted. Although the number of women and men that desired large families had declined in all regions, children remained universally valued and desired. Even in societies where women's social standing was not heavily dependent upon reproduction, the large majority of women wished to become mothers. One paper reported that in societies where women's status remained closely tied to motherhood, childlessness often represented a personal disaster; and a repudiated wife with no children, or none surviving, might be able to support herself only by prostitution.

Domestic violence, incest and rape were extreme consequences of women's lack of power. Children were also frequently victims of abuse. Too often the most basic information about the extent, frequency and severity of those problems was lacking. That lack contributed to a failure to confront those issues through public debate, programmes to help and protect victims of abuse, enforcement of social and legal sanctions and efforts to provide women with the resources that would render them less vulnerable.

The Group strongly condemned the traditional practice of female genital mutilation, or female circumcision. The practice entailed serious health risks not only at the time of the surgery, which was often done under unsterile conditions, but also later in life, when consequences could include painful and difficult intercourse, repeated surgery before and after each childbirth and obstructed labour which could lead to stillbirth and maternal death.

Women often encountered health-threatening conditions in the workplace, ranging from difficulties in continuing to breast-feed infants to sexual harassment to exposure to toxic substances, from which pregnant women and developing foetuses often faced an elevated risk. There were many practical actions that employers and Governments could take to improve conditions for women in the workplace. The paper contributed by the ILO representative summarized relevant international agreements and recommendations.

Adolescents

Young women and men received particular attention in the Expert Group discussions, because actions taken in adolescence were crucial for later life. For young women, in particular, early marriage or early motherhood could foreclose educational and employment opportunities. Very young mothers typically faced risks of maternal death much above the average, and their children also fared less well.

Child-bearing was only one aspect of teenage reproductive health. Adolescents were, in many countries, increasingly at high risk of contracting and transmitting STDs, including HIV/AIDS; and they were often poorly informed about how to protect themselves. Young women were especially vulnerable because of their subordinate social position, due jointly to their youth and their gender. The Group strongly urged Governments to promote education and provision of employment opportunities, particularly for girls; and advised Governments and non-governmental organizations to promote adolescent reproductive health, including provision of family life education with a realistic sex education component, family planning and reproductive health services and enforcement of laws regarding minimum age at marriage.

In considering adolescent motherhood and marriage, it was important to consider what choices were actually open to adolescents of all social and economic classes. Poor teenage girls might correctly conclude that attempting to achieve an alternative role would entail facing and overcoming enormous obstacles. They would therefore drop out of school, not because they were already pregnant or were being pressured into marriage, but because education was not seen as particularly useful. Even where educational or employment opportunities existed, adolescents might be poorly informed about them, and they frequently faced conflicting pressures. Governments and non-governmental organizations were urged to adopt policies and programmes that would provide young women of all social classes with real alternatives to early marriage and child-bearing.

Substantial declines in teenage marriage and fertility from traditionally high levels had occurred recently in some regions—notably Northern Africa, South-eastern and Western Asia—and levels were also quite low in Western and Northern Europe and Eastern Asia. However, in sub-Saharan Africa, Southern Asia and Latin America and the Caribbean, the level of teenage union formation and child-bearing was still quite high. Even moderate levels of teenage fertility implied that substantial fractions of women became mothers before age 20. For instance, in countries where the annual fertility rate for women aged 15-19 years was about 80 per 1,000, roughly one third of women were mothers by age 20; teenage fertility rates that greatly exceeded that level were found in most countries of sub-Saharan Africa and in parts of Asia, and most Latin American and Caribbean countries had rates of 80-140 per 1,000. Especially in areas of the world where a large proportion of teenage mothers were unmarried, such child-bearing was seen as undesirable for both the persons concerned and the society as a whole.

Family planning

The Expert Group endorsed reproductive choice as a basic right and, as such, a component of the status of women. Family planning services were also recognized as a means of improving reproductive health which deserved support. Gaining control over their fertility had the potential of opening up to women a range of new choices.

There had been notable progress in extending at least minimal family planning services in developing countries. Since 1974, there had been "a revolution" in birth control law and in administrative procedures which had in the main served to improve access to family planning services. Legal or administrative requirements still limited access to a wide range of family planning methods in some countries, and in some places women were required to obtain permission from husbands or parents before they could obtain services. However, shortages of well-trained staff, logistical problems and limited funds, rather than legal or administrative obstacles, were often the current reasons for poor access to family planning services. Recent surveys in the primarily African and Latin American countries covered so far through the Demographic and Health Surveys (DHS) programme indicated that fertility would fall by about one fourth in sub-Saharan Africa and by one third in Latin America if the current unmet need for family planning were fully met. Part of the reason that the unmet need remained high was that the number of children women desired had been declining in all regions. The number of persons of reproductive age was, however, growing rapidly. Thus, the need for more and better services had grown and had, in some countries, outpaced the growth in services provided.

Some participants strongly criticized existing family planning programmes for their tendency, in practice, to ignore the justifiable concerns of women—and men—about side-effects and other problems with contraceptive methods, for their failure to provide complete and accurate information to clients, for their tendency to dictate which method women should use instead of offering a real choice; and, in general, for their concern with achieving quantitative programme targets for numbers of "acceptors" rather than with meeting the needs of individual women and men. There was agreement that family planning programmes needed to improve quality of care and to adopt the "user's perspective" in evaluating programme services. In order to do so effectively, it was seen as necessary that programmes should involve women—who usually made up the large majority of clients—much more heavily at all levels of programme policy-making, management and service delivery, but especially at the highest levels. Recognizing that women and men needed methods that were both safe and effective and that all existing methods had drawbacks that made them unsuitable for some people, the Group also emphasized the need for development of improved methods, including a re-examination of traditional methods and the need for programmes to pay more attention to attracting men as clients.

Education and its relation to fertility and child health and welfare

The Expert Group took note of the fact that literacy and enrolment rates were increasing globally and that the difference between male and female school enrolment rates had narrowed somewhat. In 1990, UNESCO data had indicated that just over half of world youth aged 6-23 years were enrolled in school, 56 per cent for males but only 48 per cent for females. In the major less developed regions, 1990 enrolment ratios for females aged 6-23 years ranged from 32 per cent in Africa (excluding the Arab States), to 42-46 per cent in Asia and the Arab States and to 63 per cent in Latin America and the Caribbean. In the more developed regions, the ratio was 72. The enrolment ratios for both sexes had risen considerably since 1960, and most of the improvement had taken place during the first half of the 30-year period.

There was a disturbing sign, however, in the recent declines in enrolment rates for both sexes in several African countries. The Group voiced concern that programmes for structural adjustment of poorly performing economies could produce under investment or disinvestment in education and training as well as health. The Group urged international organizations and donors as well as Governments to recognize them as productive sectors of the economy, vital for the formation of a new generation of workers.

The overall educational gains between 1960 and 1990 had been larger for females than for males and the gender disparity had declined by over one third. In the developed countries, the gender disparity in primary— and secondary— school enrolment rates, which had been sizeable in 1960, had essentially disappeared by 1990. The female disadvantage hardly existed in Latin America and the Caribbean, but it remained large in Africa and Asia. In relative terms, the gender disparity in enrolment rates had been and remained largest at the upper educational levels.

Despite recent gains, in Latin America more than 20 per cent of women aged 25 or over remained illiterate, more than 40 per cent in Eastern and South-eastern Asia and as many as 70 per cent in sub-Saharan Africa and Southern and Western Asia. Thus, there had been notable progress in combating illiteracy, but poorly educated women would constitute the majority in much of the developing world for many years to come.

Recent research had confirmed the strong and far-reaching demographic effects of education on both fertility and child survival and had given some insight into the behavioural changes that were responsible for those demographic effects. Much less progress had been made in answering such questions as whether the type of education, or its amount, had consequences for fertility and child health; or the prevailing cultural setting limited or channelled the demographic effects of women's education. In that regard, several participants noted that although education might indeed give women more autonomy in some areas of household life, educated women might remain very restricted in other ways, depending upon the cultural setting. Education might, for instance, make women better able to obtain health care for their children but leave them with no say over major household expenditures or the spending of their own income. There was some evidence that in cultures where sons had traditionally been strongly preferred, educated women generally retained those preferences undiminished, which had implications for fertility and child health.

Although education had an important effect on child survival and fertility, it was also true that if fertility and child mortality were to continue to decline rapidly at the national level, the declines must be spread broadly through the population and not be confined to the highly educated. Indeed, the recent declines in both fertility and child mortality had usually occurred across the educational spectrum, although thus far without in general diminishing the often very wide differences between the more and the less educated in mortality risks or in the level of fertility. Although some populations showed a degree of convergence, in others the demographic differences between education groups had only become wider over time. Even in developed countries, education differences in fertility and child survival persisted.

In developing countries, women with secondary or higher education almost invariably had much lower fertility than less educated women, but in countries where the general level of development was low or where the general level of fertility had so far shown little decline, the impact of primary education on fertility was not uniformly the inverse. In almost all settings, and particularly where fertility differences between educational groups were large, the level of unmet need for family planning and the level of unwanted fertility were highest among the least educated. Recent research had helped clarify the effects of education on several important proximate fertility determinants, which also helped explain why the relation between education and fertility is not always strictly negative: while education led to later marriage and to increased use of contraceptive use, both of which reduced fertility, it also led to lesser observance of traditional means of birth-spacing (extended breast-feeding and, in some populations, an extended period of postnatal sexual abstinence), which tended to raise fertility.

Research on education and fertility or child survival had usually concentrated only on the amount of formal education. The possible effects of non-formal education on demographic factors had rarely been considered in empirical studies, and the Group noted that there was need to assess the demographic and other impacts of such education.

Other areas that required more research attention included the connection between the child's education and parental efforts to limit family size, and the reverse relation, namely, the impact of the number of siblings on children's education. Explanations of reasons that more affluent and better educated parents usually desired and had smaller families tended to focus on the trade-off between greater numbers of children and, in economists' terms, higher "child quality", which involved greater investment in the upbringing of each child. Direct and indirect costs of child schooling were a major aspect of such investment. Better educated parents tended to want educated children, and that might be an important factor leading to lower fertility among the better educated. At the same time, public policies that made it easier for even uneducated parents to send their children to school might have a far-reaching effect on parents' evaluation of the relative merits and feasibility of having more children or a smaller number of educated children. Such educational policies could in theory have a quicker effect on fertility than the parents' own education, since they could operate only after the educated children matured and made choices about their own child-bearing.

New research also confirmed the strong effects of mother's education on child survival, and there had been some progress in understanding how education produced that beneficial effect. Education had some effect on the prevalence—but more especially, on the treatment—of childhood diseases. The children of educated mothers were more likely to be immunized against disease, and they were much more apt to receive modern medical care when ill. Educated women were themselves more likely to have a medically trained birth attendant and to have received prenatal care and immunizations, which benefited both mother and child. Educated women were also less likely to be extremely young or old when they gave birth or to have a large number of births, all factors that had been associated with both maternal and child death. Children of more educated women were also better nourished, on average. Although better educated women also tended to be married to husbands of higher status and to live in households that were better off in material terms, the mother's education tended to be more important than those other social factors in improving child health and survival.

The effects of women's education on their own health benefited children as well, although those effects had not been as well measured as had the relation between maternal education and child survival. As a consequence of their greater likelihood of using health services, of avoiding high-risk pregnancies and of experiencing fewer pregnancies, they were considerably less likely to die in childbirth and thereby orphan their children.

Even a few years of maternal education usually had a significant effect on child survival. Results for 25 developing countries surveyed as part of the DHS programme showed that the odds of a child dying before age 2 if the mother had from one to three, from four to six or at least seven years of schooling were, respectively, 15, 35 and 58 per cent lower than those of a child whose mother had no education. Even after statistical controls for a variety of other social factors, including the father's education and occupation, children whose mothers had seven or more years of schooling had only about half the risk of dying faced by the children of the uneducated. However, the most recent research also showed that the relation between education and child survival was weaker in most sub-Saharan African countries than in other regions. The reasons for that situation remained to be determined.

Especially in developing countries, much less was known about the effect of maternal education on broader aspects of child development and welfare, including mental and emotional development, than about the effect on child survival. Positive concern for child health, beyond mere survival, was seen as one area to which researchers should devote increased attention. Doing so would require small-scale and intensive types of investigation to supplement the large sample surveys which had been the basis for most of the research linking education and other social variables to child survival. However, there was still much that could be learned through large surveys, as had been shown in recent years by the expansion of survey content, particularly in the DHS programme, into health and related areas.

Women's economic activity and demographic factors

Although women's economic contribution was greatly understated in currently available statistics, the Expert Group took note that even the available data indicated that in all parts of the world women made up substantial proportions of the population employed in the formal economy. Statistics compiled by the ILO showed that, in 1985, 37 per cent of the labour force worldwide had been female: 42 per cent in the more developed and 35 per cent in the less developed regions. In Africa, 35 per cent of the recorded labour force was composed of women; in Asia (not including China), 28 per cent; in China, 43 per cent; and in Latin America and the Caribbean, 27 per cent.

Increased opportunities in the paid labour force were generally agreed to encourage lower fertility, although the reverse was also true: lower fertility made it possible for women to participate in the labour force. However, the types of work most commonly done by women in many developing countries were not uniformly associated with lower fertility. On the contrary, poor women with large families might be driven to seek work in order to provide basic subsistence.

Incompatibility between modern sector work and child care was commonly regarded as a fundamental reason for expecting working women to have fewer children. The types of work open to poor, uneducated women, such as agricultural labour, small-scale trading and domestic labour, could often be combined with child care to some degree; and it was primarily among those engaged in paid work in the modern sector that lower fertility was observed.

There were a number of complicating factors that made it problematic to assign the work/fertility relation to any single factor, such as time conflicts between work and child care. For instance, in developing countries, alternative, affordable child care was readily available to well-educated, higher status women, who were typically those with access to well-paying jobs in the modern sector. In such settings, incompatibility between work and child care did not occur or at least was greatly reduced. Yet, it was precisely employment in the modern sector that had most consistently been associated with lower fertility, in developing as well as developed countries. Other factors that might be involved included less tangible aspects of work, particularly when employment provided a separate source of social esteem and personal fulfilment that offered women an alternative to social status based mainly on her roles as wife and mother. It was also difficult in practice to separate the effects of employment from other personal, social and cultural characteristics that might jointly influence fertility and the propensity for women to join the labour force. Such characteristics as education, which strongly affected a woman's access to good jobs, might be more important than employment itself in producing a relation between employment and fertility.

It was clear that not all jobs provided an attractive alternative to a home-centred life. Access to jobs offering good pay and enhanced status often depended upon an individual woman's education and other qualifications.

However, access to good jobs also depended upon the broader social and economic setting. Discriminatory practices that led to large gaps in the wages that women and men could earn served as an incentive for women—at least those in stable marriages—to "specialize" in domestic work and for the husband to specialize in earning income, with little of his time and energy devoted to the domestic sphere. In some societies, prevailing cultural views concerning acceptable roles for women severely constrained the job choices of even the well-educated. In such societies, small numbers of high-status women and some women that would otherwise be destitute might work outside the home, the latter in menial jobs which conferred low status in exchange for a meager livelihood.

Although some observers had pointed to women's increased participation in the labour force as a key factor in producing the extremely low levels of fertility (total fertility rates in some cases of fewer than 1.5 children per woman) that were seen in some industrialized countries, the evidence was not straightforward, and it remained indeterminate how important the growing participation in the labour force was, as compared with other forces, in producing low fertility. Although over the longer run rising rates of women's participation in the labour force in developed countries had been accompanied by fertility declines, a more detailed examination showed that trends in such participation did not correspond well to the timing of fertility increases and decreases. In addition, the countries where women were most likely to be formally employed were not necessarily those with the lowest fertility.

It was beyond dispute that in both developed and developing countries, many parents experienced stress over the competing demands of jobs and children. That was particularly true for women who continued to do most child care and housework, whether or not they also had other work. It was the total burden of those conflicting demands on women's time, as well as the contributions of men—not simply the level of participation in the labour force, or economic conditions in general—that must be the focus of attention in order to comprehend the reasons for exceptionally low fertility. One expert observed that some Nordic countries, which had taken the lead in public policies to harmonize work and family responsibilities and where men were more likely to assume some of the burden of child care and housework, currently had substantially higher fertility than such countries as Japan, Spain and Italy, where economic opportunities had been opening to women but where there was not much change in the traditional division of labour within households or much commitment through policies and programmes to easing the conflicts between formal employment, child care and housework.

It was also noted that employment opportunities might in some cases have less effect on child-bearing within marriage than on women's decisions about when, or even whether, to marry. Japan was an example of a society where increased employment of women during recent decades appeared to have had a greater effect on timing of marriage than on fertility within marriage. Whereas a woman's job might induce a male to feel that he could "afford" to marry, it could also encourage a woman to feel that she could "afford" not to marry.

There was little firm evidence about the possible relation between women's economic activity and child welfare, particularly in developing countries. On the one hand, paid work benefited children by improving the family's economic standing. There was also evidence from several settings that more of women's income than men's income was spent on child-oriented expenses, such as food, clothing and education, and less on entertainment, tobacco and alcoholic beverages. However, there was not enough evidence to tell how generally the latter findings held. In some settings, women had no control over the spending of their earnings.

A mother's involvement in market work might affect children negatively through a reduction in the time she spent caring for children and their exposure to alternative care, which for poor women in many developing countries was likely to consist of no care or care from siblings. Yet, there was very little evidence on the point. In fact, the literature suggested several mechanisms that attenuated the superficially obvious relation. In many developing countries, women engaged in work, such as small-scale trading and agriculture, which allowed them to take children to the workplace. Women might also reduce their leisure time to meet the demands of children and work. Additionally, the image of a homemaker as able to provide a warm nurturing environment, which her employed counterpart could not, underestimated the demands of domestic work on women in rural areas of many developing countries. Time lost to arduous, time-consuming tasks of household maintenance, such as gathering fuel and carrying water, was not counted as time spent in employment and indeed was nowhere reflected in commonly available statistics. Such tasks might require poor women to leave young children untended or tended by a slightly older child for long periods . There was evidence that children's health suffered under such arrangements, and there was the additional problem in the latter case that children (frequently girls) were kept away from school in order to care for younger siblings.

Actual child-care arrangements, the effects on children of different types of child care and the relation of women's market and domestic work to child care and child welfare were seen as areas that needed more research, particularly in developing countries. In considering those issues, researchers and policy makers needed to pay attention to the total burden on women's time and not restrict attention to employment as reflected in current statistical systems.

The possibility that work away from home might impede women's ability to breast-feed young children had prompted studies in a number of developing countries. These studies generally found that working women were no less likely to initiate breast-feeding than those that were not employed, but some studies found that employed women introduced supplementary foods earlier. Where supplements were prepared under unsanitary conditions, early supplementation could pose a risk to child health. Nevertheless, it was not clear from available evidence whether the health of working women's children was affected by work-induced changes in breast-feeding patterns. For one thing, as a growing number of studies examined infant-feeding patterns in more detail, it became clear that in many societies, supplements, such as water or fruit juice, were traditionally given to infants beginning at a very young age, during the period that less detailed investigations were likely to classify simply as "full" breast-feeding. Thus, the risks posed by breast-milk supplements might be quite widespread, with the mother's employment status being at most a minor factor. At a more general level, however, the benefits of breast-feeding for child health and nutrition were very well documented, and efforts should continue to encourage workplace conditions that would make it possible for women to continue breast-feeding.

The Expert Group took note that home-based and part-time employment was in some circumstances the only available way for women to earn an income and as such was a practical necessity for many poor women. However, the Group also noted that work under those conditions often involved low earnings and little or no increase in autonomy, that the equipment and substances involved in home production were sometimes hazardous and that such labour conditions often resulted in exploitation by employers.

Recognizing that increased economic productivity for women was vital for their own interests and for national development, the recommendations adopted at the meeting referred to a variety of actions that Governments and employers could and should take in order to increase the access of women to productive and remunerative employment and to protect the rights of women and men in the workplace. Policies and programmes should include measures directed to enabling parents to harmonize the demands of work and caring for children, elderly parents and other defendants, and to encouraging fathers, in particular, to assume more responsibility for child care and household maintenance. Such policies should not be directed to women employees only but should rather be framed and applied in a gender-neutral manner.

Related to those concerns was the need for better data collection about women's economic activities. Undercounting of women's employment was common, particularly for women in rural areas and those that helped run family enterprises. More generally, there was a "need for development that paid greater heed to the value of a poor woman's time. Labour-saving devices were quickly developed for men and for the better-off population as a whole. Poor working women, on the other hand, did an unenviable double shift of work for all practical purposes, so that it was often the home maintenance tasks rather than the demands of her job that took the most time and attention away from the child.

Women, population and the environment

It was agreed by the Expert Group that environmental issues were linked to population factors in a variety of ways. Although environmental issues concerned men and women alike, some environmental problems had a disproportionate impact on women. For example, certain substances employed in manufacturing or in agriculture posed heightened risks to pregnant women and to foetal development. Women's exposure to environmental toxins might also differ from men's because the type and location of daily activities differed by sex. Frequently, women had also been the first to notice environmental hazards and the first to protest publicly about them.

The Group focused particular attention on environmental problems in rural areas of developing countries and the need to involve women fully in programmes to solve those problems and to achieve sustainable development. Although population growth was by no means the only cause of environmental degradation in such areas, it was inevitably a contributing factor. As population had increased, areas suited for agriculture had become crowded, marginal lands had often been brought into production, and water resources had been depleted. Soil erosion and deforestation had resulted, and traditional ways of living in harmony with the environment had been disrupted.

Those problems could not be solved without providing means for people in those areas to escape from poverty. Nor could they be solved without a correct understanding of women's roles as de facto environmental managers and without ensuring that women should be involved at all levels of planning and execution of programmes in those areas. Particularly in poor rural areas, women's work as mothers and guardians of family health were not clearly separated in time and place from their other work; and, as stated above, statistical indicators often failed to reflect their economic contribution at all. Women's statistical invisibility in labour force data for poor rural areas, coupled with a failure to study and understand local, culturally specific gender divisions of labour, social life and rights to assets, had often led to programmes of rural development that failed to help women and sometimes undermined their traditional livelihood. It was pointed out that women must be regarded more seriously as producers and be given appropriate training and skills so that they could become more productive and thus contribute more effectively to the alleviation of family poverty, that of rural families in particular. The objective was not to remove them from the family or to create independent women's power. Rather, it was to enhance their productivity in ways that would add to their capacity and value within the community and would give them more "bargaining" power for fairer treatment by officials and family members.

II. RECOMMENDATIONS OF THE MEETING

A. Preamble

Governments and intergovernmental and non-governmental organizations have increasingly accorded high priority to women's roles and status. It has been widely accepted that women's advancement, health, education and family planning are mutually reinforcing and should be pursued simultaneously and in a holistic manner. Sustainable development cannot be achieved without the full participation of both women and men in all aspects of productive and reproductive life, including the care and nurturing of children and maintenance of the household. It is critical to recognize that gender roles are diverse and changing. National economic and demographic goals cannot be attained unless the needs of women as citizens, workers, wives and mothers are met.

The equality between men and women is proclaimed in the Universal Declaration of Human Rights. The interrelation between women and population are affirmed in the World Population Plan of Action (1974) and in the Recommendations for its Further Implementation (1984), the Nairobi Forward-looking Strategies for the Advancement of Women (1985), the Safe Motherhood Initiative (1987) and the Amsterdam Declaration on a Better Life for Future Generations (1989).

While acknowledging that some progress has been made, the Expert Group Meeting on Population and Women recognizes that numerous issues concerning women and population still need to be addressed both at the international level and at the national level. The Meeting notes that at the international level, there are several adequate instruments and guidelines, but they need to be fully implemented at the national level.

B. Recommendations

Reaffirming the provisions of internationally adopted instruments that relate to the linkage between women and population and recognizing the importance of devising practical measures that will help to empower women, the Expert Group Meeting on Population and Women adopts the following recommendations:

Recommendation 1. Governments, intergovernmental and non-governmental organizations are urged in the implementation of stabilization, structural adjustment and economic recovery programmes to recognize health and education as productive sectors which are particularly critical for women. These sectors play a fundamental role in human capital development and in the formation of future generations of workers.

Recommendation 2. Gender-based analysis should become an essential instrument in the design, implementation and evaluation of all development activities, including economic planning and population and development policy formulation. Sensitization to gender issues should be a priority in all activities, including population. Programme managers are urged to develop and utilize training materials and implement courses of training in gender issues. Governments, donors and the private sector, including non-governmental organizations and for-profit corporations, should assist with and support development of such training materials and courses.

Recommendation 3. Governments should ensure that development policies and strategies shall be assessed for their impact on women's social, economic and health status throughout the life-span.

Recommendation 4. Donors, Governments and non-governmental organizations are urged to seek culturally appropriate modalities for the delivery of services and the integration of women into population and development initiatives. They are urged to provide widespread access to information and services responsive to women's concerns and needs and to stress women's participation.

Recommendation 5. Efforts are needed to balance the representation of women and men in all areas of population and development, particularly at the management and policy-making levels, in both the governmental and the private sectors.

Recommendation 6. Governments and non-governmental organizations should promote responsible parenthood. Children are entitled to the material and emotional support of both fathers and mothers, who should provide for all their children of both sexes on an equitable basis. Governments should adopt specific measures to facilitate the realization of these rights.

Recommendation 7. Governments should strengthen efforts to promote and encourage, by means of information, education, communication and employment legislation and institutional support, where appropriate, the active involvement of men in all areas of family responsibility, including family planning, child-rearing and housework, so that family responsibilities can be fully shared by both partners.

Recommendation 8. Women that wish to terminate their pregnancy should have ready access to reliable information, sympathetic counselling and safe abortion services.

Recommendation 9. Governments should adopt measures to promote and protect adolescent reproductive health, including the teaching of family life education with a realistic sex education component, appropriate counselling and services to girls and boys. Governments are urged to work with adolescents themselves and to draw upon non-governmental organizations that have experience in this area.

Recommendation 10. So as to ensure the rights of young women to health and of young women and men to education and employment opportunities, Governments are urged to enforce laws pertaining to minimum age at marriage and to raise awareness of the importance of this issue through appropriate communication strategies.

Recommendation 11. Family planning programmes, in their efforts to reach both women and men, should be consonant with the cultural setting and sensitive to local constraints on women and should provide all aspects of quality care and services, including counselling, reliable information on contraceptive methods, informed consent and access to a wide range of contraceptives. Family planning programmes should also address infertility concerns and provide information on sexually transmitted diseases, including HIV/AIDS.

Recommendation 12. Sexually transmitted diseases have important, and often hidden, health consequences for women, increasing the incidence of reproductive tract infections with consequent risks of life-threatening ectopic pregnancy. Reproductive tract infections and genital ulcer diseases also heighten the risk of transmission of HIV/AIDS, with potentially fatal consequences for mothers and their children. Therefore, Governments and non-governmental organizations must promote safer sex, including the use of condoms, and must provide preventive, diagnostic and curative treatment to inhibit the transmission of sexually transmitted diseases.

Recommendation 13. Governments, non-governmental organizations and the private sector are urged to give priority to the adoption of measures to promote the health of women and girls. These measures should encompass the nutrition and health needs of young girls and women, women's reproductive health and the implementation of the Safe Motherhood Initiative. Priority should also be given to monitoring the impact of these measures.

Recommendation 14. Various forms of female genital mutilation are widespread in many parts of the world and cause great and continued suffering, impaired fecundity and death. Governments should vigorously act to stop this practice and to protect the rights of women and girls to be free from such unnecessary and dangerous procedures.

Recommendation 15. Governments, non-governmental organizations and the private sector should assure women and men as individuals of confidential access to safe methods of fertility regulation within the framework of an adequate health-care system.

Recommendation 16. Governments and non-governmental organizations are urged to make special efforts to improve and equalize the school enrolment and attendance of girls and boys at all levels of education. Recognizing the difficulty of some families in permitting their daughters or sons to attend school, innovative strategies need to be devised which respond to existing socio-economic and familial constraints. There is also need for increased sensitivity to young women's reasons for dropping out of formal education, whether as a result of early marriage, pregnancy or economic need. Policies and programmes must be adopted which will enable them to continue their education.

Recommendation 17. Governments and non-governmental organizations should make efforts to ensure that women of all ages who have little or no formal schooling shall be provided with special non-formal education which would assist them to gain access to remunerative employment, knowledge of their legal rights, information on family and child health, nutrition and fertility regulation and information on services for which they are eligible. This education should complement, rather than substitute for, formal schooling.

Recommendation 18. Governments and non-governmental organizations should develop culturally sensitive health education to increase the awareness of health rights of all members of the family. Efforts should also be made to achieve equal rights of access to appropriate preventive and curative health care, regardless of age, gender or family position. Such issues as rape, incest, child abuse, domestic violence and exploitation based on age and gender require special attention. Programmes that promote acceptance among men and women of equal rights in sexual relationships are required.

Recommendation 19. Taking cognizance of the interaction between extreme poverty and demographic trends, Governments are urged to strengthen women's access to productive and remunerative employment.

Recommendation 20. Governments, non-governmental organizations and the private sector are urged to develop and enforce explicit policies and practices to ensure the protection and freedom of women from gender discrimination, including economic discrimination and harassment, especially in the workplace.

Recommendation 21. Governments and private sector employers are urged to take measures to enable parents to harmonize their economic and parental responsibilities, including parental leave, child care, provisions to enable working women to breast-feed children, and measures to ensure that women and men shall exercise their right to employment without being subject to discrimination because of family responsibilities.

Recommendation 22. Governments should seek to remove all remaining legal, administrative and social barriers to women's rights and economic independence, such as limitations on the right to acquire, hold and sell property, to obtain credit and to negotiate contracts in their own name and on their own behalf.

Recommendation 23. Governments, intergovernmental and non-governmental organizations are urged to promote awareness of the crucial role women play in environmental and natural resource management and to provide information and training to women on how they can promote sustainable development. Community-based population and environment programmes should be implemented. They should involve women's participation at all levels and seek to reduce or alleviate women's workloads.

Recommendation 24. Governments are called upon to take measures to prevent the use of and exposure to hazardous substances by women. Governments and employers are urged to ensure that women doing work that is hazardous to foetal development shall be offered alternative employment upon request, without penalty.

Recommendation 25. In many countries, women take care of their husband, children and older relatives, often at the same time. Moreover, as a result of population ageing in both developed and developing countries, increasing numbers of women will be living alone, under poor conditions, or with their sons and daughters. Governments should develop adequate social security and medical care systems for all women, regardless of marital status.

Recommendation 26. Violence against women and children is widespread. Governments are required to protect women and children from all forms of violence, including rape, incest, child abuse, domestic violence and exploitation based on age and gender. Women refugees and those in circumstances of war and wherever civil rights are threatened or suspended are in special need of protection and of reproductive health care and family planning services.

Recommendation 27. Governments, international organizations, the pharmaceutical industry, the medical professions and non-governmental organizations should give urgent priority to the development and production of improved and safe contraceptives for fertility regulation and effective pharmaceutical products for protection against sexually transmitted diseases. Renewed emphasis should be placed on the development of male methods of contraception. Contraceptive research and trials of new methods should be governed by accepted ethical principles and internationally recognized standards. In particular, new methods should be tested on a range of persons in developed and developing countries who have full information and have freely agreed to participate in the testing.

Recommendation 28. While continuing data collection in existing areas, Governments and funding agencies are urged to give priority to the collection of data in areas where information is currently seriously deficient. Both large-scale surveys and more qualitative approaches are seen as valuable and complementary. Among these critical areas are:

(*a*) Structure and dynamics of the family;

(*b*) Women's, men's and children's diverse economic, domestic and resource management roles and use of time to fulfil those roles;

(*c*) Men's attitudes and behaviour regarding reproduction and other topics for which data are currently obtained mainly from women;

(*d*) Child-care arrangements;

(*e*) Unplanned pregnancy and abortion;

(*f*) Sexual abuse;

(*g*) Domestic and other forms of violence;

(*h*) Various aspects of reproductive health, including incidence of sexually transmitted diseases.

Recommendation 29. Governments, funding agencies and research organizations are urged to give priority to research on the linkages between women's roles and status and demographic processes. Among the vital areas for research are changing family systems and the interaction between women's, men's and children's diverse roles, including their use of time, access to and control over resources, decision-making and associated norms, laws, values and beliefs. Of particular concern is the impact of gender inequalities on these interactions and the associated economic and demographic outcomes.

Recommendation 30. Governments are urged to ensure that the full diversity of women's economic activities shall be properly represented in statistical systems and national accounts.

Recommendation 31. Government statistical offices are encouraged to publish a broad range of social, health and economic statistics and indicators on a gender-desegregated basis, and Governments are urged to take those statistics into account in policy and planning.

Recommendation 32. International agencies and donors are urged to increase allocation of resources for publication and dissemination of relevant documents in order to promote expanded access of national research organizations, including women's organizations, to policy-related research findings and conceptual and methodological developments.

ANNEXES

ANNEX I

AGENDA

1. Opening of the Meeting

2. Election of officers.

3. Adoption of the agenda and organization of work.

4. The value of women, women's autonomy and population trends:

   (*a*) Population and women: a review of issues and trends;

   (*b*) Family and gender issues for population policy;

   (*c*) The value of women, women's autonomy, population and policy trends;

   (*d*) Women's status and population trends in the Arab world.

5. Women, health and mortality:

   (*a*) Gender differences in health risks and use of services;

   (*b*) Maternal mortality, induced abortion and sexually transmitted diseases: impact on women's health during the fertile age;

   (*c*) Women, AIDS and sexually transmitted diseases in sub-Saharan Africa: the impact of marriage change.

6. Women, fertility and family planning:

   (*a*) Adolescent reproductive behaviour and women's status;

   (*b*) Adolescent pregnancy: focus on services, policy and practice;

   (*c*) Legal, administrative and cultural factors affecting women's access to family planning services.

7. Women's education and its demographic impact:

   (*a*) Women's education, fertility and the proximate determinants of fertility;

   (*b*) Women's education, child welfare and child survival.

8. Linkages between women's economic activity and population dynamics:

   (*a*) Women's economic activities and fertility: overview of the interactions and policy implications;

   (*b*) Women's economic roles and child health: an overview.

   (*c*) Relationship between women's economic activity and child care in low-fertility countries.

9. Population, environment and development: issues of special concern for women:

   (*a*) Women, population and the environment: a global concern;

   (*b*) Women and resource management: a critical issue in developing countries.

10. New currents and emerging emphasis in research and policy: a panel discussion

11. Adoption of the recommendations.

12. Closing of the Meeting.

ANNEX II

List of participants

EXPERTS

Alaka Basu, Institute of Economic Growth, University of Enclave, Delhi, India

Michel Caraël, Global Programme on AIDS, World Health Organization, Geneva

Colette Dehlot, Associate for Reproductive Health, The Population Council, New York

Nadia Ramsis Farah, Arab Women Center for Training and Research, Cairo, Egypt

John Hobcraft , London School of Economics and Political Science, London

Shireen Jejeebhoy, Consultant, Bombay, India

Shigemi Kono, Director General, Institute of Population Problems, Ministry of Health and Welfare, Tokyo

Cynthia Lloyd, Senior Associate and Deputy Director, The Population Council, New York

Amy Grace Luhanga, Institute of Development and Management, Gaborone, Botswana

Billie Miller, Bridgetown, Barbados

Els Postel, Faculty of Social and Behavioral Science, Leiden University, Women and Autonomy Centre, Leiden, the Netherlands

Yulfita Raharjo, Head, Centre for Population and Manpower Studies, Indonesian Institute of Sciences, Jakarta, Indonesia

Alberto Rizo-Gil, Consultant, Bogotá, Colombia

Gigi Santow, Senior Research Fellow, National Centre for Epidemiology and Population Health, The Australian National University, Canberra, Australia

Susheela Singh, Assistant Director of Research, The Alan Guttmacher Institute, New York

Marcela Villareal, Regional Advisor on Women, Population and Target Group Policies, Regional Employment Programme for Latin America and the Caribbean, Santiago, Chile

SECRETARIAT OF THE INTERNATIONAL CONFERENCE ON POPULATION AND DEVELOPMENT, 1994

Nafis Sadik, Executive Director, United Nations Population Fund (UNFPA); and Secretary-General of the Conference

Shunichi Inoue, Director, Population Division of the Department of Economic and Social Development of the United Nations Secretariat; and Deputy Secretary-General of the Conference

Jyoti Shankar Singh, Chief, Technical and Evaluation Division, United Nations Population Fund; and Executive Coordinator of the Conference

German A. Bravo-Casas, Coordinator, World Population Conference Implementation, Population Division of the Department of Economic and Social Development of the United Nations Secretariat; and Deputy Executive Director of the Conference

Joyce Bratich-Cherif, External Relations Advisor, Technical and Evaluation Division, United Nations Population Fund

UNITED NATIONS

Department of Economic and Social Development
Population Division,
Birgitta Bucht, Assistant Director
Mary Beth Weinberger, Technical Secretary of the Meeting; and Population Affairs Officer, Fertility and Family Planning Studies Section
Krishna Roy, Population Affairs Officer, Population Projects Section
Keiko Ono, Population Affairs Officer, Fertility and Family Planning Studies Section

United Nations Office at Vienna
Jacques du Guerny, Senior Social Affairs Officer, Division for the Advancement of Women

Economic Commission for Africa (ECA)
Ahmed Bahri, Chief, Population Division

Economic Commission for Latin America and the Caribbean (ECLAC)
Miriam Krawczyk, Head, Women and Development Division

Economic and Social Commission for Asia and the Pacific (ESCAP)
Nibhon Debavalya, Chief, Population Division

Economic and Social Commission for Western Asia (ESCWA)
Ahmed Abdel Ghany Abdel Raheen Al-Ayyat, First Population Affairs Officer

United Nations Centre for Human Settlements (Habitat)
Annika Tornqvist

United Nations Children's Fund (UNICEF)
Gladys Martin, Senior Health Officer, Eastern and Southern Africa Regional Office

United Nations Development Programme (UNDP)
Elizabeth Fong, Resident Representative and Resident Coordinator in Botswana
Abigail Japajapa-Lee, Department of Rural and Urban Planning, United Nations Development Fund for Women (UNIFEM), Harare, Zimbabwe

United Nations Population Fund (UNFPA)
Catherine Pierce, Chief, Women, Population and Development Branch, Technical and Evaluation Division
James Kuriah, Country Director for Botswana, Lesotho and Swaziland
Dorcas Temani, Programme Officer, Botswana

SPECIALIZED AGENCIES

International Labour Organization (ILO)
Christine Oppong, Coordinator of Population Programme, Migration and Population Branch, Employment and Development Department

Food and Agriculture Organization of the United Nations (FAO)
Zoran Roca, Population Officer, Women in Agricultural Production and Rural Development Service, Human Resources, Institutions and Agrarian Reform Division

United Nations Educational, Scientific and Cultural Organization (UNESCO)
Serim Timur, Population and Human Settlements Division

World Health Organization (WHO)
Rita Thapa, Medical Officer, Women, Health and Development

NON-GOVERNMENTAL ORGANIZATIONS IN CONSULTATIVE STATUS WITH THE ECONOMIC AND SOCIAL COUNCIL

Category I
International Planned Parenthood Federation (IPPF)
Gladys Azu, Senior Programme Officer, Sub-Regional Office for Central and West Africa

Category II
The World Conservation Union
Tabith Matiza, Wetlands Co-ordinator, Regional Office for Southern Africa

Roster
Center for Development and Population Activities
Peggy Curlin, President

OTHER NON-GOVERNMENTAL ORGANIZATIONS

Institute for Resource Development
Anne R. Cross, Regional Coordinator for Anglophone Africa and Asia

OBSERVERS

Government of Botwana
G. Charumbira
B. G. Garebakwena
Kerileng E. M. Maloantoa
Rosemary R. Mangope
W. G. Manyeneng
Marjorie N. Mohlala
Elizabeth Nombayane Mokotong
P. Molutsi
Lindiwe Myeza
Annemarie Nutt
E. Odotei
S. Pitso
C. O. Ramalefo
T. Ramatsui
T. G. G. G. Seeletso
G. Thipe
S. S. G. Tumelo
S. Walking

Institute of Developing Economies (Japan)
Yasuko Hayase

Annex III

List of documents

Document No.	*Agenda item*	*Title and author*
ESD/P/ICPD.1994/EG.III/1	-	Provisional agenda
ESD/P/ICPD.1994/EG.III/2	-	Provisional annotated agenda
ESD/P/ICPD.1994/EG.III/3	4(*a*)	Population and women: a review of issues and trends United Nations Secretariat
ESD/P/ICPD.1994/EG.III/4	4(*b*)	Family and gender issues for population policy Cynthia Lloyd
ESD/P/ICPD.1994/EG.III/5	4(*c*)	The value of women, women's autonomy, population and policy trends Els Postel
ESD/P/ICPD.1994/EG.III/6	4(*d*)	Women's status and population trends in the Arab world Nadia Ramsis Farah
ESD/P/ICPD.1994/EG.III/7	5(*a*)	Gender differences in health risks and use of services Gigi Santow
ESD/P/ICPD.1994/EG.III/8	5(*b*)	Maternal mortality, induced abortion and sexually transmitted diseases: impact on women's health during the fertile age Alberto Rizo-Gil
ESD/P/ICPD.1994/EG.III/9	5(*c*)	Women, AIDS and sexually transmitted diseases in sub-Saharan Africa: the impact of marriage change Michel Caraël
ESD/P/ICPD.1994/EG.III/10	6(*a*)	Adolescent reproductive behaviour and women's status Susheela Singh
ESD/P/ICPD.1994/EG.III/11	6(*b*)	Adolescent pregnancy: focus on services, policy and practice Billie Miller
ESD/P/ICPD.1994/EG.III/12	6(*c*)	Legal, administrative and cultural factors affecting women's access to family planning Amy Grace Luhanga
ESD/P/ICPD.1994/EG.III/13	7(*a*)	Women's education, fertility and the proximate determinants of fertility Shireen Jejeebhoy
ESD/P/ICPD.1994/EG.III/14	7(*b*)	Women's education, child welfare and child survival John Hobcraft

Document No.	*Agenda item*	*Title and author*
ESD/P/ICPD.1994/EG.III/15	8(*a*)	Women's economic activities and fertility: overview of the interactions and policy implications Marcela Villareal
ESD/P/ICPD.1994/EG.III/16	8(*b*)	Women's economic roles and child health: an overview Alaka Molwadu Basu
ESD/P/ICPD.1994/EG.III/17	8(*c*)	Relationship between women's economic activity and fertility and child care in low-fertility countries Shigemi Kono
ESD/P/ICPD.1994/EG.III/18	9(*a*)	Women, population and environment: a global concern Colette S. Dehlot
ESD/P/ICPD.1994/EG.III/19	9(*b*)	Women and resource management: a critical issue in developing countries Yulfita Raharjo
ESD/P/ICPD.1994/EG.III/INF.1	-	Provisional organization of work
ESD/P/ICPD.1994/EG.III/INF.2	-	Provisional list of participants
ESD/P/ICPD.1994/EG.III/INF.3	-	Provisional list of documents
ESD/P/ICPD.1994/EG.III/INF.4A	-	Information for participants travelling at United Nations expense
ESD/P/ICPD.1994/EG.III/INF.4B	-	Information for participants travelling at their own expense
ESD/P/ICPD.1994/EG.III/DN.1	9(*a*)	Rural women: the closing link between population and environment Food and Agriculture Organization of the United Nations
ESD/P/ICPD.1994/EG.III/DN.2	4(*b*)	A gender perspective on population issues United Nations Office at Venna
ESD/P/ICPD.1994/EG.III/DN.3	8(*b*)	Women's activity and population dynamics in Africa Economic Commission for Africa
ESD/P/ICPD.1994/EG.III/DN.4	6(*b*)	Women and family planning: issues for the 1990s International Planned Parenthood Federation
ESD/P/ICPD.1994/EG.III/DN.5	7(*a*)	Promoting women as leaders in population and development Peggy Curlin
ESD/P/ICPD.1994/EG.III/DN.6	5(*a*)	Women's participation and perspective in health issues: working notes Rita Thapa

Document No.	*Agenda item*	*Title and author*
ESD/P/ICPD.1994/EG.III/DN.7	7(*a*)	Women's education and employment and linkages with population Economic and Social Commission for Asia and the Pacific
ESD/P/ICPD.1994/EG.III/DN.8	5(*a*)	Reproductive health in the world: two decades of progress and the challenge ahead Mahmoud F. Fathalla
ESD/P/ICPD.1994/EG.III/DN.9	4(*c*)	Exploring the relationship between women's status and population dynamics with Demographic and Health Surveys data Anne R. Cross, Ann A. Way and Ann K. Blanc
ESD/P/ICPD.1994/EG.III/DN.10	7(*a*)	The impact of changes in Latin America and the Caribbean women: education, knowledge and demographic trends Economic Commission for Latin America and the Caribbean
ESD/P/ICPD.1994/EG.III/DN.11	8(*a*)	ILO standard-setting, policy studies and technical cooperation relating to population issues and women Christine Oppong
ESD/P/ICPD.1994/EG.III/DN.12	4(*a*)	Formulation and implementation of population and policies learned from technical cooperation United Nations Secretariat
ESD/P/ICPD.1994/EG.III/DN.13	7(*b*)	The impact of mother's education on infant and child mortality in selected countries in the ESCWA region Economic and Social Commission for Western Asia
ESD/P/ICPD.1994/EG.III/DN.14	9(*b*)	Population and nature conservation: advocating for conservation with a human face in Southern Africa Tabeth Matiza
ESD/P/ICPD.1994/EG.III/DN.15	4(*b*)	Does development lead to greater equality of the sexes? Helen Ware
ESD/P/ICPD.1994/EG.III/DN.16	5(*a*)	Women's and children's health: programme needs and priorities for the 1990s Gladys Martin
ESD/P/ICPD.1994/EG.III/DN.17	9(*a*)	Environmental issues of special concern to women and to children United Nations Environment Programme
ESD/P/ICPD.1994/EG.III/DN.18	9(*a*)	Rural women and poverty: the status and IFAD's evolving strategies for intervention Atiqur Rahman

Part Two

GENERAL OVERVIEW

III. POPULATION AND WOMEN: A REVIEW OF ISSUES AND TRENDS

United Nations Secretariat[*]

This paper briefly reviews a variety of issues and evidence relevant to the discussions at the Expert Group Meeting on Population and Women. It is organized into the following sections which, for the most part, follow the organization of the agenda for the Meeting: (*a*) a brief survey of milestones in the treatment of population and women's issues in the international community; (*b*) women's autonomy and equality; (*c*) health and mortality; (*d*) fertility and family planning; (*e*) education and training; (*f*) economic activity; and (*g*) women and the environment.

A. POPULATION AND WOMEN'S ISSUES IN THE INTERNATIONAL COMMUNITY

Since the end of the Second World War and the founding of the United Nations, the international community has devoted increasing attention both to women's issues and to the area of population. The chronology of major events and initiatives in these two areas of concern is displayed in box 1.

The focus on women began with the establishment of the Commission on the Status of Women by the United Nations in the year following the signing of the United Nations Charter. Growing international concern about the need to integrate women to the process of development led to the initiation of women into development activities in 1973 (Elson, 1991). The United Nations Development Fund for Women (UNIFEM) was created in 1976 as a source of financial support for initiatives related to women, especially poor, rural women in the developing countries. The years 1976-1985 were designated as the United Nations Decade for Women, and international conferences on women took place in 1975, 1980 and 1985.

In 1979, the International Convention on the Elimination of Discrimination against Women was adopted (United Nations, 1988b). By 1992, more than 100 countries had ratified this Convention. In 1982, the Committee on the Elimination of Discrimination Against Women (CEDAW) was established to monitor compliance with the 1979 Convention. A year later, in 1983, the International Research and Training Institute for the Advancement of Women (INSTRAW) came into being.

Since the close of the United Nations Decade for Women, women's concerns have been addressed at various international meetings on specific topics. These Meetings included the International Safe Motherhood Conference in 1987, in connection with which the World Health Organization (WHO) launched the Safe Motherhood Initiative, and the International Conference on Better Health for Women and Children through Family Planning (Holt, 1990). In 1991, the Global Assembly of Women and the Environment: Partners in Life took place.

Meanwhile, rapid population growth has increasingly been perceived as an important worldwide problem, and efforts to design and implement appropriate international responses have gathered momentum. In 1946, the Population Commission was established by the United Nations Economic and Social Council and still remains active, overseeing the work of the Population Division of the Department of Economic and Social Development of the United Nations Secretariat. The United Nations Fund for Population Activities (UNFPA), currently called the United Nations Population Fund, was founded in 1969, and has become a primary source of financial support for population-related activities in the developing countries. In 1974, at Bucharest,

---

[*]Prepared by Elise Jones as consultant to the Population Division of the Department of Economic and Social Development. Acknowledgement is also due Sonalde Desai for her useful comments on the draft of the paper.

Box 1. Chronology of international activities related to women and population

1946	Establishment of the Commission on the Status of Women, the Population Commission and the Population Division
1969	Founding of the United Nations Fund for Population Activities (UNFPA)
1973	Creation of the Women in Development Group
1974	World Population Conference at Bucharest and adoption of the World Population Plan of Action
1975	International Women's Year First International Women's Conference, Mexico City
1976	Launching of the United Nations Decade for Women Creation of the United Nations Development Fund for Women (UNIFEM)
1979	Adoption of the International Convention on the Elimination of Discrimination Against Women Adoption of Economic and Social Council resolution 1979/32 on strengthening of actions concerning with fulfilment of the World Population Plan of Action
1980	Second International Women's Conference, Copenhagen
1982	Establishment of the Committee on the Elimination of Discrimination against Women (CEDAW)
1983	Creation of the International Research and Training Institute for the Advancement of Women (INSTRAW)
1984	International Conference on Population, Mexico City, and adoption of the recommendations for further implementation of the World Population Plan of Action
1985	Conclusion of the United Nations Decade for Women Third International Women's Conference, Nairobi, adoption of the Nairobi Forward-looking Strategies for the Advancement of Women
1987	International Safe Motherhood Conference, Nairobi; which launched the Safe Motherhood Initiative International Conference on Better Health for Women and Children through Family Planning, Nairobi
1991	Global Assembly of Women and the Environment: Partners in Life, Miami, Florida

the World Population Conference adopted the World Population Plan of Action; and recommendations for its further implementation were adopted 10 years later at the International Conference on Population, held at Mexico City. The principal provisions of these documents pertaining to women's issues are reviewed in box 2. At the International Conference on Population and Development in 1994, one of the priority themes will be women's status and roles.

B. WOMEN'S AUTONOMY AND EQUALITY

Women's status in actuality

There is currently an impressive array of international declarations and agreements concerning women's right to equal status in many aspects of life. In addition to the 1979 Convention on the Elimination of All Forms of Discrimination against Women (referred to above), there are agreements on equal pay for work of equal value (1953), equal political rights (1954), maternity protection (1955), equality in employment (1960), equality in education (1962) and equal marriage rights (1964) (Sivard, 1985). Although there has been some real improvement in the position of women, the reality continues to fall short of even minimally acceptable standards in many parts of the world, and nowhere can women be said to enjoy complete equality with men. Evidence of women's inferior status ranges from failure to recognize the economic value of their unpaid labour to lack of access to education, and from sexual harassment in the workplace to domestic violence against women, culminating in some cases in murder. Conditions are worst where poverty exacerbates the burden of economic, social, political and legal discrimination. In addition to the vast numbers of poor women around the world, particularly vulnerable groups include single women, the young and the elderly, the disabled, migrants, refugees, abused women and members of minorities (United Nations, 1985a).

Reference is made in later sections of this paper to many issues related to equality and autonomy. This section provides a brief discussion of selected aspects of women's non-economic values and status that tend to be overlooked.

Women's life in the household and family

The demographic changes that have occurred in recent decades, combined with the process of social and economic development that has now taken hold in most parts of the world, have altered family life in fundamental ways. Where levels of living have risen, the range of opportunities for personal fulfilment available to women has usually widened. At the same time, the structure of the family has changed and traditional support arrangements within the extended family have often broken down.

Since 1970, household size has been declining in all regions except in sub-Saharan Africa (United Nations, 1989c). This decline is in part due to declining fertility, which implies smaller families and smaller kinship groups. But it is also due to changing living arrangements. In industrialized countries, the number of separate households has risen; children move out of the parental household as soon as they become adults, single people often live alone and the elderly reside independently as long as they can. Nuclear family units are more common than they formerly were in some Asian countries, although extended family groups remain the norm in Africa (United Nations, 1989e). Smaller households can mean more autonomy for women, but they also bring greater isolation.

In all areas of the world, more and more households are headed by women. In Latin America and the Caribbean, where female-headed households have long been common, almost 30 per cent of households were headed by women in the early 1980s (United Nations, 1991d). The proportion was about 24 per cent in the more developed regions, 21 per cent in Africa and 14 per cent in Asia and Oceania. Reasons for the increase in female-headed households include rising rates of marital disruption, increasing proportions of births occurring outside of marriage and migration of both males and females in search of remunerative employment. Female heads are often the sole income providers for the household and female headship is linked everywhere to poverty (United Nations, 1991d). At the same time, female-headed households are not a homogeneous group: many such households are not poor, and many of the women

Box 2. Highlights of the recommendations of the World Population Conference in 1974 and the International Conference on Population in 1984, concerning women's issues

World Population Plan of Action

The provisions of the World Population Plan of Action that concern women fall primarily into four interrelated areas: human rights; health issues; social policy; and the integration of women into the development process. The principles and objectives of the Plan established the right of couples and individuals to make reproductive decisions "freely and responsibly" (para. 14(f)), the right of women to complete integration into the development process (para. 14(h)) and the need to promote the status of women and expand their roles (para. 15(e)).

The ensuing specific recommendations elaborate upon these themes. A section on "reproduction, family formation and the status of women" contains numerous recommendations concerning family planning services, and information and education in the area of family planning, the harmonization of population policy with development programmes, educational opportunities, strengthening of the family as "the basic unit of society", equality of marriage partners, full participation of women as equals in political and economic affairs and raising women's status as a key to improvement in the quality of life (paras. 27-43). A separate recommendation calls for vigorous efforts to reduce mortality, including foetal, infant, early childhood and related maternal mortality; to reduce involuntary sterility and illegal abortion and to eliminate gender differentials in mortality (para. 24). Lastly, recommended priority areas for research include reduction of maternal mortality and mortality in early life, new methods of family planning, evaluation of the impact of family planning methods on women's health, delivery of social and family planning service, and changing family structure and gender roles (para. 78 (c,i,j,l,p)).

Recommendations for the further implementation of the World Population Plan of Action

The preamble to this set of recommendations notes that although some progress has been made worldwide since 1974 with regard to fertility decline, on the one hand and improvement in the status of women and their integration into the development process, on the other hand, much remained to be done in both areas (paras. 3(d) and 7). One section of the recommendation is devoted to the role and status of women: Governments are urged to integrate women into all phases of the development process (recommendation 5); to ensure that women shall be free to participate in the labour force (recommendation 6); to provide women with opportunities for personal fulfilment in familial and non-familial roles, including delaying the initiation of child-bearing (recommendation 7); to raise the age of marriage where it is still low (recommendation 8); to encourage the involvement of men in all areas of family responsibility; and, if they have not already done so, to ratify the Convention on the Elimination of All Forms of Discrimination Against Women. In another section, which focuses on population goals and policies, the basic right of couples and inidividuals to decide freely on the number and spacing of their children is reiterated (recommendation 30). Related actions recommended include reduction of maternal and child mortality (recommendations 17-19), encouragement of breast-feeding (recommendation 20), improvement in women's level of education (recommendation 21), support of family planning services (recommendations 25-28), provision of sex education for adolescents (recommendation 29) and development of family policies sensitive to the needs of mothers and young children (recommendation 34). In addition, Governments should make available population statistics by sex (recommendation 62) and should give priority to research on reproduction and fertility regulation and to service and operational research (recommendations 69-70).

maintaining households prefer this arrangement to the alternatives available.

Although roles and responsibilities are changing slowly, customs giving men priority in most decisions affecting the household and family continue to prevail in many parts of the world, especially in rural areas of the developing countries. Women are increasingly likely to be employed outside the home, but the division of labour within the household tends to remain the same; women do the majority of housework, care for children and often attend to family agricultural activities as well. Domestic violence, although rarely reported and therefore poorly documented, is now recognized to be common and to be perpetrated largely against women (United Nations, 1991d).

Since control over child-bearing largely determines a woman's ability to make choices concerning the use of her time and energy, and may even be a matter of life and death, reproductive rights are a particularly crucial concern for women. In some cultures, husbands, mothers-in-law and other family members have a greater say than the potential mother in fertility-related decisions. Disapproval on the part of spouses and other authority figures is frequently given as a reason for failure to use contraception. In some countries, formal authorization by the spouse is actually required before family planning services can be used (Cook and Maine, 1987).

Women's life in the public arena

Women did not have the right to vote anywhere in the world until almost the end of the nineteenth century (Sivard, 1985). Organized movements for reform had emerged around the middle of the century in a number of countries then in the process of industrialization. In 1893, New Zealand became the first country to grant women's suffrage in national elections. Three countries followed suit before the First World War and 27 more before the Second World War. After 1945, rapid progress was made, and by 1985 women had gained the franchise almost everywhere, except for those in Western Asia and the black population of South Africa. In all countries, women obtained the right to vote later than men; the lag was only one year in Australia but as much as 134 years in Peru. Even where women are legally enfranchised, social and political barriers may still restrict their participation in the electoral process, as is also the case for men.

Acquisition of the right to vote has not resulted in equal representation of men and women in positions of political power. The handful of outstanding women that have held office in recent years as heads of State or prime ministers must be regarded as exceptions that prove the rule. In 1987, women occupied between 18 and 35 per cent of the seats in the national legislatures of the Nordic countries, Eastern Europe and a few other countries (Cuba, China, Democratic People's Republic of Korea, Seychelles, Viet Nam and the former Union of Soviet Socialist Republics) (United Nations, 1991d). Between 1987 and 1990, however, there was a sharp decline in women's representation in the parliaments of Eastern Europe and the former USSR, perhaps reflecting the resurgence of traditional values currently taking place there. In other parts of the world, the number of women in national legislatures has typically amounted to fewer than 10 per cent and often fewer than 5 per cent. With regard to the ministerial level of Government, the picture is even bleaker, except possibly in the area of social affairs (United Nations, 1991d), which may more often be seen as an appropriate place for women.

Women have been somewhat more successful in local than in national politics (United Nations, 1991d). Large numbers of women are also found at the lower echelons of governmental administrative bureaucracies, as is the case generally in the service and white collar sectors of the economy. Women do not often advance to positions of responsibility, however, even when they are as well qualified as their male counterparts. Indeed, within the United Nations system itself, women are greatly underrepresented at the middle and upper professional levels. On the other hand, women have provided much of the leadership for non-governmental organizations and grass-roots movements at the community, national and international levels.

Women's legal rights

The national constitutions or other basic legal frameworks of the majority of countries now include provisions for gender equality in essential areas (Sivard, 1985). The thrust of continuing legal efforts to correct the disadvantages women faced in the past and to secure for them an equal place with men has consequently largely shifted towards translation of these general principles into practice. All too often, the concrete interventions needed to implement change have not been forthcoming, for instance, the provision of schools and teaching staff to educate girls or the enforcement of laws regarding the minimum age for marriage.

The content of legislative and judicial action has also expanded during the twentieth century to include issues of direct concern to women that had previously received little attention (Sivard, 1985). Led by trends in the developed countries, family and social matters have come increasingly under public regulation, almost always with liberalizing effects of benefit to women. These matters include divorce, family planning, job protection during pregnancy, parental leave, paternal responsibilities, child care and comparability of compensation for male and female workers. In many parts of the world, however, restrictions on women's access to land and other productive resources continue to constitute the greatest legal barrier to their advancement.

Change has generally been slowest in regions where discriminatory practices are deeply embedded in the prevailing culture, often with the sanction of religious and customary law. In Ireland, abortion is forbidden in the constitution, and divorce remains illegal. Much attention has been given to the situation of women in Muslim populations. Traditional Islamic law clearly favours men in many respects. For example, polygyny is allowed, men can divorce their wives without formality and with virtually no penalty and a woman's testimony in court is worth half that of a man (Khalidi and Tucker, 1992). At the same time, however, men and women have identical religious duties and are entitled to the same rewards, and women have absolute rights to their own property. Traditional Islamic law says little about some of the most salient issues in modern life, such as political enfranchisement and access to education, health care and employment (Khalidi and Tucker, 1991), and some progress has been achieved in these areas. Even these modest gains, however, are threatened by the recent rise of extremist movements. Custom and traditional practices also carry much weight in many countries of sub-Saharan Africa (Sivard, 1985). The 1979 Constitution of Zimbabwe forbade discrimination on most grounds but excluded gender because it was thought that this ruling could possibly be in conflict with certain entrenched interests. In Kenya, the constitutional provision on equality does not apply specifically to the inheritance of property.

C. HEALTH AND MORTALITY

General mortality

Expectation of life at birth is probably the most widely used summary measure of health conditions and level of mortality. At the World Population Conference in 1974, the targets set were to achieve an average life expectancy for both sexes combined of 62 years by 1985 and 74 years by the year 2000 in the world as a whole (United Nations, 1989d). At that time, overall life expectancy was about 58 years (table 1). By the late 1980s, it is estimated to have actually reached 64 years. Although progress in reducing mortality thus appears to have proceeded fairly well in line with the initial target, current projections suggest that it is likely to attain only about 68 years by the turn of the century, falling well short of the target for the year 2000.

In most countries and regions, women can expect to live longer than men. The sex differential is large and well documented for the developed countries. The average life expectancy for males in these countries was 70.3 years during the period 1985-1990 (table 1); for females, it was as much as 7.1 years longer, having attained 77.4 years. The sex differential has widened since the early part of the twentieth century as these countries have gone through the transition from high to low mortality (United Nations Secretariat, 1988a).

Detailed data on mortality are less complete and reliable for other parts of the world. In the develop-

TABLE 1. CRUDE DEATH RATE, INFANT MORTALITY RATE AND LIFE EXPECTANCY, THE WORLD AND MAJOR AREAS, MEDIUM VARIANT, 1950-2025

Period	*World*	*More developed regions*	*Less developed regions*	*Africa*	*Latin America and the Caribbean*	*Northern America*	*Asia*	*Europe*	*Oceania*	*USSR*[a]
					A. Crude death rate (per 1,000)					
1950-1955	19.7	10.1	24.3	26.9	15.4	9.4	24.1	11.0	12.4	9.2
1975-1980	11.1	9.4	11.7	17.6	8.6	8.5	10.7	10.4	8.8	10.0
1985-1990	9.8	9.8	9.8	14.7	7.4	8.7	9.0	10.7	8.1	10.6
1995-2000	8.6	9.5	8.4	11.9	6.6	8.8	7.8	10.3	7.9	9.5
2020-2025	7.6	10.6	7.1	7.0	7.0	9.9	7.2	11.5	8.3	9.4
					B. Infant mortality rate (per 1,000 live births)					
1950-1955	155	56	180	188	126	29	181	62	68	73
1975-1980	86	19	97	126	70	14	91	19	35	28
1985-1990	70	15	78	103	54	10	72	13	26	24
1995-2000	57	11	63	85	42	7	56	9	21	17
2020-2025	30	6	33	48	25	5	27	6	11	8
					C. Life expectancy at birth (years) *Both sexes*					
1950-1955	47.5	66.0	42.2	37.7	51.9	69.0	42.0	65.8	60.8	64.1
1975-1980	60.4	72.0	57.4	47.9	63.3	73.3	58.3	72.6	68.2	67.9
1985-1990	63.9	74.0	61.4	52.0	66.7	75.6	62.7	74.4	71.3	70.0
1995-2000	67.0	75.8	65.0	56.1	69.4	77.1	66.5	76.1	73.5	72.5
2020-2025	72.9	79.0	71.6	65.6	73.2	79.8	73.4	79.2	77.9	76.9
					Females					
1950-1955	49.0	68.6	43.1	39.1	53.5	72.0	42.7	68.0	63.0	68.5
1975-1980	62.1	75.6	58.3	49.5	65.8	77.3	58.9	75.8	71.3	73.0
1985-1990	65.9	77.4	62.8	53.6	69.5	79.2	63.9	77.7	74.5	74.2
1995-2000	69.1	79.1	66.6	57.8	72.3	80.4	67.9	79.3	76.5	76.3
2020-2025	75.4	82.1	73.8	67.4	76.3	82.9	75.5	82.2	80.8	80.4
					Males					
1950-1955	46.0	63.3	41.3	36.3	50.4	66.3	41.4	63.6	58.7	60.0
1975-1955	58.6	68.2	56.4	46.3	60.9	69.5	57.7	69.2	65.3	63.0
1985-1990	61.8	70.3	60.1	50.3	64.0	72.1	61.7	71.1	68.4	65.0
1995-2000	64.9	72.4	63.5	54.5	66.6	73.8	65.2	72.9	70.7	68.0
2020-2025	70.5	76.0	69.6	63.7	70.3	76.7	71.4	76.3	75.1	73.2

Source: World Population Prospects, 1990, Population Studies, No. 120 (United Nations publication, Sales No. E.91.XIII.4), table 17.
[a]Former Union of Soviet Socialist Republics.

ing countries, the average life expectancy at birth is estimated to have been 60.1 years for males and 62.8 years for females during the latter half of the 1980s, yielding a sex differential of only 2.7 years. Between the early 1950s and the late 1980s, the average life expectancy at birth for both sexes rose in the less developed regions, from 42 to 61 years. An analysis of 78 national life-tables for the developing countries covering the period 1945-1981 concluded that the sex differential in favour of females increased by about one year for every five-year gain in overall life expectancy (United Nations Secretariat, 1988b).

In most countries, the female advantage in survivorship holds throughout the life-span. In a number of the developing countries, however, death rates are actually higher for women than for men at most ages up to age 50 or 60 (Coale, 1991), resulting in lower female than male life expectancy at birth. Thus, in the developing countries as a whole, the sex differential in early childhood is smaller than in the developed countries. During the period 1985-1990, for example, 984 out of 1,000 girls born alive in the developed countries lived to age 5, compared with 980 boys (United Nations, 1991b). Corresponding estimates for the developing countries are 889 girls compared with 887 boys.

The less advantageous situation of women in the less developed regions, compared with that of their peers in the more developed regions, is due in part to maternal deaths and other biomedical factors that entail greater inherent risks for women than for men. Such causes of death are typically more prominent where mortality remains relatively high. In some countries, however, particularly in Eastern, Southern and Western Asia, cultural factors contribute to female mortality that is higher than would be expected in the light of their respective overall levels of mortality. A number of studies have documented preferential treatment of males with respect to feeding and health care during childhood (Das Gupta, 1989; Muhuri and Preston, 1991). In one example, the incidence of protein deficiency was found to be much higher among girls than among boys, although boys heavily outnumbered girls among those hospitalized for the condition (Lopez, 1984). It has been further observed in several instances that female survival is related to family composition; girls that had older sisters were found to be less likely to survive than those that did not, clearly revealing behavioural causes underlying this phenomenon (Das Gupta, 1989). Traditional attitudes and practices may also increase the mortality risks to adult women. Women are often the first to suffer when food resources are short. A study carried out in Punjab, India found that women were far less likely than men to receive medical care during their terminal illness; and when care was provided, it was of inferior quality to that given to men (Coale, 1991). According to a recent careful review of this issue, there are altogether about 60 million females "missing" from the populations of Bangladesh, China, Egypt, India, Nepal, Pakistan and the region of Western Asia. The estimated deficiency ranges from 2.6 per cent of all women in Egypt to 7.8 per cent in Pakistan (Coale, 1991).

Maternal health and mortality

Maternal mortality has received global attention only since 1987 when the international Safe Motherhood Initiative was launched. The term "maternal mortality" is used to refer to all pregnancy-related deaths. Among the many indicators of public health, maternal mortality currently shows the widest disparities between the developed and the developing countries. Studies on this topic are nevertheless hindered by the lack of reliable statistics for the majority of the developing countries.

Currently, very few women in the developed countries die from pregnancy-related causes. Maternal mortality ratios have dropped impressively over the past 50 years, reaching levels of 10 or fewer deaths per 100,000 births in most of these countries (United Nations, 1992). Improvements in obstetric and prenatal care, introduction of antibiotics and blood transfusion, increasing proportions of deliveries taking place in hospitals, better general health and nutritional status of pregnant women, adoption of effective means of contraception and provision of safe abortion have all contributed to the decline.

In contrast, in the less developed regions maternal mortality undoubtedly remains high. Of the 509,000 female deaths due to pregnancy-related causes estimated to have occurred annually around 1988, as many as 99 per cent took place in the developing countries (table 2). The 1988 ratio of 420 maternal deaths per 100,000 live births in the less developed regions nevertheless represented a drop of about 7 per cent from a level of 450 in 1983 (WHO, 1991b). The level varies substantially by region from over 700 deaths per 100,000 live births in 1988 in Middle Africa and Western Africa to below 200 in Central America and Eastern Asia. The main causes of maternal death are haemorrhage, anaemia, infection, toxaemia, obstructed labour and delivery, and unsafe abortion. Studies in all the less developed regions show that deaths resulting from complications of unsafe abortion contribute substantially to maternal

TABLE 2. WORLD HEALTH ORGANIZATION ESTIMATES OF MATERNAL MORTALITY, AROUND 1988

Region	Live births (millions)	Maternal deaths (thousands)	Maternal mortality per 100,000 live births	Maternal mortality per 100,000 women	Lifetime risk	Total fertility
World	137.6	509	370	39	1 in 73	3.4
Developing countries	120.3	505	420	50	1 in 57	3.8
Developed countries[a]	17.3	4	26	1	1 in 1 825	1.9
Africa	26.7	169	630	116	1 in 23	6.1
Eastern Africa	8.8	60	680	138	1 in 20	6.8
Middle Africa	3.0	21	710	135	1 in 20	6.2
Northern Africa	4.9	17	360	53	1 in 52	4.9
Southern Africa	1.3	4	270	35	i in 74	4.6
Western Africa	8.7	66	760	154	1 in 18	6.8
Asia[b]	81.2	310	380	39	1 in 71	3.4
Eastern Asia[b]	24.6	30	120	8	1 in 326	2.3
South-eastern Asia	12.5	42	340	37	1 in 77	3.5
Southern Asia	39.6	224	570	80	1 in 35	4.6
Western Asia	4.4	12	280	41	1 in 67	4.9
Latin America	12.2	25	200	22	1 in 131	3.4
Caribbean	0.8	2	260	24	1 in 122	2.9
Central America	3.5	6	160	19	1 in 150	3.7
South America	8.0	17	220	23	1 in 126	3.3
Northern America	4.0	1	12	1	1 in 4 006	1.8
Europe	6.4	1	23	1	1 in 2 288	1.7
Oceania[c]	0.2	1	600	79	i in 32	4.8
USSR[d]	5.2	2	45	3	1 in 863	2.3

Sources: World Health Orqanization, *Maternal Mortality Ratios and Rates: A Tabulation of Available Information*, 3rd ed. (Geneva, 1991), table 1. Maternal deaths and maternal mortality rates are WHO estimates; number of births in 1988 are United Nations estimates for the period 1985-1990.

NOTE: Figures may not add to totals due to rounding.

[a]Including Japan, Australia and New Zealand.

[b]Excluding Japan.

[c]Excluding Australia and New Zealand.

[d]Former Union of Soviet Socialist Republics.

mortality. Other associated factors include pregnancies at the extremes of the reproductive age span, high parity births, maternal depletion through closely spaced pregnancies, inadequate nutrition, lack of access to health services and shortage of trained birth attendants. The most favourable health outcome is achieved where women have just a few births that are well spaced and occur between their late teens and their mid-thirties.

Ironically, some of the advanced technology that is being made available to ensure better maternal health and birth outcomes in the developing countries may, at the same time, be used to the detriment of females. Ultrasound techniques, which are more and more widely used to monitor foetal health and development, as well as amniocentesis and chorionic villus sampling, which are used to detect serious genetic abnormalities, can also reveal the sex of the foetus. There is indirect evidence that in some societies where there is a strong preference for male offspring (for example, China, India and the Republic of Korea), female foetuses identified in this way have frequently been aborted. For instance, recent statistics indicate a much higher than expected ratio of male to female births, expecially among higher order births, and a sharp rise in the latter ratios during the 1980s in China and the Republic of Korea (Republic of Korea, n.d; China, 1990 and 1991).

Child health and mortality

As mothers, women have a far-reaching influence on the health of their children. The health of newborn infants is affected in many ways by the behaviour of their mothers during pregnancy. Inadequate weight gain is a common problem in the less developed regions, where many women suffer chronically from poor nutrition. In more developed regions, smoking and consumption of drugs and alcohol are matters of concern.

Survival through the first year of life is closely linked with the likelihood and duration of breast-feeding. Numerous studies in developing countries have demonstrated this relationship (Bankole and Olaleye, 1991). Infants that are wholly breast-fed are more likely to survive than those receiving supplementary nutrition. A recent comparative study of 11 countries concluded that, contrary to widespread belief, breast-feeding has not necessarily been declining in the developing world (Sharma and others, 1990). Almost all infants are still breast-fed, although the duration of exclusive breast-feeding tends to be shorter than the recommended period of from four to six months. Other studies indicate that although there have been sharp declines in some countries, such as Thailand, in many others there has been little change since the 1970s.

As the child grows, the mother is typically the primary preparer of food for the household. In the developing countries, women may also be responsible for the water-supply. Mothers often take the primary initiative in the use of well-child services, such as immunizations, and they are likely to be the decision makers concerning care when children are ill. Through these and other activities, women play a major role in hygiene and the health practices of the household (WHO, 1991c).

Unsafe abortion

Abortion occurs in all societies, either as a primary method of fertility control or as a backup to contraception. It carries minimal risk of morbidity and mortality when it is performed early in pregnancy and under modern medical conditions. In most countries where abortion is legal and in a few countries where it is illegal in principle but openly tolerated, virtually all abortions take place in favourable circumstances of this type. On the other hand, abortion is an unsafe procedure when carried out by untrained personnel or without proper sanitation. Such unfavourable circumstances prevail in most countries where abortion is either illegal; or, although legal, is inaccessible to many women.

Since clandestine abortions are, by definition, excluded from national data collection systems, only indirect estimates of the frequency of unsafe abortion can be made, and the figures are necessarily highly uncertain. A 1990 worldwide review of induced abortion suggests that the annual total number of clandestine abortions probably lies somewhere between 10 million and 22 million (Henshaw and Morrow, 1990). Maternal deaths due to abortion are sometimes used as an indicator of the level of illegal abortion, although a variety of other factors, including the poor quality of the data on causes of maternal death, can influence these figures. The annual world total of abortion-related deaths has been estimated to be in the range of 115,000-204,000 (Royston and Armstrong, 1989). Both the number of deaths and the rate per 1,000 women of reproductive age are probably highest in Southern Asia and lowest in Latin America and the Caribbean, with Africa, South-eastern Asia and Oceania, and Western Asia falling in between. In Latin America, where maternal mortality from other causes has declined considerably, complications of illegal abortion are reported to be the leading cause of death among women aged 15-39 (Royston and Armstrong, 1989).

Romania provides a striking example of the link between abortion mortality and the legal status of abortion. Romania is unusual both because of the abrupt changes that have occurred in the abortion law and because the relevant statistics are reasonably reliable. Up to 1966 abortion was legal, and because it was the primary means of fertility control, it was very common; in 1965, the maternal mortality ratio from causes related to abortion was 23 deaths per 100,000 live births (David, 1992). In 1966, most abortions were prohibited, resulting in a dramatic climb in abortion mortality. From 1982 to 1989, the ratio hovered between 118 and 151 deaths per 100,000 births. Immediately after the fall of the Ceausescu Government in December 1989, abortion was once again legalized; and even though the number of births in the denominator of the rate declined dramatically, abortion mortality immediately dropped to 57 deaths per 100,000 live births in 1990.

Contraception

Contraception has important implications for women's health. Its primary effect is unquestionably beneficial in that it avoids the risks associated with pregnancy, frequent childbirth, short birth intervals and giving birth at either extreme of the reproductive age span. Similarly, it reduces the need to resort to unsafe abortion. The extent of such indirect benefits clearly varies according to the effectiveness of the contraceptive method used. Most of the modern medical methods do carry direct risks to health, although for the large majority of women those risks are minor. One challenge for family planning programmes is to enable women that are at higher risk of serious side-effects to avoid methods that are unsuited for them, without unduly restricting access for the majority.

The fact that oral contraceptives and barrier and spermicide methods also provide some direct health benefits is less well known (Harlap, Kost and Farrist, 1991). All too often evaluation of the health implications of particular methods is influenced by myths and false rumours concerning their harmful effects. This occurs both in the developing and the developed countries. The topic of method choice is considered more fully in the section on fertility and family planning.

Female circumcision

The traditional custom of female circumcision affects the health of women in many African countries and also in parts of Asia. The international community first addressed the topic at a WHO Seminar on Traditional Practices Affecting the Health of Women and Children, held at Khartoum in 1979. Concern about the practice has mounted since that time. Considerable evidence relating to the extent and deleterious effects of the practice was presented at a seminar focusing specifically on Africa, which was organized in 1984 by the Ministry of Public Health of the Government of Senegal and the Non-governmental Organization Working Group on Traditional Practices Affecting the Health of Women and Children. In 1987 a call to eradicate the practice of female circumcision by the year 2000 was issued at another regional seminar held at Addis Ababa.

The operation involves genital mutilation, varying from a relatively mild form of clitoridectomy to far more drastic practices of excision and infibulation. The age at which the operation is customarily carried out ranges from early childhood to the time of marriage. Traditional midwives or other personnel without formal qualifications typically perform the operation but, increasingly, it may be carried out in a modern medical setting. Its harmful consequences include both sequelae of the operation itself, which is often done under unsanitary conditions and may involve unintentional damage to the urinary and reproductive systems, and long-term effects on reproduction and other aspects of physical and mental health. It has been noted that circumcised women run an increased risk of human immunodeficiency virus (HIV) infection (Carballo, 1988).

Where female circumcision is common, people often, though wrongly, attribute the practice to the teachings of Islam; it is not mentioned in the Koran (Abo, 1984), and there are many Muslim populations in which it does not occur. A variety of motivations are reported: to preserve virginity and encourage chastity, to reduce women's sexual desire; to promote cleanliness and purity; to increase fertility; to improve women's health; to further women's socialization and training; to make the woman acceptable for marriage; and to increase male sexual pleasure. Some studies suggest that the social pressure to continue the practice comes largely from older women.

Statistics on the prevalence of the practice are scattered and often anecdotal. A WHO estimate in 1984 places the total number of women who have undergone the operation at between 30 million and 74 million (Royston and Armstrong, 1989). In some countries, for example Somalia and the Sudan, virtually all adult women are reported to have been circumcised (Badri, 1984: Ismail, 1984). Although it is currently illegal in some of the countries where it has been most common, there is as yet no evidence of a substantial decline in its prevalence. A strong inverse link with the level of education has been noted, suggesting that as schooling opportunities for women improve, it is likely to be performed less often (Koso, 1987). The possibility that in the future female circumcision may more frequently be done under more sanitary medical conditions also offers some hope of mitigation of its most harmful effects.

Sexually transmitted diseases

Sexually transmitted disease (STD) is an important public health issue for both men and women. The consequences, however, are likely to be greater for women than for men (Fathalla, 1992), in part because such diseases can be asymptomatic in women or the symptoms may not be as obvious as they are in men, so that they remain unobserved. In addition, women run the risk of pelvic inflammatory disease and ectopic pregnancy, and STD is a primary cause of infertility. Some STDs are also transferable to the foetus. Young people are especially vulnerable to STDs because of the breakdown of traditional restraints on adolescent sexual activity, the likelihood of frequent changes of partner, insufficient education and experience, and lack of access to reproductive health services. Again, the burden falls most heavily on females in this age group.

STDs can be conveniently grouped under two major headings (Fathalla, 1992). The first group consists of long-known venereal diseases, such as gonorrhoea, syphilis and chancroid. The second group constitutes a second generation of STDs, including bacterial and viral syndromes, such as chlamydia, genital herpes, human papilloma virus and HIV (see below). In the more developed regions, there has been a substantial decline in the more traditional diseases during the past few decades, but infections of this type remain a serious problem in many developing countries. Diseases of the second type are widespread in all areas of the world. They tend to be difficult to diagnose and can result in chronic problems or even death. Both types of STDs are particularly prevalent in Africa.

Although STDs currently represent the most common group of notifiable diseases in most countries, their incidence is impossible to document with any precision. In 1990, WHO provided the following minimum estimates of the annual numbers of new cases worldwide for some major diseases: gonorrhoea, 25 million; genital chlamydial infections, 50 million; infectious syphilis, 3.5 million; genital herpes, 20 million; and genital human papilloma virus infection, 30 million (Fathalla, 1992).

Acquired immunodeficiency syndrome

Among the sexually transmitted diseases, acquired immunodeficiency syndrome (AIDS) requires special attention, in part because it is a lethal disease and in part because there is typically a long delay between HIV infection, which causes AIDS, and the appearance of active symptoms of the disease itself. This delay results in a substantial period during which a carrier of HIV may transmit it to others.

WHO distinguishes three patterns of HIV infection. In pattern I, which prevails in developed societies, most cases occur among homosexual or bisexual men and among urban intravenous drug users. Heterosexual transmission is infrequent, and there are not many instances of mother-to-infant transmission of the disease. In pattern II, most cases occur among heterosexuals, women are as likely to become infected as men and mother-to-infant transmission is common. This pattern is typical in countries of sub-Saharan Africa and the Caribbean. Pattern III has appeared more recently mainly in Eastern Europe, Northern Africa, the eastern Mediterranean, Asia and countries of the Pacific islands. It tends to affect persons that engage in risk behaviour, including prostitutes and intravenous drug users, and both homosexual and heterosexual transmission has been observed. WHO estimates that by 1989 more than 6 million persons were infected with HIV worldwide. Of these, approximately 2 million were women, including at least 300,000 cases among females in pattern I countries, 1,500,000 in pattern II countries and 33,000 in pattern III countries (United Nations, 1991d).

In Middle African countries, where the incidence of AIDS among women is greatest, several factors appear to contribute to the high rate of HIV infection: early age at sexual initiation; large age differences between spouses; high prevalence of HIV infection among males, which is partially driven in turn by the frequency of extramarital contacts; economic and social pressures that propel women into informal and shifting sexual relationships; and norms concerning remarriage of widows and their sexual activity, for example, the practice of levirate (Palloni and Lee, 1992). Moreover, inequalities in status between men and women inhibit women from acting in their own defence, for instance, by insisting on safe sex practices (United Nations Secretariat, 1990).

The rise in adult mortality due to AIDS can be expected to increase orphanhood and widowhood and to disrupt traditional co-residence patterns. Equally important, HIV carriers may well experience seriously deteriorating health and productivity over an extended period before they become acutely ill. Although all members of society will undoubtedly suffer in this process, the greatest burden is likely to fall on females of all ages (Palloni and Lee, 1992).

D. Fertility and family planning

Levels and trends in fertility

During the late 1980s, approximately 120.7 million births were added to the global population each year (table 3). This total represented just over 27 births per 1,000 people in the world as a whole (table 4). The total fertility rate (TFR) was estimated at that time to be 3.4 births per woman. Hence, fertility remained well above replacement level, which requires an average of about 2.1 births per woman under conditions of low mortality.

Table 3. Estimated average annual number of births and percentage change, major areas, 1975-1980 and 1985-1990[a]

	1975-1980		*1985-1990*		
Major areas	*Number of births*	*Percentage*	*Number of births*	*Percentage*	*Percentage change*
World	120 701	100.0	137 639	100.0	+14.0
Africa	20 518	17.0	26 683	19.4	+30.1
Asia	73 244	60.7	82 564	60.0	+12.7
Europe	6 894	5.7	6 385	4.6	-7.4
Latin America and the Caribbean	11 131	9.2	12 247	8.9	+10.0
Northern America	3 705	3.1	4 052	2.9	+9.4
Oceania	460	0.4	495	0.4	+7.6
USSR[b]	4 745	3.9	5 207	3.8	+9.7

Source: World Population Prospects, 1990, Population Studies, No. 120 (United Nations publication, Sales No. E. 91.XIII.4).

[a]Mediumn variant.

[b]Former Union of Soviet Socialist Republics.

The worldwide TFR of 3.4 during the period 1985-1990 nevertheless represented a decrease of about one third from a level of 5.0 in the early 1950s (table 4). Although the initial level of fertility differed strikingly between the more developed and the less developed regions, the percentage decline during the four-decade interval was nearly the same in both cases: 33 per cent, from TFR of 2.8 to 1.9, for the more developed regions; 36 per cent, from 6.2 to 3.9, for the less developed regions. There was appreciable variation, however, within these two major groupings. Among the less developed regions, TFR dropped by only 6 per cent in Africa, while it fell by as much as 40 per cent in Latin America and the Caribbean.

The pace of the decline had been more rapid in most areas of the world up to around the period 1970-1975, when it began to slacken. The decelerating trend has continued; the overall drop in TFR between the early and the late 1980s was considerably smaller

TABLE 4. CRUDE BIRTH RATE AND TOTAL FERTILITY RATE, THE WORLD AND MAJOR AREAS, MEDIUM VARIANT, 1950-2025

Period	*World*	*More developed regions*	*Less developed regions*	*Africa*	*Latin America and the Caribbean*	*Northern America*	*Asia*	*Europe*	*Oceania*	*USSR*[a]
					A. Crude birth rate (per 1,000)					
1950-1955 ...	37.4	22.6	44.6	49.2	42.5	24.6	42.9	19.8	27.6	26.3
1975-1980 ...	28.3	15.6	32.8	46.1	32.4	15.1	29.7	14.4	20.9	18.3
1985-1990 ...	27.1	14.5	31.0	44.7	28.7	15.0	27.8	12.9	19.4	18.4
1995-2000 ...	24.9	13.4	27.9	41.6	24.8	13.1	24.7	12.4	17.9	15.9
2020-2025 ...	17.5	11.9	18.6	26.0	18.4	11.7	16.1	10.9	14.0	14.1
					B. Total fertility rate (births per woman)					
1950-1955 ...	5.00	2.84	6.19	6.65	5.87	3.47	5.92	2.59	3.83	2.82
1975-1980 ...	3.84	2.03	4.54	6.54	4.36	1.91	4.06	1.98	2.79	2.34
1985-1990 ...	3.45	1.89	3.94	6.24	3.55	1.81	3.48	1.72	2.51	2.38
1995-2000 ...	3.14	1.90	3.47	5.70	3.00	1.86	3.02	1.74	2.34	2.25
2020-2025 ...	2.27	1.94	2.32	3.04	2.39	1.94	2.06	1.85	2.02	2.10

Source: *World Population Prospects, 1990*, Population Studies, No. 120 (United Nations publication, Sales No. E.91.XIII.4), table 16.
[a]Former Union of Soviet Socialist Republics.

than that between the latter 1970s and the early 1980s (Freedman and Blanc, 1991; United Nations, 1992). This deceleration is of particular concern in relation to the less developed regions, where TFR fell by only 6 per cent in the later time period, compared with 8 per cent in the earlier period.

Again, the pace and in this case even the direction of the trend during the 1980s varied within the developing world (United Nations, 1992). Much of the slow-down in the rate of decline can be accounted for by Eastern Asia, a region that is heavily dominated by the enormous population of China. Although TFR there had been much lower than in the other less developed regions (2.3 in 1980-1985 compared with 4.5 for all the less developed regions), it rose by 2 per cent during the period 1985-1990. On the other hand, the decline actually gathered momentum between the two periods in Northern Africa, increasing from 6 to 10 per cent, and in Central America, fertility dropped by as much as 12 per cent in both periods.

The transition to fertility levels at or near replacement level is a fundamental component of modernization. Currently, fertility levels near (and in some cases below) replacement level prevail in most of Europe, Northern America, most of Oceania and large parts of the Confederation of Independent States (which includes many of the former republics of the USSR). In some developed countries, reproduction has actually fallen to levels well below that needed to replace the population in the long run. TFR as low as 1.5 were first observed in Northern and Western Europe but have recently become common in Southern Europe as well. In Sweden, and possibly France, policy measures to promote child-bearing appear to be having some success in reversing the decline.

The fertility transition is well under way in Latin America and the Caribbean and in large parts of Asia; the principal exception is Western Asia, where traditional fertility levels persist in many countries. Africa is the major area where there has been the least change, although significant declines have occurred in Northern and Southern Africa. Very recently, the beginnings of fertility decline have been observed in Botswana, Kenya and Zimbabwe.

The potential for fertility decline in a population can be estimated by evaluating family size preferences and the extent of unwanted child-bearing. The questionnaires used in both the World Fertility Survey (WFS) programme and the Demographic and Health Surveys (DHS) provide information on these topics. Desired family size is usually lower than actual family size, and in most countries where comparisons over time are possible, desired family size has declined. In 15 developing countries where trends could be compared, the percentage of married fecund women that currently wanted no more children rose by an average of 10 percentage points between the late 1970s and late 1980s; the average number of children desired declined by an average of 20 per cent (Westoff, 1991). Moreover, the proportion of unwanted births appears to rise in the early stages of the fertility transition, as women's preferences change more rapidly than their actual behaviour, and then to decline in the later stages of the transition when their ability to control reproduction catches up with their desire for fewer children (Bongaarts, 1990). Even though contraceptive use has grown rapidly in many countries, on average nearly one fourth of the married women in 25 developing countries surveyed in the late 1980s had an unmet need for family planning (Westoff and Ochoa, 1991).

Nuptiality

Formal marriage is well documented in the statistics of most countries, both as an event and as a status. In many parts of the world, it serves as a satisfactory indicator of exposure to the risk of child-bearing. Important exceptions to this rule include such traditional practices as consensual and visiting unions in Latin America and the Caribbean and polygyny in many parts of Africa. In addition, especially in developed societies, sexual activity is increasing among both young single women that have never been married and women that have previously been married. For practical purposes, contemporary studies usually focus on participation in any type of sexual union that is reported in a census or survey; nuptiality is treated in this way here.

For at least several centuries, Western European societies (including Northern and Western Europe and European overseas populations in Northern America and Oceania) were characterized by late entry into motherhood, due to a relatively long interval between puberty and marriage. The average age at first marriage was typically 24 or more years for women (United Nations, 1990). Moreover, substantial proportions of women never married at all. The level of fertility was consequently much lower than it might potentially have been.

Around the middle of the twentieth century, the average age at marriage declined in most Western countries; and marriage for women became more nearly universal, reducing its restraining effect on fertility. The decrease in fertility noted above was nevertheless possible because of the widespread adoption of fertility control practices. Recently, a number of countries have experienced a renewed trend towards later formal marriage. The dampening effect that this might have had on fertility has been largely counterbalanced by the accompanying increase in sexual activity among single women and the spread of informal types of sexual union. The situation in Eastern Europe is generally similar, except that women historically married earlier and therefore tended both to begin child-bearing earlier and to have more children.

Elsewhere in the world, marriage traditionally took place at an early age, often at or even before puberty. Moreover, virtually all women married. Thus, as these societies entered the process of development, marriage imposed minimal restraint on fertility, and most women bore many children. This pattern had a profound impact on a woman's life. The negative health consequences of very early, late and frequent child-bearing have been noted above. Opportunities for education and economic activity were also curtailed. Dependence upon male members of the household tended to be the rule, especially if the woman's husband was considerably older than she, as is typically the case in many such societies.

A variety of nuptiality patterns has recently emerged in the less developed regions (United Nations, 1990). Africa, especially sub-Saharan Africa, remains a stronghold of traditional behaviour. Virtually all women marry, frequently during adolescence, and they tend to be much younger than their husbands; marriage is seen as primarily a family rather than an individual arrangement. Marriage dissolution and remarriage are common. In Latin America and the

Caribbean, the correspondence between the picture presented in the available statistics and the reality of union formation is particularly uncertain, owing to the frequency of non-legalized conjugal arrangements that may or may not be reported as unions. The data suggest that women now enter marriage at a somewhat older age than in other less developed regions, and the incidence of permanent celibacy is comparatively high. In Asia, almost all women still marry and legal union remains the predominant norm. Female age at marriage now differs considerably within this major area. In accompaniment with modernization and urbanization, women have tended to marry later. By the 1980s age at marriage was as high as 25-26 years in the most industrialized countries or areas of Eastern Asia. In many countries of South-eastern Asia and some parts of Western Asia, it has risen to 21-23 years. Elsewhere, however, particularly in Southern Asia, very early marriage tends to persist.

Adolescent fertility

It used to be common in many of the currently less developed parts of the world for girls to marry and bear children during adolescence. Where entry into marriage has been postponed to a later age, adolescent child-bearing is currently less common. Child-bearing outside of any stable or socially recognized union has increased among very young women, however, in both the more developed and the less developed regions. Very early child-bearing involves health risks regardless of the marital status of the mother. It interferes, moreover, with a woman's development as an individual in her own right. When it occurs without the social and economic support of a recognized union, the dimensions of the problem are further enlarged. International concern surrounding this issue has increased in recent decades. Since statistics are rarely available for age groups smaller than five years, investigations have generally included all women aged 15-19. The primary focus of attention, however, is on women under age 18; and where data are available, especially on women under age 15.

In the developed countries, fertility rates for age group 15-19 around 1985 ranged from 4 per 1,000 women in Japan to 78 per 1,000 women in Bulgaria (United Nations 1988a). In general, the rates in those regions had been declining since around 1970 or earlier. Differences in recent estimates of fertility rates for women aged 15-19 tend to be larger among the developing countries. There is greater variation in Africa and Asia, however, than in Latin America and the Caribbean. For Africa, the range runs from 37 per 1,000 women in Mauritius to 216 in Côte d'Ivoire; for Asia, from 7 per 1,000 women in the Republic of Korea to 239 in Bangladesh; for Latin America and the Caribbean, from 49 per 1,000 women in Martinique to 138 in Honduras (United Nations, 1989a). Trends in adolescent fertility in the developing countries are varied, but where age at marriage has risen, as in large parts of Asia, declines in adolescent fertility rates have generally been observed.

Maternal mortality is typically higher among teenagers than among somewhat older women. In some individual countries, including Bangladesh, Ethiopia and Indonesia, the incidence of deaths among women aged 15-19 is about twice as high as for women in the primary child-bearing ages as a whole (20-34 years) (United Nations, 1992). Where data are available to make the comparison, the risks for female aged 10-14 have been found to be much greater than for those aged 15-19 (United Nations, 1989a). Women under age 20 also suffer far more often than adults from injuries and other negative health consequences of childbirth, such as vesicovaginal fistula. In the developed countries that compile statistics on abortion, a high proportion of teenage pregnancies are terminated this way, with minimal threat to the woman's health. Very little is known about the likelihood of pregnant teenagers obtaining an abortion in the developing countries. Where abortion takes place under unsafe conditions, however, the health risks for young women are likely to be even higher than for older women. In addition to the health consequences for the woman herself, the offspring of teenagers typically suffer from higher levels of infant and child mortality (United Nations, 1989a).

Non-marital pregnancy among teenagers is at least partially a product of the recent rise in sexual activity before marriage. Internationally comparable statistics on sexual activity are scarce, however. The information that is available for the 1980s clearly indicates that by the time they are age 18, substantial proportions of unmarried women in both the developed and the developing countries have experienced sexual intercourse (United Nations, 1988a and 1989a).

Contraception

Voluntary control of conception emerged as one of the principal proximate determinants of fertility in most of the developed countries towards the end of the nineteenth century or early in the twentieth century. In the 1960s, new, highly effective methods of contraception were introduced, which brought about a revolution in fertility control in the developed countries and greatly facilitated the spread of contraceptive technology in the developing world.

Contraceptive use is usually evaluated in terms of overall prevalence, or the proportion of women (or married women) of child-bearing age using any contraceptive method, and the proportions using specific methods or groups of methods. For the most part, these data are collected in national-level fertility surveys that currently cover a large part of the developing world as well as most developed countries. Possible problems of data quality and of intercountry comparability must always be kept in mind, however, in interpreting the results.

By the late 1980s, an estimated 53 per cent of couples throughout the world were using contraception (table 5). In the more developed regions and in the less developed regions, the proportions were 71 and 48 per cent, respectively. The prevalence level varied substantially among the less developed regions. Use of any method remains relatively low in Africa (17 per cent of all couples), especially in sub-Saharan Africa (13 per cent). In China, on the other hand, it has reached 72 per cent, the same level as in the developed countries. Although the trend in contraceptive prevalence had been continuously upward, the pace of change appears to have slowed recently in a number of countries (Weinberger, 1991). Nevertheless, by 1991 overall prevalence in the less developed regions may well have surpassed 50 per cent (Weinberger, 1991).

The data for the late 1980s indicate that 47 per cent of all couples in the developed countries and 44 per cent of those in the developing countries were using a modern method, i.e., male or female sterilization, pill, injection, intra-uterine device (IUD) or barrier methods, including condoms. Thus, among users of any method, dependence upon modern methods was actually higher in the less developed than in the more developed regions. The female partner in 16 per cent of all couples worldwide had been surgically sterilized, as had 4 per cent of male partners. Pill use represented 7 per cent and IUD 11 per cent of all couples worldwide; pills were used more frequently than IUD in the more developed regions, however, while IUD was more common in the less developed regions. Condoms and withdrawal, which is one of the less effective methods, are used far more in the developed countries than in the developing world.

The latter two methods represent the principal currently available male methods. Lack of choice of effective male methods may be one of the reasons for the failure thus far to involve men very much in family planning (Ono Osaki, 1992). Condoms nevertheless have the unique advantage of offering considerable protection against STDs, including AIDS, as well as pregnancy, and their use is being widely promoted for this reason.

The 1984 recommendations for further implementation of the World Population Plan of Action state that all couples have a basic right to "the information, education and means" necessary to decide on the number and spacing of births (recommendation 30). The growing use of contraception is at least in part a reflection of rapidly expanding access to these services. Variation in prevalence both among and within countries is often due to differences in service availability. On a scale of 0-100, the average availability score as of 1989 was 28 for the developing countries in Africa (40 countries), 68 in Latin America and the Caribbean (20 countries) and 48 in Asia (29 countries) (table 6). In general, contraceptive availability has been increasing rapidly;

TABLE 5. AVERAGE PREVALENCE OF SPECIFIC CONTRACEPTIVE METHODS, BY MAJOR AREA AND REGION, AROUND 1987[a]

Major area and region	All methods (1)	Modern methods[b] (2)	Sterilization: Female (3)	Sterilization: Male (4)	Pill (5)	Injectables (6)	Intra-uterine device (7)	Condom (8)	Vaginal barrier methods (9)	Rhythm (10)	Withdrawal (11)	Other methods (12)
A. Percentage of couples with the wife of reproductive ages												
World	53	44	16	4	7	1	11	5	1	4	4	1
More developed regions[c]	71	47	8	4	14	–	6	13	2	9	13	2
Less developed regions	48	44	18	5	5	1	12	3	0.3	2	1	1
China	72	71	28	8	3	0.2	30	2	0.3	0.5	–	0.3
Other countries	38	32	14	3	6	1	4	3	0.3	3	2	1
Africa	17	13	1	–	7	1	3	1	0.2	2	1	1
Northern Africa	31	27	2	–	16	0.3	8	1	0.3	2	2	1
Sub-Saharan Africa	13	9	1	–	4	2	1	0.5	0.2	2	1	1
Asia and Oceania[d]	53	49	21	6	4	1	14	3	0.3	2	1	1
Eastern Asia	72	71	28	8	3	0.2	29	2	0.4	1	0.2	0.3
Other countries	40	34	16	5	4	1	4	4	0.3	2	2	2
Latin America and the Caribbean	57	47	20	1	16	1	6	2	1	5	3	1
B. Percentage of contraceptive users												
World	100	83	29	8	14	2	20	9	1	7	8	2
More developed regions[c]	100	66	11	6	20	–	8	18	3	13	19	2
Less developed regions	100	91	37	9	11	2	25	5	1	4	3	2
China	100	99	38	11	5	0.3	41	3	0.4	1	–	0.4
Other countries	100	84	36	8	16	4	12	8	1	7	5	4
Africa	100	79	9	–	40	8	18	4	1	9	5	6
Northern Africa	100	88	6	–	51	1	25	4	1	5	5	2
Sub-Saharan Africa	100	70	11	0.1	28	16	10	4	1	13	6	11
Asia and Oceania[d]	100	92	39	11	7	2	27	6	1	3	2	2
Eastern Asia[d]	100	98	39	11	5	0.3	40	3	1	1	0.2	0.4
Other countries	100	85	39	11	11	4	11	9	1	6	5	4
Latin America and the Caribbean	100	84	36	1	28	2	11	4	1	9	6	2

Source: Mary Beth Weinberger, "Recent trends in contraceptive behaviour", in *Demographic and Health Surveys World Conference, August 5-7, 1991, Washington, D.C., Proceedings,* vol. I (Columbia, Maryland, IRD/Macro International, Inc. 1991).

NOTE: These estimates reflect assumptions about contraceptive use in countries with no data.

[a]Based on most recent available survey data; average date, 1987.

[b]Including methods in columns (3)-(9).

[c]Australia-New Zealand, Europe, Northern America and Japan.

[d]Excluding Japan.

between 1982 and 1989, the average score for all the developing countries rose from 30 to 43. Much of the intercountry variation in method use can also be attributed to differences in the content of the services provided. Even in the developed countries, institutional obstacles, such as restrictive laws or

TABLE 6. AVAILABILITY OF FAMILY PLANNING SERVICES, BY MAJOR AREA AND REGION, 1980 AND 1989

Major area and region	*Number of countries*	*Availability score percentage of maximum*[a]		*Percentage of the population with easy access*[a] *to:* *Sterilization* *Female*		*Male*		*Intra-uterine device*		*Pill*		*Condom*		*Abortion*	
		1982	*1989*	*1982*	*1989*	*1982*	*1989*	*1982*	*1989*	*1982*	*1989*	*1982*	*1989*	*1982*	*1989*
						A. Countries weighted equally									
All developing countries	90	30	43	24	34	15	21	24	38	32	49	33	49	19	26
Africa	40	12	28	6	15	1	7	11	26	16	36	16	37	8	15
Northern Africa	6	25	36	14	23	0	0	25	44	33	51	30	38	18	27
Other Africa	34	10	26	4	14	1	8	8	23	13	33	14	37	6	12
Asia	29	38	48	33	41	25	34	30	44	37	49	39	46	27	29
Western Asia	11	13	30	8	18	1	12	9	35	17	40	13	31	15	10
Other Asia	18	54	60	48	56	39	48	43	50	49	55	55	56	34	40
Excluding China	17	51	57	46	54	36	45	40	48	49	53	53	53	31	37
Latin America and the Caribbean	20	53	68	47	60	28	32	42	55	57	77	56	78	30	44
						B. Countries weighted by population size									
All developing countries	90	60	72	56	65	51	57	49	62	42	69	60	70	44	50
Africa	40	13	27	5	13	1	3	11	27	17	38	17	39	10	15
Northern Africa	6	25	41	7	24	0	0	28	53	38	62	32	47	6	22
Other Africa	34	9	23	4	9	1	4	6	19	11	31	12	36	8	13
Asia	29	69	83	66	76	66	73	58	72	44	73	69	75	51	59
Western Asia	11	11	44	12	27	0	21	9	44	17	51	15	50	11	18
Other Asia	18	73	85	70	80	70	76	61	74	46	75	72	77	54	61
Excluding China	17	57	75	56	72	56	67	41	63	36	64	60	68	29	41
Latin America and the Caribbean	20	57	72	56	70	21	32	39	47	65	86	61	87	40	50

Sources: Tabulated by the Population Division of the Department of Economic and Social Development of the United Nations Secretariat from family planning availability scores in Robert Sendek and Yvette Bayoumy, Population Council Databank (version 3.0), based on country-specific estimates by Robert J. Lapham and W. Parker Mauldin for 1982 and W. Parker Mauldin and John A. Ross for 1989.

NOTES: Data for countries with estimates available at both dates. These countries contain 97 per cent of the population of developing countries.

[a]The availability score represents the sum of the scores for the specific methods. The maximum possible score is achieved if all six of the specific family planning methods shown were judged to be easily available to at least 80 per cent of the population.

[b]The percentage availability was scored on a scale ranging from 0 per cent to 80+ per cent. For countries assigned the maximum score for a particular method, it has been assumed that 90 per cent of the population had easy access to the method.

inaccessible services, often reduce contraceptive options.

In a low-fertility society, there are typically 25 or more years of a woman's reproductive life during which she is sexually active but does not want to become pregnant. As yet, however, no contraceptive is available that is highly effective and has no major drawbacks. (For a discussion of these issues, see WHO, 1991a) Hence, during a very extended period, most women face a continual choice of the lesser among evils: contraceptive methods that pose relatively little threat to health but provide inadequate protection against pregnancy; means of preventing pregnancy that are reasonably effective but carry some risk to their health; or permanent loss of the ability to bear children. The practical drawbacks of each method must also be considered; these may include expense of the product or procedure, travel to an outlet, need for frequent resupply, remembering everyday, messiness or the necessity of her partner's cooperation.

Thus, a need remains for new and improved contraceptives. One of the more disappointing trends over the past decade has been the stagnation in funding for development of new contraceptives (Lincoln and Kaeser, 1987; Mastroianni, Donaldson and Kane, 1990).

E. Education and training

Gender differences in educational attainment

National educational systems typically include three stages—the primary, secondary and tertiary levels of schooling. The operationalization of this general concept nevertheless varies greatly from one country to another, hampering both comparisons among countries and summarization across countries. Most of the data used here focus on three age groups of potential students that can be identified relatively easily in national population statistics and correspond roughly to the successive levels of education. Ages 6-11 represent the primary years, ages 12-17 represent secondary school and ages 18-23 cover the usual span of higher education. Until recently, women have universally been underrepresented at all levels of education, and especially so at the secondary and higher levels; this situation still prevails in most developing countries.

In 1990, just over half of the world youth aged 6-23 were enrolled in school (table 7). The proportion was 56 per cent for males, while for females it was only 48 per cent. The enrolment ratios for both sexes had risen considerably since 1960, with most of the improvement taking place during the first half of the 30-year period. The overall gains had been larger for females than for males, and the gender disparity had declined by over one third. Within the overall group aged 6-23, the proportions in school are highest at the primary ages and drop sharply for both sexes as age increases. Although the disparity between males and females shrinks in absolute terms as age rises, the relative disadvantage of women grows.

In the developed countries, almost three fourths of both the female population and the male population aged 6-23 were enrolled in school in 1990. The male advantage that had characterized the two older age groups in 1960 had disappeared, and virtually no gender difference in enrolment remained for any age group. For both sexes, the proportion of persons in school exceeded 9 out of 10 at ages 6-11, declined to just under nine out of 10 at ages 12-17 and then fell to just below 4 out of 10 at ages 18-23.

In the developing countries, however, the contrast by gender is still marked . In 1990, 43 per cent of females aged 6-23 were enrolled in school, compared with 52 per cent for males. Although the level for females had jumped sharply from only 26 per cent in 1960, it was not much higher in 1990 than the 1960 level for males (40 per cent). Given the rapid growth of the actual population in those age groups, the increasing proportion of females in school nevertheless represents a remarkable achievement. Among major areas of the developing world, the 1990 enrolment ratios for females aged 6-23 ranged from 32 per cent in Africa (excluding the Arab States), to 42 in Asia (excluding the Arab States), 46 in the Arab States and 63 in Latin America and the Caribbean. The female disadvantage is large and about equal in Africa and Asia, while it is almost non-existent in Latin America and the Caribbean. During the 1980s, worrisome indications of substantial declines in enrolment ratios, for both males and females, began to appear in some African countries (Kenya, Madagascar, Mozambique, Sierra Leone, Somalia, the United Republic of Tanzania and Zaire) (UNESCO, 1992). This development probably reflects the economic and political crises that have overtaken many parts of Africa.

The effects of women's lack of access to education in the developing countries in the past can be appreciated in terms of the proportions of current adult female populations that are illiterate. Recent estimates indicate that in Latin America and the Caribbean more than 20 per cent of women aged 25 or over remain illiterate (United Nations, 1991d). This fraction is over 40 per cent in Eastern and South-eastern Asia, and it is as high as 70 per cent in sub-Saharan Africa, Southern Asia and Western Asia.

TABLE 7. ESTIMATED ENROLMENT RATIOS, BY AGE GROUP AND SEX, THE WORLD, MAJOR AREAS AND COUNTRY GROUPS, 1960-1990

Major area and country group	Year	*Age group* 6-11 years Male/female (1)	6-11 years Male (2)	6-11 years Female (3)	12-17 years Male/female (4)	12-17 years Male (5)	12-17 years Female (6)	18-23 years Male/female (7)	18-23 years Male (8)	18-23 years Female (9)	6-23 years Male/female (10)	6-23 years Male (11)	6-23 years Female (12)
World total	1960	59.1	65.8	52.0	44.4	50.9	37.7	9.7	12.0	7.3	40.5	46.0	34.8
	1970	65.4	70.6	60.0	45.7	50.6	40.5	14.8	17.5	12.0	44.6	49.0	40.0
	1975	70.7	76.2	64.9	51.3	56.0	46.3	17.7	20.9	14.4	48.9	53.6	44.1
	1980	73.5	79.1	67.7	50.6	55.2	45.7	19.2	22.1	16.2	49.9	54.4	45.3
	1985	77.1	82.4	71.6	51.3	56.1	46.2	18.2	20.6	15.6	50.1	54.3	45.6
	1990	78.9	83.5	74.1	54.4	59.1	49.5	20.1	22.7	17.4	52.0	55.9	47.8
Africa	1960	31.6	39.6	23.7	17.0	23.1	11.0	1.9	3.0	0.8	18.8	24.3	13.3
	1970	40.6	47.8	33.3	25.6	32.7	18.4	4.2	6.2	2.1	26.0	32.0	20.1
	1975	48.6	55.6	41.5	31.8	39.2	24.3	6.1	8.8	3.4	31.7	37.8	25.6
	1980	60.0	66.9	53.0	42.3	50.8	33.9	8.8	12.4	5.3	40.4	47.0	33.8
	1985	57.9	63.6	52.1	44.7	53.2	36.0	10.6	14.7	6.5	41.0	47.3	34.7
	1990	56.1	60.7	51.4	42.3	48.3	36.2	10.7	13.8	7.6	39.5	44.2	34.8
Americas	1960	75.3	75.5	75.0	61.0	64.2	57.8	15.7	17.8	13.7	54.9	56.6	53.1
	1970	81.6	81.4	81.7	66.3	68.3	64.1	27.6	30.9	24.3	61.2	62.9	59.6
	1975	83.8	83.9	83.6	72.0	73.3	70.7	31.6	35.2	27.9	64.2	65.8	62.5
	1980	86.4	86.6	86.2	72.1	72.6	71.5	33.6	34.1	33.1	64.8	65.3	64.3
	1985	88.0	88.3	87.8	75.7	76.5	74.9	34.3	34.2	34.5	66.6	66.9	66.2
	1990	90.3	90.5	90.0	78.9	79.7	78.1	38.7	38.3	39.1	70.3	70.6	70.0
Asia	1960	52.2	62.2	41.7	40.7	49.2	31.7	8.6	11.1	6.0	36.6	44.0	28.7
	1970	60.4	67.7	52.7	37.5	43.6	31.0	11.1	13.9	8.1	39.2	44.9	33.1
	1975	68.2	75.6	60.4	43.8	50.1	37.1	14.3	18.0	10.3	45.1	51.1	38.7
	1980	70.6	77.9	62.8	41.9	47.9	35.6	15.8	19.7	11.6	45.6	51.5	39.3
	1985	77.2	84.4	69.9	42.3	48.1	36.2	13.8	17.1	10.3	45.5	51.0	39.7
	1990	80.8	87.2	74.1	46.6	52.8	40.2	15.9	19.4	12.1	48.0	53.2	42.4
Europe[a]	1960	86.8	86.8	86.8	60.1	62.5	57.7	12.9	15.5	10.2	54.7	56.5	52.9
	1970	89.2	89.0	89.4	70.1	71.6	68.5	22.9	25.1	20.6	62.3	63.5	61.0
	1975	89.7	89.6	89.7	74.8	75.3	74.3	25.3	26.6	24.0	63.4	64.1	62.7
	1980	90.3	90.3	90.3	76.5	75.9	77.3	25.8	26.4	25.3	63.4	63.4	63.4
	1985	89.3	89.2	89.4	80.1	80.7	79.5	27.8	27.8	27.9	64.8	65.0	64.6
	1990	89.3	89.2	89.3	83.9	84.3	83.5	32.2	32.5	31.9	68.1	68.3	67.9
Oceania	1960	88.9	89.2	88.7	60.6	63.1	58.1	8.5	11.9	4.8	57.8	59.6	56.0
	1970	94.7	96.1	93.2	71.2	73.6	68.6	12.4	16.0	8.6	61.9	64.3	59.4
	1975	95.1	96.8	93.2	74.4	75.4	73.4	17.7	21.3	13.9	64.3	66.4	62.0
	1980	97.8	99.0	96.6	71.5	71.1	71.8	19.0	21.0	17.0	64.0	64.9	63.0
	1985	96.4	97.5	95.3	75.6	75.5	75.8	20.9	21.9	19.9	64.4	64.9	63.8
	1990	98.1	99.4	96.7	75.7	75.4	76.0	24.0	24.4	23.5	65.5	66.6	64.9
Developed countries ...	1960	91.1	91.1	91.2	69.3	71.9	66.7	15.1	18.0	12.2	61.0	62.9	59.1
	1970	92.4	92.2	92.6	76.1	77.4	74.9	27.2	30.5	23.8	66.4	67.9	64.9
	1975	92.6	92.5	92.8	80.7	80.9	80.6	30.0	32.9	27.0	67.9	69.0	66.8
	1980	92.2	92.0	92.4	81.0	80.3	81.8	30.8	31.6	29.9	67.2	67.3	67.2
	1985	91.2	91.0	91.5	85.6	85.9	85.4	32.8	32.9	32.7	69.0	69.1	68.9
	1990	91.5	91.4	91.7	88.3	88.5	88.1	37.9	38.4	37.4	72.2	72.4	72.0

TABLE 7 (*continued*)

Major area and country group	Year	6-11 years Male/female (1)	6-11 years Male (2)	6-11 years Female (3)	12-17 years Male/female (4)	12-17 years Male (5)	12-17 years Female (6)	18-23 years Male/female (7)	18-23 years Male (8)	18-23 years Female (9)	6-23 years Male/female (10)	6-23 years Male (11)	6-23 years Female (12)
Developing countries ..	1960	48.1	57.3	38.6	35.1	43.1	26.7	7.5	9.6	5.2	32.9	39.7	25.7
	1970	57.8	64.5	50.8	35.8	41.9	29.4	10.1	12.7	7.5	37.6	43.0	32.0
	1975	65.5	72.4	58.4	42.5	48.7	36.0	13.6	16.9	10.1	43.6	49.2	37.6
	1980	69.6	76.3	62.5	43.0	48.9	36.8	15.6	19.1	11.9	45.6	51.2	39.7
	1985	74.2	80.7	67.5	43.8	49.6	37.7	14.3	17.4	11.1	45.8	51.0	40.3
	1990	76.5	82.0	70.6	47.3	52.9	41.5	16.1	19.2	12.9	47.7	52.5	42.8
Africa excluding 5 Arab States	1960	28.9	36.0	21.9	17.1	22.9	11.3	1.4	2.2	0.6	17.5	22.5	12.6
	1970	37.0	43.0	31.1	25.1	31.3	18.9	2.9	4.4	1.5	24.0	28.9	19.2
	1975	45.1	50.7	39.6	31.4	38.2	24.6	4.0	5.9	2.1	29.7	34.8	24.7
	1980	58.5	64.5	52.5	42.9	51.1	34.9	6.4	9.2	3.6	39.6	45.5	33.7
	1985	54.6	59.6	49.5	44.0	52.5	35.5	7.6	11.2	4.1	38.8	44.7	33.0
	1990	51.7	55.4	47.9	40.2	45.8	34.5	7.3	9.8	4.9	36.3	40.3	32.2
Asia excluding 5 Arab States	1960	52.5	62.4	42.0	41.0	49.5	32.0	8.7	11.1	6.0	36.8	44.2	29.0
	1970	60.6	67.8	53.0	37.6	43.6	31.2	11.1	13.9	8.2	39.3	44.9	33.3
	1975	68.3	75.5	60.6	43.9	50.0	37.3	14.2	18.0	10.3	45.1	51.0	38.8
	1980	70.5	77.7	62.8	41.8	47.7	35.5	15.8	19.7	11.6	45.5	51.3	39.2
	1985	77.2	84.4	69.6	42.1	47.7	36.0	13.7	17.0	10.2	45.3	50.8	39.5
	1990	80.8	87.1	74.1	46.3	52.3	40.0	15.7	19.2	12.0	47.7	52.9	42.1
Arab States	1960	39.1	50.1	27.9	18.0	25.9	9.9	3.9	6.5	1.3	22.8	30.5	14.9
	1970	51.1	62.5	39.1	28.4	38.7	17.7	8.6	12.8	4.3	32.7	42.0	23.0
	1975	61.3	73.6	48.4	35.0	44.7	24.7	13.0	18.0	7.8	39.6	49.1	29.6
	1980	68.1	78.0	57.9	42.9	52.5	33.0	16.6	21.8	11.1	45.5	53.9	36.7
	1985	71.5	79.9	62.8	49.1	58.1	39.7	19.6	24.9	14.0	50.0	57.7	41.9
	1990	74.6	81.6	67.3	52.0	60.3	43.5	21.9	26.7	16.9	53.0	59.9	46.0
Northern America	1960	100.0	100.0	100.0	94.5	98.6	90.2	30.4	33.4	27.3	80.2	82.5	77.8
	1970	100.0	100.0	100.0	89.8	91.4	88.1	48.2	53.1	43.3	80.6	82.7	78.4
	1975	100.0	100.0	100.0	94.4	94.5	94.2	48.9	54.5	43.2	80.7	82.7	78.7
	1980	100.0	100.0	100.0	90.1	89.7	90.6	48.5	47.4	49.6	76.4	75.8	77.1
	1985	100.0	100.0	100.0	97.6	97.5	97.7	53.1	50.8	55.4	80.3	79.3	81.3
	1990	100.0	100.0	100.0	97.7	98.0	97.3	63.5	61.4	65.6	85.8	85.1	86.5
Latin America and the Caribbean	1960	57.7	58.1	57.4	36.3	38.7	33.9	5.7	7.1	4.3	36.9	38.2	35.5
	1970	71.0	70.7	71.3	49.8	52.1	47.5	11.6	13.6	9.7	48.3	49.5	47.1
	1975	76.3	76.4	76.1	58.0	59.8	56.1	18.9	21.0	16.8	54.3	55.6	52.9
	1980	82.4	82.8	81.9	62.6	63.6	61.6	23.6	25.1	22.0	58.8	59.8	57.7
	1985	85.2	85.5	84.7	66.2	67.3	65.1	23.8	24.8	22.8	60.4	61.2	59.4
	1990	87.6	88.1	87.1	71.6	72.4	70.7	27.2	27.5	26.9	64.0	64.6	63.3

Source: United Nations Educational, Scientific and Cultural Organization, *Statistical Yearbook, 1991* (Paris, 1992), table 2.11.

NOTES: Not including the Democratic People's Republic of Korea and Namibia.

The countries included in the regional division in this table do not in all cases conform to those included in the geographical division established by the Population Division of the Department for Economic and Social Information and Policy Analysis of the United Nations Secretariat.

[a]Including the former Union of Soviet Socialist Republics.

Women's education and fertility

Women's education is widely recognized as a crucial determinant of reproductive behaviour (Mason, 1984; Safilios-Rothschild, 1985). Education provides women with knowledge that allows them to make informed decisions, with skills that enhance their opportunities in the wage employment sector and with exposure to new values, norms and attitudes that are likely to enhance their autonomy. For this reason, the need to improve women's education has been stressed as a means of both promoting development and reducing levels of fertility in the developing world. That view is strongly endorsed in the World Population Plan of Action. It received further support in 1984 in the recommendations for its further implementation and in the plans and programmes of the United Nations Decade for Women (1976-1985).

The relation between education and fertility has been a frequent theme in demographic literature (Holsinger and Kasarda, 1976), and a large body of research has accumulated, offering increasingly complex theories and interpretations of empirical data. Up to the mid-1970s, it was generally thought that fertility fell monotonically as the level of education increased. The classic model of the demographic transition, which hypothesized steadily declining fertility as a concomitant of socio-economic modernization, suggested a progression of this type.

An extensive review of the available empirical evidence on this topic for the developing and the developed countries published in the late 1970s, indicated that the relation between education and child-bearing was not necessarily monotonically inverse (Cochrane, 1979). Positive relations were sometimes observed in very poor, mostly illiterate rural societies. Such variations in the pattern of association showed that the negative effects of education on fertility cannot be taken for granted and stimulated in-depth exploration of the underlying causal linkages.

By the 1980s, comparable data for a large number of the developing countries participating in WFS had become available. The empirical basis for documentation of relation and development of theoretical perspectives was greatly enlarged. Cross-national studies using WFS data showed that education generally exerts a negative influence on fertility. One study covering 30 countries found an average TFR of 6.9 for women with no schooling, 6.6 for women with from one to three years, 5.5 for women with from four to six years and 3.9 for women with seven or more years. The shape and strength of the association was nevertheless contingent on level of development, social structure and cultural milieu (Cleland and Rodriguez, 1988; Jain, 1981; United Nations, 1987). This large group of surveys thus confirmed that the relation between education and fertility is not universally negative, monotonic and linear. Women with secondary schooling, however, usually have much lower fertility than those with no education or only a few years.

Women's education and the intermediate fertility variables

Growing awareness of the complexity of the effects of education on fertility led to a shift of emphasis from a description of statistical associations to investigation of the causal mechanisms that underlie the relation. Extensive research has shown that education may affect a variety of behaviour with potential either to raise or to lower fertility. In his work on the proximate determinants of fertility, Bongaarts (1978) identifies the most important such intermediate variables and evaluates the likely range of their effects. Easterlin's "synthesis framework" has proved useful in the effort to relate these effects to the development process (Easterlin and Crimmins, 1982). According to this model, fertility is determined by the supply of children, the demand for children and the cost of fertility regulation.

The supply of children refers to a couple's reproductive capacity. Education affects the various proximate determinants of fertility in different ways and thus may act either to increase or to decrease the potential biological supply of children (Singh, Casterline and Cleland, 1985). In the early stages of the demographic transition, when child-bearing is essentially "natural," or not subject to deliberate control, education is likely to raise the supply of children, in part because it tends to erode traditional practices that lower fertility, such as breast-feeding and post-partum abstinence (Lesthaeghe and Page,

1980). It may also increase fecundity and reduce spontaneous foetal deaths by improving nutrition and maternal health. At the same time, education may reduce the supply of children, mainly through the deferral of marriage, thus shortening the overall length of time during which a woman is exposed to the risk of pregnancy (Smith, 1983).

The demand for children refers to family size preferences. Much evidence exists documenting how education changes the economic and social circumstances of women's lives in such a way as to reduce the number of children they want to have. Education is also assumed to influence values and favour a normative orientation towards smaller families. Caldwell (1980), in particular, has pointed to the spread of mass education as a key factor that transforms intergenerational attitudes and economic relations within the family, leading in turn to a desire for fewer children. Women's education affects not only their fertility aspirations but also their expectations for the education of their children; better educated mothers typically look forward to higher levels of schooling for their children (Tan and Haines, 1984). The two effects are intrinsically related, since spreading family resources among fewer children leaves more available for the education of each one.

Lastly, the cost of fertility regulation refers to factors that inhibit efforts to reduce the actual supply of children to match demand, that is, the use of contraception. Possible barriers range from the ease and expense of obtaining a method to psychological restraints and aesthetic considerations that must be overcome. Education tends to reduce such costs both because it makes information more accessible and because it changes attitudes. Numerous studies have shown that education is a key factor determining contraceptive use. Education increases awareness and acceptance, and it also facilitates access. The comparative study carried out by the United Nations concluded that, within countries, contraceptive prevalence almost always increases monotonically as education rises and that even a few years of schooling usually makes a substantial difference (United Nations, 1987).

As the fertility transition proceeds in step with development, demand factors and deliberate fertility control increasingly outweigh most of the biological supply factors in determining reproductive performance. Through its impact on family size preferences and contraceptive practice, education acts more and more to lower fertility, and the expected negative relation between education and fertility is accordingly established. As educational levels rise, marriage also tends to occur later, a supply factor that reinforces these effects.

Maternal education and child health and mortality

As was true of education and fertility, the negative relation between education and child mortality is well documented in the literature. In the developing countries, child mortality appears to be more closely related to maternal education than to any other socio-economic factor (United Nations, 1985b). A recent review of data from earlier comparative studies concluded that each additional year of maternal education is associated with a decline of about 7-9 per cent in child mortality (Bicego and Boerma, 1991). It was also noted that the positive effect of better maternal education on child survival is stronger later on than during the initial months of life. The causal connections lying behind these findings remain poorly understood, however.

One important issue is the extent to which the influence of maternal education on child mortality is independent of, as opposed to merely reflecting, the effect of socio-economic status, with which it is closely linked. Two major comparative studies found that maternal education has a strong effect on a child's probability of dying net of other measures of status (United Nations, 1985b) and that this effect was stronger at ages 1-4 than during the first year (Bicego and Boerma, 1991). An in-depth study of six developing countries chosen to represent varying mortality conditions and stages of development similarly concluded that mother's education plays a predominant role in determining a child's chances of survival (United Nations, 1991a). These conclusions were confirmed in a study based on 17 DHS (Bicego and Boerma, 1991); the DHS programme provides more detailed data on children's health than was previously available. Moreover, stunting due to poor nutrition was found to be similarly related to maternal education, although in this case economic status proved to be an almost equally important determinant of faltering growth. However, the rapid declines in overall childhood mortality that characterized the period 1960-1980 cannot, apparently, be traced primarily to changes in the proportion of women that have achieved moderate and higher levels of education (Cleland, Bicego and Fegan, 1991). Child mortality has declined on each level of maternal education. At the same time, the differentials in child mortality associated with maternal education have changed little or may possibly have grown wider.

Another fundamental set of questions relates to the role of health services as an intervening variable between maternal health and child mortality. Are the children of better educated mothers more likely to survive simply because their mothers have better access to health services or because they are more likely to use the health services that are available? The implications for policy development are quite different. Empirical findings are mixed, however, and it seems possible that both kinds of causal connection may hold in different circumstances. There is, nevertheless, considerable evidence consistent with Caldwell's hypothesis that maternal education promotes utilization of existing health services by increasing women's awareness of modern ideas about health and disease, encouraging them to participate more effectively in household decision-making and enhancing their ability to interact with extrafamilial institutions (Bicego and Boerma, 1991; United Nations, 1985b).

Differentials in infant and child mortality by education of mother are by no means unique to the less developed regions. The persistence of substantial differences in such countries as the United Kingdom of Great Britain and Northern Ireland and the United States of America is a cause for concern (Cleland, Bicego and Fegan, 1991).

F. Employment and labour force participation

Gender differences in labour force participation

The economic contribution of women is greatly underestimated in the statistics on labour force participation that have been thus far in use. Most women's work at home and in agriculture, as well as in the subsistence sector in the developing countries, is not counted as economic activity. The definition of the gross national product in the United Nations System of National Accounts specifically excludes household work (United Nations, 1989c). INSTRAW is cooperating with the Statistical Division of the Department of Economic and Social Development of the United Nations Secretariat in attempting to improve the statistical collection system in this regard.

Currently available data indicate that in all parts of the world women make up substantial proportions of the population employed in the formal economy. In 1985, 37 per cent of the labour force worldwide were female (table 8). The proportion varies considerably from region to region. In the more developed regions, it was somewhat larger (42 per cent) than in the less developed regions (35 per cent). Among the developed countries, women made up a higher fraction of the labour force in those with centrally planned economies (48 per cent) than in those with market economies (39 per cent). The contrast among the less developed regions is even greater. In Africa, 35 per cent of the labour force were women; in Asia (not including China), 28 per cent; in China, 43 per cent; and in Latin America and the Caribbean, 27 per cent.

Around 1980, female workers in the developed countries were about as likely as males to be engaged in agriculture; they were much more likely than males to be working in the service sector and far less likely to have jobs in industry (United Nations, 1989c). In the developing countries, employed women were more likely than men to be in agriculture and less likely to have service jobs but, similar to the developed countries, the proportions in the industrial sector were considerably smaller for women than for men.

Data exist to compare the wage levels of women and men for 16 developed countries and 7 developing countries (United Nations, 1989c). In none of these 23 countries do women's wages equal those of men. The closest is Sweden, where women's wages came to 90 per cent of men's wages in 1986; and the disparities tend to be small in the other Nordic countries as well. At the other extreme, women's earnings were only 42 per cent of those of men in Japan and 48 per cent in the Republic of Korea.

TABLE 8. PARTICIPATION OF WOMEN IN THE LABOUR FORCE, DEVELOPING AND DEVELOPED COUNTRIES, 1970-2000

	Year	*Share of females in total labour force (percentage)*	*Females labour force distribution (percentage)*	*Annual rate of growth*	
				Male	*Female*
World	1970	35.99	100.00		
	1980	36.86	100.00	1.92	2.30
	1985	36.52	100.00	2.13	1.84
	2000	35.50	100.00	1.63	1.36
Developing countries	1970	34.37	66.98		
	1980	34.96	68.59	2.28	2.54
	1985	34.73	70.14	2.50	2.29
	2000	33.78	73.89	1.95	1.69
Africa	1970	35.95	9.24		
	1980	35.62	9.34	2.56	2.42
	1985	35.03	9.48	2.67	2.13
	2000	33.40	10.88	2.90	2.45
Asia[a]	1970	29.44	23.13		
	1980	28.51	21.88	2.20	1.74
	1985	27.98	22.01	2.49	1.95
	2000	26.70	23.37	2.20	1.85
China	1970	41.69	31.07		
	1980	43.18	32.75	2.21	2.84
	1985	43.24	33.82	2.44	2.49
	2000	43.47	33.84	1.09	1.19
Latin America and the Caribbean	1970	21.76	3.44		
	1980	26.36	4.51	2.50	5.12
	1985	26.63	4.73	2.51	2.78
	2000	27.74	5.68	2.24	2.70
Developed countries	1970	39.78	33.02		
	1980	41.83	31.41	0.94	1.79
	1985	41.55	29.86	1.04	0.81
	2000	41.51	26.11	0.49	0.49
Centrally planned economies[b]	1970	48.58	14.50		
	1980	48.33	12.95	1.26	1.15
	1985	47.57	12.12	1.11	0.50
	2000	47.50	10.59	0.55	0.59
Eastern Europe	1970	44.27	4.18		
	1980	45.67	3.57	0.14	0.71
	1985	45.73	3.36	0.55	0.60
	2000	46.33	2.98	0.51	0.69
USSR[c]	1970	50.57	10.32		
	1980	49.42	9.38	1.80	1.33
	1985	48.32	8.76	1.35	0.46
	2000	47.97	7.61	0.56	0.55

TABLE 8 *(continued)*

	Year	*Share of females in total labour force (percentage)*	*Females labour force distribution (percentage)*	*Annual rate of growth*	
				Male	*Female*
Market economies	1970	36.36	22.35		
	1980	39.30	21.62	0.70	1.96
	1985	39.31	20.69	0.93	0.94
	2000	39.36	18.09	0.45	0.46
Europe	1970	35.77	12.69		
	1980	38.51	11.63	0.23	1.41
	1985	38.54	11.04	0.75	0.78
	2000	38.81	9.46	0.24	0.33
Northern America	1970	36.14	6.04		
	1980	41.46	7.00	1.52	3.82
	1985	41.36	6.78	1.29	1.20
	2000	41.18	6.18	0.81	0.77
Japan	1970	39.03	3.62		
	1980	37.75	2.99	0.91	0.36
	1985	37.82	2.86	0.90	0.96
	2000	37.29	2.46	0.43	0.19
Oceania					
Australia-New Zealand	1970	30.94	0.35		
	1980	36.92	0.41	1.35	4.10
	1985	37.24	0.42	1.67	1.96
	2000	37.77	0.41	1.13	1.21

Source: 1989 Report on the World Social Situation (United Nations publication, Sales No. E.89.IV/1), table 6.
[a]Not including China.
[b]Currently called "economies in transition".
[c]Forner Union of Soviet Socialist Republics.

On the one hand, many characteristics of modern life propel women into employment. Improvement in education has created rising aspirations and opened opportunities. Such factors as technological innovation, the burden of international debt and changing terms of international trade, growing income disparities, changing patterns of landownership, environmental degradation, increasing likelihood of marital disruption, population growth and migration have weakened previously existing support systems, forcing women to seek new ways of maintaining themselves and their families. On the other hand, continuing discrimination prevents women from getting full reward for their effort. For instance, as discussed above, females still do not have the same educational opportunities as males in many developing countries. Women everywhere tend to be concentrated in low-paying occupations, and they do not have the same access to or control over economic and technical resources.

Women's work and fertility

The existence of a negative association between child-bearing and women's employment in developed societies is well established (Blake, 1965; Lloyd, 1991). In such countries, the more women work, the lower the level of fertility tends to be; conversely, where women have more children, the proportions in the labour force are typically smaller. The emergence of such a relation appears to be an integral part of social and economic development, which profoundly alters the costs of child-rearing, the value of women's time and personal goals and aspirations. The leading explanation for this association is the maternal role incompatibility hypothesis, according to which employment and child-rearing must compete for a woman's limited resources of time and energy (Jaffe and Azumi, 1960; Mason and Palan, 1981; Stycos and Weller, 1967; Weller, 1968).

At the individual level, the association probably results from a continuous, reciprocal process, leading to the realization or revision of a woman's intentions with regard to both employment and child-bearing during the course of her reproductive years in the light of ongoing experience and changing external conditions. The availability of the means of fertility control in such countries is an essential precondition giving women a large measure of control over their lives. While the predominant forces relating work and fertility are negative, there are also positive links between the two that may outweigh the negative effects for some women. Economic necessity may drive the mother of a large family to work, for instance.

Empirical research using data from the developing countries has led to more mixed conclusions (Lloyd, 1991; Standing, 1978 and 1983). The forces shaping the relation appear to be similar to those operating in the developed countries—need for income, desire for economic independence, job opportunities, fecundability, availability of child care etc. The balance among such factors and the extent to which role incompatibility is generated are more varied, however, and the outcomes thus differ. Moreover, because of cultural and institutional restrictions, including lack of access to family planning services, the choices available to individual women and their ability to carry them out are often very limited (Lloyd, 1991).

A large part of what is known about the interrelations between work and fertility in the developing countries comes from WFS. Under this programme, large-scale surveys of women of reproductive age were carried out in 40 developing countries during the late 1970s and early 1980s. Because the surveys used a common core questionnaire, which contained not only a detailed fertility history but also an extensive inquiry into work experience before and after marriage, the WFS data provide a unique opportunity for comparative analysis of this topic. The results have proved disappointing in some respects. The work history data were not sufficiently complete to pin down specific causal mechanisms or even to describe sequences of activities in detail (Lloyd, 1991). Some worthwhile insights have nevertheless been gained. Because of expectation that, in line with the association observed in the developing countries, women's employment might be relevant to policies directed to reducing fertility, most attention has been directed to the study of the possible negative effects of employment on fertility.

As summarized by Lloyd (1991), the principal substantive conclusions of comparative analysis of the WFS data are as follows. The relation of work to fertility varies not only among countries but among groups within a given country and across time (Lloyd, 1991). In many countries of Asia and Latin America and the Caribbean, but not in Africa, women employed in the modern sector (professional and clerical occupations) had somewhat smaller families than those not working at all; women that worked in occupations with some modern characteristics (workplace away from home, job required some training etc.) also tended to have fewer children; there was no difference between the fertility of women employed in agriculture and that of non-working women (Lloyd, 1991). The strength of any negative association between fertility and women's employment is clearly linked to the level of socio-economic development of a country: the higher the level of development, the more likely it is that the fertility of women in modern occupations will be lower than that of other women.

If employment caused women to have fewer births, it would necessarily operate through one or more of the proximate determinants of fertility; thus, empirical observation of its effects should also be possible in these areas of behaviour. The most likely candidates are nuptiality, contraception and breast-feeding. In the developed countries, employment is one of the factors associated with postponement of marriage, although the direction of causality is not clear. Evidence of an association between work experience, rising age at marriage and rising age at first birth has been found in a number of studies in the developing countries (Standing, 1983; United Nations, 1987). The relation between employment and contraceptive use is similar to the relation between employment and fertility in that it appears to depend upon type of occupation and level of development (Stoekel and Jain, 1986; United Nations, 1987). The fact that this relation is much weaker than that with fertility suggests, however, that the direction of causation is as likely to be from fertility to employment as the other way around (Lloyd, 1991). Rather than using contraception to limit child-bearing and thus to facilitate work in modern occupations, that type of job may simply be closed off to women that already have a large family. Breast-feeding tends to inhibit conception, but it can interfere with work as well, especially among women employed in the modern sector. The possibility that employment could lead to early weaning (Ferry and Smith, 1983; Nag, 1983) would tend to increase rather than decrease fertility. In sum, the variety of possible effects of employment on the proximate determinants of fertility clearly constitutes one of the reasons for the differing associations observed between employment and child-bearing itself.

Women's work, child health and family welfare

Literature on the relation between women's market work and welfare of their families, particularly that of young children, has stressed three dimensions of this relation:

(*a*) Women's paid labour force participation increases the overall family income, which benefits all family members, including young children;

(*b*) Women's independent income increases their control over resources and indirectly benefits children; and

(*c*) Employment outside the home may lead to diversion of women's time and attention away from home, which may have a negative impact on children's welfare.

The benefits of increased income have been documented in a variety of settings and require little discussion here. The latter two issues have received relatively little attention, particularly with regard to developing countries. There is some evidence that women are more likely than men to make child-related expenditures (Mencher, 1988; Thomas, 1992). If women's market work increases their power within the family and consequently allows them greater control over resources, it may result in improved child health and welfare, even when holding total family income constant. This argument, however, rests on two assumptions: first, that women's market work increases their control over resources; and secondly, that women are more likely than men to spend money in ways that benefit children. Although there is some evidence to support both propositions, more research in this area is still needed.

A mother's involvement in market work may affect children negatively through a reduction in time she spends caring for her children and their exposure to alternate care, which in many developing countries consists of no care or care from siblings (Joekes, 1989). A recent review of the literature concerning the possible links between women's market work and child nutrition in the developing countries led to two principal conclusions (Leslie, 1989). First, women's work status does not appear to be associated with infant-feeding practices in general or with the initiation of breast-feeding in particular. Employed mothers do tend to introduce supplementary nutrition sooner than those who are not employed, however, and this practice could expose children to a variety of health risks. Secondly, nutritional status (weight for age, height for age, weight for height, dietary intake) may well be less favourable among children of working mothers.

The direction of causation is nevertheless unclear. The impact of maternal employment can only be studied with reference to what family circumstances would be if she did not work. Research on family conditions that increase women's labour force participation suggest that single or divorced women, women whose husbands are employed or have very low income and women from landless families are more likely to engage in market work than women from relatively better off families. Since much of the literature fails to take into account the differing circumstances between families with an employed mother and families where the mother only works in the home, it is difficult to generalize from the findings mentioned above.

Although it is commonly assumed that women's employment increases children's exposure to alternate care, very few studies have examined this aspect directly. In fact, the literature suggests two mechanisms that attenuate this superficially obvious relation. In many developing countries, women engage in work, such as small-scale vending or working on the farm, which allows them to take children to work. Also, women may reduce their own leisure time to meet the demands of children and work (Ho, 1979). Additionally, the image of a homemaker as being able to provide a warm nurturing environment that her employed counterpart does not, underestimates the demands of domestic work on women in rural areas of many developing countries. Frequently, domestic requirements, such as fetching firewood and water, taking meals to family members on the farm and caring for livestock, induces many women to relying on other family members or neighbours to watch children for several hours a day even when they are ostensibly "not employed" (Desai and Jain, 1992). Thus, if exposure to alternate care has a negative impact on children, in many settings it occurs regardless of whether the mother is employed. Reduction of domestic drudgery (for instance, by investing in infrastructure, such as piped water and gas) may have important social benefits, by increasing the time available to women, both for the care of their children and for other income-generating activities.

Relatively few studies have examined the impact of child-care practices on the welfare of children and families in the developing countries (Joekes, 1989). Alternatives to child care provided by the mother include no care, care by other members of the household, care by family members that do not live in the same household or by other persons in the community and institutional arrangements for child care. The one clear finding relating child-care practices to child welfare concerns the strong association between use of a young child, typically an older sibling, to care for an even younger child and malnutrition in the younger child (Joekes, 1989).

These observations suggest that, particularly for poor women, demands on mothers' time for domestic work as well as paid and unpaid market work need to be more carefully and realistically assessed, in conjunction with studies of current child-care arrangements and their impact on child welfare. Provisions to promote child welfare by decreasing domestic demands on both working and non-working women and by providing higher quality child care should be undertaken along with employment promotion schemes.

G. Women and environment: issues of special concern

Population growth and the environment

Most of the recent growth in world population has occurred in the developing countries. Whereas population growth averaged 1.7 per cent per annum in the world as a whole during 1985-1990, in the less developed regions the population was increasing at 2.1 per cent per annum (United Nations, 1991c). If attention is confined to the subcategory of least developed countries, growth averaged 2.8 per cent per annum, a rate at which the population would double approximately every 25 years. Women experience this expansion directly in terms of crowded living conditions, scarcity of basic household resources and larger numbers of dependants.

Agriculture dominates the economies of most developing countries. During the early 1980s, females formed substantial proportions of the agricultural labour force in these regions: 47 per cent in sub-Saharan Africa; 25 per cent in Northern Africa and Western Asia; 40 per cent in Asia; and 19 per cent in Latin America and the Caribbean (UNEP, 1988,). For the most part, women are engaged in small-scale farming; they account for as much as 60 per cent of overall family food production (INSTRAW, 1991).

Although population growth is by no means the only cause of environmental degradation, it is inevitably a contributing factor. As population has increased, areas suited for agriculture have become crowded, marginal lands have often been brought into production and water resources have been depleted. More intensive and extensive exploitation of the land has led to soil erosion and deforestation and may have contributed to desertification. Traditional ways of living in harmony with the environment have been disrupted. The productivity of the land has actually fallen in some areas. Even where the green revolution has brought about dramatic increases in production, it has often had a negative impact on women's lives through such mechanisms as the bypassing of women in agricultural activity, exposure to chemical pollutants and even greater scarcity of water-supplies (United Nations, 1989e). Other developments, such as the introduction of cash crops in Africa, have also tended to have negative consequences for women (United Nations Secretariat, 1989).

The deterioration of rural conditions in many less developed regions has encouraged population movement into cities, where newcomers are often crowded in squatter settlements without basic public services. Migrants may also shift from one rural area to another within the same country, or they may cross national boundaries in search of better opportunities. Social networks and community supports that provide essential assistance to women in coping with the many challenges they face are destroyed. Families are often temporarily or permanently split up, with female-headed households as a common by-product.[1]

As mentioned above, the economic role of women in the informal economy as well as at home goes largely unrecognized. Unless they have "paid" jobs, most women's work is not reflected in national accounts. Because so much of their contribution is perceived as having no value, women are especially vulnerable to worsening economic conditions resulting from degradation of the environment. Further impoverishment results, which is itself invisible in national accounts, and women's health as well as that of their children is threatened.

Women as environmental managers

Much of the interaction between human life and the environment occurs within women's usual sphere of activity. In traditional societies, women plant and harvest crops, prepare food, fetch water for the household, provide fuel, collect animal fodder and dispose of waste. All of these functions bring them into immediate contact with the resource base, and they are de facto the primary persons responsible for its management. If water sources become polluted or threaten to run short, women bear the burden of bringing supplies from a more distant location. When firewood is scarce, women must either find ways in which the household can get along with less or spend additional time and effort obtaining it. Over the generations rural women have accumulated much knowledge through their daily interaction with nature; this store of experience constitutes an important resource for environmental protection and rehabilitation. In urban settings and in the developed countries, the population tends to be more removed from the environment, but even there women plan and supervise a large part of resource-based consumption.

Most development planning in the less developed regions has focused in the past on men, who occupy virtually all positions of power and own most of the property. In recent years, however, international efforts to promote sustainability and reduce environmental degradation have increasingly sought to open up the process to women. Recognition of the key roles that women play has led to a variety of innovative approaches to development strategy. For example, in some countries, access to credit, better seeds, fertilizers and agricultural extension services has been made available to female farmers (UNFPA, 1992). Elsewhere, women in urban areas have been provided with credit and training in small business management. Success stories presented at the Global Assembly of Women and the Environment in 1991 demonstrated the potential of women to bring about change at the local level with respect to energy, waste, water and environmentally friendly systems (WorldWIDE Network, 1992). Full integration of women into policy-making and large-scale action remains a challenge. The groundwork has been laid, however, by women in all areas of the world, who have spearheaded efforts to change environmentally destructive practices.

Because one of women's primary roles is the bearing and rearing of children, the slowing of population growth not only eases pressure on the environment but also benefits their lives directly. Reduction of family size improves the health of women and children; it creates opportunity for women to improve their education and to develop employment skills; it enables them to manage their immediate environment more creatively. Information about and access to family planning is thus a central component of strategies for sustainable development. Because both spouses are involved in family planning decisions, it is essential that such programmes include both men and women.

Environmental issues in the more developed regions

The developed countries have contributed disproportionately to worldwide depletion of non-renewable resources and to pollution of the air, land and water. As members of society, both women and men have a deep stake in these issues. Women, who provide much of the care for children, the ill and the elderly, were often the first to raise suspicions about the negative health effects of the extremely bad conditions in certain industrial sites in Eastern Europe and the former USSR that only recently came to general attention. Other problems associated with advanced economic development raise special questions for women themselves. Some pollutants have been shown to be hazardous to the developing foetus. Exposure to such substances in the workplace has become a controversial topic in both the developed and the developing countries. Employers have sometimes attempted to bar all women that might bear children from jobs involving risks of this type.

NOTE

[1]Topics related to migration, including issues that particularly concern migrant women, were discussed in depth at the United Nations Expert Group Meeting on Population Distribution and Migration, held at Santa Cruz, Bolivia, 18-22 January 1993.

REFERENCES

Abo, Sabib H. A. (1984). Islam's attitude to female circumcision. In *Report on a Seminar on Traditional Practices Affecting the Health of Women and Children in Africa, Dakar, Senegal, 6-10 February.* Dakar: Ministry of Public Health and Non-Governmental Organization Working Group on Traditional Practices Affecting the Health of Women and Children.

Badri, A. E. (1984). Female circumcision in the Sudan. Paper presented at the Conference on Reproductive Health Management in Sub-Saharan Africa, Freetown, Sierra Leone, 5-9 November.

Bankole, Akinrinola, and David O. Olaleye (1991). The effects of breastfeeding on infant and child mortality in Kenya. In *Demographic and Health Surveys World Conference, August 5-7 1991, Washington, D.C., Proceedings,* vol. II. Columbia, Maryland: IRD/Macro International, Inc.

Bicego, George T., and J. Ties Boerma (1991). Maternal education and child survival: a comparative analysis of DHS data. In *Demographic and Health Surveys World Conference, Washington, D.C., 5-7 August 1991, Proceedings*, vol. I. Columbia, Maryland: IRD/Macro International, Inc.

Blake, Judith (1965). Demographic science and the redirection of population policy. *Journal of Chronic Diseases* (Oxford, United Kingdom), vol. 18 (November), pp. 1181-1200.

Bongaarts, John (1978). A framework for analyzing the proximate determinants of fertility. *Population and Development Review* (New York), vol. 4, No. 1 (March), pp. 105-132.

________ (1990). The measurement of wanted fertility. *Population and Development Review* (New York), vol. 16, No. 3 (September), pp. 487-506.

Caldwell, John C. (1980). Mass education as a determinant of the timing of the fertility decline. *Population and Development Review* (New York), vol. 6, No. 2 (June), pp. 225-255.

Carballo, Manuel (1988). AIDS and female circumcision. *Interafrican Committee on Traditional Practices Affecting the Health of Women and Children Newsletter*, No. 5 (March), p. 8.

China, State Family Planning Commission (1990). *National Fertility Sample Survey (National Results).* Beijing.

China, State Statistical Bureau (1991). Preliminary tabulations from the 10 per cent sample of the 1990 population census. Unpublished.

Cleland, John G., and Germán Rodríguez (1988). The effect of parental education on marital fertility in developing countries. *Population Studies* (London), vol. 42, No. 3 (November), pp. 419-442.

Clelan, John, George Bicego and Greg Fegan (1991). Socio-economic inequalities in childhood mortality: the 1970s compared with the 1980s. In *Demographic and Health Surveys World Conference, August 5-7 1991, Washington, D.C., Proceedings,* vol. 1. Columbia, Maryland: IRD/Macro International, Inc.

Coale, Ansley J. (1991). Excess female mortality and the balance of the sexes in the population: an estimate of the number of "missing females". *Population and Development Review* (New York), vol. 17, No. 3 (September), pp. 517-523.

Cochrane, Susan H. (1979). *Fertility and Education: What Do We Really Know?* World Bank Occasional Papers, No. 26. Baltimore, Maryland: The Johns Hopkins University Press.

Cook, Rebecca J., and Deborah Maine (1987). Spousal veto over family planning decisions. *American Journal of Public Health* (Washington, D.C.), vol. 77, No. 3 (March), pp. 339-344.

Das Gupta, Monica (1989). The effects of discrimination on health and mortality. *International Population Conference, New Delhi, 1989*, vol. 3. Liège, Belgium: International Union for the Scientific Study of Population.

David, Henry P. (1992). Abortion in Europe, 1920-91: a public health perspective. *Studies in Family Planning* (New York), vol. 23, No. 1 (January/February), pp. 1-22.

Desai, Sonalde, and Devaki Jain (1992). Women's work and children's well-being in the rural Indian context. Paper presented at the Annual Meeting of the Population Association of America, Denver, Colorado, 30 April-2 May.

Easterlin, Richard A., and Eileen M. Crimmins (1982). *An Exploratory Analysis of the "Synthesis Framework" of Fertility Determination with World Fertility Survey Data.* World Fertility Survey Scientific Reports, No. 40. Voorburg, the Netherlands: International Statistical Institute.

Elson, Diane (1991). Gender issues in development strategies. Paper prepared for the Seminar on Integration of Women in Development, Vienna, Austria, 9-11 December.

Fathalla, M. F. (1992). Reproductive health in the world: two decades of progress, a new decade of challenges. Paper prepared for the Twentieth Anniversary of the Special Programme of Research, Development and Research Training in Human Reproduction. Geneva: World Health Organization.

Ferry, Benôit, and David P. Smith (1983). *Breastfeeding Differentials.* World Fertility Survey Comparative Studies, No. 23. Voorburg, the Netherlands: International Statistical Institute.

Freedman, Ronald, and Ann K. Blanc (1991). Fertility transition: an update. In *Demographic and Health Surveys World Conference, August 5-7 1991, Washington, D.C., Proceedings,* vol. I. Columbia, Maryland: Institute for Resource Development/Macro International, Inc., pp. 5-24.

Harlap, Susan, Kathryn Kost and Jacqueline Darroch Forrest (1991). *Preventing Pregnancy, Protecting Health: A New Look at Birth Control Choices in the United States.* New York: The Alan Guttmacher Institute.

Henshaw, Stanley K., and Evelyn Morrow (1990). *Induced Abortion: A World Review, 1990 Supplement.* New York: The Alan Guttmacher Institute.

Ho, Theresa J. (1979). Time costs of child rearing in the rural Philippines. *Population and Development Review* (New York), vol. 5, No. 4 (December), pp. 643-662.

Holsinger, Donald B., and John D. Kasarda (1976). Education and human fertility: sociological perspectives. In *Population and Development: The Search for Selective Interventions,* Ronald C. Ridker, ed. Baltimore, Maryland: The Johns Hopkins University Press.

Holt, Renee (1990). Women's rights: an international perspective. In *Women and the Law,* Carol N. Lefcourt, ed. Civil Rights Series. New York: Clark Boardman.

Ismail, E. A. (1984). Statement on the practice of infibulation. In *Report on a Seminar on Traditional Practices Affecting the Health of Women and Children in Africa, Dakar, Senegal, 6-10 February.* Dakar: Ministry of Public Health and Non-Governmental Organization Working Group on Traditional Practices Affecting the Health of Women and Children.

Jain, Anrudh K. (1981). The effect of female education on fertility: a simple explanation. *Demography* (Washington, D.C.), vol. 18, No. 4 (November), pp. 577-595.

Jaffe, A. J., and K. Azumi (1960). The birth rate and cottage industries in underdeveloped countries. *Economic Development and Cultural Change* (Chicago, Illinois), vol. 9, No. 1 (October), pp. 52-63.

Joekes, Susan (1989). Women's work and social support for child care in the Third World. In *Women, Work, and Child Welfare in the Third World,* Joanne Leslie and Michael Paolisso, eds. Boulder, Colorado: Westview Press.

Khalidi, Ramla, and Judith Tucker (1992). *Women's Rights in the Arab World.* Washington, D.C.: Middle East Research and Information Project.

Koso-Thomas, Olayinka (1987). *The Circumcision of Women: A Strategy for Eradication.* London; and Atlantic Highlands, New Jersey: Zed Books.

Leslie, Joanne (1989. Women's work and child nutrition in the Third World. In *Women, Work, and Child Welfare in the Third World,* Joanne Leslie and Michael Paolisso, eds. Boulder, Colorado: Westview Press.

Lesthaeghe, Ron G., and Hilary J. Page (1980). The post-partum non-susceptible period: development and application of model schedules. *Population Studies* (London), vol. 34, No. 1 (March), pp. 143-169.

Lincoln, Richard, and Lisa Kaeser (1987). Whatever happened to the contraceptive revolution? *International Family Planning Perspectives* (New York), vol. 14, No. 4 (December), pp. 141-145.

Lloyd, Cynthia B. (1991). The contribution of the World Fertility Surveys to an understanding of the relationship between women's work and fertility. *Studies in Family Planning* (New York), vol. 22, No. 3 (May/June), pp. 144-161.

Lopez, Alan D. (1984). Sex differentials in mortality. *WHO Chronicle* (Geneva), vol. 38, No. 5. pp. 217-224.

Mason, Karen Oppenheim (1984). *The Status of Women: A Review of Its Relationships to Fertility and Mortality.* New York: The Rockefeller Foundation.

_________ , and V. T. Palan (1981). Female employment and fertility in Peninsular Malaysia: the maternal role incompatibility hypothesis reconsidered. *Demography* (Washington, D.C.), vol. 18, No. 4 (November), pp. 549-575.

Mastroianni, Luigi, Jr., Peter J. Donaldson and Thomas T. Kane, eds. (1990). *Developing New Contraceptives: Obstacles and Opportunities.* Washington, D.C.: National Academy Press.

Mauldin, W. Parker, and John A. Ross (1991). Family planning programs: efforts and results, 1982-89. *Studies in Family Planning* (New York), vol. 22, No. 6 (November/December), pp. 350-367.

Mencher, Joan P. (1988). Women's work and poverty: women's contribution to household maintenance in South India. In *A Home Divided; Women and Income in the Third World,* Daisy Dwyer and Judith Bruce, eds. Stanford, California: Stanford University Press.

Muhuri, Pradip K., and Samuel H. Preston (1991). Effects of family composition on mortality differentials by sex among children in Matlab, Bangladesh. *Population and Development Review* (New York), vol. 17, No. 3 (September), pp. 415-434.

Nag, Moni (1983). The impact of sociocultural factors on breastfeeding and sexual behavior. In *Determinants of Fertility in Developing Countries,* vol. 1, *Supply and Demand for Children,* Rodolfo A. Bulatao and Ronald D. Lee, eds., with Paula E. Hollerbach and John Bongaarts. New York: Academic Press.

Ono-Osaki, Keiko (1992). Men and adolescents: unreached groups in family planning. Paper prepared for the Seminar on Planning and Implementation of Effective Family Planning/Family Health and Welfare Programmes: Some Lessons from Asian and the Pacific Region, Beijing, 17-21 March.

Palloni, Alberto, and Yean Ju Lee (1992). Some aspects of the social context of HIV and its effects on women, children and families. *Population Bulletin of the United Nations* (New York), No. 33, pp. 64-87. Sales No. E.92.XIII.4,.

Republic of Korea, National Bureau of Statistics (n.d.). Special tabulations of the 1988 Korean Fertility Survey. Unpublished.

Royston, Erica, and Sue Armstrong (1989). *Preventing Maternal Deaths.* Geneva: World Health Organization.

Safilios-Rothschild, Constantina. (1985). *The Status of Women and Fertility in the Third World in the 1970-1980 Decade.* Center for Policy Studies Working Paper, No. 118. New York: The Population Council.

Sharma, Ravi K., and others (1990). A comparative analysis of trends and differentials in breastfeeding: findings from DHS surveys. Paper presented at the Annual Meeting of the Population Association of America, Toronto, Canada, 3-5 May.

Singh, Susheela, John B. Casterline and John G. Cleland (1985). The proximate determinants of fertility: sub-national variations. *Population Studies* (London), vol. 39, No. 1 (March), pp. 113-135.

Sivard, Ruth Leger (1985). *Women: A World Survey.* Washington, D.C.: World Priorities.

Smith, Peter C. (1983). The impact of age at marriage and proportions marrying on fertility. In *Determinants of Fertility in Developing Countries,* vol. 2, *Fertility Regulation and Institutional Influences,* Rodolfo A. Bulatao and Ronald D. Lee, eds., with Paula E. Hollerbach and John Bongaarts. New York: Academic Press.

Standing, Guy (1978). *Labour Force Participation and Development.* Geneva: International Labour Office.

________ (1983). Women's work activity and fertility. In *Determinants of Fertility in Developing Countries*, vol. 1, *Supply and Demand for Children,* Rodolfo A. Bulatao and Ronald D. Lee, eds., with Paula E. Hollerbach and John Bongaarts. New York: Academic Press.

Stoekel, John, and Anrudh K. Jain (1986). Introduction and overview. In *Fertility in Asia: Assessing the Impact of Development Projects,* John Stoekel and Anrudh K. Jain, eds. London: Frances Pinter.

Stycos, J. Mayone, and Robert H. Weller (1967). Female working roles and fertility. *Demography* (Washington, D.C.), vol. 4, No. 1 (January), pp. 210-217.

Tan, Jee-Peng, and Michael Haines (1984). *Schooling and Demand for Children: Historical Perspectives.* World Bank Staff Working Papers, No. 697, Population and Development Series. Washington, D.C.: The World Bank.

Thomas, Duncan (1992). The distribution of income and expenditure within the household. Paper presented at the International Food Policy Research Institute/World Bank Conference on Intra-Household Resource Allocation.

United Nations (1985a). *Report of the World Conference to Review and Appraise the Achievements of the United Nations Decade for Women: Equality, Development and Peace, Nairobi, Kenya, 15-20 July 1985.* Sales No. E.85.IV.10.

________ (1985b). *Socio-economic Differentials in Child Mortality in Developing Countries.* Population Studies, No. 97. Sales No. E.85.XIII.7.

________ (1987). *Fertility Behaviour in the Context of Development: Evidence from the World Fertility Survey.* Population Studies, No. 100. Sales No. E.86.XII.5.

________ (1988a). *Adolescent Reproductive Behaviour*, vol. I, *Evidence from Developed Countries.* Population Studies, No. 109. Sales No. E.88.XIII.8.

________ (1988b). *Human Rights: A Compilation of International Instruments.* Sales No. E.88.XIV.1.

________ (1989a). *Adolescent Reproductive Behaviour, vol. II, Evidence from Developing Countries.* Population Studies, No. 109/Add.1. Sales No. E.89.XIII.10.

________ (1989b). *Levels and Trends of Contraceptive Use as Assessed in 1988.* Population Studies, No. 110. Sales No. E.89.XIII.4.

________ (1989c). *1989 Report on the World Social Situation.* Sales No. E.89.IV.1.

________ (1989d). *Review of Recent National Demographic Target-setting.* Population Studies, No. 108. Sales No. E.89.XIII.5.

________ (1989e). *1989 World Survey on the Role of Women in Development.* Sales No. E.89.IV.2.

________ (1990). *Patterns of First Marriage: Timing and Prevalence.* Sales No. E.91.XIII.6.

________ (1991a). *Child Mortality in Developing Countries: Socio-economic Differentials, Trends and Implications.* Sales No. E.91.XIII.13.

________ (1991b). *Population Newsletter* (New York), No. 52 (December).

________ (1991c). *World Population Prospects, 1990.* Population Studies, No. 120. Sales No. E.91.XIII.4.

________ (1991d). *The World's Women, 1970-1990: Trends and Statistics.* Series K, No. 8. Sales No. E.90.XVII.3.

________ (1992). *World Population Monitoring, 1991: With Special Emphasis on Age Structure.* Population Studies, No. 126. Sales No. E.92.XIII.2.

United Nations Secretariat (1988a). Sex differentials in life expectancy and mortality in developed countries: an analysis by age groups and causes of death from recent and historical data. *Population Bulletin of the United Nations* (New York), No. 24, pp. 65-107. Sales No. E.88.XIII.6.

________ (1988b). Sex differentials in survivorship in the developing world: levels, regional patterns and demographic determinants. *Population Bulletin of the United Nations* (New York), No. 25, pp. 51-64. Sales No. E.88.XIII.6.

________ (1989). Integrating women, environment and population into development. Paper prepared by the Population Branch of the Development Administration Division of the Department of Technical Cooperation for Development for the United Nations Population Fund Interagency Consultative Meeting on Women, Population and Environment, 6 March.

________ (1990). Interrelations between the status of women and the AIDS epidemic: a conceptual approach for intervention. Report prepared by the Division for the Advancement of Women for the Expert Group Meeting on Women and HIV/AIDS and the Role of National Machinery for the Advancement of Women, Vienna, Austria, 24-28 September.

United Nations Educational, Scientific and Cultural Organization (1992). *Statistical Yearbook, 1991.* Paris.

United Nations Environment Programme (1988). *State of the World Environment, 1988: The Public and Environment.* Nairobi.

United Nations International Research and Training Institute for the Advancement of Women (1991). Women, environment and sustainable development: seeds for a greener future. Fact sheet. Santo Domingo, Dominican Republic.

United Nations Population Fund (1992). *Women, Population and the Environment.* New York.

Weinberger, Mary Beth (1991). Recent trends in contraceptive behavior. In *Demographic and Health Surveys World Conference, August 5-7, 1991, Washington, D.C., Proceedings*, vol. 1. Columbia, Maryland: IRD/Macro International, Inc.

Weller, Robert H. (1968). The employment of wives, role incompatibility and fertility: a study among lower- and middle-class residents of San Juan, Puerto Rico. *The Milbank Memorial Fund Quarterly* (New York), vol. 46, No. 4 (October), pp. 507-526.

Westoff, Charles F. (1991). *Reproductive Preferences.* Demographic and Health Surveys Comparative Studies, No. 3. Columbia, Maryland: Institute for Resource Development/Macro Systems, Inc.

________, and Luis Hernando Ochoa (1991). *Unmet Need and the Demand for Family Planning.* Demographic and Health Surveys Comparative Studies, No. 5. Columbia, Maryland: Institute for Resource Development/Macro International, Inc.

World Health Organization (1991a). *Creating Common Ground: Women's Perspectives on the Selection and Introduction of Fertility Regulation Technologies.* Geneva.

________ (1991b). *Maternal Mortality Ratios and Rates: A Tabulation of Available Information*, 3rd ed. Maternal Health and Safe Motherhood Programme. Geneva.

________ (1991c). Women, health and development. Progress report by the Director-General to the Forty-fourth World Health Assembly. Geneva.

WorldWIDE Network (1992). Special report: findings, recommendations and action plans. *Global Assembly of Women and the Environment: Partners in Life*, issue 1 (January). Washington, D.C.

Part Three

THE VALUE OF WOMEN, WOMEN'S AUTONOMY AND POPULATION TRENDS

IV. FAMILY AND GENDER ISSUES FOR POPULATION POLICY

Cynthia B. Lloyd[*]

Implicit in the debate about population policy are certain assumptions about the family and about the roles women and men play within it. The most central of these assumptions for population policy is the long-term stability of the conjugal family as a close physical, economic and emotional unit within which children are planned, born and reared. When the policy debate centres on family planning and the supply of contraceptive methods, it is often further assumed that meeting a couple's needs for fertility regulation is synonymous with meeting the individual needs of men and women. This very assumption is implicit in the term "family planning", which frames decisions about child-bearing exclusively within a family context. Indeed, the World Population Plan of Action adopted at Bucharest in 1974 and the recommendations for its further implementation adopted at Mexico City in 1984 assert the centrality of the family as "the basic unit of society", while at the same time declaring that both couples and individuals should have "the basic right to decide freely and responsibly the number and spacing of their children" (United Nations, 1975, para. 14; and 1984b, paras. 24-25).

When the debate turns to development policies designed to affect the demand for children, in particular policies targeted to improvements in "the status of women", several additional assumptions about the roles women and men play within the family and the intra-family distribution of resources are implicit in the linkage typically drawn between rising costs of children and declining demand for children: (*a*) that improvements in women's individual livelihoods outside the family provide them with greater individual economic mobility and thus less reliance upon children and other family members for future economic support; (*b*) that fathers share with mothers joint responsibility for their children's maintenance and upbringing; and (*c*) that parents support each of their children to the same extent.

These assumptions structure the collection and analysis of demographic data and the design of population policy. The goal of this paper is to examine the empirical evidence surrounding those assumptions and to draw out the implications of that evidence for future research and policy. In so doing, a case is built for a much broader framework within which to view population issues: one in which family organization and gender relations are central. Women acting on behalf of the family are seen as agents of change in all aspects of population and development policy, whether it be the adoption of family planning, the provision of health care for children or the acquisition of independent economic livelihood. The paper argues that women cannot bring about the demographic transition alone, particularly within the context of existing family structures and gender relations in many of the current high-fertility countries. Men have much to contribute as well. Indeed, the extent of women's autonomy and men's family responsibility will likely dictate the pace at which economic and social change, as well as population policy, are able to affect demographic behaviour. The effectiveness of population policy would be much enhanced if more were known about men's reproductive and familial roles and about the way in which the costs and benefits of children are distributed.

A. THE FAMILY: WHO IS A MEMBER AND FOR HOW LONG?

The family has different meanings in different cultures but at its core in every society are parents and their biological children. Simple models of the family rely upon the assumption that these core family

[*]Senior Associate and Deputy Director, Research Division, The Population Council, New York. The author acknowledges with thanks the helpful comments from Ahmed Bahri, John Bongaarts, Susan Greenhalgh, Sawong Hong, Shireen Jejeebhoy and George Zeidenstein. Special thanks are due Judith Bruce, who has been the intellectual inspiration for the paper.

members reside together in the same household and function within a unified household economy. Parents are assumed to plan, bear and rear children jointly with a long-term view of their costs and benefits. The head of the family (often synonymous with the head of the household) is assumed to be an altruist on behalf of this core family unit, organizing production among family members (both core members and possibly others) so as to maximize efficiency and distributing resources fairly. Reality differs from this model in ways that have important implications for population and development policy.

The interconnectedness of individuals in family relationships through bonds of affection and/or obligation leads to joint decision-making, budget-pooling, cooperative work roles and altruistic parenting within a framework of culturally accepted notions about the division of rights and responsibilities by sex and generational position. As a result, families, according to the degree of their connectedness, as well as the distribution of power within them, mediate the effects of policy on intended individual beneficiaries through the redistribution of resources and responsibilities among family members. The family members with whom an individual co-resides are usually assumed to be those with whom she or he has the greatest degree of connectedness. Membership in more than one core family can complicate and potentially weaken some of these bonds—a problem for children when one or both parents are responsible for children from more than one conjugal relationship. Expectations about the duration of family relationships can be another important factor determining the strength of these bonds—a problem for women whose husbands are much older, are physically absent for long periods of time or are likely to form formally polygamous or informally consensual relationships with younger women. These three factors—co-residence, multiple membership and longevity—all affect the strength of family bonds and therefore the extent to which family members function as a unit and act altruistically towards one another.

In the following discussion, each of these three factors and the way in which each varies in different areas of the developing world is examined in turn. Family arrangements in sub-Saharan Africa often provide the most dramatic examples of deviations from the hypothetical family depicted above and thus are often used to make a point. However, the relevance here is intended to be much broader, touching as it does on the essential factors determining the strength of family ties anywhere.

Connections: residential or relational?

For a variety of reasons, a child's biological parents do not always live together. These reasons include job migration, polygamy, divorce and remarriage, as well as child-bearing outside wedlock. While this fact is widely known, it is more surprising to realize the extent of a mother's reproductive life in certain settings that are not spent living in the same household with her children's biological father(s). Table 9 gives Demographic and Health Surveys (DHS) data from the relatively few (primarily African) countries where surveys asked women not only about their marital status and marital history but also explicitly about their co-residence with a spouse.[1] The table includes estimates of the proportion of mothers' reproductive years from age 20 to age 49 spent not married, not resident with a spouse or in second or higher order marriages.[2] Among women that are mothers, the

TABLE 9. PROPORTION OF MOTHER'S REPRODUCTIVE YEARS SPENT IN DIFFERENT MARITAL AND RESIDENT STATUSES, AGES 20-49, SELECTED COUNTRIES

		Married		
			Partner resident	
Country	*Not married*	*Partner not resident*	*More than once*	*Once*
Africa				
Botswana . . .	0.45	0.12	0.04	0.39
Burundi	0.14	0.04	0.12	0.70
Ghana	0.14	0.27	0.21	0.38
Kenya	0.17	0.17	0.05	0.60
Nigeria[a]	0.05	0.16	0.10	0.69
Senegal	0.08	0.15	0.18	0.59
Sudan	0.09	0.13	0.08	0.70
Zimbabwe . . .	0.17	0.24	0.10	0.49
Asia				
Sri Lanka . . .	0.08	0.02	0.02	0.89

Source: Demographic and Health Survey standard recode tapes.
[a]Ondo State.

mothers, the estimated proportion of time during the reproductive years spent living with a first husband (in most cases the first child's father), is as low as 0.38 and 0.39 in Botswana and Ghana, 0.49 in Zimbabwe, and 0.59 and 0.60 in Senegal and Kenya, respectively. The non-co-residence of couples due to custom or migration, as well as high rates of divorce (and remarriage), weigh in as important factors in explaining these low proportions. In contrast, mothers in Sri Lanka (the only country outside sub-Saharan Africa that asked questions about spousal co-residence) spend the vast majority (0.89) of their reproductive life residing with their first husband. Thus, it is apparent that the assumption that family members live together in the same household may be appropriate in some settings but very far from reality in others.

Although physical distance between spouses does not preclude the exchange of financial support—indeed family separation is often motivated by economic reasons—distance can make economic links less secure, particularly with the passage of time. A recent review of the literature on migration points to the fact that, although the chief reason for men to migrate away from their families is to generate support for the family, the subsequent flow of remittances is typically uncertain and highly variable, often leaving women to support themselves and their children inefficiently and alone or to rely upon other family members (Findley and Williams, 1991). For example, in Lesotho, poor agricultural practices and yields have been identified as consequences of the unpredictability of remittances of male migrants to their women and children (Safilios-Rothschild, 1985). Research based on data for the United States of America shows that a father's physical presence in the home is closely linked to the extent of his financial and emotional commitment to his children (Macunovich and Easterlin, 1990; Garfinkel and McLanahan, 1986; Duncan and Rodgers, 1988; Weiss, 1984).

Financial exchange between parents is even more precarious when parents are not linked to each other through marriage, either because of child-bearing outside marriage or because of separation and divorce. The extent of a father's support for his children appears to be affected by, among other factors, his sexual access to the mother of those children. Research on child-support arrangements in the United States of America demonstrates that when parents are divorced or separated, relatively few children receive financial support from their father (Peterson and Nord, 1990). Much less information is available on fathers' contributions to children's support in cases of divorce or non-marital child-bearing in the developing countries. This situation exists mainly because so much of the data relied upon are derived from woman-based surveys, such as DHS, which link children with their biological mothers but not explicitly with their biological fathers (Lloyd and Desai, 1992).

Table 10 provides some hint of the potential scope of the problem in different societies by showing the proportion of mothers' reproductive years spent unmarried or in second or higher order marriages in a variety of the developing countries in very different areas of the world. The proportion of a mother's reproductive years after age 20 spent not currently married varies from a low of 0.04 in Tunisia to a high of roughly 0.46 in Botswana. In certain countries, women spend substantial amounts of time married to husbands that are not their first—roughly one third of a mother's reproductive years in Ghana and Liberia and slightly over one fourth in the Dominican Republic. There is substantial intercountry and interregional variation in both of these indicators; but, on average, African mothers in the sub-Saharan region spend a substantial amount of time (roughly one third) outside of marriage or in second or higher order marriages. The average for Asia and Northern Africa is less than half as much time, with Latin America falling between the two extremes. The Dominican Republic is the only country with data available from the Caribbean and it shows its own distinctive pattern, with only slightly more than 50 per cent of a mother's reproductive years spent in a first marriage.

Obviously, when parents do not live together, children cannot live with both biological parents. Even when parents do live together, however, children sometimes live apart from their parents, particularly in sub-Saharan Africa, where child fostering is common. Unfortunately, because most data collected on fostering are based on interviews with women, there has been no attempt to establish the relationship between a woman's children and her current marital partner; and, therefore, it is not possible to assess the extent to

TABLE 10. PROPORTION OF MOTHER'S REPRODUCTIVE YEARS SPENT IN DIFFERENT MARITAL STATUSES, AGES 20-29, SELECTED COUNTRIES

Area and country	Not currently married	In higher order marriages	Total
Sub-Saharan Africa			
Botswana	0.46	0.05	0.51
Burundi	0.14	0.13	0.27
Ghana	0.14	0.33	0.47
Kenya	0.17	0.06	0.23
Liberia	0.19	0.34	0.53
Nigeria[a]	0.05	0.13	0.17
Senegal	0.08	0.23	0.31
Zimbabwe	0.17	0.13	0.30
AVERAGE	-	-	0.35
Asia and Northern Africa			
Egypt	0.09	0.05	0.13
Indonesia	0.08	0.15	0.23
Morocco	0.08	0.13	0.22
Sri Lanka	0.08	0.02	0.10
Sudan	0.09	0.10	0.18
Thailand	0.09	0.09	0.18
Tunisia	0.04	0.03	0.07
AVERAGE	-	-	0.16
Latin America and the Caribbean			
Boliva	0.15	0.07	0.22
Brazil[a]	0.13	0.09	0.22
Colombia	0.21	0.09	0.30
Dominican Republic	0.20	0.26	0.47
Ecuador	0.12	0.11	0.23
Guatemala[b]	0.13	0.11	0.24
Peru	0.14	0.08	0.22
AVERAGE	-	-	0.27

Source: Demographic and Health Survey standard recode tapes.
[a]Ondo State.
[b]Based on age group 20-44.

TABLE 11. PROPORTION OF CHILDHOOD POTENTIALLY SPENT LIVING APART FROM BIOLOGICAL PARENTS, AGES 0-15 SELECTED COUNTRIES

Area and country	Away from mother	Living with mother alone	Total
Sub-Saharan Africa			
Botswana	0.28	0.26	0.54
Burundi	0.06	0.08	0.14
Ghana	0.18	0.08	0.26
Kenya	0.07	0.10	0.17
Liberia	0.29	0.10	0.39
Mali	0.12	0.02	0.14
Senegal	0.16	0.04	0.20
Zimbabwe	0.15	0.08	0.23
AVERAGE	-	-	0.26
Asia and Northern Africa			
Indonesia	0.04	0.04	0.08
Morocco	0.03	0.04	0.07
Sri Lanka	0.03	0.05	0.08
Thailand	0.07	0.05	0.12
Tunisia	0.01	0.02	0.03
AVERAGE	-	-	0.08
Latin America and the Caribbean			
Brazil	0.04	0.09	0.13
Colombia	0.06	0.13	0.19
Dominican Republic	0.13	0.14	0.27
Ecuador	0.04	0.07	0.11
Peru	0.04	0.09	0.13
Trinidad and Tobago	0.06	0.17	0.23
AVERAGE	-	-	0.18

Source: Cynthia B. Lloyd and Sonalde Desai, "Children's living arrangements in developing countries", *Population Research and Development Review* (Dordrecht, Netherlands), vol. 11, No. 3 (1992), pp. 193-216.

which children live with both biological parents. Table 11 shows the proportion of childhood years children spend away from their mother or living with an unmarried mother.[3] The proportions are strikingly different between regions, with more than one fourth of children's lives, on average, spent in these arrangements in sub-Saharan Africa, 18 per cent in Latin America and 8 per cent in Asia and Northern Africa.

To get a fuller picture of children's living arrangements, one needs household-based data. Table 12 provides an example from Ghana which shows the proportion of school-age children by age that live with both parents, mother only, father only and neither parent (Lloyd and Gage-Brandon, 1992). The proportion of school-age children living in a household without their biological father is 0.43, with as many as 0.22 of the children living in a household with neither biological parent. Although the situation in Ghana presents an extreme contrast to the traditional assumptions about the co-residential core family unit, it highlights the importance of not taking those assumptions for granted and of exploring the particular social arrangements in each setting which may lead to violations of commonly held assumptions.

TABLE 12. PROPORTION OF SCHOOL-AGE CHILDREN CO-RESIDING WITH PARENTS, BY AGE AND SEX, GHANA, 1987/88

Age group	*Both parents*	*Mother only*	*Father only*	*Neither parents*
6-11				
Boys	0.54	0.20	0.09	0.18
Girls	0.50	0.20	0.06	0.24
12-17				
Boys	0.48	0.20	0.13	0.20
Girls	0.40	0.22	0.10	0.28
TOTAL	0.48	0.21	0.09	0.22

Source: Cynthia Lloyd and Anastasia Gage-Brandon, *Does Sibsize Matter? The Implications of Family Size for Children's Education in Ghana,* Research Division Working Paper, No. 45 (New York, The Population Council, 1992).

Boundaries: exclusive or overlapping?

One reason core family members cannot all live together in the same household is that some of them may in fact be members of more than one core family. Men and women do not always form exclusive bonds which last throughout their respective reproductive years, and they have children with more than one partner. From a child's perspective, this means that the set of siblings they share with their mother may not be entirely the same as the set they share with their father. Thus, rather than functioning within a unified family economy, many children will find themselves competing with one set of siblings for their mother's resources and another set of siblings for their father's resources. Currently available women-based data do not permit one to know the prevalence of divergent sibsets among children in different settings. Again taking Ghana as an example, however, Lloyd and Gage-Brandon (1992) report that the average number of siblings school-age children share with their father is substantially greater (5.9) than the number they share with their mother (4.1), suggesting that divergent sibsets among children are not uncommon in a polygamous society or one in which divorce and remarriage are prevalent.

The fact that men's reproductive years extend over a much longer period than women's is an additional factor contributing to the phenomenon of overlapping sibsets. As a result, male and female fertility rates often diverge at older ages, with men experiencing higher fertility than women. Although little data have been collected on overall male fertility compared with female fertility, a few recent surveys conducted in Western Africa (Ghana and Mali) allow a direct comparison of the cumulative fertility of currently married women and their husbands by age. Table 13 shows the sharp divergence of the mean number of living children reported by husbands and wives that occurs at older ages in these two settings, where polygamy is common. In Mali, women end their reproductive career with 4.3-4.5 living children, while those husbands in the sample between ages 50 and 55 have, on average, 8.0 living children. In Ghana, the story is similar, with women ending their reproductive career with 5.7 living children, on average, while those husbands in the sample over age 50 had, on average, 8.5 living children. As a result, in Ghana, 36 per cent of all couples with women of reproductive age differ in their individual parity (Ezeh, 1991). Other surveys of husbands and wives have restricted their investigations to the fertility shared by the couple (for example, Côte d'Ivoire, Egypt and Thailand), precluding an analysis of the individual lifetime fertility experience of men and women.

TABLE 13. NUMBER OF LIVING CHILDREN REPORTED BY WOMEN AND WOMEN'S HUSBANDS, BY AGE, GHANA AND MALI

	Ghana (1988)		*Mali (1987)*	
Age group	*Women*	*Husbands*	*Women*	*Husbands*
40-44	5.4	5.1	4.5	5.6
45-49	5.7	6.7	4.3	8.3
50-55	–	8.5[a]	–	8.0

Sources: Ghana, Statistical Service; and Institute for Resource Development/Macro Systemns, Inc., *Ghana Demographic and Health Survey, 1988* (Accra, Ghana; and Columbia, Maryland, 1989); and Baba Traoré, Mamadou Konaté and Cynthia Stanton, *Enquête démographique et de santé au Mali, 1987* (Bamako, Mali, Institut su Sahel, Centre d'etudes et de recherches sur la population pour le developpement; and Columbia, Maryland, Institute for Recourse Development/Westinghouse, 1989.

[a]Aged 50 years or over.

Stability: long or short term?

A life-cycle perspective provides an even more dramatic view of the stability of the core family unit. What percentage of men and women will remain with the same spouse throughout their reproductive life? What percentage of children will live with both biological parents throughout their childhood years?

What percentage of children will acquire a step-parent before they become an adult? These are questions that need answers if one is to understand the family context within which reproductive decisions occur and child-rearing takes place.

Women-based surveys can only provide some of the answers because the reproductive life of men is not investigated and children's link with their biological fathers is rarely traced.[4] For example, using DHS data, the proportion of ever-married women at the end of their reproductive career (aged 40-49) that had experienced a marital disruption due to divorce, separation or widowhood can be calculated (see table 14). On average, the proportion of women experiencing a disruption is 0.36 in sub-Saharan Africa, 0.34 in Latin America and the Caribbean and 0.24 in Asia and Northern Africa. The variations between countries are particularly striking in sub-Saharan Africa, where the proportion of women experiencing a marital disruption varies from 0.07 in Mali to 0.61 in Ghana.

TABLE 14. PROPORTION OF EVER-MARRIED WOMEN AGED 40-49 WHOSE FIRST UNION HAS DISSOLVED,[a] SELECTED COUNTRIES

Country	*Proportion*	*Country*	*Proportion*
	A. Sub-Saharan Africa		
Botswana	0.32	Mali	0.07
Burundi	0.39	Nigeria[b]	0.24
Ghana	0.61	Senegal	0.42
Kenya	0.24	Zimbabwe	0.35
Liberia	0.56	AVERAGE	0.36
	B. Asia and Northern Africa		
Egypt	0.23	Sudan	0.28
Indonesia	0.37	Thailand	0.25
Morocco	0.31	Tunisia	0.11
Sri Lanka	0.16	AVERAGE	0.24
	C. Latin America and the Caribbean		
Bolivia	0.25	Guatemala[c]	0.29
Brazil[c]	0.23	Peru	0.26
Colombia	0.32	Trinidad and Tobago	0.26
Dominican Republic	0.50		
Ecuador	0.29	AVERAGE	0.34

Source: Demographic and Health Survey standard recode tapes.
[a]Marital dissolution includes widowhood, divorce, separation and remarriage.
[b]Ondo State.
[c]Based on ages 40-44.

The much richer data on women's marital histories from the World Fertility Survey (WFS) conducted from the mid-1970 to the late 1970s can be used to determine what proportion of children experienced a union disruption between their own biological parents by a certain age as well as the number of years spent with a single mother. Richter (1988) estimates that by age 15, 20 per cent of Mexican children and one third of Colombian children had experienced a union disruption or had begun life outside a union.[5] For children experiencing a period of separation between their biological parents, the average time spent with a single mother until the formation of a new union was roughly 7.4 years in Mexico and 5.9 years in Colombia. At the time of these surveys, union dissolution rates were on the rise, suggesting the possibility that the numbers of children affected in these two countries may have increased in the past decade.

Surveys that encompass the complete demographics and economics of core family units—whether they be subsumed within the same household or transcend several households—are sorely needed. One needs to know more about how membership in families changes over time; how co-residence, multiple membership and longevity affect the strength of family ties; and last, but by no means least, how men see their family roles, including the factors influencing their sense of connectedness with their families.

B. FERTILITY REGULATION: AN INDIVIDUAL OR FAMILY STRATEGY?

Couples form family units within which to bear and rear children, but at the same time, individual men and women (boys and girls) engage in sexual relations outside marital unions, which sometimes lead to pregnancy and childbirth, without planning for a family. Furthermore, some of these men and women are simultaneously spouses in marital relationships. Thus, individual needs for fertility regulation relate simultaneously to the achievement of fertility goals within families and the control of fertility outside of families. To complicate things further, husbands and wives may not share the same fertility goals for their shared family unit or for their lifetime. In such cases, differences can be resolved within the marriage if both members compromise, if one member subsumes her/his wishes to the other or if the husband or wife realizes his/her excess fertility goals with another partner outside the marriage. Differences in fertility preferences, however, can also be a cause of marital dissolution. The threat of marital dissolution is a factor determining how differences are resolved. The partner that is most dependent upon the marriage is the one most likely to defer to the preferences of the other.

Outside of marriage: who is responsible?

Research on fertility regulation behaviour has been typically based on currently married women of reproductive age. These are the women assumed to be exposed to the risk of pregnancy and childbirth and about whom data have been largely collected. Although there is growing recognition of the wide variation across societies in sex outside marriage, studies estimating current levels and projecting future trends in contraceptive prevalence throughout the world traditionally ignored the behaviour of unmarried women, for the practical reason that many surveys have not asked unmarried women about their contraceptive practice (Ross and others, 1992; United Nations, 1984a and 1989).

Estimates of unmet need (Bongaarts, 1991; Westoff, 1988), "couple-years of protection", future contraceptive demand and the costs of contraceptive commodities (Mauldin and Ross, 1992) are largely based on the assumption that unmarried women will not be sexually active.[6] Recent United Nations data (1992) on contraceptive use among unmarried women, however, show them (and their male partners) to be a potentially important group of users in many countries (table 15). Indeed, in several African countries—notably Ghana, Liberia, Mali, Togo and Uganda—use among the formerly married and/or single women exceeds use among the married group. In some sense, this finding should not be surprising, given the strong motivation of unmarried people to avoid pregnancy despite the obstacles they may face in obtaining information and supplies. Among those countries for which data are available, contraceptive prevalence among the formerly married averages roughly 0.17 in sub-Saharan Africa, 0.20 in Latin America and the Caribbean; and 0.18 in Sri Lanka and Thailand—the only Asian countries for which data are available.[7] Use among single women in Africa averages 11 per cent but is notably lower in Latin America and the Caribbean, and no data are available for Asia. When individual men and women engage in sexual activity outside a marital union, their needs for contraception are individually based rather than couple-based. An assessment of contraceptive needs requires information on the behaviour of both men and women.

TABLE 15. PROPORTION OF REPRODUCTIVE-AGE WOMEN USING CONTRACEPTION, BY MARITAL STATUS, ALL METHODS, SELECTED COUNTRIES

Area and country	*Currently married*	*Formerly married*	*Single*
Sub-Saharan Africa			
Botswana	0.33	0.30	0.27
Burundi	0.09	0.06	0.01
Ghana	0.13	0.14	0.09
Kenya	0.27	0.23	0.14
Liberia	0.06	0.13	0.13
Mali	0.05	0.07	0.01
Senegal	0.11	0.09	0.06
Togo	0.16	0.26	0.28
Uganda	0.05	0.09	0.05
Zimbabwe	0.43	0.32	0.07
AVERAGE	0.17	0.17	0.11
Asia			
Sri Lanka	0.62	0.16	..
Thailand	0.68	0.19	..
AVERAGE	0.65	0.18	..
Latin America and the Caribbean			
Bolivia	0.30	0.08	0.01
Brazil[a]	0.66	0.39	0.06
Colombia	0.66	0.29	0.04
Ecuador	0.53	0.16	0.01
Guatemala[a]	0.23	0.12	0.00
Mexico	0.53	0.23	0.01
Peru	0.46	0.12	0.02
Trinidad and Tobago	0.53	0.12	0.01
AVERAGE	0.49	0.20	0.02

Source: *World Contraceptive-Use Data Diskettes, 1991: User's Manual*, ST/ESA.SER.R/120 (New York, United Nations, 1992).
[a]Based on ages 20-44.

Rising ages at marriage have been the most important factor leading to increases in women's exposure to the risk of pregnancy outside of marriage. Table 16 shows trends over the past decade in the proportion of her reproductive years a woman spent in an unmarried state, either single, divorced, separated

TABLE 16. PROPORTION OF WOMEN'S REPRODUCTIVE YEARS SPENT UNMARRIED, AGES 15-49, SELECTED COUNTRIES

Area and country	*World Fertility Survey*	*Demographic and Health Survey*
Sub-Saharan Africa		
Ghana	0.22	0.26
Kenya	0.22	0.28
Senegal	0.13	0.19
Northern Africa		
Egypt	0.28	0.29
Morocco	0.27	0.34
Sudan	0.28	0.35
Tunisia	0.23	0.34
Asia		
Indonesia	0.28	0.27
Sri Lanka	0.37	0.36
Thailand	0.31	0.34
Latin America and the Caribbean		
Colombia	0.39	0.40
Dominican Republic	0.34	0.34
Ecuador	0.34	0.31
Peru	0.34	0.34

Sources: *Fertility Behaviour in the Context of Development: Evidence from the World Fertility Survey*, Population Studies, No. 100 (United Nations publication, Sales No. E.86.XIII.5); and Demographic and Health Survey standard recode tapes.

between ages 15 and 49. The countries included are confined to those for which both WFS and DHS data were available. In this sample of 14 countries from very different areas of the developing world, the proportion of a woman's reproductive years spent unmarried has risen from roughly 0.29 to 0.32. The variation between countries has declined as countries where women had the lowest proportions of time unmarried have experienced the most dramatic increases over the decade. Except for Senegal, where women spend less than one fifth of their reproductive years unmarried, proportions range from 0.26 to 0.40, with the most dramatic increases having occurred in Africa.

These data highlight the substantial and growing proportion of women's reproductive years that fall outside attention when the focus is exclusively on couples. The service needs of adolescent men and women are particularly noteworthy. Desirable features for such services, particularly in the African context, include a multiplicity of outlets outside the traditional maternal and child health networks, client anonymity and ease of purchase (Caldwell, Orubuloye and Caldwell, 1992). Furthermore, the growing risks of unwanted pregnancy and extra-union child-bearing point to the importance of giving greater attention to male sexual behaviour and contraceptive needs in the interest of helping them become more responsible partners.

Within marriage: who decides?

The assumption underlying estimates of unmet need is that if a married woman expresses a desire to limit fertility but is not currently using contraception, she would adopt family planning regulation if it became available. The potential influence of her husband (and/or other family members) on her contraceptive behaviour is ignored. The question is whether women and men (or other family members) share the same fertility preferences and the same attitudes towards family planning and, if not, what the implications are for contraceptive use and fertility.

Mason and Taj (1987), in a comprehensive review of the literature, found no evidence that women consistently want fewer children than men, on average. It is not always clear, however, whether questions about desired family size are interpreted by respondents to relate exclusively to the current conjugal relationship or more broadly to their lifetime which might include the possibility of multiple partners. Furthermore, agreement at the societal level may mask disagreement at the level of the couple. For example, in Ghana, only 23 per cent of couples reported the same desired family size (Ezeh, 1991). Data on fertility preferences of husbands and wives in Ondo State, Nigeria (Mott and Mott, 1985) show little agreement between husbands and wives on future fertility. The authors were led to conclude that fertility intentions, at least in this particular setting, "were essentially formed on an individual and not a family level" (Mott and Mott, 1985, p. 98). In other settings, disagreement is less extensive but none the less problematic for potentially pivotal groups of couples. For example, 20 per cent of Thai couples gave contradictory answers to the question whether more children were desired (Thailand, 1977). In Egypt, 17 per cent of urban couples and 22 per cent of rural couples gave different responses on the question on desire for more children (Egypt, 1983).

As Bongaarts (1990) points out, the implications for fertility of differences in preferences depend upon how conflicts over preferences are resolved. Fertility could be lower than would be implied from women's fertility preferences alone if child-bearing stopped when either parent wanted no more but could be higher if child-bearing proceeded until both wanted no more.

Attitudes towards family planning form an important link between fertility preferences and actual contraceptive behaviour. Even when husbands and wives agree on their fertility preferences, they may not share the same attitudes towards the actual practice of family planning. For example, in Mali, the opinion of wives and husbands were very different, with only 16 per cent of husbands and 62 per cent of wives approving of the use of family planning for limiting or spacing births (Traoré, Konaté and Stanton, 1989).

What happens when partners disagree? Data on male attitudes from Zimbabwe (Mbizvo and Adamchak, 1991) and the Sudan (Khalifa, 1988) document that men perceive that they should have the major role in the decision to use family planning. In Ghana, both men and women that participated in recent focus group discussions expressed the view that, when differences in fertility preferences occur between a husband and wife, the man's preferences usually dominate (Ezeh, 1992). A young mother from Volta region said, "When I wanted to do family planning, my husband did not allow me so I didn't do it".

Only a few studies of attitudes of husbands and wives towards family planning attempt to link these attitudes with actual behaviour. Results from the Egyptian WFS showed that husbands' fertility preferences were substantially different from those of wives and more closely linked to the woman's use of contraception (Singh, 1987). Woman-based data from metropolitan Indonesia show that a wife's perception of her husband's approval of contraceptive use was the most important determinant of a woman's actual contraceptive use (Joesoef, Baughman and Utomo, 1988). An analysis of the recent DHS in Ghana shows that the consistency of the attitudes of husbands and wives towards family planning was an important factor in the level of contraceptive use. Whereas 38 per cent of all couples in which both approved of family planning were currently using some form of contraception, fewer than 11 per cent of those where only one spouse approved were doing so (Ezeh, 1991).

It is clear that women have an important say, but not always the final say, in contraceptive use. These data show, however, that the formation of preferences, the reconciliation of differences and the specific actions that are taken by individual members of couples are the outcome of a complex negotiation process. The relative power of women in sexual relationships will depend upon their access to and control over resources, as well as upon the strength of the ties that bind their male partners to them. The types of family planning methods most suited to individual needs in terms of privacy, secrecy and the need for cooperation between partners will depend upon the nature of these relationships. The understanding of this process would be greatly enriched if one knew more about men's sense of responsibility for their sexual behaviour and their roles in reproductive decision-making and contraceptive practice. It is also important to learn more about the influence of other family members on the reproductive decision-making process.

C. The demand for children: do rising costs lead to declines in fertility?

No one denies that the costs of rearing children are rising rapidly in most areas of the developing world. Growing labour-market opportunities for women provide them with alternatives to children as sources of support and fulfilment, thus raising the opportunity cost of their time and the indirect costs of children. As economies modernize and diversify, child maintenance requires increasing access to the cash economy for the purchase of nutritious foods, essential medicines and school books and uniforms. While primary health clinics and schools are currently accessible to most parents, the direct costs of these services have been rising rapidly as many Governments seek to privatize.

With various elements of the costs of children rising, in part due to the withdrawal of government subsidies, parents may be induced to consider changes in their fertility behaviour. However, other responses are also possible. Parents may seek ways to shift some of the increased costs of child-rearing onto other relatives and older children. Fathers may seek to shift more of the costs onto mothers. Alternatively, when family resources are inadequate or credit is unavailable and when returns on child investment appear low or uncertain, parents may select only certain children to be the beneficiaries of their investments or may distribute their investments unequally. Less favoured children can stay at home, fend for themselves and help support their parents and siblings without the benefit of education or proper health care. Few Governments of developing countries make altruistic parenting institutionally compulsory (Johansson, 1991); and in many cultures the idea of equity among household members—in particular, siblings—is completely foreign.

Improved livelihood for women: who benefits?

Improvements in the status of women and the equalization of their rights with those of men were identified as essential prerequisites of effective implementation of the World Population Plan of Action in the recommendations of the International Conference on Population, held at Mexico City in 1984. Included among the recommended improvements were equalization with men of women's access to and control over resources, in particular education and employment, in the paid labour force (United Nations, 1984b). These recommendations were enthusiastically and unanimously adopted by the largely male-headed delegations of Member States of the United Nations. Their universal support suggests that they were viewed as "win-win" propositions with women having much to gain and men having nothing to lose and, perhaps, even something to gain as well.

However, unless women can capture directly for themselves the gains from improvements in education and livelihood and translate them into greater personal autonomy and economic mobility, their economic gains are likely to be dissipated within the family. The result is likely to be a reduction in men's family responsibilities, leaving women dependent upon men for essential complementary resources and dependent upon children for long-term security. Such a scenario would lead to a reduction in men's economic contribution, an increase in women's labour-market work and relatively little change in the demand for children, despite the increased personal costs of children borne by women.

There is a growing body of evidence from a variety of developing countries that women's economic activity and the bearing and rearing of children are not necessarily incompatible (Lloyd, 1991; Mason, 1985). In some cases, this may be because the burden of child care does not fall exclusively on the mother but is shared with siblings and other family members (Desai and Jain, 1992). In other cases, it may be because of the nature of the woman's work, which is often flexible in terms of scheduling and is physically proximate to the home. In still other cases, the economic demands of a growing family make it necessary for women to work despite any difficulties or costs they may encounter. Certain types of work, however, have been seen to be more difficult to reconcile with the bearing and rearing of large families—in particular, work for cash in the modern sector (Lloyd, 1991).

As a result, there has been much effort in the donor community to promote income-earning opportunities for women through training and access to credit. Indeed, some of these interventions (for example, Bangladesh, Indonesia and Thailand) have been directly linked to the design and implementation of family planning programmes (Sadik, 1990; Weeden and others, 1986). These efforts have been largely confined to individual enterprises within the informal sector for obvious reasons: it would be difficult to intervene directly in the employment practices of family enterprises, private firms or government ministries. There is evidence, however, that even women's gains from certain types of self-employment in the modern sector, specifically in commerce, do not necessarily lead to increased mobility for women in the form of business expansion, given the constraints imposed on them by family institutions and prevailing gender ideologies (Greenhalgh, 1991).

In three cases—studies drawn from very different cultural settings in Ghana, India and Thailand—Greenhalgh (1991) identifies the factors limiting women's business opportunities. With regard to vegetable vendors at Madras, women's limited physical mobility required them to depend upon men to perform crucial business transactions. Women turned over their income to the men. Business success led to the need for greater male input, with the inevitable consequence that growing businesses gradually shifted over to being male-controlled. In the case of market women in Ghana and Thailand, who had full independence in the conduct of their business, their business mobility appeared to be limited by claims made on their income by other family members. The financing of children's education was an important element of women's financial "obligations" in both case-studies. Husbands made additional financial claims in the case of Thailand, as did extended kin in the case of Ghana. In the Indian case, success on the part of women led to increasing male control; in the Ghana and Thailand cases, success on the part of women led them to take over a larger share of family obligations. In each case, men reaped the surplus from women's entrepreneurship, either directly for themselves or indirectly in the form of reduced obligations to other family members.

Further evidence of women's sense of family obligation as an important motivation for work comes from studies of autonomous female migrants. In a recent review of the literature, Findley and Williams (1991) find evidence from a variety of different settings that women migrants are often more reliable remitters than men and, despite lower incomes, remit similar proportions of their income to their families as men.

These examples make clear that, in talking about women's livelihood, it is important to identify those elements which are likely to enhance their access to and control over the necessary input into their work, as well as the profits derived from their work. Men's dominant position within the family and situational advantage in the world of work must be directly recognized in the design of interventions to enhance women's income-earning opportunities if these are to become genuine economic alternatives for women to the family as a source of economic support. More research will be needed to understand the factors that support and encourage men's economic support of families, in particular, their children, in a world in which women are playing an increasingly important role in the cash economy.

Locating the costs of children: who pays?

In an idealized traditional division of labour between mothers and fathers in the maintenance and support of their own biological children, mothers contribute their time directly to care and nurturing while fathers provide necessary material input. In societies where the support of children is not confined to the nuclear family unit, female relatives (in particular, grandmothers, aunts and older sisters) share the mother's roles and male relatives the father's roles. In the process of development, the costs of children to their parents (and other family members) inevitably rise, primarily because of increased aspirations for children's education. Children's enrolment in school involves not only direct monetary outlays but a reduction in the family labour force. How do changes in the cost of children affect the traditional division of parental and more broadly shared family responsibilities? Few studies have addressed the question but the answers are likely to depend upon, among other factors, the structure of the family and the role of family members other than parents in the support of their children.

In polygamous societies, men view wives as a source of wealth. Wives are expected to provide largely for themselves and their children through their own labour and through their access to the resources of other family members. Evidence suggests that, in sub-Saharan Africa where polygamy is prevalent, mothers provide their own food for themselves and their children (Boserup, 1970; Oppong, 1983; Joekes, 1987). In these societies, food represents the overwhelming share of the household budget. In Ghana for example, the share is roughly 70 per cent (Lloyd and Gage-Brandon, 1993a). Concrete evidence of independence of mothers and children from fathers for economic support emerges from a comparison of children's nutritional status in monogamous and polygamous unions in Ghana, Mali and Senegal. Desai (1992) found that malnutrition among children was no more apparent among children in polygamous unions than in monogamous unions, despite the fact that women in polygamous unions in monogamous unions, despite the fact that women in polygamous unions have claim to a smaller proportional share of their husband's resources than women in monogamous unions.

Because co-wives operate with a certain amount of financial autonomy and without full knowledge of their husband's resources, it is relatively easy for a man with several wives to shift a substantial share of the material costs of his children onto their mothers. This process is facilitated by the breakdown of the traditional marriage contract with the introduction of Western monogamous marriage forms in much of urban Western Africa. This has resulted in the spread of informal polygamy *deuxième bureau*, which is outside the reach of customary law and practice (Fapohunda and Todaro, 1988). The result is that men can choose the amount of support they want to provide to their children and discriminate between them according to the status of their relationship with the child's mother (Bledsoe, 1988).

In Latin America and the Caribbean, the role of the extended family in child support is not as extensive; therefore, the consequences of weaker conjugal bonds for children's welfare are more apparent. Desai (1992) shows evidence of a substantially higher prevalence of stunting among children whose mothers are in consensual unions than those in legal unions, controlling for family size and parental resources. This finding suggests lesser child investment in consensual unions, probably the result of a smaller paternal contribution in less stable unions. Cain (1984) refers to this as the "free rider" problem, in which men can father children with little, if any, economic consequences for themselves.

There is evidence of rising numbers of female-headed and maintained households in the developing countries (United Nations, 1991), causing concern that a growing proportion of children may not be receiving their full share of support from their biological fathers. However, households become female-headed for a variety of reasons. Although female-headed households with children are, on average, poorer than male-headed households, well-off women and children are found in a variety of household types. Their welfare is less conditioned by headship or even residence than by whether the costs of children are primarily borne by them or shared (Bruce and Lloyd, 1992). The growing evidence that the internal distribution of resources in female-headed households is more child-oriented than in male-headed households suggests that mothers and fathers have very different expenditure priorities. This situation may be due to the very different benefits expected by mothers and fathers from investments in their children. In a polygamous society, for example, older men can expect to be supported by younger wives while older women may have to rely largely upon the support of their own children. This material support may come in exchange for further child-care responsibilities as grandmothers become the caretakers of the next generation.

It is important to note here that suggestions of possible cost-shifting between fathers and mothers is not based on direct observation of the process but rather on observed differences in resource allocation that occur between family and household types to which men (in particular fathers) have varying degrees of commitment. No study has yet been made of the factors influencing the bargain that parents strike with each other and other family members over the division of child-rearing responsibilities or how it is renegotiated over time in response to the arrival of additional children and changing family relationships. These should be future research priorities.

Resources for children: who is the lucky child?

An implicit assumption in much research on intra-family resource allocation is that parents are altruistic towards their children—in other words, that they distribute resources "fairly" between them. A fair distribution is sometimes taken to mean the same amount of resources (both parental time and material resources) for each child and sometimes is viewed as the resources required to give each child equal opportunities or equal outcomes. The first type of distribution could lead to inequality between children according to birth order, even if equality between children was preserved at any point in time, because of the fact that children do not arrive in a family all at the same time. Given differences between children in natural endowments, the second type of distribution would imply that resources invested would not be the same but the result would be equality between children in their ultimate welfare. Both of these approaches to the distribution of resources among children would lead to the prediction that a rise in the costs of children, on average, would lead to a decrease in demand. Neither of these altruistic approaches to the intra-family allocation of resources among children would be expected to lead parents to differentiate between children on the basis of sex unless parents are thought to believe that girls and boys, given their different endowments, need different levels of resources to achieve the same ultimate level of welfare.

The negative effects of family size on child outcomes have been interpreted as the result of parents having to distribute their given resources "fairly" among more children (for example, Knodel, Havanon and Sittitrai, 1990). However, if, alternatively, parents are able to accommodate the rising costs of health care, food and education by choosing to make investments in some children but not in others, the link between rising costs and declining demand will not be as direct nor as strong. Such a strategy will involve parents in investing in quality and quantity simultaneously, hedging their bets and preparing some of their children for a modern world and some for a more traditional one. Empirical evidence of systematic differences between boys and girls within the same sibsets in various outcomes, such as mortality (D'Souza and Chen, 1980; Das Gupta, 1987), nutrition (Chen, Huq and D'Souza, 1981), child care (Levine, 1987) and educational participation and attainment (Jeejebhoy, 1992), suggests one of the ways parents may be at least partially accommodating the rising costs of children—that is, by increasing their investments in sons but not in daughters. A few studies that have explored differences in educational outcomes for boys and girls in high fertility settings according to family size have found that the negative consequences of having many siblings—or more specifically younger siblings—is much greater for girls than boys (Sathar, 1992; Lloyd and Gage-Brandon, 1992; Basu, 1992).

Not all parents can afford the luxury of being fair and one easy way to differentiate between children is according to sex. Both mothers and fathers may see very different pay-offs for investments in their sons and investments in their daughters and these will vary across societies according to marriage customs and family organization. Differential investments in sons and daughters are likely to make economic sense from a parent's perspective.

Birth order is also a factor in differential care. In some settings, older children are advantaged in relation to their younger siblings, whereas in others, they may be expected to carry an extra burden of co-parenting younger siblings. A child's value in Nepal is calculated in terms of future household needs and once those needs have been met, children become redundant (Levine, 1987). In Taiwan Province of China, the early children in large families do particularly poorly with respect to education and even worse if they are female (Parish and Willis, 1992). Foreshortened education and early marriage are often the fate of older girls from large families, with the result that patterns of early and high fertility are perpetuated and intergenerational inequality accentuated (Lloyd and Gage-Brandon, 1993a).

This section of the paper begins with the question: will rising costs of children lead to declining demand? The discussion has pointed out the ways in which the organization of families and gender relations with the family can affect the distribution of material and opportunity costs of children among family members. In settings where decision-making authority rests largely with men that do not carry the bulk of the child-rearing costs (largely borne by women), there is the likelihood of a lag in the fertility response to rising costs. The possibility that some parents will choose not to pay the costs, to shift them onto others (including their own children) or to pay them for some children only (with a preference for boys) further weakens the expected relation between rising costs and fertility decline.

Future research will need to probe the determinants of altruistic behaviour within families, particularly between parents and children. Why are women more child-centred in their expenditures than men? How could government policy induce mothers and fathers to treat their boys and girls equally? The answers to these questions would provide the framework for fairer and more effective population policy.

D. Summary and conclusions

The purpose of this paper has been to illustrate the ways in which assumptions about family organization and gender relations inform one's thinking about population policy. The empirical view of the family is needlessly limited at the moment, largely because of the biases introduced by the women-centred approach to the collection of demographic data for policy analysis. The cross-country diversity in family forms apparent in the data presented here only hint at their actual complexity, which will only be fully known once proper account is taken of father/child links, divergent sibsets and membership in multiple families. The expectations of men and women about the stability and economic cohesiveness of their own families are surely important factors influencing their family size goals and their choice of individual versus couple-based strategies for achieving those goals. Yet, there currently exist only fragmentary data on the stability of the family in different settings.

Population experts appear to have implicit faith in women's capacity to act as demographic innovators. From either a supply- or a demand-side perspective, they are seen as the persons with the most immediate stake in fertility regulation. Within a variety of family systems, however, women face constraints that limit their options outside the family and circumscribe their roles within the family. Whether the limitations be on their physical mobility, as in parts of Southern Asia and Western Asia or on their economic mobility, as in much of the developing world, the consequence is that even when the costs of bearing and rearing children are high, the benefits may also be relatively high where women have limited access to alternative sources of support. Given men's dominant position within the family, increases in the costs of children will have their most direct and immediate impacts on fertility behaviour in families where fathers carry a significant portion of the financial costs.[8] Given men's dominant position within society, improvements in women's livelihood will have the most direct and immediate impact on fertility behaviour where a fair share of women's individual economic gains can be retained for their personal benefit and not all dispersed to other family members. Lastly, given the fact that parents do not necessarily treat all children "equally" but invest in them according to expectations of return, increases in the costs of children will have their most complete impact on fertility behaviour in settings where the economic prospects for girls are as promising as for boys.

Bringing men into the picture, adding an individual perspective to the more traditional couple perspective, developing a more realistic view of "the family" in all its manifestations, gaining a sense of fairness about the process of change—these are all essential steps which will lead to more effective population policies in the 1990s and beyond. The details will have to be worked out in each individual country setting after a process of policy assessment, assumption-testing and empirical analysis, providing a critical review of gender relations and the structure and organization of families. Nothing about families should be taken for granted if these new inquiries are to yield the understanding necessary to achieve the international and national goals originally adopted in 1974 in the World Population Plan of Action.

Notes

[1]In each table, the choice of countries is dictated by the availability of data on that topic at the time the paper was written. Therefore, the selection of countries varies from table to table. Each table should be seen as illustrative and designed to demonstrate the possible range of situations that may apply.

[2]These are synthetic cohort measures which assume that mothers (women that have ever given birth to a child) would progress through their reproductive years beginning at age 20 experiencing the same residential and marital patterns at each age as mothers in each age group at the time of the survey. Obviously, some children are the product of later marriages—not the first one—so this categorization gives only a crude measure of the extent to which children's parents live apart.

[3]Some children living away from their mother may live in the same household with their biological father. On the other hand, some children that live with their mother and her spouse may not be living with their biological father. Thus, these data do not measure what one would ideally like to know, which is, what percentage of children live with both biological parents.

[4]In surveys with detailed marital and birth histories, individual children can be linked with their biological fathers.

[5]Including children born prior to a union or between unions.

[6]In those countries where all women were asked about their contraceptive practice, Maudin and Ross (1992) reclassified unmarried women reporting contraceptive use as married and their use was thus accounted for in the estimates of future contraceptive use and commodity costs.

[7]Use among the formerly married in some cases includes terminal methods actually adopted within a marital union.

[8]Indeed, in low-fertility societies, it could lead to an increase in fertility, which may be seen as desirable in some countries.

REFERENCES

Basu, Alaka Malwade (1992). Family size and child welfare in an urban slum: some disadvantages of being poor but "modern". Paper prepared for the Population Council Seminar on Fertility, Family Size and Structure: Consequences for Families and Children, New York, 9-10 June.

Bledsoe, Caroline (1988). The politics of polygamy in mende education and child fosterage transactions. In *Gender Hierarchies*, Barbara D. Miller, ed. Chicago: The University of Chicago Press.

Bongaarts, John (1990). The measurement of wanted fertility. *Population and Development Review* (New York), vol. 16, No. 3 (September), pp. 487-506.

________ (1991). The KAP-gap and the unmet need for contraception. *Population and Development Review* (New York), vol. 17, No. 2 (June), pp. 293-314.

Boserup, Esther (1970). *Woman's Role in Economic Development*. London: Allen and Unwin; and New York: St. Martin's Press.

Bruce, Judith, and Cynthia B. Lloyd (1992). *Finding the Ties that Bind: Beyond Headship and Household.* Research Division Working Paper, No. 41. New York: The Population Council.

Cain, Mead. (1984). *Women's Status and Fertility in Developing Countries: Son Preference and Economic Security*. World Bank Staff Working Papers, No. 682, Population and Development Series. Washington, D.C: The World Bank.

Caldwell, John C., I. O. Orubuloye and Pat Caldwell (1992). Fertility decline in Africa: a new type of transition? *Population and Development Review* (New York), vol. 18, No. 2 (June), pp. 211-242.

Chen, Lincoln C., Emdahul Huq and Stan D'Souza (1981). Sex bias in the family allocation of food and health care in rural Bangladesh. *Population and Development Review* (New York), vol. 7, No. 1 (March), pp. 55-70.

Das Gupta, Monica (1987). Selective discrimination against female children in rural Punjab, India. *Population and Development Review* (New York), vol. 13, No. 1 (March), pp. 77-100.

Desai, Sonalde (1992). Children at risk: the role of family structure in Latin America and West Africa. *Population and Development Review* (New York), vol. 18, No. 4 (December), pp. 689-717.

_________, and Devaki Jain (1992). *Maternal Employment and Changes in Family Dynamics: The Social Context of Women's Work in Rural South India.* Research Division Working Paper, No. 39. New York: The Population Council.

D'Souza, Stan, and Lincoln C. Chen (1980). Sex differences in mortality in rural Bangladesh. *Population and Development Review* (New York), vol. 6, No. 2 (June), pp. 257-270.

Duncan, Greg J., and Willard L. Rodgers (1988). Longitudinal aspects of childhood poverty. *Journal of Marriage and the Family* (Minneapolis, Minnesota), vol 50, No. 4 (November), pp. 1007-1021.

Egypt, Central Agency for Public Mobilisation and Statistics (1983). *The Egyptian Fertility Survey, 1980*, vol. III, *Socio-economic Differentials and Comparative Data from Husbands and Wives*. Voorburg, Netherlands: International Statistical Institute.

Ezeh, Alex C. (1991). Fertility and family planning issues in sub-Saharan Africa. In *Demographic and Health Surveys World Conference, August 5-7, 1991, Washington, D.C. Proceedings*, vol. I. Columbia, Maryland: IRD/Macro International, Inc.

_________ (1992). Contraceptive practice in Ghana: does partner's attitude matter? Paper presented at the Annual Meeting of the Population Association of America, Denver, Colorado, 30 April-2 May.

Fapohunda, Eleanor R., and Michael P. Todaro (1988). Family structure, implicit contracts, and the demand for children in Southern Nigeria. *Population and Development Review* (New York), vol. 14, No. 4 (December), pp. 571-594.

Findley, Sally E., and Linda Williams (1991). *Women Who Go and Women Who Stay: Reflections of Family Migration Processes in a Changing World.* Population and Labour Policies Programme Working Paper, No. 176. Geneva: International Labour Office.

Garfinkel, Irwin, and Sara S. McLanahan (1986). *Single Mothers and Their Children: A New American Dilemma*. Washington, D.C.: The Urban Institute Press.

Ghana, Statistical Service; and Institute for Resource Development/Macro Systems, Inc. (1989). *Ghana Demographic and Health Survey, 1988*. Accra, Ghana; and Columbia, Maryland.

Greenhalgh, Susan (1991). *Women in the Informal Enterprise: Empowerment or Exploitation?* Research Division Working Paper, No. 33. New York: The Population Council.

Jejeebhoy, Shireen (1992). Family size, outcomes for children and gender disparities: the case of rural Maharashtra. Paper prepared for the Population Council Seminar on Fertility, Family Size and Structure: Consequences for Families and Children, New York, 9-10 June.

Joekes, Susan P. (1987). *Women in the World Economy: An INSTRAW Study*. New York: Oxford University Press.

Joesoef, Mohamad R., Andrew L. Baughman and Budi Utomo (1988). Husband's approval of contraceptive use in metropolitan Indonesia: program implications. *Studies in Family Planning* (New York), vol. 19, No. 3 (May/June), pp. 162-168.

Johansson, S. Ryan (1991). "Implicit" policy and fertility during development. *Population and Development Review* (New York), vol. 17, No. 3 (September), pp. 377-414.

Khalifa, Mona A. (1988). Attitudes of urban Sudanese men toward family planning. *Studies in Family Planning* (New York), vol. 19, No. 4 (July/August), pp. 236-243.

Knodel, John, Napaporn Havanon and Werasit Sittitrai. (1990). Family size and the education of children in the context of rapid fertility decline. *Population and Development Review* (New York), vol. 16, No. 1 (March), pp. 31-62.

Levine, Nancy E. (1987). Differential child care in three Tibetan communities: beyond son preference. *Population and Development Review* (New York), vol. 13, No. 2 (June), pp. 281-304.

Lloyd, Cynthia B. (1991). The contribution of the World Fertility Survey to an understanding of the relationship between women's work and fertility. *Studies in Family Planning* (New York), vol. 22, No. 3 (May/June), pp. 144-161.

_________, and Sonalde Desai (1992). Children's living arrangements in developing countries. *Population Research and Development Review* (Dordrecht, Netherlands), vol. 11, No. 3, pp. 193-216.

_________, and Anastasia J. Gage-Brandon (1992). *Does Sibsize Matter? The Implications of Family Size for Children's Education in Ghana.* Research Division Working Paper, No. 45. New York: The Population Council.

_________ (1993a). High fertility and the intergenerational transmission of gender inequality; children's transition to adulthood in Ghana. Paper prepared for the Seminar on Women and Population in sub-Saharan Africa, Dakar, 3-6 March. Sponsored by the International Union for the Scientific Study of Population.

_________ (1993b). Women's role in maintaining households: family welfare and sexual inequality in Ghana. *Population Studies* (London), vol. 47, No. 1 (March), pp. 1-17.

Macunovich, Diane J., and Richard A. Easterlin (1990). How parents have coped: the effect of life cycle demographic decisions on the economic status of pre-school children, 1964-87. *Population and Development Review* (New York), vol. 16, No. 2 (June), pp. 301-325.

Mason, Karen Oppenheim (1985). *The Status of Women: A Review of Its Relationships to Fertility and Mortality.* New York: The Rockefeller Foundation.

_________, and Anju Malhotra Taj (1987). Differences between women's and men's reproductive goals in developing countries. *Population and Development Review* (New York), vol. 13, No. 4 (December), pp. 611-638.

Mauldin, W. Parker, and John A. Ross (1992). Contraceptive use and commodity costs in developing countries, 1990-2000. *International Family Planning Perspectives* (New York), vol. 18, No. 1 (March), pp. 4-9

Mbizvo, Michael T., and Donald J. Adamchak (1991). Family planning knowledge, attitudes, and practices of men in Zimbabwe. *Studies in Family Planning* (New York), vol. 22, No. 1 (January/February), pp. 31-38.

Mott, Frank L., and Susan H. Mott (1985). Household fertility decisions in West Africa: a comparison of male and female survey results. *Studies in Family Planning* (New York), vol. 16, No. 2 (March-April), pp. 88-99.

Oppong, Christine, ed. (1983). *Female and Male in West Africa.* London; and Boston, Massachusetts: Allen and Unwin.

Parish, William L., and Robert J. Willis (1992). Daughters, education and family budgets: Taiwan experiences. Discussion Paper Series. Chicago, Illinois: The University of Chicago, Economic Research Center, NORC: This paper refers to Taiwan Province of China.

Peterson, James L., and Christina Winquist Nord (1990). Steps to the regular receipt of child support. *Journal of Marriage and the Family* (Minneapolis, Minnesota), vol. 52, No. 3 (August), pp. 539-552.

Richter, Kerry (1988). Union patterns and children's living arrangements in Latin America. *Demography* (Washington, D.C.), vol. 25, No. 4 (November), pp. 553-556.

Ross, John A., and others (1992). *Family Planning and Child Survival Programs as Assessed in 1991.* New York: The Population Council.

Sadik, Nafis (1990). *Investing in Women: The Focus of the '90s.* New York: United Nations Population Fund.

Safilios-Rothschild, Constantina (1985). The persistence of women's invisibility in agriculture: theoretical and policy lessons from Lesotho and Sierra Leone. *Economic Development and Cultural Change* (Chicago, Illinois), vol. 33, No. 2, pp. 299-317.

Sathar, Zeba (1992). Micro-consequences of high fertility: the case of child schooling in rural Pakistan. Paper prepared for the Population Council Seminar on Fertility, Family Size and Structure: Consequences for Families and Children, New York, 9-10 June.

Singh, Susheela (1987). Additions to the core questionnaires. In *The World Fertility Survey: An Assessment*, John Cleland and Chris Scott, eds. London: Oxford University Press.

Thailand, National Statistical Office; and Chulalongkorn University, Institute of Population Studies, (1977). *The Survey of Fertility in Thailand: Country Report.* Bangkok: Economic and Social Commission for Asia and the Pacific.

Traoré, Baba, Mamadou Konaté and Cynthia Stanton (1989). *Enquête démographique et de santé au Mali, 1987.* Bamako, Mali: Institut du Sahel, Centre d'etudes et de recherches sur la population pour le développement, and Columbia, Maryland: Institute for Resource Development/Westinghouse.

United Nations (1975). *Report of the United Nations World Population Conference, 1974, Bucharest, 19-30 August 1974.* Sales No. E.75.XIII.3.

________ (1984a). *Recent Levels and Trends of Contraceptive Use as Assessed in 1983.* Population Studies, No. 92. Sales No. E.84.XIII.5.

________ (1984b). *Report of the International Conference on Population, 1984, Mexico City, 6-14 August 1984.* Sales No. E.84.XIII.8.

________ (1987). *Fertility Behaviour in the Context of Development: Evidence from the World Fertility Survey.* Population Studies, No. 100. Sales No. E.86.XIII.5.

________ (1989). *Levels and Trends of Contraceptive Use as Assessed in 1988.* Population Studies, No. 110. Sales No. E.89.XIII.4.

________ (1991). *The World's Women, 1970-1990: Trends and Statistics.* Series K, No. 8. Sales No. E.90.XVII.3.

________ (1992). *World Contraceptive-Use Data Diskettes, 1991: User's Manual.* ST/ESA/SER.R/120.

Weeden, Donald, and others (1986). Community development and fertility management in rural Thailand. *International Family Planning Perspectives* (New York), vol. 12, No. 1 (March), pp. 11-16.

Weiss, Robert S. (1984). The impact of marital dissolution on income and consumption in single-parent households. *Journal of Marriage and the Family* (Minneapolis, Minnesota), vol. 46, No. 1 (February), pp. 115-127.

Westoff, Charles F. (1988). Is the KAP-gap real? *Population and Development Review* (New York), vol. 14, No. 2 (June), pp. 225-232.

V. THE VALUE OF WOMEN, WOMEN'S AUTONOMY, POPULATION AND POLICY TRENDS

*Els Postel**

The title of this paper contains two words more than the original one suggested by the organizers of this Meeting—the author added the issue of policy. In selecting what seemed to be the most relevant issues in the context of the Meeting, the author took, as the point of departure, the needs and interests of women, particularly those living in the poor countries of the South. It was then impossible to leave population policy out of the discussion. Although it is commonly presented as a solution to existing problems, policy is in some respects part of the problem itself. Population policy is a concept with a Janus face: on the one hand, it has the potential to liberate women and provide them with the means of controlling their own sexuality and fertility; on the other hand, it brings along new forms of oppression and dependency, thus obstructing the very purpose it is meant to serve. Some people see it as the only way to save the earth, to others it is a cruel excess of Western patriarchy and capitalism. Women of the South, present at the World Women's Congress for a Healthy Planet, held at Miami, Florida in November 1991, sharply condemned population programmes as an offensive by the North to control and "depopulate" the third world.

Obviously, the field of women and population is laden with power differences, based on gender, class and the North-South opposition. It does indeed require some optimism to go in search for the better side of the Janus face. Still, this is precisely the purpose of this Meeting. The author's personal motivation is due to the experiences of many women known in Europe, Asia and Africa—heartbreaking stories of unwanted pregnancies and women desperately in need of a safe way to regulate their fertility. The other side of the coin, of course, shows the suffering of women that feel sick and depressed from inadequate contraceptives, depend upon their husband's signature for fertility regulation or have been left completely ignorant about the health aspects of the pills they use.

Against this background, this paper focuses mainly on the situation of women in the developing countries, their place in present-day discourse on population and their rights to control their own fertility. Other questions related to population, such as migration or the demographic problems of the North, are not considered here.

Section A gives a brief historical view of population policy in the context of the United Nations, looked at from a gender perspective. Section B focuses on some of the conditions that are most generally known for lowering fertility and comments on them from a viewpoint of women's interests. Section C then discusses some conceptual constraints for recognizing women's value as autonomous actors instead of instruments in development. This discussion is followed by a section on the practice of family planning and how more consideration could be given to women's autonomy. The paper ends with a summary and recommendations.

A. A GENDER VIEW ON POPULATION

In 1966, the General Assembly of the United Nations adopted a resolution in which the principle was laid down that "the family should be able to decide on its own size". A curious formulation if one tries to visualize this in a practical situation: a patriarch, sitting with his four wives in a circle to decide together whether and in whose womb the next baby will grow?

Two years later, the Proclamation of Teheran on Human Rights appeared. In that document, the right

*Faculty of Social and Behavioural Science, Leiden University, Leiden, the Netherlands.

to decide on the number of children was conferred on parents. In 1974, a new formulation was launched at the World Population Conference at Bucharest; it is the one most often quoted in documents. The relevant section states:

> "All couples and individuals have the basic right to decide freely and responsibly the number and spacing of their children and to have the information and means to do so; the responsibility of couples and individuals in the exercise of this right takes into account the needs of their living and future children, and their responsibilities towards the community." (United Nations, 1975, para. 14(f))

If one looks at it from a gender perspective, the basic assumptions behind such statements seem to be that:

(*a*) Children are born as a result of a decision-making process (husband and wife together making their choice whether first to buy a plough or a refrigerator or to have a child);

(*b*) The two individuals who make up a couple are equal partners in decision-making.

The socio-political context of procreation is thus completely ignored. In reality, sexual relationships are embedded in existing inequalities, not only of gender but also of class, ethnic affiliation, the state versus its citizens or religious leaders versus their followers. Currently, one fourth of all births are estimated to be unwanted by women. An unknown proportion of these births are the result of sexual violence and rape. To many women in the world, the very question of wanting children or not is an elusive one. It would require no less than a transformation in power relations for decision-making to become an adequate term in this connection. Official discourse on population is to a large extent degendered and detached from actual relations between living women and men. A very common form of sexism manifests itself here: the sexism that consists of pretending to speak of human beings in general, while it is evident that gender differences are a very relevant issue in the context (Eichler, 1988).

It was only in 1983 that the International Planned Parenthood Federation, after long discussions, dared to state that in the last instance women should have the right to decide on their own fertility, albeit that "free and just decision making between women and men" is always to be preferred. In the Nairobi Forward-looking Strategies for the Advancement of Women, however, the above-mentioned statement at the 1974 World Population Conference is repeated, however, in a context where the need for women to control their fertility is explicitly established (United Nations, 1985). At the same Conference, the right of women to a free choice of contraceptives was recognized. In 1990, this was restated in the Convention on the Elimination of All Forms of Discrimination Against Women.

The United Nations Fund for Population Activities (UNFPA) report, *The State of World Population 1989*, by its then new Director, Dr. Nafis Sadik, introduced the interests of women, including the unmarried and the infertile, as a major issue (Sadik, 1990a). Its main theme was the central position of women in development processes. The report calls for better health care, equal rights in family and society, better chances for women in the labour market, more access to education and control over decisions that may directly influence a woman's life. In later UNFPA reports, some of these themes recur, although somewhat less elaborated.

In spite of the growing concern for women in the international community, the discourse on population continues to be dominated by demographic projections rather than a commitment to women's interests. Conventional wisdom holds that slowing population growth is the key to solving a vast array of social, economic and environmental problems (Jacobson, 1991a). Currently, more than ever before, world attention has been drawn to the ecological disasters that threaten life on this planet. "Sustainable development" has become a common concern. In this context again, heavy emphasis is put on fertility decline as the key to survival; women tend to become instruments instead of actors in this process (see, for instance, World Bank, 1992).

The 1992 report on the state of world population (UNFPA, 1992) rightly stresses that it is hard to point to direct relations of cause and effect between global degradation of the environment, poverty and population growth in the developing countries. Still, the focus on demographics, mainly perceived as a problem of female fertility, tends to deflect attention from other aspects of human behaviour that form a threat to the health of our planet. In the Women's Action Agenda 21, issued by the World Women's Congress for a Healthy Planet, this point is made in very strong terms: "Knowing that the major causes of environmental degradation are industrial and military pollutants, toxic wastes, and economic systems that exploit and misuse nature and people, we are outraged by suggestions that women's fertility rates (euphemistically called population pressures) are to blame" (World Women's Congress, 1991).

The issue of population, in short, holds a pitfall for women if the growth of the world population is seen as the main or sole cause of disaster in this world, and women in the developing countries, by virtue of their reproductive capacity, as objects in strategies to deflect the ever-rising curves of population growth.

C. Fertility and the status of women

Ever-growing numbers of women want to control their own fertility when they acquire more control over their life, when their status is rising and when gender and power relations permit for more autonomy in a social, economic and political sense. During the past few years, much effort has been put into finding statistical correlations between lower fertility and other aspects of development, such as education, health care and higher age of marriage. No doubt, this research has contributed substantially to the understanding of processes of change. The problem with statistics, however, is that they tell little about the "hows" and "whys" behind the facts. Correlations tend to be perceived as simple causal relations, to be used as directives for influencing fertility. Although fertility regulation has a potential to raise women's status, the fact is that this purpose remains subordinate to a more powerful one: reducing population growth in the developing countries often prevents planners from relying upon women as decision makers in their own right.

During the past few years, quality of life has become more and more prominent as an issue in the development debate. The Amsterdam Declaration on a Better Life for Future Generations, a concluding document issued by the International Forum on Population in the Twenty-first Century, states quite explicitly that the "principal aim of social, economic and cultural development, of which population policies and programmes are integral parts, is to improve the quality of life of the people" (UNFPA, 1989, p.1). The challenge of the coming years, in this author's opinion, will be to apply this principle systematically in the field of women and population. Women's control over their reproduction should be a major issue in the context of human development, both for reasons of justice and for sustainability.

This section has summed up some of the main development processes usually mentioned as conducive to lower birth rates, with some comments on their potential for widening women's scope for control over their life.

Economic development and redistribution

Development in terms of growth of gross national product has often been regarded as the best way to reduce population growth. This view is rational in so far as a minimum degree of welfare is needed to provide social services, such as education and health care, to the population at large and to create a feeling of safety in life, but only if economic growth is actually allocated to these sectors.

It is interesting to note that before 1980 in some poor countries a remarkable fall in fertility rates had already taken place, even in the absence of significant economic growth and without an explicit population policy. Examples are China, Cuba, Guyana and Sri Lanka, in the 1970s; and the State of Kerala in India. A common feature of government policies in those countries during that period appears to be a combination of redistribution mechanisms, a high level of education for both men and women, and a relatively high development of their health-care system (Moore Lappé and Schurman, 1989). Rising fertility in combination with rapid economic development is to be found, for instance, in Southern Africa and Western Asia (Oman), where social inequality in terms of race and gender is prominent and women depend upon motherhood for status and even survival.

For several reasons, economic independence is a major factor in a woman's control over her own life. One of the reasons is that sexual relations, whether within or outside marriage, often takes the form of repayment for financial support given by men. Equal access of women to the labour market is thus a relevant aspect of economic development in relation to women's control over their life and fertility. Women's access to the labour market has not changed much over the years. Roughly one third of women are "working", most of them in low-paid, unskilled jobs.

So far, little research has been done into the quality of labour women want and the facilities they need to continue working in if their reproductive tasks become more intensive. Such matters as day-care centres, pregnancy leave and stimuli for fathers to take part in household activities have little priority in national or international policies.

Education

In recent years, the gender gap in education has become an issue on the international agenda. At the World Conference on Education for All held at Jomtien, Thailand in 1990, the international crisis in education, in particular as it concerns women, was officially recognized. The final Declaration of this Conference asked for priority to be given to basic education for women and girls and to the elimination of the factors that hamper the access of girls to the education system (Helleman, 1992).

For the developing world as a whole, the female literacy rate is currently three fourths that of the male. The gap has narrowed slightly in the past three decades, but much progress remains to be made. It is alarming that since the early 1970s, the proportion of government expenditure on education and health has fallen in many countries, particularly in Africa and in Latin America and the Caribbean. Everywhere in the world, enrolment of women in higher education is far behind that of men. Equality is still far from being realized.

One of the most constant statistical correlations is that between women's education and smaller families. For this reason also, more attention is now paid to this aspect of women's position. Here again, one cannot simply single out a rough statistical correlation for translation into policy guidelines. Specific needs of women in different situations should be taken into account to enhance the potential for their empowerment. Alternative "out-of-school" education programmes, open school, education at a distance, radio and television programmes can all play a more important role in the near future.

Health

Better health for infants and children is a well-known factor in fertility behaviour. The more confidence parents can have in the survival of their children, the more they will be inclined to reduce the number of births. In some countries, impressive improvements have been made in this field. Here, too, the influence of a statistical correlation with decreasing births is noticeable.

Much less attention is paid to women's health. Still, good health is one of the most important resources women have, particularly in low-income households, where they must fulfil a threefold role in production, reproduction and community management (Moser, 1989).

Reproductive health in particular is a low-priority item. Reliable records on maternal mortality are scarce, compared with those on infant mortality. Often, reproductive health is equated with only one aspect of women's lives: motherhood. Jacobson (1991b) distinguishes two more aspects: diseases of the reproductive tract, including sexually transmitted diseases, such as acquired immunodeficiency syndrome (AIDS) and syphilis; and contraceptive use, referred to below. Reproductive tract infections are a grave threat to the life of women throughout the world. Currently, these infections even cause far more deaths among women than does AIDS in men, women and children combined (Jacobson, 1991b).

Lack of access to comprehensive reproductive health care is the main reason so many women, particularly among the poor, suffer and die. Still, according to Jacobson (1991b), most illnesses and deaths from reproductive causes could be prevented or treated with strategies and technologies well within reach of even the poorest countries.

A special case can be made for women that live in situations of war or forced migration. In such circumstances, rape is a frequent occurrence and reproductive health care is virtually absent.

Communication and mobilization

Two more interconnected factors may be mentioned in this section. They are less visible in statistical evidence but probably just as important in view of women's control of their reproduction. One factor is the increase in means of communication, by which it is possible for women, even if they live in relative isolation, to envisage alternatives in lifestyle and to collect information outside the formal education system. The other is the rise of women's non-governmental organizations and networks throughout the world. This factor is of invaluable importance for sharing information, providing support and solidarity and ensuring that women's reproductive rights shall be taken into account.[1]

Besides an increasing number of local and informal networks, the formal international networks, such as the integrated set of information systems, the Women's International Information and Communication Service and the Women's Global Network on Reproductive Rights, help promote communication and give voice to women's opinions.

Family planning services

Access to modern contraception is another factor that has been mentioned both in relation to the rising status of women and as a condition for smaller family size. Family planning is estimated to account for 40 per cent of fertility decline (World Bank, 1984), and family planning programmes have been identified as one of the leading variables. This report adds: "For the single goal of reducing fertility, spending on family planning services turns out to be more cost-effective . . . than does spending on education, health . . . , and other programmes" (World Bank, 1984, p. 121). Evidently the term "human development" had not yet entered the development discourse.

A more recent influential study, covering the period 1982-1989, also stresses the impact of family planning programmes (Mauldin and Ross, 1991). In this study, a distinction is made between strong and weak programmes. "Strength" is almost synonymous with effectiveness in terms of birth control. It is defined by 30 criteria, none of which explicitly relates to users' satisfaction, let alone to women's control. Reproductive health care is scarcely mentioned and only in connection with family planning information and education. Scores for strength are based on questionnaires sent to from four to six respondents per country, all of them recruited from "program staff, donor agency personnel, local observers and knowledgeable foreigners" (Mauldin and Ross, 1991). One may wonder where the female clients are. Some features of strong programmes are obviously contrary to their interests, such as the involvement of the civil bureaucracy as responsible for the success of the programme, the use of incentives and disincentives for the adoption of family planning and the neglect of health issues.

The danger is that an efficiency approach, based on calculations of this type, will leave little room for quality assessment or for the specific needs and priorities of women, who invariably are the targets of these strategies. The consequences for the practice of population policy are further elaborated in section D.

C. THE VALUE OF WOMEN

The international women's movement, feminist authors and experts on women in development have extensively demonstrated the value of women for sustaining their families and their society. Besides their traditional roles in reproduction (child-bearing, family health care and child-rearing responsibilities), they contribute substantively to production, either in subsistence or as income-earners, and fulfil a community managing role, based on the provision of items of collective consumption and mutual exchange of services (Moser, 1989).

Positive gender conceptions, respect for and self-respect of women are key elements of a just and equitable society. As the international community begins to show a greater commitment to "human development" and human rights issues, the climate for acknowledging the value of the female half of the population should gradually improve. In practice, however, discrimination is still omnipresent. In this section, the focus is on the conceptual background of gender inequality inherent in development processes, with special reference to women's reproductive roles.

Production versus reproduction

As long as the main measure of development still is the sum of market-related activities, which are then called production, little weight is attached to reproductive activities, either in the sense of bearing children or in providing daily care. On a global level, in spite of the inclusion of various non-monetary productive activities in the United Nations and national statistics, the bulk of women's work remains invisible. Such tasks as housework, weeding of primary productive land crops and the processing, storage, transport and distribution of food from subsistence farming are still excluded from registration (Waring, 1990). In such a perspective, women can only be valued as "human resources" for production in the market. Reproductive and community managing work, because they are both seen as "natural"and non-productive, are not valued.

This view is reflected in population policy. Although much effort is put into making women accept family planning, little is done to improve their roles as providers of, for instance, family health care and community services. In view of the smaller family size, support for mastering alternative tasks, both paid and unpaid, could help women to find a new destiny in life.

Fertility as a liability

Gender concepts are changing when women's fertility is no longer seen as a source of joy and respect but rather as a weakness or an item for outside control. While in some areas (for instance, southern India) antique statues of goddesses still bear witness to people's reverence for female fertility, this attitude is rapidly changed by the new phenomena of sterilization camps (India) or mass family planning campaigns directed towards women.[2])

The question how fertility control influences the status of women in a given situation depends upon whether women are free to make their own decisions and upon the degree to which they can see alternative destinies beside that of motherhood to which they can aspire. If alternatives are offered and women's access is facilitated, fertility regulation will enhance women's value in society. If, however, they are the sole targets of an aggressive family planning programme, they can scarcely be expected to be treated respectfully in other fields. For this reason also, equal involvement and responsibility of men and women in planning their number of children should be the rule.

Reductionism in modern science

Modern scientific insights and methods are often applied to administer development processes. In spite of their pretension of objectivity, they bear the mark of an age-old patriarchal background, which is visible in much of development discourse and notably so in that on population. Recently, modern scientific thinking, as it originated in the West, has come under severe attack from the side of feminist scientists and philosophers (see, for instance, Keller (1985) for a historical-philosophical viewpoint; and Shiva (1988) for a connection with ecology). The core of the criticism they share concerns the aspect of reductionism in Western science.

Reductionism is a scientific attitude, the most relevant features of which in the context of this paper are, first, its mechanistic world view; and, secondly, its assumption that nature is uniform and manipulable. The world around is conceived as a machine, made up of similar but separate parts that can be studied and handled out of their context. The purpose of knowledge in this tradition is not so much understanding as domination. Nature is dissected into building blocks in order to manipulate them and ultimately to control and exploit the outside world.

Women, in particular their sexuality and fertility, belong to nature. Like nature, they are potentially dangerous and wild, and must be "tamed and subdued", to use the words of Francis Bacon, the father of modern science. It is easy to find the parallels in the discourse on population: the failure to see women as human beings gifted with reason and responsibility; the preference by planners for "effective contraceptives", where effectiveness is measured not in terms of users' satisfaction but with regard to control of female fertility; the lack of consideration for cultural, economic or social conditions which cause different aspirations in terms of numbers of children for different women and men.

Although few people today would still consciously adhere to the principles of science as formulated by its founding fathers in the seventeenth century, feminist and other critical philosophers have convincingly demonstrated how this powerful patriarchal ideology still permeates science and technology. Continuous critical assessment of the philosophical assumptions behind the discourse on population is needed in order to introduce the quality aspects of human life.

The power of definition

This last point, connected to the former, concerns the definition of problems. Reductionism is not an act of arbitrariness. It has to do with power and profit. The location of a problem to be tackled depends upon those with the power to define it. The world population problem, as it has been defined since the 1960s, has been formulated in the North as a problem of the poor and a problem of women. Thus far, it has been very difficult for poor women to get their needs and interests on the agenda, whether in a local or an international context. Waring (1990) aptly demonstrates the role statistics play in the process of getting things on the agenda or keeping them out of it. Items for which no statistical data are available, for instance, reproductive health problems, can easily be left out of consideration as irrelevant or anecdotal.

Definitional power lies with the predominantly male elite in society, who are living at a great distance from women working in the rice fields or in factories all day long. One does not need to believe in a global male conspiracy to assume that their reasoning is based on their own experiences and is therefore essentially androcentric. Besides, their careers and enormous financial interests are at stake, both in multilateral organizations and through the pharmaceutical industry. Without sufficient democratic control and mobilization of a countervailing power, it is highly improbable that women's issues will ever be recognized as relevant in the context of population policy.

D. WOMEN'S AUTONOMY AND THE PRACTICE OF POPULATION POLICY

> "Our choices—the term itself is misleading. We have hardly anything to choose from. How does one decide: when the choice is between the damage to the uterus by the Copper-T, and damage to the body because of repeated childbirth; when the choice is between long-term effects of injectables and implants, and the effect of a secretly performed, stick abortion; . . . when the choice is between undergoing the humiliation of sex determination tests and the daily humiliation faced in a society where only sons are counted as children; . . . when the choice is between undergoing unwanted sterilization, and remaining jobless, in want, because of lack of work otherwise . . . ." (Gupta, 1991a, p. 21)

This is a cry of distress from an Indian woman working at the Bombay Centre for Education and Documentation, quoted in Gupta (1991).

Reproductive freedom is a precondition for women's autonomy in other fields. The reverse is also true: women will not be able to gain control over their bodies as long as they have no access to and control over such resources as land, income, knowledge, education and a positive self-image. This fact is acknowledged in many recent policy documents. Equal status of women was already a forceful recommendation in the 1989 report on the state of the world population (Sadik, 1990a). Still, the execution of population policy in family planning programmes often constrains women's autonomy.

On the one hand, population policy is essentially a top-down approach, with demographic targets set at central levels. On the other hand, it has to take account of people's, particularly, women's rights; and to rely upon the whole-hearted participation of women and men. Coercion is not only reprehensible from an ethical viewpoint but in the long run also counter-productive. It appears that non-governmental and multi-purpose programmes have a better chance of realizing a participatory approach than do large-scale, single-purpose programmes. In the former case, family planning may be integrated within broader programmes of health care and socio-economic change. Even when population control is not the goal, or perhaps because of this, these programmes may be more successful than others in terms of acceptance (Hartmann, 1987).

This section has indicated some features of family planning that deserve caution for their potentially negative impact on women's autonomy.

Planning procedures

Among experts on women in development, there is general agreement that in order to integrate women's needs and interests in development activities, it is necessary for women to take part in decision-making from the very beginning. Only then will they become participants instead of passive acceptors of development policy. In the formulation of population policy and the setting up of family planning programmes, this principle is hardly applied. Neither women nor men that will be the users of family planning services in a specific country or region are normally represented in the agencies that formulate the population problem and decide on the types of solutions to be pursued. Research into the needs and opinions of potential and actual clients of family planning services is still very scarce. Contacts between agencies for population policy or family planning and non-governmental organizations or women's networks concerned with women's reproduction and health needs are few.

Numerical targets

Targets for reducing the number of births on a global level are derived from global population projections. Governments may translate their own national fertility goal into desired numbers of clients per province, district, subdistrict and even village. This is, for instance, the case in Indonesia, a country with a highly successful family planning programme in terms of reducing population growth.

As in China or India, execution of the programme is the ultimate responsibility of the local administrators. A central computer will record the results at any given moment. Several times a year, local civil servants may get a warning from the centre for being behind on their targets. Although they are not supposed to impose the programme by force, it is clear that an ambitious village or district head will use all forms of moral and material incentives to fulfil the wishes of his superiors. Neglect of the qualitative aspects of fertility regulation, notably the health aspects for women, is an almost unavoidable feature of this approach. Strikingly, although family planning is a success in terms of averted births, maternal mortality rates in Indonesia are among the highest in the world. This risk is inherent in target-oriented family planning as a separate activity. Programmes often operate under a limited mandate and their success is measured by equally limited criteria. The main yardstick of success is contraceptive prevalence, the share of women of reproductive age using birth control (Jacobson, 1991b). Local executing personnel get credit and sometimes compensation for the numbers of users they "produce", not for the amount of information given, the range of contraceptives offered for choice or any other qualitative measures. Technically, it would be possible to include more qualitative standards. This step, however, would require the commitment of Governments as well as donors. (For a guideline to quality control in service-oriented family planning programmes, see Bruce, 1990.) If the "user's perspective", as recommended by the Population Council and quoted in the 1991 report on the state of the world population (Sadik, 1992) is going to be more than a fad, systematic recording of quality-related criteria will be indispensable.

Neglect of women's health issues

Although many family planning programmes were meant originally to improve health and reduce population growth, the latter objective has often come to outweigh the former. Primary health care in general has suffered from the emphasis on population control (Hartmannn, 1987). Planners often pretend that contraception is the best way to safeguard women's health by preventing too many pregnancies. This would only be true if contraceptive services were part of a system of comprehensive health care, including wider development goals to strengthen their economic and political position.

Unfortunately, however, contraceptive services are usually offered to the exclusion of, rather than in addition to, assistance within a broader spectrum of health problems. For example, in Brazil, where 70 per cent of women with partners use some method of contraception, recent studies show that from one third to almost one half of those using the pill were at moderate or severe risk for pill use because they were smokers, were over 35 years of age, suffered from high blood pressure or heart problems, or had some other condition that put them at risk (Ford Foundation, 1991).

The side-effects of contraceptives are seldom discussed with potential users, nor are women's complaints taken seriously: medical personnel have a tendency to brush them aside as sheer "psychological" complaints. This problem is one of the items that are hard to get "on the agenda". Little research is done on a contraceptive device once it has passed its stage of trial, and clinical trials can provide only limited information (Hardon and Claudio-Estrada, 1991). Dissatisfaction turns out to be frequent wherever data are available. It may even be the main reason for stopping contraception altogether.

Contraceptive choice

Voluntary acceptance and active participation of clients is an explicit objective in population policy: "Coercion is not only incompatible with democratic values and human rights, but is ineffective in the long term" (UNFPA, 1992, p. 34). A wide range of available contraceptives is a precondition for the realization of free choice. In practice, this ideal is frustrated by several factors.

First, of course, is the problem of costs. In countries like Brazil, India and Indonesia, infrastructural problems are huge. Moreover, Governments may limit access to reversible contraceptives, such as condoms and the pill. There is a growing tendency in the developing countries, stimulated by foreign donors, to switch from the use of contraceptives that give women maximum control, such as the pill, to so-called "effective" means, that is: sterilization; intra-uterine devices; injectables; and implants. The method used most in the developing countries is sterilization (45 per cent, compared with 14 per cent in the industrialized countries). Barrier and natural methods, which in the developed countries account for nearly 52 per cent of total contraception, cover only 15 per cent in the developing countries (Sadik, 1990b). Often, the users of these methods will not even be registered as "acceptors" and thus cannot claim any of the benefits that may be conceded to official users. Although many women may actually prefer long-acting devices for reasons of comfort, or because their husbands need not be informed, they become dependent upon a health system that is often insufficiently equipped to meet medical requirements.

With regard to implants, problems have been noted in Indonesia, where since a few years ago half a million women use Norplant. In a critical report (Ward and others, 1990), the authors raise objections against the method itself and the way it is introduced. Main reservations are about insufficient sterility if it is part of a mass programme; often there is no proper pregnancy check before insertion; lack of information on the necessity of removal after five years; dangerous side-effects, especially in case of late removal; insufficient registration procedures to guarantee an adequate follow-up; and problems with early removal.[3])

A last remark on contraceptive choice concerns the striking gender bias with regard to sterilization. Female sterilization is still much more widely performed than male sterilization, even though the surgical procedure for women carries considerably greater risk, requires much more technical experience and is many times more expensive than sterilization for men (Ford Foundation, 1991).

Lack of information

Lack of sufficient information and counselling is another weak spot in many (not only the developing) countries. Often, medical staff live a—physically as well as socially—from their clients. Uninterest and even disdain may be an aspect of unequal gender and/or class relations. Recently, an Indian gynaecologist was reported to have stated that her patients in the government hospital, mainly poor women, needed implants and injectables because they don't remember to take oral contraceptives. The same attitude can be found in any hierarchical society where health care has become the privilege of a highly educated, urban medical profession.

With regard to spreading information through folders or booklets, the question of cost also is at issue. Sensitizing medical personnel and family planning experts, however, would be possible without extravagant investments.

Incentives, disincentives and coercion

Often incentives and disincentives are administered both to clients and to providers. Sterilization may be a condition for obtaining a job or other benefits. There is a sliding scale, from a travel allowance for midwives or a compensation for a few days of absence from work in the case of sterilization, to payments and to physical coercion. For poor people, financial incentives as such have a coercive character, as they are rarely in a position to refuse them.

Examples of coercion are not hard to find. In El Salvador, women were refused treatment in government health clinics unless they agreed to use contraception (Hartmann, 1987). Tubectomy is again practised in sterilization camps in India, in spite of the unfortunate experiences during the 1970s. A single surgeon may perform from 300 to 500 laparoscopies in 10 hours per day, which works out to one operation every two minutes. With the minimal care that is necessary for such an operation, only a maximum of 50 a day would be possible. It was reported that in one area as many as 1,225 women had such surgery in one day. The District Magistrate of the area proudly boasted that this was the world record for a single day (Balasubrahmanyan, 1986, quoted in Gupta, 1991b)[4].

In general, planners will perceive cases of abuse, also reported from a great number of other countries, as regrettable deviations with no more than anecdotal value. The records, however, are too many and too far-reaching not to be taken seriously. I hope to have demonstrated in this paper that these problems have a structural basis in gender and power relations.

E. Points of concern

The following issues discussed above are recommended.

(*a*) There is an urgent need for quality control to be introduced as an instrument in monitoring and assessment of population programmes;

(*b*) Systematic data collection in family planning programmes should embrace such items as range of available contraceptives, availability per area, amount of information given and by which means, number of prenatal consultations, follow-up activities and data on reproductive health care;

(*c*) Women that are potential or actual clients of family planning services should be represented in the decision-making process in all stages of the programme; autonomous women's groups for reproductive rights could play a role as intermediaries;

(*d*) Workers in population activities at all levels should be sensitized to gender issues; special gender training courses could be designed to this end;

(*e*) The quality of information, also on side-effects and health aspects of contraceptives, should be improved, through sensitizing medical personnel to this issue and through radio and television programmes geared to the needs of specific categories of women;

(*f*) Women in refugee camps and women in circumstances of war are the most frequent victims of sexual violence and rape; they should be recognized as a special target group for reproductive health care and contraceptive services;

(*g*) Special attention is needed for the issue of human rights in population activities; systematic coercion or violation of the integrity of the body should be signalized and put before an international agency or committee.

F. Summary

Population discourse has a history of striking gender blindness. During the past few years, women and women's interests have begun to appear in policy formulation but most frequently still as a subject subordinate to the goal of population control.

Worldwide, much effort has been put into identifying the statistical correlations between fertility decline and other changes in society. Once such a rough correlation has been established, it tends to become translated into general directives for policy. It would apear that it is time to look at these developments from the perspective of women, who are the main targets of this policy but had thus far had little say in it. Raising the status of women is one of the generally acknowledged factors in fertility decline. This factor relates to economic independence, women's education, health, communication and women's control over their reproduction.

Positive gender conceptions, respect for and self-respect of women are key elements of a just and equitable society. Disrespect for women, as closer to nature, is a deeply ingrained characteristic of modern scientific and technological thinking, rooted in a long-standing tradition in Western science. This way of thinking is now subject to severe criticism from feminist and other critical scientists.

The last section of this paper concerns the practice of population policy and its impact on women's autonomy. The aims of population control are hard to reconcile with the principle of women's autonomy. Family planning programmes seem to work better if they are integrated into programmes of health and socio-economic development. Strong target-oriented programmes may easily lead to neglect of women's needs and even to coercion. Few family planning programmes allow for women's active participation in decision-making, execution or evaluation. They often neglect women's needs for health care, contraceptive choice and information.

NOTES

[1]An example is given by Hartmann: "In the city of Recife, located in Brazil's impoverished Northeast, a call-in radio show candidly answers questions about contraception in a country where the subject of birth control has long been taboo. Over one hundred people call each month and letters flow in from the surrounding countryside. The question and letters are addressed to the reproductive right organization, SOS Corpo" (1987, p. 286).

[2]In Indonesia, a little boy who had learned about the blessings of contraceptives in school was seen to scold a pregnant woman in his village for what he considered to be a failure to obey the government guidelines.

[3]Recently, 18 women's organizations in India protested together against the Government's plan to introduce Norplant by "social marketing" and without sufficient medical supervision. Whatever the outcome of their struggle, at least the item will have to be openly discussed.

[4]How this work is performed in an assembly-line fashion with incredible speed and lack of care is shown in the film *Something like a War* by Deepa Dhanraj. The film deals with the national family planning programme, seen from the perspective of women, who are its primary targets. The women in this film clearly establish that population policy is an empty slogan in the absence of developmental input, such as education, health care, land reform, employment opportunities, social security and improvement in women's status.

REFERENCES

Bruce, Judith (1989). Fundamental elements in the quality of care: a simple framework. *Studies in Family Planning* (New York), vol. 21, No. 2 (March-April), pp. 61-91.

Eichler, Margrit (1988). *Nonsexist Research Methods: A Practical Guide*. London; and Boston, Massachusetts: Allen & Unwin.

Ford Foundation (1991). *Reproductive Health: A Strategy for the 1990s*. A Program Paper. New York.

Gupta, Jyotsna Agnihotri (1991a). Perceptions of women's health needs and the new reproductive technologies. *VENA Journal* (Leiden, Netherlands), vol. 3, No. 2, pp. 17-21.

_________ (1991b). Women's bodies: the site for the ongoing conquest by reproductive technologies. *Issues in Reproductive and Genetic Engineering* (Tarrytown, New York), vol. 4, No. 2, pp. 93-107.

Hardon, Anita, and Sylvia Claudio-Estrada (1991). Contraceptive technologies, family planning services and reproductive rights. *VENA Journal* (Leiden, Netherlands), vol. 3, No. 2, pp. 10-14.

Hartmann, Betsy (1987). *Reproductive Rights and Wrongs. The Global Politics of Population Control and Contraceptive Choice*. New York: Harper & Row.

Helleman, Claudine (1992). Education for women's development? *VENA Journal* (Leiden, Netherlands), vol. 4, No. 1, pp. 2-5.

Jacobson, Jodi (1991a). India's misconceived family plan. *World Watch* (Washington, D.C.), vol. 4, No. 6.

_________ (1991b). *Women's Reproductive Health: The Silent Emergency*. World Watch Paper; No. 102. Washington, D. C.: World Watch Institute.

Keller, Evelyn Fox (1985). *Reflections on Gender and Science*. London; and New Haven , Connecticut: Yale University Press.

Mauldin, W. Parker, and John A. Ross (1991). Family planning programs: efforts and results, 1982-1989. *Studies in Family Planning* (New York), vol. 22, No. 6 (November/December), pp. 350-367.

Moore Lappé, Frances, and Rachel Schurman (1989.). *Taking Population Seriously*. London: Earthscan.

Moser, Caroline (1989). Gender planning in the third world. *World Development* (Washington, D.C.), vol. 17, No. 11, pp. 1799-1825.

Sadik, Nafis (1990a). *The State of World Population, 1989: Investing in Women: Focus of the Nineties*. New York: United Nations Population Fund

________ (1990b). *The State of World Population, 1990: Choices for the New Century.* New York: United Nations Population Fund.

________ (1992). *The State of World Population, 1991: Choice or Chance?* New York: United Nations Population Fund.

Shiva, Vandana (1988). *Staying Alive: Women, Ecology and Survival in India.* New Delhi, India: Kali for Women.

Smyth, Ines (1991). The Indonesian family planning programme: a success story for women? *Development and Change (London)*, vol. 22, pp. 781-805.

United Nations (1975). *Report of the United Nations World Population Conference, 1974, Bucharest, 19-30 August 1974.* Sales No. E.75.XIII.3.

________ (1985). *Achievements of the United Nations Decade for Women: Equality, Development and Peace, Nairobi, Kenya, 15-26 July 1985.* Sales No. E.85.IV.10.

United Nations Environment Programme (1991). *Report of the Global Assembly on Women and the Environment: Partners in Life, Miami, Florida 4-8 November 1991.* Nairobi.

United Nations Population Fund (1989). Amsterdam Declaration: A Better Life for Future Generations. In *Report of the International Forum on Population in the Twenty-first Century, Amsterdam, the Netherlands, 6-9 November 1989.* New York.

________ (1992). *The State of World Population, 1992: A World in Balance.* New York.

Ward, Sheila, and others (1990). Service delivery systems and quality of care in the implementation of Norplant in Indonesia. Unpublished.

Waring, Marilyn (1990). *If Women Counted: A New Feminist Economics.* San Francisco, California: Harper Collins.

World Bank (1984). *World Developmenbt Report, 1984.* New York: Oxford University Press.

World Bank (1992). *World Development Report, 1984 and 1992. New York: Oxford University Press.*

World Women's Congress for a Healthy Planet (1991). *Report.* Miami, Florida.

VI. DOES DEVELOPMENT LEAD TO GREATER EQUALITY OF THE SEXES?

Helen Ware[*]

This paper argues that development does not necessarily result in greater equality between men and women. There are areas, such as health and education, where sooner or later the economic gains do flow on to women. But equally, there are other areas, such as legal rights, equal pay and treatment in the labour force and women's political decision-making power, where there is no necessary or clear relation between the status of women and the level of development. Although international conferences of representatives of male-dominated Governments (there are no female-dominated Governments) have been extremely reluctant to address the issue, equality for women depends not upon the level of development or the economic resources available but upon the political will of Governments and upon the cultural setting in which women have to live. Equality is not attained in a zero-sum game in which gains for women can only result from losses to men. Instead, because equality for women promotes economic growth through more effective utilization of existing resources, poor countries that opt for equity (through equal legal rights and access to economic resources) can thereby speed up the pace of development.

A. What is development?

Although ideally any definition of development should include an element covering the degree of participation by the population at large, this paper is largely concerned with development in the more conventional sense of gross national product (GNP) per capita as measured by the World Bank (1992).

An alternative measure that has more recently become available is the human development index (HDI) compiled by the United Nations Development Programme (UNDP). This index covers three key components: *(a)* life expectancy at birth; *(b)* education (adult literacy, two thirds; and mean years of schooling, one third); and (c) income. This index is even available in a gender-sensitive form which incorporates sex ratios for labour force participation and wage rates. Unfortunately, the gender sensitive variant is available for no more than 33 countries, of which only 11 are developing countries or areas (including Hong Kong, the Republic of Korea and Singapore). Thus, the index is very useful in showing the range of degrees of equality among the highly developed countries (over 90 per cent for Nordic countries, France, Australia and New Zealand, but less than 80 per cent for Italy, Japan, Portugal and Switzerland). But it is of very limited use for an examination of the situation in the developing countries where data on female labour force participation and incomes are of very low reliability. In so far as the HDI data for the developing countries can be accepted as providing some reflection of gender inequities, then Paraguay, the Philippines and Sri Lanka , all show less discrimination against women than Ireland or Japan.

B. Status of women in pre-industrial societies

The conviction that development must inevitably improve the status of women is frequently based on the belief that their status in pre-industrial societies was or is uniformly low. Such a belief is frequently based on a limited knowledge of the cultures of China and India. Both are countries where the subjugation of women among segments of the élite was raised to a high art form and where sex-selective infanticide or neglect is still sufficiently widespread to reduce the proportion of women to men significantly below 50

[*]Deputy Director General, Corporate Development and Support Division, Australian International Development Assistance Bureau, Canberra, Australia.

per cent. There is also an assumption that the status of women can be measured on a single scale, which is demonstrably false both in traditional and in industrialized societies (Whyte, 1978). High status in one area (for example, participation in economic production) is often very weakly correlated with status in another area (such as control over economic resources). Equally, the fact that a society favours polygyny or polyandry says very little about the general status of women in that society.

Although generalization is extremely difficult and fraught with anomalies, it would appear that in early traditional societies of hunter-gatherers and horticulturists, women enjoyed relative equality in many areas, while the introduction of plough agriculture, States and world religion largely served to depress the status of women in relation to men (Hendrix and Hossain, 1988). Put another way, relatively egalitarian societies, without major surpluses taken for themselves by élite groups, also tend to allow more equality for women. This situation is partially because such societies do not attach social prestige to men who can afford to keep their women secluded at home and out of the mainstream of economic life. Such a prestige system is doubly damaging, affecting both the wives and daughters of the élite and all the women lower down the social scale that are induced to evaluate their behaviour and are kept from more public roles by the fear of social stigma.

C. WAR, REVOLUTION AND THE PEACE DIVIDEND

Development only begin to raise the status of women again when women's economic and other roles once more expand outside the context of the family. Many Western societies have had the experience of seeing women's equality to men greatly improve after the demands of modern mass warfare broke down the barriers to their participation in a wide range of public and valued roles. Women have had a similar liberating experience as they participated in colonial liberation and other revolutionary movements (Wallace and March, 1991). However, the lack of any inevitable relation between development and progress for women is amply demonstrated by the extent to which, once the war or the revolution is over, women are nudged or forced back to their earlier domestic roles.

If one knew what goes wrong, why women are sent home again, there would be much understanding of the determinants of the status of women. One obvious factor is the availability of employment. When the soldiers return and there is no work for them, women are required to give up their positions in favour of the returned soldiers. Elsewhere, vast armies are retained simply because the only alternative is to discharge the men to beg in the streets. The post-cold war situation will benefit women only if the peace dividend comes first in the form of dramatically decreased arms purchases, followed by improvements of economic and social policy and only then by the discharge of the soldiers. Otherwise, there is a risk of seeing women further marginalized. Although development *per se* does not raise the status of women, women do benefit in flourishing economies where there is a strong demand for their labour (and no cultural constraints making importation of workers the preferred option, as has consistently been the case in Western Asia).

There has been considerable and understandable debate about the impact throughout the world of the employment of women by transnational corporations. However, it is important to recognize that even exploitative employment for women is a considerable advance on no employment at all and brings considerable benefits in terms of enlarging women's options (Ward, 1990). Perhaps the ultimate recognition of this was provided by the Government of Ireland, which, fearing that women's industrial work would threaten the family, selectively recruited foreign investment that provided men with jobs while using state policies to limit women's employment (Ward, 1990).

D. TWO STEPS FORWARD, ONE STEP BACK

The clearest evidence of the possibility of development and modernization being associated with a highly significant decline in the status of women in relation to men comes from such countries as the Islamic Republic of Iran and Pakistan, whose Governments are embarked on a policy of Islamization of all aspects of public life. In Pakistan, the Women's Action Forum was first established at Karachi in 1981, to speak out against a military Government which had embarked on a series of legal moves to reduce the status of women (Mumtaz and Shaheed, 1987). The

Forum was largely composed of the daughters and nieces of the élite members of the earlier women's movement who had accepted "the false assumption that the transformation of economic and social conditions automatically entails the emancipation of women" (Mumtaz and Shaheed, 1987, p. 160). As a result, the lot of the mass of rural women and of the urban poor remained unchanged. Thus, when the Government began its moves to restrict women's legal rights and access to public space (there were even restrictions on the proportion of photographs of women in newspapers), the mass of women had no reason to react because nothing was being taken away from them. Experiences in the Islamic Republic of Iran and other Islamic States have been similar. If improvements in the status of women are not spread beyond a small élite, they are extremely vulnerable to attack by neoconservatives, who can call on traditional, national and religious values to support a return to the old order of highly segregated sex roles. The mass of women will then support the neoconservatives because they associate segregation with higher status for their families and they have no experience of the benefits of liberation.

Although Islamic Governments have been the most straightforward in announcing their intentions to reduce the rights and legal status of women, conservative Governments and religious movements throughout the world have argued for a return to family values. To conservatives, family values inevitably entail women staying at home to look after large numbers of children (almost all conservatives oppose abortion, and many are ambivalent about the control over their life that contraception gives to women). There is no essential reason that the desire to support and strengthen the family should entail mothers staying home. There are many alternative models, such as mothers and fathers sharing roles or communal care for children, which avoid making women's needs subordinate to those of the other members of the family. These models are ignored, however, because they do not meet the requirement of maintaining highly segregated sex roles. Again, it would be possible to envisage a society in which women were the primary caregivers for children but suffered no loss of status thereby, but there would have to be some adjustment mechanism to give such women the same income and income-earning prospects as men and women with continuous careers. Such provision would be likely to occur only in a situation where fertility considerably below replacement level persuaded Governments of the necessity of treating child care as a task requiring high rewards.

E. From infanticide and neglect to amniocentesis

Females experience the greatest disadvantage in those cultures which practise sex-selective infanticide of females (Hausfater and Hrdy, 1984). It used to be assumed that such practices were confined to "primitive" societies. Now it is clear that there can be a mass demand for modern technology (amniocentesis) which makes it possible to determine the sex of the foetus early in pregnancy and thus to practise sex-selective abortion. Extensive data from both China and India show that this modern technology meets a modern demand to dispose of unwanted daughters. That middle-class Indians at Bombay or élite Chinese at Shanghai are prepared to go to such lengths to avoid daughters or to secure sons provides very strong testimony to the predominance of cultural effect over any development effect. These urban, industrialized cultures so discriminate against adult women that daughters are perceived as worthless burdens essentially because they do not provide the same security (and possibly religious services) for their parents in old age as do sons.

Interestingly, in Japan, which had an equally strong cultural bias against daughters in the past, the position has now changed. Since 1989, annual surveys which have asked "if you had only one child, would you rather that it is a son or a daughter", have shown a clear preference for daughters. This change reflects the fact that (*a*) daughters can now earn their own living; and (*b*) practical experience shows that in a highly industrialized consumer society daughters are more likely to provide financial and emotional support than sons. It would be very interesting to know what the situation is in Hong Kong and Singapore, areas in the Chinese tradition which have undoubtedly achieved economic success.

F. DOES DEVELOPMENT ASSISTANCE BENEFIT WOMEN?

Even where it is clear that development does not necessarily benefit women, it might well be expected that development assistance, which comprises planned input from the developed countries to the less fortunate and less technologically advanced societies, should inevitably benefit women. Unfortunately, the evidence is in and it is quite clear: development assistance does not normally improve the lot of women. This finding is true even where donors have an explicit policy of directing their assistance towards women. Indeed, some have argued that "a strictly enforced sexual division of labour, often involved with the absolute command of religious beliefs, and the maleness of public authority, appear essential to any understanding of why development seems as a rule to have had an adverse effect on the role and status of women" (UNDP, 1980, p. 7). All members of the Development Assistance Committee (DAC) of the Organisation for Economic Co-operation and Development (OECD) are agreed on the difficulty of making aid work for women, to meet their needs and advance their interests (OECD, 1992). The Committee report states that economic and political development processes have, in general, had no beneficial effect on the status of women, due in part to the way in which women were incorporated into development models or the fact that they were ignored. First, there has been a tendency to consider only one aspect of women's life. Given the numerous tasks and responsibilities of women—nurturing and/or productive work in the home and paid and unpaid work in and around the home, outside the home and in the community—such an approach is seriously flawed.

Secondly, many approaches are geared to a greater or lesser extent to integrating women into the overall development effort. The approach here is predominantly quantitative: more women must be involved to a greater extent; where this process is to take place and under what conditions are not discussed. In fact, however, women are fully integrated into the development of their country, thanks to the productive and reproductive work they perform; but because of their subordinate position they have no control over the products of their labour, their own body and their living conditions. Integration within existing institutional frameworks marginalizes their position. Strategies designed to improve the position of women cannot therefore proceed on the basis of integration as such (Netherlands, 1991, p. 230).

The Netherlands report (1991) also highlight three cultural barriers to adequate development strategies: the largely unconscious efforts of Western people to project their own cultural norms in relation to sex roles; the lack of women in the Government élite with whom donors negotiate; and a failure to accept that refusing to pass judgement on cultural elements that oppress women does not amount to objectivity but to support for an ideology that perpetuates social inequality.

There are other issues. In too many cases, women's needs are simply ignored (many infrastructure projects take little note of the requirements of people of either sex, instead focusing on abstract objectives, such as improving traffic flows or crop yields). Also, it is still true that the great majority of decision makers in the donor agencies are men; and often men that, because of the nature of their international careers and their technical backgrounds, have been little exposed to women's movements in their own countries. Lastly, for women, as for minority groups, the "trickle-across" effect does not work. Benefits to men or to ethnic or other majorities are seldom passed on or shared. Westerners tend to assume that household members inevitably share a common level of living: they fail to understand that women and men may operate in separate economies or that daughters' nutrition, health and education may be deliberately sacrificed in favour of son's welfare (Leslie, 1991) (even though the latter pattern was commonplace in Europe only a century ago).

As early as 1980, UNDP, in its review of rural women's participation in development, recognized that "while there has evolved a greater acceptance and fuller understanding of the role of women in development, difficulties are encountered in actually programming for women's participation in development" (UNDP, 1980, p.1). Women's special problems were said to be due to three main issues: (*a*) the inadequacy of the database for development planning, essentially due to the non-recording of women's work (Waring, 1988); (*b*) women's lack of access to appropriate training and education, especially extension services; and (*c*) the negative impact of technological change. In the period since that time very little has changed: women are still marginalized; and because their existing contributions to the informal economy are ignored, planning for their future participation, training and access to technology is inappropriate or non-existent.

The Indian case is typical:

"Many of the studies have shown that the adoption of modern farming methods, new cropping patterns and new technology have affected female labour adversely. The commercialization of markets and increasing role of capital and wholesale dealers in trade have virtually eliminated the traditional role of women in trade and commerce. The modernization of fishing industry and the large-scale organization of dairying, are instances in point. The displacement of female labour through the introduction of new technology, as in the case of the textile industry as against hand weaving, indicates that the labour market, as it is operating, is not neutral as between men and women." (Dube, Leacock and Ardener, 1989).

Even where projects for women in the developing countries are begun with every good intention and clear planning targets, things very often turn sour with the women sadly discovering that the promised benefits simply do not appear (Buvinic, 1984). There are a number of reasons that this so often happens:

(*a*) Planners see projects for women as part of a zero-sum game in which gains for women inevitably represent losses for men;

(*b*) Because of (*a*) and because cultural instinct tempts them this way, there is a nearly irresistible tendency for projects to deteriorate from income-generation and production-oriented focuses to welfare projects. In many cases, the failure to deliver is even worse because the net result is to add to women's workload and other burdens without any increase in their income or welfare;

(*c*) Another contributory factor is the staffing of women's projects. Too often the staff have neither the appropriate skills to impart nor the understanding of the women's situation. If they are women, they lack technical knowledge; if they are men, they lack empathy and often the motivation to push the women forward;

(*d*) The most common failure of all, however, is simply to find an income-generating activity that allows women to make money. Too little attention is given to the alternative of including women in undifferentiated or men's projects. Too often it is assumed that women have free time and can provide volunteer labour without any need for reward.

G. Women, education and equality

Beyond a certain level, high levels of national income tend to bring women educational equality with men because, first, illiteracy disappears with succeeding generations and eventually nearly all adults achieve more than a primary education. Educated men may marry illiterate women but they normally choose to educate their daughters to some extent even if not as far as their sons. It is at lower levels of development that there is the greatest scope for educational discrimination against girls. Reflecting the situation in the past, female/male illiteracy ratios for those aged 25 or over are most extreme among the Eastern Asian cultures of Hong Kong, Singapore and the Republic of Korea, where there are at least three times as many illiterate women as men (table 17). Yet these countries currently have relatively equal sex ratios at primary and secondary levels because the great majority of children finish secondary school. Discrimination still remains, however, at the tertiary level, especially in Hong Kong and the Republic of Korea.

Indeed, one of the best measures of the current and future status of women in a country is the proportion of women to men in its tertiary institutions from which the future leaders and experts are most likely to be drawn. It is not possible, however, to use the measure without caveats. As the figures for Lesotho and the United Arab Emirates indicate, in some cases girls are

TABLE 17. INDICATORS OF DEVELOPMENT AND THE STATUS OF WOMEN

Country or area	Gross national product per capita (1990 dollars) (1)	Ratio of female to male illiterates aged 25 or over (2)	Human Development Index 1990 (3)	Gender-sensitive HDI (4)	Ratio of female to male enrolment (x 100), 1985-1987 Primary (5)	Secondary (6)	Tertiary (7)
Switzerland	32 680	..	0.977	790	97	104	47
Japan	25 430	..	0.981	761	95	97	56
Sweden	23 660	..	0.976	938	97	107	89
United States of America	21 790	91	0.976	842	94	97	110
United Arab Emirates	19 860	158	..	..	94	95	139
France	19 490	..	0.969	899	94	102	97
Australia	17 000	..	0.971	879	95	99	91
United Kingdom	16 100	..	0.962	819	95	99	81
Hong Kong	11 490	382	0.913	649	91	100	53
Singapore	11 160	338	0.848	601	89	98	72
Ireland	9 550	..	0.921	689	95	105	76
Saudi Arabia	7 050	..	0.687	..	80	64	65
Rep. of Korea	5 400	341	0.871	571	94	88	43
Portugal	4 900	165	0.850	708	91	116	113
Brazil	2 680	125	0.739	..	95	..	100
Iran (Islamic Rep. of)	2 490	135	0.547	..	78	65	39
Argentina	2 370	115	0.833	..	97	112	113
Malaysia	2 320	206	0.789	..	98	96	80
Mauritius	2 250	..	0.793	..	98	90	50
Botswana	2 040	93	0.534	..	108	109	71
Tunisia	1 440	155	0.582	..	80	70	58
Thailand	1 420	236	0.685	..	93	..	..
Paraguay	1 110	164	0.637	566	92	..	..
Cameroon	960	149	0.313	..	84	61	..
Swaziland	900	112	0.458	315	98	97	62
Papua New Guinea	860	..	0.321	..	75	..	32
Côte d'Ivoire	750	..	0.289	..	70	43	..
Philippines	730	114	0.600	472	84	99	119
Zimbabwe	640	..	0.397	..	97	..	50
Egypt	600	166	0.385	..	76	65	50
Indonesia	570	192	0.491	..	93	74	48
Lesotho	530	68	0.432	..	125	148	172
Sri Lanka	470	244	0.651	518	93	..	68
Zambia	420	164	0.315	..	89	54	21
Ghana	390	133	0.310	..	78	60	21
Pakistan	380	131	0.305	..	50	37	17
China	370	226	0.612	..	93	99	89
Kenya	370	..	0.366	215	93	68	36
India	350	161	0.297	..	65	..	35
Mali	270	106	0.081	..	59	40	15
Bangladesh	210	141	0.185	..	66	39	24
Myanmar	200	213	0.385	285	..	89	64
Nepal	170	126	0.168	..	41	30	25
United Rep. of Tanzania	110	173	..	..	100	62	..

Sources and note to follow.

Table 17 (*continued*)

Sources: Columnn (1), for Myanmar and Swaziland, United Nations Developmnent Programme, *Human Development Report, 1992* (New York, Oxford University Press, 1992); for all other countries, World Bank, *World Development Report, 1992: Development and the Environment* (New York, Oxford University Press, 1992). Column (2), calculated from*The World's Women, 1970-2000: Trends and Statistics*, Series K, No. 8 (United Nations publication, Sales No. 90.XVII.3), table 4. Column (3), *Human Development Report, 1992*, human development index , table 1. Column (4), *Human Development Report, 1992*, using separate male and females estimates of life expectancy, adult literacy, mean years of schooling, employment levels and wage rages. Colums (5)-(7), *The World's Women, 1970-2000: Trends and Statistics*, table 4, except for Myanmar, secondary and tertiary, which were taken from *Human Development Report, 1992*.

NOTE: HDI = human development index.

educated in tertiary institutions in the country while boys receive higher status tertiary education internationally. More significantly, the statistics for tertiary education do not normally include the training provided for military officers, which is often the most important or essential preparation for holding positions of power in the future and is almost entirely restricted to men. Most important of all, however, the figures do not disclose the content of the tertiary education provided. In countries where only an élite of fewer than 10 per cent of the population attend tertiary institutions, it is common for women to study arts and literature in preparation not for a career but for marriage to their male fellow students, who have engaged in the study of the "harder" technical and scientific subjects (Kelly and Slaughter, 1991).

Alternatively, it is possible (as in the United States of America and in some Australian states) to reach a situation where more women than men attend tertiary institutions because the risk of unemployment is greater for young women and it is more socially acceptable for young women to stay at college looking for a marriage partner or work, while young men are under much greater pressure to get out and find a job. There is also a phenomenon whereby what were once regarded as hard male areas with good prospects rapidly decline in prestige as women move into them in significant numbers: examples are medicine in the former Union of Soviet Socialist Republics or law in Australia. It is not just that traditionally female areas are devalued—if women succeed in moving into a new area (for example, librarianship in the West), then that area itself becomes devalued. Also even within a single profession, such as law or medicine, there are those employed by the State and those in what is almost invariably better remunerated and rewarded private practice—again women very commonly are heavily overrepresented in the public sector and the lower ranks of the professions.

The economic and social benefits of educating girls are not only substantial, they are also greater than the benefits of educating boys. Women's education results in smaller and healthier families and the participation of educated women in the labour force serves to reduce poverty. Yet, paradoxically, parents' economic rationality continues to lead them to educate their sons in preference to their daughters, even where education is relatively free. This situation exists because girls can contribute more than boys to the household economy when young and then usually marry out, taking any investment in their education and their earning capacity with them. A recent World Bank study looks at ways of encouraging parents to educate their daughters. Whatever reduces the cost of education disproportionally raises the proportion of girls in school. Thus, for example, providing free primary-school textbooks in Peru resulted (controlling for all other factors) in girls being three times more likely to enrol, whereas there was no effect on boys' enrolment (Bellew, Raney and Subbarao, 1992).

Scholarships for girls may be necessary in such cultures as Bangladesh, where girls are very much undervalued. Less costly alternatives are flexible hours and calendars that allow girls to participate in household tasks. Other innovative approaches have included school child care for younger siblings, public transport, accessible water and fuel supplies, public meetings to encourage female participation, siting of girls' schools nearer to villages, improved school sanitation and hedges for girls' areas of schools, special science clubs for girls, and bonuses for women teachers in remote areas. Often a package combining these approaches is the most effective plan and shows that it is less the level of development than the political commitment to encouraging female education which counts. A situation where employment opportunities for women are better than for men can also provide encouragement for education of women.

H. Factors that facilitate women attaining equality with men

Some factors that facilitate women attaining equality with men are much easier to provide at high levels of development when economic resources are plentiful. Other factors, however, are either not dependent upon the national level of income or are actually more readily available in less industrialized societies.

Women's legal rights are not dependent upon the availability of resources but upon political will and national culture. Thus, most African countries gave women the right to vote at independence, but Switzerland only in 1971 and Iraq in 1980. Laws relating to access to contraception and abortion equally depend upon will, not resources, although access to services does reflect resource availability and allocation.

Education (as stated above) provides an excellent example of the possible interactions between culture, ideology and resources. A society or Government can decide on the resources to be allocated to different levels of education and to males and females (as well as to all the other divisions, such as urban/rural, buildings/staff or technical/arts). To take a very simple example, an élite constituting 10 per cent of the population can decide whether daughters will be educated.

The interaction between class inequalities in the distribution of resources and sexual discrimination is especially significant in the case of women's additional burdens, such as child care. Child care presents problems when neither relatives nor servants are available to release the mother for work outside the home. For more affluent women in the developing countries, servants are usually available to provide child care; for poorer women, keeping older daughters or nieces home from school is the most common solution, albeit at a cost to the next generation. Many former centrally planned economies provided highly subsidized commercial child care to free women for the labour force. Advanced market economies have yet to find a solution for child care, which, being highly labour- intensive if of high quality, tends to cost more than most women with middle or lower pay rates can afford, especially if they have more than one child (unlike hiring a servant, with public care the cost rises steeply with each additional child). Certainly for middle-class and élite women, it is easier to have a continuing career and a family in a developing country than in a developed one. Equally, it may be easier for women to make it to the top in highly stratified and/or sexually segregated societies than in more egalitarian ones. If cultural norms decree that male physicians cannot examine female patients and men cannot teach girls, then there have to be some female physicians and teachers, and possibly even professors. If political power is restricted to a highly limited group of "top families", then, in the absence of a suitable male, females may achieve power; hence the phenomenon of queens even in medieval Europe and of female prime ministers in a number of Muslim countries where the rights of ordinary women are extremely restricted.

I. Development, women's domestic roles and equality within the household

One area where statistics are understandably limited relates to the sharing of power and decision-making within households. As a rule, data for the developed countries are superior in quality and range to those for the developing countries. In this case, however, there are probably more anthropological studies of cultures regarded as exotic in the West than there are sociological or economic studies of individual interactions within families in the developed countries. Yet, all the available evidence suggests that even in these intimate settings women in the developed countries do not succeed in negotiating to achieve equality. Housework and child care are still considered the woman's responsibility even in urban areas of the most industrialized countries. Women in New York, London or Tokyo have fewer children to care for and a vast range of domestic appliances to choose from but they have not persuaded their men to share equally in domestic or child-rearing tasks. It would appear that no study anywhere in the more developed regions has found that pattern of equal sharing between husbands and wives without which there can be no true equality.

Many nineteenth century European and American feminists believed that technology as applied to domestic tasks would liberate women, both by the industrialization of such activities as food preparation and laundry and by the reduction of the time required to perform tasks still confined to the home. Instead, what has happened is that standards have risen, as with the ever-increasing frequency of the washing of clothes. The limited studies available suggest that as the wife's power (within the household) in relation to that of the husband rises with increased education and income, the household buys more outside services, such as restaurant meals, but the husband does not increase his input into the running of the household. "New" men continue to feel that a token contribution of domestic labour is sufficient. Women themselves could do much to change the situation through the way in which they raise their sons, for it is only if sons are required to make the same household labour input as daughters that equality will be achieved. As Meillassoux states: "When the emphasis is not on reproduction any more, sex differentiation fades away" (1989, p. 20).

J. Female-headed households

Because of women's economic disadvantages, in terms of access to assets and income-earning potential, female-headed households are almost invariably poorer than households headed by men. Indeed, in many societies, female-headed households contain high proportions of all of those living in poverty. In highly traditional societies, there are few female-headed households because of cultural constraints on women living without men, who are support structures which provide alternatives to women that are not members of nuclear families complete with a husband and/or father. With development, however, both the cultural constraints and the supportive structures tend to break down and many more women are found struggling alone to maintain themselves and their children (United Nations, ECA, 1984).

Development sectors, such as mining, that provide employment for men but not for women and provoke mass migration by men, who leave their families at home, play a major role in the creation of female-headed households. Thus, 47 per cent of households in Zambia are headed by women. Development in general tends to be associated, by way of changes in kin support networks, with a decrease in householdsize and an increase in the number of female-headed households (United Nations, 1991). The issue of female-headed households and the feminization of poverty had a brief period of high-profile attention but would appear to have been set aside as "too hard" in face of the society-wide problems associated with structural adjustment.

K. Women and health

Female humans have an innate biological advantage over male humans. As noted above, unless they are radically discriminated against, girl babies out-survive boy babies and women live longer than men. This is a female advantage which increases linearly with development in the absence of very marked preference shown to males (Leslie, 1991). The greatest gap between the sexes and the greatest longevity for women is found in Japan. This disparity exists despite the persistence of very considerable discrimination against women in Japan (Mioko and Jennison, 1985). Some of this discrimination, such as that legally obliging women to retire up to a decade earlier than men, may actually give an advantage to women by contributing to their good health and greater longevity.

It should always be kept in mind that any index of the status of women, such as HDI (UNDP, 1992), which incorporates a measure of women's longevity, will tend to show an advantage to women. Conversely, indices incorporating income data (which are much harder to find) will show women at a disadvantage. Even where women live longer than men, they are often less healthy; anaemia is the lot of two thirds of pregnant women and one half of non-pregnant women in Africa and in Southern and Western Asia (Leslie, 1991). It is clear that a major factor in women's health is their reproductive histories (Kane, 1991). The sad irony is that it is the women of the developed countries that have the good health to flourish through numerous pregnancies while the malnourished women of the developing countries experience repeated pregnancies and the associated high rates of maternal mortality. In the rich countries such as Australia, maternal mortality is almost entirely limited to cases of physician error.

L. Development, fertility and the status of women

Entire books can, and have been, devoted to the subject of the interrelation between women's fertility and their position in a range of spheres, such as education, employment and legal status (see bibliographies of UNESCO, 1983; and IUSSP, 1988). Their authors have focused on how to introduce changes that, while benefiting women, would have the maximum impact in reducing fertility. They have tended to assume that development *per se* raises the status of women and then to attempt to identify the precise links between improvements in women's status and fertility decline. For example, does women's education have such a strong impact because it raises women's autonomy and input into decision-making in the home? Very few writers have addressed the issue in the reverse direction by asking what impact reduced fertility has on the status of women. This gap is especially striking since it is widely recognized that a major factor in the reluctance of individual women in developing countries to limit the number of their children is the fear that fewer children will mean less social influence and a lonely and poverty-stricken old age.

In theory, gaining control over their fertility should give women an entire range of new choices (which is one reason that fathers and husbands are often so virulently opposed to birth control). Yet it is a "chicken-and-egg" problem to determine which comes first—women's desire to limit their fertility or the changes in their living circumstances that make talk of choice a much more genuine reflection of reality. The area of technology that has been of almost unalloyed benefit to women (certain defective devices being excluded) is birth control technology, even if its developers were not feminists but neo-Malthusians. For a brief period between the first spread of the pill and the intra-uterine device, and the advent of acquired immunodeficiency syndrome (AIDS), women with access to modern contraception experienced a golden age of sexual freedom without the risk of pregnancy. Undoubtedly, there were men who exploited women in this situation, but women also faced a range of choices that they had never had. Fertility control is an important component of the status of women and an element that has a meaning for women which it can never have for men. The stress placed by some feminists upon the undesirable side-effects of contraceptives and the excessive medicalization of child birth has tended to obscure the very real gains won in female autonomy and good health. Any index of the status of women should ideally include access to a choice of contraception, legal abortion and the right to choose the number of children. As the cases of Ireland and Japan show, such rights do not automatically come with economic development.

With the ageing of the population of so many industrialized countries, these regions appear to be poised on the brink of a new era of governmental pronatalism. Equality of women in this context requires that women should receive special treatment, not the negativism of restraints on contraception or employment but the positivism of access to child care without undue economic penalties and supports to make it possible for those with domestic responsibilities (whatever their sex) to pursue their careers, with or without periods out of the formal labour force (Meehan and Sevenhuijsen, 1991).

Some fear that below-replacement fertility is the inevitable outcome of gender equality, whether in Europe or the newly industrialized economies of Asia. Such a view ignores two factors. One is that pronatalist measures, such as taxation that acts affirmatively in favour of families, have been given only token support. There is also a question concerning how much divorce and remarriage, with the desire for children from each union, will contribute to raising fertility.

M. The political factor

It is difficult to overstress the importance of political will in ensuring that women shall access to the benefits of development. This does not simply mean that women need to have the vote and the right to stand for election; more importantly, it means that women need to play a vital role in decision-making at all levels. This aspect is not simply a question of equity; it is because men and women have different priorities and the less developed the country, the wider the divergence is likely to be. Often the local village level is just as or even more important than the central level. Indeed, both the developed and the developing countries have now had the experience of women prime ministers, who would appear to have done very little to improve the status of women. It would appear that for women in politics to have a feminist impact it is necessary that their numbers should reach a certain critical mass. The Nordic experience would suggest that this critical mass is close to 30 per cent.

Conversely, however, military Governments often offer very little to women, both because of their ideology which tends to stress that women should be in the kitchen and breeding the next generation, and because of their priorities, which focus on military expenditure to the neglect of virtually all forms of social expenditure. Women have much to gain from the peace dividends which should follow the end of the cold war, but only if governmental priorities are reordered to place greater emphasis on basic social expenditures on education and health.

Backing up the politicians and implementing their policies are the bureaucrats. Here again, merely having a scattering of women in the bureaucracy is not enough to secure an impact; it is necessary to have sufficient numbers of women in the senior decision-making ranks (say, at least 20 per cent). It is possible to debate whether it is more effective to have a ministry of women officers to make an impact on overall policy or individual women's bureau within each ministry to ensure that women's perspectives shall not be forgotten, whatever the topic under discussion (industry, transport or decentralized policy). What is certain that women's ministries or women's bureau will get nowhere without strong political support to allow them to overcome mass culture inertia or active opposition (Phillips, 1991).

N. Lack of political will

The reasons for a lack of political will became self-evident from the statistics on women in positions of political power (United Nations, 1991). Less than 1 in 25 of the cabinet ministers in the world is a woman, and 93 countries have no women ministers. It is true that there have been 18 women heads of Government this century, 11 of whom have headed developing countries. However, such women at the helm have done remarkably little, except as the ultimate role models, to improve the position of women in relation to men in their own country. Female heads of Government generally fall into one of two categories: (*a*) they are the widows or other relatives of notable male political figures and as such are frequently near hostages to their political supporters; or (*b*) they are political leaders that have made their own career, but most often at the cost of denying that women have interests different to men and of showing themselves to be tougher and more "masculine" than any of their male rivals. There is a very small third category of women leaders that have achieved success without denying that women have special needs, but this group would appear to be almost entirely limited to the Nordic countries where women's representation in Parliament is sufficiently common to create a feeder group of women politicians from which to choose. Strangely, although it is almost never suggested that male politicians have a bias towards representing male interests, women remain very reluctant to try to redress the balance by beginning from the presumption that the female viewpoint is just as representative as the male.

In most of the national parliaments, women represent fewer than 10 per cent of the total members. There is no simple relation between the level of development and the proportion of women among parliamentarians: women are better represented in India (8 per cent) than in the United States of America 5 per cent) and in Angola (14 per cent) and Cameroon 14 per cent) than in the United Kingdom (6 per cent) or France (6 per cent). Formerly, the centrally planned economies of Eastern Europe used to stand out as having close to one third of parliamentarians as women but the proportion of women elected has now fallen. Women tend to do better in one-party States, where the one area in which women participate at close to the one-third level in parliaments with strong powers is the Nordic countries. In contrast, in equally highly developed Japan, women make up only 1 per cent of parliamentarians.

O. Conclusion

It has been known since at least 1975 that there are many problems in ensuring that women shall have equal access to the benefits of development and that unthinking assumptions that what is good for the economy must be good for women are simply wrong. There is now a very wide range of studies of the many and varied cultural barriers to women's full participation in society and its rewards (box 3). What is lacking are solutions—successful strategies for ensuring that women shall have equal access to the benefits of development and shall avoid being unequally penalized with the unwanted negative side-effects.

Often it appears that women are only remembered when there is a need for cheap or volunteer labour. Currently, women and the environment is the theme of the year, and there is once again a pattern where women are to be loaded with new responsibilities and given inadequate resources to produce results which should be for the benefit of all. For a number of reasons, including a very justifiable awareness that one inhabitant of an industrialized country consumes more resources than 20 inhabitants of the developing countries, population issues have been relegated to a footnote to the environmental debate. Women's interests lie in ensuring that they shall be integrated as active participants at all levels in the planning and implementation of development and environmental programmes; and that their rights and access to education, health services (including a choice of family planning services) and employment and income-earning opportunities shall be recognized and realized in practical form. As has already been stressed, for women to gain such equality will require a level of political will that has yet to be demonstrated anywhere in the world (see table 17, gender-sensitive HDI); Meehan and Sevenhuijsen, 1991; NORAD, 1991; Phillips, 1991).

References

Afshar, Haleh I. (1991). *Women, Development and Survival in the Third World.* London: Longman.

__________, and Bina Garwal, eds. (1989). *Women, Poverty and Ideology in Asia: Contradictory Pressures; Uneasy Resolutions.* London: MacMillan.

Baxter, Janeen, and Diane Gibson (1990). *Double Take: The Links Between Paid and Unpaid Work.* Canberra, Australia: Australian Government Publishing Service.

Bellew, Rosemary, Laura Raney and A. K. Subbarao (1992). Educating girls. *Finance and Development* (Washington, D.C.), vol. 29 (March), pp. 54-56.

Buvinic, Mayra (1984). *Projects for Women in the Third World: Explaining Their Misbehaviour.* Washington, D.C.: International Centre for Research on Women.

Dauber, Roslyn, and Melinda L. Cain (1981). *Women and Technological Change in Developing Countries.* Boulder, Colorado: Westview Press.

Dixon, Ruth B. (1978). *Rural Women at Work: Strategies for Development in South Asia.* Baltimore, Maryland: The Johns Hopkins Press.

Dube, Leela, Eleanor Leacock and Shirley Ardener, eds. (1989). *Visibility and Power: Essays on Women in Society and Development.* Delhi, India; and New York: Oxford University Press.

Hausfater, Glenn, and Sarah B. Hrdy, eds. (1984). *Infanticide: Comparative and Evolutionary Perspectives.* New York: Aldine.

Hendrix, Lewellyn, and Zakir Hossain (1988). Women's status and mode of production: a cross-cultural test. *Signs* (Chicago, Illinois), vol. 13, No. 3 (Spring), pp. 437-453.

International Union for the Scientific Study of Population (1988). *Conference on Women's Position and Demographic Change in the Course of Development, Asker, (Oslo), 1988.* Liege, Belgium.

Kane, Penny (1991). *Women's Health From Womb to Tomb.* Basingstoke, Hamshire, United Kingdom: MacMillan.

Kelly, Gail, and Sheila Slaughter (1991). *Women's Higher Education in Comparative Perspective.* Dordrecht, Netherlands; and Boston, Massachussets: Kluwer.

Leslie, Joanne (1991). Women's nutrition. *Health Policy and Planning* (Amsterdam), vol. 6, No. 1, pp. 1-19.

Meehan, Elizabeth, and Selma Sevenhuijsen (1991). *Equality, Politics and Gender.* London: Sage Publication.

Meillassoux, Claude (1989). The pregnant male. In *Visibility and Power: Essays on Women in Society and Development,* Leela Duke, Eleanor Leacock and Shirley Ardener, eds. Delhi, India; and New York: Oxford University Press.

Mioko, F., and R. Jennison (1985). The UN Decade for Women and Japan: tools for change. *Women's Studies International Forum* (Tarrytown, New York), vol. 8, No. 2, pp. 121-123.

Mumtaz, Khawar, and Farida Shaheed, eds. (1987). *Women of Pakistan: Two Steps Forward, One Step Back?* London; and Atlantic Highlands, New Jersey: Zed Books.

Netherlands, Ministry of Foreign Affairs (1991). *A World of Difference: A New Framework for Development Co-operation in the 1990s.* The Hague.

Norwegian Agency for International Development (1991). *Mobilizing Women in Local Planning and Decision-Making: A Guide to Why and How.* Oslo, Norway.

Organisation for Economic Co-operation and Development, Development Assistance Committee (1992). *Third Monitoring Report on the Implementation of the DAC Revised Guiding Principles on Women in Development.* Paris.

Phillips, Anne (1991). *Engendering Democracy.* Oxford, United Kingdom: Polity Press.

Stamp, Patricia (1989). *Technology, Gender and Power in Africa.* Ottawa, Canada: International Development Research Centre.

United Nations (1991). *The World's Women, 1970-1990: Trends and Statistics.* Series K, No. 8. Sales No. E.90.XVII.3.

__________, Economic Commission for Africa (1984). Information Kit for Machineries on the Integration of Women in Development in Africa. Addis Ababa.

United Nations Development Programme (1980). Summary of action-oriented assessment of rural women's participation in delopment. DP/453.

_________ (1992). *Human Development Report, 1992.* New York: Oxford University Press.

United Nations Educational, Scientific and Cultural Organization (1983). *Bibliographic Guide to Studies on the Status of Women, Development and Population Trends.* London: Bowker.

Wallace, Tina, and Candida March (1991). *Changing Perceptions: Writings on Gender and Development.* Oxford, United Kingdom: Oxfam.

Ward, Kathryn (1990). *Women Workers and Global Restructuring, 1990.* New York: ILR Press, Cornell University.

Ware, Helen (1981). *Women, Demography and Development.* Canberra: Australian National University Press.

Waring, Marilyn (1988). *Counting for Nothing: What Men Value and What Women are Worth.* Wellington, United Kingdom: Allen and Unwin.

Whyte, Martin King (1978). *The Status of Women in Preindustrial Societies.* Princeton, New Jersey: Princeton University Press.

World Bank (1989). *Women in Development: Issues for Economic and Sector Analysis.* Washington, D.C.

_________. (1992). *World Development Report, 1992: Development and the Environment.* New York: Oxford University Press.

Box 3. Examples of differences between women's priorities and men's priorities

Women's priorities	*Men's priorities*
Small scale	*Large scale*
Omni buses, public transport	Private transport
Crafts	Factory production
Small loan clubs	Banks
Improvement of local markets	Major road works
Intermediate technology	State of the art technology
Use of radio (more women are illiterate)	Print media
Decentralization	Centralization
Horticulture	*Agriculture*
Improvement to traditional farming	Mechanized agriculture
Food crops	Cash crops
Small livestock around home	Ranching of large stock
Fish ponds	Freezer-plants
Village wood-lots	Major logging industry
Food-processing at village level	Factory food-processing
Health	*Health*
Preventive medicine	Irrigation schemes
Training of village health workers	Curative medicines
Family planning	Training of medical doctors
Village health centres	Town hospitals
Clean, accessible water	

Women's special needs (as cultures are currently structured)

- Child care
- Provisions for female household heads
- Legal rights to hold property, especially land

VII. A GENDER PERSPECTIVE ON POPULATION ISSUES

United Nations Office at Vienna[*]

Interrelations between population issues and those of development have received considerable attention over the past decades and the interrelations between the advancement of women and development have also been studied. It is now accepted that development in a broad sense, that is, beyond economic growth, cannot be achieved without improving the status of women. It is only recently, however, that the linkages between the three issues have been studied together rather than in isolation or two by two.

This situation is due in part to the fact that the issue of the advancement of women has demonstrated considerable vitality on both the conceptual and the operational side during the past few years. Contributions have been made from academics from both the North and the South, as well as from developmental agencies (including the United Nations system) and non-governmental organizations. This input has led to enrichment of the debate, particularly through broadening the topics examined and even to questioning the prevalent models of development, which have been shown not to be gender-neutral. Although such changes are very positive, they can also create difficulties in adjusting policies and programmes to the new considerations. The present paper does not attempt a review of developments, such as those just mentioned, but focuses rather on raising a few questions that can be formulated on the basis of some of the ongoing debates.

A. Some conceptual issues and implications in the area of population

Population experts have been collecting and analysing data on women for decades. Their work is invaluable for anyone interested in the status of women. Their practical contribution to the advancement of women is fundamental, because the provision to women of means to control their fertility is considered, to some extent, a precondition of women's advancement. Although there is change, population experts have tended to view women as objects of study rather than as subjects whose advancement is the ultimate goal. Feminists have often been critical, if not vocal, on such questions, thus sometimes disregarding the contributions to women's advancement from the population policies and programmes. Partisan approaches need to be overcome and then the dialogue that has been established between women's and population concerns can contribute not only to strengthening each area but also to national development in general. Two examples are presented here, one in the area of gender and terminology, and the other introducing the concept of empowerment of women over their life and development.

Gender and terminology

The terminology used in normal development discourse has evolved over time but is not neutral because it contains implicit assumptions which, in turn, have logical consequences for policies and programmes. For example, by focusing on the concept of status, which is a relative term defining women in relation to men, the emphasis is placed generally on eliminating discrimination, less often on catching up. Combating discrimination has traditionally implied a rather legalistic approach stressing, for example, that a woman who enjoys her rights would thus not need the consent of her husband in order to adopt family planning methods. In many cases, however, the real problem lies in de facto discrimination since many countries have taken effective measures to eliminate discriminatory legal provisions. Gender-based hierarchies attributing a lesser value to the contribution of women still have an impact in the area of population programmes. The example of the definition of "work" is a classic illustration of this situation: the debates on

[*]Division for the Advancement of Women.

the reproductive work of women are still continuing and these are essentially status issues, because the lower value given to reproductive work tends to reflect the lower status of women rather than any intrinsic value of their work. Another example is that both men and women can be considered "head of household", but in practice, if there is a man in the household, he will often be considered the head regardless of his actual relative role in the economic maintenance or decision-making in the household. In such cases, changes in definitions over time introduce difficulties in interpreting census or survey data for women; and the improvement in the status of women has also had an impact on data-collection definitions and practices.

In the case of "work" in both the formal and informal sectors, one can discuss definitions that take women's contributions into account as a form of advancement for women, but the latter example of the head of household shows that one cannot consider women in isolation, but that "gender" understood as the socially constructed and culturally variable roles that women and men play in their daily life is also an essential concept for population issues.

Gender and empowerment

Structural inequalities between genders, both within and outside the household, can have major implications in the area of population. Population activities directed to women also have consequences for men, since one cannot just modify one element in a system without this resulting in modifications for the entire system. The introduction of family planning modifies the distribution of functions both inside the reproductive roles of women and also between the production and reproductive roles within the household. Family planning messages have stressed both the many advantages for women and the family, such as better health of the mother and child, and more disposable income in the household, and also the developmental benefits for society at the national level. However, family planning has not stressed either the potential general empowerment of women or the distribution of the benefits derived from it at various levels from the perspective of women. Population policies have tended to pay more attention to their welfare contribution to women and less to their consequences in terms of empowerment. In such a context, they also have to take into account the repercussions on the status of men of such empowerment of women. Taking a narrow approach can lead to ignoring important issues in gender relations and thus reducing their effectiveness. This process requires coordination with other policies and programmes and with the women's policies and programmes.

By often assuming policies, including in the field of population, to be gender-neutral, one has generally not examined whether they could result in maintaining existing gender hierarchies rather than promoting equality. This ambiguity is understandable, since taking a clear position on such questions could be seen as going beyond narrow technical mandates and also as direct intervention in cultural norms that could provoke negative reactions. The ambiguity also has its drawbacks, resulting in ineffectiveness. In recent years, however, efforts have been made to clarify the positions and highlight empowerment. This is a complex task which requires studies and consequently resources, at both international and national levels, in view of the sociocultural dimensions of gender issues. It is also a very sensitive task because it ultimately can lead to a rethinking of development models by integrating into them human resource development and democratization. Such a rethinking is necessary because empowerment leads to a reorganization of the productive and reproductive roles not only within the family but also within the society. Simply to recommend more equal sharing within the family is to a large extent illusory if the society is not organized in a way that permits it: for example, in the developing countries sharing has a cost, which is a luxury when the strategy is focused on survival. It is thus apparent that the "advancement" of women cannot be an added dimension to other developmental activities, as is often believed, but a process at the core of society that has an impact on all developmental activities. The implications of such processes for, and the contributions of, population policies and programmes deserve to be studied at the general level and also in subnational contexts.

Empowerment requires that equality be built into all forms of human resource development from birth onward and this should encourage policies and programmes to modulate their action according to the characteristics of each new generation or cohort. By their nature, population programmes could take a lead in this area for other types of developmental activities.

B. Towards a broader concept of family planning

Traditionally, population programmes have been influenced by the basic demographic variables: birth; migration; and death. These variables have tended to be treated separately; and in view of the impact the rate of population growth can have on development in general, priority has been given to the issues surrounding fertility. This focus has meant that after studying the more immediate relations, efforts have spread to the exploration of more abstract relations and therefore to identifying possible linkages between fertility and the status of women defined by such variables as level of education and salaried employment.

Another important development has been the adoption of a gender perspective in the study of population issues, which has meant going beyond the study of women *per se* to taking into account the gender-based system in a given society. By applying a gender perspective to each of the population variables, one can gain new insights which could lead to increased effectiveness of policies and programmes. However, one can also go further and explore the possibility of a broad integration of population issues with advancement of women around an extended concept of family planning. Without any attempt at being comprehensive one can illustrate some implications for population variables and the policies built around them.

Mortality

A common criticism to health efforts for women is that they are mostly centred on maternal and child health. Operationally, such a package has made good sense, often corresponding to existing reality. Furthermore, integration with family planning has given important results. Motherhood, however, although fundamental, is but one aspect of a woman's health. A greater concern for the health of women throughout their life might lead one to explore the possibility of breaking down the concept "child" into its gender dimensions in order to avoid families later reacting differently to the sickness of daughters, compared with that of sons, and limiting the expectations for girls to their reproductive role. Women could have difficulty understanding that health problems not linked to maternity, such as caring for other sick family members or the elderly, can belong to another health organization and might be less valued. At the other end of the life course, the solutions for health problems related to the menopause and to ageing need to be identified.

Another example can be provided in relation to the acquired immunodeficiency syndrome (AIDS) epidemic. Models have shown that variables, such as the difference of age between partners, can play a significant role in increasing the risk of infection of the women. The difference of age between partners is a typical expression of difference in status since it can translate not only different sex histories but also differences in wealth and power. In such circumstances, traditional information, education and communication campaigns and the provision of condoms, although indispensable, might not be sufficient for women to insist on "safer" sex if they are not sufficiently empowered. Responses to the epidemic tend to rediscover the "caring" role of women, thus increasing their burden and endangering any advance in their status. Worse, the future of the daughters of overburdened or sick mothers can be definitively mortgaged by enrolling their assistance, rather than that of sons. One must therefore be careful that "community" responses to the epidemic do not turn out to be gender traps for women.

These few examples illustrate the fact that a gender analysis could have important organizational consequences on existing programmes, as well as considerable positive impact on their outcome.

Migration

Migration is an area where very little has been done on gender issues although demographers have highlighted sex differentials for decades, such as the general male dominance in rural-urban migration except in some regions. Gender analysis could contribute to a better understanding of the relations between migration-economic opportunities and the recognized production functions of men. Even when it is women that migrate, as in Latin America and the Caribbean, it is often linked to taking up domestic work, which is gender-determined and does not necessarily correspond to a status improvement.

People often make the decision to migrate on the basis of the economic opportunities for the men. If the wife stays behind in a rural area, she generally has no opportunity to improve her situation; and, by caring for the children in the rural areas, is in fact subsidizing urban development, reducing the need for housing, schools and social services. If the wife migrates with the husband, there still is inequality in the chances of income-earning and advancement, since the location and organization of salaried jobs can, for example, be incompatible with child care. The lower education of the wife can force her into the informal sector, so that even when she succeeds in increasing some income-earning opportunities for herself, it can result in a relative deterioration of her status in relation to that of her husband, who could more frequently be employed in the formal sector. The more recent migration of women without their spouse needs also to be examined from a gender perspective. One of the dimensions of the feminization of poverty is thus linked to migration because it is related to unequal opportunities and to the delinking of those of the husband to his family responsibilities.

Policies and programmes for urban development need to look into such issues from a gender perspective, since it appears that the results of the forces at play might not be gender-neutral. Attempts to influence these forces would have to tackle their basis in gender-related terms.

Fertility

Much has been written on fertility and family planning, and it need not be elaborated on here except to stress the need to develop in a more systematic manner the effort begun in the past few years to include gender dimensions.

The studies of the redistribution of the benefits of family planning throughout society could be examined from a gender perspective. It can be asked whether women effectively improve their status within society through family planning. This question goes beyond the study of whether economic benefits are redistributed equally between men and women to the more intangible questions, such as the trade-off between the possible economic benefits for women adopting family planning and their prestige in societies where woman's status is determined to some extent by her fertility. It can also be asked whether a woman really believes she is receiving benefits in exchange for her contribution to lowering fertility beyond the mere impact on health. This aspect implies examining the various finalities of family planning programmes from different perspectives, including from the gender perspective. In such a case, one must examine the shifts in power within the household in different stages during the life course. When one moves from the household level to that of society, one has to examine how the system formed by the gender relations is affected by the adoption of family planning in each society. To ignore such issues can lead to designing less effective policies and programmes and to misunderstanding the resistance encountered from both men and women. Techniques need to be developed to evaluate the impact of family planning beyond its immediate impact on fertility on key aspects in gender relations, such as power relations in household, distribution of benefits and burdens.

This complex task requires cooperation between different disciplines using various perspectives. The active participation of women in such studies would be part of the empowerment process because they can also assist in determining the relevant frameworks in which programmes can be designed rather than receiving what is decided as good for them.

Expanding the goal of family planning?

The preceding sections have discussed some of the gender aspects according to the traditional demographic variables to which one can add others, such as age at marriage, education, activity and residence. The question should now be asked whether gender-sensitive approaches would not lead one to consider integrating these variables into an expanded approach to family planning. This question would lead to discussing whether family planning programmes should include an introductory teaching to their clients of such issues as equality in child-rearing, encouragement to send and maintain girls in schools in order to empower them throughout their life and parental responsibility in assisting daughters opting for economic independence rather than being married. Training family planning staff to communicate on such issues both to the couple and to the extended family should become necessary. One must also examine whether there exist objections in principle to the inclusion of issues relating to migration being linked to family planning understood in a broad perspective. Other questions that would need study would include for example, how population programmes could take into account processes leading to the feminization of poverty and the problems of women heads of household, the cost of ignoring such issues without diminishing the effectiveness of population programmes and the coordination of strategies for family planning in such matters not only with the strategies developed by ministries of education and ministries of social welfare but also with those of industry or labour. Lastly, the role of national machinery for the advancement of women in such an expanded strategy would need to be defined.

If population policies can run into "glass" ceilings that limits their performance and can be related to the advancement of women, such issues need to be recognized. The introduction of gender perspectives requires a lot of rethinking of accepted models and modes of operation. It requires also experimentation and the involvement of the intended beneficiaries—both women and men. A task force could be established to organize this effort in order to produce some results in time for both the population and the women's conferences. However, one should be aware that it is also a long-term and continuing effort. It constitutes a major challenge which requires a strategic alliance between: *(a)* those concerned with the advancement of women; (*b*) those concerned with the solution of population problems; and (*c*) those concerned with general development. But it is a challenge for the benefit of all.

VIII. EXPLORING THE RELATION BETWEEN WOMEN'S STATUS AND POPULATION DYNAMICS WITH DEMOGRAPHIC AND HEALTH SURVEYS DATA

Anne R. Cross, Ann A. Way and Ann K. Blanc[*]

Since 1980, more than 100 sample surveys covering demographic and health topics have been conducted in 60 developing countries. Those countries have 3.6 billion people, or 87 per cent of the population of the developing world. In 50 per cent of those countries, the most recent survey was carried out under the Demographic and Health Surveys (DHS) programme.

The DHS programme was initiated in 1984 with the following objectives:

(*a*) To provide survey countries with data and analysis useful for informed policy choices;

(*b*) To expand the international population and health database;

(*c*) To develop in participating countries the technical skills and resources necessary to conduct demographic and health surveys; and

(*d*) To advance survey methodology.

As of early 1992, 44 surveys have been conducted in Africa, Asia, and Latin America and the Caribbean under the DHS programme. More than 260,000 women of reproductive age in 35 countries have been interviewed. In addition, seven surveys of husbands or males have been carried out (see table 18). The programme is ongoing and seven more surveys will be completed by 1993.

The DHS programme is funded by the United States Agency for International Development (USAID) and is administered by Macro International, Inc. at Columbia, Maryland. DHS is nearing the end of its second five-year phase and plans are being made to embark on phase 3 (1992-1997) in late 1992.

The DHS programme operates through implementing organizations in each participating country. Quite often these are the government statistical offices, although they can be a ministry of health and/or planning, a university, or a family planning organization. It is the responsibility of the implementing organization to carry out the survey with technical and financial assistance from DHS.

DHS policy calls for collecting data from nationally representative samples and, with few exceptions, this policy has been implemented. Standard practice also calls for employing female interviewers (except for the husband or male surveys, in which case male interviewers are preferred). It is also a DHS policy to translate the questionnaires into the major local languages in which the interviews will be conducted, in order to minimize discrepancies involved in translations made on the spot by the interviewers.

B. DEMOGRAPHIC AND HEALTH SURVEYS MODEL QUESTIONNAIRES

DHS collects basic data on household characteristics. Women of reproductive age are interviewed with a questionnaire based on one of two model or core questionnaires, the "A" questionnaire for high contraceptive prevalence countries or "B" questionnaire for low contraceptive prevalence countries. The "A" and "B" versions contain a large common set of questions and differ mainly in the number of questions devoted to the subject of contraception. Basic demographic data collected through the DHS questionnaire include: estimates of the levels of fertility and infant and child mortality; estimates of the levels of breast-feeding and other proximate determinants of fertility; measures

[*]Demographic and Health Surveys, Institute for Resource Development/Macro International Inc., Baltimore, Maryland.

TABLE 18. DEMOGRAPHIC AND HEALTH SURVEYS, 1985-1992

Area or region and country	*Year of survey*	*Respondents*	*Sample size*
Sub-Saharan Africa			
Botswana	1988	All women 15-49	4 368
Burundi	1988	All women 15-49	3 970
Cameroon[a]	1991	All women 15-49	3 871
Ghana[a]	1988	All women 15-49	4 488
Kenya	1989	All women 15-49	7 150
Liberia	1986	All women 15-49	5 239
Mali[a]	1987	All women 15-49	3 200
Nigeria	1990	All women 15-49	8 781
Nigeria, Ondo State	1986/87	All women 15-49	4 213
Senegal	1986	All women 15-49	4 415
Sudan	1989/90	Ever-married women 15-49	5 860
Togo	1988	All women 15-49	3 360
Uganda	1988/89	All women 15-49	4 730
United Rep. of Tanzania[a]	1991/92	All women 15-49	7 650
Zambia	1992	All women 15-49	6 000
Zimbabwe	1988/89	All women 15-49	4 201
Northern Africa/Western Asia			
Egypt	1988/89	Ever-married women 15-49	8 911
Jordan	1990	Ever-married women 15-49	6 462
Morocco	1987	Ever-married women 15-49	5 982
Morocco	1991/92	All women 15-49	7 000
Tunisia	1988	Ever-married women 15-49	4 184
Yemen	1991/92	Ever-married women 15-54	6 000
Asia			
Indonesia	1987	Ever-married women 15-49	11 884
Indonesia	1991	Ever-married women 15-49	22 909
Nepal, in-depth	1987	Currently married women 15-49	1 623
Pakistan[a]	1990/91	Ever-married women 15-49	6 611
Sri Lanka	1987	Ever-married women 15-49	5 865
Thailand	1987	Ever-married women 15-49	6 775
Latin America and the Caribbean			
Bolivia	1989	All women 15-49	7 923
Bolivia, in-depth	1989	All women 15-49	7 923
Brazil	1986	All women 15-49	5 892
Brazil, north east	1991	All women 15-49	6 829
Colombia	1986	All women 15-49	5 329
Colombia	1990	All women 15-49	8 644
Dominican Republic	1986	All women 15-49	7 649
Dominican Republic	1991	All women 15-49	7 320
Ecuador	1987	All women 15-49	4 713
El Salvador	1985	All women 15-49	5 207
Guatemala	1987	All women 15-49	5 160
Mexico	1987	All women 15-49	9 310
Paraguay	1990	All women 15-49	5 827
Peru	1986	All women 15-49	4 999
Peru	1991/92	All women 15-49	15 000
Trinidad and Tobago	1987	All women 15-49	3 806

[a]Surveys of husbands/males were also conducted.

of contraceptive knowledge, use and availability, and of the duration of use of contraception; and measures of the preferences for children, levels of unwanted fertility and reasons for non-use. The health data include measures of various child illnesses and treatment patterns, coverage rates for maternity care and childhood immunizations, nutritional status and infant-feeding practices. Annex I provides an outline of the contents of the two versions of the DHS questionnaire.

The DHS core questionnaire was developed during the early stages of the first phase of the project (1984-1989), with input from a broad range of potential data users representing both programmatic and academic concerns. In designing the core instrument, DHS built upon the experience of two earlier international survey programmes, the World Fertility Survey (WFS) and the Contraceptive Prevalence Survey (CPS). At the beginning of the second phase of DHS, the core questionnaire was modified on the basis of a systematic review of the experience from the first phase of the project. The most important modifications involved the incorporation in the "A" version of the monthly calendar to record fertility, contraceptive, post-partum, marriage, migration and employment histories for a period of five or six years before the DHS interview and the expansion of the information obtained on maternal and child health, including the addition of maternal anthropometry.

The use of a DHS standard questionnaire reflects the mandate of the programme to collect internationally comparable data. Standardization of the core instruments has resulted in significant savings in time and effort in the training, data processing and report preparation for the DHS programme. Although emphasizing standardization in the collection of core information, the DHS programme encourages countries to adapt the model questionnaires to meet their specific data needs. A number of supplemental modules also have been developed in response to survey country interests in obtaining information on such topics as women's employment, maternal mortality, the acquired immunodeficiency syndrome (AIDS), causes of death, sterilization, pill compliance and social marketing.

In addition to the collection of household and individual data, an important part of the DHS programme is the collection of data at the community level on the availability of family planning and health services. Service availability surveys are being fielded in most DHS countries. They collect information on the level of socio-economic development of the community, on the existence of family planning and health outreach services in the community, on the proximity of fixed facilities offering family planning and health services and on the types of services offered and other characteristics of facilities within a specified distance from the community.

C. Selected findings

The following discussion presents selected basic DHS findings with regard to women's fertility, family planning and health-care seeking behaviour. The discussion is not intended to be comprehensive but to highlight the potential as well as some of the limitations of DHS data for exploring some of the issues that the Expert Group Meeting on Population and Women will address. This brief discussion is supplemented by an annotated list of selected publications using DHS data in exploring the issues (annex II).

Women, fertility and family planning

The primary focus of DHS is on the collection of data on fertility[1] and its proximate determinants, particularly contraceptive use. These data help document sweeping changes in child-bearing behaviour in the developing countries, which have clear implications for women's status in these societies in the future. Using DHS and United Nations data, Freedman and Blanc (1991) conclude that fertility in the developing world declined by almost one third during the 15-year period from 1965-1970 to 1980-1985. Moreover, DHS data on the reproductive preferences of women indicate the potential for further fertility decline. Analyses of these data show substantial unmet need for family planning among married women of reproductive age, ranging from 11 per cent in Thailand, where use of contraception is widespread, to 40 per cent in Togo, where there is substantial interest in spacing birth but low current use (Westoff and Ochoa, 1991a). It is estimated that if all of the unmet need were to be satisfied, fertility levels would decrease by 25 per cent in sub-Saharan Africa and by

32 per cent in the Latin American countries (Westoff and Ochoa, 1991a).

The decline in fertility is linked both to increases in the age at marriage and/or first birth and to increased contraceptive use. Trends towards later age at marriage and motherhood are evident in the DHS results for many countries (Arnold and Blanc, 1990; and Adlakha and Kumar, 1991). Women and their partners are also increasingly relying upon contraceptive methods to delay and limit child-bearing. Weinberger (1991) estimates that, in the developing countries in 1991, one in two couples with the woman of reproductive age was currently using contraception, compared with fewer than 1 in 10 couples before 1965. Worldwide, there has also been a trend towards adoption of more effective methods. Currently, in the developing countries, surgical contraception is the main method, followed by the intra-uterine device and oral pills.

Although there is a clear trend towards increasing contraceptive use worldwide, DHS results document the wide variation in levels of use between and within countries. Among the 30 countries that have completed the DHS programme since 1984, the percentage of married women of reproductive age using family planning varies from 3 in Mali to 66 in Brazil and Thailand (IRD/ Macro International, 1992). Within countries, there is substantial variation in the levels of contraceptive use among women with different educational levels and between women living in urban and rural areas (Rutenberg and others, 1991). In Bolivia, for example, among urban residents, the percentage of women using contraception varied from 12 among women with no education to 49 among women with secondary or higher schooling, while among rural women, the level of use is 39 compared with 19 per cent. Looking at trends in urban/rural and educational differentials for 15 countries that had been covered by both WFS and DHS, Weinberger (1991) notes that these differentials changed very little despite overall increases in levels of use. She concludes that the "pace of future fertility decline will largely depend on growth of contraceptive practice among the less educated and in the rural areas" (Weinberger, 1991, p. 573).

One important issue is the extent to which differentials in contraceptive use are related to differences in women's access to services. The DHS service availability surveys were designed to provide data to describe the family planning, maternal and child health service environment and to examine the extent to which differential access to services underlies observed differentials in use. Using data from 13 countries that conducted service availability surveys, Wilkinson, Abderrahim and Njogu (1991) found considerable variation across countries in the level of access to services. They note that the relation between a basic indicator of access (distance to the nearest source) and use is not uniform, with availability exhibiting the clearest positive association with use in Uganda and Togo, where the service environment is poor.

Women, health and mortality

With regard to health and mortality, the focus of DHS data collection effort is largely on issues relating to child health and mortality. However, DHS does obtain information on the utilization of maternity care services. Stewart and Sommerfelt (1991) show that there is substantial variation across countries in the use of those services; for instance, in the 27 countries for which they examine DHS maternity care findings, the proportion of deliveries attended by a trained person varies from 19 per cent in Ghana to 98 per cent in Trinidad and Tobago. In the second phase of the survey, DHS also expanded data collection on women's health to include anthropometric measures (height, weight and, in some surveys, arm circumference) for women that had had a birth in the five years preceding the survey. Those data will permit analyses of differences in the nutritional status of mothers as well as their children.

In addition to collecting basic maternity care and anthropometric data, DHS has also included special modules on women's health issues in a number of countries. One of the areas in which DHS is experimenting is the collection of data needed for the estimation of maternal mortality levels (Rutenberg and Sullivan, 1991). Other more country-specific women's health issues have also been explored. For example, questions on the attitudes towards and the practice of female circumcision were included in the Sudan DHS (Kheir, Kumar and Cross, 1991).

One area of obvious interest in considering women's status issues is whether men have greater access than women to health-care services. Because DHS does not collect information on the use of health-care services by the adult population, it is not possible to look at gender biases in the provision of those services. However, with regard to the utilization of child health-care services, Arnold (1991) found that there is no evidence in the DHS results of preferential treatment of sons. He also examined DHS data on feeding practices and nutritional status for children and concluded that there was no evidence of significant discrimination against girls.

D. Strengths and limitations of the Demographic and Health Surveys

Standardized cross-sectional data-collection approaches, like DHS, have both strengths and limitations in examining the linkages between woman's status and population dynamics. The chief strength of the DHS programme is its provision of a comparable body of basic population and health data for a large number of the developing countries. In DHS, emphasis is placed on measuring fertility and child mortality levels, collecting data on the proximate determinants of fertility (including contraceptive use, marriage, breast-feeding, post-partum amenorrhoea and post-partum abstinence) and obtaining information on maternal and child health indicators. The DHS core questionnaire also includes questions relating to a number of social and economic variables, including family wealth/assets, residence and residential mobility, education, employment, ethnicity and religion, but relatively less emphasis is placed on the collection of those data.

It is the comparative paucity of information on social, cultural and economic determinants that is the greatest weakness of DHS in looking at issues relating to women's status and population dynamics. DHS works very well in measuring tangible aspects of women's life, such as child-bearing, marriage, contraceptive use and educational level, but cannot provide adequate measures of more intangible and frequently more complex aspects, such as women's autonomy or involvement in economic activity. DHS has sought to improve the collection of information on those aspects of women's life. For example, the collection of data through the calendar on a woman's employment and residential mobility during the five-year period for the survey greatly expands the possibilities for analysing the relations between those variables and fertility and contraceptive behaviour. None the less, DHS has inherent limitations in collecting retrospective data on these and other behavioural determinants. Lloyd (1991) suggests that a more fruitful approach to overcoming the weaknesses of cross-sectional surveys, such as DHS, is to turn to other research strategies, including longitudinal surveys designed to provide the in-depth contextual information needed to unravel causal relations.

ANNEX I

Contents of the core Demographic and Health Surveys questionnaire

Model A questionnaire for high-prevalence countries

Household schedule

Household listing
Water and toilet facilities
Household possessions and dwelling characteristics

Female schedule

Respondent's background
Time of interview
Childhood residence
Date of birth and age of woman
Education and literacy
Mass media
Religion and ethnicity
Household characteristics of non-usual residents

Reproduction
Lifetime fertility
Detailed birth history
Current and recent pregnancy history
Menstruation

Contraception
Knowledge and use of methods; knowledge of sources
Probes on contraceptive use

First use of contraception
Current use
Pill use
Sterilization
Source and availability of method currently used
Method preferences and problems of use
Use before the calendar period
Intentions to use contraception in the future
Source of preferred method
Media information on family planning

Pregnancy and breast-feeding

Fertility planning
Prenatal care
Tetanus toxoid
Delivery; size of newborn baby
Post-partum amenorrhoea and abstinence
Breast-feeding: ever, duration, reasons for never breast-feeding and stopping
Supplemental foods given yesterday, age when solids and liquids first introduced and frequency of breast-feeding
Duration of post-partum behaviour before the calendar period

Immunization and health

Vaccination information from written records and from the mother's recall
Fever
Cough - acute respiratory tract infection
Diarrhoea and treatment with oral rehydration therapy
Knowledge of oral rehydration therapy

Marriage

Marital status and co-residence
Date and age at marriage
Recent marriage history
Sexual activity

Fertility preferences

Reproductive intentions
Sterilization regret
Discussion on number of children and husband's preferences
Ideal family size
Ideal birth interval

Husband's background, residence and woman's work

Husband's education
Husband's work
Residential mobility
Woman's employment

Maternal and child height and weight

Checking for a bacille Calmette-Guérin scar
Weighing and measuring young children and mothers

The calendar

Model B questionnaire for low-prevalence countries

Household schedule

Household listing
Water and toilet facilities
Household possessions and dwelling characteristics

Female schedule

Respondent's background

Time of interview
Residence and mobility
Date of birth and age of woman
Education and literacy
Mass media
Religion and ethnicity
Household characteristics of non-usual residents

Reproduction

Lifetime fertility
Detailed birth history
Current and recent pregnancy history
Menstruation

Contraception

Knowledge and use of methods; knowledge of sources
Probes on contraceptive use
First use of contraception
Current use

Pill use
Source and availability of method currently used
Sterilization
Duration of current use
Intentions to use contraception in the future
Source of preferred method
Media information on family planning

Pregnancy and breast-feeding
Fertility planning
Prenatal care
Tetanus toxoid
Delivery; size of newborn baby
Post-partum amenorrhoea and abstinence
Breast-feeding: ever, duration, reasons for never breast-feeding and stopping
Supplemental foods given yesterday, age when solids and liquids first introduced, and frequency of breast-feeding
Bottle- feeding

Immunization and health
Vaccination information from written records and from the mother's recall
Fever
Cough - acute respiratory tract infection
Diarrhoea and treatment with oral rehydration therapy
Knowledge of oral rehydration therapy

Marriage
Marital status and co-residence
Date and age at marriage
Sexual activity

Fertility preferences
Reproductive intentions
Sterilization regret
Communication with husband about family planning
Discussion on number of children and husband's preferences
Post-partum attitudes
General approval of birth control
Ideal family size
Ideal birth interval

Husband's background, residence and woman's work
Husband's education
Husband's work
Woman's employment

Maternal and child height and weight
Checking for a bacille Calmette-Guérin scar
Weighing and measuring young children and mothers

ANNEX II

Abstracts from Demographic and Health Surveys publications

A. VALUE OF WOMEN, WOMEN'S AUTONOMY

Female-headed households in developing countries: by choice or by circumstances? By Keiko Ono-Osaki. In *Demographic and Health Surveys World Conference, August 5-7,* 1991, Washington D.C., *Proceedings*, vol. III.

The primary objective of this paper is to provide a more refined picture of the growing number of female-headed households by exploring the similarities and variations in the characteristics of female heads and their households. Following a global overview of the prevalence of households headed by a female, the study examines the following: (*a*) socio-demographic profile of households headed by a female; (*b*) determinants of headship; and (*c*) characteristics of households. Data are drawn from the DHS programme in Burundi, Mexico, Peru and Thailand. Empirical findings portray a generally disadvantaged condition of female heads and their households. The majority of female heads are the oldest in the household, widowed and do not have a partner in the same household. Compared with male heads, female heads tend to be older, to be the only adult in the household and to be less educated.

Fertility transition: an update. By Ronald Freedman and Ann K. Blanc. In *Demographic and Health Surveys World Conference, August 5-7, 1991, Washington D.C., Proceedings,* vol. I.

Using data from the United Nations and DHS, this paper shows that over the past 15 years, fertility in the developing world has declined by almost one third. This decline represents close to one half of the difference between the fertility rate in 1965-1970 and replacement-level fertility. The only region approaching replacement-level fertility is Eastern Asia, with a total fertility rate (TFR) of about 2.3. TFR stands at about 4-5 in South-eastern Asia and in Latin America and the Caribbean, 5-6 in Southern Asia, Western Asia and Northern Africa; and 6.4 in sub-Saharan Africa. Of particular interest to this Conference was the analysis of the effect of lower fertility on the amount of time women spend bearing and raising children. As fertility has decreased, the number of years between a woman's first and last births has also decreased (for example, from 17 to 15 years in Mexico between 1976/77 and 1987). The analysis shows that a reduction of one child in the average number of children ever born is associated with a decline of almost two years in the length of the child-bearing period. As fertility declines, the number of years women spend with a child under age 6 has also declined (from 16.2 years in 1975 to 10.5 in 1987 in Thailand).

Household structure from a comparative perspective. By Koffi Ekouevi, Mohamed Ayad, Bernard Barrère and David Cantor. In *Demographic and Health Surveys World Conference, August 5-7, 1991, Washington D.C., Proceedings,* vol. III.

This paper presents data on the age and sex structure of households, headship and size composition for 23 DHS countries. Results suggest a significant and growing percentage of female-headed households in many countries. In Botswana, the Dominican Republic, Ghana, Kenya, Togo, Trinidad and Tobago, and Zimbabwe, more than 25 per cent of households are headed by women. While some countries show the expected pattern of females progressively becoming heads of households at late adult ages, other countries, especially in sub-Saharan Africa and the Caribbean, show relatively high percentages of women as heads of households in their child-bearing years. For nine countries in which comparisons with WFS were made, the percentage of female-headed households has increased in most of the countries since the mid- to late 1970s.

Sex preference for children and its demographic and health implications. By Fred Arnold. In *Demographic and Health Surveys World Conference, August 5-7, 1991, Washington D.C., Proceedings,* vol. I.

This study finds little evidence of strong son preference among countries with DHS data, except in Northern Africa and Sri Lanka; the most common preference in most countries is a desire to have at least one daughter and one son. Although a strong sex preference for children could be a significant obstacle to fertility decline, analysis of a number of fertility-related measures shows little evidence that prevalent sex preferences are being translated into differentials in fertility behaviour. Also, DHS data refute the contention that sons may receive preferential treatment in health care and provision of healthy food. Once couples bear children, in almost all cases they seem to take equally good care of them regardless of their sex. There are few significant differences in the percentage of young boys and girls receiving immunizations, becoming ill, receiving medical assistance during an illness, being breast-fed or showing signs of being nutritionally disadvantaged.

Social class as a determinant of fertility behaviour: the case of Bolivia. By Juan Schoemaker. In *Demographic and Health Surveys World Conference, August 5-7, 1991, Washington D.C., Proceedings,* vol. I.

The author argues that the effect of social class on reproductive behaviour has been systematically overlooked by demographers. Most articles dealing with the association between socio-economic characteristics and reproductive behaviour tend to emphasize the significance of women's education. But access to education is determined to a great extent by social class, especially in the developing countries. Using DHS data from Bolivia, the author constructs a rather simple definition of social class by combining the occupation and education of ever-married respondents to create four social classes. Multiple classification analysis shows that the strong influence a woman's education has on her fertility is due in part to her social class.

Women's economic independence and fertility among the Yoruba. By Mary M. Kritz and Douglas T. Gurak.In *Demographic and Health Surveys World Conference, August 5-7, 1991, Washington D.C., Proceedings,* vol. I.

Using data from the 1986 DHS in Ondo State and a 1990 survey in rural Oyo State, this study examines the links between the changing social and gender statuses of women and several indicators of fertility attitudes and behaviour in order to determine whether those statuses are playing a role in the evolution of fertility control in south-western Nigeria. The findings suggest that a complex relation exists between women's economic independence, evolving modern social statuses and fertility processes. The fertility-related attitudes and types of behaviour of younger women are increasingly influenced by new social statuses linked to education, employment in the modern sector and urbanism. Among older women, especially those in rural areas, these modern transformations have not been common and are not exerting a major impact on fertility. As rural women's control of income and economic contributions to the household increase, recent fertility and preferences for more children tend to decrease.

B. Women's health and mortality

Direct and indirect estimates of maternal mortality from the sisterhood method. By Naomi Rutenberg and Jeremiah M. Sullivan. In *Demographic and Health Surveys World Conference, August 5-7, 1991, Washington D.C., Proceedings,* vol. III.

This paper describes the methodology of collecting information from adults in a household survey about the survivorship of their sisters to estimate maternal mortality. The method was applied in the DHS surveys in Bolivia (1988) and the Sudan (1989-1990). Results show a maternal mortality ratio of 3-4 deaths per 1,000 births in Bolivia and 5-6 per 1,000 births in the Sudan. Both estimates refer to a period about 12-14 years before the survey.

Female circumcision: attitudes and practices in Sudan. By El-Haj Hamad M. Kheir, Sushil Kumar and Anne R. Cross. In *Demographic and Health Surveys World Conference, August 5-7, 1991, Washington D.C., Proceedings,* vol. III.

The Sudan DHS conducted in 1989/90 included a number of questions about female circumcision. The survey indicated that

90 per cent of ever-married women aged 15-49 in northern Sudan are circumcised, a slight decline from previous studies. Four fifths of these women underwent the most severe (Pharaonic) circumcision in which the clitoris, labia minora and labia majora are removed. Two thirds of the circumcisions, were performed by traditional midwives. Support for female circumcision among women is widespread (80 per cent) and only begins to erode among the better educated. The social pressure to circumcise is indicated by the fact that 94 per cent of women with Pharaonic circumcision plan to circumcise their own daughters.

Maternal and child health services in Eastern and Southern Africa: progress and prospects. By F. M. Mburu and J. Ties Boerma. In *Demographic and Health Surveys World Conference, August 5-7, 1991, Washington D.C., Proceedings*, vol. II.

In this paper, data from recent national surveys in Botswana, Kenya, Uganda and Zimbabwe are used to assess the progress and prospects of maternal and child health services. The results show that Botswana has the best scores on most indicators, with small differentials between the higher socio-economic class in urban areas and the lower socio-economic class in the rural areas. Kenya and Zimbabwe have somewhat higher mortality levels and slightly lower levels of health services utilization than Botswana and urban/rural differences are marked. Child mortality is much higher in Uganda and the maternal and child health service delivery system is much less developed. Analysis by socio-economic groups within countries draws attention to the less favourable position of the urban poor, who are sometimes even worse off than the rural poor (Botswana, Kenya and Uganda).

Utilization of maternity care services: a comparative study using DHS data. By Kate Stewart and A. Elisabeth Sommerfelt. In *Demographic and Health Surveys World Conference, August 5-7, 1991, Washington D.C., Proceedings*, vol. III.

This paper looks at factors associated with tetanus toxoid immunization, antenatal care and assistance during delivery. The percentage of women receiving at least one tetanus toxoid injection during pregnancy ranged from more than 85 per cent of births in Botswana, the Dominican Republic, Kenya and Sri Lanka to fewer than 20 per cent in Egypt, Guatemala, Mali and Peru. The percentage of births in which women received antenatal care ranged from over 90 in Botswana, the Dominican Republic, Sri Lanka, Trinidad and Tobago, and Zimbabwe to fewer than 50 per cent in Bolivia, Guatemala, Mali and Morocco. Marked trends of increased use of maternity care services were not detected. Education and access to services are strongly related to utilization.

C. Women, fertility and family planning

Adolescent Women in Sub-Saharan Africa: A Chartbook on Marriage and Childbearing. Demographic and Health Surveys and Population Reference Bureau. Washington, D.C.: 1991.

This book consists of a series of charts and brief descriptions showing, for 11 sub-Saharan countries with DHS data, the extent of child-bearing among women aged 15-19. Charts show the percentage of teenagers that had given birth or were pregnant with their first child, levels and trends in fertility rates, births to teenagers as a proportion of all births, percentage married or with sexual experience, knowledge and use of family planning etc.

Availability and use of contraception: a comparative analysis. By Marilyn Wilkinson, Noureddine Abderrahim and Wamucii Njogu. In *Demographic and Health Surveys World Conference, August 5-7, 1991, Washington D.C., Proceedings*, vol. II.

The DHS programme included a special questionnaire to measure the availability of health and family planning services in 11 countries. The objectives are to describe the service environment for women and to determine if there is any association between contraceptive use, health service utilization and service availability. The findings show that availability of health and family planning services vary greatly across countries. The service environment is quite strong in the Near East/Asian countries, moderate in Latin America and relatively poor in all African countries studied, except for Zimbabwe. The relation between service availability and use is not uniform across countries; there is a positive relation in some countries and a negative or no association in others. The paper presents data on distance and time (in minutes) to the nearest source of family planning services and the percentage of women within 5 kilometres of each of several types of health facilities (hospital, clinic etc.).

Consanguinity: a major variable in studies on North African reproductive behavior, morbidity and mortality? By Alan H. Bittles. In *Demographic and Health Surveys World Conference, August 5-7, 1991, Washington D.C., Proceedings*, vol. I.

This study shows that marriage between relatives (second cousins or closer) is common in Morocco (33 per cent), Egypt (41 per cent) and Tunisia (49 per cent). Consanguinity is associated with elevated fertility and increased mortality and morbidity among progeny.

Contraceptive availability in four Latin American countries. By Luis H. Ochoa and Amy O. Tsui. In *Demographic and Health Surveys World Conference, August 5-7, 1991, Washington D.C., Proceedings,* vol. II.

This comparative analysis examines variations in contraceptive availability in Colombia, the Dominican Republic, Ecuador and Guatemala. It shows a generally favourable picture of contraceptive service availability. Both public and private sector providers occupy a significant role in servicing contraceptive demand, particularly for sterilization. Geographic access, gauged in terms of either distance or time, does not appear to be a strong influence on method-specific use levels.

Contraceptive prevalence in the year 2000. By W. Parker Mauldin. In *Demographic and Health Surveys World Conference, August 5-7, 1991, Washington D.C., Proceedings,* vol. II.

In 1980, about 40 per cent of couples in the developing countries were using contraception, compared with about one half in 1990. This study estimates that the level in 2000 will be 59 per cent of couples. Currently, about three quarters of married women of reproductive age in Eastern Asia use contraception, compared with 60 per cent in Latin America and the Caribbean, 40 per cent in Southern Asia and Northern Africa, and just over 10 per cent in sub-Saharan Africa.

The demand for family planning: highlights from a comparative analysis. By Charles Westoff and Luis Hernando Ochoa. In *Demographic and Health Surveys World Conference, August 5-7, 1991, Washington D.C., Proceedings,* vol. I.

This paper is largely a summary of a DHS comparative report. It gives estimates of unmet need (proportion of married women that say they want no more children or want to postpone their next child and yet are not using contraception) and total demand for contraception (unmet need plus current users), and examines some of the covariates of unmet need. Unmet need is greatest in sub-Saharan African countries and lowest in Brazil, Colombia, Indonesia, Sri Lanka, Thailand, and Trinidad and Tobago. Most of the unmet need in Africa is for methods to space births rather than to stop child-bearing altogether. Although the proportion of women with unmet need for family planning to limit the number of children has generally declined over time in most of the countries with two surveys, the absolute number of such women has often increased. Calculations show that if all unmet need for family planning services could be met, fertility in sub-Saharan Africa would decline by 25 per cent and that in Latin America by 32 per cent.

Differentials in contraceptive failure rates in developing countries. By Lorenzo Moreno. In *Demographic and Health Surveys World Conference, August 5-7, 1991, Washington D.C., Proceedings,* vol. I.

It has often been assumed that better educated or urban women are more likely to use contraception more effectively. This study of contraceptive failure rates in 15 DHS countries shows that in most cases, there is no evidence to support this assertion, once the type of method used, length of use, age and parity of women have been controlled. Standardized first-year probabilities of contraceptive failure suggest that women in Asian and Northern African countries are more effective users of contraceptives than their counterparts in Latin America and the Caribbean, irrespective of the type of method.

Proximity to contraceptive services and fertility in rural Kenya. By Charles R. Hammerslough. In *Demographic and Health Surveys World Conference, August 5-7, 1991, Washington D.C., Proceedings,* vol. II.

This paper supplements the 1989 DHS data for Kenya with information from a community-level survey (in which 260 of the DHS rural sample clusters were revisited) and 12 group interviews with rural and urban women's self-help groups. Results show a swift rise in the availability of family planning sources in rural Kenya during the 1980s. At the beginning of the decade, only 27 per cent of rural women lived within three hours' travel time to a source of contraception; by 1989, 87 per cent did so. The author concludes that the increase in contraceptive availability has accelerated the fertility transition by increasing the likelihood that contraceptors use efficient clinical methods.

Recent trends in contraceptive behavior. By Mary Beth Weinberger. In *Demographic and Health Surveys World Conference, August 5-7, 1991, Washington D.C., Proceedings,* vol. I.

Between 1960-1965 and 1985-1990, the United Nations estimates that the total fertility rate in the less developed regions declined by 35 per cent, from 6.1 to 3.9 births per woman. During that period, the percentage of married women of reproductive age using contraception grew from fewer than 10 to 48 per cent (53 per cent, including the developed countries). Contraceptive prevalence is estimated to be 40 per cent in Asia (excluding China, where it is 72 per cent), 57 per cent in Latin America and the Caribbean, 31 per cent in Northern Africa and 13 per cent in sub-Saharan Africa. Female sterilization is the most important single method for the world as a whole, accounting for about 30 per cent of total contraceptive practice. The intra-uterine device accounts for 20 per cent of total use, while the oral pill accounts for 13 per cent. Contraceptive use has increased in nearly all the developing countries for which trend data are available. Differentials in contraceptive use by urban or rural residence and women's education are also reported.

The role of nuptiality in fertility decline: a comparative analysis. By Arjun Adlakha and Sushil Kumar amd Mohamad Ayad. In *Demographic and Health Surveys World Conference, August 5-7, 1991, Washington D.C., Proceedings,* vol. II.

Nuptiality levels and trends are important variables in determining fertility levels and trends. Increase in age at first marriage affects fertility directly through its effect on the number of years available for child-rearing. Data on patterns of marriage (proportions single, mean age at marriage) are presented for 26 DHS countries. The data show that early marriage is more prevalent in sub-Saharan Africa than in Asia, Northern Africa or Latin America and the Caribbean. Change towards later marriage is taking place in many countries, especially in Northern Africa. In sub-Saharan Africa, the inhibiting effect of delayed marriage on fertility is generally more important than that of contraceptive use.

Use of and demand for sterilization. By Naomi Rutenberg and Evelyn Landry. In *Demographic and Health Surveys World Conference, August 5-7, 1991, Washington D.C., Proceedings,* vol. I.

Current levels of sterilization, recent trends and characteristics of potential acceptors of permanent contraception are reviewed for 26 DHS countries. Sterilization, predominantly tubal ligation, has become a major method in Latin America and the Caribbean and in South-eastern Asia, and is gaining a foothold in a few sub-Saharan African countries, but it has made few inroads in Northern Africa. In many cases, sterilization is the first and only modern method of contraception that couples use.

D. Women's education and its demographic impact

Women's education and fertility: a decade of change in four Latin American countries. By Mary Beth Weinberger, Cynthia Lloyd and Ann Klimas Blanc. International Family Planning Perspectives (New York), vol. 15, No. 1 (March 1989), pp. 4-14.

DHS data show that there has been a rapid fertility decline in Colombia, the Dominican Republic, Ecuador and Peru. In all but Peru, the gap in fertility between educated and uneducated women is narrowing. In addition to having lower fertility and desiring smaller families, women with more education generally marry later and are more likely to practise contraception than are less educated women. In all four countries, women's educational attainment has been rising rapidly enough that the increase in the proportion of more highly educated women has by itself been an important cause of fertility decline. At the same time, fertility declines within education groups have been large and in three of the four countries have contributed over half of the observed fertility decline.

E. Linkages between women's economic activity and population dynamics

Women's Childbearing Strategies in Relation to Fertility and Employment in Ghana. By Ann K. Blanc and Cynthia B. Lloyd. Research Division Working Papers, No. 16. New York: The Population Council, 1990.

This work uses data from the Ghana DHS in 1988 and the Ghana Fertility Survey in 1979/80 to examine the child-rearing strategies of Ghanaian women and, in particular, child-fostering. The latter practice is seen as a sophisticated mechanism which helps smooth out child-rearing demands over a woman's reproductive life cycle. To the extent that modernization and urbanization are affecting the traditional child-fostering, the costs of children to mothers may be expected to rise.

Note

[1]Fertility data in the DHS programme are subject to the problems of errors in dating and omission of events common to retrospective surveys. An assessment of the quality of data from 22 DHS identified problems in some surveys but concluded that the overall quality of DHS results was good (IRD, 1990).

References

Adlakha, Arjun, Sushil Kumar and Mohamed Ayed (1991). The role of nuptiality in fertility decline: a comparative analysis. In *Demographic and Health Surveys World Conference, August 5-7, 1991, Washington, D.C., Proceedings,* vol. II. Columbia, Maryland: IRD/Macro International, Inc.

Arnold, Fred (1991). Sex preference for children and its demographic and health implications. In *Demographic and Health Surveys World Conference, August 5-7, 1991, Washington, D.C., Proceedings,* vol. I. Columbia, Maryland: IRD/Macro International, Inc.

_________, and Ann K. Blanc (1990). *Fertility Levels and Trends.* Demographic and Health Surveys Comparative Studies, No. 2. Columbia, Maryland: Institute for Resource Development/Macro Systems, Inc.

Freedman, Ronald, and Ann K. Blanc (1991). Fertility transition: an update. In *Demographic and Health Surveys World Conference, August 5-7, 1991, Washington, D.C., Proceedings*, vol. I. Columbia, Maryland: IRD/Macro International, Inc.

Institute for Resource Development (1990). *An Assessment of DHS-I Data Quality*. Demographic and Health Surveys Methodological Reports, No. 1. Columbia, Maryland: Institute for Resource Development/Macro Systems, Inc.

__________/Macro International, Inc. (1992). *Demographic and Health Surveys Newsletter* (Columbia, Maryland), vol. 4.

Kheir, El-Haj Hamad M., Sushil Kumar and Anne R. Cross (1991). Female circumcision: attitudes and practice in Sudan. In *Demographic and Health Surveys World Conference, August 5-7, 1991, Washington, D.C., Proceedings*, vol. III. Columbia, Maryland: IRD/Macro International, Inc.

Lloyd, Cynthia B. (1991). The contribution of World Fertility Surveys to an understanding of the relationship between women's work and fertility. *Studies in Family Planning* (New York), vol. 22, No. 3 (May/June), pp. 144-161.

Rutenberg, Naomi, and Jeremiah M. Sullivan (1991). Direct and indirect estimates of maternal mortality from the sisterhood method. In *Demographic and Health Surveys World Conference, August 5-7, 1991, Washington, D.C., Proceedings*, vol. III. Columbia, Maryland: IRD/Macro International, Inc.

Rutenberg, Naomi, and others (1991). *Knowledge and Use of Contraception*. Demographic and Health Surveys Comparative Studies, No. 6. Columbia, Maryland: Institute for Resource Development/Macro International, Inc.

Stewart, Kate, and A. Elisabeth Sommerfelt (1991). Utilization of maternity care services: a comparative study using DHS data. In *Demographic and Health Surveys World Conference, August 5-7, 1991, Washington, D.C., Proceedings*, vol. III. Columbia, Maryland: IRD/Macro International, Inc.

Weinberger, Mary Beth (1991). Recent trends in contraceptive behavior. In *Demographic and Health Surveys World Conference, August 5-7, 1991, Washington, D.C., Proceedings*, vol. I. Columbia, Maryland: IRD/Macro International, Inc.

Westoff, Charles, and Luis Henando Ochoa (1991a). The demand for family planning: highlights from a comparative analysis. In *Demographic and Health Surveys World Conference, August 5-7, 1991, Washington, D.C., Proceedings*, vol. I. Columbia, Maryland: IRD/Macro International, Inc.

__________ (1991b). *Unmet Need and the Demand for Family Planning*. Demographic and Health Surveys Comparative Studies, No. 5, Columbia, Maryland: Institute for Resource Development/Macro International, Inc.

Wilkinson, Marilyn, Nouraddine Abderrahim and Wamucii Njogu (1991). Availability and use of contraception: a comparative perspective. In *Demographic and Health Surveys World Conference, August 5-7, 1991, Washington, D.C., Proceedings*, vol. III. Columbia, Maryland: IRD/Macro International, Inc.

Part Four

WOMEN, HEALTH AND MORTALITY

IX. GENDER DIFFERENCES IN HEALTH RISKS AND USE OF SERVICES

*Gigi Santow**

This paper reviews how the position of women affects the risks to their health and their use of health-care services, identifies some implications for the health of their children and indicates some pathways of beneficial change.

Underlying biological differences between the health of women and men are modified by behaviour and practices that are related to women's position and roles. Women's access to and use of health services are similarly modified because modern health care is often allocated according to status determined along the traditional lines of sex, age and familial role.

Despite their inferior position, women are commonly seen as the custodians of family health. It may be advantageous to both family health and the position of women to include husbands in that responsibility, and possibly other members of a wider social network.

A. RISKS TO WOMEN'S HEALTH

Differences between the health of women and men

In identifying those risks to women's health which are particularly related to their place in society, it is helpful to identify some basic underlying differences between the health risks to which women and men are exposed.

Two opposing biological factors are at work. First, a disadvantage accrues to men from the possession of a Y-chromosome (or, to be more precise, from the lack of a second X-chromosome) (Waldron, 1983). Although the evidence is sometimes contradictory, it appears that males are more vulnerable than females to the effects of harmful recessive genes on their single X-chromosome, effects that in their case are not masked by a corresponding gene on a second X-chromosome; and also that X-linked immuno-regulatory genes contribute to a greater resistance to infectious diseases for females.

Secondly, a disadvantage accrues to women from their capacity to reproduce. The most obvious example of reproductively related disadvantage is maternal mortality, men not being at risk of death caused by complications of pregnancy and childbirth. Another example is that of menstruation, which places a severe burden on women if their nutritional status is already precarious and they are anaemic. No relief comes with amenorrhoea related to pregnancy and lactation, however, since child-bearing carries very considerable burdens and risks of its own. Childbirth itself is hazardous, especially in poor countries, although even in rich countries the risks of death associated with childbirth exceed those associated with the use of contraception (Potts and Selman, 1979). Both pregnancy and lactation drain the mother's resources, particularly if, as is common in the developing world, she breast-feeds from one confinement into the next pregnancy (Bracher, 1992). Such factors may negate, or even reverse, women's innate biological advantage.

To gain insights into the actual differences between the health of women and men, it is useful to compare the sex differentials in mortality (in the absence of reliable or comparable morbidity data) of countries that are in different stages of development, whether this means the charting of differentials in one country over time or the comparison of differentials in different countries. Sex differentials in mortality are less pronounced when life expectancy at birth is short than when it is long. In the former case, when life expectancy is relatively short, the most marked divergence between women and men occurs after age 40, with women then experiencing lower mortality; before that age, women may experience similar mortality to men, or even higher mortality, undoubtedly related to the greater risks associated with reproduction in poor countries than in rich countries. In the latter case,

*Senior Research Fellow, National Centre for Epidemiology and Population Health, The Australian National University, Canberra.

when life expectancy at birth is long, females experience lower mortality than males at every age. Indeed, they enjoy a particular mortality advantage between the ages of about 10 and 40 years (Omran, 1971; Ruzicka and Kane, 1990).

In so far as rates and patterns of reproduction are culturally and socially determined and, indeed, as all aspects of life are similarly governed, it becomes very difficult to separate effects that are purely biological or genetic from those which are affected by culturally determined behaviour. More generally, there is probably no society in which health risks have not been conditioned by the relative statuses and roles of its members. The effects of some of these conditioning influences on different aspects of women's health are considered below.

Nutrition

One way in which gender distinctions are maintained and reinforced is through the differential allocation of food. As a result, it is extremely common for women to eat less, and less well, than men. The practice has been reported in widely different societies: in rural Egypt (Lane and Meleis, 1991); in rural Karnataka and Uttar Pradesh, India (Caldwell, Reddy and Caldwell, 1983; Khan and others, 1989); in Nigeria (Okojie, 1991); in Albania, Greece and Yugoslavia (Denich, 1974); and in Nepal (Gittelsohn, 1991). These studies paint a complex picture of dominance and deference arranged along lines of sex, age and familial role. In Egypt, women and girls ate the leftovers from a communal bowl after the men and boys had finished (Lane and Meleis, 1991). In southern India, male household heads and other males tended to eat first, boys tended to join any group that was eating and to obtain larger shares than their sisters, and daughters-in-law served the mothers-in-law before themselves (Caldwell, Reddy and Caldwell, 1983). Adult women ate last in Nepal; adult males received preferential treatment although they tended to be served after small children (Gittelsohn, 1991). Although it is sometimes argued, particularly by husbands, that women make up the deficit while they prepare the meals, cooking may be too public an event for much food to be consumed at that time (Caldwell, Reddy and Caldwell, 1983). Moreover, where deference and obedience are prized female attributes, women may be willing partners in this inequitable arrangement, enjoying the feeling that they are sacrificing themselves for their family's welfare (Khan and others, 1989).

Young adult women seem universally to get the worst and smallest share. These are the women most likely to be pregnant or lactating, or both, and actually to have elevated nutritional requirements for those reasons. For example, the recommended daily allowance of dietary iron in the United States of America is 10 milligrams for adult males, but 18 miligrams for women of child-bearing age (Taylor and Anthony, 1983). The nutritional deprivation of young adult women is therefore particularly critical. Moreover, it affects not only their own health but, as is examined later in more detail, the health of the foetus and the nursing child (Winikoff, 1990).

Child-bearing

The question here is not how child-bearing may adversely affect women's health but how women's status may affect the intrinsic hazards of child-bearing.

Children are everywhere valued and desired, but in the Western world a woman's position in society is unlikely to be related primarily to her fertility. This is not so in many developing countries, and women are under considerable pressure to reproduce: to provide sons for their husband or his family or clan; or to provide family workers. Where local customary practices provide for a minimum spacing between births, or where women have adopted contraception to space their births the mother is better protected from drains on her resources than where such practices do not exist or are essentially ineffective. In the latter case, however, the mother will be weakened by a continuous round of pregnancy and lactation, exacerbated by nutritional deficiencies. Various maternal depletion syndromes have been identified, involving either protein-calorie malnutrition or specific deficiencies, such as iron-deficiency anaemia or iodine-deficiency goitre (Jelliffe and Jelliffe, 1989). If pregnancy complicates iron-deficiency anaemia, the anaemia may become profound, elevating the risk of miscarriage, prematurity, perinatal morbidity and maternal heart failure (Taylor and

Anthony, 1983). The assault on women's health will be particularly severe if, because of concerns for female purity, women marry young and therefore begin bearing their children at a young age. The assault will also be exacerbated if, as is common throughout the developing world, demands for women's labour do not lessen while they are either pregnant or nursing a small child.

The question of contraception to space births is an important one. If the spacing of births is a well-established goal, then it is more likely that women will be able to substitute contraception for abstinence and that their husbands will applaud the changes in their life occasioned by their wives' adoption of "modern" behaviour. The substitution of modern contraception for post-partum sexual abstinence has been documented in a number of countries (Santow and Bracher, 1981; Bracher and Santow, 1982).

Yet, regardless of whether the deliberate spacing of births is a familiar notion, husbands may be threatened by their wives' adoption of contraception, fearing that it will allow them an unacceptable degree of sexual freedom. The statement of a participant in a focus-group study of men's attitudes to family planning in Burkina Faso exemplifies this feeling:

"For me, there is no problem. But for others, if you talk about this to them, some will say, `If I give this to my wife, maybe she will use it to her advantage and go out and do what she wants, do stupid things.' . . ." (McGinn, Bamba and Balma, 1989, p. 86).

The statement has two interesting aspects. First, the man professes not to object personally to the idea of the wife using contraception but reveals his disquiet by ascribing opposition to others. Secondly, he assumes that contraception will not be directly provided to the wife but channelled through her husband. This, indeed, is effectively the case in many countries, where a husband's approval is still legally required for his wife to use family planning services (Cook and Maine, 1987). Even where this is not so, husbands' approval may be critical for family planning acceptance. Indeed, an urban Indonesian study found that husband's approval was the strongest single predictor of the wife's use of contraception, stronger than the factors usually considered paramount, such as the wife's age, education, employment status, desire for more children and experience of child loss (Joesoef, Baughman and Utomo, 1988). The fact that the use of modern contraception, and particularly the use of condoms, is associated in many countries with premarital or extramarital sex is particularly unhelpful to its adoption within marriage. Thus, for example, Peruvian women fear their husbands' disapproval if they use contraception, since having many children is associated with faithfulness but family planning is associated with infidelity (Fort, 1989).

The ultimate reproductively related assault on women's health is maternal death. Women that die from a maternal cause, and probably most of their small children, are unrepresented in retrospective demographic surveys. Overall maternal mortality rates of 450 per 100,000 live births have been estimated for the developing countries, compared with only 30 per 100,000 in the developed countries (Belsey, and Royston, 1990). The primary causes of maternal mortality in the developing countries are sepsis, hypertensive disorders, severe anaemia and haemorrhage, all conditions that are very successfully prevented or treated in the developed countries. The picture is grimmer if maternal deaths are defined not just with respect to live births but to pregnancies in general. Induced abortion, the last resort for many desperate women, is extremely dangerous, particularly in the developing countries where it is likely to be restricted or illegal and therefore performed by untrained personnel in unsterile conditions, and to be followed by little or no after-care (Winikoff, 1990; Raikes, 1989).

Despite avoiding the risks of reproduction, the situation of the woman who has never conceived carries particular burdens. In many traditional societies, if she is fortunate enough not to be repudiated entirely by her husband, she is nevertheless doomed to a place of low status within the family and to suspicions of wrongdoing or even witchcraft; nor, of course, will she benefit from the support of children, and particularly her sons, in later life. The situation of the woman who has borne no live children, or whose children have all died, is at least as grave.

Sexually transmitted diseases and AIDS

The low-fertility belt in Middle Africa has been documented for close to 50 years (Griffith, 1963; Romaniuk, 1968). It is now known to be related to a high prevalence of sexually transmitted diseases (STDs): most importantly, to gonorrhoea, which may lead to occluded fallopian tubes, an elevated risk of life-threatening ectopic pregnancy and infertility; and secondly, to syphilis which, among other unpleasant sequelae, increases the risk of spontaneous pregnancy loss (Guest, 1978). The prevalence of STDs in the low-fertility belt is ascribed to a high level of "sexual mobility" (Frank, 1983)—to such factors as men's premarital and extramarital sexual activity during frequent work-related absences from home, institutionalized prostitution in the towns, the lack of other economic opportunities for divorcees and widows and polygyny and related post-partum sexual abstinence for wives but not for husbands (David and Voas, 1981; Frank, 1983).

More recently, there has been in sub-Saharan Africa, an explosion of acquired immunodeficiency syndrome (AIDS) in the heterosexual community. Studies have found seroprevalence rates ranging from 5 per cent (Burkina Faso) to 28 per cent (Uganda) among pregnant urban women, and rates as high as 80 per cent among female prostitutes in Kenya (de Bruyn, 1992). Throughout the world, the ratio of female to male cases is rising, but women in sub-Saharan Africa are at greatest risk, and show the highest seroprevalence (Bruyn, 1992). Many of the countries with the highest seroprevalence were formerly known for their high prevalence of STDs and there are biological and behavioural reasons why this should be so. Yet, here the similarity ends. During the 1950s, penicillin campaigns were directed in some African countries to the syphilis-like diseases, yaws and pinta (Frank, 1983) but such was their effect on gonorrhoea, which used to be "exquisitely sensitive" to penicillin (Winikoff, 1990), that primary sterility fell in some affected regions, for example, in Cameroon, and fertility rose (Santow and Bioumla, 1984). With AIDS, however, penicillin performs no magical cure.

Rural women left behind while their husbands work in urban centres may become de facto household head, despite their being denied adequate control over land and cash, and independently support themselves and their children during their husbands' absences. The husbands commonly form new sexual or matrimonial liaisons elsewhere; and if they do not abandon their wives altogether, will demand sexual relations on their visits home (Ankrah, 1991). Abandoned wives, in a no-win situation, face a host of other problems (Ankrah, 1991; de Bruyn, 1992). Those that turn to prostitution to support their families may be placing themselves at greater risk than they were from their husbands' occasional visits. Similar problems are faced by widows of AIDS sufferers if they are abandoned by their husband's kin.

Young women are placed at a particular risk in societies where, because premarital chastity is valued and opportunities for male sexual activity and marriage increase with age, the gap in age between spouses is ideally wide; older husbands are more likely to be infected than younger ones, and their young wives therefore have an elevated lifetime probability of infection, even if they themselves are monogamous (Palloni and Lee, 1990). A more general problem is that young women may be pressured into sexual activity at young ages, and with multiple partners and by older men (de Bruyn, 1992).

The basic key, therefore, is whether women have the power to refuse sex. In societies with traditionally sanctioned periods of post-partum abstinence, such refusal is presumably possible. The negotiation that goes on in such cases is exemplified by the following segments of two interviews with women in Burkina Faso:

"Q. How are you going to space your children by three years?

A. I do it my own way.

Q. How?

A. (Laugh) If my husband has a separate room and I have my room, too, I may not leave my room to go into that of my husband.

Q. But if he asks you to come?

A. Ah . . . If I know the child has made it [is big], then only do I go to him.

Q. After a delivery, how long do you wait before sleeping with the man again?

A. It takes some time at any rate. We, the women, do not want to. It is the men who want and force us, otherwise it lasts. If we get our way, we can stay a year like that. But today's men do not accept that any more. If the man does not have two wives, you know he will . . . (Laugh). At any rate, it will be difficult.

Q. If you don't want him to go to another woman, at any rate. How many moons must the child reach before you can go back to your husband?

A. Ah! At least eight to 10 moons.

Q. So, the husband must wait that long?

A. Yes, 10 moons." (Van de Walle and Traoné, 1986)

In addition, other relatives may keep an eye on the couple's sleeping arrangements and intervene, if they see fit. Lastly, not only is abstinence socially sanctioned in such cases but the bearing of a child too soon after the previous birth will attract verbal ridicule or abuse, social ostracism or even physical assault (Caldwell and Caldwell, 1981).

However, abstinence during the post-partum period is relevant to abstinence for other reasons only in that it teaches that it is possible, and at times desirable, to reject a husband's advances. Without practical evidence for the need to abstain in the person of an unweaned child, without the support or aggressive intervention of kin and without the fear of social ostracism, her task may be more difficult. Ongoing research in Nigeria suggests that in Yorubaland, where post-partum abstinence is long, women may rise to the occasion: they will refuse sex insist on a condom or leave their husbands (Orubuloye, Caldwell and Caldwell, 1992).

In contrast, where women are expected to be sexually receptive very soon after childbirth and to remain so until the next delivery, and where women are less financially independent than in Yorubaland, their power to refuse sex is undoubtedly weaker. Large proportions of surveyed women in Belize and Uganda and believed that they were at risk because they could not prevent their partners from having sex with other people, while those that dared to refuse sex or suggest that a condom be used risked accusations that they were promiscuous or themselves infected, or that they were accusing their partners of infidelity (de Bruyn, 1992).

Research on this aspect of female autonomy is still in its infancy. Valuable findings are, however, beginning to emerge. In the United States of America, focus-group research with black and Hispanic women that were recent IV drug users or sexual partners of current IV drug users, or had the human immunodeficiency virus, failed to confirm a number of commonly held notions concerning the lack of power of such women. Many reported great assertiveness in decisions regarding all aspects of their sexual activity. Barriers to condom use were not primarily related to a lack of power in sexual relationships, and a frequently reported means of enforcing condom use was the threat to withhold sex (Kline, Kline and Oken, 1992).

Female genital mutilation

A particularly unfortunate example of the relation between the status of women and the risks to their health is female circumcision. In its most severe (Pharaonic) form, it involves removal of the clitoris, labia minora and part of the labia majora, and the stitching together of the wound to leave a smooth infibulated scar with a small aperture. Further surgery is repeatedly required at marriage and before and after childbirth. Even in its mildest form (Sunna), it may lead to infection and haemorrhage.

Female circumcision is still common in many parts of the Arab world. Despite Pharaonic circumcision having been banned in the Sudan as long ago as 1946, the recent Demographic and Health Survey (DHS) reported that 89 per cent of ever-married women were circumcised, 82 per cent of them in the most severe way. The prevalence of Pharaonic circumcision has declined somewhat, from 89 per cent among women aged 45-49 to 74 per cent among women aged 15-19, yet there has been an almost corresponding increase in Sunna, from 9 to 22 per cent (Sudan, 1991). Unfortunately, since circumcision is seen as a sign of ethnic (Arab) superiority in the Sudan, in some non-Arab groups its prevalence may even be increasing (Gruenbaum, 1991).

Where it is practised, female circumcision is often wrongly believed to be enjoined by Islam. Women believe that it enhances marriageability by protecting premarital virginity and increasing the husband's pleasure. Many therefore continue to support it for their daughters and granddaughters although there are sometimes signs of tension between the generations: mothers may choose a less drastic form of operation, for example, in opposition to the wishes of grandmothers. There are also signs of opposition from men: the son of a Sudanese midwife who, like many migrant workers, had experienced the religious revival while working in Saudi Arabia, was shocked to learn, when he married, of the extent of the damage done by Pharaonic circumcision and was said to have criticized his mother for her part in it (Gruenbaum, 1991; Lane and Meleis, 1991).

The health risks posed by female circumcision are enormous. Very real dangers attend the surgery itself, which is most frequently performed without anaesthesia and in unsterile conditions, and the risk is multiplied if infibulation is practised. Vaginal tears may occur on the wedding night (Lane and Meleis, 1991). Moreover, if infibulation prevents vaginal intercourse, husbands may practise anal sex, thereby placing their wives at greater risk of contracting STDs or AIDS (De Bruyn, 1992).

Overview

In examining how women's health risks may be conditioned by their roles, it has been useful to categorize those risks under a number of separate headings. Nevertheless, the aspects of behaviour described above and the risks they pose to women's health are strongly interrelated. Both poor diet and repeated child-bearing increase the risk of anaemia. Pregnancy and childbirth are rendered more dangerous by dietary insufficiencies caused by the inequitable distribution of food, by various forms of genital mutilation and by STD infection. Moreover, both malnourishment and genital mutilation may predispose to infection, and infection may increase the risk of malabsorption of nutrients. The repudiated wife with no children, or none surviving, may be able to support herself only by prostitution.

B. Modern health care

A syncretism of health beliefs and health-seeking behaviour

A great deal of important research has addressed the reasons for underutilization of modern health services in the developing countries. Less attention has been paid to the opposite question, namely, how it is that uneducated, fairly traditional peoples have begun to use modern health services at all. After all, it is very recent in the histories of the developing countries that modern health care, however inadequate, has been made to any degree accessible to ordinary people, and the principles underlying modern health care seem largely incompatible with traditional beliefs concerning health, illness and treatment. Nevertheless, the work that has been done in this area has consistently found that traditional beliefs can coexist with modern health-care practices.

A striking example of this accommodation is the great popularity throughout the developing world of injections (Reeler, 1990). One reason advanced is that people remember the success of injection campaigns that eliminated such diseases as yaws; another is that the direct introduction of the needle into the body is compatible with traditional notions concerning the invocation of powerful outside forces; another is that the individual nature of the treatment conferred by an injection, as distinct from pills which can be shared, is consistent with a shift from a wider network of obligations to a narrower, more individualistic focus. Whatever the reasons for the popularity of injections, and it is important that they be identified because the misuse of this technology is now becoming an international public-health concern, it is clear that their popularity has little to do with an understanding of modern medicine.

The popularity of injections is only the most dramatic example of the absorption of modern medicine into traditional health beliefs. Nigerians simultaneously believed that illness and death were caused by the wish of God or jealousy leading to witchcraft; and by poor health care and health practices and lack of childhood immunization, especially in the past. Traditional healers were distrusted for treating patients only by trial and error, and because they did not give injections or perform operations. On the other hand, adult men thought that their mortality was higher than that of adult women because many men were killed by their wives, by poison or witchcraft. In the communities studied, some illnesses were thought to be amenable to modern health care, others to traditional healers and a third group to either (Okojie, 1991). The partial integration of traditional beliefs concerning disease causation into the modern health-care sector has also been reported elsewhere in Nigeria and in sub-Saharan Africa more generally (Adetunji, 1991; Schoepf, 1991); and in such different countries as Nepal (Reissland and Burghart, 1989), Pakistan (Mull, Anderson and Mull, 1990) and Indonesia (Streatfield, Tampubolon and Surjadi, 1991).

Women's access to health care and use of services

Another example of the absorption of modern health care into older and stronger patterns of belief and behaviour is that health care appears frequently to be allocated, like food, along lines of sex, age and familial role. This finding is extremely interesting, given the recency of modern health care. This recency must be borne continually in mind as one assesses the strength of gender-related barriers to the exploitation of health services. There is, once again, a situation of adjustment to a new institution but along completely traditional lines.

In the Egyptian hamlet previously mentioned, women oversaw the health of family members, deciding when a member of the family was sick and either administering home remedies or choosing additional therapy from a traditional healer, the modern health sector or a combination of the two. However, a sick person's access to therapy was determined not just by the severity of illness but by the person's status within the family. A lower status person, such as a young female, was likely to be treated only with home remedies; if assistance was sought outside the household, it was more likely to be from a traditional than a modern therapist. A higher status individual, such as a male of almost any age or an adult mother of sons, was likely to be taken directly to a private medical practitioner. Women tended to continue working when they were sick or even in the last stages of pregnancy. If the pain became too severe, then other female household members and relatives rallied around her.

Soon the men are alerted to the woman's problem and return home to find five or more women wailing like professional mourners around a woman who is rocking back and forth and crying through clenched teeth. They hasten to call on a relative or neighbour who owns a car to come and take the woman to a doctor. Men that are sick do not exhibit this type of behaviour. They seem to have access to medical care without needing to show anyone how sick they are. The women apparently to need to convince the men that they are dangerously ill before they are taken to the doctor (Lane and Meleis, 1991).

In northern India, married women tended to be less neglected than young unmarried girls or female children because their labour was recognized as important to the smooth functioning of the household. Nevertheless, the seeking of treatment was often delayed, either because of the husband's apathy or because the mother-in-law was jealous if her son appeared to be too concerned for his wife. A new bride, who had not yet borne sons or otherwise made a place for herself in her new family, often suffered greatly from such neglect. The decision to call a doctor was generally taken by men, the majority of female informants saying they had no power either to make or even influence such decisions, except in the case of complications in childbirth (Khan and others, 1989). In rural Karnataka, women were more likely to identify sickness in their husbands and urge them to seek treatment than husbands were to do the same for their wives (Caldwell, Reddy and Caldwell, 1983).

Intervention clearly hinges on a perception of need: without female relatives or neighbours, such need (as in the Egyptian example) may go unnoticed. Moreover, when health care has traditionally been seen as interventionist, rather than prophylactic, the need for intervention may go unremarked. Thus, routine but critical antenatal care was rare among the northern Indian informants a finding also of a number of much larger Indian studies (Khan and others, 1989).

In addition, issues of sequestration and modesty may create barriers to women seeking health care for themselves. In both northern India and Bangladesh, it may happen that when a woman falls sick, it is her husband or other male family member that visits a physician and obtains medicine on her behalf by describing her symptoms. A woman, or her husband, may refuse to permit a gynaecological examination by a male practitioner, leading to delays in treatment or indeed, to conditions not being treated correctly at all (Khan and others, 1989). Continuation rates of oral contraceptives were greatly improved in the Islamic Republic of Iran by giving the pill not to the wife, but to the husband to pass on to her: as the decision maker within the family, he was the appropriate person to receive contraceptives, whether they were for his own use or not (Potts and Selman, 1979).

Nevertheless, some limited change does appear to be under way. Although rural northern Indian women still preferred to be examined for gynaecological complaints by a female doctor, neither they nor their husbands were inhibited about seeing a male doctor in the city whom they did not know and would not see again. This attitude was perceived to be an enormous change over the previous 20 or 30 years, when it would have been unacceptable to both the women and their husbands unless the woman's life was perceived to be in danger (Khan and others, 1989). Similar changes are occurring in southern India, as the appropriate authorizer of health treatment shifts from the older to the younger married generation, with regard not only to the latter's own health but that of their children (Caldwell, Reddy and Caldwell, 1983).

C. The interdependence of the health of women and children

Biological factors

Just as each aspect of women's health intimately affects other aspects, so does it affect the health of her children. Iodine-deficient mothers may bear cretinous children. Poorly nourished, anaemic women bequeath poor health to their children, both *in utero* and after they are born (Winikoff, 1990). Maternal malnutrition is one of the most important contributing factors to low birth-weight babies. Resulting from intra-uterine growth retardation, this scourge of many developing countries is an indicator of stress that may lead to premature death or a lifetime dogged by disabling disease, susceptibility to infection and poor health (Jelliffe and Jelliffe, 1989). In areas on the edge of malnutrition, children from larger households are more poorly nourished than children from smaller households (Pelto and others, 1991). Children born too close together are at greater risk of death than children whose births are spaced more widely, the risk being elevated not only for the new child but for the older child deposed from the breast (Hobcraft, McDonald and Rutstein, 1983). Marasmus, a severe syndrome of protein-calorie malnutrition causing wasting and death, lies in wait for inadequately breast-fed infants; while kwashiorkor, a complex protein-deficiency syndrome, may strike the child weaned onto inadequate food (Jelliffe and Jelliffe, 1989). Thus, a gruelling round of frequent child-bearing jeopardizes not only the health of women but also that of their children.

The interrelatedness of maternal and child health has been illustrated by calculating the effects on infant, child and maternal mortality in 25 developing countries of contraception-induced changes in fertility (Trussell and Pebley, 1984). Probabilities of infant death could fall by 12 per cent if fourth and higher order births were eliminated and child-bearing restricted to ages 20-34. Infant mortality could fall by 10 per cent and child mortality by 21 per cent if births were always spaced at least two years apart.

Maternal mortality could fall by 21 per cent if fifth and higher order births were eliminated and child-bearing restricted to ages 20-39.

The health of mothers and children is bound up in other ways as well. Syphilitic mothers are more susceptible to spontaneous foetal loss: indeed, syphilis is implicated in between 35 and 50 per cent of stillbirths in Ethiopia (Winikoff, 1990). If the organism is present in the vagina during childbirth, gonorrhoea can cause an opthalmitis in newborns that may lead to blindness, and transmission is greatly facilitated if the mother also suffers from chlamydia. It has been estimated that gonococcal eye infections are more than 50 times as common in Africa as in the industrialized countries (Winikoff, 1990).

AIDS is beginning to have an even more alarming impact on children, and the situation will deteriorate before it improves. Increasing numbers of African women are becoming HIV-positive, and increasing numbers are bearing infected children that are destined to die, after considerable suffering, from paediatric HIV/AIDS. By the end of the century, under-five mortality rates in 10 Middle and Eastern African countries may exceed the United Nations projections by more than 40 per cent solely because of AIDS (Preble, 1990). The outlook for orphaned children, whether or not they are infected, is bleak. Orphanhood has always posed risks to children, particularly if they are orphaned before they are weaned, but AIDS orphans may face the additional risk of abandonment by their family (if their family still survive). Their mortality, whether they are adopted out or placed in orphanages, will be high. The effects of such dislocation or even destruction of families, compounded by an increased incidence of widowhood—what Palloni and Lee (1990) call "a complete overhaul of family arrangements"—will be felt for decades to come (Hunter, 1990).

Lastly, the health care women receive impinges directly on the health, or even the survival, of their children. An absence of antenatal care, a failure to detect a high-risk pregnancy and a failure to hospitalize women that are experiencing complications in labour place in jeopardy not only the woman herself but the child she is carrying.

Cultural, social and behavioural factors

Much of the work on the mortality of infants and children in poor countries centres on the reversal of the sex ratio of mortality that is observed in rich ones. This reversal can be very substantial and clearly reflects differential care. Where son preference is high, as indicated by considerably more mothers preferring that their next child be a son than a daughter, then the ratios of male to female infant, toddler and child mortality are likely to be unusually low, given the biological disadvantage experienced by male children in relation to females. For example, among eight developing countries with a son preference ratio of 1.5 or more, two exhibited sex ratios of infant mortality under 1.0 and an additional four had ratios no greater than 1.05; seven exhibited toddler ratios under 1.0 and seven had child ratios under 1.0 (Belsey and Royston, 1990). In rural Bangladesh, the expected sex ratio of mortality was observed only during the neonatal period, when endogenous causes (other than tetanus) can be expected to dominate; and at ages 45-64, when child-bearing no longer poses a risk and the defencelessness of old age and widowhood is not yet of overwhelming significance (Chen, Huq and D'Souza, 1981). More detailed work, which not only differentiated the mortality of boys and girls but controlled for the existence of older siblings, has shown that, in Bangladesh, while girls were subject to a 54 per cent greater mortality rate than boys, their risk was 84 per cent greater if they had older sisters and only 14 per cent greater if they did not. Thus, it is not simply that all girls were treated differently from boys, but that there was a "pattern of conscious, selective neglect of individual children" (Muhuri and Preston, 1991, p. 431).

The existence of such sex differentials in mortality indicates far more than that in many societies girls tend to fare less well than boys. In showing that some children may be better treated than others, it also shows that commitment to child welfare need not be absolute: thus, the needs of any child may go unrecognized; or, being recognized, they may go unfulfilled. These issues are considered below in turn.

Just as adult females are likely to be less well-fed than adult males, small girls are likely to suffer in contrast to their brothers. In some areas of rural Uttar Pradesh, it was even found that female babies were sometimes breast-fed for a shorter time and less intensely than male babies. In the study in question, this happened when the first child was a daughter. The parents began trying for a son, the mother conceived again and then weaned the little girl in case continuing to breast-feed would harm the new—and it was hoped, male—baby. In contrast, when the first child was a son, far from there being pressure to bear a second child, couples protected the breast-feeding period from the risk of premature weaning by means of abstinence (Khan and others, 1989).

In northern India, ordinary food appeared to be divided fairly between sons and daughters, but special, more nutritious foods went disproportionately often to sons (Das Gupta, 1987; Khan and others, 1989). Malnutrition was more prevalent in Bangladesh among girls under age 5 than among boys, and dietary surveys showed that male caloric consumption and protein consumption exceeded that of females (Chen, Huq and D'Souza, 1981). In many other countries, sex differentiation does not begin so early. Yet, the evil day cannot be indefinitely postponed, and at some point, critical for health, girls begin to take their meals with their mother (Caldwell and Caldwell, 1990).

A Nigerian study of diarrhoea in children younger than age 3 found that maternal diagnosis was affected not only by such symptoms as frequent stools and fever but by the child's age and sex: diarrhoea was significantly less often reported when the child was younger than two months (perhaps because the mothers appreciated their normal excretion of more frequent and more liquid stools); and was significantly less often reported when the child was a girl. Although the authors do not discuss the latter very significant finding, it seems to be a clear indication that differential treatment of sick children according to their sex is a far more complex matter than seeking treatment for a sick boy but not for a sick girl: in this example, a girl was simply less likely to be perceived as sick in the first place. Moreover, diarrhoeal prevalence based on maternal reports was only half that based on reports of three or more liquid or semi-liquid stools. Thus, in half the cases the question whether to seek treatment would not even have arisen, whether the child was male or female (Cogswell and others, 1991).

And what of treatment? Despite very similar under-five rates of morbidity (diarrhoeal, respiratory, skin and eye/ear infections) and despite the provision of free transport and free treatment, only three sick girls were taken for treatment for every five sick boys (Chen, Huq, and D'Souza, 1981). The same ratio obtained at ages 5-14 years. In Punjab, the expenditure on both clothing and medicine was greater for little boys than little girls (Das Gupta, 1987).

This finding is by no means an isolated instance. In northern India, despite informants' denials, direct observation showed that girls were far less likely to be taken to a village primary health centre than boys, although there was no reason to believe that levels of morbidity would have differed, or certainly not in favour of girls. In that case, the ratio was 1:4 in favour of males (Khan and others, 1989). Studies conducted in Punjab, nearly two decades apart disclosed the persistence of excess mortality of small girls despite an overall mortality decline and improvements in health care, nutrition and income (Wyon and Gordon, 1971; Das Gupta, 1987). Given both expense and competing demands on women's time, Egyptian mothers tend to delay seeking health care for their children and to delay seeking help longer for daughters than for sons (Lane and Meleis, 1991).

The point is repeatedly made in studies concerning the social aspects of health that mothers are the natural guardians of their families' health and, in particular, the health of their children (see, for example, Doan and Bisharat, 1990; Ankrah, 1991; de Bruyn, 1992). Nevertheless, although this may be the "natural" situation, the power of mothers to intervene when a child is sick may be very limited. Since women may find it difficult to obtain health care even for themselves, it is not surprising that, having recognized a need, they may find it difficult to obtain health care for their children.

Sometimes the power to intervene is limited simply by economic factors: "simply" because cultural barriers seem often to be so much more impenetrable. In Yorubaland, for example, the person (usually a parent) that chooses a particular treatment for a sick child is also the person who pays for that treatment. This is the downside of women's financial independence from men. It means that mothers are the most likely to pay for treatment for minor illnesses, but that the role of fathers becomes critical if the illness is severe and the costs therefore greater (Orubuloye and others, 1991).

Yet, just as in the case of women's own health care, incipient change can sometimes be detected. The nutritional status of Jordanian children was correlated with female autonomy as indicated by household structure (the least autonomous mothers being a daughter-in-law in an extended vertical household and the most being a co-head or head in a nuclear-family household) (Doan and Bisharat, 1990). This finding at least holds out a promise of better nutrition for some children, especially as nuclear households become more prevalent. Likewise, in northern India, the increased nuclearization of the families of young couples with some schooling has given those wives more independence in choosing what to cook and what to serve to whom, and even in persuading their husbands to seek medical help for sick children (Khan and others, 1989).

In rural Karnataka, children's illnesses were first noticed seven times more often by parents than grandparents and 10 times more often by mothers than fathers: these types of ratios, which may not be untraditional, may go some way to explaining why a child's mother is indeed the best caregiver. What has changed, however, is that the power to authorize the seeking of health care appears to have been shifting from the oldest generation to the parents of the children concerned. The decision to take children to the health centre was made by parents in almost two thirds of cases (although the decision was overruled by grandparents in one tenth of cases). Yet, mothers suggested treatment no more often than did fathers and were less likely than fathers to make decisions about treatment. Even so, when children were sick, their mothers were clearly the most distressed (Caldwell, Reddy and Caldwell, 1983).

D. A SEARCH FOR AGENTS OF CHANGE

It has been shown that even while people begin to use modern health services, they may hold fast to traditional notions of disease causation. It has also been seen that the allocation of those services may respect the traditional hierarchies based on sex, age and familial role. Ultimately, the experience of modern curative services may of itself engender change in attitudes and beliefs, and lead to greater equity in health-service use; but this feedback effect may be slow to occur. In the meantime, then, one must search for other agents of change.

Maternal education and female roles

One of the keys to improved survival chances of children in the developing countries is the education of their mother. A relation between levels of infant and child mortality, on the one hand, and maternal education, on the other, has been documented, although not without exception, in a host of fertility surveys conducted since the 1970s. Averaging the results of 34 surveys, for example, showed that children whose mother had seven or more years of schooling were subject to 45-66 per cent of the risk of death during infancy as children whose mother had no schooling, to 15-45 per cent of their risk of death during the second year of life and to 17-43 per cent of their risk from the third to the fifth years. A gradient was noticeable even if the mother had only between one and three years of schooling (Cleland and van Ginneken, 1988).

The question, of course, is why this relation should exist. The answer appears to lie neither in superior reproductive health nor socio-economic status, nor even solely in the demonstrably greater use of health services by mothers with more schooling. Nor does it lie in the actual knowledge the mother acquires at school, a number of studies having shown that traditional beliefs concerning disease causation seem to be unassailed by the experience of modern, Western-style education. One is left with a battery of possible explanations. They hinge on the confidence that education instils in a mother to cope with aspects of the modern world, to take greater personal responsibility for the welfare of her children and to assume a more important position in the family into which she marries (Caldwell, 1979; Cleland and van Ginneken, 1988). If these suppositions are correct and considerable work still remains to be done in this area, then female education is no more than a convenient proxy for a change in female status.

Nevertheless, despite overall reductions in infant and child mortality, maternal education does not eliminate sex differentials in childhood mortality, differentials that, since they are weighted in favour of male children, are clearly attributable to differential care. Indeed, because educated women are likely to want fewer children, the sex differential in both Bangladesh and Punjab has been observed to widen as the pressure increases on unwanted girls (Das Gupta, 1987; Bhuiya and Streatfield, 1991). These are both regions of traditionally strong preference for sons. What one is observing, therefore, is another instance of adaptation, with attitudes, behaviour and family structures shifting as a result of something to do with modern schooling but with completely traditional notions about the relative values of sons and daughters remaining intact.

The role of men

Women are the persons that may breast-feed their infant sons longer than their infant daughters, that later feed better food to their sons, that may be more likely to recognize that a son is sick than a daughter and that currently seem to be the major supporters of female circumcision. The discrimination of mother against daughter is mirrored in the discrimination of mother-in-law against daughter-in-law.

If one were to focus on female roles in isolation from the broader structure, one might conclude that women themselves should accept the major responsibility for maintaining many of the least desirable aspects of the traditional status quo. Yet, in behaving in the ways described above, women merely demonstrate their adherence to the only situation they know, and therefore the only one in which they feel secure. In some societies, the ultimate power for a woman comes only from being a mother-in-law and thus comes only to a mother and, indeed, a mother of sons.

Maternal and child health and family planning programmes, and public-health programmes in general, have tended to target women in their campaigns. There are simple reasons that they should do so: women are the most "natural" guardians not only of their own health but of children; they are the most directly involved with the reproductive process; and they are frequently seen also as the guardians of their family's health. Yet, this targeting of women means that, to a certain extent, the burdensome roles imposed by traditional society on its women have been reimposed on them by researchers and policy makers.

The focus on women may also mean that interventions will fail. Clear examples come from the family planning area, as has been stated, with both acceptance and continuation being strongly contingent upon the husband's having been drawn into the process. Moreover, such targeting completely ignores the realities of not only the power of ordinary, married women to care for their children and to intervene on their behalf but also of the altogether more desperate situations of women whose marriages have failed or whose husbands no longer contribute to the maintenance of their children (Whyte and Kariuki, 1991).

One reason that the role of husbands has, perhaps, been underrated by researchers is that the surveys of the 1970s (most notably those of the World Fertility Survey) that found such strong relations between child survival and maternal education did not find similarly strong relations with paternal education (Hobcraft, McDonald and Rutstein, 1984). The near ubiquity of the effect of maternal education has stimulated a great deal of valuable work in that area but may have distracted attention from other factors, especially those to do with the characteristics of husbands, that could reward some attention.

A recent study of the determinants of infant and child mortality in urban Turkey is of particular relevance in this regard (Gursoy-Tezcan, 1992). Of a range of factors that were examined for their relation with child mortality, four were of primary importance: husband's education; household composition; the woman's attitude towards abortion; and drinking and smoking by household members other than the mother. Neither the woman's own education, nor that of her parents, was of importance, undoubtedly because women's capacity to control their own behaviour was severely limited. Irrespective of their education, women were subject to their husbands' authority in all daily decisions: almost one half, for example, were not permitted to venture unaccompanied into the street; one quarter were not allowed to go shopping; one tenth were not allowed to see their own relatives.

Only one of the four factors, the woman's attitude to abortion, was a directly maternal characteristic at all. Women that most disapproved of abortion had experienced the highest child mortality, while those that approved of abortion had the lowest. Approval of abortion appears to indicate a greater degree of personal initiative and control. The fact that it had more explanatory power than female education may indicate that where women are mostly confined to the home and to family relations, their perception of a woman's proper degree of control over her own reproduction is more important for child survival than their number of years of formal schooling.

The other factors represent the influence of other people in the household. This is particularly clear in the case of smoking and drinking since, in contrast to other studies, the mother's own consumption was not included in the measure. Non-nuclear household composition, and particularly the presence of a mother-in-law, had a strongly positive effect on child mortality through its effects on decision-making concerning child care. The power of mothers to take independent action, or even to prevent traditional, possibly harmful practices, may be severely limited in the presence of her mother-in-law.

Lastly, there is husband's education. One cannot do better than to quote Gursoy-Tezcan:

> ". . . more education for the husband may mean easier access to important institutions like hospitals and to relevant health-related knowledge. Also, it may mean that the men are less dependent on the world-view imposed by their own families. More than the content of the education they have received, their years of schooling may mean an external reference point for the men and thus a break from the patriarchal constraints which also affects their wives and children. The emancipation of men by educational experience may serve women by allowing men more freedom to support the women in their own lives, which includes their reproductive choices and how they raise their children." (1992, p. 140)

One is now speaking of a new relationship between wife and husband, of a shifting of the husband's loyalties and primary interests from his family of birth to the family he formed when he married. Tellingly, some of the most compelling explanations for the impact of maternal education on child survival invoke this sort of redefinition of conjugal roles: for example, among the Yoruba, the educated woman may be more likely to challenge her mother-in-law and to win; she may also be more likely to attempt to communicate with her husband and to be successful (Caldwell, 1979). The deeply subversive nature of the companionate marriage has been noted elsewhere in this regard and also in the context of fertility decline (Caldwell, 1982).

A marked lack of communication between spouses and a great deal of misinterpretation of each other's motives, beliefs and knowledge is reported in widely disparate applications in developing countries. One particularly nice example comes from a study in Burkina Faso, which found that men believed that women knew little about family planning and would not wish to use it, and that women believed the same of men (McGinn, Bamba and Balma, 1989). In food allocation studies, men generally profess not to know what goes on in the kitchen. Here, of course, there may be a degree of self-justification or of men wishing to downplay their role in the perpetuation of dietary inequity.

The entire question of equity is an interesting one. Many of the cited studies that measured or observed preferential treatment for boys commented that mothers, fathers or other informants denied that discrimination took place. Such a denial may, of course, represent a complete lack of awareness that discriminatory behaviour exists. However, it may also suggest either that notions of equity are not alien to even quite traditional people or that they recognize equity as a modern notion that is likely to be approved by the field researchers. If either of the latter two explanations is correct, then there may be hope for behavioural change.

E. Conclusion

Women's culturally and socially determined roles have direct impacts on their health and that of their children through a complex web of physiological and behavioural interrelations and synergies that permeate every aspect of their lives. Their roles also have direct impacts on their use of health services because modern health care has been absorbed so successfully into traditional structures that it tends to be allocated, like food, along traditional lines determined by such characteristics as sex and age. Role-determined barriers to their own and their children's health often make it difficult for women to fulfil the additional role imposed upon them by public-health programmes, that of being the natural guardians of their family's health.

Some change in women's roles appears already to have occurred through the agency of Western-style schooling. Although the pathways through which education changes women are not well understood, it does seem that a redefinition of their relations within the family, with their husband and their husband's kin and probably even with their children, is of primary importance.

Apparently. therefore, one needs to look further than women. Husbands are an obvious target: bringing them into areas that are more usually viewed as the natural preserve of women, such as family planning and child health, may directly and indirectly benefit every member of the family. A direct effect could follow since husbands tend to have greater authority in the family to intervene in all areas, including that of health. An indirect effect could follow from the more collaborative nature of the marital relationship that would result, as issues concerning the treatment of children came to be matters for parents to decide on together and as balances of power began subtly to shift within the family. By allying themselves with a more powerful family member, women would less often find themselves interceding from a relatively weak position for their children and themselves with a consortium of possibly unsympathetic or even hostile relatives.

It is clear that this scenario is predicated on women having an effective spouse, which is very often not the case. Nevertheless, there is no reason that only husbands should be drawn into the general concern for family health and child care. Health programmes may find it worthwhile to target the wider community: not just mothers, but grandmothers, too; not just fathers, but uncles also. Women must gain more support either from husbands or from wider social networks if recent dramatic improvements in family health are to be maintained, let alone if they are to continue. The spectre of the social and familial disintegration consequent on the current AIDS epidemic simply adds urgency to this conclusion.

References

Adetunji, Jacob Ayodele (1991). Response of parents to five killer diseases among children in a Yoruba community, Nigeria. *Social Science and Medicine* (Elmsford, New York), vol. 32, No. 12, pp. 1379-1387.

Ankrah, E. Maxine (1991). AIDS and the social side of health. *Social Science and Medicine* (Elmsford, New York), vol. 32, No. 9, pp. 967-980.

Belsey, Mark A., and Erica Royston (1990). A global overview of the health of women and children. In *Health Care of Women and Children in Developing Countries*, Helen M. Wallace and Kanti Giri, eds. Oakland, California: Third Party Publishing Company.

Bertrand, Jane T., W. E. Bertrand and Miatudila Malonga (1983). The use of traditional and modern methods of fertility control in Kinshasa, Zaire. *Population Studies* (London), vol. 37, No. 1 (March), pp. 129-136.

Bhuiya, Abbas, and Kim Streatfield (1991). Mothers' education and survival of female children in a rural area of Bangladesh. *Population Studies* (London), vol. 45, No. 2 (July), pp. 253-264.

Bracher, Michael (1992). Breastfeeding, lactational infecundity, contraception and the spacing of births. *Health Transition Review* (Canberra, Australia), vol. 2, No. 1 (April), pp. 19-47.

_________, and Gigi Santow (1982). Breast-feeding in central Java. *Population Studies* (London), vol. 36, No. 3 (November), pp. 413-429.

Caldwell, John C. (1979). Education as a factor in mortality decline: an examination of Nigerian data. *Population Studies* (London), vol. 33, No. 3 (November), pp. 395-413.

_________ 1982). *Theory of Fertility Decline*. London: Academic Press.

_________, P. H. Reddy and Pat Caldwell (1983). The social component of mortality decline: an investigation in south India employing alternative methodologies. *Population Studies* (London), vol. 37, No. 2 (July), pp. 185-205.

Caldwell, Pat, and John C. Caldwell (1981). The function of child-spacing in traditional societies and the direction of change. In *Child-spacing in Tropical Africa: Traditions and Change*, Hilary J. Page and Ron Lesthaeghe, eds. London and New York: Academic Press.

__________ (1990). *Gender Implications for Survival in South Asia.* Health Transition Working Paper, No. 7. Canberra: The Australian National University, Health Transition Centre.

Chen, Lincoln C., Emdadul Huq and Stan D'Souza (1981). Sex bias in the allocation of food and health care in rural Bangladesh. *Population and Development Review* (New York), vol. 7, No. 1 (March), pp. 55-70.

Cleland, John G., and Jeroen K. van Ginneken (1988). Maternal education and child survival in developing countries: the search for pathways of influence. *Social Science and Medicine* (Elmsford, New York), vol. 27, No. 12, pp. 1357-1368.

Cogswell, Mary E., and others (1991). Sociodemographic and clinical factors affecting recognition of childhood diarrhea by mothers in Kwara State, Nigeria. *Social Science and Medicine* (Elmsford, New York), vol. 33, No. 10, pp. 1209-1216.

Cook, Rebecca J., and Deborah Maine (1987). Spousal veto over family planning services. *American Journal of Public Health* (Washington, D.C.), vol. 77, No. 3 (March), pp. 339-344.

Das Gupta, Monica (1987). Selective discrimination against female children in rural Punjab, India. *Population and Development Review* (New York), vol. 13, No. 1 (March), pp. 77-100.

David, Nicholas, and David Voas (1981). Societal causes of infertility and population decline among the settled Fulani of North Cameroon. *Man* (London), vol. 16, No. 4 (December), pp. 644-664.

De Bruyn, Maria (1992). Women and AIDS in developing countries. *Social Science and Medicine* (Elmsford, New York), vol. 34, No. 3, pp. 249-262.

Denich, Bette S. (1974). Sex and power in the Balkans. In *Woman, Culture, and Society*, Michelle Zimbalist Rosaldo and Louise Lamphere, eds. Stanford, California: Stanford University Press.

Doan, Rebecca Miles, and Leila Bisharat (1990). Female autonomy and child nutritional status: the extended-family residential unit in Amman, Jordan. *Social Science and Medicine* (Elmsford, New York), vol. 31, No. 7, pp. 783-789.

Fort, Alfredo L. (1989). Investigating the social context of fertility and family planning: a qualitative study in Peru. *International Family Planning Perspectives* (New York), vol. 15, No. 3 (September), pp. 88-95.

Frank, Odile (1983). Infertility in sub-Saharan Africa: estimates and implications. *Population and Development Review* (New York), vol. 9, No. 1 (March), pp. 137-144.

Gittelsohn, Joel (1991). Opening the box: intrahousehold food allocation in rural Nepal. *Social Science and Medicine* (Elmsford, New York), vol. 33, No. 10, pp. 1141-1154.

Griffith, H. B. (1963). Gonorrhoea and fertility in Uganda. *The Eugenics Review* (London), vol. 55, No. 2 (July), pp. 103-108.

Gruenbaum, Ellen (1991). The Islamic movement, development, and health education: recent changes in the health of rural women in Central Sudan. *Social Science and Medicine* (Elmsford, New York), vol. 33, No. 6, pp. 637-645.

Guest, Iain (1978). Infertility in Africa. *People* (London), vol. 5, No. 1, pp. 23-34.

Gürsoy-Tezcan, Akile (1992). Infant mortality: a Turkish puzzle? *Health Transition Review* (Canberra, Australia), vol. 2, No. 2 (October), pp. 131-150.

Hobcraft, John, John McDonald and Shea Rutstein (1983). Child-spacing effects on infant and early child mortality. *Population Index* (Princeton, New Jersey), vol. 49, No. 4 (Winter), pp. 585-618.

__________ (1984). Socio-economic factors in infant and child mortality: a cross-national comparison. *Population Studies* (London), vol. 38, No. 2 (July), pp. 193-223.

Hunter, Susan S. (1990). Orphans as a window on the AIDS epidemic in sub-Saharan Africa: initial results and implications of a study in Uganda. *Social Science and Medicine* (Elmsford, New York), vol. 31, No. 6, pp. 681-690.

Jelliffe, Derrick B., and E. F. Patrice Jelliffe (1989). *Community Nutritional Assessment with Special Reference to Less Technically Developed Countries.* Oxford: Oxford University Press.

Joesoef, Mohamad R., Andrew L. Baughman and Budi Utomo (1988). Husband's approval of contraceptive use in metropolitan Indonesia: program implications. *Studies in Family Planning* (New York), vol. 19, No. 3 (May/June), pp. 162-168.

Khan, M. E., and others (1989). Inequalities between men and women in nutrition and family welfare services: an in-depth enquiry in an Indian village. In *Selected Readings in the Cultural, Social and Behavioural Determinants of Health*, John C. Caldwell and Gigi Santow, eds. Health Transition Series, No. 1. Canberra, Australia: The Australian National University, Health Transition Centre.

Kline, Anna, Emily Kline and Emily Oken (1992). Minority women and sexual choice in the age of AIDS. *Social Science and Medicine* (Elmsford, New York), vol. 34, No. 4, pp. 447-457.

Lane, Sandra D., and Afaf I. Meleis (1991). Roles, work, health perceptions and health resources of women: a study in an Egyptian delta hamlet. *Social Science and Medicine* (Elmsford, New York), vol. 33, No. 10, pp. 1197-1208.

McGinn, Therese, Azara Bamba and Moise Balma (1989). Male knowledge, use and attitudes regarding family planning in Burkina Faso. *International Family Planning Perspectives* (New York), vol. 15, No. 3 (September), pp. 84-87 and 95.

Muhuri, Pradip K., and Samuel H. Preston (1991). Effects of family composition on mortality differentials by sex among children in Matlab, Bangladesh. *Population and Development Review* (New York), vol. 17, No. 3 (September), pp. 415-434.

Mull, Dorothy S., Jon W. Anderson and J. Dennis Mull (1990). Cow dung, rock salt, and medical innovation in the Hindu Kush of Pakistan: the cultural transformation of neonatal tetanus and iodine deficiency. *Social Science and Medicine* (Elmsford, New York), vol. 30, No. 6, pp. 675-691.

Okojie, Christiana E. E. (1991). Social dimensions of the health behaviour of rural women: findings from focus group research in Nigeria. Paper prepared for the Seminar on Measurement of Maternal and Child Mortality, Morbidity and Health Care: Interdisciplinary Approaches, Cairo, 4-7 November 1991. Sponsoredby the International Union for the Scientific Study of Population.

Omran, Abdel R. (1971). The epidemiologic transition: a theory of the epidemiology of population change. *The Milbank Memorial Fund Quarterly* (New York), vol. 49, No. 4, part 1, pp. 509-538.

Orubuloye, I. O., Pat Caldwell and John C. Caldwell (1992). *African Women's Control over Their Sexuality in an Era of AIDS.* Health Transition Working Paper, No. 12. Canberra, Australia: The Australian National University, Health Transition Centre.

Orubuloye, I. O., and others (1991). The impact of family and budget structure on health treatment in Nigeria. *Health Transition Review* (Canberra, Australia), vol. 1. No. 2 (October), pp. 189-210.

Palloni, Alberto, and Yean Ju Lee (1990). *Families, Women and HIV/AIDS in Africa.* Working Paper, No. 90-32. Madison: University of Wisconsin, Center for Demography and Ecology.

Pelto, Gretel H., and others (1991). Household size, food intake and anthropometric status of school-age children in a highland Mexican area. *Social Science and Medicine* (Elmsford, New York), vol. 33, No. 10, pp. 1135-1140.

Potts, Malcolm, and Peter Selman (1979). *Society and Fertility.* Plymouth, United Kingdom: Macdonald and Evans.

Preble, Elizabeth A. (1990). Impact of HIV/AIDS on African children. *Social Science and Medicine* (Elmsford, New York), vol. 31, No. 6, pp. 671-680.

Raikes, Alanagh (1989). Women's health in East Africa. *Social Science and Medicine* (Elmsford, New York), vol. 28, No. 5, pp. 447-459.

Reeler, Anne Vibeke (1990). Injections: a fatal attraction? *Social Science and Medicine* (Elmsford, New York), vol. 31, No. 10, pp. 1119-1125.

Reissland, Nadja, and Richard Burghart (1989). Active patients: the integration of modern and traditional obstetric practices in Nepal. *Social Science and Medicine* (Elmsford, New York), vol. 29, No. 1, pp. 43-52.

Romaniuk, Anatole (1968). Infertility in tropical Africa. In *The Population of Tropical Africa*, John C. Caldwell and Chukaka Okonjo, eds. London: Longman; and New York: Columbia University Press.

Ruzicka, Lado, and Penny Kane (1990). Health transition: the course of morbidity and mortality. In *What We Know about the Health Transition: The Cultural, Social and Behavioural Determinants of Health*, vol. I, John C. Caldwell and others, eds. Health Transition Series, No. 2. Canberra, Australia: The Australian National University, Health Transition Centre.

Santow, Gigi, and A. Bioumla (1984). *An Evaluation of the Cameroon Fertility Survey, 1978*. WFS Scientific Reports, No. 64. Voorburg, The Netherlands: International Statistical Institute.

Santow, Gigi, and M. Bracher (1981). Patterns of post-partum sexual abstinence and their implications for fertility in Ibadan, Nigeria. In *Child-spacing in Tropical Africa: Traditions and Change*, Hilary J. Page and Ron Lesthaeghe, eds. London: Academic Press.

Schoepf, Brooke Grundfest (1991). Ethical, methodological and political issues of AIDS research in Central Africa. *Social Science and Medicine* (Elmsford, New York), vol. 33, No. 7, pp. 749-763.

Streatfield, Kim, Lamtiur H. Tampubolon and Charles Surjadi (1991). Investigating health beliefs and health-related behaviour among the urban poor of Jakarta. In *The Health Transition: Methods and Measures*, John G. Cleland and Allan G. Hill, eds. Health Transition Series, No. 3. Canberra: The Australian National University, Health Transition Centre.

Sudan, Ministry of Economic and National Planning, Department of Statistics; and Institute for Resource Development/Macro International, Inc. (1991). *Sudan Demographic and Health Survey, 1989/1990*. Khartoum, Sudan; and Columbia, Maryland.

Taylor, Keith B., and Luean E. Anthony (1983). *Clinical Nutrition*. New York: McGraw-Hill.

Trussell, James, and Anne R. Pebley (1984). The potential impact of changes in fertility on infant, child, and maternal mortality. *Studies in Family Planning* (New York), vol. 15, No. 6, part 1 (November/December), pp. 267-280.

Van de Walle, Francine, and Baba Traore (1986). *Attitudes of Women and Men towards Contraception in Bobo-Dioulasso*. African Demography Working Papers, No. 13. Philadelphia: University of Pennsylvania, Population Studies Center.

Waldron, Ingrid (1983). The role of genetic and biological factors in sex differences in mortality. In *Sex Differentials in Mortality: Trends, Determinants and Consequences*, Alan D. Lopez and Lado T. Ruzicka, eds. Canberra: The Australian National University, Department of Demography.

Whyte, Susan Reynolds, and Priscilla Wanjiru Kariuki (1991). Malnutrition and gender relations in Western Kenya. *Health Transition Review* (Canberra, Australia), vol. 1, No. 2 (October), pp. 171-187.

Winikoff, Beverly (1990). Women's health in the developing countries. In *Health Care of Women and Children in Developing Countries*, Helen M. Wallace and Kanti Giri, eds. Oakland, California: Third Party Publishing Company.

Wyon, John B., and John E. Gordon (1971). *The Khanna Study: Population Problems in the Rural Punjab*. Cambridge, Massachusetts: Harvard University Press.

X. MATERNAL MORTALITY, INDUCED ABORTION AND SEXUALLY TRANSMITTED DISEASES: IMPACT ON WOMEN'S HEALTH DURING THE REPRODUCTIVE AGES

*Alberto Rizo**

A. BACKGROUND

In December 1990, the United Nations General Assembly, at its forty-fifth session, unanimously adopted the International Development Strategy for the Fourth United Nations Development Decade, to begin on 1 January 1991 (resolution 45/199). Noting that the goals and objectives of the Strategy for the Third United Nations Development Decade, the 1980s, were "for the most part unattained", the document states that "the decade should witness a significant improvement in the human condition in the developing countries and a reduction in the gap between rich and poor countries".

The halving of maternal mortality rates was one of several targets agreed upon by the international community to give special attention to women and children.

How realistic is the goal of reducing maternal mortality by one half during the last decade of the twentieth century? What impediments are there to the attainment of such a goal? What should be modified to facilitate its fulfilment? Does female reproductive health receive all the attention it deserves? Is it feasible to improve current levels significantly?

Why has maternal mortality not decreased at the pace and within the same time-frame as the death rate of children under age 5? Why are maternal deaths so numerous? The World Health Organization (WHO) estimates that there are approximately 500,000 maternal deaths in the world each year, and 99 per cent of them are in the developing countries (table 19). Why is there no reduction of maternal mortality even though the causes of maternal deaths have been identified and the technology required to reduce them to levels prevalent in industrialized countries is inexpensive and simple?

The answers are straightforward. The strategies to attain a significant reduction of maternal mortality have been known for many years and have been published after being discussed at length in conferences and congresses. The theory is not too complex, while interventions are. However, it is possible to accomplish notable advances in the reduction of maternal mortality and save the life of thousands of the 500,000 women that die each year, as is shown below.

This paper discusses some of the issues that affect women's health, particularly those related to pregnancy, childbirth and puerperium, the causes and consequences of induced abortion; and lastly, the way that sexually transmitted diseases (STDs) affect women's health, particularly during pregnancy, and what should be done to improve the current situation.

B. EXTENT OF THE MATERNAL MORTALITY PROBLEM

Of the estimated half a million women that die each year worldwide "while pregnant or within 42 days of termination of pregnancy, irrespective of the duration and site of the pregnancy, from any cause related to or aggravated by the pregnancy or its management, but not from accidental or incidental causes" (WHO, 1977, p. 764), 99 per cent die in the developing countries where 87 per cent of births take place (WHO, 1991).

The Pan American Health Organization (PAHO) estimated that in Latin America and the Caribbean

*Consultant in reproductive health, Bogotá, Colombia.

TABLE 19. CHANGES IN MATERNAL MORTALITY, AROUND 1983 AND 1988

Region	*Live births* 1983 (millions)	*Live births* 1988 (millions)	*Maternal deaths* 1983 (thousands)	*Maternal deaths* 1988 (thousands)	*Maternal mortality* 1983 (per 100,000 live births)	*Maternal mortality* 1988 (per 100,000 live births)
World	128.3	137.6	500	509	390	370
Developing countries	110.1	120.3	494	505	450	420
Developed countries[a]	18.2	17.3	6	4	30	26
Africa	23.4	26.7	150	169	640	630
Eastern Africa	7.0	8.8	46	60	660	680
Middle Africa	2.6	3.0	18	21	690	710
Northern Africa	4.8	4.9	24	17	500	360
Southern Africa	1.4	1.3	8	4	570	270
Western Africa	7.6	8.7	54	66	700	760
Asia[b]	73.9	81.2	308	310	420	380
Eastern Asia[b]	21.8	24.6	12	30	55	120
South-eastern Asia	12.4	12.5	52	42	420	340
Southern Asia	35.6	39.6	230	224	650	570
Western Asia	4.1	4.4	14	12	340	280
Latin America and the Caribbean	12.6	12.2	34	25	270	200
Caribbean	0.9	0.8	2	2	220	260
Central America	3.7	3.5	9	6	240	160
South America	8.0	8.0	23	17	290	220
Northern America	4.0	4.0	1	1	12	12
Europe	6.6	6.4	2	1	27	23
Oceania[c]	0.2	0.2	2	1	300	600
USSR (former)	5.2	5.2	3	2	50	45

Sources: For maternal deaths and maternal mortality rates, World Health Organization, *Maternal Mortality Ratios and Rates: A Tabulation of Available Information,* 2nd and 3rd eds. (Geneva, 1986 and 1991); for number of births in 1983, estimates for 1980-1985 from *Demographic Indicators of Countries: Estimates and Projections as Assessed in 1980* (United Nations publication, Sales No. E.82.XIII.5); for number of births in 1988, estimates for 1985-1990 from *World Population Prospects, 1990,* Population Studies, No. 120 (United Nations publication, Sales No. E.91.XIII4).

NOTE: Figures may not add to totals due to rounding.

[a]Including Japan, Australia and New Zealand.

[b]Excluding Japan.

[c]Excluding Australia and New Zealand.

alone 1 million maternal deaths might occur during the period 1980-2000 if the mortality trend observed in the 1980s was not improved (PAHO, 1986a). On the other hand, should mortality figures improve by some 50 deaths per 100,000 live births per annum, as has occurred in Cuba and Costa Rica, the number of estimated deaths would be merely 60,000. The gain in terms of human life saved would be enormous.

Not all the regions nor all the countries of the world show the same levels of maternal mortality. WHO statistics for maternal mortality established that the risk of a woman dying for causes related to the maternity process was 1 in 23 in Africa, 1 in 71 in Asia, 1 in 131 in Latin America, 1 in 2,228 in Europe and 1 in 4,006 in Northern America (WHO, 1991).

In the rural areas of Bangladesh, maternal mortality is 600 per 100,000 live births, while in the Central American countries or the Andean region, this figure could, perhaps, be about 200 per 100,000 births. In contrast, in Australia, Canada or Japan, the maternal mortality rate is approximately 26 per 100,000 births.

Despite the fact that maternal mortality has been experiencing a downward trend in almost all the developing countries, figures continue to be elevated (between 100 and 800 deaths per 100,000 births), the decrease observed is not sufficiently rapid and the causes of maternal mortality remain the same through the years. Hence, there is reason for concern by the international community, particularly since the International Conference on Safe Motherhood, held at Nairobi, Kenya in February 1987.

C. Measuring maternal mortality

Determining the level of maternal mortality continues to pose problems that are yet unsolved, despite efforts by such agencies as WHO. In 1986, WHO called on all developing countries to produce reliable estimates of maternal mortality by 1995. The problem can be attributed in part to the poor quality and limited coverage of information gathered by the statistical systems in place.

Maternal mortality statistics should be collected and compiled as accurately and completely as possible, not only to use them as simple assessments of the state of that health problem but also to direct attention more generally to the population under study. In this context, efforts by WHO to publish *Maternal Mortality* (WHO, 1991) as a periodical are worth highlighting.

The basis for estimating maternal mortality is the death certificate, on which maternal deaths are underrecorded not only in the developing countries but in most countries. This deficiency is caused by several factors—either the death certificate was not filled in by qualified personnel, or the person that completed it was not the treating physician or the local authorities did not enforce death registration before the burial. Physicians frequently make mistakes when they complete a death certificate. For example, "sepsis" or "hypovolemic shock" are often entered as causes of death in women of fertile age. These conditions need to be linked to child-bearing, which is the true cause of the woman's death. Very often, however, the statistical offices simply code the cause of death as death by "septicaemia" or by "haemorrhage", thus contributing to significant underrecording.

Such studies as the Inter-American Mortality Investigation conducted by PAHO in 1965 and similar investigations used a careful review and verification of each death certificate, consulting with parents or acquaintances of the deceased, and showed that the existing system of coding and processing of information indiscriminately was a questionable practice. Bureaux of statistics, have, nevertheless, continued to process inadequate mortality records which lead to serious underreporting of such events as maternal deaths. Maternal mortality is underestimated in the range of 100-200 per cent in metropolitan areas. What can then be said in the case of rural areas or small cities?

Another frequently observed problem in the developing countries is the length of time bureaux of statistics take to process and report on such events as maternal mortality. It often takes from three to five years for programme managers to learn about official maternal mortality statistics, which undoubtedly affects the decision-making process and delays solutions.

Last but not least is the way in which maternal mortality is estimated. It is well known that statistics on maternal mortality reports do not reflect the true rates but only the ratios. The denominator currently used is the number of live births per 10,000 or 100,000 per annum. The maternal mortality ratio measures obstetric risk.

In order for the maternal death indicator to be the actual rate, the denominator used should reflect the number of women exposed (ages 15-49) to the risk of dying from causes related to pregnancy. For practical intents, this figure is difficult to determine; thus, the reason for using the maternal mortality ratio is to facilitate management and to standardize information. Using the number of live births as denominator omits all women whose pregnancies terminate in abortion, and this is one limitation of this statistic. Despite its apparent simplicity, however, using a ratio instead of the actual rate does not fully resolve the issue of inadequate registration, as in many countries not only are deaths underrecorded but births are not adequately registered.

Maternal mortality can also be measured by the lifetime risk of dying from complications of pregnancy. The risk of a woman dying as a result of a given pregnancy in the developed countries stays about 1 in 2,000. An African woman's lifetime risk is often greater than 1 in 20 (WHO, 1991).

Maternal deaths registered in hospitals, used to determine mortality ratios, are a non-permanent substitute for the universal registration of death, which every country should have. Many home deliveries are not promptly reported, despite the interest displayed by local authorities in implementing this requirement. Community-based registration systems, which rely upon the participation of midwives and community organizations, do contribute to improved coverage, but quality control is often a problem and, notwithstanding the efforts made, these records are also incomplete.

The situation described above enables one to conclude that maternal mortality and its specific causes may need to be assessed by special investigations, as was the case with the Inter-American Mortality Investigation and similar studies carried out since that time. Those studies should complement and never substitute for vital statistics.

Population-based surveys have gained popularity in recent times, and the sisterhood method, which is an extension of the sibling-survivorship method of estimating early adult mortality, appears to be promising, as the data requirements are modest and the information can be obtained with a few minutes of interviewing time. The calculation of mortality risk is also simple and can be done by hand with a basic tabulation of the data on sisters arrayed by age of the respondents (Boerma and Mati, 1989).

Surveyed persons are asked whether a female member of the household died during some reference period and, if so, whether the death was associated with pregnancy or childbirth. Bolivia, Egypt, Ethiopia and the Sudan are some of the countries where this approach has been put into practice. A recent article concludes that "where the interest is in estimating in some detail the level, recent trends and distribution of maternal deaths according to age and parity, the direct approach is a rich source of data on these issues" (Rutenberg and Sullivan, 1991, p. 1679).

D. Does pregnancy entail risks for women today?

Despite what has been taught by several generations of medical educators in the world, that pregnancy should not be considered an illness, the truth is that pregnancy is not free from risks that might produce permanent damage, nor should death be ignored as an unwanted outcome.

It has been proposed that the various risks that are associated with or complicate pregnancy should be classified into four main categories: (*a*) pre-existing risks, such as age, parity, marital status, weight and residence; (*b*) risks associated with pregnancy (anaemia, infections, Rh factor incompatibility, toxaemia, haemorrhage etc.); (*c*) risks associated with existing conditions, such as tuberculosis, malaria, acquired immunodeficiency syndrome (AIDS), cardiorenal disease and structural abnormalities; and (*d*) risks associated with delivery, such as prolonged delivery, dystocia, infection, haemorrhage and premature rupture of membranes.

Several risks (poverty, adolescence, first pregnancy) frequently coexist in the same person and aggravate the condition significantly. Some risks may not be avoided despite strict monitoring during a normal pregnancy. For instance, the need for an emergency Caesarean section resulting from foetal suffering due to clamping and/or tying of the umbilical cord, is difficult to predict at the primary health care level.

Studies conducted in various areas of the world (for example, Walker and others, 1986; Kwast, Rochat, and Kidane-Mariam, 1986; Alauddin, 1986) have contributed to a better understanding of the different risk factors presented by women dying from causes associated with pregnancy, delivery or post-partum. Some of the most important risk factors are discussed below.

Age

The risk of maternal mortality is greater at both extremes of reproductive life. The British Confidential Enquiries found that the rates of true maternal deaths per 100,000 pregnancies are lowest for age group 20-24 and dramatically higher for ages 40 or over, with a relative risk of 16.5. In a study conducted in Chile, Mexico and Venezuela, it was found that maternal mortality increased with the age of the mother to over 300 per 100,000 births and that the mortality of women in age group 15-19 was higher than at ages 20-29, thus producing a J-shaped mortality curve. This result is due to the fact that there is a higher incidence of placenta previa or toxaemia among women at either extreme of the reproductive ages, which also increases the risk of serious complications, including death, during pregnancy and delivery.

Adolescent pregnancy

There has been an explosive increase of pregnancies among adolescent women in the developing countries and in the United States of America. Fertility rates for age group 15-19, for example, has reached an unprecedented level of 189 births per annum per 1,000 women in Senegal, 173 in Nigeria, 137 in Jamaica, 104 in Mexico and 112 in the Syrian Arab Republic. The percentage of women giving birth before age 20 was 63 in Kenya, 49 in Pakistan, 44 in the Dominican Republic, 57 in Jamaica and 41 per cent in Mexico (Liskin and others, 1985).

In some countries, early pregnancy in adolescents accounts for more than one fourth of the obstetric bed occupancy by young mothers. Although child-bearing by women under age 20—adolescent fertility—is not a new phenomenon in world history, there is increasing concern about its adverse health, social, economic and demographic effects. This situation is generally the result of disrupted homes, unstable unions and lack of opportunities; it particularly affects the low-income segment of the population.

Despite discrepancies among investigators as to whether there is a higher risk of morbidity and maternal death in adolescents aged 15 or over, compared with women aged 20 years or over, they agree that during the adolescent years, both women and men should be preparing themselves to face adulthood, whether it be by studying, learning skills or holding a job, which will provide them an opportunity for progress and personal development.

Early pregnancies represent a setback which hampers possibilities for the young mother to develop her potential fully and constitutes a risk to the health and survival of the child, as the probability of illness or death dramatically increases in children of young mothers. The effects go beyond her offspring, as fathers, other members of the adolescent's family and the society itself are affected.

Resources of the social sectors to meet the needs of adolescent pregnancy and child-bearing do not exist in government budgets. If funds are earmarked for this purpose, they are insufficient and are generally taken from equally or more important line items.

Effect of parity on maternal mortality

One of the most well-known risks of maternal mortality relates to the child-bearing experience the woman has had (parity); it has been established that maternal mortality is higher in women with more than four children. Several studies carried out in Latin America show that prenatal problems concurrently increased with the number of pregnancies. Likewise, eclampsia was greater as the number of pregnancies increased. It is frequently observed that uterine prolapse, haemorrhage and infection have a higher incidence among the multipara. This indicates that one of the variables requiring more careful attention in maternal mortality prevention programmes is that related to the number of previous deliveries or pregnancies the woman has experienced.

Pregnancy and delivery complications, such as toxaemia, anaemia, bleeding, dystocia and prolonged and difficult labour, are more frequent among teenage women. In most Latin American countries, for example, child-bearing and abortion are ranked in the top five causes of death for women aged 15-19. The situation in Bangladesh, India and Sierra Leone is not different.

Pregnancy-related complications

It was mentioned earlier that a series of pathological conditions might develop concomitantly with pregnancy or that health problems pre-existing at the time of pregnancy aggravate the health of the pregnant woman and place her in a risky situation. Some of the most common problems are those related to nutrition and anaemia (iron or folic acid deficiencies) during pregnancy. Bleeding, the risk of spontaneous abortion or premature birth and pre-eclampsia are important causes of morbidity and mortality during pregnancy.

The way food is shared within the family, particularly if there are small children and it is solely the husband who is the breadwinner, places the woman in an unfavourable situation. Her caloric and protein intake will rarely be adequate for health, because she leaves little or no food for herself after having shared it with her children and husband.

This situation is made worse by the extra calorie requirements of pregnancy. In the developing countries, a chronically malnourished woman usually performs heavy tasks that worsen her condition, as well as that of the foetus, and place her in a category of extreme risk and vulnerability.

Maternal malnutrition has critical health and development significance; unfortunately, it has received little attention by Governments thus far. Many countries interrupt their supplementary food programmes for lack of funds, and such programmes have limited coverage or are heavily dependent upon international assistance, which sometimes is not sustained and therefore produces a limited impact.

Pregnancy affects not only the woman's health but also that of the foetus. Food supplement programmes for pregnant women (providing flour, enriched oil and grain) have been evaluated on the basis of the child's weight at birth or the mother's capacity to breast-feed for some time. What also might be required is an assessment of the long-term effects of those food programmes in helping improve women's health throughout the world, especially where much of women's reproductive ages is spent pregnant or breast-feeding. A chronic psychological and physical depletion seriously affects these women and their integration in the productive process.

In countries where malaria is prevalent, thousands of pregnant women are exposed to miscarriage and premature births, which, as is well known, increase the risk of death.

Infectious diseases caused by bacteria, virus or fungi, tuberculosis; or non-infectious conditions, such as gestational diabetes, hypertension, musculoskeletal alterations, short stature, cardiorenal diseases and toxaemia, haemorrhage, slow weight gain and Rh factor incompatibility, all contribute to complicating the course of a pregnancy and placing the mother in a high-risk category requiring constant surveillance and care at an intermediate or third-level health-care facility. Lifestyle and use of such substances as alcohol and tobacco also affect women during pregnancy.

Given the importance of abortion and STDs for maternal health, they are discussed below in sections G and I, respectively.

The most frequent causes of maternal mortality

In countries with high maternal mortality rates, the most frequent causes are abortion, haemorrhage, toxaemia and infection. The leading cause of death varies from country to country. For example, in Argentina, the leading cause is abortion; in the United States of America, post-partum complications; in Brazil, toxaemia; in Ethiopia, abortion; in Egypt, haemorrhage.

Indirect causes include a vast number of conditions, which significantly vary from one country to the next. Ill-defined causes are also frequent. Hepatitis, epilepsy, anaemia, rabies, respiratory diseases, neoplasm etc. are often found to be indirect causes of maternal death.

It is worth mentioning that in countries having experienced political unrest and violence, such as Chile, Colombia, El Salvador and Lebanon, there have been reports of maternal deaths due to causes unrelated to pregnancy (Gil, 1991). There are opinions in favour of recording such cases as maternal deaths, as the pregnancy could have prevented such a victim from reacting in time and may have lessened her ability to protect herself.

Other pre-existing risks influenced by the socio-economic condition of women

Maternal mortality is linked to different social and economic factors, such as illiteracy, place of residence in the rural area, lack of health care, poverty, lack of public services, overcrowding, unstable unions and abandonment of the woman by the spouse or partner, delivering the baby at home, lack of prenatal and post-partum care, past experience in infant or child death, and a history of one or more abortions. In some cultures, female circumcision has adverse implications for women's health, particularly during their reproductive period (for a brief discussion, see section F).

More than one factor may coexist in the same person and therefore multiply the risk of complications and death of the woman during pregnancy, childbirth, or during the post-partum period.

E. Use of health services during pregnancy, delivery and post-partum: the importance of prenatal care

Service demand by pregnant women has been studied by different authors (for example, Leslie and Gupta, 1989). Service demand is influenced by the user's profile (user factors) and by the type of services available (service factors).

User factors, such as the educational level, age and parity of the woman, play an important role when she requests health-care services, as better educated or urban and higher income women may find it less difficult to look for early prenatal care, are most likely to give birth at the hospital; and experience fewer complications during pregnancy, at birth and post-partum. User factors explain why adolescents experience difficulties when they think about visiting a health facility, as they are uneasy about the "establishment" represented by the health centre or they simply do not find a good reason for prenatal care as services are completely unfamiliar and are therefore not trusted.

On the other hand, frequently noted service factors concern accessibility, cost, quality of care available and staff attitude. The Demographic and Health Surveys (DHS) carried out in many developing countries are beginning to include information on service delivery to women of reproductive age. This information will help administrators and programme officers understand and decide which issues need to be addressed.

Surveys including questions about services may have to cope with technical difficulties that may affect quality, such as the recall bias which influences response validity. It is worth noting that even though some information is available in the second round of DHS, it seems necessary to work further on the questionnaires used to assess use of maternal and child services, user perception of such services etc. (DHS, 1991).

There are not many controlled studies of service provision as a means of reducing maternal mortality. None the less, there are some results that might help explain the reasons that prenatal care is beneficial to pregnant women's health. Kwast, Rochat and Mariam (1986) found maternal mortality rates of 6.2 per 1,000 in women with no prenatal care, while those women that had received care had rates of 2.4 per 1,000 ($p < 0.01$).

In a survey of 22,774 consecutive hospital births at Zaria in northern Nigeria, Harrison found that for those women that had received prenatal care, the risk of death was 25-30 per cent below the overall rate for the lowest risk age/parity group (Harrison, 1979).

In 1980, the coverage of prenatal care was 37 per cent in Zimbabwe, 35 in Indonesia, 52 in El Salvador, 76 in the Republic of Korea and 98 in China. These figures have improved since then: for example, the percentage of recent births where the mother received prenatal care ranged from over 90 in Zimbabwe, Sri Lanka and the Dominican Republic, to 70-73 in Nigeria and fewer than 50 in Mali, Bolivia, Morocco and Guatemala (DHS, 1991).

The study conducted by Kwast, Rochat and Mariam (1986) at Addis Ababa found that prenatal care alone would have averted about one third of the deaths recorded in the study.

It has also been reported that women that attended prenatal control clinics from four to six times during pregnancy and during delivery had fewer complications during pregnancy and delivery than women that had received care only once or twice. The primary objectives of prenatal care are early diagnosis of abnormalities and the detection of asymptomatic, potentially threatening conditions in either mother or foetus, such as premature birth, intra-uterine growth retardation, and maternal and perinatal mortality.

Low educational level, poverty, stressful physical activities, rearing of several children and difficult access (distance, other barriers) to prenatal care are the most frequent causes observed for the low demand (or low use) of such care by a considerable number of women in the developing countries (Leslie and Gupta, 1989).

What has been said for prenatal care also holds true for post-partum and technical care at childbirth. Despite the progress made by almost every country, not all deliveries are taken care of by skilled personnel. For instance, childbirth attended by a trained person ranges from more than 85 per cent of births in Sri Lanka, Trinidad and Tobago and the Dominican Republic to fewer than 33 per cent in Burundi, Mali, Morocco and Guatemala (DHS, 1991). Even when women give birth in hospitals and clinics or are attended by skilled providers, some die in such institutions. Many maternal deaths originate at home when women give birth under precarious conditions.

A maternal mortality study carried out at Menoufia in northern Egypt during the period 1981-1983 (Saleh, 1987), showed that 112 (29 per cent) of the 385 maternal deaths occurred during labour at home and 227 (59 per cent) during the post-partum period. These maternal deaths could have been prevented had the women either made use of the available hospital facilities or been attended by a skilled health-care provider in the area (Saleh, 1987).

Home deliveries by unskilled providers may result in prolonged labour, ruptured uterus, foetal suffering and irreversible brain damage, severe birth trauma, haemorrhage, infection and delayed treatment for non-lethal conditions that may become serious if left unresolved.

It is worth noting that in some Latin American countries visited by the author, a large proportion of maternal deaths occurred at third-level health-care institutions. The most reasonable explanation for this situation is that because the facilities have better resources, high-risk women in extreme conditions are referred, which makes it impossible to reverse the clinical status before they die. None the less, in many mortality review sessions attended by the author, significant omissions and inadequate management of the cases were observed. These lapses occurred especially during night shifts, weekends and holidays, when unskilled staff were on duty, and support and close supervision of obstetricians, anesthesiologists and other personnel with experience in treating obstetric emergencies were not available. These situations demand responsible attitudes and should give way to conducting studies where the iatrogenic factor in in-hospital maternal deaths is examined in order to learn and adopt the necessary corrective measures. The situation described above may be equally prevalent in many other places.

Lastly, it should also be stressed that despite the importance given to appropriate maternal and child health care in recent years, such services have room to grow in almost all the developing countries. In several Latin American countries, childbirth coverage does not exceed 40 per cent.

Of the 385 maternal deaths studied between 1981 and 1983 at Menoufia, Egypt (Saleh, 1987), 227 (59 per cent) occurred during the post-partum period. Haemorrhage and infections were the most common causes and were the result of home deliveries attended by unskilled providers. The importance of post-partum care must be emphasized from the time of the first prenatal consultation, and maintained throughout the pregnancy. Towards this end, the nursing staff, social workers, health promoters, traditional birth attendants, the staff at the Registrar's Office and community agents, all play an important role in prevention and should become fully involved.

Every woman in the post-partum period and every newborn should receive close follow-up care by the health system, since it is during this period that serious risks may affect both mother and child. It must be kept in mind that many of the women that die during the post-partum period may not have been considered high-risk cases during the prenatal period. As a result, they perhaps delivered at home and possibly were attended by unskilled personnel insufficiently familiar with last-minute complications; hence the need for these women to receive careful monitoring during the post-partum period.

F. Circumcision and women's health

According to International Planned Parenthood Federation estimates, in those countries where female circumcision is carried out, there currently exist over 100 million women and girls that have undergone some form of female genital mutilation and are at risk of immediate and long-term medical and other complications.

The former complications include infection, haemorrhage and structural modifications that affect urinary function. Late complications include difficulties in passing menses, keloid scar formation, repeated infections and marital problems deriving from difficulties in the consummation of marriage. Obstetric problems can lead to gynaecological conditions that result in secondary sterility and may contribute to divorce.

Efforts to give women the power to deal with the problem of this form of female genital mutilation should continue.

G. Induced abortion and women's reproductive health

Induced abortion continues to be a serious public health problem in most developing countries. Although it is not generally considered a method of family planning, it is nevertheless definitely a method of fertility regulation that women have used from time immemorial and to which they will continue to turn, whatever the risks (Sai and Nassim, 1989).

Because they lack access to safe abortion care, approximately 200,000 women die every year from complications of unsafe abortion; many more are seriously injured. Ninety-nine per cent of those needless deaths and injuries occur in the developing world. The Safe Motherhood Conference held at Nairobi in 1987 concluded that:

> "Illegal abortion from unwanted pregnancies causes some 25-50 per cent of these [maternal] deaths, simply because women do not have access to the family planning services they want and need, or have no access to safe procedures or to humane treatment for the complications of abortion." (Mahler, 1987, p. 670)

Unwanted pregnancy and induced abortion occur in every society and affect women throughout their reproductive years. Thirty-two per cent of women in the world live under restrictive abortion laws, with 10 per cent living in areas where abortion is not legal in any circumstances. It is estimated that some 20-30 per cent of all pregnancies in the world terminate in an abortion.

The number of induced abortions in a country where abortion is illegal cannot be determined. Estimates of abortion-related deaths in the developing countries range from 50 to 100 per 100,000 procedures. With computer simulations, the possibility of rates as high as 1,000 per 100,000 has been shown.

Where abortion is not legal, official statistics compile only information on abortions treated at hospitals where women with severe complications go for health-care services. Abortions thus accounted for represent variable proportions ranging from one of every three deliveries to from two to five abortions per delivery. In those Latin American countries where abortions are illegal, numerous procedures are induced in doctors' offices and/or in private clinics, and they are never reported. Information is available only in the event of complications following the procedure.

Studies conducted in some countries have omitted from the maternal death statistics the deaths resulting from abortions. Mortality rates are up to 50 per cent lower than the actual rate (Kenyatta National Hospital, 1977/78); Egyptian Government, 1987; Nigeria, Ahmadu Bello University Hospital, 1964-1972).

In Chile and in Trinidad and Tobago, 50 women per million aged 15-44 died from causes associated with illegal abortion during the 1970s. In Mauritius, 66 women per million died, while 87 per million died in Paraguay. Between 1980 and 1985, 31 per cent of all maternal deaths in Bangladesh were due to abortion, 25 per cent in Ethiopia and 17 per cent in Zambia and the United Republic of Tanzania (Herz and Measham, 1987). Deaths resulting from abortions accounted for almost half of all deaths that occurred in 1978 and 1987 in a major hospital at Rio de Janeiro (La Guardia and others, 1990).

In those countries where abortions are legal, the rates range from a maximum of 112 per 1,000 women of reproductive age (former USSR) to a minimum of 5 per 1,000 in the Netherlands. In the developed countries, death resulting from legal abortions amount to 0.6 death per 100,000 procedures. The procedure is performed on an out-patient basis through vacuum aspiration. Uterine evacuation in those countries is now safer than pregnancy and childbirth.

Causes and consequences of induced illegal abortions

Among the many reasons women interrupt a pregnancy, the unwanted pregnancy stands out. In African countries, the percentages of married women that want no more children range from 49 in Kenya and 33 in Zimbabwe to 17 in Liberia and Mali. In the Latin American and Caribbean countries, the picture is not too different from that in Africa.

The non-use of contraceptives, inadequate use or the failure rates inherent to modern and traditional contraceptives result in unwanted pregnancies which often end in an illegal induced abortion. For instance, global failure rates, including sterilization, vary substantially from one country to the next, from a minimum of 2 per cent in Thailand and 3 per cent in Indonesia, to a maximum of 16 per cent in Peru and 19 per cent in Bolivia (Moreno and Goldman, 1991). This is an important reason for a woman to seek an abortion. There are other circumstances that increase the risk of an abortion, such as multiparity, adolescence, poor birth-spacing, poverty and overcrowding. It is, none the less, puzzling to find that despite poverty, many women disburse large sums of earned or borrowed money for an abortion.

Women that seek an abortion in countries where they are illegal recognize that they are running a tremendous health risk. Such risk increases as the capacity to pay for the procedure decreases. The illegal abortionists have no training and use elementary techniques and inadequate instruments, which frequently leads to severe complications, often requiring radical surgery in young women. Death is not an unusual outcome. Numerous studies have been conducted worldwide to document the cost of abortion not only in terms of human lives but in the suffering of thousands of orphan children and families (Paxman and others, 1993). Health care provided in hospitals to infected post-abortion patients and women that are anaemic or in shock because of an abortion generally takes up a large portion of the resources available for regular obstetric cases.

Despite the situation described above and the evidence of a dramatic reduction of maternal abortion mortality when legislation is less restrictive, heated debates on the advantages and disadvantages of changing the laws exist almost everywhere this is proposed. Disputes between the anti-abortion group and the supporters of free choice continue in the final years of the present decade and rather than decreasing, appear to intensify as time passes by.

H. WHAT THEN SHOULD BE DONE?

The Safe Motherhood Conference stated that "there exist low-cost effective and available interventions that can have a major impact in reducing maternal mortalities and morbidities if these interventions are specifically planned and practiced as a priority" (Mahler, 1987, p. 670). It is unlikely, however, that these and other available options will be fully implemented until significant changes occur in policy makers' and health system administrators' thoughts on the abortion issue. This goal will most likely be achieved when the society's perception of the value of women evolves from its current stand.

Much has been said on the contribution of family planning to the prevention of maternal mortality and abortion. Contraception has the ability to decrease the risk of unwanted pregnancies and thus the need to resort to induced abortion (Herz and Measham, 1987). On the other hand, widespread acceptance of family planning may not bring down levels of maternal mortality, as is seen in Brazil, Colombia and Mexico, where the death ratios remain well above 100 per 100,000 live births, in spite of contraceptive prevalence of 50-65 per cent of women of reproductive age.

Although doubts as to the effectiveness of family planning in reducing maternal mortality have been expressed, Fortney (1987) believes that family planning as well as better obstetric care may help reduce abortion deaths in the least developed countries.

A pro-active approach to abortion care has been proposed that involves acknowledging that the problem exists, addressing family planning and abortion-related needs and planning in order to provide the highest quality, most comprehensive care permitted by law. Training of staff in abortion care; use of existing techniques and technologies, such as vacuum aspiration; implementation of referral and transport systems; procurement of commodities and supplies, and monitoring and coordination of services need to be undertaken in order to better serve women in need.

Administrators and policy makers need to acknowledge the magnitude of the problem of unsafe abortion and then implement interventions such as those described in box 4.

Pending changes that will close the gap between how women cope with an unwanted pregnancy and the current abortion legislation, the pro-active approach addresses the need for treating abortion where it remains illegal.

Contraception by itself seems unsatisfactory, whether for fertility reduction in a population or for safe birth control for individuals. Even couples that use highly effective methods are subject to failures over an extended period of time. Thus, contraception alone is not sufficient to prevent unwanted births (Tietze and Henshaw, 1986). The need for legal change continues to exist, whatever the contemporary public opinion and the political climate, as the incidence of induced abortion and maternal deaths remain high.

I. Sexually transmitted disease as a risk factor for maternal mortality and morbidity, infertility and pregnancy loss, and infant mortality and morbidity

Although sexually transmitted diseases have been known since ancient times, they have recently gained special relevance with the AIDS epidemic. Both sides of the problem coexist when STDs and how they affect the reproductive life of the couple are taken into consideration. On the one side, they are a significant cause of infertility and deprive men and women of the faculty to reproduce. Moreover, STDs are an important cause of morbidity among women during pregnancy and intergestational periods. These diseases produce lethal effects not only in the woman but also the child during gestation, at the time of delivery and then during the post-partum period (Meheus, 1988).

For many years, health sciences students were taught the effects on human beings of the 25 or more germs that cause STDs. They learned the clinical symptoms, the causative agents, the epidemiology and the means of making an accurate diagnosis and treating such diseases. They were also made aware of control measures to stop transmission and limit harm not only to the individual or his/her sexual partner but also to the community at large. AIDS has shown in merely a few years that the traditional approach used to prevent STDs has not been effective and, on the contrary, this is an epidemic with unforeseeable repercussions.

Two recent publications (Dixon-Maeller and Wasserheit, 1991; and Elias, 1991) propose a restatement of the traditional approach to examine STDs; it is suggested that STDs should not be considered individually as in the past but should be grouped in clinical syndromes (such as reproductive tract infection or genital ulcer disease) to facilitate a more integral approach to the problem, as well as to assist in identifying resources and specific initiatives to deal effectively with them. The author considers this approach to be valuable and hence will try to follow that format.

In almost all countries, STDs have had a low profile in reproductive health programmes. A close look at the way health programmes are organized in developing countries confirms the almost absolute lack of coordination between family planning services, prenatal care and clinics for STDs wherever they exist. Prenatal care programmes have traditionally screened pregnant women with the Venereal Disease Research Laboratories test for syphilis. Maternity clinics have used antibiotic-based ophthalmic solutions for the prevention of gonococcal ophthalmia of the newborn. These are very limited interventions, given the vast array of problems derived from STDs that can affect the child and his mother.

Programmes for STDs, where they exist, have been erroneously used to detect such diseases in high-risk groups (e.g., prostitutes, military garrisons, jails), overlooking the fact that women not involved in the sex trade might also be infected during their reproductive years by their husband or sexual partner. This neglect has resulted in many women throughout the world having suffered severe complications, such as pelvic inflammatory disease, infertility and sterility, congenital infections or cervical cancer (Meheus, 1988).

Health programme administrators and directors reportedly have not given reproductive tract infections a high priority because: (*a*) they are not lethal; (*b*) they are costly and difficult to treat; (*c*) they relate

Box 4. Pro-active health care by system level		
Preventive care	*Treatment for abortion complications*	*Pregnancy termination services allowed by law*
	Community level	
* Provide health education about unwanted pregnancy and unsafe abortion. * Provide family planning information and education. * Provide some family planning services and commodities.	* Recognize signs of abortion complications. * Provide timely referral to the formal health-care system.	* Provide information to women on the available services and how to obtain them.
	Primary level	
* All the activities listed at the community level. * Provide post-abortion family planning counselling and services or referrals.	* Diagnose abortion complications (physical exams, pelvic exam and laboratory tests). * Resuscitate patients and prepare them for treatment or referral, if needed. * Perform uterine evacuation (using vacuum aspiration or manual vacuum aspiration) during 12 weeks of gestation. * Initiate other available treatments (such as fluid replacement or antibiotic therapy) as required. * Provide timely referral and transport as required.	* Assess uterine size (duration of gestation) and perform diagnostic procedures listed for treatment of abortion complications for this level. * Perform elective pregnancy terminations (using vacuum aspiration or manual vacuum aspiration) during the first trimester.
	First referral level	
* Same as listed above	All activities listed above plus: * Perform uterine evacuation during the second trimester. *Treat such conditions as haemorrhage, sepsis and uterine perforations. * Provide timely referral and transport for severe complications (e.g., renal failure).	* Perform terminations as allowed by law in the first and second trimester.
	Second and third levels	
* Same as listed above	*Perform uterine evacuation for all patients with abortion complications.	* Perform pregnancy termination to the extent allowed by law and for high-risk patients.

to patterns of sexual behaviour that are not totally understood, have been the subject of little investigation and are highly sensitive and difficult to modify; and (*d*) they can adversely affect a good programme. Each of these points can easily be refuted as STDs—for example, cervical cancer—can in fact be fatal. If detected in time, they may be successfully treated (except for AIDS). Moreover, adequate information, counselling and communications can contribute to modify behaviour; and a programme is so much the better if it helps solve problems affecting the client's health.

STDs can be grouped into four main categories: (*a*) reproductive tract infections, which include vaginitis, cervicitis and pelvic inflammatory diseases that can affect the lower and upper reproductive tract; (*b*) genital ulcer diseases, such as herpes, syphilis and chancroid; (*c*) sexually transmitted disease malignancies, such as cervical cancer; (*d*) human immunodeficiency virus (HIV) and AIDS.

Reproductive tract infections attack both the lower reproductive tract, as in the case of trichomoniasis and candidiasis, or bacterial vaginosis, and the upper tract, as with chlamydia or gonorrhoea. The first group can also affect the newborn and favour the entrance of HIV; and the latter can lead to infertility, ectopic pregnancy or chronic pelvic pain, a condition that affects a considerable number of women throughout the world. Chlamydia and gonorrhoea produce congenital infection and cause foetal wastage and low birth weight.

Genital ulcer diseases (syphilis, herpes, donovanosis, lymphogranuloma, venereum, chancroid etc.) affect the lower reproductive tract and also facilitate the entry of viruses such as HIV, and may infect the foetus and the newborn. These diseases are not easily diagnosed and particularly in women, they may be overlooked. The final diagnosis of genital ulcer disease generally requires a microscope and specific cultures or serological tests. Herpes genitalis is a recurrent disease, for which there currently is no known cure.

STD malignancies are represented by cervical cancer, whose aetiology is linked to the human papilloma virus transmitted by sexual contact. Likewise, the hepatitis B virus, also sexually transmitted, has proved to be associated with hepatic cirrhosis and hepatocellular carcinoma.

HIV/AIDS is currently the leading cause of morbidity and death in young women and children. These diseases are now recognized as an international health problem of extraordinary scope and unprecedented urgency, and the scenario is predicted to become much worse before an improvement can be seen.

WHO projects that by 1992, an additional 1.5 million women and 500,000 children will be infected with HIV and over 1 million will have developed AIDS (Chin, 1990). In the major cities of the Americas, Western Europe and sub-Saharan Africa, AIDS is now the leading cause of death for women between ages 20 and 40 years; and in some central African cities, up to 40 per cent of women aged 30-34 were found to be HIV-infected. The proportion of pregnant women that are HIV-positive ranges from 10 to 20 per cent in many African countries. By the end of 1992, about 4 million infants will have been born to women infected with HIV and nearly 1 million of those babies also will be HIV-infected (Chin, 1990).

AIDS is threatening the health gains that have been achieved in the developing world. Most Governments have now committed to the urgent and complex challenge of AIDS. Safe sex seems to be the most feasible alternative today to reduce the risk for women of acquiring HIV. Intercourse only with an uninfected partner, abstinence and/or using condoms consistently and correctly have been advocated to stop the epidemic.

J. Conclusions and proposals to improve women's health during the reproductive years

Maternal mortality

Maternal mortality continues to affect the health of women, children and families, particularly in the developing countries. The major causes of maternal mortality were identified long ago and in most cases are preventable. Early detection of risks and treatment of anaemia, the management of reproductive tract infections with adequate antibiotics, supplementary protein and calories for women with nutritional deficiencies during pregnancy and the early management of haemorrhage are cost-effective interventions.

Likewise, appropriate care during childbirth by qualified personnel, timely transfer of any person with possible complications to a better equipped centre, the use of formats for the early detection of risk factors, the organization and implementation of maternal mortality committees and contraception with modern methods to prevent unwanted pregnancies are effective interventions that do not require budgets that go beyond the possibilities of countries facing high maternal mortality.

Women's health programme officers might implement such interventions as those given below:

1. Make an early assessment of expected pregnancies in a given area or region, which is now possible with DHS or census data that permit an estimation of pregnancies using fertility rates by region. Health personnel would have a better grasp of how many pregnant women need to be provided with adequate prenatal and delivery care;

2. Encourage family planning and expand provision of effective contraceptives by promoting them during prenatal care. Implementing post-partum and post-abortion contraceptive services in every maternity ward is feasible and highly beneficial;

3. Implement simple data-collection systems that will permit early detection of risk factors and yield basic data in order to introduce corrective measures to identify persons at high risk and to manage risks effectively;

4. Train medical and nursing staff in the management of normal and high-risk pregnancies and in the adequate management of induced abortions;

5. Provide maternal health units with the necessary equipment, instruments and supplies to handle low- and moderate-risk patients effectively;

6. Organize maternal health committees in every hospital with childbirth services. Every maternal complication or death of a woman of reproductive age should be assessed to establish the causes and determine action;

7. Integrate the network of state and local surveillance systems and try to improve the epidemiology of maternal mortality;

8. Provide the pregnant working woman with legal protection from the Government and society through laws that guarantee rights in the event of discrimination;

Induced abortion

With regard to induced abortion, the following points can be made:

1. Maternal mortality resulting from illegal induced abortions is a tragedy that also affects the health of thousands of children and their families;

2. Behind illegally induced abortion, unwanted pregnancies stand. Many of these pregnancies could be prevented by accessible, safe and effective contraceptive methods.;

3. Health-care personnel must be skilled in the techniques and procedures for the management of obstetric emergency situations and induced abortions. For example, the use of vacuum equipment should be standard in every childbirth centre and shock management should be mastered. The training of personnel should be complemented with provision of equipment to primary health care and referral centres and with the establishment of guidelines and standard procedures;

4. Abortion surveillance systems should be implemented to improve epidemiological information.

5. The liberalization of abortion legislation is an effective measure for reducing maternal mortality resulting from illegally induced abortion. Attempts to modify legislation are subject to long and bitterly fought debates that may be worth experiencing before legal change occurs;

6. A pro-active approach proposed for coping with induced abortion is worth considering.

Sexually transmitted diseases in women of reproductive age

As concerns STDs, some comments and recommendations are given below:

1. STDs that affect women's health during their reproductive years are a serious problem, with unforeseen repercussions, in most developing countries;

2. STDs are troublesome, affect the sexual life of the couple and can kill or seriously handicap the child as well as the mother;

3. Education for the prevention of STDs is a key element in programmes against such diseases;

4. Male condoms, female condoms and the combined use of condoms and Nonoxinol 9 spermicides are all effective programme components that reduce the incidence of STDs;

5. Guidelines and standard protocols for the adequate treatment of STDs and the prevention and management of those still incurable, are a must;

6. Safe sex should be promoted by all Governments as an effective public-health strategy for reducing STDs;

7. Family planning programmes should include activities for the promotion, prevention and treatment of STDs;

8. Continued education of health personnel in the management and prevention of STDs is imperative;

9. Participation of the education sector in creating healthy habits and in promoting safe sex by mass media are important steps in the fight against STDs;

10. Research and development to identify quick, inexpensive and specific means for the diagnosis of STDs should be continued and expanded;

11. Research should continue for the development of effective vaccines against STDs and pharmaceutical products should be available for the treatment of such diseases.

12. The involvement of women's organizations in programmes for the prevention of STDs offers promise and should be encouraged.

K. Conclusion

The health of women, particularly in the developing countries, continues to be severely affected by a series of conditions leading to risk situations during pregnancy and childbirth. Illegally induced abortions and STDs are serious risks as well.

Given that developing countries have mortality and morbidity patterns that increasingly combine preventable and treatable health problems with such diseases as cancer and chronic disorders, those countries are now faced with a dilemma, not at all easy to solve, as to where resources should be channelled in order to attain the best possible results.

The promotion of safe sex for the prevention of STDs, the reduction of maternal mortality and the proactive approach to induced abortion are feasible, relatively inexpensive and cost-effective.

Family planning is not only a human right but also a duty for men and women in the fight against maternal mortality and the prevention of abortion. Family planning programmes may also contribute importantly to the prevention of STDs. Education for the prevention of such diseases continues to be the backbone of all efforts implemented to reduce their magnitude and to limit their spread.

Because maternal mortality, abortion morbidity and mortality, and STDs tend to affect most heavily the low-income sectors in every society, those problems have adverse effects on development and the well-being of individuals, entire families and societies.

The unbroken cycles of disability and death produced by the conditions described above should and can be effectively addressed. They represent severe problems that affect large numbers of people for which interventions of established efficacy can be provided at low cost.

REFERENCES

Alauddin, Mohammad (1986). Maternal mortality in rural Bangladesh: the Tangail District. *Studies in Family Planning* (New York), vol. 17, No. 1 (January-February), pp. 13-21.

Boerma, J. Ties, and J. K. G. Mati (1989). Identifying maternal mortality in developing countries. *Studies in Family Planning* (New York), vol. 28, No. 5 (September-October), pp. 213-221.

Chin, James (1990). Current and future dimensions of the HIV/AIDS pandemic in women and children. *The Lancet* (London; and Baltimore, Maryland), vol. 336, No. 8709 (28 July), pp. 221-224.

Demographic and Health Surveys (1991). *Demographic and Health Surveys World Conference, August 5-7, 1991, Washington, D.C., Proceedings*, vols. I-III. Columbia, Maryland: IRD/Macro International, Inc.

Dixon-Mueller, Ruth, and Judith Wasserheit (1991). *The Culture of Silence: Reproductive Tract Infections among Women in the Third World.* New York: International Women's Health Coalition.

El Dareer, Asma (1982). Women, Why Do You Weep? *Circumcision and its Consequences*. London; and Westport, Connecticut: Zed Press.

Elias, Christopher (1991). *Sexually Transmitted Diseases and the Reproductive Health of Women in Developing Countries.* Programme Division Working Paper, No. 5. New York: The Population Council.

Fortney, Judith H. (1987). The importance of family planning in reducing maternal mortality. *Studies in Family Planning* (New York), vol. 18, No. 2 (March-April), pp. 109-114.

Gil, E. Personal communication.

Harrison, K. A. (1979). Nigeria. *The Lancet* (London; Baltimore, Maryland), vol. II for 1979, No. 8154 (8 December), pp. 1229-1232.

Harsburgh, C., and others (1987). Preventive strategies in sexually transmitted diseases for the primary care physician. *Journal of the American Medical Association*, vol. 258, No. 6.

Herz, Barbara Knapp, and Anthony R. Measham (1987). *Iniciativa de la maternidad sin riesgo: medidas propuestas.* Washington, D.C.: The World Bank.

Kheirs, El Haj Hamad M., and others (1991). Female circumcision: attitudes and practices in Sudan. *Demographic and Health Surveys World Conference Proceedings*, vol. III. Columbia, Maryland: Institute for Resource Development, Westinghouse.

Kwast, Barbara E., Roger W. Rochat and Widad Kidar-Mariam (1986). Maternal mortality in Addis Ababa, Ethiopia. *Studies in Family Planning* (New York), vol. 17, No. 6 (November-December), pp. 288-301.

La Guardia, and others (1990). A ten year review of maternal mortality in a municipal hospital in Rio de Janeiro: a cause for concern. *Obstetrics and Gynecology* (New York), vol. 75, pp. 27-90.

Leslie, Joanne, and Geeta Rao Gupta (1989). *Utilization of Formal Services for Maternal Nutrition and Health Care in the Third World.* Washington, D.C.: International Center for Research on Women.

Liskin, Laurie, and others (1985). *Youth in the 1980's: Social and Health Concerns.* Population Reports, Series M, No. 9. Baltimore, Maryland: The Johns Hopkins University, Population Information Program.

Mahler, Halfdan (1987). The Safe Motherhood Initiative: a call to action. *Lancet* (Baltimore, Maryland; and London), No. 8534(21) (21 March), pp. 668-670.

Meheus, A. (1988). The worldwide impact of sexually transmitted diseases on reproductive health. In *Reproductive Health and Technology Issues and Future Directions*. Baltimore, Maryland: The Johns Hopkins University.

Moreno, Lorenzo, and Noreen Goldman (1991). Tasas de falla de anticonceptivos en países en desarrollo: encuestas de demografía y salud. *Perspectivas internacionales en planificación familiar* (New York), special issue.

Omran, A. (1985). Fecundidad y salud. In *La experiencia latinoamericana*. Washington, D.C.: Pan American Health Organization.

Pan American Health Organization (1986a). Elementos básicos para el estudio y la prevención de la mortalidad materna. *Boletín Epidemiológico de la OPS* (Mexico City), vol. 7, No. 5/6.

__________ (1986b). *Boletín Epidemiológico de la OPS* (Mexico City), vol. 7, No. 5/6.

Pathfinder Fund/The Population Council (1989). Memorias Conferencia Internacional sobre Fecundidad en Adolescencia en America Latina y el Caribe.

Paxman, John M., and others (1993). The clandestine epidemic: the practice of unsafe abortion in Latin America. *Studies in Family Planning* (New York), vol. 24, No. 4 (July/August), pp. 205-226.

Royston, Erica, and Sue Armstrong, eds. (1989). *Preventing Maternal Deaths.* Geneva: World Health Organization.

Rutenberg, Naomi, and Jeremiah M. Sullivan (1991). Direct and indirect estimates of maternal mortality from the sisterhood method. In *Demographic and Health Surveys World Conference, August 5-7, 1991, Washington D.C., Proceedings,* vol. III. Columbia, Maryland: IRD/Macro International, Inc.

Sai F. T., and J. Nassim (1989). The need for a reproductive health approach. In "Women's health in the third world: the impact of unwanted pregnancy", A. Rosenfield and others, eds. *International Journal of Gynecology and Obstetrics* (limerick, Ireland), Supplement No. 3, pp. 103-113.

Saleh, Saneya (1987). Maternal mortality in Menoufia, Egypt, 1981-1983. In *High Risk Mothers and Newborns,* Abdel R. Omran, J. Martin and B. Hamza, eds. Switzerland: Ott Publishers.

Senderowitz, Judith S., and John M. Paxman (1985). *Adolescent Fertility: Worldwide Concerns.* Population Bulletin, vol. 40, No. 2. Washington, D.C.: Population Reference Bureau.

Starrs, Ann (1987). *Preventing the Tragedy of Maternal Deaths.* A report on the International Safe Motherhood Conference, Nairobi, Kenya, February 1987; co-sponsored by the World Bank, World Health Organization and United Nations Fund for Population Activities. Washington, D.C.: The World Bank.

Tietze, Christopher, and Stanley K. Henshaw (1986). *Induced Abortion: A World Review, 1986.* New York: The Alan Guttmacher Institute.

United Nations (1982). *Demographic Indicators of Countries: Estimates and Projections as Assessed in 1980.* Sales No. E.82.XII.5.

__________ (1991). *World Population Prospects, 1990.* Population Studies, No. 120. Sales No. E.91.XIII.

United States of America, Centers for Disease Control (1989). 1989 sexually transmitted disease treatment guidelines. *Morbidity and Mortality Weekly Report* (Atlanta, Georgia), vol. 38, No. S-8 (1 September).

Walker, Godfrey A., and others (1986). Maternal mortality in Jamaica. *The Lancet* (London; and Baltimore, Maryland), vol. I for 1986, No. 8479 (1 March), pp. 486-488.

Walsh John, and Kenneth S. Warren (1979). Selective primary health care: an interim strategy for disease control in developing countries. *The New England Journal of Medicine* (Boston, Massachusetts), vol. 301, No. 18 (1 November), pp. 967-974.

World Health Organization (1977). *Manual of the International Statistical Classification of Diseases, Injuries, and Causes of Death,* vol. 1, 9th rev. Geneva.

__________ (1986). *Maternal Mortality Ratios and Rates: A Tabulation of Available Information.* 2nd ed. Geneva.

__________ (1991). *Maternal mortality. A Global Factbook.* Compiled by Carla AbouZahr and Erica Royston. Geneva.

XI. WOMEN, AIDS AND SEXUALLY TRANSMITTED DISEASES IN SUB-SAHARAN AFRICA: THE IMPACT OF MARRIAGE CHANGE

Michel Caraël[*]

Although the three routes of transmission of the human immunodeficiency virus (HIV)—sexual, perinatal and parenteral—are universal, the patterns of HIV spread are highly diverse between and within countries and over time.

The acquired immunodeficiency syndrome (AIDS) was originally thought of as a man's disease, because it was first identified in homosexual men and in male IV drug users in the early 1980s. It took several years to realize that from the beginning of the pandemic both men and women had been equally infected with HIV in sub-Saharan Africa. It took another two or three years to realize that women are particularly affected by the HIV epidemic because of biological, sociocultural, economic and status factors that render them more vulnerable to HIV infection than men.

Because the predominant mode of HIV transmission is sexual, many of the sociocultural determinants and the measures for preventing sexual transmission of HIV and other sexually transmitted diseases (STDs) are the same. Furthermore, there is a strong association between the occurrence of HIV and the presence of other STDs. Increasing evidence suggests that some STDs, particularly genital ulcer disease, facilitate the acquisition and transmission of HIV. It is ironic that AIDS, which is one of the few sexually transmitted syndromes with no current curative therapy, has recently done more to focus attention on the importance of STDs in health and in reproductive health than have all the data showing that STDs were classed among the six most important public-health problems, particularly for women.

This paper briefly reviews the epidemiology of HIV and STDs in sub-Saharan Africa. It focuses on the interrelations between HIV and STDs and on the influence of cultural factors and sexual behaviour that promote their diffusion.

The epidemic of HIV and other STDs in Rwanda provides a case-study to illustrate the importance of commercial sexual relationships and to examine the relation of the epidemic to nuptiality and marital status.

B. The HIV epidemic

Global estimates and projections of the HIV epidemic

Heterosexual transmission is the predominant mode of HIV spread throughout the world. In industrialized countries, heterosexual transmission has increased slowly but steadily since the mid-1980s, especially in urban populations with high rates of STDs or IV drug use.

The World Health Organization (WHO) estimates that close to 1.5 million adults developed AIDS during the 1980s; of these, over 350,000 were women. The 1990s will be the decade of the AIDS case, with a major mortality impact on women and children. By the year 2000, it is estimated that the number of AIDS cases will be equal in men and women.

Worldwide, WHO estimates that from 9 million to 11 million adults are currently infected with HIV and that over one third are women; more than 1 million are infants and children. If current trends continue, WHO estimates that by the year 2000 from 30 million to 40 million adults will be infected with HIV and the male-to-female ratio will be 1.3:1. According to Chin (1990), there may be a cumulative total of over 6 million maternal AIDS orphans.

Although precise estimations and long-term projections cannot be made with great certainty, all epidemiological studies point to continuing large increases in

[*]Global Programme on AIDs, World Health Organization, Geneva, Switzerland.

HIV seroprevalence levels in most developing countries and to substantial increases in total numbers of women and children infected.

Estimates and epidemiology of HIV in sub-Saharan Africa

WHO estimates that in Africa in 1992 there were nearly 1 million adult AIDS cases and a cumulative total of 6.6 million HIV infections, about half being women. About two thirds of HIV infections are found in nine countries of Eastern and Middle Africa.

By the year 2000, about 5 million women and 5 million men that are HIV-infected will still be alive, and there will be a cumulative total of over 6 million maternal AIDS orphans that would have been under 15 years of age at the time of their mother's death.

The epidemiology of HIV-1 and HIV-2 has been extensively reviewed in recent articles (Nkowane, 1991; Torrey and Way, 1990; Caraël and Piot, 1989b). The seroprevalence rates in selected groups of people in different countries vary enormously: among those attending STD clinics, rates were from 3 to 62 per cent; among prostitutes from 2 to 90 per cent. In the general population, rates from 0.5 to 18 per cent were reported. The distribution of seroprevalence by age is bimodal, with a peak under age 2 and a peak between ages 20 and 30. The distribution reflects sexual transmission between adults and vertical transmission from mother to child. In populations where HIV is mostly transmitted by heterosexual contact, a considerable proportion of fecund women are infected by the virus. In the large cities of Eastern and Middle Africa, between 0.5 and 33 per cent of them are seropositive. For this reason, perinatal infection is more and more frequent, as is shown in the seropositivity levels reaching 12 per cent in children aged 0-4 years in urban areas of Rwanda.

The probability of perinatal transmission ranges from 30 to 40 per cent. Much of this mother-to-infant transmission occurs during pregnancy and delivery; recent evidence suggests that the risk of HIV transmission through breast-feeding is substantial among women that become infected during the breast-feeding period and is lower among women already infected at the time of delivery (van de Perre and others, 1991).

Although heterosexual transmission of HIV is the predominant mode of HIV infection for African women, it is essential not to ignore the effect of unsafe blood transfusions and the use of inadequately sterilized injection equipment. The likelihood of HIV transmission through blood transfusion, a common treatment of anaemia or obstetric complications, is higher among children under age 5 and women of child-bearing age. Testing for HIV antibodies in blood donations, which has been introduced in the majority of African countries, will probably prevent more cases of HIV infection in Africa than in industrialized countries. Use of unsterile needles, syringes and skin-invasive equipment is thought to account for a very small part of HIV infections in this part of the world.

In the absence of longitudinal studies of cohorts of HIV-infected people, the relation between HIV prevalence and mortality has been estimated empirically for the short term; Chin's model (1990) estimates that with every 10 per cent increase in HIV prevalence among sexually active adults, the adult mortality rate (ages 15-49) will increase by about 5 per 1,000 within five years. Where the adult crude mortality rate is on the order of 5 per 1,000 (an average for Africa in the absence of AIDS), a 10 per cent HIV prevalence rate implies a doubling of the mortality rate, while a 20 per cent HIV prevalence implies treble the deaths normally expected.

AIDS has been shown to be the leading cause of mortality in adults at Abidjan (De Cock and others, 1991) and in child-bearing women at Kigali where HIV/AIDS now accounts for 90 per cent of all deaths (Lindan and others, 1991).

However, any long-term projection of the socio-demographic impact on AIDS depends upon a greater understanding of sexual behaviour and upon assumptions of behavioural change.

C. The burden of STDs and their sequelae in Africa

The following data on the epidemiology of STDs in Africa throw light on possible HIV patterns. Prevalence levels for the different diseases were obtained from pregnant women that sought prenatal care.

For *Neisseria gonorrhoeae*, the prevalence rates among pregnant women, generally from urban areas, vary from 1 to 15 per cent, with a mean of 5 to 10 per cent (Schulz, Cates, and O'Mara, 1987).

For *Chlamydia trachomatis,* other studies have suggested that the prevalence is about 5-8 per cent. The incidence rate of chlamydia infections, the most common cause of urethritis, could be similar or even higher than that of gonorrhoea (Meheus, Reniers and Collet, 1986). Infection from this disease is often asymptomatic among women and is asymptomatic among only about 25 per cent of men.

The prevalence rates for *Treponema pallidum,* which is responsible for syphilis, are on the order of 3-19 per cent (Meheus, Reniers and Collet, 1986) but the techniques that have been used to calculate those rates have serious limitations and interpreting them is difficult. Syphilis is responsible for 12-25 per cent of genital ulcers (Mabey, 1986). With syphilis prevalence of about 10 per cent among pregnant women, 5-7 per cent of all pregnancies end either by spontaneous abortion/miscarriage in the first months or with perinatal or infant mortality; 1 per cent of the newborns will have clinical signs of congenital syphilis (Schultz, Cates and O'Mara, 1987). Gonococcal ophthalmia of the newborn is 50 times higher in Africa than that in industrialized countries (Galega, Heymann and Nasah, 1984).

The sexually transmitted *Haemophilus ducreyi,* which is responsible for chancroid, and for 30-50 per cent of genital ulcerations, has an incidence about the same as that of syphilis (Lancet, 1982). The relative frequency of genital ulcers is high due to chancroid, to venereal lymphogranulomas and to inguinal granulomas. Other STD agents, such as *Herpes simplex* virus, *Trichomonas vaginalis* and *Condylomata acuminata*, are equally widespread, but their prevalence is not well known.

The best known effects of STDs are their consequences for primary and secondary infertility among men and women (Retel-Laurentin, 1974; Cates, Farley and Rowe, 1985). It is estimated that secondary infertility may be from two to three times more common than primary sterility (WHO, 1990). From 40 to 85 per cent of cases of infertility among women can be traced to pelvic inflammatory disease (PID) (Meheus, Reniers and Collet, 1986).

The annual incidence of PID reaches 3-4 per 1,000 in certain regions of Africa, compared with 1 per 1,000 in other major areas (Muir and Belsey, 1980). The difference can be explained by the high prevalence of chlamydiae, gonoccoci and genital infections at the time of childbirth. Another important consequence of PID is the risk of pregnancies that begin outside the uterus: it has been estimated that 1 out of 25 pregnancies in women with PID were ectopic, compared with 1 out of 147 among members of a control group (Meheus, Reniers and Collet, 1986).

Do STDs burden women more than men in sub-Saharan Africa?

Transmission of STD pathogens that cause a discharge or reside in genital secretions (e.g., gonococci, chlamydiae, trichomonads, HIV) is reported to be more efficient from male to female than from female to male (Ehrardt and Wasserheit, 1991).[1] In addition, women infected with STD are far more likely than men to be asymptomatic and when symptoms do occur, they are generally less obviously attributable to STDs. But the argument here is less epidemiological—incidence or prevalence —than related to long-term sequelae and social and psychological consequences. It is clear that STDs and their resulting reproductive tract infections compromise women's ability to achieve and sustain pregnancy; and lead to infertility, ectopic pregnancy and chronic pelvic pain for non-pregnant women and to foetal wastage, low birth weight and congenital infection when reproductive tract infection occurs during pregnancy.

Fertility performance—bearing and rearing children—is so central to women's status in most African societies that STDs are provoking divorce, marital instability and sexual mobility, which further enhance the spread of these diseases. The reproductive function itself is so important to the status of the individual woman and to the two kinship groups concerned that the status of adulthood for women is almost completely contingent on motherhood and the last instalments of bride-wealth payments are often transferred only upon the birth of the first child (Lesthaeghe, 1989).

Furthermore, presentation to a public STD clinic may be so shameful that it is not considered a viable option. Alternative remedies, such as douches or intravaginal preparations, often mask rather than cure infections.

Sociocultural perceptions of STDs in women are not well known. People with little schooling or low income rarely use what Westerners would regard as sound health methods for prevention or modern treatment once symptoms develop. Why they fail to seek treatment is unclear. Studies sometimes mention, often anecdotally, that symptoms of STDs in men are considered banal or mundane types of illnesses or a rite of passage to manhood for an adolescent boy (Griffith, 1963; Bennett, 1962); hence, several months may go by before men seek treatment for symptoms considered minor. They are similarly less likely to seek treatment for their female sexual partners.

There is evidence, however, that the health, social and economic consequences of STDs, knowledge about the sources of the diseases and how to treat them, and whether sexual partners are informed are women's topics that remain largely unexplored.

D. STDs as a biological risk factor for HIV transmission

Sexual transmission is thought to be facilitated biologically by the presence of a sexually transmitted disease. It quickly became clear that STDs have probably facilitated the transmission of HIV (van de Perre and others, 1988; Caraël and others, 1985; Kreiss, Caraël and Meheus, 1988). Seropositivity for HIV has been associated in Africa with genital ulcers, *T. pallidum* and *C. trachomatis* (Kreiss and others, 1986; Greenblatt and others, 1988; and Simonsen and others, 1988). A prospective study among 422 clients of prostitutes has shown that men with genital ulcer diseases more frequently seroconverted to HIV than clients with urethritis (Cameron and others, 1989). Although men ordinarily are more effective transmitters of HIV to women than vice versa, those data suggested a high rate of HIV transmission from women to men with an active STD. Genital ulcers and the agents that cause them—chancroid, syphilis and genital herpes— may contribute to the infectiousness of HIV in a seropositive person of either sex and/or to the susceptibility of the person not already infected with it. Furthermore, at Kinshasa, 450 HIV-negative female prostitutes were followed for two years, during which time 12 per cent seroconverted. Gonorrhoea, chlamydial infection and trichomoniasis were significantly associated with HIV seroconversion (Laga, Nzila and Goeman, 1991). These results, if confirmed, are of particular importance because such non-ulcerative diseases are far more common than genital ulcer diseases. Conversely, because of its impact on the host immune response, HIV seropositivity can lead to altered clinical manifestations of those STDs and increase their spread.

Other studies suggest that any conditions that increase the number of lymphocytes in the female genital tract, such as STD that elicit an inflammatory response, may potentiate the risk of HIV transmission (van de Perre and others, 1988).

These factors reinforce the need for effective control programmes for STDs and a better understanding of the sexual and social behaviour that is critical in determining the spread of sexually transmitted infections.

E. Social determinants of STDs

There are nearly 2,000 references on STDs in Africa and on the relation between sexuality and health (Barton, 1988). Most of those works focus on the clinical aspects of these diseases, laboratory techniques for studying them and the difficulties in diagnosing and treating them. Moreover, many of the studies describe the rate of STDs among patients that have come to specialized services or family planning clinics: people that may not be representative of the general population. A serious drawback to this apparent richness of materials is that few are concerned with the behavioural or sociocultural underpinnings of STDs, especially the relation between such diseases and forms of nuptiality. Even studies on STDs that do address behaviour seldom touch on social status and nuptiality. Such oversights clearly reflect a lack of concern among clinicians and epidemiologists about the topic of nuptiality, although it is obviously important to their work.

The sociological variables used most often in studies on STDs, such as age, sex, income, education, occupation and marital status, appear to be useful for overall characterization of differences in the prevalence of these diseases. But they have proved to be weak correlates of STDs because they are used as substitutes or proxies for more precise risk factors that are rarely incorporated directly: age at the beginning of sexual activity as an indicator of the duration of exposure, number and type of sexual partners; detailed marital status; use of condoms; and the timeliness and efficacy of the treatment of STDs. Of major importance are the types of sexual union into which persons enter: different types of unions, with their related social status, obligations and expectations for partners and their families, have different implications for the range of sexual experiences that occur before and outside the union—elements that are important for understanding sexual behaviour and the prevalence of STDs. Relationships of marriage and parenting provide the person with a sense of meaning and purpose as well as a set of important obligations. In turn, the sense of meaning and the obligations affect the person's motivations, lifestyle and health behaviour (Umberson, 1987). Marital status is probably one of the major determinants of women's status.

The complexities of conjugal partnerships and roles in the family are crucial to present concerns for understanding the transmission of STDs and HIV. Unfortunately, both anthropological and demographic studies often view marital status categorically: people may be married, divorced, widowed or single. Few studies have considered polygamous unions, other forms of partnership or the importance of concubines, mistresses, *deuxième bureaux* (second offices), "outside wives" etc. Standard survey procedures often fail to capture the complexity and diversity of unions, particularly in urban settings: a man that has a customary marriage in a rural setting, cohabits in the city with a regular partner and sometimes stays with more casual partners may be classified simply as "married". The "legal" union classification masks semi-regular or occasional sexual relations which are crucial for the epidemiology of STDs and HIV.

STDs and nuptiality

Patterns of transmission of STDs have been linked to marriage patterns. For example, multiple marriages, either simultaneously or in sequence have been linked to greater risk than marriages with one partner. A recent study conducted in Cameroon, Kenya and the Sudan showed that women married more than once and women in polygamous unions were more frequently infertile than monogamous women in their first unions (Larsen, 1989). In some instances, these differences in conjugal and STD patterns may be linked to ethnic affiliation. A rural study in Uganda (Arya, Taber and Nsanze, 1980) compared the adults in the Teso region, where gonorrhoea was widespread and fertility was low, with those in Ankole region, where gonorrhoea was rare and fertility was high. Teso women were more likely to have had more than one marriage than the women from Ankole (33 versus 10 per cent). But it is not clear whether marriage was the cause or the effect. The greater number of marriages among Teso women could have derived from a greater proportion of infertile women (20 per cent of Teso women versus 2 per cent of Ankole women), with sterility rapidly leading to remarriage.

Although some attention has been given to ethnic patterns of transmission of STDs, urban correlates have drawn the most attention. In the study in Cameroon, Kenya and the Sudan, the education of the woman and her husband and the husband's profession were not significantly associated with the level of infertility. In contrast, STD levels were higher in cities than in rural settings, especially in the capitals. According to Larsen (1989), the higher prevalence of venereal diseases in the cities probably reflects more prostitution.

Quite apart from prostitution *per se*, however, the duration of urban residence appears to be an important correlate of STDs. A study in Kenya examined the sociodemographic predictors of contracting gonorrhoea (Verhaghen and Gemert, 1972): 444 urban male patients that came to a clinic for gonorrhoea were compared with a similar group without gonorrhoea. Multivariate analysis, controlling for age, indicated that correlates for whether a man had gonorrhoea were a long period of residence in the city and the lack of cohabitation with a wife or regular partner. Marital status as such was not significant (40 per cent in both groups were married), but cohabitation did appear to lower the risk of contracting gonorrhoea. Only 9 per cent of those with gonorrhoea lived regularly with their wives, compared with 19 per cent of those without gonorrhoea.

The rates of incidence (that is, the number of new cases during a given time period) of STDs are generally much higher in the city than in rural areas but because rural areas lack laboratories and qualified health personnel, it is sometimes difficult to determine the STD levels in rural areas (Arya and Lawson, 1977). Such diseases are usually less common in rural settings and are less easily treated there than in the city; their prevalence (number of cases in a defined population at a specific point in time) can thus be higher even though the incidence may be low. In the city, the situation is often the inverse—a low prevalence accompanied by a higher incidence—because there is more contagion but diseases are treated more readily. In Cameroon, for example, the prevalence rate of gonorrhoea among women in their reproductive years was estimated at 14 per cent in Yaoundé and at 22 per cent in rural areas (Nasah and others, 1980). When the interchange between city and countryside is extensive, or when circular migrations often take people far from their home communities, the rural setting can itself constitute a vast reservoir of STDs (Arya, Taber and Nsanze, 1980).

Like those of migration, the mechanisms of infection may be circulating and complex: young adults—men and, less commonly, women—migrate to the city to look for jobs to amass money for bridewealth or other marriage expenses and then return to their rural homes to marry. In those cases, STDs are contracted in the city through casual sexual relations or relations with prostitutes and are introduced into the rural populations. In other cases, the circulation involves only rural locales: young Fulani men of northern Cameroon, for example, who travel abroad in order to solidify a social network, often have sexual partners among divorced or married women (David and Voas, 1978).

The urban environment has been described as a place where behaviour is more individualistic, customary rules governing marriage are disappearing and acculturation is intensifying especially because of schooling and the diffusion of Western models of behaviour. Yet, stereotypical dichotomies of "urbanization, individualism and modernity" versus "village, community and tradition" obscure the fact that far from losing their ethnic or cultural identities, urban residents often adapt them to the demands or constraints of the new environment. Cultural practices can continue to define sexual and marital options (Parkin, 1966). Sexual freedom in the cities is thus not necessarily brought about by the abandonment of custom or transgression of control on their sexuality but may represent the adaptation of customary rules to a new environment. For example, respect for a long-lasting period of long post-partum female sexual abstinence after a birth, which is supported in rural settings by polygamy, may induce urban husbands to contract sexual relations outside of marriage with "free" (unmarried) women. One study found that the longer the duration of the post-partum abstinence at Ibadan, Nigeria, the more common were STDs (Caldwell and Caldwell, 1983).

Although part of the rise in STDs can result from adaptations to new environments, the notion of a "crisis" of disaster or social disintegration, can be applied to critical events that sharply intensify the spread of STDs. Wars, migration flows and economic crises—events that rupture social structures and break norms—are often associated with an increase in STDs (Hart, 1974). The vast sexual market in certain African cities, therefore, may be less a response that is culturally determined by a tradition among particular groups than the result of ruptures brought about by a series of society-wide misfortunes and subsequent efforts by persons to cope. More generally, widespread underemployment, the build-up of rural poverty resulting in an increase of migrants to cities and the dearth of opportunities that women face when divorced or abandoned pregnant by occasional partners (Robertson and Berger, 1986) can also be viewed as crisis situations leading to the spread of STDs and HIV.

Lesotho illustrates an extreme situation where massive male emigration leads to the absence of a large proportion of the adult male population; this long-term imbalance has as corollaries late marriage, the decline of polygamy, an increase in marital dissolution and frequent sexual relations outside of marriage (Timaeus and Graham, 1989). In a national survey based on a sample of 1,582 persons (Lesotho, 1989) 45 per cent of the men and 29 per cent of the women that were sexually active reported casual and commercial sexual relations during the preceding 12 months: vaginal/urethral discharge and pain for several days, as an approximate measure of gonorrhoea, was about 25 per cent. So common, apparently, are sexual exchanges among married adults because of the male partner's absence that married people or people that had been married reported that they had been treated in the past 12 months for those symptoms more often than sexually active single people (20 and 14 per cent, respectively).

For the epidemiology of STDs in Africa, it is probably the prostitutes and their clients, and the secondary contacts of their clients that run the greatest risks of infection. Little proposes as a definition of a prostitute a person "whose means of livelihood over a period of time depends wholly on the sale of sexual services and whose relationship with a customer does not extend beyond the sexual act" (1973, p. 84). This definition of the prostitute-client relationship is not entirely satisfactory and covers only one limited aspect of an often complex, ongoing relationship, although an important component is always the financial aspect.

The definitions of prostitution commonly employ obscure numerous problems in the African context. Under this rubric are grouped specific practices that do not necessarily bear the same meaning from one culture to another. And the concepts of sexuality, sexual relations and sexual partners are themselves relative and culturally specific, as are the exchange networks, the relationships between clients and prostitutes, and the place that they occupy in the sum total of sexual exchange. The data that follow often suffer from lack of clarity of the concepts used but they reflect, none the less, a specific aspect of the epidemiology of STDs.

Sexual relations with prostitutes are cited as a probable source of STD infection by 50-90 per cent of male patients: 50 per cent at Khartoum (Taha and others, 1979); 62 per cent in Ethiopia (Plorde, 1981); 84 per cent of the students at the University of Kampala (Arya and Bennett, 1974); 90 per cent of the patients at Butare (Meheus, De Clerq and Prat, 1974). At Nairobi, 90 per cent of male patients with gonococcal gonorrhoea declared that they had acquired their infection at the time of sexual contact with prostitutes (Plummer, 1988). By comparison, fewer than 30 per cent of male STD patients in Europe and in the United States of America stated prostitutes as the probable source of their infection (Turner and Morton, 1976; Potterat and others, 1980).

Those data suggest that in Africa, particularly in Eastern and Middle Africa, the relationships of men with prostitutes play a central role in the spread of STDs in urban areas. At Nairobi, a study among three groups of prostitutes (Kreiss and others, 1986) of high, medium and low socio-economic status showed that their numbers of clients per day were, respectively, 0.3, 5.0 and 5.6. The prevalence of gonorrhoea among them was 16, 28 and 46 per cent, respectively. Seventy per cent of the prostitutes studied had at least one STD. The mean time for reinfection by *N. gonorrhoeae* was 12 days.

Few studies have related prostitution patterns to local kinship organization and the relative position of women. In the strictly patrilineal societies of Eastern Africa, the wife possesses only minor personal belongings and has no independent source of income; female market activities are limited or non-existent. It is not surprising to find that in such societies, the majority of prostitutes are divorced, widowed or women abandoned with young children.

F. Knowledge and perceptions of AIDS

Current knowledge of attitudes and behaviour related to HIV/AIDS is limited, especially when related to gender issues. Presented here are some results of the surveys of knowledge, attitudes, beliefs and practices (KABP) based on nationally representative samples of adult men and women in selected countries of Africa. Sample sizes range from 1,600 to 3,000 and the age range is 15-44. All these surveys sponsored by the Global Programme on AIDS (GPA) of WHO were conducted by teams of national investigators during the period 1989-1991.

Knowledge of AIDS is generally high (table 20). Women are more likely than men to believe in HIV casual transmission (through shaking hands, sharing clothing, food and eating utensils, coughing, sneezing and insect bites), showing that a large proportion of women tend to extend to AIDS explanatory models developed in relation to other illnesses.

Women are less likely than men to discuss AIDS with family or with friends. Knowledge and communication are usually higher in cities among youth and persons with higher education.

Knowledge and reported use of condoms is significantly lower among women than men, highlighting the fact that men are probably using condoms in commercial sexual relations to protect themselves from STDs and that women are using them in the context of fertility control. The WHO/GPA data indicate that despite widespread awareness of AIDS, knowledge and use of condoms is still very low.

Large proportions of men and, to a lesser extent, of women perceive themselves "at risk of AIDS" (except in Mauritius). There is no evidence of widespread denial (table 21). In men, there is a positive association of higher risk perception with high-risk behaviour.

Classification of sexual relationships is extremely complex, especially in cross-national surveys. In the surveys, all sexual relationships that had lasted a year or more were classified as regular partnerships. At the other extreme, sexual encounters involving the giving or receipt of money or gifts were defined as commercial sex. The intermediate category was termed "casual sex". Commercial sex during the preceding 12 months varied from 1 to 19 per cent among men and from 0 to 15 per cent among women (table 21). Casual sex was highly prevalent among men, from 3 to 38 per cent, and to a lesser extent among women, from 1 to 28 per cent. The overall male-to-female ratio for engaging in casual sex was between two and three, except in Côte d'Ivoire, Mauritius and Togo, where it was even greater. A large difference between men and women in the prevalence of commercial sex is to be expected, because of the imbalanced ratio of female prostitutes to clients. For casual sex, a greater equality might be anticipated. This suggests that male and female respondents may interpret questions differently and that women may underreport the number of casual partners.

In most countries, the frequency of casual sex increases with urban residence and levels of schooling, particularly for men. Being single, separated, divorced or widowed, and being in free or cohabiting unions were associated with a higher frequency of casual sex (Caraël and others, 1991), a point that is further discussed below.

G. The case of Rwanda: HIV and nuptiality

The HIV epidemic in Rwanda is probably older than in other regions. A retrospective study found that already in 1982, 12 per cent of blood donors from Kigali were infected with HIV (Sontag, 1986). In 1987, a national study (Rwandan HIV Seroprevalence Study Group, 1989) established that HIV seroprevalence was 18 per cent in urban areas for the general population and 30 per cent among people aged 26-40. In rural settings, the prevalence was 1 per cent for the general population and 3 per cent among people aged 26-40.

In Rwanda, at any age, women were more likely to be HIV-infected than men. In the national HIV seroprevalence survey in Rwanda, women in urban areas were significantly more infected than men, when all ages are taken together (20.7 versus 15.5 per cent; $p < 0.05$). In Burundi, women in both urban and rural areas were significantly more infected than men (table 22). This difference in the rates of infection by sex could be due to an HIV transmission rate that is higher from men to women and the fact that infected men have greater numbers of partners than infected

TABLE 20. KNOWLEDGE OF AND DISCUSSION ABOUT AIDS, AND KNOWLEDGE AND USE OF CONDOMS, BY SEX, SUB-SAHARAN AFRICAN COUNTRIES

Knowledge and discussion	*Burundi*	*Central African Republic*	*Guinea-Bissau*	*Côte d'Ivoire*	*Kenya*	*Lesotho*	*Mauritius*	*Togo*
Percentage that have heard of AIDS								
Male	97	87	77	94	92	98	95	73
Female	96	78	72	86	90	98	88	56
Percentage that believe AIDS can be transmitted by:								
Sexual contact								
Male	99	96	94	91	85	96	97	94
Female	99	94	90	89	83	96	92	94
Casual contact								
Male	23	46	52	69	25	47	69	73
Female	27	41	45	81	27	50	70	79
Mean score of "discussion among family"								
Male	0.86	..	0.48	..	0.66	..	0.17	0.33
Female	0.70	..	0.33	..	0.64	..	0.23	0.23
Mean score of "discussion among friends"								
Male	1.3	..	0.95	..	1.1	..	0.75	0.64
Female	0.93	..	0.63	..	0.95	..	0.38	0.29

TABLE 21. PERCEIVED PERSONAL RISK IN COMMERCIAL AND CASUAL SEX, BY SEX, SUB-SAHARAN AFRICAN COUNTRIES

Perception	*Burundi*	*Central African Republic*	*Guinea-Bissau*	*Côte d'Ivoire*	*Kenya*	*Lesotho*	*Mauritius*	*Togo*
Percentage that have heard of condoms								
Male	63	54	71	54	71	79	92	54
Female	52	38	61	29	63	75	76	47
Percentage that have ever used condoms								
Male	15	20	31	28	15	15	39	13
Female	6	6	11	9	9	7	27	5
Percentage that perceive their personal risk to be somewhat or very likely								
Male	59	77	48	54	33	43	22	50
Female	52	79	34	37	28	33	21	53
Percentage that reported in the past 12 months								
Commercial sex								
Male	4	13	11	11	11	19	1	8
Female	1	5	2	8	7	15	0	1
Casual sex								
Male	8	3	39	31	21	38	9	20
Female	2	1	28	4	10	22	1	3

TABLE 22. HIV SEROPOSITIVITY IN ADULT POPULATION, BY SEX AND RURAL OR URBAN RESIDENCE, BURUNDI, 1989
(*Percentage*)

	Rural		*Urban*	
Age group	*Women* (*N* = *479*)	*Men* (*N* = *470*)	*Women* (*N* = *1,831*)	*Men* (*N* = *1,834*)
15-24	..	..	14.4	5.5
25-34	0.9	0.4	23.9	12.8
35-44	..	..	20.9	13.2
All	0.9	0.5	19.2	10.2

Source: Adapted from Burundi, *Enquête nationale de séroprévalence au VIN* (Bujumbura, Burundi, PNLS and World Health Organization, 1990).

women. Other possible factors include differences in exposures as a result of the age difference in infection rates (older men having sex with younger women) and similarly differences in age and gender-specific prevalence of STDs.

The national survey in Rwanda also found that divorced, separated or widowed people, and people living in informal unions were more likely to be HIV-infected than those living within marriage (table 23). A cohort study at Kigali in 1988, based on a representative study of 1,469 sexually active women aged 17-45 (Lindan and others, 1991), found an even clearer difference in terms of marital status and HIV infection: while only 22 per cent of married women were seropositive, 54 per cent of widows, divorcees and separated women were seropositive, as were 48 per cent of single people, and 35 per cent of women living in informal marriages. Similar results were shown at

TABLE 23. HIV SEROPOSITIVITY IN ADULT AGED 14 YEARS OR OVER, BY MARITAL STATUS AND RURAL OR URBAN RESIDENCE, RWANDA, 1987

	Percentage seropositive	
Marital status	*Rural* (*N* = *441*)	*Urban* (*N* = *1,529*)
Single	6.3	25.4
Married	0.4	13.0
Common-law union	3.3	27.4
Widowed, divorced separated	4.5	29.5
All statuses	2.0	21.8

Source: Adapted from data of the Rwandan HIV Seroprevalence Study Group, 1989.

Sassandra, Côte d'Ivoire, where women in free unions showed a relative risk of seropositivity of 7.1 compared with married women.

In Rwanda, civil, religious and customary marriage have been declining for more than a decade although the change cannot be clearly measured because of lack of precise data that separate marriages from free unions. The latter relationships, for instance, were included in the category of non-legitimate unions, as were polygamous unions. Civil or customary marriage implies the payment of the bride-wealth that links the families of the bride and groom and gives the patrilineage certain rights over the children. In former times, a couple married under customary procedures settled in a separate dwelling near the husband's parents with a parcel of land. Bride-wealth allowed the family to establish an equilibrium in the marriage exchange; the wealth received for girls permitted young men to marry. The total diminution of agricultural lands in Rwanda, the increase in population density and general poverty have considerably transformed the marriage system and have led to informal unions (Wils, Caraël and Tondeur, 1987).

Free unions or "common-law" marriage with regular or irregular cohabitation, without payment of the bride-wealth, have become widely accepted; yet they have a low status in Rwandan society and they exert fewer constraints on male sexual behaviour than formal legal marriages. Many free unions are transformed into formal marriages with the passage of time, the birth of children and the accumulation of a bit of financial capital, but others end in dissolution. In Rwanda in 1984, free unions represented 41 per cent of first unions; civil marriages, 44 per cent; and customary marriages, 15 per cent (Rwanda, 1985).

Lindan and others (1991) found that women in free unions generally had more infections than married women, after controlling for age (table 24). Furthermore, for a cohabitation lasting less than six years, women whose husband or partner had a higher monetary income were at greater risk of HIV seropositivity, compared with women with very low income, regardless of the nature of the union. Informal unions were, on average, shorter in duration than legal marriages and were more often associated with lower income (56 versus 29 per cent; $p < 0.001$). In addition, women in informal marriages more often declared that their unions were non-monogamous than married women (38 versus 24 per cent; $p < 0.001$). They were also more likely to report more than one regular union in their life. Both of those factors are associated with higher HIV seropositivity (table 25).

TABLE 24. HIV SEROPOSITIVITY IN WOMEN AGED 17-45, BY MARITAL STATUS, LENGTH OF UNION AND PARTNER'S INCOME, KIGALI, RWANDA, 1988
(Percentage)

	Length of union	
Marital status and income	*Less than six years*	*More than six years*
Married (N = 613)		
Lower income	24	16
Higher income	35	17
Common-law union (N = 568)		
Lower income	38	16
Higher income	52	39

Source: Christina Lindan and others, "Knowledge, attitudes, and perceived risk of AIDS among urban Rwandan women: relationship to HIV infection and behavior change", *AIDS* (London), vol. 5, No. 8 (August, 1991), pp. 993-1002.

NOTE: Income lower or higher = + or - 10,000 Rwandan francs (RF).

TABLE 25. PROPORTION OF HIV-SEROPOSITIVE WOMEN, BY NUMBER OF LIFETIME SEXUAL PARTNERS AND PERCEIVED RELATIONSHIP, RWANDA, 1988[a]
(Percentage)

Number of partners and perceived relationship	*Monogamous relationship*	*Non-monogamous relationship*[b]
One lifetime sexual partner	21 (N = 408)	36 (N = 246)
More than one	38 (N = 85)	51 (N = 253)

Source: Adapted from Christina Lindan and others, "Knowledge, attitudes, and perceived risk of AIDS among urban Rwandan women: relationship to HIV infection and behavior change",AIDS (London), vol. 5, No. 8 (August), pp. 993-1002.

[a]N = 992, excluding 21 per cent of women that did not know the status of their relationships; 12 per cent of them were seropositive.

[b]Non-monogamous relationships included women cohabiting with a spouse/regular partner with other partners (76 per cent), those cohabiting and reporting other partners (3 per cent) and sexually active women reporting other partners (21 per cent).

Informal unions reflect several marriage strategies. For a couple that is not doing well financially, informal unions represent a period of temporary cohabitation or a definitive union. For men with a high income, on the other hand, they constitute temporary liaisons. These men either "accumulate" women by issuing multiple marriage promises and by continuing to seek other partners for a marriage that is socially more advantageous or practise a discreet form of polygyny in a society that is predominantly Christian, without taking on the obligations that are traditionally attached to polygynous marriage. For women, free unions, though far from ideal, are preferable to divorce or separation; marriage options for women are reduced after the first union and are often responses to economic necessity. What resources women obtain from these unions allow them to become less dependent upon their parents. The evolution towards a greater range of forms of marriage resulting from different economic constraints has been described in other contexts (Cherlin and Chamratrithiyong, 1988; Comaroff and Roberts, 1977).

The increase in informal unions seems also to be associated with a general rise in the age at first marriage or union. Between 1976 and 1983, the mean age of entry into a union for women rose from 18.6 to 22.0 years (Rwanda, 1985). Men in urban areas may delay marrying because of higher levels of schooling, lack of financial resources and greater access to sexual partners outside marriage.

The apparent increase in age at entry into the first union for women accompanied a surprising decline in the mean age at first pregnancy (from 21.3 to 19.5 years) between 1978 and 1988. In addition, pregnancies in single women represented about 10 per cent of annual births in the prefecture of Butare in 1988 (Rwanda, 1989), a fact that supports the thesis that the age at which sexual activity begins is independent of the increase in the age of entry into the first union.

In urban areas, the high proportion of sexually active single men, both immigrants and residents, has important consequences in terms of sexual behaviour and STDs. Two groups in particular, blood donors and military personnel from Kigali, declared that they had had between 9 and 11 different sexual partners during the preceding year, the majority being prostitutes (Caraël and Piot, 1989b). A multivariate analysis indicated that the men most likely to have sex with prostitutes were single and slightly older (25-29 versus 20-24 years). Having a higher than average income was also associated with more contact with prostitutes. These data suggest that for men that can afford these services, going to prostitutes represents an important element in men's sexual transactions.

The role of prostitutes and their clients in the dynamics of an epidemic of STDs was illustrated by a retrospective analysis of the medical records of annual cohorts of the military contingent from Kigali between 1981 and 1986 (Caraël and Piot, 1989b). In 1981, 20 per cent of the recruits had been treated for STDs after two years of service; this proportion increased to 60 per cent in 1986. The soldiers enlisted after 1981 acquired similar rates of infection more quickly. Thus, 60 per cent of the 1984 recruits had been treated for such a disease after only two years of service and the per capita incidence of STDs also increased. Because there is no evidence that sexual behaviour in this particular group changed during five years, it was very clear that STD infection rates among the group of prostitutes near the military camp had risen because of increased infection among the soldiers.

A study at Butare, Rwanda (van de Perre and others, 1985 and 1976) analysed risks of HIV infection among prostitutes and their clients. The prostitutes were age 24 on average; they had a mean of two children and 82 per cent were single. They had practised their profession for an average of four years. They declared a monthly median of 44 partners, and only 5 per cent regularly used condoms. The results showed a positive serology for syphilis among 58 per cent of the prostitutes and 40 per cent of the clients (6 and 4 per cent, respectively, among the women and men of a control group); an immunofluorescence test indicated a positive reaction to *C. trachomatis* among 94 per cent of prostitutes and 25 per cent of clients. In this context, an outbreak of HIV became an immediate epidemic; 88 per cent of prostitutes and 28 per cent of clients were seropositive. The likelihood of being seropositive increased significantly with the number of contacts with the prostitutes. The median number of prostitutes that those clients saw each year was 31, compared with three sexual partners per year among members of the control group. In such a situation, the dynamic of HIV infection extends far beyond those target groups.

A study among 124 couples (Caraël and others, 1988), of whom one or both partners were infected by HIV, found that in nearly half of the cases, one of the two partners had previously been in at least one union (table 26). Compared with 150 seronegative couples, the male partners of infected couples were more likely to have: (*a*) experienced long periods of sexual activity before entering their first union (7.2 versus 4.6 years); (*b*) had contact with prostitutes (81.5 versus 27.3 per cent); (*c*) had a higher frequency of contacts (2.1 versus 1.5 per month); and (*d*) had a history of STD in the two preceding years (64.5 versus 15.3 per cent). Furthermore, they were more likely to have travelled frequently to the interior of Rwanda (25 versus 6 per cent, with more than one week per month) events that may have created opportunities for contact with casual sexual partners.

The women in the infected couples were more often in free unions (65 versus 48 per cent). But the seropositive women, like seropositive men, were more likely to have experienced more than one regular union (31.4 versus 5.3 per cent). Compared with women in seronegative couples, these women were more often in polygamous unions (20 versus 3 per cent).

Polygamy apparently intensified two risk factors: (*a*) the man's accumulation of several sexual partners; and (*b*) the women's likelihood of having been in other unions. But although the women in the infected couples were more likely to report episodes of STDs (47.6 versus 11.3 per cent), the study concluded that the risk factors for STDs/HIV infection in the unions were principally those related to male sexual behaviour.

An intervention among a representative sample of 1,458 child-bearing women in the same city, consisting of educational video, HIV testing and counselling, and distribution of free condoms and spermicide was evaluated during two years of follow-up (Allen and others, 1992). Only 7 per cent of the women reported ever trying condoms before the intervention, but 22 per cent reported condom use one year after HIV testing; comparable figures for spermicides were 2 and 10 per cent. HIV-seropositive women were more likely to adopt condom use than HIV-seronegative women (36 versus 16 per cent).

TABLE 26. HIV-SEROPOSITIVE AND HIV-SERONEGATIVE COUPLES, BY SOCIODEMOGRAPHIC VARIABLES AND RISK BEHAVIOUR, KIGALI, RWANDA, 1986

Sociodemographic variables and bahaviour	*Seropositive couples (N = 124)*	*Seronegative couples (N = 150)*
Age, median (years)		
Men	32.2	31.9
Women	26.2	26.5
Age at first sexual intercourse (years)		
Men	18.7	19.7
Women	19.4	19.0
Duration of premarital sexual activity, median (years)		
Men	7.2	4.6[a]
Women	0.6	0.3
Duration of union, median (years)	5.6	5.3
Monogamous union (percentage)	79.8	96.7[b]
First union (percentage)		
Men	73.4	82.0
Women	68.6	94.7[b]
Parity, median (n)	2.2	2.7
History of STD in past two years (percentage)		
Men	64.5	15.3[b]
Women	47.6	11.3[c]
Male sexual contacts with prostitutes (percentage)	77.9	27.3[b]

Source: Adapted from Michel Caraël and others, "Human immunodeficiency virus transmission among heterosexual couples in Central Africa", *AIDS* (London), vol. 2, No. 2 (June 1988), pp. 201-205.

NOTE: STD = sexually transmitted disease.

[a] $p<0.01$.

[b] $p<0.001$.

Predictors of condom use for the sample included whether the male partner received HIV testing and counselling and having a non-monogamous relationship. Of concern was the finding that HIV-seronegative women with untested partners were the group least likely to use condoms and the rate of HIV seroconversion in this group was more than twice that for women whose partners were tested and counselled. In areas where the epidemic has spread to groups that may not realize they are vulnerable because of partner behaviour, enhancing the perception of risk should be a goal of future intervention.

H. CONCLUSION

Based on the observations made in urban areas of Rwanda and other cities of Eastern Africa and Middle Africa, the following generalization can be suggested: the greater the imbalance in sexual freedom between men and women, the more rapid the progress of the HIV/STD epidemic (Caraël and others, 1987). When men are not constrained, yet the virginity of young girls and the faithfulness of married women remain norms, single men commonly seek the services of prostitutes. Once they are married, moreover, a large percentage may continue to frequent prostitutes. The rapid spread of HIV infection among prostitutes is intensified by their numerous sexual partners—between 500 and 1,500 clients per annum—and by the high prevalence of STDs among clients. This high prevalence in turn increases the rates at which prostitutes infect a variety of other clients of different ages and social networks (for example, rural migrant workers or young men in search of money in cities) and results eventually in the contamination of the clients' regular female partners. These particular characteristics of its transmission may help explain why HIV infection spreads at an exponential pace, as it has at Kigali, Kampala, Lusaka and Nairobi (Caraël and Piot, 1989b).

These situations of rapid evolution of HIV/STD infection should be compared with other cultural contexts where, paradoxically, sexual liberty for both sexes actually limits the spread of HIV infection. In that case, men turn to commercial sexual relations less often, meaning that there is little concentration of numerous sexual partners around a small number of women. The fluidity of sexual relations and the diversity of possible unions—*deuxième bureau*, mistresses etc.—slows the development of both the HIV and other STD epidemics and confines them to limited networks. The HIV epidemic at Kinshasa, Zaire, which has stabilized at the level of 5-6 per cent of the adult population during the past five years, probably corresponds to this latter model.

The important point to stress is that urban situations themselves do not necessarily intensify transmission of HIV/STDs. Rather, inequalities in male and female social status and sexual behaviour, and particularly the double standard in urban areas where men marry late and may accumulate casual partners as a sign of status or most probably as a transgression of traditional control on their sexuality (which still exists in many rural areas) while women are expected to be faithful to one partner, appears to be a social structure that is particularly susceptible to the AIDS epidemic. In such a context, women do not have any control of resources for decision-making, particularly in the sexual relationship. In urban societies that allow women to adopt a variety of marital strategies and that facilitate, through the flexibility of forms of unions, their entry or re-entry into marriages, whether monogamous or polygamous, may even keep the spread of HIV from becoming an epidemic.

Whereas this study has examined some effects of forms of union on STD and HIV epidemics, the possible effect of the perception of the HIV epidemic on conjugal behaviour is relevant as well. No specific study so far has attempted to evaluate this question. None the less, a shift towards monogamous unions and a greater stability of unions as a response to the threat of the epidemic seems unlikely in urban contexts of economic decline where conjugal strategies become elements of survival for individuals. The change that appears to be more likely and, indeed, has already appeared in several surveys on sexual behaviour is the shift towards more protective behaviour (the use of condoms) within relations that are strictly commercial (van de Walle, 1990; Caraël and others, 1991). This change could reduce the incidence of HIV and STDs without eliminating them altogether. Should that happen, infection by HIV would become another item on the list of endemic tropical diseases.

Specific recommendations on HIV/STD

First, sex education should be initiated early in life to encourage deep reflection on male and female roles in society in order to reduce discrimination against women. Sex education has often focused mostly on women, whose risks from sexual activity are greater than men's. Education, information and access to the means for prevention of STDs/HIV should be provided, beginning in adolescence. This aspect is part of sex education but merits separate mention. Appropriate sex education may reduce the incidence of STDs by warning against risky sexual behaviour, but this is not enough to prevent transmission among sexually active adolescents and adults. Appropriate protection, such as condoms, will significantly reduce the risk of all STDs, from the less severe vaginitis to cervical cancer and AIDS. Information on condoms, and on their correct use, and training on skills to negotiate their use should be part of the curriculum.

Secondly, there is a need to emphasize the improvement of STD services since, traditionally, not enough attention has been given to the provision of adequate and accessible services for the prevention and control of STDs. In many countries, these services have not been adequate because, like most of the health sector, they have been understaffed and underfunded. In addition, they have often been stigmatized. This attitude has made it difficult for large segments of the population, particularly women and vulnerable social groups, such as female prostitutes, to use STD services when needed. The ratio of men to women using such services often exceeds 10:1. It is therefore imperative to destigmatize STD services and to widen the range of service delivery points to include a variety of other health settings, such as family planning clinics, maternal and child health clinics, general urology clinics, dermatology clinics, pharmacies, and public and private hospitals. Special efforts should also be made to ensure that the services are more accessible to those practising behaviour leading to high-frequency transmission of HIV and STDs.

Thirdly, it is important to take into account the special needs of women, who are often not in the position to take decisive action in the domain of sexual relationships, and encourage partner notification. In addition, most of the sexually transmitted diseaes in women tend to be asymptomatic and hard for a woman to recognize and seek treatment. Thus, an improvement in women's access to health services in general, and STD services in particular, would be crucial to protect not only their sexual health and fertility but also their overall health and well-being.

Fourthly, in addition to improving access to services, it is important to improve information and education activities for HIV and AIDS prevention. People engaging in high-risk sexual practices and/or their partners are likely to be in one-time or repeated contact with STD services; those services therefore provide an excellent opportunity to reach this key audience not only with diagnosis and treatment but also with education. STD clinics and services can be used to provide open, relevant, specific and targeted prevention and care messages to persons at risk of both AIDS and STDs at a time when they are in most need.

Information, education and communication activities on AIDS and STDs should not be concentrated on the latter services alone. Other communication and education channels (including the mass media, outreach, health-care settings and institutional networks and sex education in schools) should not be overlooked, especially as they raise public awareness of AIDS and STDs and provide a broader context for the acceptance and reinforcement of the information provided through the STD services. In addition, they can provide information to those that, for legal, cultural, access, economic or other reasons, do not visit such services but seek treatment through other sources or do not seek them at all.

The content of the educational messages should be carefully planned, making sure that it is adequate to the needs of the target audiences and is perceived as relevant by them. There is also a need to find ways that more effectively use information, education and communication strategies to improve health-seeking behaviour among persons engaging in risky practices and/or their partner.

Lastly, it is also important to stress the role of condom promotion and distribution because this is the best tool currently available for the prevention of both AIDS and STDs among sexually active populations. Notwithstanding all the difficulties, much more should be done in the area of condom promotion and procurement to ensure both availability of good quality and affordable condoms to all those in need and increased use of condoms by all those at risk of STD and HIV infection. Family planning services should include AIDS/STD prevention and condom provision in their activities.

NOTES

[1] The relative efficiency of male-to-female compared with female-to-male HIV transmission is still debated. Results from cross-sectional and longitudinal studies of couples consisting of one HIV-infected partner show a 20 per cent transmission rate from infected men to their female sexual partners. Data of transmission from infected women to their male sexual partners are not consistent, ranging from no transmission to less than 10 per cent (Padian, Shibaski and Jewell, 1991). The important fact is that in most of the studies, HIV male-to-female transmission is consistently higher and that acquisition of HIV infection from a sex partner was not correlated with frequency of intercourse with the infected partner. This finding suggests that in absence of advanced disease and of facilitating risk factors, such as STDs, transmission is less likely to occur. However, the hetegeroneity of infectiousness suggests that certain HIV strains are transmitted after only one or a few encounters, while others are not despite multiple unprotected episodes. This variability increases the risks associated with multiple partners because the random chance of being exposed to a high-frequency transmitter increases (Holmberg and others, 1989). Other biological factors that are suspected to facilitate sexual transmission of HIV are duration of HIV infection and/or more advanced clinical stage, sexual intercourse during menses and possibly lack of circumcision in men. However, STDs are suspected to play a much more important role in HIV transmission or acquisition.

[2]Prostitutes often represent an extremely mobile group; at Mombasa, Kenya, they came from 40 different ethnic groups and seven countries of Western Africa; 40 per cent of them had lived in the city for less than one year (Verhaghen and Gemert, 1972).

REFERENCES

Allen, S., and others (1992). Confidential HIV testing and condom promotion in Africa: impact on HIV and gonorrhea rates in a representative sample of urban women. To be published in the *British Medical Journal* (London).

Arya, Om Prakagh, and Francis J. Bennett (1974). VD control: a case study of university students in Uganda. *International Journal of Health Education* (Geneva), vol. 17, No. 1, pp. 53-65.

Arya, Om Prakagh, and J. B. Lawson (1977). Sexually transmitted diseases in the tropics: epidemiological, diagnostic, therapeutic and control aspects. *Tropical Doctor* (London), vol. 7, No. 2 (April), pp. 51-56.

Arya, Om Prakagh, S. R. Taber, and H. Nsanze H. (1980). Gonorrhea and female infertility in rural Uganda. *American Journal of Obstetrics and Gynecology* (St. Louis, Missouri), vol. 138, No. 7 (1 December), pp.929-932.

Barton, T. (1988). Sexually-related illness in Eastern and Central Africa: a selected bibliography. In *AIDS in Africa: The Social and Policy Impact*, Norman Miller and Richard C. Rockwell, eds. Lewiston, New York: The Edwin Mellen Press.

Bennett, F. J. (1962). The social determinants of gonorrheoa in an East African town. *East African Medical Journal* (Nairobi, Kenya), vol. 39, No. 6, pp. 332-342.

Burundi (1990). *Enquête nationale de séroprévalence au VIH.* Bujumbura: PNLS and World Health Organization

Caldwell, John C., and Pat Caldwell (1983). The demographic evidence for the incidence and cause of abnormally low fertility in tropical Africa. *World Health Statistics Quarterly* (Geneva), vol. 36, No. 1, pp. 2-34.

Cameron, D. W., and others (1989). Female to male transmission of human immunodeficiency virus type I: risk factors for seroconversion in men. *The Lancet* (London; and Baltimore, Maryland), No. 8660 (19 August), pp. 403-407.

Caraël, Michel, and Peter Piot (1989a). HIV infection in developing countries. In *Health Interventions and Mortality Change in Developing Countries,* Allan G. Hill and D. F. Roberts, eds. Supplement 10 to *Journal of Biosocial Science* (Cambridge, United Kingdom). Cambridge: Parkes Foundation.

_________ (1989b). Le SIDA en Afrique: aspects épidémiologiques et sociaus. In *Mortalié et société en Afrique,* Gilles Pison, Etienne Van de Walle and Mpembele Sala-Diakanda, eds. Institut national d'études démographiques, Travaus et documents, Cahier No. 124. Paris: Presses universitaires de France.

Caraël, Michel, and others (1985). Socio-cultural factors in relation to HTLV-III/LAV transmission in urban areas in Central Africa. Abstract 05.1. In *The First International Symposium on AIDS in Africa.* Brussels.

_________, and others (1987). Le SIDA en Afrique. In *Le SIDA: rumeurs et faits.* Paris: Les éditions du Cerf.

_________, and others (1988). Human immunodeficiency virus transmission among heterosexual couples in Central Africa. *AIDS* (London), vol. 2, No. 2 (June), pp. 201-205.

_________, and others (1991). Research on sexual behaviour that transmits HIV: the GPA/WHO Collaborative Surveys, preliminary findings. In *Seminar on Anthropological Studies Relevant to the Sexual Transmission of HIV, Sonderborg, Denmark, 19-22 November 1990.* Sponsored by the International Union for the Scientific Study of Population.. Liege: Ordina Press.

Cates, W., T. M. M. Farley and P. J. Rowe (1985). Worldwide patterns of infertility: is Africa different?. *The Lancet* (London; and Baltimore, Maryland), No. 8455 (14 September), pp. 596-598.

Cherlin, A., and A. Chamratrithirong (1988). Variations in marriage patterns in central Thailand. *Demography* (Washington, D.C.), vol. 25, No. 3 (August), pp. 337-353.

Chin, James (1991). Global estimates of AIDS cases and HIV infections:1990. *AIDS* (London), vol. 4, Supplement 1, pp. 277-283.

Comaroff, J. P., and S. Roberts (1977). Marriage and extra-marital sexuality. *Journal of African Law Digest* (Addis Ababa, Ethiopia), vol. 21, No. 1, pp.97-123.

David, Nicholas, and David Voas (1978). Societal causes of infertility and population decline among the settled Fulani of North Cameroon. *Man* (London), vol. 16, No. 4 (December), pp. 644-664.

De Cock, K., and others (1991). AIDS: the leading cause of adult death in the West African city of Abidjan, Ivory Coast. *Science* (Washington, D.C.), vol. 249, No. 4970 (17 August), pp. 793-796.

Erhardt, J., and J. Wasserheit (1991). Age, gender and sexual risk behavior for STD in the United States. In *Research in Human Behavior and Sexually Transmitted Diseases in the AIDS Era,* Judith N. Wasserheit, Seqvi O. Aral and King K. Holmes, eds. Washington D.C.: American Society for Microbiology.

Galega, F., D. F. Heymann and B. T. Nasah (1984). Gonococcal ophtalmia neonatorium: the case for prophylaxis in tropical Africa. *Bulletin of the World Health Organization* (Geneva), vol. 62, No. 1, pp. 95-98.

Greenblatt, R. M., and others (1988). Genital ulcerations as a risk factor for human immunodeficiency virus infection. *AIDS* (London), vol. 2, No. 1 (January), pp. 47-50.

Griffith, H. B. (1963). Gonorrheoa and fertility in Uganda. *The Eugenics Review* (London), vol. 55, No. 2, (July) pp. 103-108.

Hart, Gavin (1974). Factors influencing venereal infection in a war environment. *British Journal of Venereal Diseases* (London), vol. 50, No. 1 (February), pp. 50-68.

Holmberg, Scott D., and others (1989). Biologic factors in the sexual transmission of human immunodeficiency virus. *Journal of Infectious Diseases* (Chicago, Illinois), vol. 60, No. 1 (1 July), pp. 116-125.

Kreiss, Joan K., M. Caraël and A. Meheus (1988). Role of sexually transmitted diseases in transmitting human immunodeficiency virus. Editorial. *Genitourinary Medicine* (London), vol. 64, No. 1 (February), pp. 1-2.

Kreiss, Joan K., and others.(1986). AIDS virus infection in Nairobi prostitutes: spread of the epidemic to East Africa. *The New England Journal of Medicine* (Boston, Massachusetts), vol. 314, No. 7 (3 February), pp. 414-418.

Laga, M., M. Nzila and J. Goeman (1991). The interrelationship of STD and HIV infection: implications for the control of both epidemics in Africa. *AIDS* (London), No. 5, supplement, pp. S55-S63.

Lancet (1982). Chancroid. Editorial. *The Lancet* (London; and Baltimore, Maryland), No. 8301 (2 October), pp. 747-748.

Larsen, U. (1989). Levels and differentials of sterility. In *Reproduction and Social Organization in Sub-Saharan Africa,* Ron Lesthaeghe, ed. Berkeley: University of California Press.

Lesotho (1989). *Knowledge, Attitudes, Beliefs and Practices about AIDS: National Survey.* Lesotho: National AIDS Programme and World Health Organization.

Lesthaege, Ron, ed. (1989). *Reproduction and Social Organization in Sub-Saharan Africa.* Berkeley: University of California Press.

Lindan, Christina P., and others (1991). Knowledge, attitudes, and perceived risk of AIDS among urban Rwandan women: relationship to HIV infection and behavior change. *AIDS* (London, vol. 5, No. 8 (August), pp. 993-1002.

Lindan, Christina P., and others (1992). Predictors of mortality among HIV-infected women in Kigali, Rwanda. *Annals of Internal Medicine* (Philadelphia, Pennsylvania), vol. 116, No. 4 (15 February), pp. 320-328.

Little, Kenneth Lindsay (1973). *African Women in Towns: An Aspect of Africa's Social Revolution.* London and New York: Cambridge University Press.

Lourdes D' Costa, J., and others (1985). Prostitutes are a major reservoir of sexually transmitted diseases in Nairobi, Kenya. *Sexually Transmitted Diseases* (Philadelphia, Pennsylvania), vol 12, No. 2 (April-June), pp. 64-67.

Mabey, David C. W. (1986). Syphilis in sub-Saharan Africa. *African Journal of Sexually Transmitted Diseases* (Nairobi, Kenya), (October), pp. 61-66.

Meheus, A., A. De Clercq and R. Prat (1974). Prevalence of gonorrheoa in prostitutes in a Central African town. *British Journal of Venereal Diseases* (London), vol. 50, No. 1 (February), pp. 50-52.

_________, J. Reniers and M. Collet (1986). Determinants of infertility in Africa. *African Journal of Sexually Transmitted Diseases* (Nairobi, Kenya), (October), pp. 31-36.

Muir, D. G., and M. A. Belsey (1980). Pelvic inflammatory disease and its consequence in the developing world. *American Journal of Obstetrics and Gynecology* (St. Louis, Missouri), vol. 138, No. 7 (1 December), pp. 913-928.

Nasah, B. T., and others (1980). Gonorrhea, trichomonas and candida among gravid and non gravid women in Cameroon. *International Journal of Gynecology and Obstetrics* (Limerick, Ireland), vol. 14, pp. 48-52.

Nkowane, B. (1991). Prevalence and incidence of HIV infection in Africa: a review of data published in 1990. *AIDS* (London), No. 1, supplement, pp. S7-15.

Padian, Nancy, S. C. Shiboski and N. P. Jewell (1991). Female-to-male transmission of HIV. *Journal of the American Medical Association* (Chicago, Illinois), vol. 266, No. 12 (25 September), pp. 1664-1667.

Parkin, David (1966). Types of urban African marriage in Kampala. *Africa: Journal of the International African Institute* (Edinburgh, Scotland), vol. 36, No. 3 (July), pp. 269-285.

Plorde, Diane S. (1981). Sexually transmitted diseases in Ethiopia: social factors contributing to their spread and implications for developing countries. *British Journal of Venereal Diseases* (London), vol. 57, No. 6 (December), pp. 357-362.

Plummer, F. (1988). Unpublished data.

Potterat, John J., and others. (1980). Gonococcal pelvic inflammatory disease: case-finding observations. *American Journal of Obstetrics and Gynecology* (St. Louis, Missouri), vol. 138, No. 7 (1 December), pp. 1101-1104.

Ratnam, Attili V., and others.(1982). Syphilis in pregnant women in Zambia. *British Journal of Venereal Diseases* (London), vol. 58, No. 6 (December), pp. 355-358.

Retel-Laurentin, A. (1974). *Infécondité en Afrique noire: maladies et conséquences sociales.* Paris: Masson.

Romaniuk, Anatole (1967). *La fécondité des populations congolaises.* Paris: Mouton.

Robertson, Claire, and Iris Berge, eds. (1986). *Women and Class in Africa.* New York: Africana Publishing Co.

Rwanda (1988). *Enquête national connaissances, attitudes et croyances à l'égard du Sida.* Kigali: PNLS and World Health Organization.

Rwanda, Office national de la population (1985). *Enquête nationale sur la fécondité, 1983.* Kigali.

__________ (1989). *Aspects socio-culturels des grossesses no désirées des jeunes filles rwandaises de la préfecture de Butare, Rwanda.* Kigali.

Rwandan HIV Seroprevalence Study Group (1989). Nationwide community-based serological survey of HIV-1 and other human retrovirus infections in a Central African country. *The Lancet* (London; and Baltimore, Maryland), vol. I for 1987, No. 8644 (29 April), pp. 941-943.

Schulz, K. F., W. Cates, Jr. and P. R. O'Mara (1987). Pregnancy loss, infant death and suffering: legacy of syphilis and gonorrhoea in Africa. *Genitourinary Medicine* (London), vol. 63, No. 5 (October), pp. 320-325.

Simonsen, J. Neil, and others (1988). Human immunodeficiency virus infection among men with sexually transmitted diseases: experience from a center in Africa. *The New England Journal of Medicine* (Boston, Massachusetts), vol. 319, No. 5 (4 August), pp. 274-278.

Sontag, D. (1988). Unpublished data.

Taha, O. M., and others (1979). Study of STDs in patients attending venereal disease clinics in Karthoum, Sudan. *British Journal of Venereal Diseases* (London), vol. 55, No. 5 (October), pp. 313-315.

Timaeus, J., and W. Graham (1989). Labor circulation, marriage and fertility in Southern Africa. In *Reproduction and Social Organization in Sub-Saharan Africa,* Ron Lesthaeghe, ed. Berkeley: University of California Press.

Torrey, Barbara B., and Peter O. Way (1990). *Seroprevalence of HIV in Africa: Winter 1990.* Center for International Research Staff Paper, No. 55. Washington, D.C. United States Bureau of the Census.

Turner, E. Barbara, and R. S. Morton (1976). Prostitution in Sheffield. *British Journal of Venereal Diseases* (London), vol. 52, No. 3 (June), pp. 197-203.

Umberson, Debra (1987). Family status and health behaviors: social control as a dimension of social integration. *Journal of Health and SociaBehavior* (Washington, D.C.), vol. 28, No. 3 (September), pp. 306-319.

United Nations (1991). *World Population Prospects, 1990.* Sales No. E.91.XIII.4.

Van de Perre, Philippe, and others (1985). Female prostitutes: a risk group for infection with human T-cell lymphotropic virus type III. *The Lancet* (London; and Baltimore, Maryland), No. 8454 (7 September), pp. 524-526.

_________, and others (1987a). HIV antibodies in a remote rural area in Rwanda in Central Africa: an analysis of potential risk factors for HIV seropositivity. *AIDS* (London), vol. 1, No. 4, pp. 213-215.

_________, and others (1987b). Risk factors for HIV seropositivity in selected urban-based Rwandese adults. *AIDS* (London), vol. 1, No.4, pp. 207-211.

_________, and others (1987c). Seroepidemiological study on STD and hepatitis B in African promiscuous heterosexuals in relation to HTLV-III infection. *European Journal of Epidemiology* (Stuttgart, Germany), No. 1, pp. 14-18.

_________, and others (1988). Detection of HIV p17 antigen in lymphocytes but not epithelial cells from cervicovaginal secretions of women seropositive for HIV: implications for heterosexual transmission of the virus. *Genitourinary Medicine* (London), vol. 64, No. 1 (February), pp. 30-33.

_________, and others (1991). Postnatal transmission of human immunodeficiency virus type 1 from mother to infant. *The New England Journal of Medicine* (Boston, Massachusetts), vol. 325, No. 9 (29 August), pp. 593-598.

Van de Walle, Etienne (1990). The social impact of AIDS in sub-Saharan Africa. *The Milbank Memorial Fund Quarterly* (New York), vol. 68, Supplement, pp. 10-32.

Verhaghen, A. R., and W. Gemert (1972). Social and epidemiological determinants of gonorrhoea in an East African country. *British Journal of Venereal Diseases* (London), vol. 48, No. 4 (August), pp. 277-286.

Wils, W., M. Caraël and G. Tondeur (1987). *Le Kivu montagneux: surpopulation, malnutrition et érosion des sols.* Bruxelles: Académie Royale des Sciences d'Outremer.

World Health Organization (1990). Unpublished data.

XII. WOMEN'S PARTICIPATION AND PERSPECTIVES IN HEALTH ISSUES: WORKING NOTES

*Rita Thapa**

Women are not only users but also major providers of health care in both formal and non-formal[1] sectors. They form the majority of health workers: community health workers; traditional birth attendants; midwives; nurses; laboratory and research workers; doctors; and many others. Most of the births in developing countries take place under the care of traditional birth attendants. The proportions of female health workers in the formal health system range from 24 per cent in some developing countries to 72 per cent in some developed countries (Pizurki and others, 1987). The proportion of female doctors ranges from 3 to 30 per cent in developing countries and from 8 to 70 per cent in developed countries (WHO, 1991d). Women are natural health educators. They contribute substantively to the food and nutrition supply of the family. By virtue of their dual role as providers and users of reproductive health care, women are uniquely endowed to bring a more balanced user-provider perspective, thus assuring a better quality and utilization of maternal and child health and family planning services (MCH/FP).

Women's participation and perspective in health relates to their rights, responsibilities and empowerment in all aspects of health development. Operationally, it means enabling women's participation, by incorporating their needs and feelings, in the planning, implementation and evaluation of all aspects of health development. In short, women's participation forms the very cornerstone of achieving Health for All by the Year 2000 (WHO, 1978).

Over the years, the World health Organization (WHO), through its programme on women, health and development, has made considerable progress towards improving the status and role of women in health. Among the important outcomes are: the promotion, collection and dissemination of gender-specific health data; the promotion of women's perspectives, participation and leadership in health and development; and the promotion of women's role and status in health and health-related matters from family to national decision-making levels. Through resolution WHA42.42, a network of multisectoral teams consisting of representatives of women's organizations, the Government's focal points on women in development and managers of national MCH/FP programmes, has been established in 32 countries covering six WHO regions (WHO, 1992b). Building the capacity of multisectoral team action on promoting women's leadership and participation in MCH/FP has been its main objective, in both substantive and methodological terms. The teams in 10 of those countries have initiated research action on promoting women's leadership and participation in matters related to MCH/FP.

A. Why women's participation and perspectives matter

Existing research information, though limited, highlights the importance of the role of women health workers in improving user-provider relations and incorporating users' feelings in delivering MCH/FP services. A recent review of workers' performances in Bangladesh indicated that female workers spent more time with family planning clients, were more likely to recommend a range of family planning methods and were less likely to push women to sterilization (Phillips and others, 1986). Compared with physicians, nurses were more likely to change the family planning method used, possibly an indicator of concern for users' perspectives. The study also showed that with "conscientious and caring workers" and with involvement of local women and men, the percentage of women in Matlab using contraceptives rose from 7 to 33 per cent within 18 months (Phillips and others, 1988).

*Maternal and Child Health, Family Planning and Population, Division of Family Health, World Health Organization, Geneva, Switzerland.

Fauveau and others (1991) report that in a community-based study in Matlab, posting midwives at the community level and empowering them to refer complex cases and/or treating complications in the home brought about a 68 per cent reduction of maternal mortality in only three years.

A recent World Bank country study on gender and poverty in India notes some health improvements due to empowerment of women and traditional birth attendants (*dai*) in rural areas of India. One is the provision of safe delivery kits to mothers so that at the time of delivery, regardless of the *dai*'s presence, the umbilical cord can be cleanly cut and cared for, reducing the risk of neonatal tetanus. The other innovation is the provision of an additional incentive (money) for *dais* to attend and report births (World Bank, 1991).

B. Women's situation and role in health

A brief analysis of the situation and role of women in MCH/FP will provide insight into the current types and levels of women's participation and perspectives in health care. The priority issue is their health during childhood and their reproductive years, for it affects not only women's immediate and strategic health needs but also those of their children both born and unborn. Furthermore, the issues relating to MCH/FP[2] concern the health of two thirds of the total population in developing countries, thus decisively affecting the attainment of the Health for All and the common goals of the United Nations Children's Fund (UNICEF), the United Nations Population Fund (UNFPA) and WHO.

The second evaluation of the Global Strategy for Health for All indicates that despite some progress in the provision of health care, equity and social justice remain a distant goal. The health situation of women remains precarious and in some situations is worsening (WHO, 1992a).

Despite the steady decline in infant and child mortality, and despite the biological advantage of females (girls are more resistant to infection and malnutrition), the mortality rate of the female child is higher than that of the male child in a number of developing countries (WHO, 1991d). In a number of developing countries, mortality among girls in age group 2-5 is commonly higher than that of boys in the same age group (United Nations, 1991). Analysis of sex-specific mortality by cause in Latin America and the Caribbean has found an excess of female mortality among children aged 1-4 years, with more girls than boys dying from diseases preventable by immunization (Gomez, 1991).

Several studies have suggested that the existing higher mortality rates of the girl child in many developing countries are not due to poverty or biological reasons, but simply to son preference, leading to discriminatory treatment of girls in terms of food provision and even parental care (Waldron, 1987). Coale (1991) estimates the total number of missing females as a result of such discriminatory practices is about 60 million (Drèze and Sen, 1989). In view of this situation, incorporation of sex-disaggregated databases should become a routine practice in any child survival programme, especially in developing countries.

In all developing countries, coverage of prenatal care and attended child birth by trained personnel appears to have improved, but the number of women dying from complications related to pregnancy and childbirth in those countries remains unchanged. The slight upward trend in maternal mortality in parts of Africa and Asia during 1983-1988 reflects, *inter alia*, the deteriorating economic and health conditions of women (WHO, 1991c). Ninety-nine per cent of some 500,000 annual maternal deaths take place in the developing world, which accounts for 86 per cent of the world births. Such a high rate of maternal deaths for women in developing countries reflects the cumulative health effect of women's unequal access to and control over maternal and child health care from childhood onward.

Despite women's major role in the production and preparation of family food, more than 50 per cent of pregnant women worldwide suffer from nutritional anaemia, one of the leading causes of maternal mortality and low birth weight (WHO, 1992a).

Furthermore, women's inadequate access to quality care during pregnancy and childbirth in developing countries results in a large number of infant deaths.

This is because more than 50 per cent of infant deaths in developing countries occur within the first month after birth (Rutstein, 1983), mostly due to preventable health problems related to pregnancy and childbirth.

Despite the well-known benefits of timing, spacing and control of births on maternal and child mortality, as many as 300 million women of reproductive age in developing countries do not have access to modern methods of family planning. Demographic and Health Surveys indicate that although 9 out of 10 women wish to space births two years apart or more, only two thirds are able to do so. It is estimated that if women desirous of spacing births had the means to do so, about 50 per cent of maternal mortality and 21 per cent of child mortality could be prevented (UNFPA, 1992). A current WHO estimate indicates that 20-40 per cent of maternal deaths are caused by complications of unsafe abortion, which is an indicator of women's inaccessibility to modern family planning methods.

Despite the fact that the lowest rates of infant and maternal deaths occur among women aged 18-35 years, the percentage of first births to women under age 20 varies from more than 20 per cent to more than 50 per cent in developing countries. The proportion of married women under age 20 varies from fewer than 10 per cent in developed countries to up to 70 per cent in some developing countries, where marriage is often the only socially acceptable option for most women (WHO 1991d).

The percentage of infants that are exclusively breast-fed for from four to six months varies from fewer than 5 per cent to more than 80 per cent in developing countries (WHO, 1991b). The benefits of exclusive breast-feeding on children's and women's health are recognized by an increasing number of countries, both developed and developing. What is also becoming clearer is that attainment of the goal of exclusive breast-feeding for from four to six months, with continued partial breast-feeding, will require mobilizing sustained support to women, both within and outside their homes, with multisectoral actions based on multisectoral perspectives.

The acquired immunodeficiency syndrome (AIDS) pandemic has hit women in both developed and developing countries. It is estimated that by the year 2000, 75-80 per cent of human immunodeficiency virus (HIV) transmission will be through heterosexual intercourse, with no difference in adult infection rates between men and women (WHO, 1991a). In developing countries, this situation means a double burden for women: suffering from AIDS and caring for AIDS victims in the family. At the same time, most women in developing countries are not in a position—socially, culturally and economically—to be able to negotiate condom use with their partners.

An equally important issue is that despite women's multiple contributions to health, very few women, including female physicians, hold decision-making positions, even in those countries where women make up the majority of doctors. Women have participated in health and development but only passively, without equitable access to and decision-making roles in health resources. This situation has in turn affected their efficiency, effectiveness and decision-making as users and providers of health care.

Health, as a multisectoral entity, cannot be viewed without considering the trend in women's socio-economic situation. Although the gross national product has grown globally, women in developed and developing countries have become poorer. During the past 20 years, poverty among rural women has increased by 48 per cent, while that among rural men rose by 3 per cent (IFAD, 1992).

Although a steady improvement in school enrolment and adult literacy is taking place throughout the world, the number of illiterate women increased from 543 million in 1970 to 597 million in 1985, while that of men rose from 348 million to 352 million (United Nations, 1991). In view of the strong inverse relation between women's literacy, fertility, and maternal and child mortality, the increased illiteracy among women is a serious impediment to achieving the goal of Health for All.

In short, women's greater vulnerability to illiteracy, poverty, passivity, uncontrolled fertility, preventable diseases and premature death is not only due to their biomedical and general socio-economic situation but is largely due to the visible and invisible discrimination women suffer throughout life. The existing de facto discrimination against women in health and development is the single most important issue affecting women's health status; its elimination, in all aspects of health, should therefore constitute the single common perspective of all women worldwide.

C. But why de facto discrimination against women?

At this juncture, a brief analysis of the origin of this paradox might be useful in the search for elimination of discrimination against women. Although the reasons for women's poor health status and their exclusion from decision-making roles can be found in many factors, including the non-participatory orientation of medical education and health-care systems, in the final analysis, the underlying cause derives from the socially constructed gender roles of man and woman. Historically, gender-based division of work has created unequal relations between a man and a woman. Over time, this inequality has resulted in the lower health, social, economic and political status of women, those described as the "second sex" by Simone de Beauvoir. Unlike biological roles in procreation, however, gender roles between men and women can change, between societies and over time, even within the same culture. Existing evidence from within and outside the same cultures has shown that changing gender roles to a more equitable level has a positive effect on women's and children's health.

D. What constitutes women's perspectives and participation?

Against this backdrop of the global situation and the role of women in health, the next question relates to what constitutes women's perspectives and participation in MCH/FP. There is no such thing as a single "women's perspective". There could be as many "women's perspectives" as there are cultures between and within countries. In the same way, the mode of participation could vary from country to country, depending upon social, cultural and political systems. But by using the universally advocated principle of gender equity in health and development and through a collective effort, a common ground for promoting women's equity could be worked out.

As users of health services, women's perspectives would relate to a host of factors assuring their equitable access to and control over the means of MCH/FP. Among those factors, the most important could be listed as follows:

(a) Technical information and economic resources;

(b) Food, education, health care and self-esteem at family level;

(c) Physical proximity and scheduling of MCH/FP clinics;

(d) Health information provided in the language and symbols women understand;

(e) Opportunities for informed choice;

(f) Local women's perceptions and feelings about childbirth, spacing of births, child care, sense of privacy/decency, breast-feeding and safety of family planning methods, as well as other MCH/FP interventions, such as tetanus toxoid, safe delivery kits and hospital delivery;

(g) User-provider relations;

(h) Economic ability of women to meet the cost of and time spent in MCH/FP services;

(i) Cultural and social ability to seek health care outside the household;

(j) Approval and involvement of husband or male members of family in MCH/FP.

Likewise, women's perspectives as providers could relate to equal access to and control over:

(a) The MCH/FP technologies and decision-making roles in health and related sectors;

(b) Skills and educational opportunities;

(c) Participation as planners and implementers and evaluators;

(*d*) Gender awareness and orientation about user needs;

(*e*) Building technical competence in MCH/FP at all levels, including that of traditional birth attendants;

(*f*) Equal pay for equal work in health—as a means of livelihood;

(*g*) Gender awareness and education for men and women in leadership positions in health and related sectors;

(*h*) Collection, dissemination and use of gender-specific data on all aspects of MCH/FP programmes, including education and training programmes.

In this context, women's participation should constitute those activities which would enable women to exercise their rights and responsibilities as providers and users of MCH/FP. Although the operational definition of those activities varies according to country-specific situations, the recommendations emanating from the global network of multisectoral teams established under the WHO/UNFPA interregional project reflect the general definition based on common perspectives. Qualitative and quantitative improvement of delivery systems of MCH/FP is one of the important common perspectives emanating from this global multisectoral network. Operationally, they have been defined as follows. By involving women's groups and their perspectives, undertake:

(*a*) Integrated planning and implementation of primary health care based on health systems services;

(*b*) Training and retraining of more health workers;

(*c*) More precise and gender-specific health information collection and utilization;

(*d*) Participatory evaluation and monitoring;

(*e*) Awareness-raising and involvement of women and women's organizations and assistance to communities to identify their needs;

(*f*) Increased use of local resources and also local operational research for local solutions, including the linkages between non-governmental organizations and the Government in the delivery of services and education;

(*g*) Modification of medical and nursing/midwifery education to integrate women's perspectives;

(*h*) Strengthening of intersectoral coordination and collaborative action.

The activities can be summarized into a key phrase "empowerment of women as major actors in MCH/FP", which would require an integrated approach by all related sectors/agencies from the planning phase onward. However, there are a number of constraints of which the most important are insufficient country-specific information, experiences and tools for integrating women's participation and perspectives into MCH/FP-related sectors, lack of budget within MCH/FP and inadequate sectoral and donor coordination, especially at operational levels.

E. Conclusion: the challenges

In conclusion, the emerging issues can be summarized as follows. Can the development catalysts working in health and health-related sectors:

(*a*) Take the first step to organize themselves as a team by involving the women's sector, both governmental and non-governmental, and by adopting a cooperative rather than a competitive approach directed to achieving the common Health for All goals related to women and children?

(*b*) Collaborate as a team to choose a particular health problem that affects women's immediate and strategic needs; and, through a gender-based analysis, to ascertain what each sector could do as part of its overall objectives towards solving the chosen problem concerning the quality and utilization of MCH/FP?

(*c*) Identify, within the overall objectives, the actions that would promote women's perspectives and participation in related activities directed to solving the chosen problem?

(*d*) Formulate a corresponding package of indicators to monitor in each sector the level and type of women's participation in related activities, women's share of benefits, the effect on the problems chosen to be solved and the effect of increased women's participation and perspectives on the sectoral objectives?

(*e*) Disseminate and utilize the information with a view to improving the situation and role of women in health and other health-related sectors?

The answers to these challenges must come from within the persons involved in the effort, from their own situations where women suffer discrimination from birth onward and from their individual and institutional commitment to change this situation. The answers to these questions should be found through participatory problem-solving action research at country level—designed, implemented and evaluated by a local multisectoral team consisting of a women's group and members of health or other related sectors. Such problem-solving action research should be closely linked with the related sectoral programmes so that the research findings could be used to improve the performance of respective programmes in gender equity. Mobilization of more resources with greater coordination from all sectors concerning MCH/FP should thus become essential, especially at operational level, if this goal is to be realized.

Notes

[1]The term "non-formal" is used here to cover the health care provided by, for example, family members in the home, lay health workers, traditional birth attendants and self-help agencies, including clinics and dispensaries established and run by women (usually for women exclusively).

[2]The term "maternal and child health and family planning" is viewed here holistically as extending far beyond the narrow confines of medical technologies and health services. It refers to the inherent interrelations between the social, political, economic, environmental, nutritional, legal and health situations of women in society.

References

Bruce, J. (1989). *Fundamental Elements of the Quality of Care: A Simple Framework*. New York: The Population Council.

Coale, Ansley J. (1991). Excess female mortality and the balance of the sexes in the population: an estimate of the number of "missing females". *Population and Development Review* (New York), vol. 17, No. 3 (September), pp. 517-523.

Drèze, Jean, and Amartya Sen (1989). *Hunger and Public Action*. WIDER Studies in Development Economics. Oxford, United Kingdom: Clarendon Press.

Fauveau, V., and others (1991). Effect on mortality of community-based maternity care programme in rural Bangladesh. *The Lancet* (London; and Baltimore Maryland), vol. 338, No. 8776 (9 November), pp. 1183-1186.

Gómez, E. (1991). Sex discrimination and excess female mortality among children in the Americas. Paper prepared for the 18th NCIH International Conference, Arlington, Virginia, United States of America.

International Fund for Agricultural Development (1992). Report on rural women living in poverty. Paper prepared for the Summit on the Economic Advancement of Rural Women, Geneva.

Phillips, James F., and others (1986). Worker-client exchanges and the dynamics of contraceptive use in rural Bangladesh. Paper prepared for the Annual Meeting of the Population Association of America, San Francisco, California, 3-5 April.

_________ (1988). Determinants of reproductive change in a traditional society: evidences from Matlab, Bangladesh. *Studies in Family Planning* (New York), vol. 19, No. 6 (November-December), pp. 313-334.

Pizurki, Helena, and others (1987). *Women as Providers of Health Care*. Geneva: World Health Organization.

Rutstein, Shea Oscar (1983). *Infant and Child Mortality: Levels and Trends and Demographic Differentials*. World Fertility Survey Comparative Studies, No. 24. Voorburg, Netherlands: International Statistical Institute.

United Nations (1991). *The World's Women, 1970-1990: Trends and Statistics*. Series K, No. 8. Sales No. E.90.XVII.3.

United Nations Population Fund (1992). *The State of World Population 1992: A World in Balance*. New York.

Waldron, Ingrid (1987). Patterns and causes of excess female mortality among children in developing countries. *World Health Statistics Quarterly* (Geneva), No. 40.

World Bank (1991). *Gender and Poverty in India*. A World Bank Country Study. Washington, D.C.

World Health Organization (1978). *Primary Health Care: Report of the International Conference on Primary Health Care, Alma-Ata, USSR, 6-12 September 1978*. Geneva.

_________ (1991a). Global Programme on AIDS: database. WHO/GPA/RES/SFI. Geneva.

_________ (1991b). Infant and young child nutrition: progress and evaluation report; and Status of implementation of the International Code of Marketing of Breast Milk Substitutes. Report by the Director-General. EB89/28. Geneva.

_________ (1991c). New estimates of maternal mortality. *Weekly Epidemiological Record* (Geneva), No. 66, pp. 345-352.

_________ (1991d). Women, health and development: progress report of the Director-General. A44/15. Geneva.

_________ (1992a). Implementation of the Global Strategy for Health for All by the Year 2000: second evaluation and eighth report on the world health situation. EB89/10. Geneva.

_________ (1992b). *The Work of WHO, 1990-91: Biennial Report of the Director-General*. Geneva.

_________, United Nations Children's Fund and United Nations Population Fund (1990). *Common Goals for Women and Children*. New York.

XIII. WOMEN'S AND CHILDREN'S HEALTH: PROGRAMME NEEDS AND PRIORITIES FOR THE 1990s

*Gladys Martin**

The health problems of women came into the limelight during preparatory seminars, conferences and the celebrations of the International Women's Year in 1975. Since that time, there have been international and national conferences on women's health during which several declarations, resolutions and recommendations were adopted. Operationalizing and implementing them has been slow and the few small-scale successful projects undertaken are little known. Another important point to note is that viable data on morbidity and mortality of women in the developing countries and their health-seeking patterns are almost non-existent, except in special small-scale studies of particular diseases (Rathgeber, 1992), and from incomplete health facility data. Demographic and Health Surveys have also provided useful data in the countries that have undertaken them.

Most of the data presented during the Safe Motherhood and the Better Health for Women and Children conferences in 1986 are still the most recent. Hence, it is not possible to show trends in women's and maternal health status over the past few years. It is, however, true to say that the health status of women in most African countries is deteriorating because of persisting high fertility (figure I), the increasing poverty of households (the large number of female-headed households, especially in rural areas and periurban slums), wars, in- and out-migration, drought and famine, the negative impact of structural adjustment policies, debt payments and a deteriorating health-care system. The human immunodeficiency virus (HIV) and the acquired immunodeficiency syndrome (AIDS), drug-resistant malaria and the excessive workload of women aggravate the situation.

The order of magnitude of diseases in children has changed dramatically in most of the developing countries. Measles, pertussis and neonatal tetanus, which used to be the major killers of children under age 5, no longer feature among the top five killers in Africa, except in those countries which have not attained Universal Child Immunization (UCI), that is, at least 80 per cent coverage (75 per cent for African countries) with the six antigens by one year of age and those with low coverage areas.

A. Health problems of children

Mortality rates for infant and children under age 5 have been decreasing over the years, although the rates of decline have been rather slow in most of the developing countries (figure II). To achieve the goal of the World Summit for Children—a one-third reduction of 1990 rates or a decline to 50 and 70 per 1,000 live births for infant and under-five mortality, respectively, by the year 2000—the rates of decline must be increased up to sixfold. The major direct causes of infant and child deaths are acute respiratory infections, particularly pneumonia; diarrhoeal diseases, malaria, vaccine-preventable diseases, malnutrition, perinatal pathologies and accidents. Most of the unnecessary deaths and the disease burden can be prevented through application of existing, low-cost effective technologies and the provision of health information to parents and child caretakers. Data on son preference and the higher morbidity and mortality rates in girls under age 5 are mainly from Asia. This issue may be very subtle in Africa and needs to be studied, especially in the light of the increasing trend towards smaller family size and family planning.

Over 3 million people each year have been saved from deaths due to the vaccine-preventable diseases and over 1 million saved from diarrhoeal diseases,

*Eastern and Southern Africa Regional Office, United Nations Children's Fund.

Figure I. Total fertility rate by level of under-five mortality rates, 1990

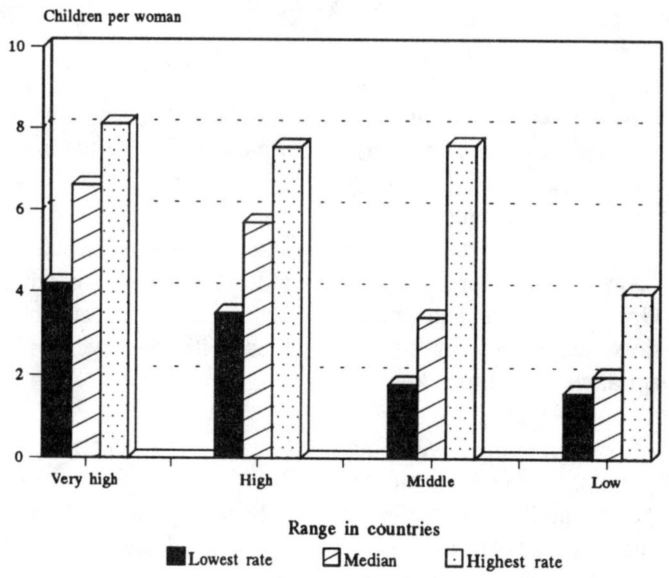

Source: United Nations Children's Fund, *The State of the World's Children, 1992* (New York, Oxford University Press, 1992).

Figure II. Trends in under-five mortality rates, median rates for groups of countries

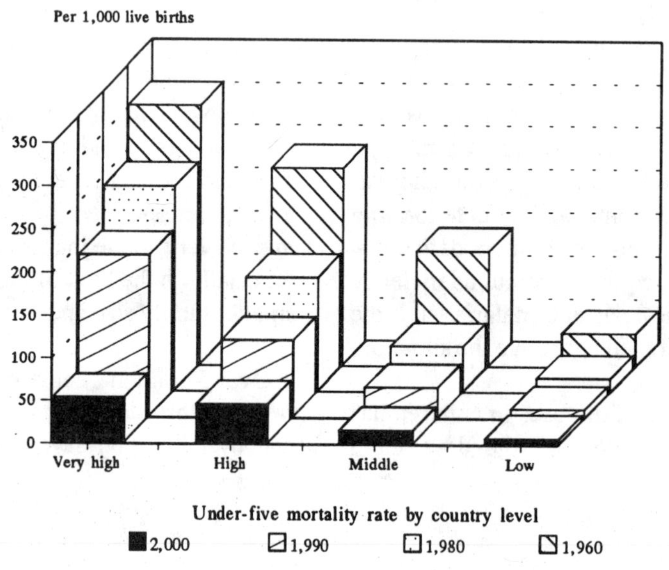

Source: United Nations Children's Fund, *The State of the World's Children, 1992* (New York, Oxford University Press, 1992).

through increased access to safe vaccinations, oral rehydration therapy and some improvement to health-care services (UNICEF, 1992b). Unfortunately, HIV/AIDS is already showing signs of reversing this positive trend. It is estimated that AIDS-related deaths will increase infant mortality rates by 20-40 deaths per 1,000 live births. The increase in the incidence of malnutrition, acute respiratory infection and diarrhoea is already evident. The mortality rate of mothers from AIDS will further increase the death rate of orphans.

Age group 5-14, usually considered the healthiest period, is fast becoming endangered. They are exposed to accidents and tropical diseases as the participate in educational, leisure and occupationa activities (caring for animals and fetching water, fuel and food in developing countries). The tropical diseases contracted may go untreated and may cause severe complications during adolescence and womanhood. Girls are particularly at risk because of harmful traditional practices, such as circumcision; early, usually forced marriages; and the increasing tendency for men to seek sexual relations among girls as young as nine years. A study from Uganda showed a male-to-female ratio of AIDS in age group 14-19 of 1 to 6 (figure III), which indicates that the girls might have been infected between the ages of 9 and 14 years.

Figure III. Women's health status, selected indicators by level of under-five mortality rates, 1980-1990

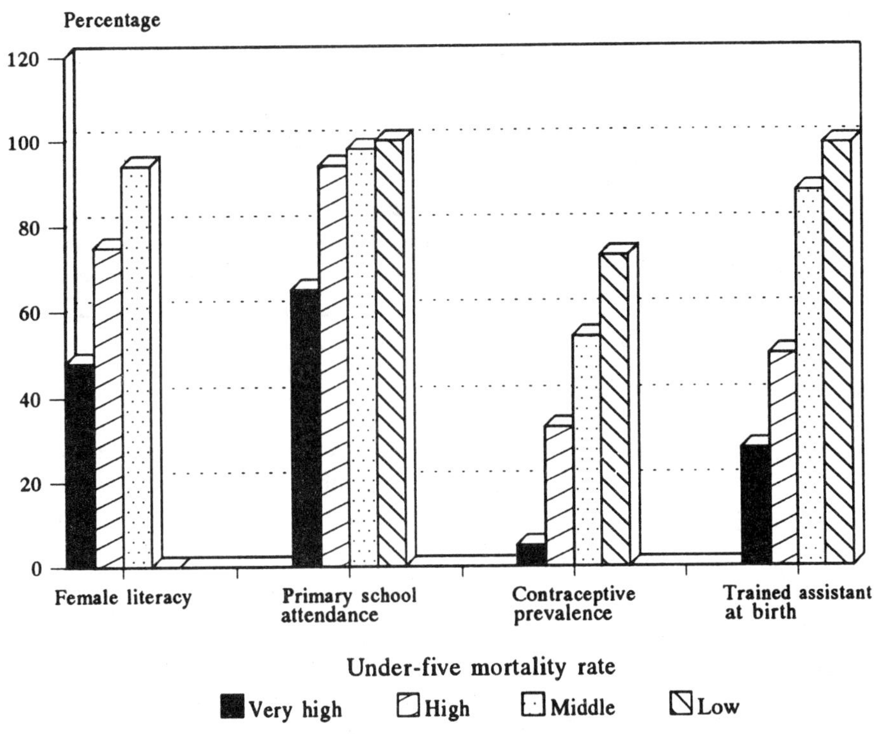

Source: United Nations Children's Fund. *The State of the World's Children, 1992* (New York, Oxford University Press, 1992).

B. Health problems of women

Whenever reference is made to women's health problems and needs, the direct causes of maternal morbidity and mortality are most often considered. Pregnancy-related causes account for about 20-25 per cent of deaths of women aged 15-44 years in the developing countries, while they constitute only about 2 per cent of deaths in the same age group in the developed countries. The reasons for this very marked difference are multiple. Four of them, "too early, too many, too soon, too late", exist in varying proportions in different countries. The major immediate causes of maternal deaths are haemorrhage, sepsis, dystocia, eclampsia and anaemia. Other factors are illegal abortions of unwanted pregnancies, ignorance of need for early and regular antenatal/delivery and post-partum care, limited access to services that are usually of poor quality and demotivating rapport between health personnel and their clients. For every maternal death, recent findings show that there are not 12-15 but 100 women suffering from pregnancy and childbirth-related complications, such as prolapse of the uterus, bladder and rectum; fistulae and other sequelae of physical and mental trauma.

Adolescent females are at particularly high risk of developing pregnancy-related complications and death because they do not usually seek nor receive adequate antenatal care, they tend to procure abortions under unsafe conditions and they are in most cases anaemic and undernourished. They are also at risk of contracting sexually transmitted diseases (STDs), including HIV infection. Insufficient attention has been given to their health status in general. They may be undergoing mental stress arising from misunderstandings between generations, inappropriate and excessive workload, parental discrimination *vis-à-vis* their brothers, sexual harassment and broken homes.

Health services, especially maternal care and family planning, are not usually accessible (socially, culturally and financially) to adolescent females; and in several countries they need parental consent in order to avail themselves of the services. They do not usually benefit from social, educational and rehabilitative services for children on the street because many of these runaway and/or abandoned girls may be lulled into prostitution by older women or maltreated as housemaids.

Most women in the developing countries begin pregnancy in a compromised state. Anaemia is common and prevalence rates among pregnant women may be over 66 per cent, with more severe forms occurring in areas highly endemic for malaria and helminths. Screening for anaemia and malaria are rarely done; neither are drugs always available for prophylaxis and treatment.

Women suffer from communicable and non-communicable diseases prevalent in the environment in which they live and work. Chronic bronchitis and cor pulmonale have been linked to exposure to smoke while cooking and performing other household chores (WHO, 1992a). STDs are usually undiagnosed and untreated, and present later as severe complications. Gender-sensitive studies of the tropical diseases are generating new evidence that these diseases have severe biological and psychosocial consequences for women, not only during pregnancy but in adolescence and other periods of their lives, thus preventing them from fulfilling their productive and reproductive functions (Rathgeber and Vlassoff, 1992). Nutritional deficiencies are also more severe in girls and women because of taboos, increased demand dictated by their physiological state and excessive workload. The precarious health status of mothers from childhood or during reproductive life, compounded with poor quality care during pregnancy and delivery, contributes to 30-40 per cent of infant deaths.

Deaths from cancers of the breast and cervix are increasing, even though these cancers are curable if diagnosed and treated early. About 500,000 women develop cervical cancer every year. Cancer of the lung, colon and uterus were found to be from two to three times more frequent in women in mining districts, compared with those in non-mining districts in Czechoslovakia. Female genital mutilation is still being practised in some countries, thus endangering the general and reproductive health of women. However, the increasing campaign being launched by non-governmental organizations may be protecting more girls from this practice.

As more women become involved with social, political and economic activities, they are exposed to environmental hazards and may become victims of physical, sexual and substance abuse. Osteoporosis and post-menopausal symptoms are beginning to receive more attention in the developed countries because the older female leaders and managers are becoming more vocal about their health and symptoms. Elderly women in the developing countries also require such needs to be addressed, especially as they continue to toil under difficult conditions in order to meet the basic needs of their families and themselves.

Studies from the industrialized countries also show that women complain more of illness and tend to seek medical care more often than men because they are more sensitive and react more to the physiological and pathological changes they experience (Rathgeber and Vlassoff, 1992). Data from the developing countries are few and contradictory; but, in general, although women have more contacts with health services for their children and other family members, they tend to repress their feelings of illness, give their own reasons for their symptoms or seek care from other providers rather than from health facilities.

C. Programme needs

Although maternal and child health (MCH) services have had a positive impact on the health status of children under age 5, the same cannot be said for mothers and other women. Coverage of antenatal services varies from 60 to 100 per cent in the developing countries but most women attend only once, usually in the second or third trimester, and receive inadequate and sometimes inappropriate care. Even when the quality of care is good, it is administered too late after severe complications have set in. Up to 80 per cent of deliveries occur at home without assistance from trained workers. Complications and deaths go undetected and unreported. In spite of available technologies, maternal mortality (figure IV) and morbidity rates remain very high. The World Summit

Figure IV. Maternal mortality rate by level of under-five mortality rates, 1989-1990

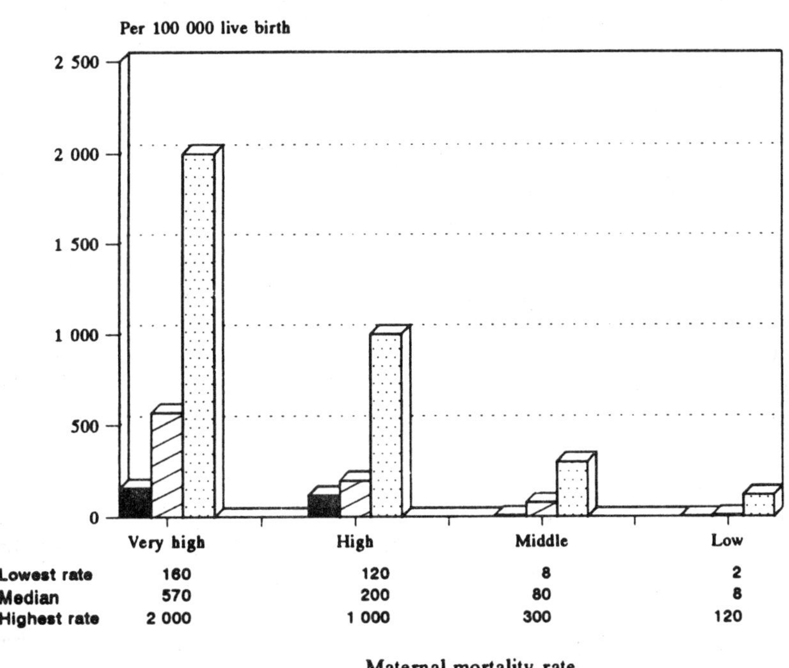

Source: United Nations Children's Fund, *The State of the World's Children, 1992* (New York, Oxford University Press, 1992).

goals that are linked to health interventions are reduction of maternal mortality rates by 50 per cent, reduction of nutritional deficiencies, an increase of information to and acceptance of family planning and increasing access to antenatal and delivery care. Other pathologies, such as the tropical diseases, classical STDs and HIV/AIDS, identified during situation analysis for the National Programme of Action formulation are also to be addressed.

Safe motherhood and reproductive health initiatives address the broader concept of women's health that includes the underlying and basic factors. However, the intervention programmes, like maternal and child health and family planning (MCH/FP) services, also tend to focus on the immediate pregnancy-related problems and female fertility control. These approaches will no doubt reduce maternal deaths but the incidence and prevalence of complications and chronic disability will not be substantially affected because the underlying and basic high-risk factors are not usually addressed.

Gender-sensitive research has taken the argument much further to look at women's health within the framework of how both women's productive and reproductive contributions to development affect their health, their relations with others and their views of themselves. It stresses that women should be seen as individuals with personal health needs (Vlassoff and Bonilla, 1992; Turshen, 1991a).

Raikes, Shoo and Brabin (1992) categorize women's health needs under three headings: reproductive health needs; women's other health needs; and women's socio-economic needs relating to health. Access to sufficient quantities of clean water and information/support for acquiring food security are rightly included here, even though they are not provided by health services, because of their direct and indirect impact on health status. Access to legal abortion is still a moot point among some agencies and Governments. Strong emphasis is put on both information and services and the need for men to be knowledgeable about women's health and needs. The specific activities under each category are not new and have been regrouped differently in several documents; for example, in the forward-looking strategies by WHO (1985) in the report on the appraisal and achievement of the United Nations Decade for Women.

Situation analysis, monitoring and evaluation are very important activities in all stages. The United Nations Children's Fund (UNICEF) identifies four major areas: more reliable information on all aspects of the situation of children and women; close monitoring of the achievement of the targets set for the period; better analysis and utilization of country experience; assessing the impact and cost-effectiveness of programmes and of innovative programme components (UNICEF, 1990a).

D. Strategic priorities

Strategies for combating major childhood diseases have been developed and are being applied to varying degrees in the developing countries. The challenge to vaccinate 80 per cent of children at age 1 by 1990 was taken up worldwide; and even though not all countries achieved the target, significant increases were made and several lessons learned. Among them are the need for formulation of programmes with well-defined strategies, objectives and targets; monitoring systems; and activities that include training, information, communication and mobilization. Resources were provided mainly from external sources, which raises the issue of sustainability. Several programmes were vertical, hence, the new strategy, UCI plus, proposed by UNICEF to integrate such activities as vitamin and iron supplementation, effective growth monitoring and promotion into vaccination programmes. Lessons learned from the Expanded Programme on Immunization/UCI activities should be used in strengthening programmes for the control of diarrhoeal, acute respiratory and nutrition deficiency diseases.

Malarial control is being simplified and low-cost effective measures developed. Insecticide-impregnated nets and other materials are being accepted as an effective affordable and sustainable intervention for malarial control.

Some of the major constraints to promoting the health and social status of girls and women are lack of awareness of the magnitude of the problem, women's subordination, poverty, large gaps between legislation and application of laws, lack of funding of women's promotional activities; underdeveloped social systems, particularly the health-care system; and non-involve-ment of women in decision-making. Among the priority strategies are:

(a) *Strengthening health-care systems and increasing access.* Health systems in the developing countries have been deteriorating and are being overloaded by AIDS cases. Governments are unable to provide quality care through the health systems. The Bamako Initiative and the district health focus are among the approaches adopted by the African ministers of health to revitalize health systems within primary health care in order to provide essential, quality health-care packages to communities, especially to women and children. Some of the goals for 1990 can be achieved in an integrated health-care system that is co-managed and sustained by the providers, such as Governments and non-governmental organizations, and the users—the community. Funds generated should be managed and used at the source. Some of the Bamako Initiative projects have been evaluated and they showed very positive and promising results (McPake, Kara and Mills, 1991);

(b) *Empowerment of women.* Women are the main utilizers (for their families and themselves) and providers of health services. They need to be better informed, trained, motivated and supported. They need to be encouraged to take leadership/decision-making roles on their own or, whenever necessary, with their male partners. Longwe and Clark (1990) discuss female subordination and women's increased risk to HIV/AIDS and present a framework for combating it in AIDS control programmes. This principle should be applicable to all women's programmes;

(c) *Reaching the unreached.* Women and children cannot be reached because of physical, financial and social barriers as well as time constraints. Marked disparities in the health status of women and access to care exist in rural and urban areas and different socio-economic groups. Strategies have to be developed and resources made available to those unfortunate women and children that live in difficult circumstances in rural and urban areas.

(d) *Baby-friendly initiative.* This programme, launched jointly by WHO and UNICEF, is to promote correct breast-feeding practices and accelerate the implementation of the breast-milk substitute code. Breast-feeding is advantageous to children, mothers, families and the country. Health facilities should be both baby- and mother-friendly so as to give childbirth and motherhood the dignity it deserves;

(e) *Legal measures.* Laws that protect women during pregnancy and lactation and from environmental or occupational hazards, misuse; and physical, sexual and mental abuse should be revised and measures taken to enforce them;

(f) *Involvement of women's organizations.* These organizations constitute enormous resources and supportive forces for programme development, implementation and monitoring, as well as for mobilizing action. Programmes will be better sustained if women are involved at all stages. They need special training for their roles and tasks;

(g) *Intersectoral and inter-agency collaboration.* Resources are scarce and small vertical projects are usually targeted to the same population. Inter-agency collaboration should bring about effective use of resources through joint planning with governmental and non-governmental partners. The integration of donor-funded activities within national programmes of action will yield greater impact.

E. Conclusion

Twenty-seven years after the declaration of the United Nations International Women's Year and the Decade for Women, it is very disappointing to note that the health status and well-being of women have not improved. If anything, there has been some deterioration, considering the devastating effects of HIV/AIDS and the unstable political and socio-economic environment in which women and children live. Many more women are the head of household and most of them fall within the realms of the poor.

Women should be seen not as targets for population control programmes (Turshen, 1991b) nor as vehicles through which other goals should be achieved, but as the primary beneficiaries of development programmes (Vlassoff and Bonilla, 1992). The issues of women, health and development were reviewed at the technical discussion of the Forty-fifth World Health Assembly (WHO, 1992c), and once again the need for generating more gender-specific data and country-specific information was reiterated. It was strongly recommended that Governments should establish effective mechanisms to address women's health issues in a holistic manner and within a national agenda for action on women's health.

The goals of the 1990s for women and children (World Summit for Children, 1990) and other specific national goals identified in national programmes of action are challenges that should be addressed within a revitalized, integrated health system. If women themselves play major roles, their life can be saved and the goal of 50 per cent reduction of maternal deaths and disabilities could become a reality by the year 2000. Improved health, nutritional and social status of girls and women will also have a positive impact on child survival and development, especially the perinatal and neonatal pathologies. Increased survival and better health of children will motivate women to reduce their number of pregnancies and enable them to live a healthy, productive life as an equal partner in development.

References

Longwe, S. H., and C. Clark (1990). Proposed methodology for combating women's subordination as a means towards improved AIDS prevention and control. Paper prepared for the Expert Group Meeting on Women and HIV/AIDS and the Role of a National Machinery for the Advancement of Women. Vienna.

McPake, B., H. Kara and A. Mills (1991). Experience to date of implementing the Bamako Initiative: a review and five country studies. London School of Hygiene and Tropical Medicine, Department of Public Health and Policy, Health Policy Unit.

Raikes, Alamagh, R. Shoo and L. Brabin (1992). Gender-planned health services. Paper prepared for the WHO/TDR/ESR Consultation on Women and Tropical Diseases, Oslo, Norway.

Rathgeber, Wijeyaratne P., ed. (1992). *Women and Tropical Diseases.* Co-sponsored by the United Development Programme, the World Bank and the World Health Organization Special Programme for Research and Training in Tropical Diseases. Ottawa, Canada: International Development Research Centre.

Rathgeber, E. M, and C. Vlassoff (1992). Gender-planned health services: a new research focus. Paper prepared for the WHO/TDR/ESR Consultation on Women and Tropical Diseases, Oslo, Norway.

Turshen, Meredith, ed. (1991a). Introduction. In *Women and Health in Africa*, Meredith Turshen, ed. Trenton, New Jersey: Africa World Press.

_________ (1991b). Taking women seriously: towards demographic health care in Africa. In *Women and Health in Africa*, Meredith Turshen, ed. Trenton, New Jersey: Africa World Press.

United Nations Children's Fund (1990a). Medium-term plan for the period 1990-1993. United Nations Children's Fund Executive Board, 1990 Session. E/ICEF/1990/3. New York.

_________ (1990b). Safe Motherhood. United Nations Children's Fund Executive Board, 1990 Session. E/ICEF/1990/L13. New York.

_________ (1992a). Health and revitalization of health services issue. Bamako Initiative Management Unit and Child Survival Unit. New York.

_________ (1992b). *The State of the World's Children*, 1992. New York: Oxford University Press.

Vlassoff, C., and E. Bonilla (1992). Gender differences in the determinants and consequences of tropical diseases: what do we know? Paper prepared for the WHO/TDR/ESR Consultation on Women and Tropical Diseases, Oslo, Norway.

World Health Organization (1985). *Women, Health and Development, 1985.* A report by the Director-General. WHO Offset Publication, No. 90. Geneva.

_________ (1992a). Report of the 1992 technical discussion on women, health and development to the Forty-fifth World Health Assembly. Geneva.

_________ (1992b). Resolution on women, health and development. Forty-fifth World Health Assembly. WHA 45.25. Geneva.

_________ (1992c). Women's health: across ages and frontier. Background document to the technical discussion, Forty-fifth World Health Assembly, May 1992.

World Summit for Children (1990). World Declaration and Plan of Action for Implementing the World Declaration on the World Summit for Children. In *First Call for Children.* New York: United Nations Children's Fund.

Part Five

WOMEN, FERTILITY AND FAMILY PLANNING

XIV. ADOLESCENT REPRODUCTIVE BEHAVIOUR AND WOMEN'S STATUS

*Susheela Singh**

Adolescent reproductive behaviour has recently been the focus of a substantial amount of research and policy and programme formulation throughout much of the world. The issue has attracted research attention for at least 20 years, but interest has grown noticeably since the early 1980s, especially in developing countries. A major conference was held at Mexico City in 1985 on the subject of adolescent reproductive behaviour in the Latin American region, reflecting the interest existing at that time. More recently, in March 1992, the Inter-African Conference on Adolescent Health: Adolescent Health in Sub-Saharan Africa, the first major conference on teenagers in Africa, was held at Nairobi. Much of the recent surge in discussion and research has sprung from concern about the current level and recent trends in early sexual activity, adolescent marriage and child-bearing. But adolescent reproductive behaviour is also the result of broad changes in societal values, which have led to a redefinition of expectations for young people in the society as a whole. Both male and female teenagers in all social groups are now expected to attain some minimum level of education and to form part of the workforce during some stages of their lives.

Early marriage and child-bearing among adolescent women is not a new phenomenon. It is only relatively recently, however, that it has been defined and widely recognized as a social problem. The reasons for the upsurge of interest in the question are varied. The issue first attained prominence in the United States of America as premarital sexual activity and pregnancy among unmarried teenagers began to increase noticeably. Child-bearing by teenagers, especially unmarried teenagers, was seen to have undesirable consequences for the young woman, the infant and society as a whole. But in addition, a high proportion of pregnant teenagers in the United States chose to terminate their pregnancies by abortion, increasing the likelihood that all behaviour related to reproduction during the teenage years would be viewed as a social problem. Furthermore, the fact that most teenage births were occurring among poorer women also supported the perception that action should be taken to reduce pregnancy and child-bearing among teenagers, as one means of breaking the cycle of poverty.

In the developing world, marriage and child-bearing among adolescents became a focus of attention for some of the same reasons and for some different reasons. Data measuring the level of child-bearing and marriage formation among young women have become available in a large number of developing countries since the mid-1970s, which has made it possible to formulate the issue so that the extent and relevance of the problem to each society could be evaluated. From the government policy maker's point of view, it is important that educational attainment and job training be improved in the population as a whole, as a basic prerequisite of economic development. This goal would require delaying marriage and motherhood to the late teenage years, if not later. In addition, the thesis that child-bearing by very young teenagers (usually defined as under age 17) is associated with poorer outcomes for both the infant and the mother has encouraged Governments to argue for reducing all child-bearing among teenagers. A further justification for delaying the first birth is to increase the average length of generations and therefore contribute to reducing population growth. Lastly, in some countries, and especially in cities, the question of adolescent reproductive behaviour has also gained attention because an increasing proportion of young women are entering consensual unions, as well as engaging in sexual relationships outside any union. As a result, pregnancy is probably rising among some subgroups; and even if child-bearing is not on the rise, abortion may be increasingly prevalent among single young women. Moreover, to the extent that both consensual unions (which have a higher probability of breakup) and premarital child-bearing result in single women

*The Alan Guttmacher Institute, New York.

having to support their children, any delays in the timing of the first birth have the potential of reducing the burden that teenage motherhood might place on society.

How has the interrelation between adolescent child-bearing and women's status been viewed, within this recent focus on the reproductive behaviour of adolescent women? From the beginning, some researchers and policy makers were interested in the issue of delaying adolescent child-bearing because of its likely interrelation with women's status and roles. Even though the implications for women's status were not spelled out in detail, they were nevertheless felt to be valid underpinnings of the work of researchers, policy makers and service providers in both developing and developed countries. For example, those arguing for better contraceptive services for teenagers did so for many reasons that were related to improving the status of women. Avoiding pregnancy and birth at an early age was seen as necessary in order to enable teenagers to accomplish other goals, all of which have long-term implications for their health, status and roles. These goals include completing physical growth before the onset of child-bearing; reaching a stage of psychological maturation at which the young woman has developed a concept of herself as an individual and is therefore capable of assuming an equal role in decision-making when she enters a marital union; being mature enough to accept and fulfil the responsibilities of taking care of a family and completing some minimum level of schooling and/or gaining some job-related training. Part of the motivation behind much research and policy formulation in this area was the hypothesis, now backed up with data, that the great majority of young women were not consciously choosing to have a birth when they did but were doing so because of others' expectations of them, because of a lack of knowledge and ability to plan and because of a lack of more attractive alternatives to motherhood.

Research from these perspectives provides information about the likely effects of early marriage and early child-bearing on women's lifetime status and roles. To the extent that early reproductive behaviour affects life chances for teenagers, it will later affect many aspects of their status as women.

A. Variation in early marriage and early child-bearing

It is important to look at levels and trends in early marriage and child-bearing, because these are indicators of the scale of their overall potential effect on women's status. Knowledge of the absolute level and of the direction of changes in this behaviour would influence the effects on women's status that one expects to find and the hypotheses that one may want to test. In addition, it is also relevant to know whether early marriage and child-bearing is behaviour that tends to be concentrated in certain social groups.

Regardless of the measure of teenage reproductive behaviour that is used, there is clearly a great deal of worldwide variation in levels of early reproductive behaviour. The proportion of women aged 15-19 in a union, the proportion that have had at least one child, the age-specific fertility rate (ASFR) and the proportion of fertility that occurs to women aged 15-19 are all possible measures of the extent of reproductive behaviour among adolescent women. Selected measures are presented in table 27.

The level of child-bearing among teenagers is very low in several large countries in Eastern Asia, with ASFR of fewer than 10 births per 1,000 women aged 15-19, and moderately low in most countries of Northern, Western and Southern Europe, in Canada and in Australia and New Zealand; with ASFR typically ranging between 10 and 30. Even with their very low total fertility rates (TFR), teenage births are a relatively small proportion of total fertility , fewer than 2 per cent in Eastern Asia and between 2 and 8 per cent in most of the other countries in this group. It is this group of countries that also has a quite low proportion of teenage girls married, fewer than 2 per cent in Eastern Asia and in some Northern and Western European countries, and under 7 per cent in most of the other countries in this group. It is clear that although a small minority of teenage women in these countries do begin child-bearing and marriage under age 20, it is a relatively uncommon pattern.

However, the teenage birth rate is noticeably higher in a few developed countries, including much of Eastern Europe, the former Union of Soviet Socialist Republics, a few countries in Southern Europe and the

TABLE 27. INDICATORS OF TEENAGE MARRIAGE AND CHILD-BEARING, MOST RECENT DATA FROM EARLY 1980S AND MID-1980S[a]

Major area, region and country or area[b]	Percentage of women aged 15-19 ever married (1)	Singulate mean age at marriage (2)	Age-specific fertility rate, ages 15-19 (3)	Proportion of fertility to ages 15-19[c] (4)	Total fertility rate (5)
Africa					
Eastern Africa					
Burundi	6.5	21.9	52	3.8	6.9
Comoros (4)	..	..	135	9.6	7.0
Djibouti (5)	..	..	..	..	6.6
Ethiopia (4)	60.9	17.1	115	8.2	7.0
Kenya (1)	20.1	21.0	152	11.3	6.7
Madagascar	..	..	125	9.5	6.6
Malawi..	..	..	168	10.8	7.8
Mauritius	10.7	23.8	41	10.8	2.0
Mozambique	52.4	17.6	131	10.1	6.5
Réunion	..	25.8	49	9.1	2.7
Rwanda (4)	12.7	21.2	77	4.5	8.5
Somalia (4)	..	..	108	7.3	7.4
Uganda (1)	40.8	19.0	187	12.8	7.3
United Republic of Tanzania (4)	37.6	19.1	138	9.9	7.0
Zambia (4)	31.7	19.4	153	10.6	7.2
Zimbabwe (1)	19.8	20.7	109	9.7	5.5
Middle Africa					
Angola (5)	..	..	..	..	6.4
Cameroon (2)	49.0	18.8	187	14.6	6.4
Central Africa Republic (4)	46.8	18.4	195	15.7	6.2
Chad (5)	..	..	..	..	5.9
Congo (4)	25.7	21.9	107	9.1	5.9
Gabon (5)	..	..	..	..	4.5
Guinea	..	..	..	..	5.5
Zaire	..	..	..	..	6.3
Northern Africa					
Algeria	23.6	21.0	43	3.6	6.0
Egypt	22.4	21.4	83	8.8	4.7
Libyan Arab Jamahiriya (5)	..	..	..	..	7.2
Morocco (1)	12.8	24.0	49	5.3	4.6
Sudan (1)	15.9	24.1	69	6.9	5.0
Tunisia	6.9	24.3	30	3.4	4.4
Southern Africa					
Botswana[d] (1)	7.3	26.4	125	12.5	5.0
Lesotho (2)	25.9	20.5	102	8.8	5.8
Namibia (5)	..	..	..	..	6.1
South Africa (5)	5.6	25.7	..	..	4.8
Swaziland (4)	..	..	117	8.5	6.9

TABLE 27 (*continued*)

Major area, region and country or area[b]	*Percentage of women aged 15-19 ever married* (1)	*Singulate mean age at marriage* (2)	*Age-specific fertility rate, ages 15-19* (3)	*Proportion of fertility to ages 15-19*[c] (4)	*Total fertility rate* (5)
Western Africa					
Benin (2)	45.5	18.3	151	10.6	7.1
Burkina Faso (5)	..	..	..	..	6.5
Cape Verde (4)	..	..	78	8.3	4.7
Côte d'Ivoire (2)	52.1	18.9	216	14.6	7.4
Gambia (4)	..	..	200	15.6	6.4
Ghana (1)	24.4	20.2	124	9.7	6.4
Liberia (1)	36.0	20.2	184	14.6	6.3
Mali (1)	75.4	16.4	201	15.0	6.7
Mauritania (2)	39.0	19.6	154	12.4	6.2
Niger (5)	..	..	..	..	7.1
Nigeria (2)	40.3	19.1	173	13.8	6.3
Senegal (1)	43.5	19.4	159	12.0	6.6
Sierra Leone (4)	..	..	212	16.3	6.5
Togo	40.6	18.5	127	9.8	6.5
Asia					
Eastern Asia					
China	..	22.4	9	2.0	2.3
Hongkong	2.1	26.6	6	2.1	1.4
Japan	1.1	25.8	4	1.2	1.7
Mongolia (5)	..	..	..	..	5.3
Republic of Korea	0.9	24.7	7	1.8	2.0
South-eastern Asia					
Brunei Darussalam	8.2	25.0	..	..	..
Cambodia (5)	..	..	..	..	5.1
East Timor (5)	..	..	..	..	5.8
Indonesia	18.8	21.1	75	11.0	3.4
Lao People's Democratic Rep. (5)	..	..	..	..	6.7
Malaysia	10.3	23.5	21	2.8	3.8
Myanmar (4)	16.8	22.4	43	4.6	4.7
Philippines	14.3	22.4	47	4.9	4.8
Singapore	2.3	26.2	8	2.7	1.5
Thailand	17.5	22.7	52	11.3	2.3
Viet Nam	..	..	..	..	4.2
Southern Asia					
Afghanistan	..	..	..	..	7.6
Bangladesh	68.8	16.7	239	19.6	6.1
Bhutan	..	..	..	..	5.9
India	44.2	18.7	86	9.8	4.4
Iran (Islamic Rep. of) (4,5)	34.3	19.7	133	11.9	5.6
Nepal	50.8	17.9	94	7.8	6.0
Pakistan	31.1	19.8	99	8.4	5.9
Sri Lanka	10.4	24.4	38	6.8	2.8

TABLE 27 (*continued*)

Major area, region and country or area[b]	*Percentage of women aged 15-19 ever married* (1)	*Singulate mean age at marriage* (2)	*Age-specific fertility rate, ages 15-19* (3)	*Proportion of fertility to ages 15-19* (4)	*Total fertility rate* (5)
Western Asia					
Bahrain	..	..	..	..	7.0
Cyprus	4.6	24.2	28	5.8	2.4
Democratic Yemen[e] (5)	..	..	..	..	6.8
Iraq (4,5)	33.0	20.8	90	6.7	6.7
Israel	6.8	23.5	21	3.4	3.1
Jordan	12.9	22.8	49	3.7	6.6
Kuwait	18.1	22.4	57	6.2	4.6
Lebanon (5)	..	..	..	..	3.8
Syrian Arab Republic (2)	24.9	21.5	123	8.3	7.4
Turkey	21.8	20.7	68	8.3	4.1
United Arab Emirates	..	..	..	..	5.3
Yemen[e]	60.5	16.9	178	10.5	8.5
Europe					
Eastern Europe					
Bulgaria	17.8	..	81	21.3	1.9
Czechoslovakia	8.0	21.7	51	12.7	2.0
German Democratic Rep.[f]	4.2	21.7	44	12.9	1.7
Hungary	16.1	21.0	48	14.0	1.7
Poland	4.8	22.8	32	7.0	2.3
Romania	16.0	..	58	13.8	2.1
Northern Europe					
Denmark	1.1	25.6	10	3.4	1.4
Finland	2.2	24.6	13	4.0	1.6
Ireland	2.3	23.4	17	3.4	2.5
Norway	2.4	24.0	18	5.2	1.7
Sweden	0.7	27.6	11	3.2	1.7
United Kingdom					
England and Wales	4.5	23.1	30	..	1.7
Scotland	5.0	22.5	31	..	1.7
Northern Ireland	4.0	22.6	29	..	1.7
Southern Europe					
Albania (5)	..	..	..	..	3.4
Greece	13.9	22.5	41	12.1	1.7
Italy	4.6	23.2	17	6.0	1.4
Malta	..	..	..	..	1.9
Portugal	8.9	22.1	28	8.2	1.7
Spain	5.6	23.1	..	..	1.6
Yugoslavia	11.5	22.2	41	10.3	2.0
Western Europe					
Austria	4.2	23.5	23	8.0	1.4
Belgium	5.3	22.4	16	5.3	1.5
France	1.9	24.5	10	2.8	1.8
Germany, Federal Rep. of	3.6	23.6	9	3.3	1.3
Luxembourg	4.4	23.1	12	4.1	1.4
Netherlands	2.7	23.2	7	2.3	1.5
Switzerland	1.6	25.0	6	2.1	1.5

TABLE 27 (*continued*)

Major area, region and country or area[b]	*Percentage of women aged 15-19 ever married (1)*	*Singulate mean age at marriage (2)*	*Age-specific fertility rate, ages 15-19 (3)*	*Proportion of fertility to ages 15-19 (4)*	*Total fertility rate (5)*
Latin America and the Caribbean					
Caribbean					
Barbados (3)	21.2	..	64	16.0	2.0
Bahamas (3,4)	..	..	70	12.1	2.9
Cuba (3)	28.8	19.9	88	24.2	1.8
Dominican Republic (1)	21.8	21.4	104	13.7	3.8
Guadeloupe (3)	..	26.6	34	6.8	2.5
Haiti (2,3)	20.3	21.8	87	6.8	6.4
Jamaica (3,6)	52.3	18.0	114	19.7	2.9
Martinique (3)	..	..	35	7.6	2.3
Puerto Rico	16.8	22.3	66	13.8	2.4
Trinidad and Tobago (1)	24.8	20.8	84	13.5	3.1
Central America					
Costa Rica	15.5	22.2	96	13.7	3.5
El Salvador	30.0	20.1	129	14.7	4.4
Guatemala (1)	28.3	20.5	139	12.4	5.6
Honduras	29.2	20.0	138	12.3	5.6
Mexico (1)	19.9	22.1	94	12.4	3.8
Nicaragua	22.7	20.2	132	12.0	5.5
Panama	21.5	21.3	94	15.2	3.1
South America					
Argentina	10.3	22.9	82	12.4	3.3
Bolivia (1)	16.6	22.1	94	9.4	5.0
Brazil (1)	14.2	23.2	78	11.8	3.3
Chile	9.2	23.6	59	12.3	2.4
Colombia (1)	14.2	23.2	78	11.8	3.3
Ecuador (1)	19.3	21.9	91	10.6	4.3
Guyana (2,3)	28.0	20.0	103	16.1	3.2
Paraguay (1)	15.4	22.3	97	10.1	4.8
Peru (1)	12.9	23.7	83	10.1	4.1
Suriname (3,5)	..	..	106	17.7	3.0
Uruguay	12.8	22.4	66	16.5	2.0
Venezuela	20.7	21.2	101	14.0	3.6
Northern America					
Canada	6.7	23.1	23	7.1	1.6
United States of America	8.8	23.3	52	14.4	1.8
Oceania					
Australia	4.3	23.5	27	7.0	1.9
New Zealand	6.7	22.8	32	8.4	1.9
Melanesia					
Fiji (2)	12.0	21.8	61	9.5	3.2
Papua New Guinea	..	..	..	..	6.0
USSR (former)	9.5	21.8	44	9.1	2.4

Sources and notes follow.

Table 27 (*continued*)

Sources: The primary sources, except where otherwise indicated, are: for columns (1) and (2), *Patterns of First Marriage: Timing and Prevalence* (United Nations publication, Sales No. E.91.XIII.6); for columns (3) and (5), *World Population Monitoring, 1991: With Special Emphasis on Age Structure,* Population Studies, No. 126 (United Nations publication, Sales No. E. 92.XIII.2), tables 32 and A.2.

These supplementary sources are indicated after the country or area name by a numeral in parentheses:

1. Demographic and Health Survey for the country.
2. World Fertility Survey for the country.
3. Jean-Pierre Guengant, "Demographic transition in the Caribbean: an attempt at interpretation", paper presented at the Seminar on Fertility Transition in Latin America, Buenos Aires, Argentina, April 1990; sponsored by the International Union for the Scientific Study of Population.
4. *Adolescent Reproduction Behaviour*, vol. II, *Evidence from Developing Countries*, Population Studies, No. 109/Add.1 (United Nations publication, Sales No. E.89.XIII.10).
5. *World Population Prospects, 1990*, Population Studies, No. 120 (United Nations publication, Sales No. E.91.XIII.4).
6. Carmen McFarlane and Charles Warren, "1989 Jamaica Contraceptive Prevalence Survey, draft of final report"; Kingston, Jamaica, The National Family Planning Board of Jamaica, 1989.

[a]In a few cases, data are for the mid-1970s, when no more recent information was available.

[b]A numeral in parentheses following a country or area name indicates the supplementary source.

[c]Column (4) is the proportion of total fertility as measured by the synthetic cohort measure, the total fertility rate, that is to women aged 15-19. It is equal to the age-specific fertility rate for ages 15-19 divided by the sum of age-specific fertility rates for those aged 15-49.

[d]Not including stable non-cohabiting unions. According to the Demographic and Health Survey report (1988), 64 per cent had ever had sexual intercourse and the singulate mean age at first intercourse was about 17 years.

[e]On 22 May 1990, Democratic Yemen and Yemen merged to form a single State. Since that date they have been represented as one Member of the United Nations with the name"Yemen". For some statistical data which predate the merger, it has been necessary to refer occasionally to the former States of Yemen and Democratic Yemen.

[f]Through accession of the German Democratic Republic to the Federal Republic of Germany with effect from 3 October 1990, the two German States have united to form one sovereign State, As from the date of unification, the Federal Republic of Germany acts in the United Nations under the designation "Germany". For some statistical data which predate the unification, it has been necessary to refer occasionally to the former States of the Federal Republic of Germany and the German Democratic Republic.

United States of America (rates typically ranging between 40 and 60 births per 1,000 women). Interestingly, rates of a similar level are found in some developing countries, especially in the regions of Northern Africa, South-eastern Asia and Western Asia. The teenage ASFR ranges between 40 and 55 in Algeria, Jordan, Myanmar, Morocco, the Philippines and Thailand, and is fewer than 40 in a few developing countries, such as Malaysia, Sri Lanka and Tunisia). Births to teenagers form a larger proportion of total fertility in the developed countries, with teenage ASFRs of 40-60, because of their very low TFRs (typically 1.5-2.0 children per woman). In many cases, 12 per cent or more of total fertility in these countries is to teenagers; and in Bulgaria, it is as much as 21 per cent. By comparison, the developing countries with moderate teenage fertility still have relatively high TFRs of 3.0-6.0 or more children, with the result that teenage fertility as a proportion of the total ranges between 3 and 8 per cent (only in Thailand, with TFR of 2.3, does the level reach 11.3 per cent).

In most of the rest of the world (mainly the developing countries), ASFR among teenagers aged 15-19 is much higher. It is moderately high (70-100) in much of South America, the Caribbean and South-central Asia, very high (100-150) in most of sub-Saharan Africa and some of Central America, and exceptionally high in a few countries in the same regions (Bangladesh has the highest rate, 239 per 1,000 teenagers per annum). In general, these are countries with very high TFRs, yet teenage fertility as a proportion of the total is moderately high in most cases. The range of 10-14 per cent includes most of those countries, but a few have exceptionally high proportions of total fertility to teenagers: Cuba (24.4 per cent); Jamaica (19.7 per cent); and Bangladesh (19.6 per cent). In this very large group of countries, a fairly high proportion of teenagers are also married; and the singulate mean age at marriage (SMAM) is relatively low. However, the Caribbean and South America are somewhat different in that marriage is not as prevalent as it is in sub-Saharan Africa and Southern Asia, and a substantial number of teenage child-bearing occurs outside of marriage.

Still, it is worth bearing in mind that even in the countries with a moderate teenage fertility rate, a fairly high proportion of young women are involved in such behaviour: ASFR of about 50 per 1,000 teenagers per annum means that about 20 per cent of young women will have had their first child before they reach age 20. This proportion is by no means insignificant. Typically, in South America, with teenage ASFRs of about 80 per 1,000 women, about one third of women have their first birth under age 20; in Guatemala, with ASFR of about 130 per 1,000, about half of all young women have their first child by that age (Singh and Wulf, 1990). Thus, in countries with even higher rates, the vast majority of women become mothers during adolescence. It is clear that, except in the Eastern Asian, Western European and Northern European regions, child-bearing during the teenage years is either a somewhat common or a very common occurrence.

Although current levels of teenage reproduction and marriage have important implications for a woman's status, trends in this behaviour may also affect the weight that should be assigned to this factor in relation to other influential factors. Estimates of recent trends in the level of teenage fertility can be ventured, based on countries that have had good quality data for the past 10-20 years (United Nations, 1992). Teenage fertility has declined markedly in some developing countries, notably in Northern Africa, Western Asia, South-eastern Asia and even in a few Southern Asian countries, for example, Pakistan. Many of these declines were accompanied by increases in the mean age at marriage.

In other areas of the world, declines are less obvious, and some increases have also occurred. The decline in India has been quite small; and from the 1970s to the 1980s, there was an increase in Bangladesh (United Nations, 1992). Declines in sub-Saharan Africa are also quite small and in most cases, the actual level remains quite high: for example, in Kenya, ASFR for ages 15-19 dropped from 178 in the early 1970s to 152 in the mid- to late 1980s, and a similar change occurred in Senegal. In the Caribbean and South America, the level of teenage fertility either remained almost constant between the 1970s and the 1980s (Barbados, Bolivia, Costa Rica, Guatemala, Peru, and Trinidad and Tobago), increased in a few instances (Argentina, Brazil, Haiti and Uruguay), or changed relatively little (almost all of the other countries). A few countries did have noticeable declines in absolute terms, even though their current level is still high (Cuba, Honduras, Mexico and Panama). In the case of the Caribbean and South America, the absence of any great change in teenage fertility for most countries is especially remarkable because total fertility declined greatly during this period (Chackiel and Scholnik, 1990). The great difference in trends in both teenage marriage and teenage fertility that is observed between Northern African, South-eastern Asian and Western Asian countries, on the one hand, and Latin America and the Caribbean, on the other hand, suggests that differences in social values and social organization may account for variation in the likelihood of change in teenage reproductive behaviour. It is clear that a large overall fertility change is not necessarily accompanied by an equivalent decline in teenage child-bearing. Instead, it may be accomplished by a very early cessation of child-bearing, frequently achieved by means of a woman becoming sterilized by the time she is in her mid-twenties to late twenties. Even where declines from especially high levels (for example, from ASFR of 120 or more) have occurred, it is not at all certain that these declines will continue. Certainly, in the Caribbean and South America, teenage child-bearing has remained at a moderately high level (70-90) even where total fertility has declined to quite low levels (TFRs of about 2.0-4.0).

It is also possible that some of the declines that have occurred so far may be reversed. Premarital sexual activity may increase somewhat, given changes in social values and in parental control over adolescents, declines in the age at menarche and increases in the age at first union. Although little firm data are available on trends in premarital sexual activity, the impression of researchers is that it is rising in Latin America and the Caribbean (Wulf, 1986). Changes in social values in large urban centres in sub-Saharan Africa and South-eastern Asia are also believed to be leading to increases in premarital sexual activity, pregnancy and possibly child-bearing among adolescents.

In summary, substantial recent declines in teenage marriage and child-bearing from traditionally high levels have occurred in some regions (Northern Africa, South-eastern Asia and Western Asia). Additionally, levels are very low in other regions (Western and Northern Europe, Eastern Asia), where teenage marriage and child-bearing either now affects only a small minority of women, or will soon do so.

However, the current level of teenage union formation and child-bearing is clearly still very high in some regions of the world, namely, Southern Asia, sub-Saharan Africa, and Latin America and the Caribbean. In most of those regions, awareness of the negative implications of widespread teenage marriage and motherhood for women and for society is increasing. In addition, even though the level is moderate in some other regions (including some developed countries), teenage child-bearing accounts for a relatively large proportion of total fertility; and especially in areas of the world where much of it occurs among unmarried women, it is perceived as a social problem for both the persons concerned and the society as a whole. In the two groups of countries where this is the case, the prevalence of teenage marriage and/or child-bearing is high enough to affect any proportion, from a large minority up to the majority of women.

B. Reasons for early union formation and child-bearing

This section describes some of the more fundamental factors that have been identified as contributing to an early beginning of reproductive behaviour. However, it is clear that at the microlevel, when short-run trends within countries are considered, explanation of such trends is necessarily more complex than those fundamental factors would indicate. The foregoing discussion illustrates some of the major differences across the main regions of the world in levels of early marriage and child-bearing during the teenage years. Meaningful explanations for worldwide variation in reproductive behaviour should be able to link regions with similar levels of behaviourial prevalence to common cultural, economic and social factors.

From a functional perspective, high mortality, which was typical in developing countries until the past few decades, is the primary reason for early entry into union and subsequent early fertility, simply because a large average family size is needed for the survival of the community. An early beginning of reproduction ensures that the maximum level of fertility shall be achieved, although if conditions change, means to decrease fertility may be introduced (abstinence, contraception, abortion, infanticide) (Davis and Blake, 1956). If age at entry into union is late, it is impossible to make up the lost potential fertility.

Secondly, within this perspective, a large family size is economically rational in a traditional agrarian society with a subsistence economy that is predominantly based on familial production (Caldwell, 1976). What Caldwell calls the "superstructure", family structure and fertility behaviour, is accommodated to meet overriding economic needs. The costs and care of children are shared by the extended family, making it possible for women to bear a large number of children, who then become productive at quite young ages.

Cain (1989) highlights another structural factor that was much more applicable to developing countries than to developed countries, which supports the demand for a large family and hence, an early beginning of family formation. This is the fact that the State or community does not provide for support during old age, so that individuals are responsible for their own security when they become unproductive; therefore, adults ensure their future welfare by having many sons. Because the burden of support falls exclusively on sons, fertility has to be much higher than it would otherwise be if children of either sex could fill this role. The risks involved in not following the pattern of having a large family are great for the woman, as well as for the family as a whole. Even if a woman is employed, she may not be able to predict at the time she is making reproductive decisions whether she can accumulate enough assets to be self-supporting in old age (Dixon-Mueller, 1989). In contrast, there is a fairly high degree of certainty that some of one's children will be willing and able to provide support during old age.

The mechanisms for ensuring that almost all women shall marry and that they shall marry young are many and varied, depending upon the country and social group. Where individual couples that are to be married are not expected to be financially independent or have their own residence, marriage is more feasible and therefore occurs earlier and more universally than where residential and financial independence is the norm (Dixon, 1971). Even where early marriage is feasible, it may not be desirable. Desirability is ensured by a social organization that rewards those that marry young, and their families, and penalizes those that do not. The penalties that accompany childlessness, such as social isolation and stigma, and the loss of opportunities for economic support and social mobility, are probably strong enough to produce compliance by almost all families. It has been argued that even though objectively it may be in parents' best interests to marry their children later rather than earlier, societal norms that are usually internalized by parents will make them comply. In addition, sanctions (religious obligations, community pressure) usually exist to enforce compliance (Davis and Blake, 1956).

Another important mechanism that helps to support early marriage and child-bearing is the rigid sex-role system that exists in most developing countries. Permissible roles for women are those of wife and mother, which means that women derive status from these roles only. This system may exist even in situations where women in practice perform other roles, such as worker on the family farm or productive worker within the household. Because women are assigned status within the family or the society only through their roles of wife and mother, it follows that families will seek to move women into these roles as early as it is feasible.

Some of the conditions that have traditionally justified this pattern of behaviour have changed in most countries. For example, mortality has declined worldwide, some societies have moved from being largely rural and agrarian to having most people living in cities and the average level of education has risen substantially. As a result, in many countries, bearing a large number of children is no longer necessary to women for survival or economic well-being; and in other countries this becomes true only within specific social groups. However, the social organization has not changed as quickly as have material circumstances. The case of many parts of Latin America and the Caribbean, where substantial social and economic change has occurred during the past several decades, is a good example of how adolescent child-bearing can remain at a quite high level and may even increase as a proportion of all fertility (Singh and Wulf, 1990). The fact that fertility among adolescents failed to decline in proportion to the overall drop in fertility may be due to a combination of persistence of elements of a traditional social organization mixed with the increasing acceptance of more Westernized values and behaviour.

A further important point is that although demographic, social and economic change has occurred throughout the world, affecting almost all countries, it is clear that living conditions and opportunities have not changed to the same extent for all segments of society within countries. When adolescent marriage and child-bearing patterns are studied for subgroups within countries, large variations become evident. Among the less educated and the rural population subgroups, adolescents have a higher rate of both union formation and child-bearing (Singh and Wulf, 1990). Where poverty can be measured, adolescent reproduction is found to be higher among the poorer segments of society (Henriques and others, 1989; Singh, 1986). The positive association between poverty and adolescent reproduction has become more noticeable where some degree of social and economic change has been achieved and overall fertility has declined. As an increasingly large segment of a society benefits from economic change, adolescent child-bearing becomes more concentrated in the poorer segments of society. However, this situation may coexist with high levels of sexual activity overall, and depending upon differential levels of contraceptive use, high levels of pregnancy and abortion among the better-off segments of society.

The question whether poverty is itself a basic underlying cause of the low status of women has been raised. In general, one needs to study the status of women by looking within social classes, that is, to try to determine whether women's status is different from that of men within their own social class. Although there is no question that in general women have a lower status in relation to men even in non-poor social classes, it is possible that poverty can exacerbate the low status of women, since viable alternative roles for women are particularly scarce in poor communities. Moreover, even if community beliefs condone women's assumption of roles other than wife and mother, the occupational structure may not provide women opportunities to pursue these roles. And even when women supplement family income by working, because their income is variable over time and generally lower than men's, society continues to view them primarily as wives and mothers. Poor teenage girls may correctly perceive that attempting to achieve an alternative role will entail facing and overcoming enormous obstacles; they will therefore drop out of school because education is not seen as particularly useful, rather than because they are already pregnant or because they are being pressured into marriage (Levy, Chataigne and Guengant, 1992). In contrast, among the better-off segments of society, where alternative opportunities are more likely to exist or be created, teenagers are more likely to perceive these options as being attainable and are therefore more likely to pursue a course of action (staying in school, avoiding child-bearing) that would make it possible for them to take advantage of such opportunities.

The possibility that poor young women may consider having a child to be an attractive alternative to their current situation has been discussed in the context of adolescent child-bearing in the United States. Within poor communities, social support for young mothers may continue and although there may be no active encouragement or pressure by the family for a teenager to have a child, motherhood and the baby are valued once the event has occurred. Moreover, given the very high prevalence of teenage child-bearing (the annual ASFR among black teenagers in the United States is about 90 per 1,000 and about one third have had a child before age 20), it is likely that early child-bearing, occurring mainly among unmarried teenagers, may not be stigmatized. In general, most teenagers, including those that are disadvantaged, do not plan to become pregnant; however, once the pregnancy occurs it may be welcomed overoptimistically because the negative consequences are underestimated (Trussell, 1988). Some small-scale studies found that pregnant teenagers show poorer self-esteem and greater defensiveness, feelings of inadequacy and family conflict than non-pregnant teens (Zongker, 1977).

A comparative analysis of teenagers in the United States of America with those in selected Western European countries highlighted the important point that sexual activity among teenage girls in Europe was at least as high as that in the United States, and yet the pregnancy rate (both abortions and births) was much lower (Jones and others, 1985). European women that began sexual relationships during their teenage years apparently had a more practical outlook. They sought and could obtain contraceptive supplies and use them effectively. The authors of this study hypothesize that American teenagers were much less open in accepting their sexuality (reflecting attitudes in the society itself) and therefore did not take immediate steps to avoid pregnancy.

In summary, the traditional social structural supports for early marriage and child-bearing are long-standing and strong. Indeed, these structural factors are still dominant in some countries. However, even when the effects of urbanization and modernization begin to be felt, changes in the cultural and social organizational supports for a traditional pattern of early marriage and child-bearing often lag behind. Thus, even though an early pattern of child-bearing may become dysfunctional, it may continue to be practised. In other countries, where these underlying factors have either changed substantially or remained rather static, but the emphasis on education has risen greatly, or other changes have occurred in values and norms, declines in teenage child-bearing are observed. However, even when norms and values about women's roles change and alternative roles become possible in some social groups, there may not be a uniform pattern across all social groups. The poor are likely to benefit less from such changes, and the pattern of early child-bearing is likely to persist longer and may even be viewed by some as adaptive to their very limiting conditions of life. Even in better-off subgroups, other counteracting changes may occur simultaneously with the improvements noted above and cause some stabilization in the level of early child-bearing, and perhaps even cause an increase. Examples of such changes include declines in parental control, changing norms concerning premarital sexual activity and possibly unmarried motherhood, and a lengthening of the period between menarche and marriage.

C. Relation between early marriage and child-bearing and women's status

In discussing the relation between early marriage and child-bearing and women's status, it is very important to distinguish the various aspects of teenage reproductive behaviour, because their impact on women's status will differ greatly. The term "adolescent pregnancy" is often used broadly to encompass sexual activity, union formation, pregnancy and child-bearing. However, each of these types of behaviour is unique and can have different effects on women's status. It may be argued that sexual activity and pregnancy, in and of themselves, are not the behaviour that will have major effects on women's status. This is not to say that such behaviour may not have some impact on the health of the teenager but that the importance of these two types of behaviour for women's status is much smaller than that of marriage and child-bearing. Some possible negative aspects of sexual relationships at an early age are the likelihood that the participants have begun under pressure or even force and that the risk of sexually transmitted diseases may be great, because younger teenagers tend to have less knowledge and power in a sexual relationship. Pregnancies that are terminated by abortion will not have the long-run impact that having a child would, but the event and the decision-making process are bound to be important points in the teenager's life that at least temporarily distract her from pursuing long-term goals. Despite these kinds of effects, it is the formation of a stable union, whether or not it is a legal marriage, and more significantly, having a child at a young age, that are likely to have the greatest impact on the teenager's life chances and on her status in the long term.

Although most current research does not directly address the implications for the status or role of women of early outset of reproductive behaviour, some effort has been devoted to ascertaining the extent to which any early reproductive behaviour, but especially motherhood, influences outcomes that are used as proxy measures of women's status. For example, the question of the direction of the relation between high school drop-out and early motherhood is relevant for understanding the relation between early motherhood and the status of women. In-depth research along these lines has been done mostly in the United States of America, with less being done in the developing countries so far. However, awareness of such issues as these is increasing in the developing countries.

Impact of early marriage or consensual union on women's status

Early entry into a union may have some impact on a woman's status independent of the fact that it may also lead to early motherhood. Having to adapt to the new role of wife, especially if it is combined with moving out of her own family network, greatly increases the probability that a young woman will have little say in decisions and little chance to exercise independent action. The young woman is subject to family control as she moves from the role of protected daughter to that of a protected wife. Fostering a weak marital bond is one means that social groups have of ensuring that the young wife shall remain in a subservient status within her new family. This pattern is more dominant in areas where an extended family structure is common, such as in the Southern Asia but it probably occurs in a less extreme form in other regions as well. This pattern of control may exist even where early marriage does not necessarily result in early motherhood, and it may even characterize women that marry at a somewhat older age (over 20) to a lesser extent, because of long-standing attitudes and values concerning the role of women. What is more, early marriage will most likely coincide with leaving school, because it is likely that education will not be viewed as necessary for, and may even be seen as incompatible with, the new role of a wife that the young woman will be assuming. The interrelation of education and early reproductive behaviour is discussed below in more detail.

A large age difference between the two partners (e.g., the male partner is more than five years older than the female, who is under age 20 at the time the union is formed) is also likely to increase the probability that the union will lead to a woman's loss of control and to her having little power in decision-making within the household. A large age difference may have an effect similar to that of early marriage and change of residence, even if the new couple forms an independent nuclear household. The greater knowledge and experience of the male partner gives him an important advantage at the beginning of the union, an advantage which may be difficult to overcome. Large age differences are typical in Africa and are not unusual in Latin America (Casterline, Williams and McDonald, 1986; United Nations, 1990).

Premarital sexual relationships in Latin American and the Caribbean, and in urban areas in sub-Saharan Africa and the United States, are often not accompanied by co-residence and therefore probably will not have nearly the same effect in limiting the woman's role in decision-making concerning her own life. She is also likely to be still living with her own family, or in some cases, living independently. The extent to which young women are free to engage in sexual relations and voluntarily choose to do so may be seen as indicative of a higher status for women. The remaining question then is whether female teenagers, at a very young age, are knowledgeable and practical enough to use contraception to avoid pregnancy and sexually transmitted diseases. Because it is the female who will bear most of the burden of deciding how to resolve the pregnancy and of bringing up the child if she decides to have one, the freedom to choose to engage in sexual relations is somewhat unreal if she is unable to protect herself adequately.

Possible impact of early motherhood on women's status

The strongest impact of early motherhood on women's status is hypothesized to occur indirectly, through the fact that it may curtail education and/or work experience that the young woman would otherwise have had some chance of achieving. Although there are many mechanisms through which education and employment in non-family work can affect the status of women, a few that are believed to be especially important are given below:

(a) Education may enable a woman to conceptualize family size and reproduction as something apart from tradition and culture, something that may be within her control. As Dixon puts it: " . . . the knowledge alone of the possibility and means of [planning births] . . . gives women the power to shape their lives in ways undreamed of by those who have never questioned the inevitability of their childbearing . . . " (1975, p. 3);

(b) Education and access to the outside world also make it more feasible for a woman to look for and find means of contraception;

(c) Education increases the chance that a woman will find work that is better paid and has more potential for developing a career;

(d) Education may lead to paid work, thus enabling a woman to achieve a degree of economic independence by contributing to the family income. Earning power also gives a woman some measure of power in family decision-making;

(e) Education alone may increase a woman's power within the family because the woman is more knowledgeable about options in terms of purchases, schooling and so on, and is more able to understand and make choices.

These interrelations, however, are only relevant where women have a high probability of pursuing education beyond the early years of child-bearing and where an early birth limits chances of staying in school (Dixon, 1975). They are not relevant where most women marry very early, and young women have little or no control over the decision to marry or stay in school. The extremes (teenagers understand their options and are able to exercise a choice versus the situation in which they have little or no control over decisions concerning their education, marriage and child-bearing) are approximated in some countries or some social groups within countries. However, intermediate situations are also very common. For example, teenagers may not clearly perceive or understand their options, even where they have some possible choices; or even though parents may have little control or be in favour of continued schooling, economic necessity may lead teenagers to leave school; or girls may understand their options and be free to choose to stay in school but because of insufficient motivation or knowledge of how to prevent pregnancy, they become pregnant, drop out of school and have a child. It is easy to conceive of many other intermediate situations.

Research that improves understanding of the events that lead to early motherhood would make the development of interventions to prevent it more feasible. In addition, information on the process of decision-making that the individual teenager goes through would contribute to better understanding of the relation between early motherhood and school drop-out. However, research on this question is inconclusive because the available data are rarely sufficiently detailed.

One example of research on an intermediate situation is that of Levy, Chataigne and Guengant (1992), carried out in Guadeloupe. Although the general pattern in Guadeloupe is that the majority of teenage girls stay in school and avoid child-bearing during their teenage years (ASFR is currently quite low, about 35), the minority that are poor do not. The authors argue that because of poverty and the overall lack of opportunities, girls will drop out of school even before entering a marital union or becoming pregnant. Having dropped out of school, girls are then likely to contract early unions and soon have their first child. It is unlikely that parental control causes young women in Guadeloupe to leave school and begin a union and have a child—indeed, the wish of parents is probably the opposite. Instead, the authors suggest that the perception that there are no viable alternatives, given their poverty, is the underlying reason for school drop-out.

Research in the United States that examines the timing of events and follows teenage mothers over time allows one to assess better the importance of early child-bearing in terms of life chances. One study found a strong relation between delaying the timing of the first birth and the probability of completing secondary school (Mott and Marsiglio, 1985). This relation was found for Whites, Blacks and Hispanics. It should be noted that some teenage mothers do eventually obtain their secondary—school credentials through the General Educational Development equivalency programme. The older the age at first birth (during the teenage years), the more likely the teenage mother was to have graduated. A second study (Furstenburg, Brooks-Gunn and Morgan, 1987), which was longitudinal, followed up 300 urban black teenage mothers over 15 years. This study found that this group of women were disadvantaged compared with peers that bore children later, but within the group of young mothers there was great variability in many measures of "success". This variability was caused in part by variation in background factors, such as parental education and number of siblings; characteristics of the individual, such as personal competence and educational motivation; and the availability of services, such as a school for pregnant teenagers that stressed the importance of finishing school and delaying further births was available.

Also looking at black, urban, poor teenagers, Geronimus (1987) argues that it is rational for this subpopulation to have children at a young age because social expectations favour early child-bearing and some of these births are wanted and because birth outcomes are healthier and family support is more readily available during adolescence than at a later age. However, underlying this argument is the assumption that the countervailing advantages of delaying the first birth for the young women themselves do not balance or outweigh these factors. It implies an acceptance of the premise that there is no viable way out of the circular pattern of teenage motherhood and poverty for this population subgroup.

In one writer's review of the research on teenage pregnancy in the United States, the importance of a young woman's perception of the advantage of deferring parenthood is mentioned (Trussell, 1988). The author notes that this perception is heavily influenced by "her present circumstances and her belief in her future". Although an adolescent may be aware that having a child will jeopardize her life chances, she may feel helpless to alter her fate. Conflicting values of teenagers and their parents surrounding sexual intercourse also mitigate against planning for and effectively using contraception to avoid pregnancy. Research in the United States clearly supports the hypothesis that early child-bearing lowers long-term educational attainment and economic status. However, this relation is not a fixed one and outcomes will vary among women that have their first child as a teenager.

Other aspects of women's status that may be related to early child-bearing

Other areas in which early motherhood may have an impact on women's status have also been mentioned. The high negative correlation between the age at beginning child-bearing and completed family size suggests that, independent of other factors, a woman that has her first child at an early age may have less control over fertility and presumably over decision-making surrounding family size.

In addition, very early child-bearing is argued to have negative effects on the health of both the woman and her infant. However, research (reviewed by Makinson, 1985) suggests that when compared with births to older women, many of the differentials that have been found are due more to the fact that teenage births are mostly first births and are more likely to be births to women that are socio-economically disadvantaged in the first place. At least some of the remaining disadvantage to young mothers is also due to inadequate prenatal care, rather than any factor inherent in the age of the mother. Although some evidence suggests that when background variables are controlled, maternal age is linked to a small degree to cognitive development, there is no conclusive evidence of a link to impaired social or emotional development or to an increased likelihood of infants suffering non-accidental injuries.

The importance of education and employment for women will most likely rise, given the current demographic pattern of an increasingly early cessation of child-bearing in many developing countries, and given economic necessity. This pattern is evident in Latin America, where most women are having their last child at an increasingly early age—the late twenties or early thirties. Child-rearing will continue to occupy most women for about six years after the birth of the last child. Even though an average of from three to four children implies that the average woman will be mainly involved in child-rearing for about one third of her reproductive life (Weinberger, Lloyd and Blanc, 1989), it is still true that less time will be spent on child-rearing from about the mid-thirties on for most women. The decline in family size is of relatively recent origin and it will take some time for awareness of its implications for the changing role of women to become widespread. As recognition of the implications grows, however, the need for a larger economic role for women should also be acknowledged.

D. Conclusion

It is clear that the causal relation between women's status and early marriage/child-bearing is reciprocal. In other words, the relation can be circular and reinforcing: societal perception of acceptable roles for women means that women will engage in the roles of wife and mother at a young age; and early marriage/motherhood in itself largely precludes the possibility of seeking or developing any other alternative roles. Even when the situation changes for some social groups, it is still true that the overall perception of women's roles is unlikely to change for other groups because alternatives are scarce or non-existent.

Attempts to help women to break out of this self-perpetuating cycle involve changes in either (or preferably both) of two important factors: broadening the perception of what are acceptable roles for women (that is, providing more opportunities for women to engage in alternative roles); and encouraging a delay in the age of entry into marriage and motherhood. Of course, an increase in the availability of alternative roles itself represents an improvement in the status of women. However, in conditions of economic stagnation or slow growth, this goal may be very difficult to achieve; in addition, it may not be a sufficient condition for the improvement of women's status, because norms of behaviour must also change in order for women to be able to take advantage of improved opportunities. Delaying the initiation of reproduction and marriage is also difficult to achieve, given pre-existing patterns of behaviour; and even if it is achieved (for example, indirectly, as a result of societal emphasis on keeping girls in school), it too is certainly not a sufficient condition for improving the status of women. At the very least, however, the delay should facilitate such an improvement by buying young women time in which to achieve greater physical and emotional maturation and, potentially, self-identification, as well as greater power in interpersonal relations and in decision-making within the family.

The two approaches are themselves interrelated: to best enable women to take advantage of increased opportunities (e.g., in the labour force), they will need improved education and training. Moreover, in order to stay in school for more years, the age at marriage and motherhood must be delayed. This is not to say that schooling and reproduction are mutually exclusive. The longitudinal study of a sample of black, urban teenagers in the United States discussed above showed that where the attendance of adolescent mothers in school is tolerated and even encouraged, and resources are available to enable young mothers to return to school after delivery (such as economic and social support by their family, provision of child care and governmental programmes that provide some financial support), it is possible to increase greatly the chances that teenage mothers' will complete secondary school (Furstenberg, Brooks-Gunn and Morgan, 1987). However, this possibility is unlikely to be an option for the majority of developing countries, even if only the cost of the support services is considered.

A wide range of types of programmes and approaches have been tried, mainly in the United States, to improve the situation of adolescents. Although such programmes have several aims, one of their central goals is to improve the ability of adolescents in disadvantaged social groups to plan their births. Less emphasized approaches are counseling and help with completing high school, seeking further training and finding employment, but these are interconnected with reproductive planning and are, at least, as important. There is a need for more attention to these diversified goals. Althoughe the more comprehensive types of programmes (often including not just health-related services but also counseling on many topics and even recreational activities) cost a great deal and may not seem very applicable to developing countries, aspects of these programmes may be adapted and used even in poorer countries. The comprehensive programme Centro de Orientación para Adolescentes (CORA) at Mexico City has successfully pioneered youth participation in counselling and provision of services and is viewed as an ideal model in the Latin American context.

At the minimum, improved access to contraceptive services for young and unmarried women and men is a necessary facilitator of change in the status of women. When young women do begin to remain in school in large proportions and the age at first marriage is delayed, the prevalence of premarital sexual activity is likely to rise. Depending upon the cultural context of sexuality, the extent of parental control and sanctions on such behaviour, there will be a greater or lesser need for family planning services for unmarried adolescents.

The discussion in this paper highlights some very large gaps in knowledge in this area. The need for more information ranges from "simpler" topics such as remedying the lack of basic data on teenage reproductive behaviour in a number of countries in Africa (see table 27), to resolving the disagreements among researchers about the interrelation between teenage marriage and child-bearing and educational attainment, for example. Some of these disagreements over the relation within a single cultural context, such as the United States, as well as those that are more broad-based, are often due to a lack of data. However, many more disagreements will arise because of the great variation in the social and cultural contexts surrounding adolescents and their reproductive behaviour. And, of course, these differences imply that the impact on women's status will vary equally widely. These wide variations make the need for more specific information on individual countries and social groups even more evident. It cannot be assumed, for instance, that programmes that work in one area will necessarily work in another, even if the problem seems to be similar.

However, early marriage and child-bearing are only two among many factors that are highly related to women's status. These two factors are particularly relevant to attempts to improve women's status because they are closely tied to educational attainment. As pointed out earlier, however, many countries are still in the stage where more fundamental changes are needed, since the degree of parental control over female children may mean that the choice between education and marriage and child-bearing may not even exist. What is more, even if change is achieved (e.g., in those societies or social groups within societies where teenage child-bearing and marriage are declining or already very low), it does not necessarily follow that the change is an entirely positive one for women. For example, if women work full time but still continue to carry by far the greater share of housework and child-rearing responsibilities, this may be seen as a new form of slavery (Davis, 1977) rather than an improvement in women's status. While one hopes to achieve social change in this area, one must bear in mind that such change is not only difficult to achieve but also that however influential adolescent reproductive behaviour, it is only one of many other factors that are highly related to women's status.

REFERENCES

Cain, Mead (1989). Family structure, women's status and fertility change. *In International Population Conference, New Delhi*, vol. 1. International Union for the Scientific Study of Population, Liège, Belgium.

Caldwell, John C. (1976). Toward a restatement of demographic transition theory. *Population and Development Review* (New York), vol. 2, No. 3/4 (September/December), pp. 321-366.

Casterline, John B., L. Williams and P. McDonald (1986). The age difference between spouses: variations among developing countries. *Population Studies* (London), vol. 40, No. 3 (November), pp. 353-374.

Chackiel, Juan, and Susana Scholnik (1990). América Latina: gransición de la fecundidad en el período, 1950-1990. Paper presented at the Seminar on Fertility Transition in Latin America, Buenos Aires, April. Sponsored by the International Union for the Scientific Study of Population.

Davis, Kingsley (1977). The theory of teenage pregnancy in the United States. Preliminary Paper Series, No. 10. Berkeley: University of California, International Population and Urban Research.

__________, and Judith Blake (1956). Social structure and fertility: an analytic framework. *Economic Development and Cultural Change* (Chicago), vol. 4, No. 3 (April), pp. 211-235.

Demographic and Health Surveys and Population Reference Bureau (1991). *Adolescent Women in Sub-Saharan Africa: A Chartbook on Marriage and Childbearing*. Washington, D.C.: Population Reference Bureau.

Dixon, Ruth B. (1971). Explaining cross-cultural variations in age at marriage and proportions never marrying. *Population Studies* (London), vol. 25, No. 2 (July), pp. 215-233.

__________ (1975). *Women's Rights and Fertility*. Reports on Population/Family Planning, No. 17. New York: The Population Council.

Dixon-Mueller, Ruth (1989). Patriarchy, fertility and women's work in rural societies. In *International Population Conference, New Delhi*, vol. 2. Liége, Belgium: International Union for the Scientific Study of Population.

Furstenberg, Frank F. Jr., J. Brooks-Gunn and S. Philip Morgan (1987). Adolescent mothers and their children in later life. *Family Planning Perspectives* (New York), vol. 19, No. 4 (July/August), pp. 142-151.

Geronimus, Arlene T. (1987). On teenage childbearing and neonatal mortality in the United States. *Population and Development Review* (New York), vol. 13, No. 2 (June), pp. 245-279.

Guengant, Jean Pierre, Tirbani Jagdeo and Denise Richards (1991). Teens in a changing society: Saint Lucia. Port-of-Spain, Trinidad.

Economic Commission for Latin America and theCaribbean/Centro Latino-americano de Demografia. Mimeographed.

Henriques, Maria Helena, and others (1989). *Adolescentes de Hoje, Pais do Amanha: Brasil.* New York: The Alan Guttmacher Institute.

Jones, Elise F., and others (1985). Teenage pregnancy in developed countries: determinants and policy implications. *Family Planning Perspectives* (New York), vol. 17, No. 2 (March/April), pp. 53-63.

Levy, Maryse, Claudine Chataigne and Jean-Pierre Guengant (1992). Determinants et consequences immédiates de maternités chez les jeunes mères en Guadeloupe. Paper presented at the Colloque fecondité et insularité, Réunion, May.

Makinson, Carolyn (1985). The health consequences of teenage fertility. *Family Planning Perspectives* (New York), vol. 17, No. 3 (May/June), pp. 132-139.

Mott, Frank, L., and William Marsiglio (1985). Early childbearing and completion of high school. *Family Planning Perspectives* (New York), vol. 17, No. 5 (September/October), pp. 234-237.

Singh, Susheela (1986). Adolescent pregnancy in the United States: an interstate analysis. *Family Planning Perspectives* (New York), vol. 18, No. 5 (September/October), pp. 210-220.

__________, and Deirdre Wulf (1990). *Today's Adolescents, Tomorrow's Parents: A Portrait of the Americas.* New York: The Alan Guttmacher Institute.

Trussell, James (1988). Teenage pregnancy in the United States. *Family Planning Perspectives* (New York), vol. 20, No. 6 (November/December), pp. 262-272.

United Nations (1989). *Adolescent Reproductive Behaviour*, vol. II, *Evidence from Developingp Countries.* Population Studies, No. 109/Add.1. Sales No. E.89.XIII.10.

_________ (1990). *Patterns of First Marriage: Timing and Prevalence.* Sales No. E.91.XIII.6.

_________ (1991). *World Population Prospects, 1990.* Population Studies, No. 120. Sales No. E.91.XIII.4.

_________ (1992). *World Population Monitoring, 1991: With Special Emphasis on Age Structure.* Population Studies, No. 126. Sales No. E.92.XIII.2.

Weinberger, Mary Beth, Cynthia Lloyd and Ann Klimas Blanc (1989). Women's education and fertility: a decade of change in four Latin American countries. *International Family Planning Perspectives* (New York), vol. 15, No. 1 (March), pp. 4-14.

Wulf, Deirdre (1986). Teenage pregnancy and childbearing in Latin America and the Caribbean: a landmark conference. *International Family Planning Perspectives* (New York), vol. 12, No. 1 (March), pp. 17-21.

Zongker, Calvin (1977). The self-concept of pregnant adolescent girls. *Adolescence* (San Diego, California), vol. 12, No. 4 (Winter), pp. 477-488.

XV. ADOLESCENT PREGNANCY IN THE AMERICAS AND THE CARIBBEAN

Billie A. Miller[*]

In Latin America and the Caribbean, the early family planning programmes of the 1950s and the 1960s were directed primarily to women that had already embarked upon motherhood, women that had already given birth to some children and lost some to spontaneous and induced abortion, stillbirth and early childhood diseases. Priority was given to arresting repeated pregnancies and pregnancy-related morbidity and mortality among post-adolescent women, who would ordinarily have been part of the workforce. There was strong economic motivation to contract women's reproductive output in order to expand their productive output—even though at that time the true economic value of women's work was grossly underestimated and consequently undervalued.

Those early programmes were almost exclusively launched by non-governmental organizations in an era when Governments were openly hostile to family planning or, in a few cases, were prepared to permit others to interface between them and the Church in the provision of services. Crisis intervention was the hallmark of the day and the point at which family planners that intervened was decidedly in the post-adolescent age group. It would have appeared more urgent in 1958 to try to persuade a woman not to have her seventh or eighth child than to try to persuade an adolescent to postpone her first or even her second pregnancy. Therefore, although teenage fertility was high, it was overlooked in favour of high fertility among older women in their twenties and thirties as targets for family planning.

Teenagers were left to fend for themselves in the manner in which they acquired sex education; in the procurement of contraceptives, of guidance counselling or of induced abortions; and in the rearing of their own children, especially as the extended family began to decline as a consequence of urbanization and other socio-economic pressures. This situation is still true for teenagers some 30 years later.

Despite the slowing effect of overpopulation on the development process, improved education and health services, especially those provided for young children, helped to enhance the status of women. This improvement was observed earlier in the Caribbean than in Latin America. Education became free, universal and eventually mandatory through primary and, in the Caribbean, secondary stages. Access to health care, especially maternal and child health, through community-based clinics and generally improved public-health services, including sanitation, clean water and immunization, did more to reduce maternal and infant morbidity and mortality than any other single factor.

During the 1970s and early 1980s, it became apparent that despite the improved indicators of mortality rates and total fertility rates, adolescent fertility rates were escalating. In some countries in Latin America and the Caribbean, they were higher than the non-adolescent rates—and they still are. Adolescents continued to be a neglected majority among the young.

Family planning associations and Governments had come to recognize many realities by this time. The nexus between population and development could no longer be ignored: that family planning saved lives was an inescapable truth and special attention would have to be focused on adolescent fertility as a matter of urgency. Available data were forcing acceptance of the need for change—change which had to be carefully managed in order to produce positive results. Theories about sole causative factors had to be rethought and read together with a number of variables and interdependent considerations and imperatives.

In this context, other realities had to be faced. A plethora of studies and surveys disclosed that: (*a*) adolescents were reaching puberty earlier; (*b*) sexual activity began as early as puberty; (*c*) there was a high incidence of promiscuity among adolescents (often

[*]Member of Parliament, Bridgetown, Barbados, and president of International Planned Parenthood Federation/Western Hemisphere Region, Regional Council.

with older partners); (*d*) by the late 1980s it was all being compounded by the acquired immunodeficiency syndrome (AIDS).

Yet Governments gave only lip-service to the admittedly unacceptably high incidence of teenage pregnancies. Adolescents were still left to fend for themselves; and it should be borne in mind that little or no family life education was taught formally in schools or informally in the homes, no sale or access of contraceptives to adolescents was permitted, no counselling or termination-of-pregnancy facilities were available to them (particularly serious in view of the rising rate of abortion among adolescents), no encouragement of post-partum resumption of education was offered and the question of parental consent for anything was not entertained.

National government and international agency policy changes were not always for the better. For example, abortion legislative changes in Northern America represented loss of freedom of reproductive choice. Everywhere in Latin America and the Caribbean, population dynamics were not yet integrated into national planning ministries; and health was still regarded as an exclusively social sector concern, with no productive sector impact or linkage.

By the late 1980s and in the early 1990s, AIDS began to generate new and different perspectives on the age-old problem of adolescent fertility. When AIDS was added to early sexual activity and rampant promiscuity among teenagers, the tragic results commanded the attention of parents and policy makers alike. World Health Organization (WHO) data put the issue beyond doubt in 1990, when it was reported that the per capita incidence of AIDS was highest in the world in the Americas; and within the Americas, was highest in some small Caribbean islands, where the greatest number of reported cases and recorded deaths was in age group 15-29. The obvious conclusion was that the disease was being contracted by adolescents while they were still in the school system. For the first time adolescents came into high focus. This triggered a rapid and, in some countries, a sudden liberalization of attitudes towards family life education. Voices that had long opposed the introduction of family life education into schools were now heard insisting that it had to begin at the primary level and must begin immediately. They were careful to point out that the family life education syllabus should have a realistic sex education component. The teachers' manual, *Teaching of Human Sexuality in Caribbean Schools*, which had been prepared and published by the Caribbean Family Planning Affiliation several years before, was in great demand.

Long-time proponents of the teaching of family life education from primary schools upward were understandably sceptical as to how long the panic-inspired enthusiasm would last. They wondered if, like the sudden and dramatic increase in condom sales, it, too, would subside and plateau out at levels not much higher than the pre-panic demand. Access to contraceptives for adolescents, mainly condoms and other barrier methods, was another spin-off from the fear of human immunodeficiency virus (HIV) infection and AIDS.

The positive reaction to the spread of this new "plague"of the late twentieth century was welcomed by family planners but there was a negative aspect as well. The media attention and money being channelled to AIDS prevention, treatment and care was diverting market share away from other sexually transmitted diseases (STDs) and reproductive tract infections, which were prevalent among adolescents. STDs and reproductive tract infections traumatize the lives of many, many more people than AIDS but the difference is, of course, that AIDS is always fatal. It is a fatal threat to men and women during their productive years and, in the case of women, in the reproductive process itself. Family planners are deeply concerned that AIDS is in danger of derailing progress in family planning, other STDs and reproductive tract infections. It is an interesting observation that several family planning associations and clinics, because of the initial overwhelming public reaction to the advent of HIV and AIDS, found great difficulty in recognizing it as another STD which required and merited their attention. The patients were often one and the same.

It would be impossible to discuss adolescent fertility without reference to the current debate on induced abortion in Latin America and the Caribbean and in Northern America. The ongoing struggle led by the Planned Parenthood Federation of America in the United States of America for freedom of reproductive choice has its equally vibrant but different counterpart in Latin America. The Caribbean is poised somewhere in between the two continental strategies. Safe motherhood is the preferred strategy being pursued in Latin countries which are strongly influenced by the Catholic church. It should not be construed as an initiative designed exclusively to appeal to mothers to the exclusion of the nulliparous. Rather. it should be viewed and promoted as a vehicle for family life education, particularly for young girls.

In the United States of America, adolescent pregnancy and child-bearing looms in the centre of a range of other demonstrations of alienation that plague large percentages of teenagers, those that drop out of school, engage in violence and other criminal acts, suffer mental disorders, abuse drugs and alcohol, attempt suicide, are disabled by injuries or die. These American adolescents are bombarded by messages on television, in the movies and in magazines that glorify casual unprotected sexual intercourse as glamorous, portray alcohol and cigarettes as symbols of maturity and hold out the accumulation of consumer goods as the measure of success and status.

The rate of births in the United States is unmatched in the rest of the industrialized world. The average age of first intercourse of American teenagers is 16.2 for girls and 15.7 for boys. By age 15, 13 per cent of white boys and 6 per cent of white girls have had intercourse, compared with 45 per cent of black boys and 10 per cent of girls. More than one fifth of all first pregnancies happen in the month after the "first time" and half occur within six months. Three fourths of all unintended teenage pregnancies happen in adolescents that do not use contraception. Among sexually active girls aged 15-19, 15 per cent had never used contraception and more than 50 per cent did not use it at first intercourse. Almost one third of all sexually active adolescents continue to have sexual intercourse without using any birth control devices whatsoever. In the United States, birth rates for white teenagers alone are higher than those for teenagers in any other Western country; the figures for black teenagers are three times the rates for Whites.

In both the United States and the Caribbean, small sample surveys found that numbers of girls experience their first intercourse involuntarily as victims of rape and incest. Sexual child abuse is believed to be far more widespread than the number of cases coming to light would suggest. In addition, many young adolescents are impregnated not by teenagers but by adult males.

Currently, one in six babies born in the United States is born to a school-age mother. There are 1.3 million children living with teenage mothers, half of them unmarried. Another 6 million children under age 5 are living with mothers that were adolescent when they gave birth.

In 1992, the International Planned Parenthood Federation reported that adolescent pregnancy in Brazil had been relatively neglected and was getting worse. Teenagers in Brazil are experiencing increasing economic difficulties, prevailing negative attitudes towards sex reinforced by the mass media and widespread ignorance of contraceptive methods. The 1980 census showed that the number of adolescent pregnancies had trebled in a decade. In 1990, some sources counted more than 1 million pregnant adolescents. Of these, 75 per cent could not identify one contraceptive method. It is also estimated that approximately 400,000 women have died from abortion-related causes, half of them adolescents. In 1980, statistics showed that in age group 15-19, death during pregnancy was the sixth highest cause of death.

In neighbouring Chile, a 1988 survey found that 65 per cent of adolescent boys and 35 per cent of girls had had at least one sexual experience before marriage. However, only one in five young women in 1986 had used contraception at first intercourse, resulting in one in six children being born to adolescent mothers (compared with one in nine in 1966). The point has been made that young people today live in a society that is surrounded by sexual messages but fails to provide the knowledge or tools necessary to practise responsible and safe sex.

Research by Tirbani Jagdeo of the Caribbean Family Planning Affiliation headquartered in Antigua showed that most adolescents became pregnant out of ignorance, even though they knew of at least one method of contraception. Dr. Jagdeo pointed out that teenage girls became pregnant not so much because they wanted to but more because they were misinformed about basic contraceptive and reproductive issues. For want of proper sex education, which was not available in the home or in the school, they tended to adopt a contraceptive method only after the first pregnancy. Studies conducted in the Caribbean showed that among sexually active women contraception was lowest among teenagers. Studies also disclosed that in those communities where sexual activity began in the very early teens, very few girls used a contraceptive method at the beginning of their sexual career. Later surveys revealed a changing pattern of behaviour. Teenagers today are twice as likely to use a contraceptive at first intercourse as they were 10 years ago. These changes have been greatly influenced by improved access to family life education and the generally improving status of women as they assumed their rightful place in the development process. These findings serve to underscore and emphasize the need for access to and availability of safe, convenient and reliable contraceptive methods to be made easier for young Caribbean citizens.

In Barbados, a Medical Termination of Pregnancy Act was passed by Parliament in 1983 but had little impact on the number of teenage pregnancies, which continued to rise. So, too, did the number of abortions, to the extent that Jean-Pierre Guengant, a Guadeloupan demographer, suggested in 1990 that the low fertility of Barbados, currently below replacement, could not be explained by the contraceptive prevalence rate which was about 50 per cent. He stated that one must assume virtually as many abortions as live births in order to obtain consistent results, and further suggested that there were about as many abortions as live births in Cuba, Barbados and, possibly, Antigua; and between 25 and 50 per cent of the number of live births in Martinique, Aruba, Curaçao and Puerto Rico. These research findings pose the question whether family planning programmes have been as successful in terms of contraception as in terms of abortion, which is not a service offered by family planning associations.

Adolescents play a starring role in these scenarios. They are often forced to choose between having a child and their education, their job and sometimes their health because of the high health risks for teenage mothers. Adults in the roles of parents, teachers, Governments, the Church and non-governmental organizations continue to be judgmental and derogatory, and talk down to or at adolescents, but little is actually being done. A strenuous effort must be made to persuade the medical profession, the pharmaceutical industry and Governments of the need for reliable contraceptives specially designed for adolescents. They would have to be accessible, inexpensive, effective and user-friendly in terms of ease of usage and low risk to health.

The implementation of stabilization programmes and structural adjustment policies in Latin America and the Caribbean has exacerbated the difficulties encountered by family planners in their endeavour to reduce adolescent pregnancies and rein in adolescent fertility. Social sector cut-backs, which invariably begin with health and education, are misguided and destructive of the programmes meant to answer the tragically expressed unmet need of teenagers. As contradictory as it may seem, structural adjustment does not facilitate family planning nor curb teenage pregnancies. Even in those countries where remarkable success has been achieved in lowering the birth rate and in decreasing infant and maternal mortality and morbidity rates, the incidence of adolescent fertility remains unacceptably and embarrassingly high.

Having considered the persistent problem of adolescent pregnancy together with the negative impact of AIDS, abortion and the current recessionary environment, it would appear that the subject for immediate and urgent attention is the knowledge/use gap. Innovative and effective means must be found to close it. The need has been clearly established for family life education with a realistic sex education component to be taught in schools from the primary stage onward. Adolescents themselves should be consulted about this matter which concerns them so intimately. There is a body of opinion which holds that new sexual attitudes and behaviour are already evolving for the twenty-first century.

Why are teenagers treated as a subgroup of ordinary humanity? Millions of dollars are spent educating them about everything except their sexuality. Why is it thought that teenagers do not need sex education—education about something that could derail all of the other aspects of formal education?

Much talk on family life education has been bandied about and it seems to mean different things to different people. What is meant here are the following points:

(a) Family life education needs to be institutionalized so that it is scheduled into the curricula of schools rather than being left entirely in the hands of overburdened guidance counsellors or taught on an ad hoc basis;

(b) Teachers need to be trained in family life education;

(c) Local family planning associations should be a very useful resource base for the design and implementation of the family life education syllabus.

Creative programmes can be devised. In Latin America and the Caribbean, television "soap operas", newspaper cartoons and comic strips have been produced and are playing to keen audiences, especially the adolescents, who cannot help but hear the family planning message. Youth Parliamentary Debates were a special success story. A series of those debates was organized in several Caribbean countries, including Antigua, Barbados, Dominica, Grenada, Guyana, Jamaica, Saint Kitts and Nevis, Saint Lucia, Saint Vincent and the Grenadines, and Trinidad and Tobago.

In the debates, teenagers from schools and youth groups debated resolutions calling for the inclusion of family life education in the schools at primary and secondary levels. In most of the countries, the debates took place in the national House of Parliament with the permission of the Speakers of the House, who were very cooperative. The youth parliamentarians democratically elected themselves to be government and opposition Members of Parliament and were guided by Standing Orders (rules of debate) very similar to the real Standing Orders that govern the real parliaments in each country. The debates presented a rare opportunity for the public to hear young people speak out on issues which concerned them. For a while, adults listened to youth rather than talked down to them. Recommendations, ideas and opinions offered by the students were often revealing and enlightening. The debates centred around teenage pregnancy in the first series and AIDS in the second—both in the context of family life education. They were carried live on radio in each country and edited televised versions were later screened for public viewing. Several real-life parliamentarians, including prime ministers, speakers, ministers, governors-general and community leaders, attended in the public galleries together with hundreds of schoolchildren supporting their school's representative in the national youth parliament. Women played a far larger role in the youth parliaments in all of the participating countries than they do in the actual parliaments. The end results were that youth were sensitized, parliamentarians were made more aware, the Church was supportive, the media was involved and the public was impressed with the need to put the issue high on its agenda.

There were other more specific positive results, which included legislation for the introduction of family life education in schools in Saint Lucia; the submission for discussion of national population policies in the parliaments of some countries, including Saint Lucia and Trinidad and Tobago; the appointment of a youth parliamentarian to the National AIDS Task Force in Trinidad and Tobago, and the spontaneous growth of teenage peer counselling groups in schools. The format of the Youth Parliament has been adopted by the Governments of Barbados, Dominica, Grenada, and Trinidad and Tobago as a means of eliciting the views and ideas of young people on issues of national importance. The teaching of family life education has been stepped up in most countries of the Caribbean as a way of countering traditional socialization, ignorance and lack of sex education among adolescents.

Teenagers have to be persuaded to postpone that first pregnancy especially in the face of 20-40 per cent unemployment. They have to be taught that their health and education are more often than not put in jeopardy by too early pregnancy and childbirth. They should not have to choose between aborting a child or aborting their education, and sometimes both. These are cruel choices which teenagers, being children themselves, are ill equipped to make. Teenagers are for the most part unemployed and unemployable, having no skills—thus, teenage pregnancies increase the burdens on already economically hard-pressed extended families.

This paper is not proposing that family life education by itself is the only real solution to the intractable and much neglected problems of adolescent pregnancy and fertility. Rather, it is suggesting that family life education can be a point of departure whether it is taught in the school, the home or the community. The geopolitical realignments taking place in the North while the South continues to languish in debt crisis, structural adjustment and poverty are not guaranteed to give priority to the subject under discussion. Neither in the North nor in the South do teenagers have any political power to articulate and protect their reproductive rights and their rights to information and safe services related to pregnancy. Life is about choice and change. If teenagers are to be expected to change their sexual behaviour, they will have to be afforded the opportunity for their choice to be informed and they will need to be consulted about how the change can be effected. Adults are not expected to complete this great task but neither are they at liberty to abstain from it.

XVI. LEGAL, ADMINISTRATIVE AND CULTURAL FACTORS AFFECTING WOMEN'S ACCESS TO FAMILY PLANNING

*Amy Grace Luhanga**

The United Nations has since 1945 promoted the improvement of the status of women through change, raising awareness of the situation of women throughout the world. The equal rights of men and women were enshrined in the Preamble of the United Nations Charter, which legally established gender equality as a fundamental human right for the first time. Throughout the world, discrimination against women has been based on deep-rooted cultural beliefs and traditional practices. In order to correct the situation, the international community resorted to different measures. However, in seeking for remedies, possible areas that encourage discrimination and affect the advancement of women had to be identified. One key area that was identified is health and family planning.

Indeed, it is recognized that the age at which a woman marries and begins having children, the size of her family and her ability to control her fertility are vital factors in determining not only her health and socio-economic status but also that of her family and the community as a whole.

Lower fertility is argued to be a means to improve the levels of living for all and to help meet national development goals. On the other hand, rapid population growth is seen as a major contributor to or the cause of high unemployment, crowded cities, pollution, inadequate housing, poor sanitation, continued illiteracy and insufficient public services. Consequently, the international community is giving more attention to the need for laws and policies that can slow this growth. Health laws and policies are among them; and, indeed, some considerations focus on the benefits of children. In the developing countries, it is estimated that one half of all births pose a high risk to the health of both mother and child, as births occur to women that are too old or too young, or that have had too many previous births or whose current birth occurs too soon after another birth. If births could be controlled so that they occur to women aged 18-35 and no woman would have more than four children with births at least two years apart, a large proportion of infant deaths and maternal deaths would be avoided. That is, family planning can substantially reduce high rates of sickness and death among women and children and create a healthy, happy community.

If the international community recognizes the role of family planning in the advancement of women and international development strategies, what has it done to promote family planning?

A. THE INTERNATIONAL COMMUNITY AND FAMILY PLANNING

The view that family planning is a basic human right is not new. It has been in existence since early 1950s, when the international community stated that knowledge of planned parenthood was a fundamental right. In many areas of the world, family planning has been denied to people through restrictive laws, policies or cultural and religious practices, or because of lack of access to information and services. On the other hand, the increasing complexity of population policies and family planning programmes has given rise to many ethical and legal issues. Because of those factors, the international community decided to promote and protect family planning as a basic human right.

In 1952, the International Planned Parenthood Federation (IPPF) was founded and its Constitution was ratified in 1953. Article 1 of the IPPF Constitution recognizes knowledge of planned parenthood to be a fundamental human right, a belief that has remained with the organization ever since. This may have been the first time such a right was enunciated at the international level. In 1966, the United Nations General Assembly adopted resolution 2211(XXI) on

*Lecturer/ Consultant, Legal Services, Institute of Development Management (Botswana, Lesotho and Swaziland).

the principle that "the size of the family should be the free choice of each individual family".

However, it was at the International Conference on Human Rights at Tehran in 1968, that the international community really expressed this view in a proclamation concerning the right to family planning which provides in article 16 that "Parents have a basic human right to determine freely and responsibly the number and spacing of their children."

Since 1968, the international community has reaffirmed this right but with further elaboration. The Proclamation on Human Rights confined the right to "parents" but the scope was later widened, first to include "all couples" and then to "all individuals". That is, the conceptual change has established the right to decide on child-bearing as a personal prerogative. At Bucharest in 1974, the World Population Conference adopted the World Population Plan of Action, which affirms that:

> "All couples and individuals have the right to decide freely and responsibly the number and spacing of their children and to have the information, education and means to do so; the responsibility of couples and individuals in the exercise of this right takes into account the needs of their living and future children, and their responsibilities towards the community." (United Nations, 1975, para. 14(f))

Family planning was reaffirmed as a basic human right in 1984 by the International Conference on Population held at Mexico City, which also emphasized the right to choice of family size without coercion and the right to choice of method, which "should include all medically approved and appropriate methods of family planning" (United Nations, 1984, p. 24).

One major factor that was considered at both of these conferences is the recognition that for women, access to family planning services opens the way to many other benefits. A woman's control over her own fertility is the freedom from which other freedoms flow.

In 1989, at Amsterdam, the International Forum on Population in the Twenty-first Century called for stronger family planning and maternal and child health services in both the public and private sectors. Indeed, since the Amsterdam Declaration for a Better Life for Future Generations, support for greater emphasis on population activities has been given by all bodies, including the United Nations Population Fund (UNFPA) and other United Nations organizations.

Several international agreements, including the International Strategy for the Fourth United Nations Development Decade and the 1990 World Summit for Children, endorsed the view that population growth and fertility are critical for development.

For the first time, targets in fertility and family planning for the next decade are part of international development strategies. It is recognized that reaching those targets will be critical for development and even for human survival in the next century.

Therefore, the international community has undoubtedly taken steps to promote and protect family planning as a right of an individual. However, how much has been achieved in practice, especially since Bucharest?

B. Promotion and protection of family planning as a basic human right

Before discussing whether the objectives of the international community concerning family planning have been achieved or not, there is a need to address the concept "family planning services". Most people think that family planning services concern only the provision of contraceptives, whereas they include:

(a) The right to have ready access to information, education and services for fertility regulation, which includes infertility as well as related issues, such as venereal diseases; and

(b) The right to make decisions about reproductive behaviour, including whether to have children, when and how many.

One needs to be well informed and educated in responsible parenthood in order to make a sound decision about fertility. At the same time, it is useless to inform and educate people about fertility if they do not have ready access to the services.

Prior to 1974

At the Bucharest Conference, most developing countries, especially those in sub-Saharan Africa and the Arab States, believed that they were not ready for population policies and that development was the best contraceptive. Most policy makers and planners were unaware of the seriousness of the population situation in their country and its consequences for socio-economic development, due to a lack of analysed population data. The only countries in Africa and the Arab region that had explicit population policies were Egypt, Ghana, Kenya, Mauritius and Tunisia.

Meanwhile, the countries of Asia and the Pacific led the way in formulating and implementing population policies. Between the 1950s and early 1960s, several Governments, notably those of India, Pakistan and the Republic of Korea, realized that in order to achieve socio-economic objectives, they ought to reduce their rapid population growth. By 1974, 17 Asian countries had adopted population policies and almost all countries had family planning programmes.

In Latin America and the Caribbean, the Governments were hardly involved in population activities nor did they have an interest in population policies attuned to the social goals of development. However, the attitude changed about 30 years ago, with almost all Governments undertaking the formulation of policies and the implementation of population programmes.

After 1974

Most countries that had the negative attitudes towards population policies after the Bucharest Conference had changed their perceptions markedly by 1984, and those which had previously had policies decided to strengthen them. By 1991, only four of the 170 countries had limited access to family planning services and 144 provided either direct or indirect support to family planning programmes. Indeed, at the World Summit for Children in August 1990, 70 Heads of State called for an extension of family planning services to all that wanted them.

In other words, the world has by and large recognized the importance of family planning in socio-economic development. The results of the World Fertility Survey programme, however, show that many millions of people throughout the world still do not have ready access to family planning. Why is that the case when almost all countries have accepted family planning as a necessity for socio-economic development and/or have established population policies and are supporting family planning programmes either directly or indirectly?

C. Factors contributing to successes and failures in planning services

Several factors contribute to the successes and failures of family planning services. The main contributory factors are: *(a)* political commitment; *(b)* legislation and policies; *(c)* administrative measures; and *(d)* attitudes (cultural and religious).

Political commitment

As stated earlier, most countries have either formulated new population policies or strengthened existing policies that recognize the role of family planning in national development and in the advancement of women's status. However, without political commitment no population policy can succeed. Political commitment here refers to:

(*a*) *Political statements*. Political leaders should affirm publicly their support of family planning. Such affirmations increase staff morale, commitment and personal effort. Moreover, other agencies accept the programme as legitimate, at the same time reassuring current and potential clients;

(*b*) *Political structure*. The closer to the political leadership, the more family planning programmes are valued and therefore the easier it is to mobilize necessary resources;

(*c*) *Political participation*. Political leaders should take an interest in the key positions of and give continuing support to programme implementers.

Almost all developing countries have not only formulated national population policies, but their political leaders have time and again made strong statements on population policies and family planning. Furthermore, they have become involved in the programmes, working together with those who implement them.

Most Governments have established high-level units to formulate, coordinate or monitor population policies and family planning to ensure that population policies and family planning programmes shall be implemented.

Legislation and policies

In some countries, such as Ecuador, Mexico, Peru and Yugoslavia, the Constitution guarantees the right of individuals to choose the number and spacing of children. In China, Portugal and Turkey, the Constitution requires the Governments to provide family planning services.

Almost all sub-Saharan African countries do not have legislation that directly refers to the right to family planning. Instead, Government policies, administrative guidelines or instructions have been issued. For example, in 1987, the Government of Botswana issued guidelines; and one of them gives "the right to all persons of reproductive age regardless of marital status, to determine for themselves how many children to have and when to have them".

Other areas commonly covered by administrative regulations are distribution and importation of contraceptives; public education and information, including young people; and monitoring of the safety and effectiveness of contraceptives.

While considering relevant legislation, it is worthwhile to touch on legislation relating to women's status. Women have always been regarded as minors and therefore incapable of making decisions, including decisions on whether to have children, when and how many and what methods of fertility control to use. However, the international community has long recognized that women without fertility control would never be able to improve their socio-economic status; and conversely, failure to improve their socio-economic status would affect their fertility management. The extent to which this occurs may depend upon how accessible these socio-economic improvements are to women. Many countries have taken legal measures to improve the status of women and specifically to enhance women's opportunities for education and employment and women's ability within and outside marriage to hold property, enter into contracts and carry on business. Most constitutions prohibit sex discrimination.

The ease of policy and legal reforms should, however, not be exaggerated. New ideas usually are slowly accepted. Priorities shift frequently to reflect different national needs. Indeed, for any policy or law to be reformed or effectively implemented, opinions and attitudes need to change.

In many countries, policy makers are confronted with customs and traditions that make reform or implementation difficult. In sub-Saharan Africa, for example, Governments have a difficult task of fashioning a legal system that can reconcile the forms and principles of the inherited legal systems with the principles of customary law.

Consequently, millions of women, mostly in developing countries, have found themselves having children they did not want.

Legislation, including administrative regulations, instructions and guidelines, would normally follow policy statements. However, in some cases, it never happens. Nevertheless, positive legislation ensures effective implementation of policies.

Since 1974, there has been a revolution in birth control law and practice, which has expanded the use of contraceptives. Changes in laws and policies have expanded contraceptive use by:

(a) Broadening the categories of workers allowed to supply contraceptives;

(b) Legalizing distribution of contraceptives;

(c) Allowing public information and advertising of contraceptives;

(d) Providing services and education to all who need them including women and young people;

(e) Easing import requirements;

(f) Ensuring effectiveness and safety of contraceptives and their distribution.

These changes have permitted effective distribution of contraceptives through private and public sectors. In developing countries, the majority of contraceptive users obtain services from the public sector, whereas in developed countries, the majority use the private sector.

While discussing contraceptives, it is important to refer to two other sets of laws on fertility regulation, that is, the laws on voluntary sterilization and abortion.

Sterilization

Voluntary sterilization has become the most widely used method of fertility control throughout the world. There are countries where voluntary sterilization: *(a)* is permitted by statutes, decrees or regulations; or *(b)* is permitted because there is no law prohibiting it; or *(c)* is of uncertain legality because of the ambiguity of the law where "intentional bodily injury" is forbidden; or *(d)* is illegal under the written law.

Since 1974, there has been a trend throughout many areas of the world to reduce or remove restrictions on voluntary sterilization and to clarify its legality. There have been new laws, regulations and court decisions not only legalizing it but also permitting women to use the method without anyone's consent. However, in order to avoid abuse and knowing of the irreversibility of the method, Governments do establish informed consent procedures and penalties for coercion, and set age, parity and other requirements on who may obtain voluntary sterilization.

Abortion

Abortion has been a controversial issue in many countries, including developed countries. In most legal systems, abortion had been either completely banned or permitted in special cases, particularly if it is done in order to save the life of the mother.

During the past two decades, several countries amended their laws through legislation and/or court decisions legalizing abortion or extending the permission to cover such situations as rape, incest and socio-economic problems. Changing laws, however, does not guarantee implementation, due to attitudes based on cultural and religious beliefs. Therefore, in some countries where laws have been changed, doctors and prospective clients have faced hostility from their communities.

Administrative measures

Since 1974, the international community, through such organizations as UNFPA, non-governmental organizations, such as IPPF; and individual Governments, has been working on various population programmes. The majority of the developing countries now see population policy as necessary to meet the challenge of high population growth, economic hardship and the environment. Hence, the establishment of population policies. However, population policies without active promotion of the ideas of family limitation and birth-spacing and information on the availability of different services would have proved futile. Information and education on critical choices affecting population growth, socio-economic development and, in particular, fertility management, are essential to providing an effective and successful family planning programme. Governments therefore agreed, as a matter of urgency, to make universally available the information, education and means to assist couples and individuals to achieve their desired number of children.

Fortunately, in accepting the need for population policies, the international community and individual countries also began to provide general information about family planning. Consequently, contraceptive acceptance rose in the developing countries. Throughout the world, women are having fewer children now than they did 20 years ago. Between 1970 and 1991, fertility rates declined from an average of 2.6 to 1.7 births per woman in the more developed regions and from a range of 5-7 to a range of 3-6 in the less developed regions. In the least developed countries, however, fertility rates have only recently begun to decline. Sub-Saharan Africa shows only a small drop over the past 20 years after decades of very high rates.

Indeed, at an average of 6.2 births per woman, fertility rates in this region remain much higher than those in any other region.

Despite the high acceptance of modern family planning techniques, it is, nevertheless, worth noting that acceptance and use of family planning methods are uneven. Many millions of people throughout the world still do not have ready access to family planning. Most lack an appropriate range of methods and follow-up services. It is reckoned that births would be fewer by about one fourth in Africa and about one third in Asia and in Latin America and the Caribbean if women were able to have only the number of children that they desire. The World Fertility Survey and other surveys conducted during the 1970s, 1980s and early 1990s show that majority of women in many developing countries say they do not want more children but are not using any form of family planning. In Brazil, it has been reported that nearly one third of married women resort to an illegal and expensive sterilization operation because they have no easy and accessible alternatives. In Kenya, although half of all married women said they wanted no more children, another 26 per cent said they would like to wait at least two years before having another child; yet, only 27 per cent use contraception.

Most national development plans emphasize family programmes as the primary government intervention to lower fertility. Indeed, many Governments have specific family planning goals in contraceptive prevalence and acceptance, establishment of clinics and distribution points. Most Governments support family planning services either directly or indirectly.

However, most Governments in the developing world have failed to meet their goals because of: *(a)* costs; *(b)* lack of personnel and backup facilities; *(c)* transportation; *(d)* communication; *(e)* attitudes; and *(f)* lack of coordination.

Attitudes

It is common to see new ideas gaining acceptance slowly. Government policies may shift frequently to reflect different national needs. However, it would be difficult for any policies and laws to be reformed or effectively implemented without first changing the opinions and attitudes of people.

Despite much legal change in the direction of fertility control and sexual equality, there still remains a wide gap between law and fact. Policy makers and implementers of policies and laws in most countries are confronted with customs, traditions and religious beliefs that make reform and implementation difficult. This is particularly true where laws and policies call for social change, as in improving women's status or making family planning services and information easily available to all.

D. Conclusion and recommendations

During the past 20 years, most countries have been trying to move in the directions recommended at the Conferences at Bucharest and Mexico City. They have generally succeeded or partially succeeded in the following areas: *(a)* formulating explicit policies to lower fertility; *(b)* embodying population policies in constitutions, development plans and/or laws; *(c)* establishing national population commissions or other coordinating units; *(d)* providing funds from within and without to carry out programmes; *(e)* modifying laws to strengthen family planning information, education and services; and *(f)* improving the legal status of women by removing barriers to education, gainful employment, greater participation in national life and, most importantly, family planning.

Despite these successes, however, the world has still a lot to offer to women, especially the millions that up to now have had no ready access to family planning. As indicated earlier, a woman cannot manage her life without controlling her fertility nor can she play any useful role in development. Therefore, it is recommended that the international community and individual countries should work together so that:

(a) Family planning information, education and services are brought closer to all the people, particularly women;

(b) High-quality services and a wide variety of family planning methods are provided;

(*c*) Family planning services are integrated into all health services and are made a priority in development plans;

(*d*) Services are made more widely available through all possible means, including the private sector and individual communities;

(*e*) All discriminatory laws and practices that restrict the rights of women and girls are eliminated in order to improve their status; improving the status of women helps increase voluntary family planning; and

(*f*) Up-to-date reports on the progress of fertility programmes in individual countries are shared by the international community at regular intervals.

References

Church, Cathleen, and Judith S. Geller (1990). *Voluntary Female Sterilization: Number One and Growing*. Population Reports, Series C, No. 10. Baltimore, Maryland: The Johns Hopkins University, Population Information Program.

Cook, Rebecca J. (1987). Human rights and infant survival: a case of priorities. *Columbia Human Rights Law Review* (New York), vol. 18, No. 1 (Fall-Winter), pp. 1-41.

Grubb, A. (1988). Participating in abortion and the conscientious objector. *The Cambridge Law Journal*, vol. 47.

__________, and D. Pearl (1987). Sterilisation and the courts. *The Cambridge Law Journal*, vol. 46.

International Planned Parenthood Federation (1976). *Family Welfare and Development in Africa: Proceedings of the IPPF Africa Regional Conference*. London.

__________ (1983). *The Human Right to Family Planning*. London.

__________ and International Women's Rights Action Watch (1991). *Reproductive Rights: How Signatories to the United Nations Convention on the Elimination of all Forms of Discrimination against Women are Measuring Up*. London.

International Women's Rights Action Watch (1991). *The Women's Watch* (London), October.

__________ (1992). *The Women's Watch* (London), January.

Jacobson, Jodi L. (1987). *Planning the Global Family*. Worldwatch Paper, No. 80. Washington, D.C.: Worldwatch Institute.

__________ (1990). *The Global Politics of Abortion*. Worldwatch Paper, No. 97. Washington, D.C.: Worldwatch Institute.

Population Crisis Committee (1988). *Country Ranking of the Status of Women: Poor, Powerless and Pregnant*. Population Briefing Paper, No. 20. Washington, D.C.

Sadik, Nafis, ed. (1991a). *Population Policies and Programmes: Lessons Learned from Two Decades of Experience*. New York: United Nations Population Fund.

__________ (1991b). *The State of World Population, 1990: Choices for the New Century*. New York: United Nations Population Fund.

__________ (1992). *The State of World Population, 1991: Choice or Chance*. New York.

United Nations (1975). *Report of the United Nations World Population Conference, 1974, Bucharest, 19-30 August 1974*. Sales No. E.75.XIII.3.

__________ (1984). *Report of the International Conference on Population, 1984, Mexico City, 6-14 August 1984*. Sales No. E.84.XIII.8.

__________ (1985). *Report of the World Conference to Review and Appraise the Achievements of the United Nations Decade for Women: Equality, Development and Peace, Nairobi, Kenya, 15-26 July*. Sales No. E.85.IV.10.

__________ (1988). Convention on the Elimination of All Forms of Discrimination against Women. In *Human Rights: A Compilation of International Instruments*. Sales No. E.88.XIV.1.

__________ (1991a). *Women: Challenges to the Year 2000*. Sales E.91.I.21.

__________ (1991b). *The World's Women: Trends and Statistics, 1970-1990*. Series K, No. 8. Sales No. E.90.XVII.3.

United Nations Population Fund (1987). *Better Health for Women and Children through Family Planning*. New York.

__________ (1990). *Population Issues: A Briefing Kit*. New York.

__________ (1991). *Population Issues: A Briefing Kit*. New York.

__________ (n.d.). *Meeting the Population Challenge*. New York.

__________ (n.d.). *Safeguarding the Future*. New York.

__________, and Harvard University Law Library (1988). *Annual Review of Population Law, 1985*, vol. 12. New York: UNFPA.

World Bank (1988). *Toward Sustained Development in Sub-Saharan Africa: A Joint Programme of Action*. Washington, D.C.

XVII. WOMEN AND FAMILY PLANNING: ISSUES FOR THE 1990s

*International Planned Parenthood Federation**

The non-governmental sector can be a powerful, leading force both in showing the way to new directions in family planning and in dealing with women in development issues. An interest in combining these two concerns, women's issues and family planning, is a most appropriate focus of attention for the Expert Group Meeting on Population and Women. It is also important for the Expert Group Meeting on Family Planning, Health and Family Well-being to consider them and for the 1994 International Conference on Population and Development to include them in its conclusions and recommendations. Programmes of all sectors—Governments, multilateral and non-governmental organizations, and even commercial programmes—can benefit from addressing women's concerns in family planning directly.

A. Evolution of the linkage between women's issues and family planning

As world Governments and specialists look back over the past 40 years of research and action in the population field, they can recognize a clear evolution in the approaches that have been used to address women's issues. As the end of the millennium approaches, it is important to look back in order to draw all the lessons that can be learned from the efforts and results to date. Based on that history, it is possible to look ahead with firmer conclusions and guidelines about what must be done in the future. In the first half of the twentieth century, pioneers in the United States of America, the United Kingdom of Great Britain and Northern Ireland, Sweden, India and elsewhere struggled to gain legal and popular approval for their efforts to introduce contraception and to address both women's health problems and poverty concerns (Suitters 1973; PPFA, 1991). Increased scientific and political awareness shaped most work on family planning in the second half of the century; a simple analysis of the evolution of these approaches includes the stages described below.

Stage I. Macrolevel approach in early days of population research

Demographers originally focused their analyses on the consequences of rapid population growth (cf. Coale and Hoover, 1958). Individuals and their behaviour were not yet recognized as crucial in most population work. Population "bomb" and "explosion" were dominant metaphors, and aggregate level statistics were of primary interest. There was little room to consider individuals in general, and women in particular, in these frameworks (Wiarda and Helzner, 1981).

Stage II. Research turning to determinants of fertility

Demographers began to investigate the characteristics that influence family size and fertility regulation, such as urban/rural residence and ethnicity. There was increasing recognition both in research and in service delivery programmes that reducing fertility rates required changes in a person's behaviour, and in a sensitive, intimate area of his or her life.

Stage III. Impact of the United Nations Decade for Women on family planning programmes

The United Nations Decade for Women, 1975-1985, saw two major programme thrusts: the involvement of family planning programmes in income-generating projects for women; and the beginning of a definition of a "user's perspective" in family planning service delivery (Bruce, 1980). The former programme, income generation, eventually tapered off as evaluations showed multiple problems when a family planning agency ventured outside its area of comparative advantage (Eilbert, 1990); while the latter, explicit

---

*London, United Kingdom of Great Britain and Northern Ireland.

attention to consumers, flourished and evolved further into a "quality of care" perspective (see section B).

Stage IV. Gender perspective in reproductive and sexual health

In recent years, substantially more attention has been paid to the needs, preferences and perspectives of family planning clients, most of whom are women, worldwide. In addition, thinking has expanded to include looking at women as resources for solving health problems rather than only as "acceptors" of services. This view means addressing not only issues of gender balance among those in decision-making roles but also the status, training and responsibilities of women in their roles as health and family planning providers. The tools of gender analysis are being adapted specifically to apply to reproductive health and family planning services.

B. WOMEN AND FAMILY PLANNING ISSUES FOR THE 1990S

As the world population community looks ahead to the challenges of the future, areas that should be addressed include the areas discussed below.

Quality of care from the clients' perspective

Six elements of quality have been widely accepted as valuable tools for diagnosing problems and pointing towards needed improvements in family planning service delivery (Bruce, 1990). These elements are: choice of contraceptive methods; information provided to users; technical competence of providers; client-provider relations; mechanisms to encourage continuity; and appropriateness and acceptability of services (Helzner and Kopp, 1991). There is a gap between survey results worldwide which show, on one hand, high proportions of women responding that they want to delay or limit child-bearing; while, on the other hand, a smaller percentage is actually using any contraceptive method. The persistence of clandestine abortion, despite its often negative health consequences, is another indicator of women's desire to avoid unwanted or mistimed pregnancies. Improving the quality of programmes is one way to try to bridge the gap between stated demand and actual behaviour, increasing contraceptive use and thus lowering abortion rates. Those couples with very strong motivations to contracept are already doing so in many places. Therefore, family planning services now need to be as “user-friendly” as possible, in order to overcome the obstacles that may be perceived by non-contracepting couples that do not desire additional pregnancies but have not yet made use of existing services or have tried but dropped out.

Counselling and sexuality

Family planning information has too often been a one-way flow, from provider to client, and has focused on imparting facts (what methods exist, how they work etc.) rather than on exploring clients' feelings. Research has shown that counselling clients beforehand on possible side-effects of methods and how to handle them can actually increase contraceptive continuation rates. Ideally, clients should feel that the provider is supportive, a good listener and open to questions both at the first visit and subsequently. Family planning service providers have often separated their work from any discussion of sexuality; this omission is less tolerable in an age when awareness is growing that sexual behaviour and the choice of contraceptive method can, together, prevent or further the spread of sexually transmitted diseases (STDs) including the acquired immunodeficiency syndrome (AIDS).

Power dynamics between women and men

At the level of an individual couple engaging in sexual activity, power issues often exist. These issues can affect each partner's risk of contracting STDs and, for the woman, can strongly influence the risk of pregnancy. For family planning methods that are coitus-related (barrier methods, such as condom, spermicide, diaphragm and even the so-called "natural" methods involving periodic abstinence), success depends upon the willingness in many cases, of both parties to rein in sexual behaviour, at least temporarily. At times this behaviour is not within the woman's control, just as her male partner's use of a condom (with her and/or other sex partners he may have) depends upon his willingness to cooperate. Even when a contraceptive is not coitus-related (pill, intrauterine device (IUD), injection, implant), there may well be power struggles around the use of any method at all or over such matters as the woman's ability to achieve sexual gratification when she seeks it and to avoid sexual contact when she so prefers. Ideally, from a woman's perspective, family planning can be part of a comprehensive effort to transform power relations in the family, the community and society (Dixon-Mueller, 1988; Helzner and Shepard, 1990). The way in which programmes train their staff, arrange referrals to other services and link with other organizations can help in addressing these power dynamics within couples.

A reproductive and sexual health approach

Family planning has been addressed, in some areas, as an isolated service. Many women would prefer to have it set within a context of reproductive health (Ford Foundation, 1991; Jacobson, 1991) or sexual health (Gordon and Kanstrup, 1992; Porter, 1992). This context means that, besides showing concern about preventing unwanted pregnancy, programmes might address health problems, such as reproductive tract infections, STDs of all types including human immunodeficiency virus (HIV) and AIDS, sexual malfunction, infertility and/or abortion. Each of these problems has been carefully addressed in a wide variety of materials. Reproductive tract infections not only cause discomfort but can lead to debilitating conditions if left untreated (Dixon-Mueller and Wasserheit, 1991; Germain, 1991). Like reproductive tract infections, the presence of STDs may be important in a woman's choice of a contraceptive method (contraindicating IUDs or favouring condoms, for example). The managers of family planning services can choose to address these concerns either with their own resources or by setting up effective referral systems; in either case, there are implications for training staff and counselling clients. The severe consequences of HIV transmission and the current lack of woman-controlled contraceptives that combat HIV mean that a reproductive health approach would also promote the idea of ensuring that researchers in contraceptive technology shall make it a priority to develop a woman-controlled virucide to kill HIV. Thus, at the service delivery level, in programme management and design, and even in contraceptive technology research, a reproductive or sexual health approach would have implications for the context, image, quality and effectiveness of family planning from a woman's perspective.

Gender analysis of family planning programmes

The tools of gender analysis were originally developed to help planners and managers in such areas as agricultural development, where women are more likely to be invisible, than in family planning programmes. Nevertheless, evidence from efforts to adapt gender analysis to population activities of all types indicates that the exercise is useful. While gender analysis and awareness for family planning programmes has begun at primary level in some population organizations, a great deal more awareness-building is required until greater sensitivity is demonstrable. Among the leaders in this field are the United Nations Population Fund (UNFPA, 1989 and 1990), the International Planned Parenthood Federation (IPPF) and the Population Council. Both as sensitization for staff to issues that may not be sufficiently recognized or valued and as a technical input to programme design and evaluation, gender analysis can produce more effective use of resources and better results. The gender analysis framework includes: *(a)* analysis of division of labour (activities carried out, by sex); *(b)* analysis of decision-making; and *(c)* analysis of access to, and control over, resources.

The results are then applied to project design, using gender as a technical variable with concrete programme applications. This approach contrasts strongly and positively with the older, more marginal approach of funding income-generation activities for women through family planning agencies. With gender analysis, health programmes can retain their "comparative advantage" and still seek to increase benefits to women at all levels of their programmes.

Attention to women as clients, providers and decision makers

Studying the links between "status of women" and fertility is an academic approach in which few action-oriented programmes are involved. Carrying out advocacy activities with Governments and other institutions to "improve the status of women" is a broad, outward-looking exercise for a family planning agency. In the 1990s, it is crucial for all organizations—non-governmental organizations and others—involved in family planning to look inward as they review their roles with regard to women. This view means examining women's participation at three levels:

(a) As clients, through quality of care approaches and, where possible, client committees or other mechanisms to ensure client input on services;

(b) As service providers, for example, helping women staff on the front lines of service delivery (whether full time in a clinic or part time at home as a community-based distributor) to improve their status and self-esteem (Pizurki and others, 1987); and

(c) As decision makers, at senior staff levels and on boards of directors and advisory bodies of family planning programmes.

Over the years of modern family planning programmes, women's perspectives have not often been sought and their actual contributions and perspectives have not always been recognized sufficiently. Remedying these deficiencies can make family planning more acceptable and can help close the gap between unmet need and actual use.

Strengthening of links between population and family planning agencies and women's organizations

During the early decades of population programme implementation, there seemed little motivation or encouragement for women's groups and family planning specialists to collaborate. This situation existed, first, because the way in which the population issue was framed, primarily in terms of demographic impact or "population control", left little room for advocates of the health or human rights rationales; and, secondly, because many women's organizations in the South first blossomed during the United Nations Decade for Women (1975-1985) and are only now reaching the point where interests and activities in the areas of family planning and reproductive health seem appropriate to them. The conditions appear to be right for the remainder of the decade of the 1990s to become a golden age of communication and cooperation between institutions involved in family planning and groups promoting women's rights and health concerns (Germain and Ordway, 1989). The agendas of both sides would benefit from a carefully nourished effort to promote linkages at many levels—local, national, regional and worldwide. The potential for identifying substantial overlap of interests is there, but the collaboration is not likely to happen automatically. Both through the International Conference on Population held at Mexico City in 1984 and through the Conference on Women in 1995, the United Nations family of agencies can specifically recommend such efforts at linkages and collaboration to Governments and non-governmental organizations alike. Although non-governmental organizations are likely to be able to lead the way in trying out various models of collaboration, the scale of such experiences should not stop there but should be addressed by public and research institutions as well. This call for collaboration is even more important now that the discussion about population issues emerging from parts of the environmental movement is cast, once again, largely in terms of the consequences of rapid population growth. Many women's groups are not comfortable with this top-down approach and may feel the need to reconsider some of their steps towards working in and supporting reproductive health issues if women's rights, women's health, women's sexuality and a true women's perspective in the design and implementation of programmes are not consciously reaffirmed. It is hoped that as preparation for the International Conference on Population and Development proceeds, both the Expert Group Meeting on Population and Women and the Expert Group Meeting on Family Planning, Health and Family Well-being will address the importance of strengthening links between women's organizations and population/family planning agencies, recognizing the differences that have led to conflict in recent years and specifically identifying possible approaches for the remedy of those conflicts.

C. Conclusion

This paper has, first, examined some of the historical developments shaping the course of the evolution of linkages between women's issues and population/family planning concerns. There were logical reasons that such links have developed primarily in the 20 years since the World Population Conference at Bucharest in 1974, with most of the real progress coming only in the past decade. Now that the groundwork has been laid for such linkages, a number of approaches are worth exploring in the 1990s and beyond. Seven of them are highlighted here: quality of care from the client's perspective; counselling and sexuality; power dynamics between women and men; a reproductive and sexual health approach; gender analysis of family planning programmes; attention to women as clients, providers and decision makers; strengthening of links between population and family planning agencies and women's organizations. Separately or in combination, these approaches can lead to higher levels of contraceptive use, higher levels of client satisfaction, better health for women and their children (including a reduction in the transmission of STDs), and more self-esteem and participation for women.

References

Bruce, Judith (1980). Implementing the user perspective. *Studies in Family Planning* (New York), vol. 11, No. 1 (January-February), pp. 361-363.

__________ (1990). Fundamental elements of the quality of care: a simple framework. *Studies in Family Planning* (New York), vol. 21, No. 2 (March-April), pp. 61-91.

Coale, Ansley J., and Edgar M. Hoover (1958). *Population Growth and Economic Development in Low-income Countries*. Princeton, New Jersey: Princeton University Press.

Dixon-Mueller, Ruth (1988). Redefining family planning: feminist perspectives on service delivery. Paper presented at the Annual Meeting of the Population Association of America, New Orleans, Louisiana, 21-23 April.

__________, and Judith Wasserheit (1991). *The Culture of Silence: Reproductive Tract Infections among Women in the Third World*. New York: International Women's Health Coalition.

Eilbert, Kay W. (1990). *Planned Parenthood and Women's Development: A Review of Projects*. London: International Planned Parenthood Federation.

Ford Foundation (1991). *Reproductive Health: A Strategy for the 1990s*. A Program Paper. New York.

Germain, Adrienne (1991). *Reproductive Tract Infections in Women in the Third World: National and International Policy Implications*. New York: International Women's Health Coalition.

__________, and Jane Ordway (1989). *Population Control and Women's Health: Balancing the Scales*. New York: International Women's Health Coalition.

Gordon, Gill, and Charlotte Kanstrup (1992). Sexuality: the missing link in women's health. *IDS Bulletin* (Brighton, United Kingdom), vol. 23, No. 1, pp. 29-37.

Helzner, Judith F., and Bonnie Shepard (1990). The feminist agenda in population private voluntary organizations. *Women, International Development and Politics: The Bureaucratic Mire*, Kathleen Staudt, ed. Philadelphia, Pennsylvania: Temple University Press.

Helzner, Judith F., with the collaboration of Susan Zoe Kopp (1991). Quality of care in family planning: perspectives from the International Planned Parenthood Federation/Western Hemisphere Region. Background paper prepared for the World Bank Policy Paper on Effective Family Planning Programs Series. Unpublished. New York: IPPF/WHR, Inc.

Jacobson, Jodi L. (1991). *Women's Reproductive Health: The Silent Emergency*. Worldwatch Paper, No. 102. Washington, D.C.: Worldwatch Institute.

Pizurki, Helena, and others (1987). *Women as Providers of Health Care*. Geneva: World Health Organization.

Planned Parenthood Federation of America (1991). *A Tradition of Choice: Planned Parenthood at 75*. New York.

Porter, Mary (1992). Sexual health. *Planned Parenthood in Europe* (London), vol. 21, No. 1, pp. 2-4.

Suitters, Beryl (1973). *Be Brave and Angry: Chronicles of the International Planned Parenthood Federation*. London: IPPF.

United Nations Population Fund (1989). *Gender Analysis for Project Design*. New York.

__________ (1990). *Incorporating Women into Population and Development: Knowing Why and Knowing How*. New York.

Wiarda, Ieda Siqueira, and Judith F. Helzner (1981). *Women, Population and International Development in Latin America: Persistent Legacies and New Perceptions for the 1980's*. Amherst, Massachusetts: University of Massachusetts.

Part Six

WOMEN'S EDUCATION AND ITS DEMOGRAPHIC IMPACT

XVIII. WOMEN'S EDUCATION, FERTILITY AND THE PROXIMATE DETERMINANTS OF FERTILITY

*Shireen J. Jejeebhoy**

Although it is widely argued that the enhancement of women's education is critical for fertility reduction, the evidence for this effect is neither as general nor as strong as is often implied and the processes through which this effect occurs are quite diverse (Cochrane, 1979 and 1983; United Nations, 1987). The pattern of the relation varies by region of the world, level of development and time. It is also affected by cultural conditions, notable among which is the position women occupy in the traditional kinship structure.

The purpose of this paper is to summarize the relation of female education to fertility and to outline the pathways through which women's education affects fertility and its proximate determinants in developing countries. The paper updates Cochrane's (1979) review of what is known about this relation in two ways. First, it re-examines the relation in the light of the enormous amount of data generated during the 1980s. Secondly, and more important, it sketches the links between education and other aspects of women's status which may together impinge on fertility and its proximate determinants.

The multiple effects of education on women's situation are obvious. Some effects are generally applicable to men and women, others are uniquely applicable to women. Among the former group, education affects access to knowledge, information and new ideas; it enhances overall efficiency, market opportunities and social status; it also changes attitudes and behaviour. Additionally striking is the role of education in enabling women to assume more power in traditional patriarchal family settings. Especially important for the purposes here are the links of education to the following unique but interrelated attributes of women's situation, which are observed to be critical in effecting changes in fertility: their decision-making autonomy in the home; their exposure to the outside world; their conjugal family orientation; and their control over resources.

Through one or more of these effects on women's situation, education is expected to affect fertility: by affecting the supply of children or the number of children a couple can have, the demand for children or the number of children a couple wants and the motives underlying this number; and the costs of fertility regulation, in terms of money, time and social attitudes (Easterlin, 1978; Easterlin and Crimmins, 1985). In this way, education has the potential both to increase fertility and to reduce it; the strengths of these opposing effects vary considerably, depending upon the cultural and development contexts.

The paper begins with a brief review of gender-specific trends in literacy and school enrolment in the developing world (section A). Thereafter, the discussion turns to the relation of education to fertility. First, trends in the direct relation are reviewed (section B). Then the ways in which education has been observed to influence other aspects of women's situation, with demographic repercussions are examined (section C). The effects of education, through changes in the situation of women, on each of the three intervening mechanisms are then discussed: on the supply of children (section D); the demand for children (section E); the unmet need for contraception (section F); and fertility regulation and obstacles to it (section G). Section H sets forth the major intervening pathways through which education affects fertility in different

---

*Consultant, Bombay, India. This research is to be expanded into a larger review of the effect of female education on fertility, sponsored by the International Union for the Scientific Study of Population. The author wishes to express gratitude to Karen Oppenheim Mason, Jyoti Moodbidri and Mary Beth Weinberger for their valuable comments and suggestions on earlier drafts, and to David Rose, Phyllis Tabusa and R. T. Randeria, and their respective staff, for help in bibliographical searches and to Shantha Rajgopal for research assistance.

stages of the transition. Section I then summarizes the main points and policy implications of the paper.

A. Trends in educational attainment

The developing world is characterized by considerable heterogeneity in terms of culture, development and fertility. Although most countries in the less developed regions have strong patriarchal cultures that stress women's reproductive role, important cultural distinctions exist. For example, although traditionally women in Latin America have had considerable autonomy in decision-making, exposure to the outside world and control over resources, even here, gender inequalities are apparent (LeVine and others, 1991). Women in sub-Saharan Africa have considerable autonomy in certain well-marked but limited spheres (Kritz and Gurak, 1991). Those in the northern part of Southern Asia and in the Islamic countries have the least control over their lives, make few decisions and have limited freedom of movement and control over resources (see Dyson and Moore, 1983, for example). Development levels also vary; per capita income levels, for example, range from less than $100 to $2,500. Fertility rates also vary: total fertility rates (TFR) range from a low of about 2.0 to a high of about 8.0 (World Bank, 1992).

In addition, the developing world displays wide variations in literacy and enrolment levels. Not only the levels of female literacy and enrolment but also rates of growth and gender disparities in these indicators vary widely from region to region. Tables 28 and 29 show these measures of education by gender and region of the developing world. Two points are noteworthy:

(a) Steadily increasing literacy rates and enrolment ratios over time suggest a shift in the educational distribution of women; this changing distribution itself may have implications for fertility decline;

(b) There is a loose inverse conformity between educational levels of females and gender disparities in educational attainment. Latin America and the Caribbean, and Eastern and South-eastern Asia exhibit the highest levels of female literacy and enrolment, and also the narrowest gender disparities in enrolment. In contrast, Western and Southern Asia and Northern and sub-Saharan Africa exhibit the lowest female literacy rates and enrolment ratios and also the sharpest gender disparities. Wide gender disparities in educational attainment are a hint of wide disparities in social and economic reliance up on children, as is shown below, and also have implications for fertility.

B. Women's education and fertility: the direct relation

At the global level, the relation between women's education and fertility is clearly inverse and usually more inverse than the relation with men's education. Zero-order correlations for more than 100 developing countries show a strong and significant negative association between educational and fertility measures (table 30). But at lower levels of aggregation, evidence of the relation is far less uniform and it is evident that education does not automatically reduce fertility in all circumstances and that a variety of patterns of this relation can exist, as in shown in figure V. In fact, a case can be made for a foam of transition in the relation of female education to fertility.

As far as the direct relation goes, the evidence suggests five major points of interest:

(a) In early stages of development, a small amount of education can increase or at best have a negligible negative effect on fertility;

(b) It is largely in countries with higher levels of development that the familiar inverse relation is observed;

(c) In most societies, there is a threshold level of education, beyond which strong differentials in fertility are generated;

(d) Although the inverse relation persists, differentials once more begin to narrow at later points in development;

(e) On balance, the impact of female education on fertility is stronger than either that of male education or other household socio-economic characteristics.

Positive and curvilinear relation

In early stages of development, in the poorest and least literate societies, the evidence for a uniformly inverse relation is shaky, especially once urban or rural residence is controlled. Here, a little education appears to lead to higher fertility and one is likely to observe a curvilinear or reversed U-shaped relation.[1] Of the 35 World Fertility Survey (WFS) countries classified by level of development (United Nations, 1987), one finds that 12 of the 16 countries classified as middle-low and low developed have clearly curvilinear relation (another two show no relation and only two show an inverse relation). In contrast, only 7 of the 19 countries classified as high and middle high on the development scale show non-linear relation. There is also a region-specific pattern, which may well be related to level of development: of the 37 countries classified by region, a non-linear (reversed U-shaped or no relation) is evident in 10 of 12 African countries, 7 of 12 Asian countries and 2 of 13 Latin American countries. Evidence of non-linearity comes also from other, in settings as diverse as Sierra Leone (Bailey, 1986), Mexico (Holian, 1984) and rural Pakistan (Sathar and others, 1988).

Inverse relation

The familiar inverse relation occurs at a later stage of development (Cochrane, 1983). Inverse relation were observed, for example, in a majority (12 of 19) of the more economically advanced of the developing countries covered by WFS compared with only 2 of 16 less economically advanced countries (United Nations, 1987). A study of WFS and Demographic and Health Surveys (DHS) data from 15 countries, using somewhat different educational and fertility classifications than the United Nations study (Rodríguez and Aravena, 1991), suggests that inverse relation were observed in only five countries in the 1970s, compared with eight in the 1980s, as is shown in figure V.

TABLE 28. ADULT LITERACY RATES, LESS DEVELOPED REGIONS, 1970 AND 1990

	Literacy rates				*Sex ratio: literate females per 100 literates males*	
	1970		*1990*			
Region	*Male*	*Female*	*Male*	*Female*	*1970*	*1990*
Total	52.5	32.3	74.2	53.7	61.6	72.4
Number of countries or areas	(91)	(90)	(85)	(85)	(90)	(85)
Africa						
Northern Africa	42.5	12.8	61.3	34.7	29.9	58.8
Sub-Saharan Africa[a]	39.2	27.1	64.4	43.6	46.6	58.4
Asia						
Eastern Asia[b]	94.2	83.8	84.5	63.2	80.8	74.0
South-eastern Asia[c]	76.0	60.7	87.3	73.1	71.9	78.0
Southern Asia[d]	46.7	29.2	59.0	32.0	37.8	52.3
Western Asia[e]	57.3	36.0	79.0	57.8	45.5	71.1
Latin America and the Caribbean	75.3	69.1	86.6	82.7	90.2	94.2

Sources: For literacy rates, United Nations Children's Fund, *The State of the World's Children, 1991* (New York, 1992); for enrolment ratios, United Nations Educational, Scientific and Cultural Organization, *Statistical Yearbook, 1990* (Paris 1991); both weighted by population size in the nearest available year.

[a]Data not available for Ethiopia, Namibia and South Africa, 1970 and 1990; Mauritania, 1970; and Malawi and Mauritius, 1990.

[b]Data not available for China and the Democratic People's Republic of Korea, 1970; and Hong Kong and Mongolia, 1990.

[c]Data not available for Cambodia and Viet Nam, 1970; and Singapore, 1990.

[d]Data not available for Bhutan, 1970.

[e]Data not available for Oman, 1970 and 1990; and Israel, 1990.

[f]Data not available for Nicaragua, and Trinidad and Tobago, 1990.

TABLE 29. ENROLMENT RATIOS, LESS DEVELOPED REGIONS, 1986-1989

Region	*Primary-school enrolment* Primary enrolment ratio 1986-1989 Male	Female	Sex ratio: females per 100 males, 1986-1989	*Secondary-school enrolment* Secondary enrolment ratio, 1986-1989 Male	Female	Sex ratio: females per 100 males, 1986-1989
Total	112.3	95.7	85.2	45.9	34.5	75.2
Number of countries or areas	(92)	(93)	(92)	(92)	(92)	(92)
Africa						
Northern Africa[a]	87.8	67.9	77.3	54.8	41.7	76.1
Sub-Saharan Africa[b]	68.7	57.1	83.1	22.4	13.7	61.2
Asia						
Eastern Asia[c]	139.8	124.8	89.3	52.5	40.1	76.4
South-eastern Asia[d]	111.6	106.8	95.7	47.8	42.7	89.3
Southern Asia	103.0	75.6	73.4	44.7	26.2	58.6
Western Asia[e]	111.4	94.4	84.7	58.5	38.2	65.3
Latin America and the Caribbean[f]	110.0	108.7	98.8	46.9	52.0	110.9

[a]Data not available for primary and secondary school in Libyan Arab Jamahiriya, 1986-1989.

[b]Data not available for primary school in Angola and Guinea-Bissau, 1960; and in Gabon, Namibia, Rwanda and Zimbabwe, 1986-1989; and secondary school in Gabon, Liberia, Namibia, Somalia, South Africa and Zambia.

[c]Data not available for primary school in China and the Democratic People's Republic of Korea, 1960.

[d]Data not available for primary school in Cambodia, 1960 and 1986-1989; and in Viet Nam, 1960.

[e]Data not available for primary school in Oman, the United Arab Republic and Yemen, 1960.

[f]Data not available for primary school in El Salvador, and Trinidad and Tobago, 1960; and in Brazil, 1986-1989; and secondary school in the Dominican Republic.

TABLE 30. RELATION BETWEEN EDUCATION MEASURES AND FERTILITY, AND SELECTED INTERVENING VARIABLES: ZERO-ORDER CORRELATIONS FOR 100 DEVELOPING COUNTRIES

	Literacy rates				*Enrolment ratios*			
	1970		*1990*		*1989*		*1989*	
Variable	*Males*	*Females*	*Males*	*Females*	*Males*	*Females*	*Males*	*Females*
Crude birth rate	-0.6848	-0.6060	-0.5753	0.5939	-0.5373	-0.6604	-0.7329	-0.8030
Total fertility rate	-0.6589	-0.6207	-0.5446	0.5815	-0.4801	-0.5822	-0.6197	-0.6990
Age at marriage	-0.6409	0.5079	0.6007	0.5886	0.4054	0.5798	0.5462	0.6337
Infant mortality rate	-0.6801	-0.5512	-0.6890	-0.6780	-0.6245	-0.7547	-0.7677	-0.8174
Couple-protection rate	-0.4275	0.3759	0.3572	0.3553	0.3442	0.3573	0.5281	0.4975

Sources: *The World's Women, 1970-1990: Trends and Statistics,* Series K, No. 8 (United Nations publication, Sales No. E.90.XVII.3); and United Nations Educational, Scientific and Cultural Organization, *Statistical Yearbook, 1990* (Paris, 1991).

NOTE: All correlations are significant at the 0.001 level.

Figure V. The effect of women's education on marital fertility: a comparison of patterns observed from the World Fertility Survey and the Demographic and Health Surveys, selected countries

A. Africa

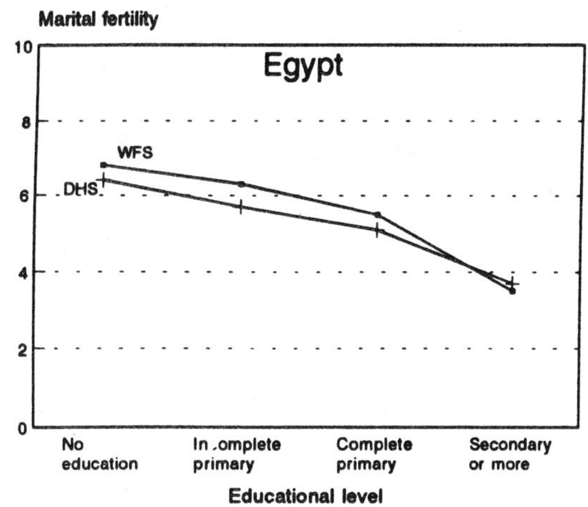

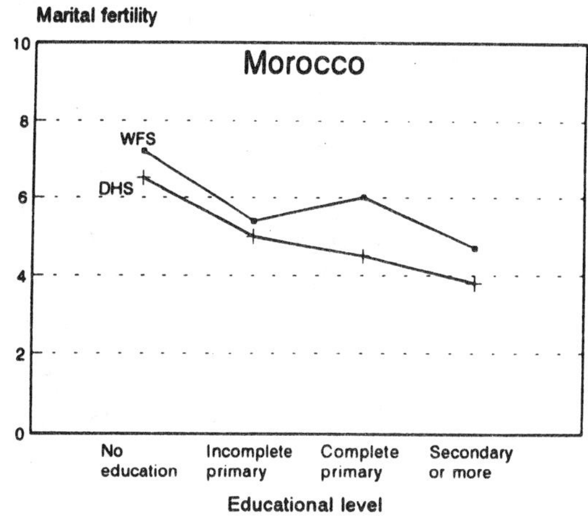

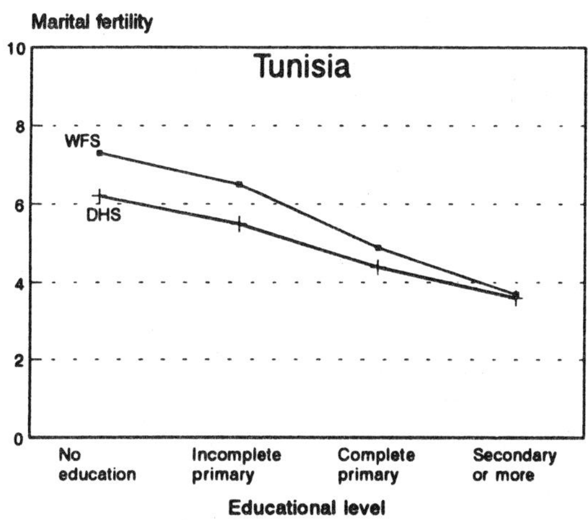

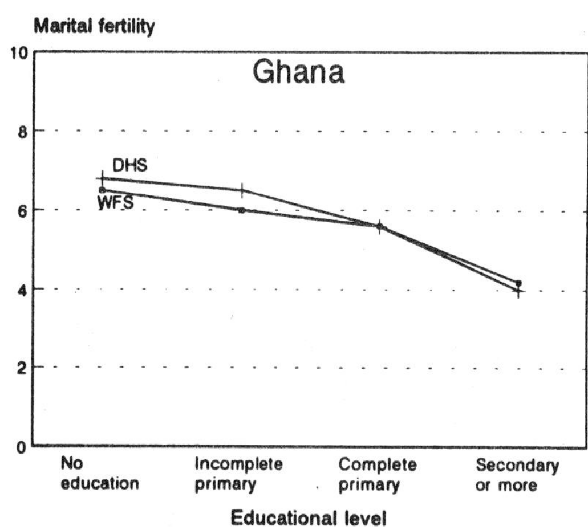

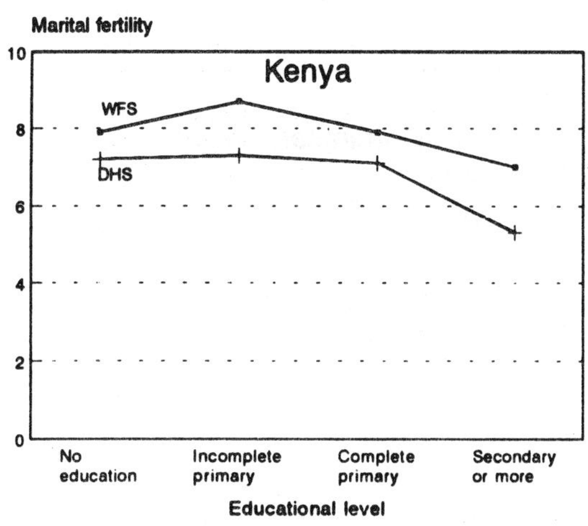

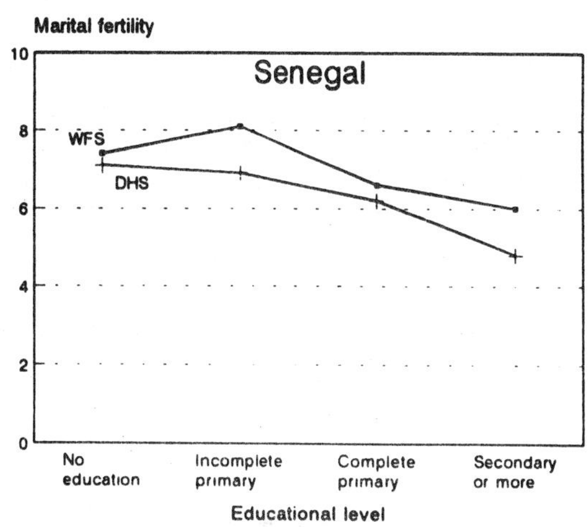

Figure V (*continued*)

B. Asia

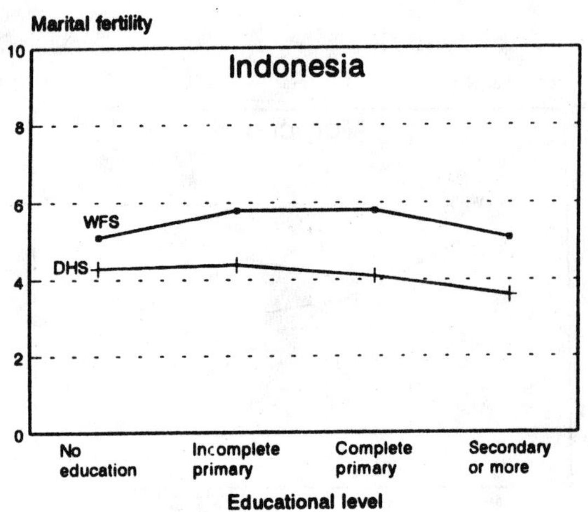

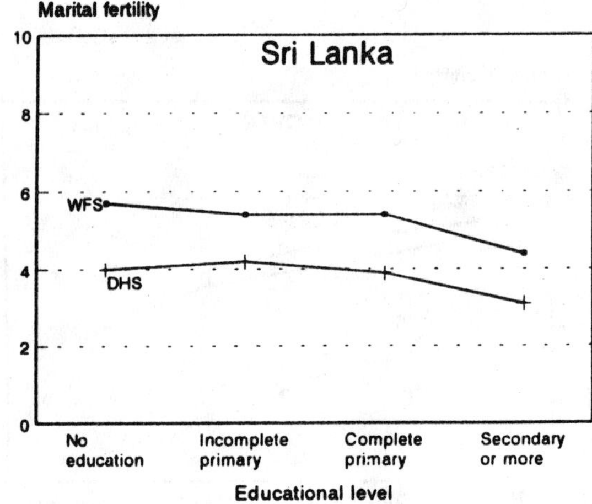

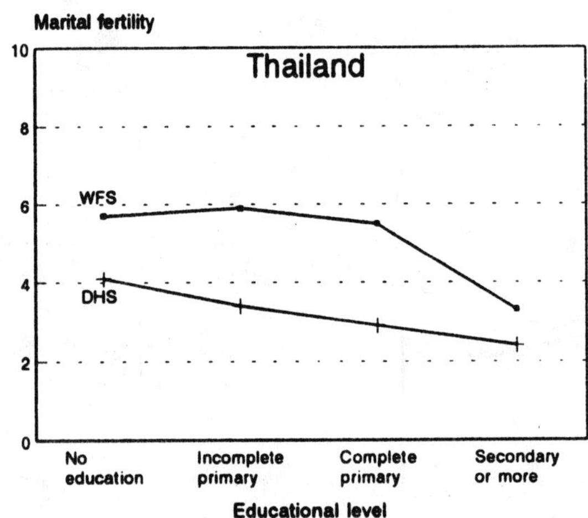

C. Latin America and the Caribbean

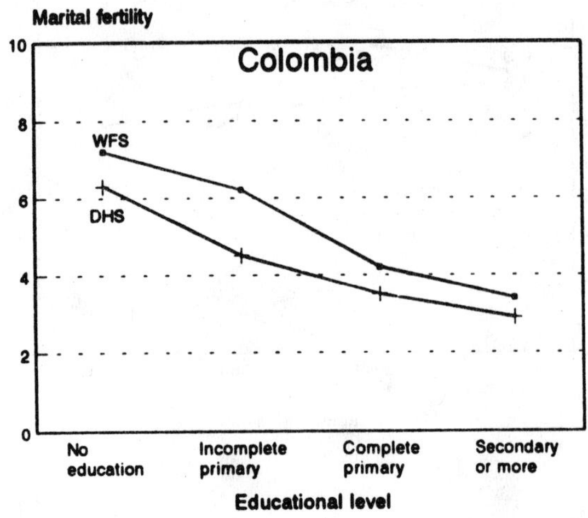

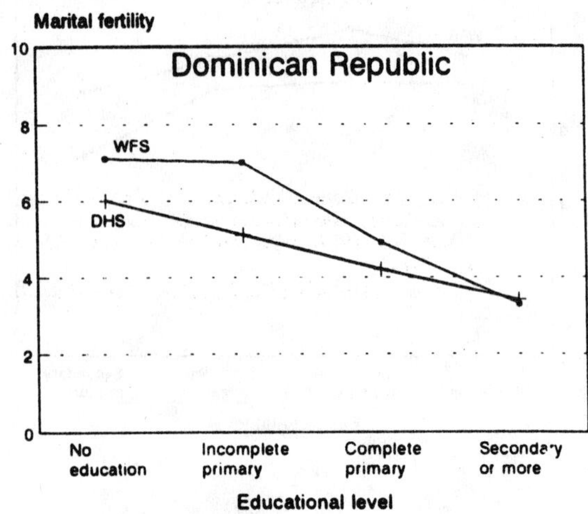

Figure V (continued)

C. Latin America and the Caribbean (continued)

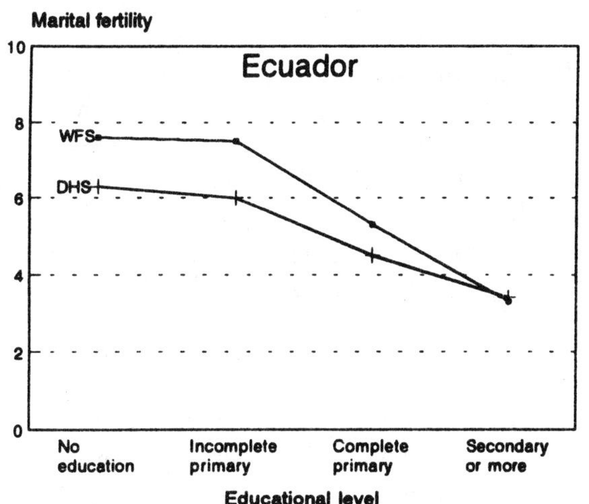

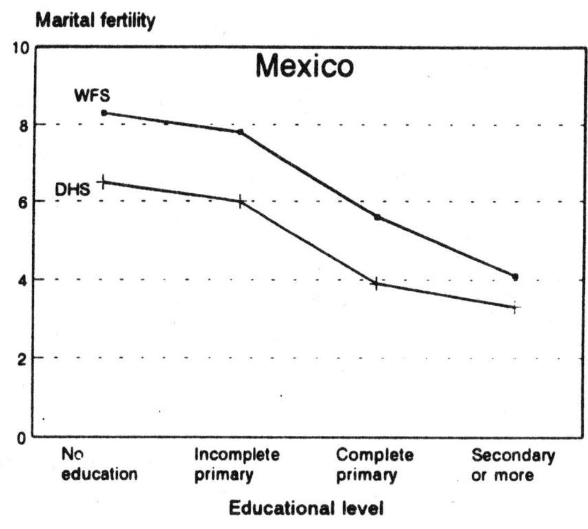

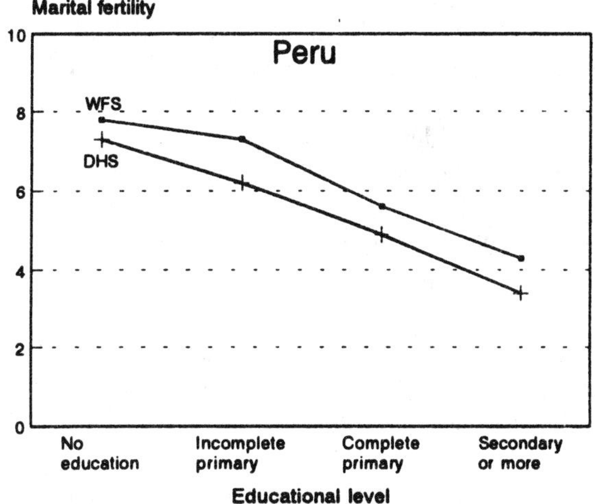

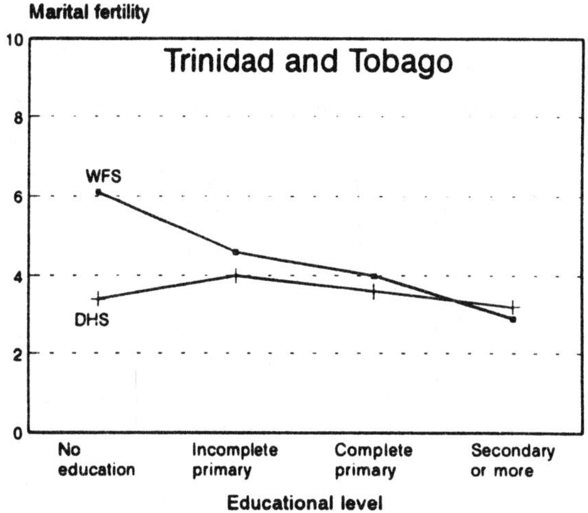

Source: Germán Rodrígues and Ricardo Aravena, "Socio-economic factors and the transition to low fertility in less developed countries: a comparative analysis", *in Demographic and Health Surveys World Conference, August 5-7, 1991, Washington, DC, Proceedings,* vol. I (Columbia, Maryland, IRD/Macro International, Inc., 1991)

Note: DHS = Demographic and Health Surveys; WFS = World Fertility Survey.

Evidence that the curvilinear relation turns inverse over time comes also from a study of successive cross-sections of women in Tamil Nadu, India (Jejeebhoy, 1991). Here, the effect of five years of education was to increase fertility marginally at an early point (1970) in time and to reduce it by over half a child 10 years later.

Does a country need to achieve a particular level of development before an inverse relation is observed? A look at income levels of countries with and without monotonic relation between education and fertility suggests that this is so (Cochrane, 1983). Countries with per capita income levels of $510 or less in 1978 exhibit curvilinear relation; all those with per capita income levels of $740 or more show inverse ones. Such evidence lends empirical support to the argument that the pattern of the relation of education to fertility varies considerably by level of development.

Even within countries, better developed regions and urban areas are systematically more likely to report inverse relation than are lesser developed or rural areas. For example, a study in Nigeria (Adewuyi and Isiugo-Abanihe, 1986) reports a positive association between maternal education and fertility in the less economically advanced northern region and an inverse relation (after primary schooling) in the more developed southern region. In a similar vein, the cross-sectional impact of female education on fertility tends to be more consistently inverse in urban areas than in rural (Cochrane, 1983; Holian, 1984). And evidence from Peru shows that community-level influences also play an important role conditioning the pattern of the relation: the impact is more sharply inverse in areas of high levels of community development and education and reversed U-shaped in areas with poor community characteristics (Tienda, 1984).

Threshold levels of education

It is frequently observed that the effect of a small amount of education—lower or upper primary—is negligible but beyond a threshold level of education (middle, secondary) the effect of maternal education on fertility becomes uniformly inverse, as confirmed by various studies (Rodríguez and Aravena, 1991; United Nations, 1987; Caldwell, 1982). In other words, a primary-school education has little effect on fertility; the break comes later, most often at the level of some secondary school or about seven years of education (United Nations, 1987) or among women that have completed primary school (Rodríguez and Aravena, 1991). This pattern is evident in diverse settings, as is shown from both the WFS and DHS programmes and from other data from Pakistan (secondary school, Kazi and Sathar, 1986), rural Maharashtra (middle school, Jejeebhoy, 1992) and Java and Bali (Achmad, 1980). The pattern is found even in the more economically advanced countries of the developing world, for example, Colombia (Florez, 1989, complete primary), Mexico (Holian, 1984, complete primary), Peru (Tienda, 1984, secondary) and Sri Lanka (Fernando, 1977, junior secondary).

Narrowing of the relation

Lastly, at late stages of the transition, differentials narrow once more and this is most perceptible today in the most developed of the less developed regions, Latin America and the Caribbean (Bongaarts and Lightbourne, 1990; Weinberger, Lloyd and Blanc, 1989). Studies comparing WFS and DHS results show that although the relation is inverse at both times, roughly 10 years apart, differentials in the total fertility rate, which were very wide during the 1970s, have narrowed considerably, largely resulting from major declines at the lower end of the educational spectrum, where, there was no evidence of fertility decline in the 1970s. This change is evident for a number of countries, as is shown in figure V.

Impact of female education compared to that of male education or household socio-economic characteristics

Although some of the effect of maternal education on fertility is undoubtedly related through other factors, such as family income, husband's occupation and husband's education, evidence suggests that women's education influences fertility more strongly than either husband's education (United Nations, 1987; Cochrane, 1979 and 1983; Rodríguez and Cleland, 1981; Zanamwe, 1988)[2] or household socio-economic characteristics (United Nations, 1987; LeVine and others, 1991).

The United Nations study (1987) shows that the contrast between the highest and lowest educational categories amounted to 73 births per 1,000 woman-years when controlled for age and marital duration; this figure was reduced to 56 when residence was controlled and further to 39 when husband's education was also controlled.[3] In fact, wife's education emerged as the most decisive influence even after controlling for residence, husband's education, husband's and wife's occupation, and marriage duration and age at marriage in 15 countries covered by WFS (United Nations, 1987; Weinberger, 1987) and in every single region, except the Caribbean, when controlling for husband's education and socio-economic status. A comparison of WFS and DHS data from 15 countries finds that after adjusting for residence and husband's education, the average effect of female education was reduced from -2.7 to -1.6 children in the 1970s (WFS) and from -2.3 to -1.1 children in the 1980s (DHS), suggesting a continued strong independent effect of maternal education (Rodríguez and Aravena, 1991). These findings are consistent with the idea that it is women's situation, knowledge, attitudes to child-rearing and to children rather than their socio-economic status that influences reproductive behaviour most strongly.

C. How education affects the situation of women

Education sets off important changes in women's situation in that which then impinge on fertility and mortality.[4] The rest of this paper goes beyond the direct effect and examines the pathways through which education affects fertility in order to understand why these patterns occur. These channels are summarized in table 31. Specifically, from the available evidence, it is hypothesized that education leads to at least four changes in the situation of women, which then affect fertility, both inadvertently through supply of children (column (1), rows 1-4); or volitionally through demand for children (column (1), rows 5-11) and contraceptive cost factors (column (1), rows 12-14). These changes in turn affect, both positively and negatively, a variety of intervening and proximate determinants of fertility, as is seen in column (2) of table 31. The direction of the effect of these intervening variables on fertility is set out in column (3), and column (4) presents the direction of the overall effect of education on fertility through these various pathways.

The four ways in which education affects the situation of women are outlined in column (1) of table 31 and are described below.

Decision-making autonomy

Educated women are freer to make decisions in the domestic spheres most relevant to them, notably with regard to child health and internal food distribution but also sometimes more generally, depending on the culture (for Southern Asia; Caldwell, Reddy and Caldwell, 1982; Basu, 1989; for Latin America, LeVine and others, 1991; Acuna, 1981). Also, with greater education comes more self-confidence and a greater ability to demand her dues; hence, educated women tend to be taken more seriously by their families and by such outsiders as care providers (LeVine and others, 1991; Caldwell, Reddy, and Caldwell, 1983; Streatfield, Singarimbun and Singarimbun, 1986). And educated women are better equipped to resist pressures from the patriarchal family (Hsiung, 1988). However, the range of issues over which educated women have autonomy probably varies by the culture and level of education. An important observation made by Caldwell, Reddy and Caldwell (1982) is that although educated women make decisions on child health and other aspects of behaviour related to their conjugal family, they do not usually control other behaviour, such as the sexuality of unmarried women or decisions about major purchases. This limited decision-making authority is consistent with the patriarchal family structure that characterizes most developing countries; even in Latin America, the husband is expected to dominate in domestic life in terms of decision-making and even exerting force over the wife (LeVine and others, 1991).

Control over resources

Consistent with greater autonomy, educated women may have greater control over material resources. This control comes from two sources: first, and more frequently observed, better educated women are more likely to have access to and control over family resources, particularly in the domestic sphere (Basu,

TABLE 31. HYPOTHESIZED EFFECTS OF MATERNAL EDUCATION ON FERTILITY THROUGH CHANGES IN THE SITUATION OF WOMEN AND THE INTERVENING FACTORS AFFECTING FERTILITY

	Effect of maternal education on intervening variables		*Effect of this intervening variable on children ever born*	*Effect of maternal education on children ever born through specific intervening variable*
Intervening factors	*Through (1)*	*Direction (2)*	*(3)*	*(4)*
Supply of children				
1. Age at marriage	a,b,o	+	-	-
2. Breast-feeding	a,c,d	-	-	+
3. Post-partum abstinence	a,c,d	-	-	+
4. Child mortality	a,b,c,d	-	+	-
Demand for children				
5. Desired family size	a,b,c	-	+	-
6. Son preference	a,b,c	-	+	-
7. Children's labour contribution in childhood	a,b,c	-	+	-
8. Children's financial and residential support in adulthood	a,b,c	-	+	-
9. Children as a source of prestige	b			
10. Economic costs of children	a,b,c	+	-	-
11. Time and opportunity costs	a,b,c	+	-	-
Fertility regulation and obstacles to use				
12. Method awareness	c	+	-	-
13. Approval	a	+	-	-
14. Spousal communication	a,d	+	-	-
15. Contraceptive use	a,b,c,d	+	-	-

NOTE: a = decision-making autonomy; b = control of resources (family, own); c = knowledge of and exposure to modern world; d = husband and wife closeness; o = direct, other.

1989 and 1990; LeVine and others, 1991). In highly patriarchal settings, this access may be limited to resources for the treatment of child illness or purchase of daily foods. Where gender disparities are smaller, access may extend both to major purchases and investments as well as to property and assets. With greater access to resources comes a greater economic self-reliance among better educated women and a correspondingly lesser reliance upon children.

The second source of control over resources is educated women's economic independence and control over their own incomes. It is frequently argued that education opens economic opportunities for women and increases their participation in the wage sector. The evidence for this is quite shaky, however, except in certain parts of Latin America (Wainerman, 1980), and then only for certain kinds of work. In other regions, where the labour market continues to be sex-segmented and opportunities for women's work limited, education has less impact. For example, evidence from Southern Asia (Sathar and Kazi, 1990) and even Mexico (LeVine and others, 1991) shows that work is most typically poverty-driven and is unrelated or even negatively related to education, except at the highest levels. Few women work out of choice, most begin to work after having several children; economically, their household income is far exceeded by that of non-working women and the majority of them would give up work if their financial position improved (Sathar and others, 1988; Sathar and Kazi, 1990). In fact, women's status in Pakistan is observed to improve only with 10 or more years of education and with employment in professional or salaried positions outside the home.

Knowledge, exposure to the modern world

Better educated women are less fatalistic and are more exposed to television and reading materials. As a result, they have better access to modern ideas and information about a variety of subjects, ranging from family health and hygiene to child-rearing to the appropriateness of large numbers of children, to contraception and other non-traditional behaviour and lifestyles; (Vlassoff, 1982; Streatfield, Singarimbun and Singarimbun, 1986; Acuna, 1981; Basu, 1989; LeVine and others, 1991, for Mexico). They may also be conceded more freedom of movement, which in itself would expose them to non-familial contacts and new ideas. Even here, however, there is evidence that little education does not necessarily improve knowledge of the outside world or change traditional attitudes, especially in a society in which women's movement is curtailed (Vlassoff, 1980).

Husband-wife closeness

Educated women are more likely to forge a closer relationship with their husbands, implying greater social equality and emotional intimacy between spouses, a greater loyalty to the conjugal unit rather than to the larger extended family network and a child orientation (Nigeria, Omideyi, 1990; South India, Caldwell, Reddy and Caldwell, 1983; Mexico, Levine and others, 1991). This closeness tends to strengthen women's ability to challenge the authority of family elders in a variety of areas, ranging from contraception to abstinence and from child-rearing patterns to the timing and spacing of births.

In brief, maternal education primarily influences women's exposure to new ideas, their domestic autonomy, access to resources and husband-wife intimacy. How these changes affect the intervening and proximate determinants of fertility is discussed below.

D. Women's education and inadvertent factors affecting the supply of children

Education affects the supply of children in at least four quite unintentional ways (rows 1-4 of table 31), that is, as a result of changes in behaviour that were not deliberately undertaken to affect fertility: *(a)* education delays entry into marriage; *(b)* there is a decline in the duration and intensity of breast-feeding among more educated women; *(c)* traditional postpartum abstinence taboos are less likely to be observed among educated women; and *(d)* education is associated with lower infant and child mortality. As suggested in column (4), rows 1-4, through reduced breast-feeding and adherence to abstinence taboos, education has the potential to increase fertility, other things being equal; through increased age at marriage and improved child survival, to reduce it.

Better educated women marry later

There is a remarkable consistency in research findings of a positive relation between female education and their age at marriage as is seen in the zero-order correlations for more than 100 developing countries presented in table 30. Two explanations for this relation have been offered: *(a)* it invokes the autonomy route (table 31); and *(b)* it suggests a more mechanical connection. Neither suggests that marriage is delayed with the specific intention of reducing fertility.

The first argument suggests that education grants young women a greater autonomy, which allows them to challenge such norms as arranged marriages or at least to veto family choices of potential husbands (Dixon, 1975; see Mason review, 1984; Goldstein, 1970), thereby lengthening the search for a husband and delaying age at marriage. In a different vein, if education generates new employment opportunities for unmarried girls, women may defer early marriage in favour of increased participation in the labour force. In Mexico, for example, better educated women deliberately maintained a longer courtship period so that they could work and save enough money to establish a nuclear residence as soon after marriage as possible (LeVine and others, 1991). In areas where benefits of this labour force participation accrue to parents, it is possible that parents themselves will be more motivated to postpone their daughters' marriages.

But education does not necessarily change attitudes towards marriage. For example, studies of young Indian women (Kumari, 1985; Vlassoff, 1980) observe highly traditional attitudes to marriage even among the educated. But even in settings in which traditional attitudes and norms persist among the educated, there is a tendency for better educated women to marry later. To some extent, the mere fact of schooling may deter parents from marrying off their daughters. In many cultures, in response to the demand from educated men for literate wives, female education has become an asset in arranging a good marriage (Minturn, 1984, for Rajasthan, India) and indeed the major justification for delaying marriage beyond menarche (Mhloyi, 1991). In turn, the longer a young girl is kept in school, the longer she will remain out of the net of marriage negotiations. Negotiations for the marriage of an educated daughter are far more time-consuming (the pool of available better educated potential husbands is smaller) and dowry requirements greater than for an uneducated daughter, thereby mechanically increasing the age at marriage (for Southern Asia, see Caldwell, Reddy and Caldwell, 1982). Hence, it is postulated that the mechanical effect is at least as strong as, if not stronger than, other female status changes in raising the age at marriage of educated females.

Whatever the underlying motivation, the fact is that educated women are systematically more likely to delay marriage (United Nations, 1987) and this is as true of sub-Saharan Africa (Kaufmann, Lesthaege and Meekers, 1987; Mhloyi, 1991; for Kinshasa, Shapiro and Tambashe, 1991) as it is of Latin America and the Caribbean, Eastern Asia or Southern Asia (United Nations, 1987; Le Vine and others, 1991; Alsuwaigh, 1989; for Saudi Arabia; Sathar and others, 1988; Jejeebhoy, 1992). In fact, results from 38 WFS countries suggest that the singulate mean age of marriage is almost four years higher among women with at least seven years of schooling as among uneducated women. Again, however, pronounced differences are found at the higher extremes, that is, between women with from four to six years and more than seven years of education.

Duration of breast-feeding and post-partum abstinence

Prolonged breast-feeding and post-partum abstinence have been two mechanisms that have traditionally kept fertility relatively low in many regions of the developing world. Education has frequently been observed to erode these mechanisms, resulting in an increase in fertility. For example, as seen in row 2, columns (1) and (2), of table 31, the exposure to the outside world that accompanies education can evoke new ideas on infant-feeding practices and lead to a reduction in lactation. The tightening of the conjugal bond may lead to reluctance to adhere to traditional, long periods of post-partum abstinence. And in strong patriarchal structures, personal decisions in the areas of breast-feeding and abstinence practices of the next generation may be among the earliest concessions made to an educated daughter-in-law (Caldwell, Reddy and Caldwell, 1982).

DHS, WFS (Sharma and others, 1990; United Nations, 1987; Smith and Ferry, 1984) and other survey results representing a variety of cultures[5] show a consistent decline in breast-feeding durations with increased education. Differences between least and most educated women averaged 7.5 months and ranged from 2 to 15 months in the 1970s (35 WFS countries; United Nations, 1987). After 10 years, comparable DHS data from 11 of those countries (Sharma and others, 1990) continue to show an inverse relation, although differentials have narrowed. Other things being equal, this finding implies shorter durations of post-partum amenorrhoea and shorter natural birth intervals for better educated women. However, a new trend is emerging in several countries: the recent focus on breast-feeding has led better educated women to breast-feed for longer durations than lesser educated women (for example, Trinidad and Tobago, Peru, Indonesia, among developing countries, as well as the United States of America and other developed countries).

Extended periods of post-partum abstinence have been an important mechanism through which fertility has been controlled, particularly in sub-Saharan Africa, but also in parts of Southern Asia.[6] Better educated women are systematically more likely to abandon post-partum abstinence taboos (columns (1) and (2), row 3. For example, the median duration of abstinence reported in a study in urban Nigeria declined from 22.5 months among uneducated women to 7.6 months among post-secondary school educated women. And in relation to illiterate mothers, the risk of terminating abstinence is 1.67, 2.42 and 3.27 for mothers with primary, secondary and post-secondary education, after controlling for other factors (Oni, 1985). In part, long periods of post-partum abstinence have been tolerated in sub-Saharan Africa because of polygamy and the availability of other wives (Oppong and Abu, 1987) and there is some evidence (for Cameroon, Kritz and Gurak, 1989) that better educated women resist polygamous unions. In other words, a traditional check on fertility in this context has been relaxed among better educated women and unless offset by increased contraception, would lead to increased fertility among them.

Education improving infant and child survival

The effect of women's education on child mortality is probably its most pervasive and consistently observed effect ("boringly inverse", Cochrane, Leslie and O'Hara, 1982). Female autonomy, access to family resources and exposure to the outside world are argued to be key factors explaining this relation (table 31, columns (1) and (2), row 4). Even a small amount of education affects child mortality levels. From recent DHS, there is evidence that child mortality declines are perceptible from primary school onward (Boerma, Sommerfelt and Rutstein, 1991) and zero-order correlations from more than 100 developing countries suggest a significant negative association between educational measures, particularly primary and secondary school enrolment ratios and the infant mortality rate (table 30).

Educated women tend to be less fatalistic about illness, more aware of nutrition (Jensen and Juma, 1989, for Kenya) and more knowledgeable about hygiene and preventive health practices (Bicego and Boerma, 1991). They are more likely to know of modern treatments for child illnesses, such as oral rehydration therapy (Boerma and others, 1990). They are also more concerned with hygiene. For example, the Mexico study (LeVine and others, 1991) observed that regular hand-washing was far more common among educated mothers than others. A study from Ghana observed that even when source of water is controlled, educated mothers tend to have the lowest child mortality; this finding is attributed to their better sanitation practices (Stephens, 1984).

Equally important, educated women are more likely to use appropriate health care, whether antenatal care, immunization or timely and appropriate medical attention to sick children (Bicego and Boerma, 1991; LeVine and others, 1991). There is also evidence of a more equitable treatment of sons and daughters and a more equitable distribution of food by better educated mothers, although Cleland and van Ginneken (1988) could not identify this as a major pathway in the link between female education and child mortality. In short, educated women are more able to manipulate their environments, know their rights and demand attention, challenge their in-laws with their knowledge, have access to family resources which would enable purchase of services and drugs, communicate with husbands about treatment of sick children and so on.

There are two conditions under which the link between maternal education and child survival is weakened: in societies with female seclusion; or a strong son preference. As argued earlier, under these conditions, unfavourable to women, even educated women are unlikely to get independent access to health care. And where strong son preference exists, even educated women are seen to discriminate against higher order daughters in health care and feeding practices (as compared with sons and eldest daughters) (Das Gupta, 1987).

As in the case of fertility, women's education is far more important in explaining child mortality and, to a lesser extent morbidity, than are residence, husband's occupation and education (Caldwell, 1979; Rodríguez and Cleland, 1981). One review of multivariate studies from various countries (Cochrane, Leslie and O'Hara, 1982) observes that the effect of mother's education on infant and child mortality is about twice that of father's education. The effect of education is considerable: cross national evidence suggests that each one-year increment in maternal education is associated with a 7-9 per cent decline in childhood (under-five) mortality (Cleland and van Ginneken, 1988). Another estimate (Cochrane, Leslie and O'Hara, 1982) suggests that a 1 per cent increase in female literacy will reduce infant mortality by 0.5 death per 1,000.

Improved child survival has both a mechanical and a behavioural effect on fertility. Mechanically, especially in societies where extended breast-feeding is practised, improved infant mortality implies longer birth intervals and therefore a slower pace of child-bearing, other things being equal. Deliberate modifications of behaviour, however, arise from one's own-child mortality experience and one's perceptions of the likelihood of child deaths: the tendency to replace dead children or to produce more than the desired number of children to ensure a buffer in case of mortality. Through any of these effects, the improved child survival that accompanies education would lead to lower fertility (table 31, column (4), row 4).

Overall supply side-effects

The inadvertent effects of maternal education on fertility are both positive (through diminished breast-feeding and post-partum abstinence and possibly higher fecundity) and negative (through improved child survival and especially through increased age at marriage), as is seen in table 31, column (4), rows 1-4. The strengths of these effects vary with cultural contexts and different levels of education. On balance, when the fertility-enhancing effects of education, through reduced breast-feeding and abstinence durations, are not sufficiently offset by fertility-reducing effects, such as increased marital age, reduced child mortality and increased contraception, fertility undoubtedly increases—and this explains the increased fertility of women with a small amount of education observed earlier.

E. Women's education, family size preferences and the structure of demand

Education also results in deliberate changes in behaviour, changes that involve a volitional component with a specifically fertility-oriented intent on the part of the educated woman. The negative effect of education on family size desires is well established, although for the most part the effect of education on actual fertility tends to be more sharply inverse than its effect on family size desired. Education reduces parental demand for children for many reasons, as is seen in table 3, column (2), rows 5-11. It tends to raise the perceived cost of children and to reduce parents' reliance upon them; it changes attitudes towards small family-size norms and exposes the educated to new ideas and alternatives. In Caldwell's terms (1982), the direction of wealth flows from children to parental and higher generations becomes reversed and better educated parents will want fewer children.

The developing world exhibits considerable variation in the number (United Nations, 1987) of children desired. Desired family size is highest in sub-Saharan Africa (6-9), followed by Western Asia (5-6), Northern Africa (4-5), Eastern and Southern Asia, and Latin America and the Caribbean (3-5), roughly following the pattern of regional differences in educational attainment seen in table 28. Although levels vary by region, a similar pattern is evident in all regions. Mean-desired family size generally decreases systematically with increased female education (table 31, column (2), row 5), although once again, as in the case of actual fertility, the break occurs for women with some secondary education. In general, the effect of education on desired family size is sharpest in areas where overall desired family size is high—notably sub-Saharan Africa and Western Asia—and lowest in some Caribbean, Southern Asian and Eastern Asian settings, where the difference between the extreme educational categories is one child or less (United Nations, 1987).[7]

Family-size desires are dictated by a variety of motives, all of which are felt, undoubtedly, by women and men; some, however, are felt more intensely by women. Important motives underlying family-size desires include the strength of the son preference; the extent of women's dependence upon reproduction for social acceptance and upon children (or sons) for economic security; and the costs that child-bearing imply, both financial and time. That high-fertility motives will erode with education seems clear. How fast this erosion occurs, however, depends upon the extent to which the kinship structure allows educated women to assume non-traditional roles.

Strength of the son preference

Few regions of the developing world value their daughters as much as they value their sons. This situation was evident from the enrolment figures seen earlier, where boys are consistently more likely to be educated than girls. It is also seen more directly from WFS and other surveys. Only 10 out of 38 WFS countries (United Nations, 1987) display an equal sex preference or preference for daughters over sons and eight of these are in Latin America and the Caribbean. In contrast, WFS reports a weak son preference in Africa, although a study by Orubuloye (1987) suggests it could be quite strong (60 per cent of all men and half of all women want four sons and two daughters). Very strong son preference is observed in Chinese cultures (Greenhalgh, 1985; Hsiung, 1988) and in Southern Asia where sons represent between three fifths and three fourths of total desired family size (Khan and Prasad, 1983).

Evidence on the effect of maternal education on son preference is sparse. To the extent that education gives women greater independence and control over resources, and to the extent that it frees them to override the decisions and controls of other family members and makes them less reliant upon sons for future flows of economic assistance, education is expected to lead to a more equal preference for sons and daughters, as is shown in table 31 (columns (1) and (2), row 6.

There is evidence, however, that the cultural preference for sons is at best weakly eroded as a result of education, especially in traditional rural settings of Southern Asia, where sons continue to be a woman's only ticket to security in her husband's home and to material support in the future. A national survey in India (Operations Research Group, 1990) finds that among women with up to some secondary education, family size preferences overwhelmingly favour sons; it is only among women with a secondary-school education that preferences are balanced. Education also makes a difference in women's determination to produce a second son: while a quarter of uneducated and primary-school educated women would be prepared to have three or more daughters in this endeavour, this proportion declined to 18 and 7 per cent among women with higher levels of education. At least in this rural setting in Southern Asia, the evidence is that cultural preference for sons is eroded only after a relatively high level of education has been achieved. That educated women will resort to the abortion of their female foetuses to ensure their desired number of sons attests to relatively unyielding son preference. How rapidly education diminishes the preference for sons depends to a large extent upon the underlying kinship structure and the costs and values attached to children of each sex.

Maternal reliance upon children

There is evidence that better educated women are less likely to rely upon children—on their labour contribution in childhood and their economic and residential support in adulthood—and upon reproduction to legitimize their position in their husband's homes.

Children's labour contribution in childhood

With the increasing importance of schooling for children, the traditional reliance upon children's labour contributions from an early age on the family farm and in housework has diminished in most developing countries (see, for example, Caldwell, Reddy and Caldwell, 1982; Caldwell, 1979; Makinwa-Adebusoye, 1991). Because better educated parents (here, women and men have similar concerns) have higher educational aspirations for their children, they are more likely to reduce the labour contribution of their children in all kinds of activities (table 31, column 2, row 7). Exposure to modern ways of child-rearing may lead educated parents to expect less from children in terms of labour but to focus rather on children's schooling, on the one hand, and leisure on the other. Educated women may be better equipped to challenge the authority of household elders on the subject of child labour; and certainly where they control household resources, they are in a stronger position to ensure that children shall be freed from work responsibilities. Evidence from rural Maharashtra, for example, (Jejeebhoy, 1992) indicates that both expected and actual labour support from sons declined significantly with maternal education, even after controlling for husband's socio-economic position. Labour support from daughters in housework showed a more modest decline, however, largely because housework is not seen as competing with school time and because girls are not expected to take school as seriously as are their brothers.

Children's financial and residential support in adulthood

Traditionally, children are most highly valued as their parents' main source of economic and residential support in the future, even though the flow of wealth between parents and children is not always upward. Education is associated with increased options in terms of old age and other support, so diminishing the dependence upon children for the future (table 31, columns (1) and (2), row 8). As women gain relative autonomy and control over family resources, their dependence upon male family members and, consequently, their need for sons for future support is expected to diminish (Cain, 1982).

The evidence for this effect is mixed. At early stages of modernization, the old-age security motive for children appears to abate relatively little in response to changes in education *per se*. Strongly held old-age-support motives for children can and do coexist with lower desired family size and lower fertility, as seen in settings as diverse as Africa (Makinwa-Adebusoye, 1991) and Asia. Although educated women may be relatively less likely to acknowledge this motive for large number of children, there is evidence that children, albeit fewer and better educated, continue to be desired for old-age residential and economic security even among educated women (for evidence among the Yoruba, see Akande, 1989). Evidence from Karachi (Sathar and Kazi, 1990) and rural Maharashtra (Jejeebhoy, 1992) concur that maternal education is virtually unrelated to expectations about old-age economic and residential support from sons (an almost universally expressed expectation). This suggests that in strong patriarchal cultures with relatively limited economic opportunities for women and strong seclusion norms, even educated women continue to rely on their sons. At Karachi, the turning-point comes with 10 or more years of education, and even so, for fewer than half of all women. The fact that better educated women continue to rely upon their children for the future does not, apparently, play an important role in determining their family-size preferences or fertility.

Children as a source of prestige

In societies as diverse as sub-Saharan Africa, and Eastern, South-eastern and Southern Asia, fertility is a means of legitimizing a woman's position in her marital family (Makinwa-Adebusoye, 1991; Akande, 1989; Hsiung, 1988; Karve, 1965). Childlessness is deeply feared and is sufficient justification for taking on a second wife or for desertion. In fact, Makinwa-Adebusoye argues that in sub-Saharan Africa, the need for a large family as a means for women to legitimize their status in their husband's family is a far more important motive for high fertility than is the economic rationale. To the extent that education grants women access to other sources of prestige (economic independence, for example), frequent child-bearing may become less important as the only means of deriving prestige, as is tentatively suggested in table 31, row 9. But empirical evidence of this relation is unfortunately lacking; on the contrary, the traditional pattern in sub-Saharan Africa suggests that even considerable economic independence coexists with a fear of childlessness and high family-size desires, making it questionable whether other sources of prestige are really a substitute for large numbers of children.

Costs of large numbers of children

Better educated parents want better educated and "higher quality, more expensive" children. This involves greater financial costs, usually borne by both parents as well as greater time and opportunity costs, invariably borne by the mother.

Economic costs

Economic costs of children are felt by both women and men, although in some cultures, in different ways. In all cultures, however, the major economic cost of children is certainly education. In fact, the growing recognition of the importance of education for children and their costs are held to be the most important factor swinging the flow of wealth away from parents and an important precondition for the fertility transition (Caldwell, 1982). Since educated parents aspire to have educated children, this cost becomes a major deterrent to high fertility, as seen in table 31, columns (1) and (2), row 10). And, of course, to the extent that better educated women enjoy more effective decision-making and control over family resources, they can ensure high-quality, well-educated and costlier children.

Evidence from Southern Asia (Pakistan and India) shows that systematically larger proportions of children of more educated women were currently in school or had achieved educational milestones, although the relation was stronger for sons than for daughters. In Africa, where child-rearing costs were not traditionally borne entirely by parents (Makinwa-Adebusoye, 1991), as a result of high public investment in education, the practice of fostering out children and relying upon older siblings and other relatives for child-rearing costs; the deteriorating economic situation accompanied by more expensive aspirations for children (and probably a limit to the willingness of better-off relatives to share child costs) has led better educated women disproportionately to assume the responsibility of meeting these costs, more independently of the kin network. Both in settings where women assume a direct role in meeting child costs and in those where their role is more passive, educated women have higher and more costly aspirations for their children and frequently cite costs as a major disincentive for large numbers of children.

Time and opportunity costs

More specifically affected by maternal (as opposed to parental) education are time and opportunity costs of children as seen in table 31, columns (1) and (2), row 11. The higher the woman's education, the higher is her potential wage and opportunities for modern sector work and the more she forgoes to rear children as opposed to engaging in wage-earning occupations. This link is less important in most of the less developed world because child-care substitutes are readily and cheaply available (see, for example, Sathar and Kazi, 1990).

Education, however, changes women's perceptions of the amount of maternal time and attention needed by children, thereby making children more time-intensive, as noted in a recent study in Mexico (LeVine and others, 1991). For example, this study finds that better educated Mexican women are more likely to see young infants as capable of communication and child care as labour-intensive, requiring a great deal of maternal attention. Similarly, Mason and Palan (1981) in Malaysia, and Oppong and Abu focused biographies in Ghana (1987), found that better educated women define the maternal role as requiring greater personal attention, deterring women from high fertility. In short, these studies show empirically that maternal education, through exposure to new ideas and a greater ability to make and implement decisions, is associated with a more labour-intensive style of mother-child interaction, requiring more time and energy, and making women unwilling to bear many children (table 31, row 11).

Summary

Although education appears to be inversely related—after the attainment of the familiar threshold—to family size preferences, the strength of the effect and the motives underlying the effect vary. The effect of education on the labour contribution of children in childhood and the perceived costs of child-rearing appear to be more uniformly observed than other effects, including the old-age security motive and the extent of son preference (where son preference is traditionally high).

It is worth speculating on why the strength of the effect varies from study to study. It can be argued that the speed with which educated women will change their reliance upon children is closely linked with their autonomy and access to family resources, notably the spheres in which they have autonomy. Where education grants women increased self-reliance or leads them to prefer more labour-intensive child-rearing practices (as in Mexico) one might expect its effect on desired fertility to be quite sharp. However, if, as was shown earlier, educated women derive autonomy in limited spheres, such as deciding on the duration of post-partum abstinence, child health care and so on, rather than more generally, even educated women with some autonomy cannot be expected to reduce their reliance upon children easily and the effect on desired family size may not be as sharp.

G. Women's education and unmet need

Even when actual or potential family size equals or exceeds the desired number, large numbers of women do nothing to prevent unwanted further pregnancies. Evidence from a number of countries shows that educational differentials in desired family size are not as wide as differentials in actual fertility, suggesting that in many settings, the most important effect of education is to enable women to prevent unwanted pregnancies.

The extent to which actual family size exceeds desired family size defines the level of unwanted fertility and is best reflected by the experience of women aged 40 or over that have essentially completed their child-bearing. The evidence on the effect of maternal education on unwanted fertility suggests a number of patterns. An analysis of WFS data (United Nations, 1987) observes that it is only in the most developed of the developing countries and in the Latin American and Caribbean region that better educated women have systematically lower levels of unwanted fertility. Evidence over time from seven Latin American and the Caribbean countries (Colombia, Costa Rica, Dominican Republic, Ecuador, Jamaica, Peru, and Trinidad and Tobago) shows that while educational differences in wanted fertility are quite narrow, it is better educated women's ability to prevent unwanted fertility which accounts for the more impressive observed fertility differences by education, both in the 1970s (WFS) and in the 1980s (DHS) (Bongaarts and Lightbourne, 1990). Education tends to generate much narrower differences in wanted than in actual fertility in this region (Weinberger, Lloyd and Blanc, 1989). Obviously, better educated women in these countries know more about fertility regulation and are better able to exercise their preferences.

At lower levels of development and in other regions, the pattern is curvilinear, with smaller proportions of uneducated and highly educated women, compared with women with from one to six years of schooling, reporting an unwanted birth. This finding presumably reflects the higher desired family size of uneducated women, and the greater ability to achieve—that is, not overshoot—their preferences among the highly educated. Lastly, in sub-Saharan Africa, where, as a result of high desired family size, unwanted fertility levels are much lower than in any other region, the relation of education to unwanted fertility is actually positive; that is, better educated women are more likely to have experienced it.

More consistent patterns emerge when one considered unmet need, that is, the proportion of couples that want no more children but are not practising contraception. The effect of maternal education on the level of unmet need usually is inverse (Westoff and Pebley, 1981; Westoff and Moreno, 1989; Westoff and Ochoa, 1991). For example, WFS and DHS evidence for Latin America and the Caribbean suggests that while an average of 40 per cent of uneducated women have an unmet need for family planning, it is only 13 per cent for women with higher education.

H. Women's education, fertility regulation and obstacles to contraception

Factors underlying the persistence of unmet need reflect a range of social, psychological and economic barriers to the use of contraception, many of which are rooted in women's sociocultural situation. Women's education is expected to influence their access to modern knowledge and new ways of life and hence the extent to which they know and approve of and can engage in such new forms of behaviour as contraception (table 31, rows 12-15). In addition, women's education, by fostering a strengthening of the conjugal unit, breaks down barriers to communication between spouses on contraception. Above all, the enhanced autonomy in domestic decision-making which women gain as a result of education leads them to act upon their lower family-size preferences through the use of contraception, even when this behaviour contradicts the preferences of family elders.

Knowledge and approval of deliberate fertility control

There is ample evidence of the link between education and contraceptive knowledge and approval and fertility (table 31, rows 12 and 13). For example, the DHS results in sub-Saharan Africa (Botswana, Burundi, Kenya, Liberia, Mali, Nigeria and Senegal), Northern Africa (Morocco and the Sudan, Asia (Sri Lanka and Thailand), and Latin America and the Caribbean (Colombia, Ecuador, and Trinidad and Tobago) indicate a systematic increase in knowledge of modern contraceptive methods by education. In these data, even a little education significantly enhances knowledge levels in every single country. Similarly, the proportions approving of family planning increase monotonically with education; evidence of this increase is available from a variety of DHS and other surveys (Operations Research Group, 1990).

Spousal communication

Education is expected to encourage greater intimacy between spouses; and one manifestation of this is a tendency to discuss such previously forbidden subjects as sexual behaviour, contraception and the number of children to have. There is a good deal of evidence in support of this argument (for example, DHS data from Oyo and Ondo States in Nigeria (Kritz and Gurak, 1991); a 1989 survey from India (Operations Research Group, 1990). Better spousal communication in turn is expected to increase contraceptive use and lower fertility (table 31, row 14).

Contraceptive use

As a result of the effect of education on both demand and regulation cost factors, education is positively related to contraceptive prevalence, both at the macrolevel, as is seen in table 30, and at the household level.[9] At the household level, for example, the United Nations review of education and fertility (1987) observed large educational differentials in contraceptive practice, after controlling age: the percentage of women with seven or more years of schooling that were practising contraception was about 24 points greater than the level for women with no education. Moreover, even a few years of education makes a difference: the mean percentage using contraception was about nine points higher for women with from one to three years of schooling, compared with uneducated women. These results are essentially corroborated by the addition of more recent DHS data from 15 countries, which suggest a uniformly positive relation between female education and contraceptive use. A review of a number of DHS findings in sub-Saharan Africa also observes that contraceptive prevalence rates rise notably especially among women with primary schooling or more (Kritz and Gurak, 1989).

Although most studies support a positive link between maternal education and contraceptive use (table 31, row 15), there are some conditions under which this link is observed to be relatively weak (Cochrane, 1979; United Nations, 1987). One possible explanation is the presence of a strong family planning programme, directed to the least educated and poorest sections of the population (Weinberger, 1987). A study of two provinces in China, one more educated than the other, observed a convergence in fertility rates between the two provinces and attribute this absence of a differential to unusually powerful family planning programme efforts, focused most strongly in the less developed province (Sichuan) (Freedman and others, 1988). Similarly, a number of cross-sectional studies in India observe a consistently negative association between women's education and sterilization, the method most vigorously promoted by the programme (Operations Research Group, 1990).

I. Decomposition of the education-fertility relation in different stages of the transition

Many multivariate studies that examine the relation of women's education to fertility have concluded that women's education exerts an independent effect on fertility even when such factors as household income and husband's education are controlled (United Nations, 1987; Cleland and Wilson, 1987). Fewer studies, however, have tried to decompose the effects of education through the major proximate and other intervening variables.

That schooling has a powerful and pervasive effect on reproductive behaviour is undisputed. But more important from a policy point of view is how much education, what the various paths are and so on. Many studies observe that the fertility-reducing effect of marriage and contraception increases with education and the fertility-enhancing effect of post-partum insusceptibility diminishes. For example, Bulatao (1984) argues that marriage delay and reductions in breast-feeding have roughly offsetting effects early in fertility transition, whereas contraception leads to large fertility declines later. An empirical decomposition of these effects using data from urban Nigeria finds that fertility was inhibited most powerfully by post-partum insusceptibility among uneducated and even up to secondary-school educated women; among women with post-secondary-school education, the strongest effect was through marriage, while contraception had the weakest effect at each point (Oni, 1985). Another decomposition, in relatively lesser developed rural Maharashtra attributes more than 60 per cent of the difference in the fertility of uneducated and middle and secondary-school educated women, respectively, to differences in age at marriage; the positive effects through post-partum amenorrhea and abstinence are largely offset by the negative effect through demand for children and deliberate fertility control (Jejeebhoy, 1992). And an analysis of WFS data from two more developed regions, Sri Lanka and Colombia (Easterlin and Crimmins, 1985) attributes about half of the differential (effect of an additional 10 years of schooling) to increased marital age, about a third to increased fertility control and the rest (13-14 per cent) in the reverse direction to shorter periods of breast-feeding and lower levels of secondary sterility.[10]

A study of successive cross-sections of women in Tamil Nadu (Jejeebhoy, 1991) offers support to this pattern. At an early point in the transition, the effect of a shift to completed primary school has a marginally positive effect on children ever born (0.07); now two thirds of the total effect is attributed to natural fertility factors, 29 per cent to delayed marriage and 11 per cent to increased contraception. After 10 years, the overall effect has turned inverse (0.55); and the underlying proximate determinants are more similar to those for Sri Lanka and Colombia observed above—42 per cent is attributed to delayed marriage, 40 per cent to increased fertility control and 18 per cent to natural fertility factors.

These studies provide evidence that in early stages of development, the primary effect of education is through inadvertent fertility-enhancing factors (table 31, rows 2-3); thereafter, through delayed marriage (row 1), an inadvertent but fertility-depressing factor; this effect gradually weakens and is probably overtaken by the effects through deliberate demand-related factors (tables 31, rows 5-15). And as far as women's status changes are concerned, Sathar and Mason (1989) suggest that at Karachi greater opportunity costs, reduced costs of regulation and greater autonomy of better educated women each play at least a limited role in explaining why schooling influences fertility.

What does all this mean in terms of the role of women's education? Some (Cleland and Wilson, 1987) point out that a small amount of education is more likely to change attitudes and aspirations than economic realities. Along the same lines, it has been observed in Southern Asia that educated women at first obtain autonomy over limited, non-economic aspects of their lives (child care, breast-feeding and post-partum abstinence) rather than over broader economic issues. Other things being equal, these changes are unlikely to set off changes in women's demand for children and practice of contraception (Caldwell, Reddy and Caldwell, 1983); hence, one will not observe the expected negative effect of education on fertility. Rather, the more inadvertent consequences of education on women's situation, through shorter periods of post-partum insusceptibility and through delayed marriage, will prevail, resulting in a curvilinear or moderately negative relation of education to fertility. Of these two intervening pathways, the evidence from the diverse examples cited above, as well as such other studies as that of Achmad (1980) in Java and Bali and those cited in Cochrane's review (1983) strongly support the view that the most important effect of female education on fertility in the less developed regions probably operates through delayed age at marriage.

It is when economic realities for women become more secure and their decision-making authority more comprehensive that the effects of education through a lower desired family size and increased contraception become important for fertility. The stage at which this occurs depends largely upon the cultural context or the traditional situation of women in respect to economic and other forms of self-reliance. As a result, Kritz and Gurak (1989) and Sathar and Kazi (1990), for example, hypothesize that although the relation of maternal education to family formation in sub-Saharan Africa or Pakistan is similar to that in Eastern and South-eastern Asia, and in Latin America and the Caribbean, the levels of education required to effect a change in fertility in the latter group may be higher. This conclusion is consistent with Mason's suggestion (1988) that the pre-existing nature of women's position affects the pace at which mass educational efforts will have an effect on fertility. Where the pre-existing situation grants women autonomy over family decisions and economics, as in parts of Latin America, for example, even a little education may have a dampening effect on fertility. Where the traditional kinship structure assigns little independence to women, as in Southern Asia and to a lesser extent, sub-Saharan Africa, high levels of education may be necessary to affect family-size preferences and contraception.

One might argue that in strongly patriarchal settings, the effect of primary-school education acts mainly to provide women a limited autonomy which results in a loosening of traditional checks on fertility, on the one hand, and an improvement in child survival, on the other. The relative strengths of these two effects then determine the effect of a small amount of education on fertility. At the next stage, education reduces fertility moderately, an effect explained by age at marriage. It is only at the highest level of education (secondary and beyond) that the truly volitional aspects of the education-fertility relation come into play. Now the strength of both delayed marriage and weaker motives for large numbers of children serve to offset other pro-fertility effects and account for a more sharply negative relation.

J. Summary and conclusions

This review has offered qualified support for the widely held belief that improvements in female education will reduce fertility. The author says "qualified" for a number of reasons. The cross-sectional relation between education and fertility is uniformly inverse only in certain stages of the fertility transition and after a threshold level of education has been attained. The strength with which women's education affects their fertility is largely conditioned by the overall development and cultural context of the society and hence, wide regional variation is observed. The evidence concurs with Mason's suggestion (1988) that variations in the pace of educational expansion and resulting changes in reproductive attitudes and behaviour may both be conditioned by the position that women occupy in the traditional kinship structure of a society. Four main conclusions emerge from this review:

(a) There appears to be a systematic shift in the effect of maternal education on fertility in the course of the fertility transition, from curvilinear at the earliest stages to uniformly and sharply inverse during periods of rapid fertility decline to a flatter inverse relation in late stages;

(b) Despite the ambiguities in early stages of the transition, it is evident that beyond a threshold level of education, most commonly identified as from six to seven years or some secondary schooling, the effect of maternal schooling on fertility is almost always negative;

(c) During the early stages of the transition, it is inadvertent forces that determine the shape of the relation of education to fertility, that is, the effects of education on diminished periods of breast-feeding and abstinence and on delayed age at marriage, which are not intended to reduce fertility. In fact, in much of the developing world today, the main effect of education on fertility continues to be through postponement of marriage. It is only in later stages that volitional factors, such as lower desired family size and increased contraception, become the primary channels through which education affects fertility. Even here, desired family size may fall as a result of education, without corresponding declines in such motives for child-bearing as the need for children for old-age support;

(d) The impact of women's education on their fertility is greatest when education offers women more than a limited role in family decisions and access to resources. Where a woman's role in family affairs is

limited to deciding on her breast-feeding and abstinence behaviour, on the treatment of sick children and even veto rights over prospective husbands, education is unlikely to have a strong impact on fertility. Moreover, where it does, it will be through forces not intended to have an effect on fertility. It is when the economic realities begin to change, that is, when education provides women with decision-making authority in a broader realm and greater access to and control over the family's resources, that fertility is likely to turn sharply downward.

This review also points to at least three policy concerns:

(a) It has been shown that literacy and enrolment rates are increasing globally, which means that the proportion of uneducated women will continue to decline, although poorly educated women will constitute the majority in much of the developing world. Rather than relying upon the shift in the educational distribution to reduce fertility (because some degree of fertility decline can be anticipated as a result of this change), rapid fertility decline will depend as well upon changes in the behaviour of less educated women. Fertility levels of highly educated women in many countries are already quite low, leaving little room for further decline. On the other hand, among less educated women, fertility and family-size preferences continue to be high. As has been seen in many settings unwanted fertility is high among these women. In almost all settings, the level of unmet need is highest among the least educated. Thus, fertility is unlikely to decline rapidly unless programmes are established that help to address the unmet need of less educated women.[11]

(b) In the early stages of development, the impact of primary education on fertility is not uniformly inverse. One policy implication of this finding is that the current focus on universal primary education may not be sufficient to induce changes in fertility behaviour. This finding suggests a need for innovative and culturally sensitive strategies to extend the exposure of girls to education and greater investments in female schooling;

(c) The pathways through which education affects fertility and the pace at which this effect occurs appear to be varied. There is, however, convincing evidence that education sets off a number of changes in women's situation which tend to create an environment conducive to demographic changes. It is not simply the greater domestic decision-making autonomy, or the greater control of resources, or the exposure to the modern world or closer husband-wife ties that individually affect fertility behaviour; nor does the effect arise simply through delayed marriage, reduced costs of contraception or higher costs of children. Rather, each of these processes plays a role—at different times, in different cultures—in mediating the effect of women's education on their fertility. The evidence suggests that even where economic opportunities for women are limited or health and family planning services weak, more than a primary-school education for women can result in both lower fertility and improvements in their situation in the family and outside.

Notes

[1]Cochrane (1979) observed an inverse relation in only 49 per cent of the cross-tabular studies reviewed and a significant inverse relation in only 31 per cent. With the inclusion of data from a series of developing countries, WFS results from 38 developing countries (United Nations, 1987) suggest an inverse relation in even fewer cases. The effect of education on children ever born to women aged 40-49 was inverse in only 18 of the 37 countries for which data were available; but reversed U-shaped in 16 and unrelated or positively related in another three.

[2]Cochrane (1979) observes that although 56 per cent of studies relating women's education to fertility reported an inverse relation, this was so for only 31 per cent of those relating men's education to fertility (79 per cent and 32 per cent in age adjusted relation).

[3]The relation with female education remained significant in 23 countries, compared with 30 countries when no controls were applied (husband's education was significant in 27, but this included a number of significant positive associations). Rodríguez and Cleland (1981) estimate the effects of education and other variables on fertility using dummy variables and regression; they find that there is a difference of 1.9 children between uneducated women and those with a secondary education, compared with a difference of 1.3 children for males.

[4]Caldwell (1982) argues that it is predominantly the fact of education rather than its content that is important. In some cases, of course, content is also important, particularly when it is determined by religion, for example, Catholic or Islamic; for example, evidence from the 1960s in the United States of America and even more recently in developing countries (Bailey, 1986) suggests a positive relation between education and fertility among women educated in Catholic schools.

[5]For Zimbabwe, Mhloyi, 1991; for Lagos, Lesthaeghe, Page and Adegbola, 1981; for Kuwait, Al-Bustan and Kohli, 1988; for Malaysia, Othman, 1985; for urban Nigeria, Oni, 1985.

[6]See, for example, Oni, 1985; Lesthaeghe, Page and Adegbola, 1981; and Caldwell and Caldwell, 1981, for urban Nigeria; and Caldwell, Reddy and Caldwell, 1982, for India.

[7]Educational differentials in desired family size are not as pronounced as those in actual fertility; nor do they correspond very well with the largest differentials in actual fertility (United Nations, 1987). Once sub-Saharan Africa, where uneducated women report exceptionally high preferences, is excluded, the relation between level of development and mean desired family size, in any educational category, is weak.

[8]For Nigeria, Makinwa-Adebusoye, 1991; for Zimbabwe, Mhloyi, 1991; for Asia, Casterline, 1991; for Pakistan, Sathar and others, 1988; and for India, Jejeebhoy, 1992.

[9]Since contraception is so much a function of age, marital duration and children ever born, it is important that this relation be estimated with controls for at least one of them.

[10]A subnational examination of the proximate determinants of total fertility rate using data from 29 WFS, which sheds light on the relative effects of education through each of the three proximate determinants (marriage, contraception and lactation), finds that the fertility difference between the two lowest educational strata was attributed to the effect of contraception rather than marriage; at middle and secondary levels, the contribution of nuptiality exceeded that of contraception. This generalization applies both to regional groups and sets of countries defined by stage of the transition. At the same time, the contribution of post-partum insusceptibility increased with education, suggesting a fertility-enhancing effect, other things being equal. This effect, however, was weaker than the fertility-depressing effects described above, perhaps because post-partum abstinence, overall fecundity and sterility differences and abortion were not included. Only in select instances did the magnitude of the fertility-enhancing forces match those of marriage or contraception: for the two lowest strata in Africa, the Americas and countries with no or recent declines (Singh, Casterline and Cleland, 1985).

[11]Investment in improved female education is probably the most frequently suggested alternative to family planning programmes as a means of reducing fertility. Cochrane (1988) estimated the costs of births averted directly through improved female education and compared them with corresponding costs through family planning programmes; the results suggest that the cost of a birth averted through education far exceeds that averted through family planning in most countries. In reality, of course, there is no either/or solution but this exercise serves as a note of caution to those advocating various indirect policies to reduce fertility.

References

Achmad, Sulistinah Irawati (1980). *A Study of the Relationship between Educational Attainment and Fertility Behaviour of Women in Java and Bali.* Tallahassee, Florida: Florida State University.

Acuna, O. M. (1981). La mujer en la familia y el valor de los hijos. In *Seminario Nacional de Demografía, Dirección General de Estadística y Censos.* San José, Costa Rica: Departamento de Publicaciones.

Adewuyi, A. A., and U. C. Isiugo-Abanihe (1986). *Regional Patterns and Correlates of Birth Interval Length in Nigeria.* International Population Dynamics Program Research Note, No. 107. Canberra: The Australian National University.

Akande, B. (1989). Some socio-cultural factors influencing fertility behaviour: a case study of Yoruba women. *Biology and Society* (London), vol. 6, No. 4 (December), pp. 165-170.

Al-Bustan, Mahmoud A., and B. R. Kohli (1988). Socio-economic and demographic factors influencing breast-feeding among Kuwaiti women. *Genus* (Rome), vol. 44, No. 1/2 (gennaio-giugno), pp. 265-278.

Alsuwaigh, Sihan A. (1989). Women in transition: the case of Saudi Arabia. *Journal of Comparative Family Studies* (Calgary, Canada), vol. 20, No. 1 (Spring), pp. 67-78.

Bailey, Mohamed (1986). Differential fertility by religious group in rural Sierra Leone. *Journal of Biosocial Science* (Cambridge, England), vol. 18, No. 1 (January), pp. 75-85.

Basu, Alaka Malwade (1989). Culture and the status of women in north and south India. In *Population Transition in India,* S. N. Singh and others, eds. Delhi, India: B. R. Publishing Corporation.

__________ (1990). Cultural influences on health care use: two regional groups in India. *Studies in Family Planning* (New York), vol. 21, No. 5 (September/October), pp. 275-286.

Bicego, George T., and J. Ties Boerma (1991). Maternal education and child survival: a comparative analysis of DHS data. In *Demographic and Health Surveys World Conference, August 5-7, 1991, Washington D. C., Proceedings,* vol. II. Columbia, Maryland: IRD/Macro International, Inc.

Boerma, J. Ties, A. Elisabeth Sommerfelt and Shea O. Rutstein (1991). *Childhood Morbidity and Treatment Patterns.* Demographic and Health Surveys Comparative Studies, No. 4. Columbia, Maryland: Institute for Resource Development/Macro International, Inc.

Boerma, J. Ties, and others (1990). *Immunization: Levels, Trends and Differentials.* Demographic and Health Surveys Comparative Studies, No. 1. Columbia, Maryland: Institute for Resource Development/Macro International Inc.

Bongaarts, John, and Robert Lightbourne (1990). Wanted fertility in Latin America: trends and differentials in seven countries. Paper prepared for the Seminar on Fertility Transition in Latin America, sponsored by the International Union for the Scientific Study of Population Committee on Comparative Analysis of Fertility and Family Planning, in cooperation with Centro Latinamericano de Demografia and Centro Nacional de Poblactíon, Buenos Aires, Argentina, April.

Bulatao, R. A. (1984). *Reducing Fertility in Developing Countries: A Review of Determinants and Policy Levers.* World Bank Staff Working Paper, No. 680. Washington D. C.: The World Bank.

Cain, Mead (1982). Perspectives on family and fertility in developing countries. *Population Studies* (London), vol. 36, No. 2 (July), pp. 159-175.

__________ (1984). *Women's Status and Fertility in Developing Countries: Son Preference and Economic Security.* Centre for Policy Studies Working Papers, No. 110. New York: The Population Council.

Caldwell, John C. (1979). Education as a factor in mortality decline: an examination of Nigerian data. *Population Studies* (London), vol. 33, No. 3 (November), pp. 395-413.

__________ (1981). The mechanisms of demographic change in historical perspective. *Population Studies* (London), vol. 35, No. 1 (March), pp. 5-27.

__________ (1982). *Theory of Fertility Decline.* London: Academic Press.

__________, and Peter McDonald (1982). Influence of maternal education on infant and child mortality: levels and causes. *Health Policy and Education* (Amsterdam), vol. 2, pp. 251-267.

Caldwell, John C., P. H. Reddy and Pat Caldwell (1982). The causes of demographic change in rural South India: a micro approach. *Population and Development Review* (New York), vol. 8, No. 4 (December), pp. 689-727.

_________ (1983). The social component of mortality decline: an investigation in South India employing alternative methodologies. *Population Studies* (London), vol. 37, No. 2 (July), pp. 185-205.

Caldwell, Pat, and John C. Caldwell (1981). The function of child-spacing in traditional societies and the direction of change. In *Child-spacing in Tropical Africa: Traditions and Change*, Hilary S. Page and Ron Lesthaeghe, eds. London and New York: Academic Press.

Casterline, John B. (1991). Fertility transition in Asia. Paper presented at the Seminar on the Course of Fertility Transition in sub-Saharan Africa, Harare, November. Sponsored by the International Union for the Scientific Study of Population and the University of Zimbabwe.

_________, and others (1984). *The Proximate Determinants of Fertility*. World Fertility Survey Comparative Studies, Cross-National Summaries, No. 39. Voorburg, Netherlands: International Statistical Institute.

Cleland, John G., and J. K. van Ginneken (1988). Maternal education and child survival in developing countries: the search for pathways of influence. *Social Science and Medicine* (Elmsford, New York), vol. 27, No. 12, pp. 1357-1368.

Cleland, John G., and Christopher Wilson (1987). Demand theories of the fertility transition: an iconoclastic view. *Population Studies* (London), vol. 41, No. 1, (March), pp. 5-30.

Cochrane, Susan H. (1979). *Fertility and Education: What Do We Really Know?* World Bank Occasional Papers, No. 26. Baltimore, Maryland: Johns Hopkins University Press.

_________ (1983). Effects of education and urbanization on fertility with Paula E. Nallubach and John Bongaarts. In *Determinants of Fertility in Developing Countries*, vol. 2, *Fertility Regulation and Institutional Influences*, Rodolfo A. Bulatao and Ronald Lee, eds., New York: Academic Press.

_________ (1988). *The Effects of Education, Health, and Social Security on Fertility in Developing Countries*. Policy, Planning, and Research Working Papers, No. 93. Washington, D.C.: The World Bank.

_________, and Samir M. Farid (1989). *Fertility in Sub-Saharan Africa: Analysis and Explanation*. World Bank Discussion Papers, No. 43. Washington D.C.: The World Bank.

_________, Joanne Leslie and Donald J. O'Hara (1982). Parental education and child health: intracountry evidence. *Health Policy and Education* (Amsterdam), vol. 2, pp. 213-250.

Dixon, Ruth (1975). *Women's Rights and Fertility*. Reports on Population/Family Planning, No. 17. New York: The Population Council.

Das Gupta, Monica (1987). Selective discrimination against female children in rural Punjab, India. *Population and Development Review* (New York), vol. 13, No. 1 (March), pp. 77-100.

Dyson, Tim, and Mick Moore (1983). On kinship structure, female autonomy and demographic behaviour in India. *Population and Development Review* (New York), vol. 9, No. 1 (March), pp. 35-60.

Easterlin, Richard A. (1978). The economics and sociology of fertility: a synthesis. In *Historical Studies of Changing Fertility*, Charles Tilly, ed. Princeton, New Jersey: Princeton University Press.

_________, and Eileen M. Crimmins (1985). *The Fertility Revolution: A Supply-Demand Analysis*. Chicago, Illinois: The University of Chicago Press.

Fernando, Dallas F. S. (1977). Female educational attainment and fertility. *Journal of Biosocial Science* (Cambridge, United Kingdom), vol. 9, No. 3 (July), pp. 339-351.

Florez, Carmen E. (1989). Changing women's status and fertility decline in Colombia. In *International Population Conference, New Delhi*, vol. 1. Liège, Belgium: International Union for the Scientific Study of Population.

Freedman, Ronald, and others (1988). Education and fertility in two Chinese provinces: 1967-1970 to 1979-1982. *Asia-Pacific Population Journal* (Bangkok), vol. 3, No. 1 (March), pp. 3-30.

Goldstein, Rhoda L. (1970). Students in saris: college education in the lives of young Indian women. *Journal of Asian and African Studies* (Leidan, Netherlands), vol. 5, No. 3 (July), pp. 193-201.

Greenhalgh, Susan (1985). Sexual stratification: the other side of "growth with equity" in East Asia. *Population and Development Review* (New York), vol. 11, No. 2 (June), pp. 265-314.

Holian, John (1984). The effect of female education on marital fertility in different sized communities of Mexico. *Social Biology* (Madison, Wisconsin), vol. 31, No. 3/4 (Fall-Winter), pp. 298-307.

Hsiung, Ping-chun (1988). Family structure and fertility in Taiwan: an extension and modification of Caldwell's wealth flows theory. *Journal of Population Studies* (Taipeh, Taiwan Province of China), vol. 11 (June), pp. 103-128.

Jejeebhoy, Shireen J. (1991). Women's status and fertility: successive cross-sectional evidence from Tamil Nadu, India, 1970-80. *Studies in Family Planning* (New York), vol. 22, No. 4 (July/August), pp. 217-230.

_________ (1992). Maternal education and fertility behaviour: rural Maharashtra, India, 1983/84. Paper prepared for the Population Division of the Department for Economic and Social Information and Policy Analysis of the United Nations Secretariat. New York.

Jensen, An-Magritt, and Magdallen N. Juma (1989). *Women, Childbearing and Nutrition: A Case Study from Bungoma, Kenya*. Oslo, Norway: Norwegian Institute for Urban and Regional Research.

Karve, Irawati 1965. *Indian Kinship Systems: Kinship Organisation in India*. 2nd ed., rev. Bombay: Asia Publishing House.

Kaufmann, Georgia, Ron Lesthaege and Dominique Meekers (1987). Marriage patterns and change in sub-Saharan Africa. In *The Cultural Roots of African Fertility Regimes: Proceedings of the Ife Conference, 25 February - 11 March 1987*. Ife, Nigeria: Obafemi Awolowo University, Department of Demography and Social Statistics.

Kazi, Shanaz, and Zeba A. Sathar (1986). Productive and reproductive choices: report of a pilot survey of urban working women in Karachi. *Pakistan Development Review* (Islamabad), vol. 25, No. 4, pp. 593-608.

Khan, M. E., and C. V. S. Prasad (1983). *Family Planning Practices in India: Second All India Survey*. Baroda, India: Operations Research Group.

Kritz, Mary M., and Douglas T. Gurak (1989). Women's status, education and family formation in sub-Saharan Africa. *International Family Planning Perspectives* (New York), vol. 15, No. 3 (September), pp. 100-105.

_________ (1991). Women's economic independence and fertility among the Yoruba. In *Demographic and Health Surveys World Conference, August 5-7, 1991, Washington D.C., Proceedings*, vol. I. Columbia, Maryland: IRD/Macro International Inc.

Kumari, Raj (1985). Attitude of girls towards marriage and a planned family. *Journal of Family Welfare* (Bombay, India), vol. 31, No. 3 (March), pp. 53-60.

Lesthaeghe, Ron, Hilary J. Page and O. Adegbola (1981). Child-spacing and fertility in Lagos. In *Child-Spacing in Tropical Africa: Traditions and Change*, Hilary J. Page and Ron Lesthaeghe, eds. London: Academic Press.

LeVine, Robert A., and others, (1991). Women's schooling and child care in the Demographic Transition: a Mexican case study. *Population and Development Review* (New York), vol. 17, No. 3 (September), pp. 459-496.

Makinwa-Adebusoye, Paulina (1991). Changes in the costs and benefits of children to their parents: the changing cost of educating children. Paper presented at the Seminar on the Course of Fertility Transition in sub-Saharan Africa, sponsored by the International Union for the Scientific Study of Population and the University of Zimbabwe, Harare, November.

Mason, Karen Oppenheim (1984). *The Status of Women: A Review of its Relationships to Fertility and Mortality*. New York: The Rockefeller Foundation.

_________ (1988). The impact of women's position on demographic change during the course of development: what do we know about the issue? In *Conference on the Position of Women and Demographic Change in the Course of Development, Asker (Oslo)*. 1988: Statistical Papers. Sponsored by the International Union for the Scientific Study of Population.

_________ (1990). Does women's status influence the decline of fertility in third world countries? Paper presented at the University of Southampton, November.

_________, and V. T. Palan (1981). Female employment and fertility in Peninsular Malaysia: the maternal role incompatibility hypothesis reconsidered. *Demography* (Washington, D.C., vol. 18, No. 4 (November), pp. 549-575.

Mhloyi, Marvellous (1991). Fertility transition in Zimbabwe. Paper presented at the Seminar on the Course of Fertility Transition in Sub-Saharan Africa, Harare, November. Sponsored by the International Union for the Scientific Study of Population and the University of Zimbabwe.

Minturn, L. (1984). Changes in the differential treatment of Rajput girls in Khalapur: 1955-1975. *Medical Anthropology* (New York), vol. 8, No. 2 (Spring), pp. 127-132.

Omideyi, Adekunbi Kehinde (1990). Women's position, conjugal relationships and fertility behaviour among the Yoruba. *African Population Studies,* vol. 4 (August), pp 20-35.

Oni, Gbolahan A. (1985). Effects of women's education on postpartum practices and fertility in urban Nigeria. *Studies in Family Planning* (New York), vol. 16, No. 6 (November-December), pp. 321-331.

Operations Research Group, India (1990). *Family Planning Practices in India - Third All India Survey*, vol. II. Baroda, India.

Oppong, Christine (1983). Women's roles, opportunity costs, and fertility. In *Determinants of Fertility in Developing Countries,* vol.1, *Supply and Demand for Children*, Rodolfo A. Bulatao and Ronald Lee, eds., with Paula E. Nallubach and John Bongaarts. New York: Academic Press.

_________, and Katharine Abu (1987). *Seven Roles of Women: Impact of Education, Migration and Employment on Ghanaian Mothers.* Geneva: International Labour Organization.

Orubuloye, Oyetunji (1987). Values and costs of daughters and sons to Yoruba mothers and fathers. In *Sex Roles, Population and Development in West Africa*, Christine Oppong, ed. London: James Currey; and Portsmouth, New Hampshire: Heinemann.

Othman, A. (1985). The contraceptive role of breastfeeding by educational attainment: an assessment based on Malaysian fertility and family survey. *Malaysian Journal of Reproductive Health* (Kuala Lumpur), vol. 3, No. 1 (June), pp. 77-83.

Rodríguez, German, and Ricardo Aravena (1991). Socio-economic factors and the transition to low fertility in less developed countries: a comparative analysis. In *Demographic and Health Surveys World Conference, August 5-7, 1991, Washington D.C., Proceedings,* vol. I. Columbia, Maryland: IRD/Macro International Inc.

_________, and John Cleland (1981). Socio-economic determinants of marital fertility in twenty countries: a multivariate analysis. *World Fertility Survey Conference 1980: Record of Proceedings,* vol. II. Voorburg, Netherlands: International Statistical Institute.

Sathar, Zeba A., and Karen Oppenheim Mason (1989). Why female education affects reproductive behaviour in urban Pakistan. Paper presented at the International Union for the Scientific Study of Population General Conference, New Delhi, September.

Sathar, Zeba A., and Shahnaz Kazi (1990). Women, work and reproduction in Karachi. *International Family Planning Perspectives* (New York), vol. 16, No. 2 (June), pp. 66-69 and 80.

Sathar, Zeba A., and others (1988). Women's status and fertility change in Pakistan. *Population and Development Review* (New York), vol. 14, No. 3 (September), pp. 415-432.

Shapiro, David, and Oleko Tambashe (1991). Women's employment, education and contraceptive behaviour in Kinshasa. Paper presented at the Seminar on the Course of Fertility Transition in Sub-Saharan Africa, Harare, November. Sponsored by International Union for the Scientific Study of Population and the University of Zimbabwe.

Sharma, Ravi K., and others, (1990). A comparative analysis of trends and differentials in breastfeeding: findings from DHS surveys. Paper presented at the Annual Meeting of the Population Association of America, Toronto, Canada, 3-5 May.

Singh, Susheela, John B. Casterline and John Cleland (1985). The proximate determinants of fertility: sub-national variations. *Population Studies* (London), vol. 39, No. 1 (March), pp. 113-135.

Smith, David P., and Benoit Ferry (1984). *Correlates of Breastfeeding*. World Fertility Survey Comparative Studies, No. 41. Voorburg, Netherlands: International Statistical Institute.

Streatfield, K., M. Singarimbun and I. Singarimbun (1986). *The Impact of Maternal Education on the Use of Child Immunisation and other Health Services.* International Population Dynamics Program Research Note on Child Survival, No. 8CS. Canberra: The Australian National University.

Stephens, P. Wolanya (1984). *The Relationship between the Level of Household Sanitation and Child Mortality: An Examination of Ghanaian Data.* African Demography Working Paper, No. 10. Philadelphia: University of Pennsylvania, Population Studies Center.

Tienda, Marta (1984). Community characteristics, women's education, and fertility in Peru. *Studies in Family Planning* (New York), vol. 15, No. 4 (July/August), pp. 162-169.

United Nations (1987). *Fertility Behaviour in the Context of Development: Evidence from the World Fertility Survey.* Population Studies, No. 100, Sales No. E.86.XIII.5.

_________ (1991). *The World's Women, 1970-1990: Trends and Statistics.* Series K, No. 8. Sales No. E.90.XVII.3.

United Nations Children's Fund (1992). *The State of the World's Children, 1991.* New York: Oxford University Press.

United Nations Educational, Scientific and Cultural Organization (1991). *Statistical Yearbook, 1990.* Paris.

Vlassoff, Carol (1980). Unmarried adolescent females in rural India: a study of the social impact of education. *Journal of Marriage and the Family* (Minneapolis, Minnesota), vol. 42, No. 2 (May), pp. 427-436.

_________ (1982). The status of women in rural India: a village study. *Social Action* (New Delhi, India), vol. 32, No. 4 (October-December), pp. 380-407.

Wainerman, Catalina H. (1980). The impact of education on the female labour force in Argentina and Paraguay. *Comparative Education Review* (Chicago, Illinois), vol. 24, No. 2, part 2 (June), pp. S180-S195.

Weinberger, Mary Beth (1987). The relationship between women's education and fertility: selected findings from the World Fertility Surveys. *International Family Planning Perspectives* (New York), vol. 13, No. 2 (June), pp. 35-46.

_________, Cynthia Lloyd and Ann Klimas Blanc (1989). Women's education and fertility: a decade of change in four Latin American countries. *International Family Planning Perspectives* (New York), vol. 15, No. 1 (March), pp. 4-14.

Westoff, Charles F., and Lorenzo Moreno (1989). The demand for family planning: estimates for developing countries. Paper prepared for the Seminar of the Committee on the Comparative Analysis of Family Planning and Fertility in Tunisia, June. Sponsored by the International Union for the Scientific Study of Population.

Westoff, Charles F., and Luis H. Ochoa (1991). *Unmet Need and the Demand for Family Planning*. Demographic and Health Surveys Comparative Studies, No. 5. Columbia, Maryland: Institute for Resource Development/Macro International Inc.

Westoff, Charles F., and Anne Pebley (1981). Alternative measures of unmet need for family planning in developing countries. *International Family Planning Perspectives* (New York), vol. 7, No. 4 (December), pp. 126-136.

World Bank (1992). *World Development Report, 1992: Development and the Environment*. Oxford, United Kingdom: Oxford University Press.

Zanamwe, L. (1988). The relationship between fertility and child mortality in Zimbabwe. In *African Population Conference, Dakar, Senegal*, vol. 2. Liége, Belgium: International Union for the Scientific Study of Population.

XIX. WOMEN'S EDUCATION, CHILD WELFARE AND CHILD SURVIVAL

John Hobcraft[*]

This paper concerns the consequences of a mother's education for the health of her children, where health is interpreted in its broadest sense as complete physical, social, emotional, developmental and environmental well-being. However, a number of limitations must be noted at the outset.

First, most of what is said here relates to formal schooling of the mother, variously measured by years of schooling, highest level of schooling achieved or literacy. Yet, much important information relevant to the well-being of the child is imparted to the mother from other sources, including informal education, health education programmes, exposure to the media and interaction with relatives and peers. The efficacy, or otherwise, of these other forms of health education (including potential misinformation) may be conditioned by the level of formal education that the mother has achieved (as well as many other factors).

Secondly, the assessment of the true consequences of maternal education is an almost impossible task, since many important correlates of child health are often unavailable as controls in analyses. Thus, almost all that can be said about the links between formal schooling for mothers and the health outcomes of their children must be regarded as indicative of associations, rather than causal links. Where such associations are strong and persistent across many cultures and studies, it is more plausible, but almost never proven, that the association is real. Moreover, evidence is being assembled concerning differences in knowledge, attitudes and practice in health care of children according to the level of maternal education that are consistent with the hypothesized pathways for the influence of education of the mother on child health.

Thirdly, the demographic literature on links between maternal education and child survival is much more detailed than the literature on other aspects of child health or welfare. Consequentially, disproportionate emphasis is given to those areas that are well documented, such as child mortality, although increasing information is becoming available concerning differentials in knowledge, attitudes and practice in the arena of child health. What must be borne in mind, though, is that even in the poorest countries a majority of children survive, so that the positive health of those survivors is of great importance for the future well-being of their societies.

This point is well made by the title *The Twelve Who Survive* (Myers, 1992), which refers to the 12 out of every 13 children born in the world in 1991 that would survive to their first birthday. How can their coping strategies in later life be affected by their mother's education? Can this act as a buffer against the worst effects of abject poverty to alter the life chances of the children into their own adulthood? Lasting associations of differing levels of maternal education for their children can be documented for some developed societies, but to the author's knowledge, long-term prospective studies are not yet available for developing countries. Thus, although one might expect lasting consequences of maternal education for the complete well-being of their surviving children, there is little hard evidence to support this speculation for poorer countries. Nevertheless, there is a formidable body of evidence concerning links of maternal education to at least the physical well-being of children and some concerning their mental development.

A. A SKETCH OF EVOLVING KNOWLEDGE AND CONCERNS

This section sketched the background to the concerns of this paper, indicating the origins and some of the major threads of research during the 1980s on links

[*]Professor of Population Studies and Centre for the Study of Global Governance, London School of Economics.

between maternal education and child survival. Three main arenas of research are identified. First, there are cross-national studies at the macrolevel. Secondly, a welter of information have been emerging at the microlevel from national retrospective surveys, predominantly the World Fertility Survey (WFS) (more recent important evidence from the programme of Demographic and Health Surveys (DHS) is required in later sections). Thirdly, a number of subnational and often very small-scale studies have been conducted to elucidate the pathways through which maternal education influences child survival. Good recent reviews of this literature are given by Ware (1984), Cleland and van Ginneken (1989), Caldwell (1990) and Cleland (1990).

The importance of mother's education for child survival, through pathways other than enhanced socio-economic status, was brought into focus by Caldwell's seminal paper on Nigeria (1979). This paper argues that education of women play an important role in determining child survival even after control for a number of other factors, such as the socio-economic characteristics of the husband, including his own educational level and his occupation. Caldwell suggests several pathways whereby mother's education might enhance child survival. In increasing probable order of importance (according to Caldwell) these pathways are: a shift from "fatalistic" acceptance of health outcomes towards implementation of simple health knowledge; an increased capability to manipulate the modern world, including interaction with medical personnel; and a shift in the familial power structures, permitting the educated woman to exert greater control over health choices for her children.

There is a tradition of cross-national analysis at the national level that tries to obtain insights into the relative importance of a range of factors in determining national mortality levels. Some of this literature also focuses on child (or more usually infant) mortality. One of the more careful studies of infant mortality in this respect is that of Flegg (1982). He concludes that developing countries "which place a low priority on enhancing women's education and achieving a more equal distribution of incomes are unlikely to accomplish a rapid fall in their infant mortality rates" (Fleff, 1982, p. 454). An influential study that was analytically less careful, but much richer in interpretation, is that of Caldwell (1986). He also stresses the importance of female education and of commitment to equality, especially in health provision, among the countries that were "super-achievers" in health for their levels of gross national product per capita. A further example of an important and influential study based upon macrolevel indicators for provinces within Kenya is given by Mosley (1985) who demonstrates powerful associations of child mortality with levels of female education and levels of poverty.

During the 1980s, factual knowledge concerning the associations between maternal education and child survival at the microlevel expanded considerably as a result of the WFS programme (for example Hobcraft, McDonald, Rutstein, 1984) and from a United Nations study (1985) that used both survey and census data. Both of these major studies showed that increased levels of mother's education are associated with improved chances of child survival in a wide range of developing countries. (Hobcraft, McDonald, Rutstein covers 28 WFS countries, and the United Nations study covers 15 countries; there is some overlap in coverage). This association usually survived controls for a number of other socio-economic variables, including the husband's education and occupation. The former study demonstrated that socio-economic differentials in child survival widen with increasing age of the child and found the greatest consistency in fitted models for mortality between ages 1 and 5, where there were strong suggestions that a model that included terms for both mother's and father's levels of education and for father's occupation had widespread applicability. The United Nations explored a wider range of covariates and found that, on average, about half of the gross effect of maternal education survived as a net effect after controls. They also found that the association of maternal education and child survival was approximately the same in rural and urban areas, which is seen as consistent with Caldwell's hypothesized pathways, whereas the husband's educational level was associated with greater child survival advantage in urban areas. Both studies suggest that the associations between mother's education and child survival are somewhat weaker in sub-Saharan Africa than in Asia or, particularly, in Latin America and the Caribbean (where socio-economic differentials are generally larger). Hobcraft, McDonald and Rutstein (1984) also suggest that the husband's socio-economic characteristics (especially education) are slightly more strongly associated with improved child survival in the sub-Saharan African countries. Both studies also suggest that there is no threshold level of maternal education that needs to be reached before advantages in child survival began to accrue; even a small amount of education is usually associated with improved chances of child survival and the gains generally increased with increasing levels of education. (There were some exceptions where children of the uneducated appeared to have better survival chances than those born to women with from one to three years of education; Hobcraft, McDonald and Rutstein (1984) suggest that this finding might result from data deficiencies). There is also overwhelming evidence that the strong and persistent associations of infant and child mortality with birth-spacing are barely mediated by maternal education; nor is the reverse the case.

During the 1980s, a number of small-scale studies also tried to elucidate the pathways involved in lowering the mortality of children born to more educated mothers. Findings from these studies often appear contradictory, although it is possible that what is beginning to be accumulated is evidence that different pathways are important in differing cultures.

Lindenbaum (1990) stresses the apparent role of greater cleanliness among educated women in explaining differentials in child mortality in Bangladesh. Cleland (1990) reviews the very mixed international evidence on reported incidence of diarrhoeal episodes by levels of maternal education (including some further studies on Bangladesh). This review suggests that the greater cleanliness, if it exists, often fails to translate into lower frequency of diarrhoeal episodes.

A second pathway to receive considerable attention is the role of education in ensuring that the mother utilizes health services for her children. Again, Cleland concludes that "education may have a modest effect on health knowledge and beliefs, but a pronounced effect on the propensity to use modern medical facilities, and adopt modern health practices, because of a closer social identification with the modern world, greater confidence at handling bureaucracies or a more innovative attitude to life among women who have some experience of school" (1990, p. 412).

A third pathway is that maternal education may be associated with greater emphasis on child quality, perhaps ensuring that fewer children shall be more likely to survive, have greater food and human capital investments and thus become higher quality citizens, being healthier, better educated, more affluent and emotionally better developed. Evidence for this thesis is scant, although LeVine and others (1991), in a small study in Mexico, suggest that better educated mothers expect earlier intellectual and emotional development of their children. Moreover, Chavez, Martines and Yaschine (1975) suggest that nutrition can play a critical role in making children more active, demanding and independent, thereby gaining more attention from the mother. However, there are also possible indications that educated mothers may become more effective at discriminating against little valued children. For example, Das Gupta (1990) found that the relative excess mortality of second and later daughters was greater for the children of the more educated mothers.

A final pathway to receive attention is perhaps best referred to as the empowerment of women through education. Cleland (1990) identifies three components to this empowerment, which he terms "instrumentality, social identification and confidence". Instrumentality is the ability to manipulate and feel control over the outside world. Social identification is concerned with engagement with modern institutions and bureaucracies. Greater confidence permits the interaction with such officials and bureaucracies. Caldwell's original concerns with women's education altering power structures within the family should also be considered here. Most evidence for this pathway is indirect and can be summarized thus. Educated women make greater use of health services for themselves and their children; hence, they are empowered.

Despite a decade of attention to pathways, the evidence is still not clear as to which pathways are important where and even leaves room for doubt as to whether the strong associations of child survival and access to health care with levels of women's education are causal. For example, the study by Da Vanzo and Habicht (1986) strongly suggests that little of the overall change in infant mortality in Malaysia from 1946 to 1975 could be attributed to changes in maternal education at the microlevel, even though a strong cross-sectional relationship was apparent at different points in time. Ewbank and Preston (1990), and Woods, Watterson and Woodward (1989), have extended findings on links between child mortality and maternal education to around 1900 in the more developed region and suggest that the weaker associations observed were due to the lack of access to facilities and to modern medical knowledge that were simply unavailable at that time. However, studies that have tried to examine the links between maternal education and service accessibility in determining health outcomes in the third world have had very mixed success in elaborating such links.

B. Life events of the mother with consequences for children

There are a number of associations with education of women that are not widely considered in the demographic literature on child survival (and child welfare, such as it exists). First, educated women tend to marry later and to have their first births later. If this delay moves the first birth beyond the teenage years, especially beyond age 18, the women themselves are more likely to survive the hazardous first birth and the first-born child is also more likely to survive. A United Nations study (1994) summarizes the excess risk for first-born children to teenage mothers as being about 40 per cent, when averaged across 25 DHS.

Educated women generally experience lower rates of maternal mortality, both a per birth and as a result of having fewer children. Loss of a mother can be potentially disastrous for her children's survival chances and for their future welfare, although elaborate fostering mechanisms exist in parts of sub-Saharan Africa. Regrettably, information on the differentials in maternal mortality by educational level is scant, as is evidence on the consequences for the children. Part of the reason for such limited information is that retrospective surveys and population censuses, the main source of national-level information on survival, only include surviving women. Nevertheless, there is the possibility of exploiting census reports on children ever born and surviving to men (rather than women) cross-tabulated by responses on spousal survival to address this issue.

Graham (1991) gives estimated lifetime risks of maternal death. In a typical sub-Saharan African country, the overall level of maternal mortality is about 650 per 100,000 live births. With a total fertility of about 6.0 births per woman, this translates into a lifetime risk of maternal mortality of about 1 in 20. If an educated woman experiences maternal mortality at about 300 per 100,000 live births and has an average of four children, her lifetime chance of death would be only 1 in 70. Put another way, 50,000 out of every 1,000,000 families where the mother was uneducated would be motherless; for educated mothers, some 14,000 families would be motherless. If one assumes, for simplicity, that the mothers that die average 3.5 and 2.5 children, respectively, at the time of their death, there would be 175,000 motherless children in the 1,000,000 families with uneducated mothers and 35,000 motherless children in the 1,000,000 families with educated mothers. If maternal mortality were lowered to a still rather high and unacceptable level of 100 per 100,000 live births, with each surviving mother averaging 3.0 births, the lifetime risk for the woman is reduced to about 1 in 330, and there might only be 6,000 maternal orphans in 3,000 motherless families among a 1,000,000 families. Although these figures are illustrative, they do show that very large differences can arise in levels of orphanhood. (For this illustration, risks of maternal death are assumed to be unvarying with age or parity, which leads to an understatement of probable true differentials; women are assumed to have 1.2 times as many pregnancies as births).

Since uneducated mothers tend to have larger families when they do survive and to begin child-bearing earlier, their children are more likely to suffer the excess mortality risks associated with child-bearing too early or too late.

An element in determining the survival of the mother and the birth outcome is likely to be the extent to which the mother receives prenatal care, tetanus toxoid vaccination and quality of assistance at delivery. New evidence is beginning to accumulate especially from DHS on differentials in such care before and around the time of delivery, although much analysis remains to be done. Stewart and Sommerfelt (1991) provide summary information on these variables for 25 DHS, but their multivariate analysis only covers three countries (Bolivia, Egypt and Kenya). Overall levels of prenatal care vary substantially from 25 per cent of births in Morocco to more than 90 per cent in Botswana, the Dominican Republic, Sri Lanka, and Trinidad and Tobago, and Zimbabwe, for Bolivia, Egypt and Kenya, these levels are 45, 53 and 77 per cent, respectively. The percentages of deliveries attended by a trained person are also highly variable, from fewer than 33 per cent in Burundi, Guatemala, Mali and Morocco, up to 90 per cent or more in the Dominican Republic, and Trinidad and Tobago, with the three study countries being at 42, 35 and 50 per cent respectively. Women had received tetanus toxoid during fewer than 20 per cent of their pregnancies in Egypt, Guatemala, Mali and Peru; in more than three fourths of their pregnancies in Botswana, Kenya, and the Dominican Republic, Sri Lanka and Zimbabwe; the percentages were 20, 12 and 89 respectively, in Bolivia, Egypt and Kenya.

Stewart and Sommerfelt (1991) show large differences according to the woman's level of education for prenatal care in Bolivia and Egypt, but much smaller ones in Kenya. After control for several other variables (urban/rural residence, a possessions index, husband's education, parity, age at delivery, multiplicity of birth and prior family planning use), the woman's own educational level emerged as the most powerful predictor of prenatal care for Bolivia and Egypt and as weakly significant for Kenya (where only urban/rural residence proved a significant predictor). The association of prenatal care with the woman's education was more powerful in urban areas than in rural areas for both Bolivia and Egypt. A more elaborate comparative analysis by Bicego and Boerma (1991) found huge, but immensely variable, differentials in the extent of failure to receive prenatal care by level of education. After controls for an index of economic status and a range of biodemographic variables, the risk of receiving no prenatal care was from 55 to 1,300 per cent higher among uneducated women than those with no education. Since prenatal care did little to account for mortality differentials, it is by no means clear what to make of these vast differences in access.

In all three countries studied by Stewart and Sommerfelt (1991), educated women were much more likely to be attended by a trained person at delivery. Once again, these associations remained powerful after control for the same set of other factors, being strongest in Bolivia. For both Bolivia and Egypt, the net association with the woman's level of education was the largest source of difference, whereas urban/rural differences were again marginally stronger in Kenya. Once again, the association with the woman's education was more powerful in urban areas for Bolivia and Egypt.

Differentials in tetanus toxoid immunization by level of woman's education were small for both Egypt and Kenya, but quite substantial for Bolivia. No multivariate analysis was pursued by Stewart and Sommerfelt (1991) on this outcome. However, Bicego and Boerma (1991) show remarkable differences between urban and rural strata in the relation between female education and non-use of tetanus toxoid during pregnancy. The educational advantage seems to be much greater in rural areas than in towns. Bicego and Boerma speculate that immunization is (correctly) perceived as unnecessary by the educated urban elite, but that female education provides the knowledge and the means to access such health interventions in rural areas.

C. Maternal education and child survival: new evidence

Much fresh evidence on associations between maternal education and child survival is appearing from the analysis of DHS data. Results from three substantial comparative studies are summarized here. The first is an attempt to assess the changing role of socio-economic differentials over time, using data from WFS and DHS in countries where both occurred (Cleland, Bicego and Fegan, 1991). The second draws upon a comparative study of DHS data which is mainly concerned with the consequences of the timing of births for child survival (United Nations, 1994). The third is a valuable comparative study focused explicitly on maternal education and child survival, which also provides important insights into pathways and child welfare as discussed in the following section (Bicego and Boerma, 1991).

Macrolevel evidence

Cleland, Bicego and Fegan (1991) examine results for 12 countries where both WFS and DHS were carried out and ask how much convergence there had been in socio-economic differentials over time. In most of the 12 countries, there had been a substantial decline in child mortality over the 20 years from around 1965 to around 1985, with the median decline being 50 per cent. Only northern Sudan showed a decrease of less than one third. Moreover, the pace of decline for mortality risks between ages 1 and 5 was typically about twice that for infant mortality (although this finding probably implies similar absolute declines). Since socio-economic differentials are larger in childhood than in infancy, such an age pattern of decline might be expected to be associated with a narrowing of these differentials. However, this proved not to be the case.

Both around 1975 and around 1985, children of uneducated mothers were about 40 per cent more likely to die during their first five years of life than those born to mothers with primary education. This relative excess mortality was more consistent for the later DHS and more variable for the earlier WFS. A comparison of the excess mortality of children born to mothers with primary education contrasted with those with secondary or higher education, which was only possible for 6 of the 12 countries, suggested a widening differential, with mortality risks being approximately halved for the secondary or higher group around 1985. This widening of differentials may simply reflect changing composition of the secondary and higher group, with increasing proportions going beyond the minimal levels.

Cleland, Bicego and Fegan (1991) also pose the question to what extent changing socio-economic composition might have been responsible for mortality declines over the roughly 20-year period from around 1965 to around 1985. Despite some major changes in the socio-economic structures over this period, the percentage of child mortality reduction attributable to the change in levels of maternal education was 10 per cent or fewer in 7 of the 12 countries considered, about one fifth in Indonesia, the Dominican Republic and Mexico, and about one third in Ecuador and Peru. During that period, Indonesia saw massive changes in the educational composition of births, with only 28 per cent of births being to mothers with some schooling around 1965 and fully 82 per cent some 20 years later. Such a change can only happen once. It is clear, that other factors were largely responsible for the major decline in child mortality that took place in Indonesia, even in this time of massive socio-economic change.

The inescapable conclusion seems to be that maternal education, while conveying distinct individual advantage, is not substantially responsible for lowering child mortality. Thus, the results from macrolevel studies, which regularly suggest the importance of levels of women's schooling for infant and child mortality, are undoubtedly partially capturing information about overall development levels from this indicator. Nevertheless, female education seems to be a more sensitive indicator of development than male education (although only just), at least in the context of child survival.

Multivariate analysis

The United Nations study (1994) discusses results from several multivariate analyses for 25 DHS, which incorporate mother's education as one of the covariates of child mortality (taken here as survival to age 2). The general conclusions concerning the associations between maternal education and survival to age 2 do not differ substantially among the various models considered. The gross effects of mother's education are altered very little by controls for the timing and spacing of births, which is the major concern of the study. This finding serves to confirm earlier conclusions from WFS data. The greatest attenuation of the gross effects occurs for the "socio-economic" model, which incorporates mother's education, father's education, father's occupation and region of residence as the covariates of survival to age 2. Information on women's occupation or work status is not easily used in these comparative analyses (see Hobcraft, McDonald and Rutstein, 1984, for example), because the information available is often extremely limited, women often do not work and definitions of women's work status apparently differ in unpredictable ways across WFS and probably DHS. It is the results from the "socio-economic" model that are considered briefly here.

Table 32 shows the average odds ratios for groups of countries resulting from fitting logistic models to predict the chance of survival to age 2 for each country in turn. The first panel shows the average gross odds ratios (that is without control for the other socio-economic variables). In gross terms, the overall average odds of dying before age 2 for a child born to a mother with seven or more years of education are only 42.5 per cent compared with the children of uneducated mothers. The extreme contrasts for the other socio-economic factors are smaller, with the odds ratio being 56.6 per cent for the children of fathers with seven or more years of education compared with those whose fathers are uneducated and 56.3 per cent for the contrast between children of professional and clerical worker fathers and those whose fathers are in agriculture and fishing. Thus, there is apparently greater differentiation by maternal education than by the other factors.

Examining the overall average values for the net odds ratios, one sees that all are attenuated somewhat by the control for the other factors shown and for region within country. However, the attenuation is mild for mother's education, with the most advantaged group of children having odds of death that average only half of those for the most disadvantaged group on this dimension. The attenuation is much greater for the father's education and his occupation, with the odds of death for the most advantaged group only about 80 per cent of that for the least advantaged. These findings strongly suggest that maternal education exerts the most powerful influence on child survival among the few socio-economic variables considered here.

This conclusion is confirmed by a more detailed examination of the results for individual countries, which is summarized in table 32. The parameters associated with the effects of maternal education are far more likely to be statistically significant, with 19 countries reaching a 5 per cent level and 14 being significant at the 1 per cent level for the contrast between the most educated and the least educated groups. Five of the six countries for which this contrast is not significant are in sub-Saharan Africa (Botswana, Ghana, Mali, Uganda and Zimbabwe); the other exception is Trinidad and Tobago, which has the smallest sample size. Moreover, the odds ratios for the children whose mothers have had only from four to six years of education reach statistical significance more frequently than do those associated with any of the father's characteristics. Similar conclusions can be drawn from the magnitude of the odds ratios associated with the variables considered. In the majority of countries, the odds ratios associated with parents having higher socio-economic status are below 1.0, but this occurs more frequently for all categories of mother's education. Even more importantly, very few odds ratios are below 0.6 for the father's characteristics (only one or two in each category, suggesting chance occurrences); yet, fully 18 of the 25 countries have net odds ratios below this level for the contrast between the children with the most educated and least educated mothers. The net odds ratios for this contrast are always below 0.5 in the countries of Latin America and the Caribbean; and always below 0.6 in the few Northern African and Asian countries included here.

Weak effects in sub-Saharan Africa

However, only three of the sub-Saharan African countries have odds ratios for the extreme maternal education contrast that are below 0.6 (Burundi, Senegal and Togo); the remaining seven include Kenya and Liberia at just over 0.6; Mali, Zimbabwe, Botswana and Uganda at about 0.75-0.8; and Ghana at 0.95.

Earlier studies (e.g., Hobcraft, McDonald and Rutstein, 1984; and United Nations, 1985) indicated that the association of child survival with maternal education was weaker in sub-Saharan African countries than elsewhere, but the findings here are more powerful. One can only speculate about the reason for this substantial difference.

First, the apparently weaker effect of maternal education on child survival does not arise simply because of lower penetration of education in African countries, because several of the countries considered here have quite advanced educational systems. More than one third of births in Botswana, Ghana, Kenya and Zimbabwe occurred to mothers with seven or more years of education during the period of 2-15 years preceding DHS used in the analysis. Only Sri Lanka and Trinidad and Tobago exceed these proportions that are relatively highly educated. Of course, several of the sub-Saharan African countries included

TABLE 32. AVERAGE ODDS RATIO FOR REGIONAL GROUPS, SOCIO-ECONOMIC MODEL

Regional group and number of countries	*Mother's education* 1-3	4-6 (years)	7+	*Father's education*[a] 1-3	4-6 (years)	7+	*Father's occupation*[b] Manual	Sales and service	Professional and clerical
Gross									
Northern Africa (3)[c]	0.791	0.655	0.341	8.851	0.808	0.466	0.870	0.803	0.599
Sub-Saharan Africa (10)[d] .	0.916	0.766	0.562	0.953	0.797	0.652	0.844	0.791	0.610
Asia (3)[e]	0.979	0.663	0.409	1.139	0.783	0.493	0.771	0.906	0.505
Latin America and the Caribbean (9)[f]	0.750	0.524	0.305	0.880	0.752	0.524	0.837	0.712	0.529
Overall (25)	0.849	0.653	0.425	0.939	0.781	0.566	0.834	0.779	0.563
Net[g]									
Northern Africa (3)[c]	0.880	0.830	0.486	0.951	0.912	0.708	0.868	0.881	0.856
Sub-Saharan Africa (10)[d] .	0.988	0.827	0.680	0.940	0.817	0.773	0.939	0.895	0.803
Asia (3)[e]	1.020	0.721	0.544	1.136	0.863	0.717	0.965	0.921	0.862
Latin America and the Caribbean (9)[f]	0.790	0.600	0.384	0.901	0.905	0.850	1.087	0.920	0.853
Overall (25)	0.902	0.725	0.518	0.950	0.863	0.782	0.989	0.907	0.835
Ratio (net/gross)									
Northern Africa (3)[c]	1.113	1.267	1.427	1.117	1.128	1.518	0.997	1.097	1.429
Sub-Saharan Africa (10)[d] .	1.078	1.080	1.210	0.986	1.025	1.186	1.112	1.131	1.317
Asia (3)[e]	1.042	1.087	1.329	0.997	1.102	1.455	1.252	1.016	1.705
Latin America and the Caribbean (9)[f]	1.053	1.145	1.259	1.024	1.204	1.620	1.298	1.293	1.612
Overall (25)	1.063	1.110	1.219	1.012	1.104	1.380	1.187	1.165	1.483
Number of countries									
Statistical significance									
1 per cent	2	8	14	0	2	6	1	0	1
5 per cent	5	10	19	2	4	7	2	4	5
Values of odds ratios		(of 25)			(of 24)			(of 21)	
<1.0	20	23	25	16	20	23	13	19	19
<0.6	0	6	18	1	1	2	0	0	2
		(of 25)			(of 24)			(of 21)	

Source: John Hobcraft, "Child spacing and child mortality", in *Demographic and Health Surveys World Conference, August 5-7, 1991, Washington, D.C., Proceedings,* vol. II (Columbia, Maryland: IRD/Macro International, Inc., 1991).

NOTE: Reference categories (with odds of 1,000) were no education for mother and father, agricultural and fishing occupations.

[a]Not available for Mexico.

[b]Not available for Egypt, Liberia, Mexico and Togo.

[c]Including Egypt, Morocco and Tunisia.

[d]Including Botswana, Burundi, Ghana, Kenya, Liberia, Mali, Senegal, Togo, Uganda and Zimbabwe.

[e]Including Indonesia, Sri Lanka and Thailand.

[f]Including Bolivia, Brazil, Colombia, Dominican Republic, Ecuador, Guatemala, Mexico, Peru, and Trinidad and Tobago.

[g]Including control for regional group.

in the analysis have very low levels of education: fewer than 7 per cent of births occurred to women with seven or more years of education in Burundi, Mali, Senegal and Togo. But this is also the case for Guatemala and Morocco. So, the low differentiation in child survival by maternal education in sub-Saharan Africa cannot be ascribed to fundamental structural differences.

Caldwell (1990) draws attention to the much greater autonomy of women in sub-Saharan Africa than in many Asian and Muslim societies. He might thus go on to argue that the effects of maternal education for child survival are weaker in sub-Saharan Africa because the key empowerment aspects within the family are less relevant. But this argument ignores the even greater differentiation in Latin America and the Caribbean, where women also have considerable autonomy.

Several of the sub-Saharan African countries considered here have significant levels of child-fostering or of labour migration. Perhaps, these aspects of child-care practice, including the level of surrogate care, interact with mother's education in a way that means that a few years of education leads to higher risks of child death than for the children of uneducated mothers, for example, by disrupting traditional practices.

Perhaps, health infrastructures are weaker in sub-Saharan Africa, thereby inhibiting the ability of more educated women to take advantage of their human capital in the health environment. But, once again, this argument can hardly be applied throughout the diverse range of sub-Saharan African societies considered here. Botswana, Kenya and Zimbabwe have fairly low levels of child mortality by third world standards, with fewer than 100 children per 1,000 dying by age 5 (see Hobcraft, 1991); these countries have achieved mortality levels that are comparable to those achieved in the other regional groups considered here. Undoubtedly, many of these sub-Saharan countries do have very high levels of child mortality; among the 25 DHS countries considered, the only countries with estimated under-five mortality levels of more than 150 per 1,000 for the 15 years preceding the surveys come from this region: Mali (295); Liberia (232); Senegal (223); Burundi (192); Uganda (184); Togo (160); and Ghana (153). But Burundi, Senegal and Togo are the only three countries of the region that do exhibit low odds ratios of death (<0.6) for the children of the most educated group of mothers compared with those born to uneducated mothers, and Liberia is only just above this level.

Ghana and Uganda, in particular, experienced periods of unusually extreme hardship during the 15 or so years covered by this analysis. Perhaps the very weak association of child mortality with mother's educational level in these two countries is in part a reflection of these experiences? The following section discusses recent evidence on differentials in health-service utilization and nutritional status: perhaps sub-Saharan African countries achieve a greater homogeneity of provision of whatever health services they have, possibly associated with outreach programmes of immunization overcoming the traditional advantage associated with having an educated mother?

One further possibility that must be mentioned is the issue of data quality. The weak associations with levels of maternal education do not simply occur for the poorest and least educated sub-Saharan African societies. Is there any reason to suppose that reporting of child mortality is worse in Botswana and Zimbabwe, relatively advanced societies in this context, than in Senegal or Togo? This explanation also seems implausible.

Thus, despite a clearly weaker association between levels of maternal education and child survival in sub-Saharan Africa, it has only been possible to speculate as to the reasons for this finding. A number of plausible explanations have been raised here, but none was found convincing. This issue will be a focus of further research.

Further multivariate analysis

Next, the results of the comparative analysis by Bicego and Boerma (1991), covering experience from up to 17 DHS, is briefly examined. This study fitted logistic regression models to neonatal mortality and hazards models to mortality from ages 1-24 months. Only births during the five or six years preceding the surveys were included in the analyses, mainly because they go on to examine health-service utilization information which was only covered for recent births. The main focus of the analysis was on maternal education and child survival. Countries were divided into two groups: those with sufficient numbers of births occurring to women with secondary or higher levels of education (Bolivia, Colombia, Dominican Republic, Egypt, Ghana, Guatemala, Kenya, Sri Lanka, Thailand, Uganda and Zimbabwe), where three education groups were maintained (no education, primary, and secondary); and those with lower levels of education (Burundi, Mali, Morocco, Senegal, Togo and Tunisia), where only the contrast between mothers with no education and those with some was maintained. The analyses consisted of the estimation of a series of models, which progressively introduced "blocks" of control variables. Only the coefficients for maternal education are presented. The first model simply includes maternal education as an explanatory variable, giving the "gross" effects. The second model controls further for whether the household has piped water and some kind of latrine and for an index of household economic status, derived from information on possession of a radio or television, of motorized transport and a non-dirt floor in the dwelling unit. The third model introduced controls for birth order, preceding birth interval length and age of the mother at birth—"bio-demographic" or "family formation" controls. Their fourth model includes indicators as to whether the mother received prenatal care and tetanus toxoid during the relevant pregnancy. A final model introduces an interaction between the maternal education effect and rural/urban residence in order to assess whether the relation is different.

Bicego and Boerma (1991) confirm once again that neonatal mortality is generally less sensitive to maternal education than mortality in the next 23 months of life. But they also note that Bolivia, Burundi Colombia and Mali provide exceptions to this generalization. In contrast to United Nations study (1985), they find a stronger relation of maternal education with child survival in towns than in rural areas. Whether this contrast in findings is related to Bicego and Boerma not controlling for paternal education or to their only interacting maternal education with urban-rural residence remains open to question. Recall that the United Nations (1985) found no difference between urban and rural areas in the relation of child mortality to maternal education, but did find stronger effects for father's education in urban areas; they also fitted separate models to the rural and urban strata, thereby interacting all variables with urban or rural residence. Bicego and Boerma (1991) see education as being more important in towns partially because of the greater complexity of bureaucracy and social structure and partially because urban-dwellers may more easily escape traditional family power structures, enabling them to make more effective use of educational advantage. Somewhat curiously, they see their finding as indicating that education is not important for overcoming problems of physical access to services, since the advantage is not greater in low-access rural areas; but a certain density of service provision may be essential for any access and this may occur more easily in towns.

The gross effects of maternal education on child survival were substantially reduced (by 30-50 per cent) by controls for the economic index and prior use of health services. This finding suggests that a sizeable fraction of the gross effect of maternal education on child survival is operating to capture more general socio-economic advantage, although more than half of the effect is not attributable to these indicators.

Controls for family formation patterns generally slightly increased the advantages of higher maternal education for child survival, although there were exceptions. Only Kenya showed a large increase in the education effects, suggesting that the less educated have the most favourable patterns of family formation there. In general, though, the association of these family formation variables with maternal education proves weak, as in many other studies.

Addition of the health-service use indicators reduced the net maternal education effect in most countries, but only substantially so in Bolivia, Dominican Republic and Zimbabwe (and, perhaps, Morocco). Of course, this prior health-service utilization is at least partially attributable to the mother's education, so that the indirect effect of maternal education through these indicator variables should still be properly accounted as part of the total effect of maternal education on child survival. What is being captured here is thus one of the pathways through which higher education leads to better child survival.

D. The health and well-being of children

DHS has also provided considerable body of new information on differentials in the health status of children. Information is collected on use of prenatal care, tetanus toxoid immunization during pregnancy, and type of care at time of delivery for all births during a five or six-year period preceding the surveys. For surviving children only, further information is collected concerning height and weight, extent of immunization, childhood morbidity and treatment patterns. Once again, this rich mine of information has been only partially digested to date.

Growth faltering

Bicego and Boerma (1991) continue their comparative analysis referred to in the preceding section to provide useful information on maternal education and growth faltering for children aged 3-23 months at the time of the surveys. Low height for age ("stunting") is widely regarded as indicative of adaptation to routine and chronic malnutrition but not as a key indicator of being at risk of death. Thus, the study of stunting is likely to provide important indicators of the likely longer term health of children into adulthood and perhaps indicate probable future small stature with potential higher risk of low-birth-weight babies and consequent higher risks of child mortality. Bicego and Boerma find that stunting in early life is strongly related to maternal education but not as strongly as mortality risks between 1 and 24 months. Control for the index of economic status reduces the excess risks for the children of the less educated mothers by about 50 per cent, suggesting that economic status is important in determining long-term nutrition. However, even after controlling for economic status, children of women with no education are at least twice as likely to be stunted in Colombia, the Dominican Republic and Thailand as children of secondary-school educated women. It would be interesting to have these analyses further controlled for the socio-economic characteristics of the father (for example education and occupation).

Low weight for age is usually more closely associated with likely future mortality, reflecting short-term nutritional crises to a greater extent than stunting. Bicego and Boerma (1991) found that the gross relation of being underweight is of the same order of magnitude as that for mortality between 1 and 24 months. But control for the index of economic status reduces these effects more substantially (by close to 60 per cent on average), such that the net effects of maternal education on low weight for age are a little weaker than the net effects on stunting.

Control for prior use of health services only accounts for about 10 per cent of the excess risk of being underweight and about 20 per cent of the effect for stunting. These findings suggest that the greater propensity to use health services among the educated mothers, whether as a result of education *per se* or other related factors, does not play a critical role in determining or reducing growth faltering, although, it may, play a small part.

Immunization

Some of the information on differentials in immunization of children is discussed below (see Boerma and others, 1990). The DHS results serve to reiterate and confirm the huge changes under way in the coverage of immunization. Among children aged 12-23 months at the time of DHS, about 80 per cent were reported to be fully immunized (Bacillus Calmette-Guérin, three Diphtheria Pertussis-tetanus, three or more polio and measles) in Botswana, Tunisia and Zimbabwe; about two thirds in Kenya and Sri Lanka; and more than half in Brazil, Colombia, Egypt and Morocco. Fewer than 20 per cent of such children were fully immunized in Bolivia, Guatemala, Liberia, Mali and Senegal; about one third in Ghana, Peru, Thailand and Uganda; and 44 per cent in Burundi.

Among children born to mothers with at least secondary schooling, more than 90 per cent of those aged 12-35 months at the time of DHS had ever been vaccinated in 20 of the 23 countries considered by Boerma and others (1990). The only exceptions were Liberia and Uganda (both at 88 per cent) and Mali. But the children of uneducated women were far less likely to have ever been immunized, although levels still exceeded 90 per cent in nine countries. Fewer than three fourths of such children had ever been immunized in Bolivia, Ghana, Liberia, Mali, Senegal, Thailand and Uganda. The difference in immunization coverage between children of the uneducated and those of the educated was less than 10 percentage points in 10 of the 23 countries and only exceeded 20 percentage points in Bolivia, Ghana, Liberia, Mali, Senegal, Thailand and Uganda. Increased coverage of ever-immunization of children can only narrow these differentials.

Information on specific immunizations in Boerma and others (1990) is restricted to children aged 12-35 months with a health card. Fractions of the population covered by health cards vary enormously and there are often large differentials in such coverage by the mother's level of education. In general, the extent of coverage by health cards increases with level of mother's education and often quite substantially. For example, the extent of coverage increases by at least 25 percentage points from children of uneducated mothers to those of secondary educated mothers in the Dominican Republic, Ghana, Senegal and Thailand. But coverage decreases with increasing education of mother in Botswana and Zimbabwe, and drops away for children born to mothers with secondary schooling in several other countries. This makes differentials in immunization levels among those with a health card extremely hazardous to interpret.

As a general rule, more than 90 per cent of children with a health card have received their first DPT immunization. This coverage level only drops below 90 per cent in Liberia (62) and Egypt (86) for children born to mothers who had primary education; and for children of uneducated mothers in Liberia (68), Egypt (76), Bolivia (82) Senegal (83) and Brazil (88). Differentials are thus generally small, with the few exceptions noted here. But coverage among this group with health cards for the third DPT vaccination is much more variable. Even for children born to women with secondary or higher education, fewer than 80 per cent received DPT3 in Bolivia, Burundi, Guatemala, Liberia m and Senegal. Among children of uneducated women with health cards, 80 per cent or more received DPT3 in Botswana, Kenya, Thailand, Tunisia, Sri Lanka and Zimbabwe. Differentials in coverage by level of maternal education were thus generally small for these countries. However, these differences spanned over 30 percentage points in Ghana, Senegal, Uganda and Brazil, and were also in excess of 20 percentage points in Bolivia, Colombia. Egypt, Liberia, Morocco,and Peru.

Measles immunization for children with a health card reached about 90 per cent of those with uneducated mothers in Botswana, Tunisia and Zimbabwe, but was fewer than 80 per cent in the 17 other countries covered by Boerma and others (1990). Education differential in extent of measles vaccination were usually in the 10-20 percentage points range, but were lower in Botswana, Burundi, Tunisia and Zimbabwe, reversed in Guatemala and Thailand. It was slightly above the 20 percentage point level in Egypt, Ghana and Kenya.

In many countries, immunization levels have increased very rapidly over recent years. As saturation levels are reached, socio-economic and other differentials in coverage inevitably become small. How far the very high and even coverage by levels of maternal education in Botswana and Zimbabwe play a role in producing the low-mortality differentials remains an open but intriguing question. The outreach nature of mobile vaccination teams undoubtedly serves to reduce the access advantages normally associated with socio-economic advantage, including maternal education. Perhaps, one is beginning to see the results of a new "radical egalitarian" form of health provision in parts of Africa, which is achieving smaller differentiation by socio-economic status than in a classic case like Sri Lanka (Caldwell, 1986); and perhaps this equality of treatment is being achieved medically, despite the lack of the same political will for equality. Or perhaps this change is just reflective of major and rapid development. Answering these questions further is a fascinating topic but beyond the scope of the current paper.

Morbidity and treatment

Differentials in the prevalence of diarrhoea during the two weeks preceding DHS for children aged 6-23 months are given by Boerma, Sommerfelt and Rutstein (1991). The differentials in reported incidence of diarrhoea show unexpected features and are often somewhat counter-intuitive. The varied pattern of these differentials no doubt reflects a combination of differing propensities to report, the salience of diarrhoeal episodes for the mother and real differentials in incidence. In 5 out of 23 countries studied, the prevalence of diarrhoea was considerably higher (at least 20 per cent) among children of uneducated women than among those born to mothers with primary schooling, but prevalence was also lower for four countries by 10 per cent or more. In 14 of the 23 countries, children of primary-school mothers had a diarrhoea prevalence that was more than 20 per cent higher than that for children of mothers with secondary schooling; in only one country was the difference more than 10 per cent in the opposite direction. These differentials by education of the mother, especially the contrast associated with secondary schooling, were among the largest and most consistent of a wider range that were examined, including possession of a radio, piped drinking water and toilet facility. The greater strength of association of reported incidence of diarrhoea with maternal education than with these other variables is strongly suggestive that Cleland's (1990) dismissal of Lindenbaum's (1990) hypothesis was both unfounded and premature, since he was using the same DHS evidence.

There are massive variations in the extent of knowledge concerning oral rehydration salts (ORS) packets among mothers of differing educational levels, although some countries provide notable exceptions. In Botswana, Egypt, and Zimbabwe, more than 90 per cent of all mothers had heard of ORS packets; not surprisingly, educational differentials are small in these countries. At the other extreme, fewer than half of the mothers had heard of ORS packets in Burundi, Mali, Togo and Uganda. In Peru, only 25 per cent of uneducated mothers had heard of ORS, contrasting with 89 per cent of those with secondary schooling: a difference of 64 percentage points. The range was about 50 percentage points in Guatemala, Mali and Uganda, and also more than 40 points in Bolivia, Burundi and Ghana. Thus, differentials in knowledge of ORS by mother's education are among the most dramatic found.

The fraction of diarrhoeal episodes to children aged 1-59 months in the two weeks preceding DHS that were treated with ORS packets was nevertheless fairly low for all levels of education of the mother. About 40-50 per cent of diarrhoeal episodes for children of mothers with secondary schooling were so treated in Botswana, Colombia, the Dominican Republic, Ghana, Thailand, Togo, and Trinidad and Tobago. Elsewhere, the levels of ORS treatment among secondary-school mothers were lower still, being fewer than 15 per cent in Brazil, Liberia, Mexico, Peru and Uganda. Educational differences were small in Botswana, where more than 40 per cent of children of all educational groups received ORS treatment. Differentials were absolutely large (over 20 percentage points) in the Dominican Republic and Togo and relatively large in a number of other countries.

Information on prevalence of fever in the four weeks preceding DHS was only collected for 10 sub-Saharan African countries and Colombia (Boerma, Sommerfelt and Rutstein, 1991). The differentials in reported prevalence of fever by mother's education are typically small. Overall prevalence levels are low in Botswana, Burundi and Zimbabwe, being less than 10 per cent. Elsewhere, the reported prevalence of fever is much higher, being more than 30 per cent and in excess of 50 per cent for Liberia; the figure for Senegal is also high, at 61 per cent, but reflects a question on incidence of malaria during the previous cold season. The low reported prevalence of fever in Burundi increases with increasing education of the mother. From moderate to significant gradients in the expected direction emerge for Senegal, Togo and Uganda.

More educated mothers are generally more likely to take children with a fever to a medical facility; some 90 per cent do so in Botswana, where there is little differentiation. Differential use of medical facilities for feverish children is greatest in Ghana (33 percentage points) and in Togo and Colombia (both at 21 percentage points). Exception for Botswana, about 25-50 per cent of uneducated mothers took a feverish child to a medical facility, contrasted with about 50-75 per cent of mothers with secondary schooling.

By and large, there is strikingly little variation by level of mother's education in the prevalence of a cough or rapid/difficult breathing in the four weeks preceding DHS, although overall reported prevalence levels vary dramatically among societies. Prevalence of a cough etc. in the four-week reference period is reported for more than 40 per cent of children in Egypt, Liberia, Zimbabwe, Bolivia and Ecuador, and for fewer than 10 per cent of children in Mali and Togo. Prevalence increases with increasing maternal education in Egypt.

Resort to medical facilities for treatment of coughs etc. is high in Botswana (82 per cent) and Kenya (66) and low in Burundi (36), Togo (33) and Bolivia (22); elsewhere, the range is 40-55 per cent. Educational differentials in accessing medical treatment for coughs are small in Botswana, Kenya and Zimbabwe, being less than 12 percentage points. But differentials are large (more than 20 percentage points) in Bolivia, Colombia, Egypt and Ghana, and nearly 40 percentage points in Togo.

E. Conclusion

With the striking exceptions of Botswana and Zimbabwe (for which some information is missing), there is fairly clear evidence of differentiation according to the level of the mother's education in the prevalence but more especially in the treatment of childhood diseases. By and large, educated mothers do appear to be somewhat more successful at reducing the prevalence of diarrhoeal diseases, but their children seem equally at risk of fevers and coughs. Educated mothers are notably better informed about ORS packets and generally more likely to make use of these for diarrhoeal episodes. Educated mothers are also generally more likely to access medical facilities for treatment of diarrhoeal episodes, fevers and coughs. It is not possible to assess how far these differentials translate into better chances of survival for the children, since this information is only obtained for surviving children. Equally, one can at the moment only speculate as to how far these differences, especially in treatment, translate into the improved nutritional status of children of educated women.

Similarly, more educated women are more likely to have initiated immunization and even more likely to have ensured that their children shall be fully vaccinated. Again, one cannot assess from DHS data how far these differences translate into a mortality advantage, since this information is only collected for surviving children, although DHS II extends coverage. More educated women are also more likely to have received prenatal care, to have been immunized with tetanus toxoid during pregnancy and to have their deliveries attended by trained personnel. Some evidence suggests that some of the survival advantage accruing to the children of more educated mothers is mediated through better prenatal care and tetanus toxoid vaccination.

More educated women also marry and enter motherhood later and have fewer children. As a consequence of their greater likelihood of accessing health services, of avoiding high-risk pregnancies and of experiencing fewer pregnancies, they are considerably less likely to die in childbirth and thereby orphan their children, with deleterious consequences.

More educated women also have fewer stunted children, who will be disadvantaged in later life through their adaptation to low nutritional input, for example, by producing lower birthweight children of their own.

The evidence of improved survival chances of children with increasing education of the mother has been shown to be very strong across time and culture, although some exceptions which ought to be the focus of greater scrutiny do exist. This paper has discussed, but failed to resolve, the apparently weaker association in several sub-Saharan African countries. The literature that tries to disentangle the pathways through which survival and health advantage accrues to children born to more educated mothers remains inconclusive.

Of course, as has been regularly stressed throughout this paper, one can still not be sure that the associations of all of these key factors in child health with maternal education are causal. It has been shown that associations are often attenuated by control for a limited range of other factors. Control for key unmeasured factors might reduce these associations with mother's education to negligible levels. However, one must beware accepting such findings without careful thought, because the additional factors may simply be capturing the pathways through which maternal education operates to produce differing health outcomes.

The discussion has largely neglected issues of the role of maternal education in broader child development and welfare, mainly because the knowledge of a literature on such topics is scant. However, LeVine and others (1991) illustrate some of these broader concerns for a small study in Mexico, as does the assessment by Myers (1992). The neglect of child welfare and development issues is not because they are taken to be unimportant. On the contrary, the author feels that this arena of positive health concerns for children in the developing world should become the next major focus of demographer's attention, following on the gradual spread into broader health concerns as evidenced by recent DHS and a widespread literature on small-scale and anthropological studies to which adequate attention has not been given here.

Evidence from the more developed region strongly suggests important developmental advantages for children of more educated mothers—the move towards "quality" children and away from emphasis on basic survival. Educational differentials in survival certainly persist in the developed world (Valkonen, 1987) and a massive literature assesses disadvantages and relative welfare of children in relation to mother's education among other explanatory variables (see, for just one example, Robins and Dickinson, 1985).

References

Bicego, George T., and J. Ties Boerma (1991). Maternal education and child survival: a comparative analysis of DHS data. In *Demographic and Health Surveys World Conference, 5-7 August 1991, Washington D.C., Proceedings*, vol. I. Columbia, Maryland: IRD/Macro International, Inc.

Boerma, J. Ties, A. Elizabeth Sommerfelt and Shea O. Rutstein (1991). *Childhood Morbidity and Treatment Patterns.* Demographic and Health Surveys Comparative Studies, No. 4. Columbia, Maryland: Institute for Resource Development/Macro International Inc.

_________, and others (1990). *Immunization: Levels, Trends and Differentials.* Demographic and Health Surveys Comparative Studies, No. 1. Columbia, Maryland: Institute for Resource Development/ Macro Systems, Inc.

Caldwell, John C. (1979). Education as a factor in mortality decline: an examination of Nigerian data. *Population Studies* (London), vol. 3, No. 3 (November), pp. 395-413.

_________ (1986). Routes to low mortality in poor countries. *Population and Development Review* (New York), vol. 12, No. 2 (June), pp. 171- 220.

_________ (1990). Cultural and social factors influencing mortality levels in developing countries. In "World population: approaching the year 2000", Samuel H. Preston, ed. *The Annals of the American Academy of Political and Social Science* (Newbury Park, California), vol. 510 (July), pp. 44-59.

Chavez, A., C. Martinez and T. Yaschine (1975). Nutrition, behavioral development and mother-child interaction in young rural children. *Federation Proceedings*, vol. 34, No. 7, pp. 1574-1582.

Cleland, John G. (1990). Maternal education and child survival: further evidence and explanations. In *What We Know about the Health Transition: The Cultural, Social and Behavioral Determinants of Health*, vol. I, John Caldwell and others, eds. Health Transition Series, No. 2. Canberra, Australia: The Australian National University, Health Transition Centre.

_________, and Jeroen van Ginneken (1989). Maternal schooling and childhood mortality. In *Health Interventions and Mortality Change in Developing Countries*, Allan G. Hill and D. F. Roberts, eds. *Supplement No. 10 to Journal of Biosocial Science* (Cambridge, United Kingdom). Cambrfidge: Parkes Foundation.

Cleland, John G., George T. Bicego and Grea Fegan (1991). Socioeconomic inequalities in childhood mortality: the 1970s compared with the 1980s. In *Demographic and Health Surveys World Conference, 5-7 August 1991, Washington, D. C., Proceedings*, vol. I. Columbia, Maryland: Institute for Resource Development/Macro International, Inc.

Das Gupta, Monica (1990). Death clustering, mother's education and the determinants of child mortality in rural Punjab, India. *Population Studies* (London), vol. 44, No. 3 (November), pp. 489-505.

Da Vanzo, Julie, and Jean-Pierre Habicht (1986). Infant mortality decline in Malaysia, 1946-1975: the roles of changes in variables and changes in the structure of relationships. *Demography* (Washington, D.C.), vol. 23, No. 2 (May), pp. 143-160.

Ewbank, Douglas C., and Samuel H. Preston (1990). Personal health behaviour and the decline in infant and child mortality: the United States, 1900-1930. In *What We Know about the Health Transition: The Cultural, Social and Behavioral Determinants of Health*, vol. I, John Caldwell and others, eds. Health Transition Series, No. 2. Canberra, Australia: The Australian National University, Health Transition Centre.

Flegg, A. T. (1982). Inequality of income, illiteracy and medical care as determinants of infant mortality in underdeveloped countries. *Population Studies* (London), vol. 36, No. 3 (November), pp. 441-458.

Graham, W. J. (1991). Maternal mortality: levels, trends, and data deficiencies. In *Disease and Mortality in Sub-Saharan Africa*, Richard G. Feacham and Dean T. Jamison, eds. Oxford, United Kingdom; and New York: Oxford University Press.

Hobcraft, John N. (1991). Child spacing and child mortality. In *Demographic and Health Surveys World Conference, 5-7 August 1991, Washington, D.C., Proceeding*, vol. II. Columbia, Maryland: Institute for Research Development/Macro International, Inc.

_________, John W. McDonald and Shea O. Rutstein (1984). Socioeconomic factors in infant and child mortality: a cross-national comparison. *Population Studies* (London), vol. 38, No. 2 (July), pp. 193-223.

LeVine, Robert A., and others (1991). Women's schooling and child care in the Demographic Transition: A Mexican case study. *Population and Development Review* (New York), vol. 17, No. 3 (September), pp. 459-496.

Lindenbaum, Shirley (1990). Maternal education and health care processes in Bangladesh: the health and hygiene of the middle classes. In *What We Know about the Health Transition: The Cultural, Social and Behavioral Determinants of Health*, vol. I, John Caldwell and others, eds. Health Transition Series No. 2. Canberra, Australia: The Australian National University, Health Transition Centre.

Mosley, W. Henry (1985). Will primary health care reduce infant and child mortality? A critique of some current strategies, with special reference to Africa and Asia. In *Health Policy, Social Policy and Mortality Prospects*, Jacques Vallin and Alan Lopez, eds. Liège, Belgium: Ordina Editions.

Myers, Robert G. (1992). *The Twelve Who Survive: Strengthening Programmes of Early Childhood Development in the Third World.* London and New York: Routledge.

Robins, Philip K., and Katherine P. Dickinson (1985). Child support and welfare dependence: a multinominal logit analysis. *Demography* (Washington, D.C.), vol. 22, No. 3 (August), pp. 367-380.

Stewart. Kate, and A. Elizabeth Sommerfelt (1991). Utilization of maternity care services: a comparative study using DHS data. In *Demographic and Health Surveys World Conference, 5-7 August 1991, Washington, D.C., Proceeding*, vol. III. Columbia, Maryland: Institute for Resource Development/ Macro International, Inc.

United Nations (1985). *Socio-economic Differentials in Child Mortality in Developing Countries.* Population Studies, No. 97. Sales No. E.85.XIII.7.

_________ (1994). *The Health Rationale for Family Planning: Timing of Births and Child Survival.* Sales No. E.95.XIII.3.

Valkonen, T. (1987). Social inequality in the face of death. In *European Population Conference: Issues and Prospects.* Helsinki, Finland: Central Statistical Office of Finland.

Ware, Helen (1984). Effects of maternal education, women's roles and child care on child mortality. In "Child survival: strategies for research", W. Henry Mosley and Lincoln C. Chen, eds. *Population and Development Review* (New York), vol. 10, supplement, pp. 191-214.

Woods, R. I., P. A. Watterson and J. H. Woodward (1989). The causes of rapid infant mortality decline in England and Wales, 1861-1921, part II, *Population Studies* (London), vol. 43, No. 1 (March), pp. 113-132.

XX. WOMEN'S EDUCATION AND EMPLOYMENT AND LINKAGES WITH POPULATION

Economic and Social Commission for Asia and the Pacific[*]

Advocacy for women's equality has been under way for more than three decades. In 1946, the United Nations Commission on the Status of Women was formed to monitor the situation of women to promote women's rights around the world. In 1952, the Commission initiated the Convention on the Political Rights of Women, which was the first global mandate granting women equal political rights under the law—the right to vote, hold office and exercise public functions. In 1957 and 1962, conventions were initiated on the equality of married women, guaranteeing them equal rights in marriage and in dissolving marriage, respectively. In 1967, there was a Declaration on the Elimination of Discrimination against Women. The year 1975 was declared International Women's Year and the World Conference on Women proclaimed 1976-1985 as the United Nations Decade for Women: Equality, Development, Peace. Agencies were requested for the first time to collect thorough statistical information on women. In 1979, the United Nations General Assembly adopted the Convention on the Elimination of All Forms of Discrimination Against Women. In 1980, the World Conference on Women held at Copenhagen adopted the Programme of Action for the Second Half of the United Nations Decade for Women: Equality, Development, Peace. Agencies were requested to prepare the most recent data and time-trend analyses on the situation of women. In 1985, the World Conference at Nairobi reviewed progress during the decade for women and adopted the Forward-looking Strategies for the Advancement of Women.

In other fields, concern for the status of women is also evident. The World Population Plan of Action focuses on all aspects of women's lives, including education, employment and political participation, as well as their domestic and maternal roles. Two aspects that had received major attention, particularly in the context of population policy, were education and labour force participation. This attention is justified not only because of the lack of opportunities for education and employment of women compared with men but also because of the implications of women's education and employment for population dynamics.

A. Women's education and its demographic impacts

Education affects demographic processes—fertility, mortality and migration—in a number of ways. Empirical evidence suggests that women's education has a more profound effect on fertility compared with men's, the educational level of the wife being more strongly correlated with a couple's fertility than the educational level of the husband. Indeed, it has been argued that the educational level of females is the strongest and most consistent predictor of fertility (Murdoch, 1980). Women's education helps to postpone the age at marriage and/or child-bearing both because early marriage would conflict with staying in school and because education leads to better knowledge of, attitude towards and practice of family planning. Women's education is also associated with greater opportunities for employment outside the home and greater domestic power in decision-making (Mason, 1984).

Most studies indicate a negative relation between the level of women's education and their fertility; that is, fertility declines with an increase in the level of women's education (Goldstein, 1972; Rodríguez and Cleland, 1981; and Jain, 1981). This inverse relation tends to be strongest when such factors as husband's education, women's employment, type of education and place of residence are not controlled

[*]Bangkok, Thailand.

(Selvaratnam, 1988b). However, a number of studies indicate that the extent to which women's education influences fertility depends upon the level and type of education. Evidence from many countries in Asia suggests an inverted U-shaped relationship. For instance, in India, the inverse relation between education and fertility occurs only after matriculation (Rao, 1979). In the Philippines and Indonesia, the majority of studies appear to support the inverted U-shaped relation between wife's education and fertility (Concepción and Smith, 1977; Canlas and Encarnación, 1977; Hull and Hull, 1977). In the Philippines, the relation occurs among mothers that have completed the sixth or seventh grade of school (Concepción, 1974). In Thailand, for most of the various national surveys from 1969 to 1979, an inverse association is apparent between educational attainment and both the expected and the preferred number of children, while a direct association is evident between education and the percentage practising contraception (Knodel, Debavalya and Kamnuansilpa, 1981). In Malaysia, the negative relation between education and fertility was observed to be significant only for women with seven or more years of education (Chander and Palan, 1977). A detailed study of interaction effects (Tan, 1981) found that the negative impact of education on fertility was mediated through its positive relation with husband's occupation, monthly family income, age at marriage and contraceptive-knowledge score and its negative relation with net marital duration.

Lim (1984 and 1991), quoting Cochrane and Ware, shows that there are at least 20 ways in which education may affect fertility levels in either a positive or a negative fashion. In an individual cultural context, it is sometimes debatable whether the relation assumed should be positive or negative. For example, while the cost of alternative child-rearing or domestic help may be relatively high in Malaysia and Singapore, these services are still inexpensive and widely available in Indonesia, the Philippines and Thailand. In the Asian context, the following key considerations may be identified:

(a) Under what conditions would education not serve to reduce fertility? Especially in the poorer Asian countries with lower levels of literacy, education may at first serve to raise fertility by improving health and by lowering marital instability (Hull, 1979);

(b) What is the threshold level beyond which education will reduce fertility? How much education is needed and over what period of time? There is little evidence of a single threshold level; the exact turning-point apparently depends upon the nature of traditional cultures, the level of development and the mechanisms through which education affects fertility. Available evidence tends to suggest that it may be only after a primary level of education that there is a negative impact on fertility, that it may take at least a generation before education exerts its impact because it must also be associated with changes in cultural attitudes which take time (United Nations, ESCAP, 1982, citing the case of Sri Lanka) and that education tends to have a more dramatic impact upon women's lives and fertility in Muslim countries rather than in other settings. Kirk (1971) found that the national-level correlation between female education and fertility was -0.55 in South-eastern Asia, -0.71 in Latin America and the Caribbean and -0.81 in 15 Muslim countries;

(c) What are the relative contributions of male and female education to the reduction of fertility? The general tendency is to find that female education has a considerably stronger and more consistent effect than male education on fertility levels, especially where education raises the woman's evaluation of her own worth and provides her with alternative roles. Although female education tends to be inversely related to fertility, male education can be positively related (for Pakistan, Khan and Sirageldin, 1975; for Bangladesh, Noman, 1983);

(d) What are the mechanisms through which education reduces fertility? Patterns of work outside the home and age at marriage tend to be the first areas where female education leaves its mark, with fertility reduction following later. However, timing of the first two or three births after marriage may well not be much affected by education or by later age at marriage. An earlier cessation of child-bearing is likely to be the key longer term effect of education and delayed age at marriage. Such an effect would take time to show up. Many studies have also shown a direct relation between female education and knowledge,

approval and practice of family planning. But again, the nature of causation is not clear—is the positive relation due to a greater motivation among educated women to reduce family size or simply to their greater access to information and family planning services? Education may also affect son preference; as education makes women more aware of their own worth, the desire for male children may decline.

B. Women's employment and population change

It has often been argued that participation of women in the labour force contributes to lower fertility through such factors as delayed marriage, increased education, reduction of preferred family size and increased adoption of family planning practices. Hence, there has been a tendency to recommend that an effective way to reduce national birth rates is to increase women's employment (Concepción, 1974). However, a review of evidence does not support these conclusions fully. The inverse relation between women's employment and fertility appears to be strong in most developed countries but tends to be either weak or absent in many developing countries. Besides, in the developing countries the probability of an inverse relation appears to be higher in the urban than in the rural areas, and in the modern than in the traditional sectors of the society (Selvaratnam, 1988a and 1988b).

A number of studies in developing countries suggest that the relation between women's employment and fertility is either not significant or is absent in the case of women that work as unpaid family workers in "cottage industries", agriculture and other family-based enterprises, but that the relation is strongly inverse for women engaged in non-domestic, non-familial enterprises and non-agricultural employment. (These studies were, however, conducted during the 1960s and 1970s.) This finding indicates that participation in the labour force *per se* may not be so important as the type of employment in which women are engaged. Equally important is the compatibility or incompatibility of a woman's employment with her maternal role, the assumption being that women's employment "away from home" is more incompatible with their maternal role than family-based work (Safilios-Rothschild, 1985).[1]

In Thailand, analytical results indicate that the relation between labour force participation and fertility is produced by several causal relation, and there is remarkably little "pure" relation between cumulative fertility and current work status. Nevertheless, there is an "employee-white collar" effect: that is, women in the modern labour force tend to have lower fertility, presumably because the opportunity cost of children is high and work and child care are not compatible in urban areas. These women, with a high level of education, tend to work outside the home, and the nature of their work not only makes for a conflict of maternal and occupational roles but also may influence attitudes towards practising contraception and reproductive behaviour in general (Debavalya, 1977 and 1983).

The participation of women in the labour force is mainly affected by social factors such as women's status and also by some demographic factors. Indeed, the fact that in most countries of the region, the reported female labour force participation rates are substantially lower than the male rates could be explained in part by demographic factors. For example, in rural societies women are still largely responsible for domestic work and child-rearing; therefore, they are not as free as men to enter the labour market. On the other hand, in societies where it is difficult to combine child care with wage employment outside the home, women often withdraw from the labour force on marriage or child-bearing (United Nations, ESCAP, 1986).

Marriage is also an obstacle to the continued education of women; the younger the average age at marriage, the sooner females terminate their schooling. The lack of education and adequate training in turn hampers the opportunities for the employment of women. In fact, the pattern of high fertility in most developing countries means that women are burdened with the task of frequent child-bearing as well as the responsibility of caring for and rearing the many children they produce. Since alternative arrangements, such as day-care centres, for assisting women with their family responsibilities are not available in most developing countries, women are engaged full-time in their traditional roles and are not free to upgrade their knowledge and skills or to participate in economic activities, particularly wage employment.

However, in the rural agrarian setting in many countries, it is often possible for the mother to combine children with work on the farm or other family-operated enterprises because of the availability of extended family, kin and neighbourhood support networks for child care, and the location of farm work and market activity near the home (Mahajan, 1987). On the other hand, large family size may compel a woman to seek employment in order to augment family incomes to support the large number of children (Srinivasan and Bardhan, 1988).

C. Some research and policy needs

The relation between women's education and fertility is not yet conclusive. More studies should be conducted, particularly in regard to the key issues raised above. Under what conditions would education not serve to reduce fertility? What is the threshold level beyond which education will reduce fertility? How much education is needed and over what period of time? What are the mechanisms through which education reduces fertility?

The causal relation between women's education and women's employment, on the one hand, and fertility and other demographic factors, on the other hand, are still not clear. Research in this direction should be encouraged.

With the continued and determined efforts of all concerned, it is obvious that women's role and status are changing. For long-term planning purposes, studies to trace the time-paths of the impacts of this change in women's situation on demographic factors and development processes should be attempted.

The integration of women into development should not be interpreted as being the same as efforts to bring women into the labour force. Large proportions of women, especially in poor countries, are already working in various capacities, a phenomenon in effect long before the conscious efforts of development planners to increase women's employment. What is often overlooked is that entering into wage employment does not necessarily lead to an increase in the social status of women; on the contrary, it often means the assumption of a double or even treble workload (working in the home, caring for children and working on the subsistence farm and/or in wage employment) (Lim, 1991).

It is generally accepted that women's status and roles, education, employment and fertility behaviour are interrelated. Thus, one of the policy concerns that needs to be recognized is that women's status and roles cannot be treated as separate or apart from their demographic role and that this combination of roles in production and reproduction is pivotal in the whole development process. It should be noted, however, that promoting women's education by extending secondary and higher education to increasing proportions of women will greatly increase women's opportunities to participate in development. It will do this, for example, by raising the status of women and by enabling them to work in professional fields. Another result of this aspect of national development could be a significant reduction in the fertility levels of the country as a whole over the long term.

Note

[1]In the rural setting of developing countries, a woman's employment, whether paid or unpaid, has little impact on fertility for two reasons. First, the value of large numbers of children still remains strong. Secondly, the nature of the employment engaged in (mostly agricultural or cottage-industry type), is compatible with her role as mother, as she can keep the young children with her or entrust them to other family members while she is at work. On the other hand, in an urban setting, a woman's employment is, or is likely to be, incompatible with her maternal role, because invariably that employment is outside her home and no alternative arrangements are available for taking care of her young children while she is away at work. However, an urban woman worker is more likely to learn about birth control and to have relatively easy access to family planning services.

References

Canlas, D. B., and J. Encarnación, Jr. (1977). Income, education, fertility and employment: Philippines, 1973. *Philippine Review of Business and Economics* (Metro Manila), vol. 14.

Chander, R., and V. T. Palan (1977). *Malaysia Fertility and Family Survey, 1974: First Country Report*. Kuala Lumpur: Department of Statistics.

Concepción, Mercedes B. (1974). Female labour force participation and fertility. *International Labour Review* (Geneva), vol. 109, No. 5-6 (May-June), pp. 503-517.

_________, and Peter C. Smith (1977). *The Demographic Situation in the Philippines: An Assessment in 1977*. Papers of the East-West Population Institute, No. 44. Honolulu: East-West Center.

Debavalya, N. (1977). *Female Employment and Fertility: Cross sectional and Longitudinal Relationships from a National Sample of Married Thai Women*. Population Studies Paper, No. 24. Bangkok: Chulalongkorn University, Institute of Population Studies.

_________ (1983). *Economic Activities of Thai Women: As Assessed in the 1980 Population Census*. Bangkok: Office of National Economic and Social Development Board and Chulalongkorn University, Institute of Population Studies.

Goldstein, Sidney (1972). The influence of labour force participation and education on fertility in Thailand. *Population Studies* (London), vol. 26, No. 3 (November), pp. 419-436.

Hull, Terence, and Valerie Hull (1977). The relation of economic class and fertility: an analysis of some Indonesian data. *Population Studies* (London), vol. 31, No. 1 (March), pp. 43-57.

Hull, Valerie (1977). *The Woman's Place: Social Class Variations in Women's Work Patterns in a Javanese Village*. Population Studies Center Working Paper, No. 25. Yogyakarta: Gadjah Mada University.

Jain, Anrudh (1981). The effect of female education on fertility: a simple explanation. *Demography* (Washington, D.C.), vol. 18, No. 4 (November), pp. 577-595.

Khan, M., and I. Sirageldin (1975). Education, income and fertility in Pakistan. *Economic Development and Cultural Change* (Chicago), vol. 27, No. 3 (July).

Kirk, Dndley (1971). New demographic transition? In *Rapid Population Growth: Consequence and Policy Implications*. Baltimore: The John Hopkins University Press; National Academy of Sciences.

Knodel, John, Nibhon Debavalya and Peerasit Kamnuansilpa (1981). *Thailand's Continuing Fertility Decline*. Institute of Population Studies, Paper No. 40. Bangkok: Chulalongkorn University.

Lim, Lin Lean (1984). The role of women in population and development in Asian countries. In *Population Policies in Asian Countries: Contemporary Targets, Measures and Effects*, Hermann Schubnell, ed. Centre of Asian Studies, Occasional Papers and Monographs, No. 57. Lubeak, Germany: The Prager Foundation; and Hong Kong: University of Hong Kong.

_________ (1991). Women, population and development. Paper prepared for the Inter-Country Training Workshop on Population, Human Resources and Development Planning, organized by the International Labour Organization and Nihon University, 10-21 December. Mimeographed.

Mahajan, Inez Wyngaards (1987). Family related responsibilities of women workers and diversification of training and employment. In *Diversification of Women's Employment and Training*. Bangkok: International Labour Organization, Regional Office for Asia and the Pacific.

Mason, Karen Oppenheim (1984). *The Status of Women: A Review of its Relationships to Fertility and Mortality*. New York: The Rockfeller Foundation.

Murdoch, William W. (1980). *The Poverty of Nations: The Political Economy of Hunger and Population*. Baltimore, Maryland: The John Hopkins University Press.

Noman, Ayesha (1983). *Status of Women and Fertility in Bangladesh*. Dhaka: Bangladesh University Press.

Rao, Kamala (1979). Status of women: factors affecting status of women in India. In *ILO Sub-regional Seminar on Status and Role of Women in the Organized Sector*. Bangkok: International Labour Organization, Regional Office for Asia and the Pacific.

Rodríguez, German, and John Cleland (1980). Socio-economic determinants of marital fertility in twenty countries: a multivariate analysis. In *World Fertility Survey Conference, 1980: Record of Proceedings*, vol. II. Voorburg, Netherlands: International Statistical Institute.

Safilios-Rothschild, Constantina (1985). *The Status of Women and Fertility in the Third World in the 1970-1980 Decade*. Center for Policy Studies Working Paper, No. 118. New York: The Population Council.

Selvaratnam, S. (1988a). Population change and women's development. In *Frameworks for Population and Development Integration*, vol. 1, *ESCAP Regional Perspectives*. Asian Population Studies Series, No. 92, Bangkok: Economic and Social Commission for Asia and the Pacific.

_________ (1988b). Population change and education. In *Frameworks for Population and Development Integration*, vol. 1, *ESCAP Regional Perspectives*. Asian Population Studies Series, No. 92. Bangkok: Economic and Social Commission for Asia and the Pacific, pp. 163-192.

Srinivasan, T. N., and Pranab K. Bardhan, eds. (1988). *Rural Poverty in South Asia*. New York: Columbia, University Press.

Tan, B. A. (1981). Socio-economic factors affecting fertility. Paper presented at the Population Studies Unit Seminar on Integrating Population with Development. Kuala Lumpur, Malaysia: University of Malaya. Mimeographed.

United Nations, Economic and Social Commission for Asia and the Pacific (1982). *Regional Seminar on Strategies for Meeting Basic Socio-Economic Needs and for Increasing Women's Participation in Development to Achieve Population Goals*. Bangkok.

_________ (1986). *Status of Women in Asia and the Pacific Region*, Series 1, *Women in the Economy: Employment*. ST/ESCAP/417. Bangkok.

XXI. THE IMPACT OF CHANGES ON WOMEN IN LATIN AMERICA AND THE CARIBBEAN: EDUCATION, KNOWLEDGE AND DEMOGRAPHIC TRENDS

Economic Commission for Latin America and the Caribbean[*]

This brief paper presented for discussion at the Expert Group Meeting on Population and Women addresses only two of the many important aspects of the current debate on how to improve the integration of women into development: first, the main changes undergone by women in Latin America and the Caribbean in recent decades and their current situation, with special emphasis on agenda item 6, "Women's education and its demographic impact"; and secondly, the proposed discussion of certain ideas or areas of interest for future exploration of the topic, taking into account the various prevailing scenarios in the region and the Economic Commission for Latin America and the Caribbean (ECLAC) proposal on changing production patterns with social equity (United Nations, ECLAC, 1990a).

Although ECLAC takes a systemic approach to the subject of women's integration, in view of the close interdependence of the various aspects of their situation and the problem of development, priority has now been given to the topic of education as probably the clearest way to illustrate this interdependence. This sector also best reflects the changes that have taken place in the situation of women in this major area as a result of the massive incorporation of the Latin American and the Caribbean women into the formal educational system at all levels. In relation to the specific objectives of this Meeting, education is a factor that seems to be strongly associated with changes in demographic trends, especially fertility. Moreover, in the ECLAC proposal, education and knowledge are regarded as basic pillars of changing production patterns with social equity, of which the consideration of women's integration into the new types of educational paradigms is a fundamental part (United Nations, ECLAC and UNESCO, 1992).

As in the case of other United Nations bodies and specialized agencies, the activities of the regional commissions relating to the integration of women have been carried out through the instruments adopted by the Organization for this purpose. From the beginning, these activities have played a central role, through the following three functions: support of country actions in the form of studies, diagnostic evaluations and recommendations; coordination of activities with other organizations of the United Nations system, in accordance with their respective work programme; and implementation of specific actions, such as projects, technical assistance or generation and dissemination of new knowledge. ECLAC began its studies concerning women in compliance with its resolution 321 (XV), adopted in 1973, and thus became a leader in this field at the regional level. In 1977, it adopted the Regional Plan of Action for the Integration of Women into Latin American and Caribbean Development, which deals with the living conditions of the Latin American and the Caribbean women as they relate to the development problem of countries, and its recommendations were in line with the preferred development models for the region in the 1970s. From that perspective, practically speaking, the regional position was oriented towards the vulnerable women's sectors, especially the low-income sector. Through its actions, ECLAC sought to incorporate the women's dimension into the overall issue of the economic and social development of the region and to expand on certain less familiar aspects of the subject in order to promote the general improvement of the situation of women. Thus, besides carrying out periodic, comprehensive diagnostic evaluations for purposes of policy-making, ECLAC studied aspects relating to the status of women in such fields as legislation, culture, migration,

[*]Santiago, Chile.

youth, the low-income urban sector, socialization in the home environment, labour and employment, new technologies and human resources training.

A. The situation of women in Latin America and the Caribbean in relation to education and its demographic impact

The situation of women in Latin America and the Caribbean has changed enormously over the past four decades. Their ever-increasing presence in education and in the workforce, the legal consolidation of their citizenship in respect of the right to vote and their growing social acceptance in the political arena and public life are transformations whose importance has transcended the economic and social spheres and is beginning to be expressed in changes in cultural behaviour. Advances in medicine—which have reduced the risks inherent in childbirth and raised life expectancy in the region from 51.8 in 1950-1955 to 66.6 in 1985-1990—and in birth control, have provided to the women of the region with totally new options in terms of life opportunities and the possibility of exercising their rights. The Latin American and Caribbean region is extremely heterogeneous, and the significant internal differences that affect the specific condition of women, depending upon their socio-economic level or whether they are rural or urban, have an impact on the speed of these seemingly irreversible changes (United Nations, ECLAC, 1990a).

The first change in the situation of women is reflected in demographic figures. Latin America is passing through a phase of demographic transition, represented by a decline in both fertility and mortality. In the 1980s, the average annual growth rate was 2.2 per cent, and it was expected to reach 1.9 per cent in the 1990s, while the number of children per woman would have declined from an average of 5.9 in 1950-1955 to 3.6 in 1985-1990, with the lowest fertility rate being found among urban, educated women (CELADE, 1991). Child-bearing age is increasingly concentrated (70 per cent) in the middle range of ages, 20-35 years. Proportions of pregnancies in high-risk groups are still 25 and 30 per cent, with a significant increase in teenage pregnancies and a reduced number of pregnancies in older women. Multiparity has declined, but 50 per cent of women still have more than the critical limit of four children. It is difficult to find reliable data on birth-spacing, in view of a lack of figures on actual abortions (PAHO, 1990).

The use of contraceptives in Latin America and the Caribbean varies considerably: 7 per cent in Haiti, 23-27 per cent in Bolivia, Guatemala and Nicaragua; and 70 per cent in Costa Rica and Puerto Rico. Most variation appears to be correlated with socio-economic level, educational level, adolescence, level of development of the country and the prevailing health policy. The most frequently used method is female sterilization, and 80 per cent of contraceptive use in general is accounted for by women (PAHO, 1990).

Poverty is a fundamental topic in a region where "the feminization of poverty" has become a commonplace, and it should certainly receive priority attention in the design of demographically oriented educational policies, since this sector of women has little access to the most elemental options. It is true that in Latin America and the Caribbean, as in the rest of the world even where sanitary and nutritional conditions are adequate and peacetime conditions prevail, male mortality rates are higher than female rates at any age and women live longer than men in general. It is in the poorest sector, however, that an excess of female mortality occurs as a result of preventable causes. In early childhood, these causes are of malnutrition (72 per cent), influenza and pneumonia (64 per cent), bronchitis, emphysema and asthma (56 per cent), measles (50 per cent), whooping cough (50 per cent) and specific and non-specific intestinal infections. The main causes of female mortality between ages 15 and 44 are complications related to pregnancy, childbirth and the post-partum period, with an enormous difference among countries, depending upon living conditions and health coverage. (The rate in Paraguay is 111 times higher than that in Canada.) Maternity-related mortality and morbidity vary a great deal among the countries of the region and reach their peak between developed and developing countries, especially due to the following causes: abortion; toxaemia; haemorrhage; and post-partum complications. Anaemia and malnutrition are other major causes of mortality associated with pregnancy and cultural factors within families, but they are fundamentally correlated with poverty. In Latin America and the Caribbean, it is difficult to separate the analysis of the situation of women from the topic of poverty, since the majority of women are poor—a fact that the crisis made even more abundantly clear. Despite poverty, the changes that have taken place have had a much more important impact on the women of the region than the figures show. That sexuality can be separated from reproduction and that with a certain margin of safety a woman can decide whether to have children are very recent phenomena on the Latin American scene. Although these changes are more visible in the middle- and upper-class urban-educated strata, the choice-oriented model is beginning to permeate all social sectors, as shown by the Demographic and Health Surveys conducted in the 1980s, in which a large number of births are characterized as "unwanted" (CELADE, 1992).

In the educational sphere in Latin America and the Caribbean, enrolment rates continue to rise, with a tendency towards parity. Achievements with regard to access to education have been noteworthy, although they have not had such a strong impact on access to the labour market or on income levels. Currently, more than half the women between ages 15 and 19 have completed primary education. In higher education, women represented approximately 45 per cent of enrolment in 1985, and in 40 per cent of the countries the number of women enrolled exceeded that of men. On the other hand, female illiteracy rates in 1985 still fluctuated between 19.2 and 48 per cent in rural areas. The distribution of women according to area of study has varied little. While the proportion of women in engineering careers has increased by 8 per cent, the percentage of women studying the social sciences and pedagogy continues to fluctuate between 60 and 70 per cent. At the same time, women in the region have fewer opportunities to reach higher academic positions, and more years of study are required of them than of men in order to have access to the same occupations. Wage discrimination is equivalent to about four years of formal education and declines as educational level rises. It is important to note, lastly, that gender discrimination persists in the textbooks used in the region (United Nations, ECLAC and UNESCO, 1992).

Education exerts a strong influence on demographic trends, affecting the variables that produce changes in these trends. The educational level of the population, which is associated with improvements in living conditions, has played a basic role in the decline of infant mortality. Many studies exist on the relation between the educational level of the mother and the variables of fertility and infant mortality, showing an inverse correlation in all cases. In general, it is agreed that education affects reproductive behaviour, especially in terms of the formation and spread of attitudes, values and beliefs associated with desired family size. Trends in the region show that women with more schooling tend to marry later and have fewer children. In terms of policy-making, however, education cannot be considered a direct tool for designing short-term policies, since its immediate effects depend upon the content of the education offered and upon interactions with the rest of the social system (United Nations, ECLAC and UNESCO, 1992).

It is important to take into account that the mass entry of women into the educational system occurred between the 1950s and 1980s, at a time when Latin America and the Caribbean was experiencing a sustained expansion in terms of the formal educational system and of scientific and technological research capacities and human resources training. This development took place together with an intense urbanization process, accompanied by migration to the cities and a considerable increase in the participation of women in the workforce. The expansion of formal education, although very widespread, accentuated the existing heterogeneity among countries and was not accompanied by a qualitative improvement, a fact that is reflected, for example, in the repeater rates, which are among the highest in the world (46 per cent in the first grade). The deterioration in the quality of education, which was exacerbated in the 1980s, was due, among other factors, to poor living conditions, the decline in the number of teachers, a reduction of public spending on education and outdated curricula.

Two aspects must be borne in mind in attempting to improve the situation of women. First, the content of education, which, although it favours their integration in an early stage, by giving them access to universally shared codes, later reverts to the reinforcement of stereotypes as to their role in society and distorts their incorporation into the workforce. Secondly, despite all the educational and training achievements, the capabilities for improving human resource training are uncertain, and a major effort will be required in order to address the new issues involved in international integration, making profound changes with the aim of linking the educational system to development needs, including gender-specific needs.

B. FUTURE PROSPECTS

The past decades have witnessed not only the modification and enrichment of the debate on women's role in society but also fundamental changes in the concept of the development process as such. Until very recently, development was considered essentially a process of economic growth; today, its integration with social issues is accepted as inevitable. This change means that the welfare of populations and the quality of life of individuals are becoming an integral part of the debate on development. All of the foregoing change constitutes a theoretical and conceptual advance that allows for a much better articulated and more meaningful linkage of gender issues with the problems of society as a whole. The idea that development benefits, or hurts, men and women in a differentiated way is much more widely accepted in the current context. One important step forward in the analysis of demographic impact in relation to women is that the concept of "woman" is no longer approached merely as an empirical reference to the biological condition of one of the sexes, but rather as a social construct relating to gender that extends beyond the biological difference between the sexes to include the entire set of standards for the behaviour and attitudes accepted and expected from each of the sexes. In the early 1970s, the "populationist", "developmental" and "egalitarian" approaches referred to very different points of view and perspectives on actions to improve the situation of women. Today, the existence of consensual instruments in the United Nations and the convergence of various perspectives despite their varying emphases, allow for much greater and more effective strides towards the future, as is shown by the various plans of action of United Nations organizations and the results of a number of regional and international conferences.

The backdrop for the subject of women today and their relation to development is undergoing profound changes, including changes in the relation between the developed and the developing countries. The contemporary regional context is one of increasingly extensive economic internationalization and extraordinarily rapid changes in various fields of knowledge, including science, technology and economics. Scientific advances, which are applied almost simultaneously to technology, are producing changes whose key elements are competitiveness, technical progress, innovation and intellectual added value. This form of modernity, which already characterizes some countries, gives primacy and centrality to their ideas and values. This form of modernity, however, means neither greater harmony nor greater equity. The breakdown of ideological polarization and the consideration of democracy as an almost inherent component of human development have been accompanied by wider gaps between economic and social issues, by exclusionism and by the physical deterioration of large segments of the population and of the planet itself. For Latin America and the Caribbean, modernity is not an option but a virtual obligation. Globalization processes are irreversible and must be voluntary if they are to help create an environment of greater liberty, democracy and equity. The problems arising from adjustment processes and the critical situation of large segments of the population highlight the need to supplement theoretical advances with programme proposals. The decades prior to the crisis, despite all their constraints and failings, created expectations of social mobility and integration into society, especially for women and young people, who must now cope with situations of extreme economic fragility (United Nations, ECLAC, 1990a and 1990b).

With respect to the issue of gender, it is equally impossible to continue to act according to past models in any sphere. In the debate on the future, it is important to eliminate dichotomies and to look at development processes from a fresh perspective that comprises an understanding of their ambivalences and contradictions. It is particularly important at this time to develop the capacity to elaborate viable programmes that can be converted into concrete policies (ECLAC, 1991).

It has been stressed that the changes that Latin America and the Caribbean has undergone require a new conception of the future in all of its aspects. In this context, ECLAC has set forth a proposal on changing production patterns with social equity, consisting of a set of ideas on regional options for the future based on an evaluation of the impact of the crisis. The basic aim is to bring about the transformation of production structures in a context of growing social equity. Emphasis is placed on the possibility of achieving economic development in a democratic context and on the premise that the sustainability of such development can only be ensured through better distribution of its benefits, that is social equity. The proposal has three basic goals: international competitiveness, which calls for changing production patterns in the countries concerned; the capacity and opportunity for innovation that unites the objectives of efficiency and equity; and the creation or multiplication of possibilities for collective action and interregional cooperation. The proposal is "systemic", as it comprises a combination of different actions and modalities.

According to this proposal, social equity is one of the essential objectives of development processes. From the viewpoint of the integration of women into development, social equity is presumed to exist at two levels. First, since women belong to various socio-economic groups, equity is related to issues of redistribution, changing production patterns and appropriate and adequate provision of social services. Secondly, gender equity is linked to the integration of women into development through more equal participation in the labour market, education and sociopolitical activity, but it also refers to the cultural transformations required if women are truly to enter the third millennium in conditions of effective parity with the men of their generation.

The central idea orienting this linkage is that in Latin America and the Caribbean, the problem is not the integration of women into development, but rather the way in which they are integrated and their incorporation into development strategies and policies, which have not taken them into account.

In sectoral policies and in any plan for the future, the role of education will be essential. However, its transformation is equally essential. Currently, education in the region is out of step with reality and with regional needs, in terms of not only its content but also its perspectives and methods. In Latin America and the Caribbean, which is rich above all in human resources, education for the future must constitute an ongoing but flexible process of training that promotes open-mindedness and greater autonomy and stimulates creativity and innovation. In this type of education, women will have more options and probably greater success, since the traditional backgrounds of many women demand that they show considerable flexibility.

The formulation of educational policies for women requires another type of support. Despite their evident desirability, measures that allow for the equitable participation of women must continue to be emphasized. Principal among these are measures concerning reproduction, which take the form of mother and child care, protection of pregnant women and flexible working hours. Child care, on the other hand, still is not assumed to be an inevitable obligation of all human societies. Integrated policies must be designed in this area to unite the coordinated efforts of the public, private, business and community sectors and to explore flexible options and combinations of various resources to ensure that children of the region whose mothers are obligated to work shall receive the necessary specialized care. Another issue with significant repercussions on the living conditions of women is household work. Although it has to some degree been recognized that household work has a measurable economic value which can be evaluated and which is greater than normally supposed, little has been done to date in terms of concrete measures to lighten the burden, to socialize it to the extent possible or to turn it into a socially shared activity.

Lastly, it is important to point out, at least in the context of Latin America and the Caribbean, that educational policies concerning the exercise of the reproductive rights of women and men must be directed to both sexes.

References

Centro Latinamericano de Demografía (1991). Población y transformación productiva con equidad. Santiago, Chile. Unpublished.

__________ (1992). Política de población: una perspectiva de América Latina y el Caribe. Santiago, Chile.

Pan American Health Organization (1990). *Health Conditions in the Americas, 1190 Edition*, vol. I. Scientific Publication, No. 524. Washington, D.C.

United Nations, Economic Commission for Latin America and the Caribbean (1990a). *Changing Production Patterns with Social Equity: The Prime Task of Latin American and Caribbean Development in the 1990s*. Santiago, Chile. Sales No. E.90.II.G.6.

_________ (1990b). *Los grandes cambios y la crisis: impacto sobre la mujer en América Latina y el Caribe*. Santiago, Chile. Sales No. S.90.II.G.13.

_________ (1991a). Activities of the ECLAC secretariat from 1 July 1988 to 31 May 1991 relating to the integration of women into the economic and social development of Latin America and the Caribbean. LC/L.626(CRM.5/3. Santiago, Chile.

_________ (1991b). Women in Latin America and the Caribbean: the challenge of changing production patterns with social equity. LC/L.627(CRM.5/4). Santiago, Chile.

_________, and United Nations Educational, Scientific and Cultural Organization. Regional Office for Education in Latin America and the Caribbean (1992). *Education and Knowledge: Basic Pillars of Changing Production Patterns with Social Equity*. LC/G.1702(SES.24/4 and Corr.1). Santiago, Chile.

XXII. THE IMPACT OF MOTHERS' EDUCATION ON INFANT AND CHILD MORTALITY IN SELECTED COUNTRIES IN THE ESCWA REGION

Economic and Social Commission for Western Asia[*]

This paper discusses some of the available analytical studies on the impact of the effects of paternal and maternal education on the levels and differentials of infant and child mortality in the region of the Economic and Social Commission for Western Asia (ESCWA).

The analytical tools were: *(a)* descriptive analysis; *(b)* bivariate regression analysis; *(c)* multivariate regression analysis; and *(d)* risk groups introduced through the multivariate regression analysis. These case-studies are discussed: *Egyptian Fertility Survey, 1980* (Egypt, 1983); *Pregnancy Wastage and Infant Mortality, Egypt, 1979-1983* (Egypt, 1987); *Jordan Fertility Survey, 1976* (Jordan, 1979); and *Jordan Demographic Survey, 1981* (Jordan, 1983).

A. BACKGROUND

Recently, many studies have suggested that child mortality in developing countries is associated more closely with maternal education than with any other socio-economic factor (Behm, 1980; Caldwell, 1979; and Cochrane, 1980, cited in United Nations, 1985). It is not unexpected that in the absence of other variables, a child's probability of dying is inversely related to the mother's years of schooling. What has impressed many analysts is the strength and persistence of the association when other socio-economic as well as more proximate variables are controlled.

Although the importance of maternal education is now widely recognized, questions remain concerning the magnitude and nature of its effect in different settings. The degree of effect of maternal education may work through other socio-economic variables the value of which are established later in life; for example, much of the importance of mother's education could result from the ability of a better educated woman to attract a husband who earns more, a factor that appears to operate in some areas where men have begun to recognize the desirability of having an educated wife (Lindenbaum and others, 1983, cited in United Nations, 1985).

B. EGYPTIAN FERTILITY SURVEY, 1980

Descriptive analysis

According to the mortality rates, during the period 1975-1979 there is a strong association between the mother's education and survival of her children. A woman's education tends to denote higher socio-economic status than would an equivalent educational level for a man. This situation exists because women are less likely than men to be educated and a woman is usually married to a man with the same or a higher level of education than herself.

This indication is reflected in the education differentials in infant and child mortality. The children of illiterate women have a marginally better chance of survival than those born to women whose husbands are also illiterate. At the other extreme, the lowest level of infant and child mortality is to be found among the children of women with at least secondary education, fewer than 1 in 10 of whom die during the first five years of life. Of special note are the superior survival chances between ages 1 and 5 for children of women with at least primary education (table 33).

Table 34 shows that there are similar interregional education differentials in infant and child mortality. Mother's education appears to have the most impact at Cairo (the capital) and Alexandria, where 1 in 5 children born alive to illiterate women had died in the first five years of life, compared with 1 in 13 of those born to women with at least primary education.

[*]Social Development and Population Division, Amman, Jordan.

TABLE 33. INFANT AND CHILD MORTALITY DURING THE FIVE YEARS BEFORE THE FERTILITY SURVEY, EGYPT, 1975-1979

Mother's level of education	*Neonatal*	*Post-neonatal*	$_1q_0$	$_5q_0$	$_4q_1$
Illiterate, no schooling	65	75	140	205	75
Illiterate, some schooling	51	82	133	192	67
Can read and write	51	78	129	160	60
Primary school	(42)	(49)	(91)	(122)	(34)
Secondary school	44	44	88	(99)	(13)

Source: Egypt, *The Egyptian Fertility Survey, 1980,* vol. II (Cairo, Central Agency for Public Mobilisation and Statistics, 1983), p. 59.

NOTE: Figures in parentheses were based on fewer than 500 children exposed.

TABLE 34. REGIONAL ESTIMATES OF INFANT AND CHILD MORTALITY DURING THE 10 YEARS BEFORE THE FERTILITY SURVEY, BY MOTHER'S EDUCATION, EGYPT, 1970-1979

	Cairo and Alexandria		*Lower Egypt*		*Upper Egypt*		*All*	
Mother's level of education	$_1q_0$	$_5q_0$	$_1q_0$	$_5q_0$	$_1q_0$	$_3q_0$	$_1q_0$	$_5q_0$
Illiterate	137	198	116	193	184	271	146	225
Can read and write	(104)	(147)	111	(188)	(187)	(282)	127	196
Primary school + ...	58	77	86	(129)	(138)	(168)	81	110
All	11d66	113	188	185	272	138	282	

Source: Egypt, *The Egyptian Fertility Survey, 1980,* vol. II (Cairo, Central Agency for Public Mobilisation and Statistics, 1983), p. 60.

NOTE: Figures in parentheses were based on fewer than 500 children exposed.

The proportion of children surviving is not meaningful unless some control for the period over which the child has been exposed to the risk of dying is introduced; the simplest way to control for this is a proxy, such as maternal age. More sophisticated indirect techniques make much finer adjustments. In table 35, the proportion of children surviving adjusted for maternal age could be examined. The differential in child survival by the wife's educational background and urban/rural residence is given in table 35. In general, the higher the education, the higher the child survival. This pattern is sharpest and most uniform for the wife's education in rural areas. The proportion of children dying among children of rural mothers with secondary education and above is only 38 per cent of that of unschooled women; in urban areas, the comparable figure is 61 per cent (table 35).

Bivariate analysis: mortality differentials[1]

Another study, employing a bivariate analysis of the 1980 Egyptian Fertility Survey (Ashy and others, 1983) found that differentials in infant and childhood mortality rates by the mother's education (out of different investigated social status indicators) in Egypt are generally similar to those found in other populations (table 36). When the mother's or the father's education is used as a measure of status, a pronounced inverse relation is observed with each age-interval mortality rate. For example, the infant mortality rate (IMR) for mothers with no schooling is 158 and is about 89 per cent greater than the rate of 84 for mothers with six or more years of schooling. Similarly, the neonatal mortality rate of mothers with no schooling is greater by 91 per cent, the post-neonatal rate is

TABLE 35. PROPORTION OF CHILDREN SURVIVING, BY EDUCATION OF WIFE, EGYPT, 1980

Education of wife	*Urban*		*Rural*		*Total*	
	Unadjusted	*Adjusted for age*	*Unadjusted*	*Adjusted for age*	*Unadjusted*	*Adjusted for age*
Illiterate, no school	82	82	76	77	78	78
Illiterate, some school	81	82	79	79	80	82
Literate, no certificate	83	81	82	82	83	80
Primary school	89	90	85	86	88	89
Secondary school/university	91	89	91	91	91	87
TOTAL	84		78		80	

Source: Egypt, *The Egyptian Fertility Survey, 1980,* vol. II, *Fertility and Family Planning*; and vol. III, *Socio-economic Differentials and Comparative Data from Husbands and Wives* (Cairo, Central Agency for Public Mobilisation and Statistics, 1983).

TABLE 36. INFANT AND CHILD MORTALITY RATES BY MOTHER'S EDUCATION FOR BIRTHS BETWEEN 1970 AND 1975, EGYPTIAN FERTILITY SURVEY, 1980

Mother's education	*Mortality rates per 100 persons exposed*[a]				*Persons exposed*	
	Neonatal mortality	*Post-neonatal mortality*	*Infant mortality*	*Childhood mortality*	*Neonatal, post-neonatal and infant mortality*	*Child mortality*
None	68.5	89.1	157.6	68.8	9 942	4 449
1-5 years	60.3	84.9	145.1	69.2	4 065	1 793
6+ years	35.8	47.8	83.6	32.8	1 424	609
TOTAL	63.3	84.2	147.5	65.7	15 431	6 851

[a]The analysis of neonatal, post-neonatal and infant mortality excludes births that occurred within one year of the date of interview. The analysis of childhood mortality excludes births that occurred within five years of the date of interview.

greater by 86 per cent and the childhood mortality rate is greater by 108 per cent than the corresponding rate for mothers with six or more years of schooling.

Multivariate analysis: net effects[2]

Post-neonatal mortality

In a multivariate analysis, it was observed that the post-neonatal mortality rate decreased significantly with an increase in mother's education. When mother's education changed from illiterate to six or more years of schooling, post-neonatal mortality decreased by 46.2. For such a change in mother's education, the risk of post-neonatal death was only 0.71 times as great for mothers with six or more years of schooling than that of illiterate mothers (table 37).

Infant mortality

Results for infancy—that is, neonatal and post-neonatal periods combined—are presented in table 38. Among the given socio-economic factors, mother's education has a significant effect on infant mortality. Expressed in terms of the relative risk ratio, for a change in mother's education category from "illiterate" to six or more years of schooling, the infant mortality is reduced by 26 per cent.

Childhood mortality

Unlike infant mortality, mother's education did not show any significant net effect on child mortality (table 39).

TABLE 37. NET EFFECTS OF MOTHER'S EDUCATION ON POST-NEONATAL MORTALITY, EGYPTIAN FERTILITY SURVEY, 1980

	Regression results by model			
	Model II: socio-economic variables		*Model III: demographics plus socio-economic variables*	
	Beta coefficient	*Standard error*	*Beta coeffient*	*Standard error*
Intercept	2.511[a]	0.095	1.061	0.604
Mother's education				
None	0.184	0.139	0.133	0.138
1-5 years	0.174[b]	0.071	0.130[c]	0.072
6+ years	0.358[b]	0.117	0.263[b]	0.118
Number of observations	11 263		11 263	
Model chi-square	19.67[b]		316.69[a]	
Degrees of freedom	10		15	
D statistics	0.002		0.027	

Source: For *D* statistic, F. Harrel, *The Logist Procedure: SAS Supplement Library Users Guide*, 1980 ed. (Carry, North Carolina, SAS Institute, 1980).

NOTE: The regression models were fitted with the maximum likelihood procedure so the standard R^2 statistic could not be computed. However, the *D* statistic, which has an interpretation similar to R^2, was computed.

[a]Significant at 1 per cent level.
[b]Significant at 5 per cent level.
[c]Significant at 10 per cent level.

TABLE 38. NET EFFECTS OF DEMOGRAPHIC AND SOCIO-ECONOMIC FACTORS ON PROBABILITIES OF INFANT MORTALITY, EGYPTIAN FERTILITY SURVEY, 1980

	Regression results by model			
	Model II: socio-economic variables		*Model III: demographics plus socio-economic variables*	
	Beta coefficient	*Standard error*	*Beta coefficient*	*Standard error*
Intercept	1.923[a]	0.073	1.304[a]	0.486
Mother's education				
None	0.193[b]	0.110	0.137	0.112
1-5 years	0.125[c]	0.057	0.84	0.058
6+ years	0.358[a]	0.094	0.221[c]	0.096
Number of observations	11 961		11 961	
Model chi-square	59.63[a]		563.42[a]	
Degrees of freedom	10		15	
D statistics	0.005		0.045	

Source: For *D* statistics, F. Harrel, *The Logist Procedure: SAS Supplement Library Users Guide*, 1980 ed. (Carry, North Carolina, SAS Institute, 1980).

NOTE: The regression models were fitted with the maximum likelihood procedure so the standard R^2 statistics could not be computed. However, the *D* statistic, which has an interpretation similar to R^2, was computed.

[a]Significant at 1 per cent level.
[b]Significant at 5 per cent level.
[c]Significant at 10 per cent level.

TABLE 39. NET EFFECTS OF DEMOGRAPHIC AND SOCIO-ECONOMIC FACTORS ON PROBABILITIES OF CHILD MORTALITY, EGYPTIAN FERTILITY SURVEY, 1980

	Regression results by model			
	Model II: socio-economic variables		*Model III: demographics plus socio-economic variables*	
	Beta coefficient	*Standard error*	*Beta coefficient*	*Standard error*
Intercept	2.950[a]	0.165	0.251	1.040
Mother's education				
None	0.028	0.222	0.034	0.224
1-5 years	0.073	0.115	0.054	0.117
6+ years	0.045	0.190	0.020	0.191
Number of observations	5 336		5 336	
Model chi-square	21.66[b]		80.25	
Degrees of freedom	10		15	
D statistics	0.004		0.015	

Source: For *D* statistic, F. Harrel, *The Logist Procedure: SAS Supplement Library Users Guide*, 1980 ed. (Carry, North Carolina, SAS Institute, 1980).

NOTE: The regression models were fitted with the maximum likelihood procedure so the standard R^2 statistic could not be computed. However, the *D* statistic, which has an interpretation similar to R^2, was computed.

[a]Significant at 1 per cent level.

[b]Significant at 5 per cent level.

B. PREGNANCY WASTAGE AND INFANT MORTALITY SURVEY, EGYPT, 1980

Examination of differentials in infant mortality by major socio-economic and bio-demographic variables was done using both tabular and multivariate analysis of the data of the Pregnancy Wastage and Infant Mortality Survey[3] (Egypt, 1987b). Out of the examined variables, differentials in infant mortality by demographic and reproductive characteristics of the mother showed a substantial and strong impact on infant mortality. Differentials in infant mortality by educational attainments of both parents, occupation of the father, mother's work status and some other socio-economic variables were examined. The overall general pattern of the relation between infant mortality and education is negative.

The probability of dying in infancy decreases with increases in levels of education of both the mother and the father. Better educated mothers (secondary or more) have an infant mortality rate that is only one third of that of illiterate women (44 versus 127 per 1,000). Parent's education showed a greater impact on post-neonatal than on neonatal mortality.

Mother's educational status, as mentioned above, is an indicator of level of knowledge about child and health care and is associated with household income level; thus it is one of several socio-economic measurements that may affect infant deaths.

Table 40 shows the expected inverse relation between infant mortality rates and mother's educational status. More educated mothers (those with secondary schooling or more) have the lowest IMR (44), while illiterate mothers have IMR that is almost three times as large 127. The differences are largest for post-neonatal mortality rates, but the same pattern is observed for neonatal mortality as well (Egypt, 1987a).

C. THE JORDAN FERTILITY SURVEY, 1976; AND JORDAN DEMOGRAPHIC SURVEY, 1983

The case of Jordan (Hill, 1991) is one of a series of studies on socio-economic differentials in child mortality using similar data and analytical methods carried out under the auspices of the United Nations Secretariat. A multivariate model was used to examine relation between child mortality and selected socio-economic variables.

TABLE 40. NEONATAL, POST-NEONATAL AND TOTAL INFANT MORTALITY RATES, BY EDUCATIONAL LEVEL OF MOTHER

Mother's education	*Neonatal*	*Post-neonatal*	*Total*	*Number of births*
Illiterate	58.4	72.9	127.0	8 989
	(4.4)	(3.7)	(5.5)	
Literate	38.6	42.7	79.6	829
	(7.3)	(7.9)	(11.2)	
Primary/preparatory	34.3	51.3	83.8	525
	(9.2)	(11.7)	(15.4)	
Secondary or more	25.9	18.2	43.5	735
	(6.7)	(4.9)	(8.4)	
A. Chi-square tests for effects by educational level of mother				
X^2	26.1[a]	52.9[a]	76.1[a]	–
df	3	3	3	–
B. Within regions				
Urban governorate				
Illiterate	35.2	68.2	101.0	1 109
Literate	35.1	54.5	87.7	228
Primary/preparatory	37.0	33.0	68.8	189
Secondary or more	25.4	9.8	34.9	315
Urban lower				
Illiterate	28.8	73.4	100.1	729
Literate	23.3	39.7	62.0	129
Primary/preparatory	12.3	25.0	37.0	81
Secondary or more	35.7	5.3	40.8	196
Rural lower				
Illiterate	56.8	70.4	123.2	3 838
Literate	36.3	33.5	68.5	248
Primary/preparatory	29.9	76.9	104.5	134
Secondary or more	27.8	71.4	97.2	72
Urban upper				
Illiterate	39.5	95.2	130.9	886
Literate	30.5	39.4	68.7	131
Primary/preparatory	12.3	62.5	74.1	81
Secondary or more	14.2	28.8	42.6	141
Rural upper				
Illiterate	87.4	70.4	151.6	2 427
Literate	86.0	47.1	129.0	93
Primary/preparatory	125.0	85.7	200.0	40
Secondary or more	0	0	0	11
C. Chi-square tests for interactions of mother's educational level with region				
X^2	9.8[b]	17.6[b]	12.9[b]	–
df	12	12	12	–

[a]Significant at 0.001.
[b]Not significant at 0.05.

The conceptual framework for this study is described in detail elsewhere (Behm, 1987). Child mortality is seen as the final outcome of a continual interaction between child and its environment. The role of parental education may be summarized as follows:

Higher levels of parental education may be expected to be associated with lower child mortality. Exposure to disease may be reduced by better hygienic practices and other behaviour, resistance may be increased by better nutrition (although countered by possible reductions in breast-feeding) and greater use of immunizations, and severity may be reduced by the appropriate use of curative or palliative measures. If household income is adequately controlled for, one should probably expect the mother's education to be relatively more important than the father's education, since in most societies the mother has more immediate involvement in child care. If income is not adequately controlled for, however, father's education and household income are likely to be strongly related, and the father's education may appear to be highly important. In some societies in which the possibilities for independent female action are limited, the husband's education may also be of importance to determining the use or otherwise of preventive and curative health services.

In this study, a multivariate model is used to estimate the relation between a set of socio-economic indicators and an indictor, standardized for exposure to risk of death, of the child mortality experience of the children of each currently married woman. Similar models are estimated using both 1976 and 1981 data sets in order to explore possible changes in the relation over time.[4]

Results of the regression model

Ordinary least squares regression was used to estimate the relation between the child mortality indicator, MORT, and a number of independent, categorical variables represented by dummy variables. Separate equations were estimated for each data set, 1976 and 1981.

Values of MORT were calculated for each survey as follows: first, an estimate of the probability of dying by age 5, ${}_5q_0$, was obtained by averaging the national-level mortality estimates derived from the proportions dead of children ever born by duration of marriage groups 0-4, 5-9 and 10-14, using the Coale-Demeny South family mortality pattern. The values of ${}_2q_0$, ${}_3q_0$, ${}_5q_0$ and ${}_{10}q_0$ corresponding to the estimated, q were found. The estimation equations were then used in reverse, using the observed ratios of average parity by duration group, to estimate expected proportions dead in each duration group. Results are shown in table 41.

TABLE 41. STANDARD VALUES OF THE PROBABILITY OF DYING BY AGE 5, ${}_5q_0$ AND THE EXPECTED PROPORTIONS DEAD, BY DURATION OF MARRIAGE, JORDAN, 1976 AND 1981

Measure	*Duration of marriage (years)*			
	0.4	*5-9*	*19-14*	*15-19*
Jordan, 1976				
Probability of dying by age 5, ${}_5q_0$		0.093		
Expected proportion dead	0.067	0.081	0.088	0.093
Jordan, 1981				
Probability of dying by age 5, ${}_5q_0$		0.077		
Expected proportion dead	0.056	0.068	0.072	0.076

Source: Kenneth Hill, "Jordan", in *Child Mortality in Developing Countries: Socio-economic Differentials, Trends and Implications* (United Nations publication, Sales No. E.91.XIII.13), table 29.

For each woman, the expected proportion dead, given her duration of marriage, was then multiplied by her number of children ever born to obtain the expected number of children dead. MORT is then calculated as the ratio of actual number of children dead divided by the expected number.

The independent variables used were categorized as shown in table 42; the deleted or reference category was the category expected to show the lowest child mortality. As an attempted control on trend effects, a variable representing duration of marriage was used. The four categories used were 0-4 years (the reference category) and 5-9, 10-14 and 15-19 years. Regression results are summarized in table 42, which shows for each survey the population mean for each category (the proportion of the reported children falling in the category) and its coefficient in the regression equation.

The results are in line with expectations, as education is clearly strongly related to child mortality. The children of mothers with less than six years of education have clearly higher mortality risks than children with well-educated parents, and the higher mortality risks extend to children of parents with primary and even some secondary schooling, in an attenuated form. The regression coefficients are similar for both surveys and suggest that a little bit of education has little effect on lowering mortality (the coefficients for education categories "none" and 1-5 years are similar for both the mother and the father), that education of the mother and of the father have independent effects of similar size, that there is no clear evidence that the relation between child mortality and paternal education has changed in the recent past and perhaps that maternal education of between 6 and 11 years has a slightly greater effect on reducing child mortality than paternal education in the same range.

TABLE 42. RESULTS OF MULTIVARIATE REGRESSION, JORDAN, 1976 AND 1981

	1976 Survey		*1981 Survey*	
Variable	*Mean*	*Regression coefficient*	*Mean*	*Regression coefficient*
MORT	1.031	..	1.132	..
Mother's education				
None	0.547	0.402[a]	0.456	0.505[a]
1-5 years	0.151	0.398	0.183	0.486[a]
6-8 years	0.200	0.053	0.194	0.247[a]
9-11 years	0.048	0.070	0.090	0.114[a]
12 years or more	0.054	b	0.077	b
Father's education				
None	0.141	0.354[a]	0.191	0.392[a]
1-5 years	0.279	0.383[a]	0.221	0.362[a]
6-8 years	0.296	0.293[a]	0.255	0.299[a]
9-11 years	0.121	0.078	0.140	0.216[a]
12 years or more	0.163	b	0.193	b
Constant	-	0.638	-	0.506
R^2	-	0.028	-	0.026
Number of cases (births)	-	9 771	-	33 154

Source: Kenneth Hill, "Jordan", in *Child Mortality in Developing Countries: Socio-economic Differentials, Trends and Implications* (United Nations publication, Sales No. E.91.XIII.13), table 30.

[a]Significantly different from zero at 5 per cent level.

[b]Reference category.

Table 43 shows regression coefficients for models including residence and education variables; models 2 and 4 include, in addition, occupation indicators. In comparison with table 42, the child-mortality reducing effects of both maternal and paternal education are substantially lessened in both magnitude and significance, the reduction being somewhat larger for paternal education than for maternal education.

It is sometimes suggested in the literature that important interactions exist between place of residence

TABLE 43. REGRESSION COEFFICIENTS FOR MODELS INCLUDING RESIDENCE AND EDUCATION, AND INCLUDING AND EXCLUDING OCCUPATION VARIABLES, JORDAN, 1976 AND 1981

Variable	*1976*				*1981*			
	Model 1	*Model 2*	*Model 3*	*Model 4*	*Model 1*	*Model 2*	*Model 3*	*Model 4*
Education (years) ...	*Mother*		*Father*		*Mother*		*Father*	
None	0.601[a]	0.398[a]	0.596[a]	0.376[a]	0.792[a]	0.778[a]	0.721[a]	0.693[a]
12 or more	b	b	b	b	b	b	b	b
	1976				*1981*			
Constant	0.534	0.810	0.629	0.925	0.523	0.493	0.679	0.590

Source: Kenneth Hill, "Jordan", in *Child Mortality in Developing Countries: Socio-economic Differentials, Trends and Implications* (United Nations publication, Sales No. E.91.XIII.13), table 31.
[a]Coefficient is significantly different from zero at 5 per cent level.
[b]Reference category.

and other variables included in child mortality models. In order to examine this issue in the case of Jordan, the basic model shown in table 42 was applied for urban and rural areas separately. For these applications, separate urban or rural estimates of child mortality, obtained from proportions dead of children ever born to currently married women classified by duration of marriage, were used to compute the dependant variable. If important interactions exist, one should expect to see substantial differences between urban and rural coefficients. The coefficients are shown in table 44. A number of points arise from table 44. First, the

TABLE 44. SUMMARY RESULTS OF MULTIVARIATE REGRESSIONS, JORDAN, 1976 AND 1981

Variable	*1976 Survey regression coefficient*		*1981 Survey regression coefficient*	
	Urban	*Rural*	*Urban*	*Rural*
MORT	0.979	1.018	1.176	1.022
$_5q_0$	0.091	0.113	0.069	0.097
Mother's education				
None	0.379[a]	0.897	0.557[a]	0.335[a]
1-5 years	0.377[a]	0.999	0.515[a]	0.343[a]
6-8 years	0.043	0.539	0.279[a]	0.086
9-11 years	0.087	0.181	0.122[a]	0.049
12 or more years	b	b	b	b
Father's education				
None	0.311[a]	0.378[a]	0.395[a]	0.398[a]
1-5 years	0.401[a]	0.333[a]	0.361[a]	0.381[a]
6-8	0.306[a]	0.277[a]	0.349[a]	0.223[a]
9-11 years	0.008	0.411[a]	0.155[a]	0.366[a]
12 or more years	b	b	b	b
Constant	0.727	0.002	0.461	0.775
R^2	0.026	0.029	0.030	0.014
Number of cases (births)	7 355	2 416	23 277	9 877

Source: Kenneth Hill, "Jordan", in *Child Mortality in Developing Countries: Socio-economic Differentials, Trends and Implications* (United Nations publication, Sales No. E.91.XIII.13), table 32.
[a]Significantly different from zero at 5 per cent level.
[b]Reference category.

1976 rural model has a negative constant, indicating negative child mortality for the reference group of women. The number of women in this model with high education is probably so low that the regression fit has been distorted. Secondly, the effects of maternal education show no clear pattern for both 1976 and 1981; in 1976, maternal education appears to be more protective of children in rural areas than in urban, but in 1981 the opposite is the case. Thirdly, for paternal education, there does seem to be a pattern; in urban areas, paternal education seems to be protective for nine or more years of schooling, whereas in rural areas there is little difference by level of schooling until 12 or more years.

One further interaction was examined, that between maternal and paternal education. The specific question considered was whether a large positive or negative difference in education between fathers and mothers reduced the overall effect of education on child mortality. Two dummy variables were specified, one which would be zero unless the mother had an educational level at least two categories higher than that of the father, and the second that would be zero unless the father had an education level at least two categories higher than that of the mother. These two variables were included with the variables found to be consistent and often significant, namely, residence, mother's education and father's education. Results are shown in table 45. In 1981, large differentials in

TABLE 45. REGRESSION COEFFICIENTS FOR MODELS, INCLUDING RESIDENCE, MATERNAL EDUCATION, PATERNAL EDUCATION AND SPOUSAL EDUCATIONAL DIFFERENTIAL, JORDAN, 1976 AND 1981

	Regression coefficients	
Variable	*1976 Survey*	*1981 Survey*
Residence		
Rural	0.132[a]	0.075[a]
Urbanl	b	b
Mother's education		
None	0.532[a]	0.325[a]
1-5 years	0.478[a]	0.343[a]
6-8 years	0.123	0.131[a]
9-11 years	0.064	0.056
12 or more years	b	b
Father's education		
None	0.159	0.611[a]
1-5 years	0.174	0.555[a]
6-8 years	0.220a	0.377[a]
9-11 years	0.026	0.260[a]
12 or more years	b	b
Mother with greater education		
2 or more categories	-0.319	0.071
Other	b	b
Father with greater education		
2 or more categories	-0.205[a]	0.212[a]
Other	b	b
Constant	0.541	0.437
R^2	0.027	0.024

Source: Kenneth Hill, "Jordan", in *Child Mortrality in Developing Countries*: *Socio-economic Differentials, Trends and Implications* (United Nations publication, Sales No. E.91.XIII.13), table 33.

[a]Significantly different from zero at 5 per cent level.

[b]Reference category.

educational levels between spouses do appear to be associated with higher child mortality risks, especially when the male has the higher level of education. Using the 1976 data set, on the other hand, large educational differentials between spouses are associated with lower child mortality risks. The picture is thus not consistent, and given the problems of multicollinearity involved, no conclusions can be drawn.

Identification of child survival risk groups

The regression models estimated in the preceding section can be used to identify risk groups for children according to the characteristics of their families. In identifying risk groups, the study focuses on two characteristics, place of residence and education of mother, in order to define risk cells with numbers of children in the samples of 100 or more. Table 46 shows risks expressed in terms of the probability of dying by age 5, ${}_5q_0$, obtained by converting the value of MORT estimated by the relevant regression model into a ${}_5q_0$ on the basis of the average value of ${}_5q_0$, the average value of MORT and the regression coefficients and constant.[5] The risk categories used are: very high, more than 30 per cent above the national average; high, from 11 to 30 per cent above the national average; average, from 10 per cent below to 10 per cent above the national average; low, from 11 to 30 per cent below the national average; and very low, more than 30 per cent below the national average.

Using this classification, there are no very high-risk mothers or children. The high-risk group in 1976 consists of children born to mothers in rural areas with less than completed primary education, constituting 19 per cent of both children born and women. For 1981, however, this category of high risk also includes the children of women in urban areas with no education, raising the size of the group to 64 per cent of children and 52 per cent of mothers. The average risk group is made up of children of the remaining women with less than completed primary education. The low-risk group consists of the children of rural women with less than completed secondary education and of urban women with 6-8 years of education, accounting for about 20 per cent of all women, but only about 14 per cent of children. The very low risk group is made up of the children of women with completed secondary education or tertiary education, plus those of urban women with 9-11 years of education; the children in this category comprise only some 6-9 per cent of all children.

The results given in table 46 show that there are large differentials in child mortality risks between different segments of the population of Jordan. However, these differentials are not as large as those found in some other parts of the developing world. For example, in 1976, the risk of death by age 5 for children born to women in the most disadvantaged group, rural women with no education, was about 2.5 times that of the most advantaged group, women with 12 or more years of education living in urban areas. It should also be noted that the actual risk of dying by age 5 for children in the most disadvantaged group in 1981 was fewer than 100 per 1,000 live births, a relatively low figure for a developing country. On the other hand, structural factors have resulted in redistribution of children within risk groups, such that the high-risk group in 1981 included 64 per cent of all children born, an increase from only about 20 per cent in 1976.

As a conclusion from the Jordan study, the most interesting feature of education results is that a small amount of education, either of fathers or of mothers, has little effect on child mortality risks; not until primary school has been completed does education reduce risks appreciably. This finding suggest that substitutes for formal education, such as adult literacy campaigns, may have little effect on child survival. The child mortality models account for very little of variance of the mortality indicator being used, but this result is to be expected given the characteristics of the mortality indicator.

The results of the analysis show the existence of substantial child mortality differentials by urban or rural residence and parental education. The child of a woman with no education living in a rural area, for example, is estimated to have between two and three times the risk of dying of the child of a woman with completed secondary education living in urban area. The differentials in child mortality risks do not appear to have changed appreciably in the recent past; each risk group appears to have experienced approximately equal percentage declines in child mortality.

TABLE 46. CATEGORIES OF RELATIVE CHILD MORTALITY RISK BY RISK FACTOR, JORDAN, 1976 AND 1981

Residence and mother's education	1976 Survey $_5q_0$	1976 Survey Percentage of total: Births	1976 Survey Percentage of total: Women	1981 Survey $_5q_0$	1981 Survey Percentage of total: Births	1981 Survey Percentage of total: Women
A. Very high risk[a]						
	None	None	None	None	None	None
B. High risk[b]						
Rural None	0.116	18	17	0.095	23	20
Rural 1-5 years	0.115	1	2	0.089	3	3
Urban None	..	..	..	0.089	38	29
C. Average risk[c]						
Urban None	0.102	50	40	..	..	..
Urban 1-5 years	0.101	11	11	0.084	13	12
D. Low risk[d]						
Rural 6-8 years	0.079	1	2	0.068	2	3
Rural 9-11 years	0.071	<1	<1	0.054	1	1
Urban 6-8 years	0.065	12	17	0.063	11	14
E. Very low risk						
Rural 12 or more years	0.062	<1	<1	0.041	<1	<1
Urban 9-11 years	0.057	3	5	0.048	5	8
Urban 12 or more years	0.048	3	6	0.036	4	9

Source: Kenneth Hill, "Jordan", in *Child Mortality in Developing Countries: Socio-economic Differentials, Trends and Implications* (United Nations publication, Sales No. E.91.XIII.13), table 34.

[a]More than 30 per cent above the national average.

[b]11-30 per cent above the national average.

[c]90-110 per cent of the national average.

[d]11-30 per cent below the national average.

[e]More than 30 per cent below the national average.

Notes

[1]The analysis of differentials is restricted to births that occurred in the 10-year period preceding the survey, from 1970 to 1979. This restriction was applied to minimize the bias that arises from the truncation effect. Also, the use of the most recent data minimizes the problem of memory and recall laps that may be existing in the data.

[2]The approach followed is that of Sullivan, Adlakha and Suchindran (1983). Results are presented separately for the neonatal, post-neonatal, infant and childhood age intervals. For each age interval, a logistic regression model was used to investigate the effect of the selected factors on mortality.

[3]The Central Agency for Public Mobilisation and Statistics in Egypt conducted the Pregnancy Wastage and Infant Mortality Survey in three rounds, 1979, 1981 and 1983, in collaboration with the United Nations Fund for Population Activities (UNFPA).

[4]The basic form of the model is:

$$MORT = b_o + b_i . x_i + e$$

Where MORT is the exposure-standardized indicator of mortality experience at the individual level, b_o is the intercept (the level of MORT when all x_i are equal to zero); and b_i is the incremental effect on MORT over b_o of having mother with characteristic x_i, for n such characteristic. MORT is a continuous variable with a mean of approximately 1, whereas the x_i are all categorical variables, the possession or otherwise of the characteristic.

[5]The mortality risks shown in table 44 were calculated from regression equations including only the two variables, maternal education and residence, shown in the table. The coefficients for the equations were as follows:

Variable	*Jordan Fertility Survey, 1976*	*Jordan Demographic Survey, 1981*
Constant	0.534	0.523
Residence	0.154	0.084
Education 1-5	0.101	0.187
Education 6-8	0.019	0.398
Education 9-11	0.582	0.708
Education 12 or more	0.601	0.792

References

Ashy, Hosni Soliman M., and others (1983). *Levels, Trends and Differentials of Infant and Child Mortality in Egypt: Proceedings of the International Conference on Fertility in Egypt.* Organized by the Central Agency for Public Mobilisation and Statistics and the International Statistical Institute (World Fertility Survey), 20-22 December. Cairo: Central Agency for Public Mobilisation and Statistics.

Behm, Hugo (1987). The determinants of child survival: an analytical frame of reference. Paper prepared for the United Nations Meeting on the International Collaboration Study of Geographic and Socio-economic Differentials in Early-age Mortality, New York, 7-9 December.

Egypt, Central Agency for Public Mobilisation and Statistics (1983). *The Egyptian Fertility Survey, 1980*, vols. II and III. Cairo.

_________ (1987a). *Maternal Health and Infant Mortality in Egypt.* Cairo.

_________ (1987b). *Pregnancy Wastage and Infant Mortality, Egypt, 1979-1983.* Cairo.

Jordan (1979). *Jordan Fertility Survey, 1976: Principal Report.* Amman: Department of Statistics.

_________ (1983). *Jordan Demographic Survey, 1981: Principal Report.* Amman: Department of Statistics.

Harrell, F. (1980). *The Logist Procedure: SAS Supplement Library Users Guide*, 1980 ed. Carry, North Carolina: SAS Institute.

Hill, Kenneth (1991). Jordan. In *Child Mortality in Developing Countries: Socio-economic Differentials, Trends and Implications.* New York: United Nations. Sales No. E.91.XIII.13.

Sullivan, J. M., A. L. Adlakha and C. M. Suchindran (1983). Levels, time trends and determinants of infant and child mortality in Jordan. Paper presented at the Annual Meeting of the Population Association of America, Pittsburgh, Pennsylvania, 14-16 April.

United Nations (1985). *Socio-economic Differentials in Child Mortality in Developing Countries.* Population Studies, No. 97, Sales No. E.85.XIII.7.

_________, Economic and Social Commission for Western Asia (1989). *Infant and Child Mortality in Western Asia.* Baghdad.

XXIII. PROMOTION OF WOMEN AS LEADERS IN POPULATION AND DEVELOPMENT

*Peggy Curlin**

In much of the developing world today, to be a woman is to be at risk for lifelong poverty, poor health, illiteracy and premature death. The low social, economic and political status of women is the context in which a lifetime of deprivation is played out.

Not only do women constitute the majority of the poor adults in the world, they lack the resources and power to change what to many must seem to be their destiny. Women own only 1 per cent of the land and earn just 10 per cent of the total world income. Yet, they perform 60 per cent of the work and in some areas grow 60-80 per cent of the food. Women are the sole breadwinners in from one fourth to one third of the families in the world. In every country, households headed by women are the poorest.

Throughout the world, women's health is viewed almost exclusively in relation to their child-bearing role. Yet, more than two thirds of pregnant women in developing countries receive no formal prenatal care, and at least 500,000 women die each year from pregnancy-related causes. Moreover, for every maternal death, there are more than 100 women that suffer complications that threaten their life and the life of their child. This means that more than 62 million women annually—roughly 40 per cent of all women pregnant at any given time—suffer pregnancy-related complications before, during and after birth, including haemorrhage, sepsis, anaemia, hypertension and obstructed labour.

A woman's health and well-being are compromised from birth by the fact of gender. The overriding preference for male children leads to poor nutrition for girls, limited or no educational opportunities and a host of more subtle discriminatory actions that together deny girls a sense of their own worth and the option to fulfil their potential beyond being a wife and mother. The gender gap in education has a devastating effect on the aspirations and opportunities of young women. Of the 949 million illiterate people in the world, almost two thirds are women. In all of the lowest income countries, women's literacy lags behind men's, in most cases by a significant percentage; and far fewer girls than boys attend school.

The costs of failing to make significant improvements in the health, economic and educational status of women are high: uncontrolled population growth; high infant and child mortality; weakened economies; a deteriorating environment and a poorer quality of life for all. As the 1992 edition of the *State of World Population* says, "There can be no sustainable development for anyone without development for women" (UNFPA, 1993, p. 13). The report also states:

> "The connection between the status of women and the pace of development is becoming increasingly clear. Economic growth and improvement in the quality of life have been fastest in those areas where women have highest status, and slowest where they face the greatest disadvantages" (UNFPA, 1992, p. 13).

The Center for Development and Population Activities (CEDPA), in recognition of the position of women at the nexus of all sectors of development, focuses on the empowerment of women at all levels of society to be full partners in development. Research and experience show that women must gain control of their fertility to be effective partners in development; to achieve this control, they must have adequate health, education and income-generating opportunities and services. Therefore, the CEDPA model of development is a comprehensive model of training, local action and technical support that targets family planning, health, and human development services for women as the most effective avenues to foster change at the community level. To make the maximum

*President, Center for Development and Population Activities, Washington, D.C.

impact and to provide services to those most in need, CEDPA focuses on the pivotal role women play as leaders and potential leaders of family planning, health and development programmes.

Decisions about conception and contraception take place in a social, economic and cultural context. When the status and education of women are higher, use of family planning is higher and fertility is lower. Fertility is related to all aspects of a woman's life—education, health, employment and the well-being of children. CEDPA was among the first agencies to promote the linkage of women's reproductive health and other sectors of development in specific programmatic ways: by training women to be policy makers in family planning and other health and human services sectors, by supporting programmes in income-generation and health to sustain and promote family planning services at the community level, by linking family planning services to development programmes, and by supporting programmes for adolescent girls and boys to form attitudes and types of behaviour that will be conducive to delayed pregnancy and increased options.

The multilevel CEDPA development model links training and action at the community level and promotes the formulation and implementation of policies favourable to women. The model is based on the concept that trained managers are a country's best development resource, the catalyst that brings policies, programmes, resources and people into action to reach a goal. More than 3,600 professionals from developing countries in the fields of health, human service, and family planning have participated in the CEDPA management training programmes since 1975. They form a worldwide network with a high level of commitment to the mission and goals of CEDPA to empower women. Training is followed by support of selected projects developed by training participants, called "alumnae". The community-level, community-run projects supported by CEDPA are run by women and are focused on women. They address problems and needs identified by those experiencing them at the grass roots. As a result of this basis in the community, CEDPA projects are well targeted to needs, make efficient use of resources and are adaptable to changing conditions. CEDPA provides resources and technical assistance to promote the success of projects, including technical transfer, institution-building support, training of trainers and development of local and regional networks of CEDPA alumnae.

Recent studies of the CEDPA training model concluded that it is an effective tool to empower women to become change agents. An evaluation of the CEDPA training programme in 1990 at the request of the United States Agency for International Development, Office of Women in Development, found that CEDPA graduates went back to their country with renewed confidence to undertake larger tasks and issues, confidence that led to greater productivity and skill in the work setting and to further responsibility and promotion. Further, the replication throughout the world of CEDPA training programmes "could result in graduates having a national impact on development in many countries.

In 1991, a study sponsored by the Interregional and Non-Governmental Organizations Programmes Branch of the United Nations Population Fund (UNFPA) reported that training graduates assume positions of greater leadership and that training results in institutional growth and contributes to national change. The survey of one third of CEDPA training graduates during the period 1986-1989 found that 85 per cent increased their professional responsibilities after training and 90 per cent expanded their professional network. Two thirds instituted new programmes in their organizations that they developed during training and 62 per cent applied management strategies learned during training to improve their organizations. It is clear that CEDPA management training is a practical means to implement change.

With an increasing number of CEDPA alumnae in senior-level positions and a growing network of alumnae, policy-level activities have been taking place that reflect the CEDPA philosophy of empowerment of women as change agents. In 1987, with the sponsorship of UNFPA, women leaders from Southern Asian countries gathered at Kathmandu, Nepal, for a conference on options for a Better Life for Young Women. They recommended that the plight of girls in the region be made a priority. Heeding their request, the South Asian Association for Regional Cooperation declared 1990 to be the Year of the Girl Child, marking a major achievement for CEDPA alumnae in the region. The Association subsequently declared the 1990s to be the Decade of the Girl Child. The declarations have generated a number of studies and publications documenting the disadvantages of females in Southern Asia. In order to ensure follow-up action, CEDPA supported establishment of a Policy Advisory Group of CEDPA alumnae and conference delegates.

A major strength of the CEDPA development model is that it is replicable at the community and country levels. In India, Prerana, a private voluntary organization on the outskirts of New Delhi, is involved in community development with a strong emphasis on community participation. Following participation in CEDPA training programmes, Prerana linked with CEDPA in 1983 as Prerana Associate CEDPA. CEDPA provides funding for community-level projects and assists Prerana in developing proposals and monitoring and evaluating project activities. Prerana now plays a role for organizations in India similar to the role that CEDPA once played for Prerana. Serving as an extension of CEDPA in the region, Prerana helps small but effective groups in remote areas to respond to community needs. In Nepal, a similar project has evolved. The CEDPA Nepal Country Office was established by a CEDPA alumna and now has an active training programme for managers; it supports and monitors 10 projects that integrate health, income-generation, literacy, family planning and other services directed to women.

With its focus on women as leaders and organizations run by and for women, CEDPA works in partnership with women throughout the world. CEDPA has pioneered a women-to-women approach to development. This approach involves women at all levels of project design and implementation and often targets women and children as the main beneficiaries of programmes. The women-to-women approach has been remarkably effective in family planning. In the traditional societies where CEDPA has concentrated its efforts, women may not be comfortable discussing family planning and may be reluctant to visit a health-care professional for these services. In India, Mali, Turkey and elsewhere, CEDPA has implemented innovative programmes in which women family planning motivators from local communities discuss family planning options with potential clients in the privacy of their homes. This approach is effective in overcoming barriers to family planning acceptance, especially among low-parity women. CEDPA-supported projects employ a women-to-women approach that is sensitive to traditional values, stresses education and counselling, and builds private sector partnerships with development institutions that include family planning among a variety of services.

For example, the Gujarat State Crime Prevention Trust at Ahmedabad, India, is a non-governmental organization established in 1979 to improve the quality of life in the urban slums through social welfare programmes, including adult education centres, preschools and day-care centres, and counselling centres. The Trust developed a women-to-women programme that has been successful in reaching the isolated and illiterate women of the slums through outreach workers that are members of the same ethnic groups as those in the community. The project has increased the use of contraception in the community from 12 to 61 per cent, largely as a result of the women-to-women approach.

The Gujarat project and others like it in Africa, Asia, Eastern Europe, and Latin America and the Caribbean are proof that sensitive community-based approaches to population and development can increase the use of family planning and enable women to improve their life and the life of their family. The knowledge exists to overcome the crippling barriers that keep women trapped and perpetuate the tragic cycle of poverty, illiteracy and sickness. Now this knowledge must be translated into action.

REFERENCE

United Nations Population Fund (1992). *The State of World Population, 1997: A World in Balance*. New York.

Part Seven

LINKAGES BETWEEN WOMEN'S ECONOMIC ACTIVITY AND POPULATION DYNAMICS

XXIV. WOMEN'S ECONOMIC ACTIVITIES AND FERTILITY: OVERVIEW OF THE INTERACTIONS AND POLICY IMPLICATIONS

Marcela Villarreal[*]

The interactions between women's participation in the labour force and fertility have been addressed for some time in the demographic and economic literature (e.g., Bumpass and Westoff, 1970; Collver and Langlois, 1962; Jaffe and Azumi, 1960; Pratt and Whelpton, 1958; Standing, 1978), not only out of sheer academic interest but also because of their strong policy implications. In recent years there have been important conceptual and methodological contributions that have helped to explain the nature of the relation and the array of factors that condition it, shedding new light on how to approach it for policy and action purposes. Whereas much effort was once dedicated to the assessment of causality—that is, whether fertility causes changes in actual or intended labour force participation or vice versa—and to the determination of the direction of the relation, attention should now focus on narrowing down the contexts and precise circumstances in which the relation holds and can be acted upon.

Concomitant with an historical increase in the levels of women's participation in the labour force, especially in modern sector occupations, there have been significant decreases in fertility that have led to the postulation of a relation between women's work and their demographic behaviour. The relation could operate in both directions, for women that work or intend to work may want to limit their fertility in order to be able to do so without role conflicts, but at the same time women that have many children may experience additional pressure to enter the labour force to produce additional income for their maintenance. Moreover, women with few or no children might have an additional incentive to engage in the labour force to develop non-familial roles.

Whereas findings from developed countries are concordant in showing a negative relation, with working women consistently having smaller completed family sizes than non-working women (see Kasarda, Billy and West, 1986), studies carried out in less developed regions document a negative or positive relation or even the absence of a relation, between female labour force participation and fertility (for a review of more than 50 such studies, see Standing, 1978. Far from presenting inconsistent or contradictory results, this evidence brings to the fore the complex nature of the relation and underlines the importance of understanding the factors that condition its occurrence.

In recent years, there have been a number of theoretical and methodological developments that help explain the nature of the relation. Among them are the concept of the status of women, the appraisal of the importance of social, economic and geographical heterogeneity, the knowledge of the undercounting of women's work, the acknowledgment of the relevancy of using the household as a unit of analysis, the awareness of and means to measure the segmentation of markets, and the development and/or application of techniques such as two-stage least squares (2SLS) and event-history analysis. Sections A-J examine some of the most relevant factors that influence the fertility-work relation in the context of a developing country. Section K then provides an overview of the policy implications that emerge from such analysis.

[*]Regional Adviser for Population, Women and Target Group Policies, Programa Regional del Empleo para América Latina y el Caribe International Labour Organization, Santiago, Chile.

A. STATUS OF WOMEN

The status of women is, perhaps, the one concept that has contributed most in recent times to the understanding of population dynamics while providing an effective means for action on demographic variables. In this sense, it constitutes a true conceptual leap.

The demographic implications of the status of women began to attract attention in the mid-1960s (Blake, 1965; Ridley, 1968; Dixon, 1975). Since then, a wealth of literature has focused on the theoretical links of women's status with fertility and mortality (Mason, 1984; Anker, Buvinic, Youssef, 1982; Safilios-Rothschild, 1982, 1985a and 1985b; Deere, Humphries and León de Leal, 1982), and empirical studies illustrating such links have proliferated (e.g., Safilios-Rothschild, 1985a and 1985b; Cain, 1984; Sathar and others, 1988).

Participation in the labour force has been singled out as the most important determinant of women's status (Javillonar and others, 1979; Safilios-Rothschild, 1985a and 1985b), for it can give women an independent source of income (Cain, Khanam and Nahar, 1979), thus enhancing domestic autonomy and producing a more egalitarian distribution of power in the household whenever women have access to and control over their earnings. Safilios-Rothschild (1985a) argues that the most effective way to increase women's status is to increase their share of paid employment.

An improvement of women's status arising from their labour market insertion depends upon the type of job to which they have access. Although modern sector or professional occupations do provide sources of income that enable an increase in independence and autonomy, insertion constricted by economic necessity in low-productivity jobs can have the effect of decreasing status, for it entails a double work burden and increases the number of hours worked while providing but a meagre income. Although economic development may increase the share of women in modern occupations, evidence showing a growing proportion of women in the informal sector in the developing world indicates that economic development does not guarantee, *per se,* an increase in women's status.

Closely associated with labour force participation is education, another of the core building blocks of women's status. A high educational attainment is in fact related to entry into the labour market into a status-enhancing job. By increasing women's opportunity costs, education provides a further incentive to enter and remain in the labour force. Moreover, by developing intellectual capacity, education gives women a sense of worth and achievement and allows them to interact more equally with men, contributing to bridge the gap between the genders. It supplies varied sources of information and motivates women to develop interests other than child-bearing (Germain, 1975; Holsinger and Kasarda, 1976; Rosen and LaRaia, 1972).

Another central component of women's status is equality between the sexes. In a general sense, such equality refers to access to and control over resources, in all spheres of society. The legal aspect is essential for it sets the basis for equitable access to resources, including land and property.

Both education and participation in the labour force provide environments where inequality can be reduced. Furthermore, higher equality in education contributes to lower inequality in the workplace. Societies (and couples) in which relation between the genders are more egalitarian tend to have lower levels of fertility (Caldwell, 1982). Women's autonomy, self-esteem, economic independence and feelings of worth, achievement and control over their bodies are associated with lower fertility and more consistent and successful fertility regulation (Dixon-Mueller, 1989; Oppong, 1982a; Eriksen, Yancey and Eriksen, 1979; Scanzoni, 1975; Rainwater, 1965).

The components of women's status are closely related among themselves and each of them independently as well as jointly bear a strong relation with fertility. Policies to increase women's status will have a direct effect on the reduction of fertility, while providing the context for a negative work-fertility relation.

B. Poverty conditions

It is only fairly recently that the methodologies to quantify poverty gaps have become widely employed in economic and sociological research and in Government plans endeavouring to eradicate extreme poverty (Altimir, 1978; Kaztman, 1988; United Nations, ECLAC, 1991a and 1991b). Such methodologies are powerful tools for a fuller understanding of the dynamics of developing country situations.

It is well known that fertility is higher among low-income groups.[1] Likewise, it is the poorest women that bear the most acute problems associated with their participation in the labour force. They are more likely to be unemployed or to be employed in the lowest paying, lowest productivity, most unstable jobs. In fact, data for Latin America and the Caribbean show that participation rates among destitute women were significantly lower than those for other poor or non-poor women.[2] Among men the same holds true but in much smaller proportions.

Poor women's low labour-market participation rates arise from several factors: the domestic work burden, which is greater among poorer women for they do not have access to domestic help or to home appliances that save labour; the greater difficulty of caring for children in the absence of adequate child-care facilities; the greater number of children frequently present in the poorest households; the higher incidence of open unemployment and of hidden unemployment due to discouragement; the weak incentive to participate provided by the low levels of remuneration available for low educational attainment and poor training skills; and the gap between women's and men's earnings for similar type of work (Villarreal, 1991). For destitute women, working outside the home can entail a high opportunity cost due to the double work burden that results and the emotional or financial costs of leaving children unattended.

The differences in economic activities among women of diverse strata, as well as the differences in their demographic responses call attention to the variations in the relation between labour force participation and fertility by strata, as well as to the different needs in policy orientations. For example, a study in Bolivia that tested several work situations found that among the poorest women the largest fertility differential was between women that worked in the formal sector versus those working in the informal sector. Among non-poor women, the largest differential was between working versus non-working women (Villarreal, 1991). Creating employment in the modern sector for destitute women will have a greater fertility impact (on the women with the highest fertility) than simply opening job opportunities or targeting programmes in the informal sector.

Having more members and fewer resources, the demographic dynamics of poor households make them likelier to transmit their conditions of poverty on to the next generation (Uthoff, 1990).[3] Providing status-enhancing jobs for poor women has a twofold effect on the reduction of poverty: *(a)* it decreases their fertility, which will aid in breaking the intergenerational transmission of poverty; and *(b)* it offers an opportunity for the household to surmount the poverty line, for an additional adult income-earner increases the total household income per capita to levels above destitution.

C. Contextual heterogeneity

There are tremendous differences in the contexts in which women realize their productive and reproductive roles in the developing world. The context itself plays a part in the determination of the interaction between such roles. Caldwell (1980) shows the importance of the advent of mass education and the importance of the spread of Western values for a decline in fertility. The relation between women's work and fertility will take different shapes depending upon the cultural context and the stage of the demographic transition in which the country or region is at the time.

An extensive literature shows significant fertility differentials between urban and rural areas, socio-economic strata and ethnic origins. Labour force participation and other economic activities vary in their patterns among such groups (see, for example, Vlassoff, 1986; Alam and Casterline, 1984). By generating mobility among different settings, migration can be a factor in combining cultural contexts.

During the 1960s and 1970s, when the largest migration flows in Latin America and the Caribbean took place, a high proportion of the women living in the cities had been born in a rural area. The cultural setting for them was quite different from the current situation, in which a majority of Latin American and Caribbean women have been born and raised in an urban milieu. In such cases, the norms and values of the background may affect behaviour in fertility and/or work in spite of living in an urban area. There is a large heterogeneity present in third world societies. This heterogeneity may account for differences in demographic and/or labour responses and must be considered in policy formulation.

D. Undercounting of women's work

One of the most prominent obstacles to the assessment of a relation between women's participation in the labour market and their demographic responses is the accounting of women's economic activities. Women's work has been systematically undercounted (see Benería, 1982; Recchini de Lattes and Wainerman, 1986; Dixon-Mueller and Anker, 1988; Wainerman and Recchini de Lattes, 1981), especially in rural areas and in traditional activities such as those of the informal sector. These activities are precisely where ambivalent or inconclusive results with regard to the relation between women's work and fertility have been found. As Safilios-Rothschild (1977) points out, the very self-perception of working or not working may be directly related to the mother-wife role identification and thus bias the data for the work-fertility relation that is sought to be clarified.

Although data-collection techniques have been criticized (Anker, 1983) and improvements proposed for different data sources and regions (Wainerman, 1992; Anker and Anker, 1988), the lack of means and/or political commitment to add or change questionnaire items precludes the amelioration of the measurement of women's work. A better assessment of women's economic activities is needed both to increase the accuracy of national income accounts and to have an adequate knowledge basis to formulate realistic and efficient policy.

E. Household as unit of analysis

Early approaches to viewing demographic behaviour as a household response (Becker, 1981) assume the household to be a homogeneous and harmonious unit where rational decisions about fertility and other behaviour are made. Although this view is scarcely applicable to third world countries, where fertility responds to entirely different dynamics, focusing on the household rather than on the individual can prove to be a useful tool for both understanding and policy purposes. More than individual choice, fertility as well as labour force participation may reflect socio-economic structural characteristics as well as internal relationships between household members.

Understanding the relationships among different household members is essential for efficient policy purposes. For example, it has been documented that one of the most frequent reasons for poor Latin American women not to use modern contraceptive methods is their husband's objection. An effective family planning demand-raising policy should therefore direct awareness-creation efforts to husbands. Furthermore, as the proportion of female-headed households tends to increase sharply, along with their percentage among the poorest groups, these become a priority group for action purposes. Their demographic dynamics, as well as their labour insertion, is different from those of households headed by men and these households therefore have distinct policy needs.

F. Type of work

The type of work in which women engage is key to understanding the relation it bears to their fertility. The positive relation documented in the literature more frequently than not occur in rural settings (Standing, 1978), where the main occupations women engage in are agricultural.

The proportion of the labour force engaged in informal sector occupations increased strongly in Latin America and the Caribbean during the 1980s (PREALC, 1991) and other major area have also been registering upward trends in this regard. Throughout the developing world, women's participation in this sector is disproportionate and has been increasing more than that of men. In addition, women are also more likely to engage in unpaid family work. A United Nations study (1985), which separates modern and traditional jobs in 38 developing countries found significant fertility differentials by type of work. In spite of this evidence and of the characteristics of informal employment, in which role incompatibility between mothering and economic activity is minimized and women's status is not enhanced, this sector of the economy is rarely considered in the analyses of the relation between women's work and fertility.

The reasons for engaging in economic activity are related to the type of work. Women that work out of economic necessity are more likely to do so in lower status occupations and are more likely to have lower levels of education. On the contrary, women that work for personal fulfilment and satisfaction tend to belong to a higher economic stratum and to have higher levels of education. In this latter case, a strong negative relation between labour force participation and fertility is common, while in the former it is not certain.

Related to the reasons to work is the desire to do so. The literature has referred to this point as work commitment, suggesting that high commitment will limit a woman's number of children (Freedman, Whelpton and Campbell, 1959; Whelpton, Campbell and Patterson, 1966; Safilios-Rothschild, 1972; Tickamyer, 1979). Whereas the commitment focus may be relevant for explaining the contradictions in findings of studies relating women's work to fertility (Safilios-Rothschild, 1972), the approach of type of work offers an operational advantage in that it is easily measurable from available data sets.

Other variables that are related to the relation between women's work and fertility with respect to the type of work are the number of hours worked (full-time or part-time work) and the career possibilities available.

G. Role incompatibility

The time conflict that arises for a woman who has to care for children and to work is one of the main explanations that have been offered to understand the ways in which labour force participation can affect fertility or that fertility can affect labour-market behaviour (Stycos and Weller, 1967; Jaffe and Azumi, 1960). Role incompatibilities may rise from such time conflicts as well as from normative incongruities, i.e., when cultural preferences disapprove of working roles for mothers or married women (Kasarda, Billy and West, 1986).

Attitudes towards working mothers have been changing, especially in developed countries, and moving towards greater acceptance. Rising demands for female labour fostered a transition in women's economic roles and with it, a decline in the normative restrictions against married women's working (Oppenheimer, 1970 and 1973). In developing countries it has been documented that in conditions of economic need the financial contribution that women can make legitimizes their leaving the home and fosters the acceptance of women's non-familial roles (Safa, 1988; Benería and Roldán, 1988).

Where substitute child care is readily available or when women do not have to leave their homes to perform the economic activity, role incompatibility does not occur and thus does not condition the relation with fertility (Bean, Swicegood and King, 1985; Standing, 1983; Mason and David, 1971). As stated above, the type of work is closely related to the existence of role incompatibility. Whereas traditional agricultural or informal sector jobs can be performed while caring for children, modern sector occupations pose a conflict in both spatial and temporal terms.

The absence of child-care substitute caregivers (either familial or institutional) does create a conflict and may limit the number of children a woman has so that she can participate in the labour force and develop her career plans. In contrast, women that want large families may not enter or may drop out of the workforce in order to rear them.

Role incompatibility is related to socio-economic stratum, especially in developing countries where women from the middle class or above can find relatively inexpensive domestic help to harmonize the mother/worker roles, leading to substantially higher participation rates for them than for poor women (Harper, 1991). Both low-paying informal sector jobs and high-paying middle- or upper-class occupations can thus coincide in not generating a role incompatibility. In such cases, the relation with fertility is determined in stronger proportions by other factors, such as education.

Because status-enhancing jobs are frequently those incompatible with child-rearing, while occupations that do not enhance women's status tend to be compatible, it is likely that the crucial factor in accounting for the relation with fertility is status enhancement of work rather than role incompatibility.

H. Education

Educational attainment is strongly related to both fertility and labour force participation. Higher levels of education among women are directly related to reduced fertility as well as to increased participation in the workforce (Cochrane, 1979; Safilios-Rothschild, 1985a). The independent effect of education on fertility is among the strongest that has been documented in the literature, and operates once a certain threshold number of years in the educational system has been passed. Education has the important effect of delaying age at marriage, which is central to fertility determination for it shortens exposure to pregnancy. Likewise, participation in the labour force can also cause a delay in marriage, in particular when it responds to a desire to work for personal satisfaction. Moreover, education is associated with different timings for life cycle events related to fertility: highly educated women tend to have their first child at an older age and to have longer birth intervals (Marini, 1984; Rindfuss, Bumpass and St. John, 1980).

Education also exposes women to modern sex-role orientations (Kasarda, Billy and West, 1986), aids in development of psychological traits that favour the use of family planning methods and fosters more egalitarian relation between the genders (Caldwell, 1980; Villarreal, 1989).

Another aspect that is frequently alluded to in accounting for the relation between education, work and fertility is the opportunity cost (see Oppong, 1982b and 1983). Increased levels of education for women will raise their opportunity costs of foregoing employment. The higher the wage possibilities for a woman, the likelier she is to enter the labour force and to stay longer in it.

Lastly, educational attainment is closely connected to the type of work to which a woman can have access, which is in turn related to work commitment and role compatibility, as was seen before. Education is thus related directly to both fertility and labour force participation, constituting one of the most important mediating factors in the relation. Because it is essential in securing a status-enhancing job, it is a *sine qua non* for a negative work-fertility relation.

I. Family planning

Knowledge and practice of family planning is strongly related to higher levels of education and to labour force participation and, of course, to fertility. Although findings for both developed and developing countries report a positive association between education and use of contraceptives (Berent, 1982; Lightbourne, Singh and Green, 1982; Miró and Rath, 1965), the link between labour force participation and use of family planning is positive in developed countries (Blake, 1965; Davis, 1967) but not necessarily so in developing countries (Bamberger, del Negro and Gamble, 1976). In the latter countries, greater modern contraceptive use is associated with the type of job, much as role incompatibility also is. While occupations in the modern industrial sector that must be performed away from home are associated with a higher use of family planning, agricultural or informal sector jobs are not.

Both education and a modern sector job provide the environment, resources and incentives to learn about and use contraception by removing myths and misinformation concerning family planning and promoting awareness of the benefits of small families. They thus increase knowledge, desire and ability to practise family planning methods efficiently (Kasarda, Billy and West, 1986). Moreover, such methods aid in making fertility and work plans compatible. Education and participation in the modern sector labour force enhance women's status. Concomitantly, increased female status helps to expand and sustain family planning efforts (Oppong and Haavio-Mannila, 1979).

J. Methodological concerns

Unlike the relation between education and fertility, in which, in general, the former is mostly completed when the latter begins, fertility behaviour and labour force participation take place simultaneously, each one affecting decisions and actions in the other sequentially, with or without a time-lag. Methodologically, this situation poses a number of problems for, in the first place, the simultaneity of the relation requires a dynamic approach which is much more difficult to handle technically. Moreover, available data sets usually do not provide the necessary information for such analysis. Ideal data sets for this purpose are longitudinal (following the same respondents over their reproductive and productive lifetimes), but these sets are very costly and require an inordinate amount of time to complete. Some researchers have used sequential data (Gurak and Kritz, 1982), constructed from a one-time recollection. The advantages concerning explanatory power that this type of model offers offset the problems of recall errors that it entails. As awareness of the limitations of the static approach becomes widespread (Gurak and Kritz, 1982; Rosenzweig, 1976; West, 1980; Cramer, 1980), the use of a dynamic approach becomes essential (Kasarda, Billy and West, 1986).

While the technique of two-stage least squares (Smith-Lovin and Tickamyer, 1978) and simultaneous equation models (Magdalinos and Symeonidou, 1989) have been used to handle simultaneity, the ideal methodology to study the work-fertility relation is event-history analysis (see Tuma and Hannan, 1984). The shortcoming of the latter methodology is its data constraints.

The choice of variables to measure fertility and labour force participation involves many problems. Most current measures of women's work lead to the undercounting of their economic activity, especially in developing countries. In addition, most studies use data on current employment status, which may have little or no relation with work history, and it is such history and not current status that bears a strong relation with demographic behaviour.

Information on other work variables held to be at the core of the work-fertility relation is scarcely ever gathered. Frequently used data sources, such as household surveys and censuses, do not touch upon them. Such is the case for commitment to work, motivation, involvement and sex-role orientation (Kasarda, Billy and West, 1986).

With regard to fertility, the most frequent measure is the woman's number of live births up to the moment of the survey. Because this measure says nothing of completed fertility (unless the woman is past child-bearing age), methodological problems arise and spurious findings may result concerning the work-fertility relation. Event-history analysis is the only method to date that makes a provision for this case by developing a way to deal with right-censored events.

K. Policy implications

The current level of knowledge about women's work-fertility relation, although certainly incomplete, has a number of important policy implications. Policy should be approached both from global and sectoral perspectives, as well as at the programme level. Global policy, pursuing an overall goal to integrate population and development aspects, should enhance the synergy resulting from mutually supportive actions in population and other development sectors (Sadik, 1989). At the global level, an integrated effort to reduce gender inequality in all spheres is needed. The improvement of women's access to and control over social resources demands actions of different nature: *(a)* to eliminate institutionalized discrimination including the right to own property and land; *(b)* to ensure equality of opportunity in the access to high-status jobs and equal pay for equal jobs; (c) to value women's work and activities and to make women legitimate recipients of social policy benefits; *(d)* to ensure women's representation in power and decision-making positions. All these actions are related to the enhancement of the status of women, a goal that should be incorporated in all action programmes and plans, not only because its improvement constitutes a development goal in and of itself but also due to its effects on lowering fertility and child mortality.

Providing status-enhancing jobs for poor women is a powerful tool to contribute to eradication of poverty, both because of its effect on lowering fertility and thus in diminishing the intergenerational transmission of poverty and because the additional income can pull the household out of poverty. As the number of poor women with access to such jobs augments, the country will increase its chances of reducing the proportion of its population living below the poverty line. For this purpose, Governments should strive to offer equal opportunities to women for access to full-time formal sector jobs with decision-making possibilities and career development opportunities.

Training for women should likewise be geared to modern sector jobs. Because such jobs are incompatible with child-bearing, the effect on fertility will be stronger than promoting jobs that do not impose that restriction. Educational scholarships and employment training should centre on skills that allow entrance and foster remaining in the modern sector (Harper, 1991).

The marked difference in women's labour force participation rates by socio-economic stratum calls attention to the need to address such diversity and its causes explicitly in policy design. Adequate child care, be it institutional or community-based, is essential to boost the poorest women's access to paid employment in status-enhancing jobs. Other measures to encourage poor women's incorporation in the labour market are training and remuneration policies.

When the social and economic consequences of the incorporation of women, especially poor women, into paid employment are fully grasped, child care will be seen as a social necessity and not purely the responsibility of individual women. Regulations on the provision of child care should explicitly avoid discriminatory consequences for women's work. In the developing world, some Governments have passed legislation requiring businesses that employ more than a certain number of women to build a day-care centre. This type of legislation may act as a hindrance to employing women because it raises the costs of the female labour force. Day-care facility regulations should thus cover all workers.

A comprehensive wage policy can help to intensify the fertility deterrent effect from the labour market (Harper, 1991). The larger the wage gap between the genders, the earlier women marry (Smith, 1981), the larger their completed family size and the less they participate in the labour force (Sprague, 1988; Semyonov, 1980). Eliminating gender inequalities in labour force returns constitutes one essential step to approaching equality in the society and is central not only to advance changes in fertility but to the development process itself.

At the sectoral level, efforts to reduce differences between the sexes in educational attainment, as well as to ensure that women shall complete at least a minimum threshold number of years in the system, will have strong and direct effects on fertility and on women's labour force participation. Moreover, it will have a bearing on the work-fertility relation by producing the conditions in which it is negative. Increasing levels of education among women is the necessary ground for the efficiency of policies to foster status-enhancing female employment.

Within the educational system, it is easier to overcome gender discrimination than in the labour market. However, if the elimination of discrimination is seen as a process, efforts undertaken within this realm will percolate into other social spheres and, with a lag, they can create more equitable gender conditions in the labour force.

For the design and implementation of policy and programmes that incorporate the interests of women, it is essential that development planners themselves receive training and education on the way to integrate women into the decision-making process, a feat that needs reinforcement in their own lives and attitudes to be achieved (Sadik, 1989).

Notes

[1]Recent studies report wide fertility differentials among the destitute poor. See, for example, Patiño, Caicedo de Cardozo and Ranjel (1985) for Colombia; Gabriel (1991) for Honduras; and Villarreal (1991) for Bolivia.

[2]A study using data for Bolivia found that while the labour force participation rate for destitute women was 21.7, that for other poor women was 35.2 and for non-poor, 48.1. Men's rates ranged from 52.5 to 68.9 (Villarreal, 1991). Similar findings have been reported for Chile, Colombia, Costa Rica, Honduras, Peru and Venezuela.

[3]Children from poor households have far less chance of acquiring the educational and nutritional profile that will secure them productive employment. They enter the labour force at earlier ages. Moreover, as Buvinic (1990) shows for a number of Latin American and Caribbean countries, daughters of single mothers have a higher probability of becoming pregnant teenagers.

References

Alam, I., and J. B. Casterline (1984). *Socio-economic Differentials in Recent Fertility.* World Fertility Survey Comparative Studies: Cross-national Summaries, No. 33. Voorburg, Netherlands: International Statistical Institute.

Altimir, O. (1978). *La dimensión de la pobreza en América Latina.* Cuadernos de la CEPAL, No. 17, Santiago, Chile.

Anker, Richard (1983). *Female Labour Force Activity in Developing Countries: A Critique of Current Data Collection Techniques.* Population and Labour Policies Programme Working Paper, No. 136. Geneva: International Labour Organization.

__________, and M. Anker (1988). *Improving the Measurement of Women's Participation in the Egyptian Labour Force: Results of a Methodological Study.* Population and Labour Policies Programme Working Paper, No. 163. Geneva: International Labour Organization.

Anker, Richard, Mayra Buvinic and Nadia H. Youssef, eds. (1982). *Women's Roles and Population Trends in the Third World.* London: Croom Helm.

Bamberger, M., M. del Negro and G. Gamble (1976). Employment and contraceptive practice in selected barrios of Caracas. In *Recent Empirical Findings on Fertility: Korea, Nigeria, Tunisia, Venezuela, Philippines.* Occasional Monograph Series, No. 7. Interdisciplinary Communications Program. Work Agreement Reports. Washington, D.C.: Smithsonian Institution.

Bean, F. D., Gray Swicegood and A. King (1985). Role incompatibility and the relationship between fertility and labour supply among Hispanic women. In *Hispanics in the U.S. Economy,* George J. Borjas and Marta Tienda, eds. Orlando, Florida: Academic Press.

Becker, Gary S. (1981). *A Treatise on the Family.* Cambridge, Massachusetts: Harvard University Press.

Benería, Lourdes (1982). Accounting for women's work. In *Women and Development: The Sexual Division of Labour in Rural Societies,* Lourdes Benería, ed. New York: Praeger.

__________, and Martha Roldán (1988). *At the Crossroads of Class and Gender.* Chicago, the Illinois: University of Chicago Press.

Berent, Jerzy (1982). *Family Planning in Europe and USA in the 1970s.* World Fertility Survey Comparative Studies: Cross-national Summaries, No. 20. Voorburg, Netherlands: International Statistical Institute.

Blake, Judith (1965). Demographic science and the redirection of population policy. *Journal of Chronic Diseases* (Oxford, United Kingdom), vol. 18 (November), pp. 1181-1200.

Bumpass, Larry L., and Charles F. Westoff (1970). *The Later Years of Childbearing.* Princeton, New Jersey: Princeton University Press.

Buvinic, Mayra (1990). *La vulnerabilidad de los hogares con jefatura femenina: preguntas y opciones de política para América Latina y el Caribe.* Santiago, Chile: Economic Commission for Latin America and the Caribbean.

Cain, Mead T. (1984) *Women's Status and Fertility in Developing Countries: Son Preference and Economic Security.* Center for Policy Studies Working Paper, No. 110. New York: The Population Council.

__________, Syeda R. Khanam and Shamsun Nahar (1979). Class, patriarchy, and women's work in Bangladesh. *Population and Development Review* (New York), vol. 5, No. 3 (September), pp. 405-438.

Caldwell, John C. (1980). Mass education as a determinant of the timing of fertility decline. *Population and Development Review* (New York), vol. 6, No. 2 (June), pp. 225-255.

__________ (1982). *Theory of Fertility Decline.* London: Academic Press.

Centroo Latino Americano de Demografía (1991). Proyecciones de población por estrato socio económico. Santiago, Chile. Mimeographed.

Cochrane, Susan H. (1979). *Fertility and Education: What do We Really Know?* World Bank Staff Occasional Papers, No. 26. Baltimore, Maryland: The Johns Hopkins University Press.

Collver, Andrew, and Eleamor Langlois (1962). The female labor force in metropolitan areas: an international comparison. *Economic Development and Cultural Change* (Chicago, Illinois), vol. 10, No. 4 (July), pp. 367-385.

Cramer, J. C. (1980). Fertility and female employment: problems of causal direction. *American Sociological Review* (Washington, D.C.), vol. 45, No. 1, pp. 167-190.

Davis, Kingsley (1967). Population policy: will current programs succeed? *Science* (Washington, D.C.), vol. 58, No. 3802 (10 November), pp. 730-739.

Deere, Carmen Diana, Jane Humphries and Magdalema León de Leal (1982). Class and historical analysis for the study of women and economic change. In *Women's Roles and Population Trends in the Third World,* Richard Anker, Mayra Buviníc and Nadia H. Youssef, eds. London: Croom Helm.

Dixon, Ruth B. (1975). *Women's Rights and Fertility.* Reports on Population/Family Planning, No. 17. New York: The Population Council.

Dixon-Mueller, Ruth (1989). Patriarchy, fertility and women's work in rural societies. In *IUSSP International Population Conference, New Delhi,* vol. 2. Liège, Belgium: International Union for the Scientific Study of Population.

__________, and Richard Anker (1988). *Assessing Women's Economic Contribution to Development.* Training in Population, Human Resources and Development Planning Series, No. 6. Geneva: International Labour Organization.

Eriksen, Julia A., William L. Yancey and Eugene P. Eriksen (1979). The division of family roles. *Journal of Marriage and the Family* (Minneapolis, Minnesota), vol. 4, No. 2 (May), pp. 301-313.

Freedman, R. C., P. L. Whelpton and A. A. Campbell (1959). *Family Planning, Sterility and Population Growth.* New York: McGraw-Hill.

Gabriel, J. (1991). Honduras: caracteristicas socio-demográficas y económicas de la población según grado de pobreza,1990. Santiago, Chile: Centro Latinoamericano de Demografía. Mimeographed.

Germain, Adrienne (1975). Status and roles of women as factors in fertility behavior: a policy analysis. *Studies in Family Planning* (New York), vol. 6, pp. 192-200.

Gómez, E. (1980). Trabajo femenino y fecundidad; antecedentes de investigación y perspectivas teóricas. Paper presented to the Seminario de Análisis y Capacitación de la Encuesta Mundial de Fecundidad, Santiago, Chile, 18 August.

Gurak, Douglas, and Mary M. Kritz (1982). Female employment and fertility in the Dominican Republic: a dynamic perspective. *American Sociological Review* (Washington, D.C.), vol. 47, No. 4 (December), pp. 810-818.

Harper, C. (1991). Fertility and female participation in the labour force. Santiago, Chile: Programa Regional del Empleo para América Latina y el Caribe. Mimeographed.

Holsinger, Donald B., and John D. Kasarda (1976). Education and human fertility: sociological perspectives. In *Population and Development: The Search for Selective Interventions*, Ronald G. Ridker, ed. Baltimore, Maryland: The Johns Hopkins University Press.

Jaffe, A. J., and K. Azumi (1960). The birth rate and cottage industries in underdeveloped countries. *Economic Development and Cultural Change* (Chicago), vol. 9, No. 1, part I (October), pp. 52-63.

Javillonar, Gloria L., and others (1979). *Rural Development, Women's Roles and Fertility in Developing Countries: A Review of the Literature.* Durham, North Carolina: Research Triangle Institute and South East Consortium for International Development.

Kasarda, John D., John O. G. Billy and Kirsten West (1986). *Status Enhancement and Fertility.* Orlando, Florida: Academic Press.

Kaztman, R. (1989). La heterogeneidad de la pobreza: el caso de Montevideo. *Revista de la CEPAL* (Santiago, Chile) (abril).

Lightbourne, Robert E. Jr., and Susheela Singh, with Cynthia P. Green (1982). *The World Fertility Survey: Charting Global Childbearing.* Population Bulletin, vol. 37, No. 1. Washington, D. C.: Population Reference Bureau.

Magdalinos, M., and H. Symeonidou (1989). Modelling the fertility-employment relationship: simultaneity and misspecification testing. *European Journal of Population* (Amsterdam) (October), pp. 119-143.

Marini, Margaret (1984). Women's educational attainment and the timing of entry into parenthood. *American Sociological Review* (New York), vol. 49, No. 4 (August), pp. 491-511.

Mason, Karen Oppenhein (1984). *The Status of Women: A Review of its Relationships to Fertility and Mortality.* New York: The Rockefeller Foundation.

__________, and S. A. David (1971). *Social and Economic Correlates of Family Fertility: A Survey of the Evidence.* Durham, North Carolina: Research Triangle Institute.

Miró, Carmen A., and Ferdinand Rath (1965). Preliminary findings of comparative fertility surveys in three Latin American cities. The *Milbank Memorial Fund Quarterly* (New York), vol. 43, No. 4, part 2, (October), pp. 62-68.

Oliveira de, O., and B. García (1990). Work, fertility and women's status in Mexico. *Development* (Rome), No. 3/4, pp. 152-158.

Oppenheimer, Valerie Kincade (1970). *The Female Labor Force in the United States: Demographic and Economic Factors Governing its Growth and Changing Composition.* Population Monograph Series, No. 5. Berkeley: University of California.

__________ (1973). Demographic influence on female employment and the status of women. In *Changing Women in a Changing Society*, Joan Huber, ed. Chicago, Illinois: The University of Chicago Press.

Oppong, Christine (1982a). *Familial Roles and Fertility: Some Labour Policy Aspects.* World Employment Programme, Research Working Paper, No. 124. Geneva: International Labour Office.

__________ (1982b). *Maternal Role Rewards, Opportunity Costs and Fertility.* World Employment Programme. Geneva: International Labour Organization.

__________ (1983). Women's roles, opportunity costs and fertility. In *Determinants of Fertility in Developing Countries*, vol. 1, *Supply and Demand for Children*, Rodolfo. A. Bulatao and Ronald. D. Lee, eds., with Paula E. Hollerbach and John P. Bongaarts, eds. New York: Academic Press.

__________, and Elina Haavio-Mannila (1979). Women, population and development. In *World Population and Development: Challenges and Prospects*, Philip M. Hauser, ed. New York: Syracuse University Press.

Patiño, C. A., E. Caicedo de Cardozo and M. Ranjel (1988). *Pobreza y desarrollo en Colombia: su impacto sobre la infancia y la mujer.* Bogotá, Colombia: United Nations Children's Fund.

Pratt, L., and P. K. Whelpton (1958). Extra-familial participation of wives in relation to interest in and liking for children, fertility planning, and actual and desired family size. In *Social and Psychological Factors Affecting Fertility*, vol. 5, Pascal K. Whelpton and Clyde V. Kiser, eds. New York: The Milbank Memorial Fund.

Programa Regional del Empleo para América Latina y el Caribe (1991). *Empleo y equidad: el desafío de los 90.* Santiago, Chile: International Labour Organization.

Rainwater, Lee (1965). *Family Design, Marital Sexuality, Family Size and Contraception.* Chicago, Illinois: Aldine.

Recchini de Lattes, Zulma, and Catalina Wainerman (1986). Unreliable account of women's work: evidence from Latin American census statistics. *Signs* (Chicago, Illinois), vol. 11, No. 4, pp. 740-750.

Ridley, Jeanne C. (1968). Demographic change and the roles and status of women. *Annals of the American Academy of Political and Social Science* (Newbury Park, California), vol. 375 (January), pp. 15-25.

Rindfuss, Ronald R., Larry L. Bumpass and Craig St. John (1980). Education and fertility: implications for the roles women occupy. *American Sociological Review* (Washington, D.C.), vol. 45, No. 3 (June), pp. 431-447.

Rosen, Bernard C., and Anita L. LaRaia (1972). Modernity in women: an index of social change in Brazil. *Journal of Marriage and the Family* (Minneapolis, Minnesota), vol. 34, No. 2 (May), pp. 353-360.

Rosenzweig, Mark R. (1976). Female work experience, employment status and birth expectations: sequential decision-making in the Philippines. *Demography* (Washington, D.C.), vol. 13, No. 3 (August), pp. 339-356.

Sadik, Nafis (1989). Old challenges and new areas for international co-operation in population. *Population Bulletin of the United Nations* (New York), No. 27, pp. 125-135. Sales No. E.89.XIII.7.

Safa, Nelean I. (1988). Women and industrialisation in the Caribbean. In *Women, Employment and the Family in the International Division of Labor*, Sharon Strichter and Jane L. Parpart, eds. London: MacMillan Press.

Safilios-Rothschild, Constantina (1972). Relationship between work commitment and fertility. *International Journal of Sociology of the Family* (New Delhi), No. 2 (March), pp. 64-71.

__________ (1977). The relationship between women's work and fertility: some methodological and theoretical issues. In *The Fertility of Working Women: A Synthesis of International Research*, Stanley Kupinsky, ed. New York: Praeger.

__________ (1982). Female power, autonomy and demographic change in the third world. In *Women's Roles and Population Trends in the Third World*, Richard Anker, Mayra Buvinic and Nadia H. Youssef, eds. London: Croom Helm.

_________ (1985a). *Socioeconomic Development and the Status of Women in the Third World.* Center for Policy Studies Working Papers, No. 112. New York: The Population Council.

_________ (1985b). *The Status of Women and Fertility in the Third World in the 1970-1980 Decade.* Center for Studies Working Papers, No. 118. New York: The Population Council.

Sathar, Zeba A., and others (1988). Women's status and fertility change in Pakistan. *Population and Development Review* (New York), vol. 14, No. 3 (September), pp. 415-432.

Scanzoni, John H. (1975). *Sex Roles, Life Styles and Childbearing: Changing Patterns in Marriage and the Family.* New York: Free Press.

Semyonov, Moshe (1980). The social context of women's labour force participation: a comparative analysis. *American Journal of Sociology* (Chicago), Illinois, vol. 86, No. 3 (November), pp. 534-550.

Smith, S. K. (1981). Women's work, fertility, and competing time use in Mexico City. In *Research in Population Economics*, vol. 3, Julian L. Simon and P. H. Lindert, eds. Greenwich, Connecticut: Jai Press.

Smith-Lovin, Lynn, and Ann R. Tickamyer (1978). Nonrecursive models of labor force participation, fertility behavior and sex role attitudes. *American Sociological Review* (Washington, D.C.), vol. 43, No. 4 (August), pp. 541-557.

Sprague, Alison (1988). Post war fertility and female labour force participation rates. *Economic Journal* (London), vol. 98, No. 393 (September), pp 682-700.

Standing, Guy (1978). *Labour Force Participation and Development.* Geneva: International Labour Organization.

_________ (1983). Women's work activity and fertility. In *Determinants of Fertility in Developing Countries*, vol. 1, *Supply and Demand for Children,* Rodolfo A. Bulatao and Ronald D. Lee, eds., with Paula E. Hollerbach and John Bongaarts. New York: Academic Press.

Stycos, J. Mayone, Ronald D. Lee and Robert Weller (1967). Female working roles and fertility. *Demography* (Washington, D.C.), vol. 4, No. 2 (April), pp. 210-217.

Tickamyer, Ann R. (1979). Women's roles and fertility intentions. *Pacific Sociological Review* (Beverly Hills, California), vol. 22, No. 1 (January), pp. 167-184.

Tuma, N. B., and M. T. Hannan (1984). *Social Dynamics. Models and Methods: Quantitative Studies in Social Relations.* San Diego, California: Academic Press.

United Nations (1985). *Women's Employment and Fertility: A Comparative Analysis of World Fertility Surveys for 38 Developing Countries.* Population Studies, No. 96. Sales No. E.85.XIII.5.

United Nations, Economic Commission for Latin America and the Caribbean (1991a). *La equidad en el panorama social de América Latina durante los años ochenta.* Santiago, Chile.

_________ (1991b). *Magnitud de la pobreza en América Latina en los años ochenta.* Estudios e Informes de la CEPAL. Santiago, Chile.

Uthoff, Andreas (1990). Población y desarrollo en el Istmo Centroamericano. *Revista de la CEPAL* (Santiago, Chile), No. 40 (abril), pp. 139-158.

Villarreal, M. (1989). Status of women, education, and attitudes toward fertility and female labor force participation among Costa Rican adolescents. Unpublished doctoral dissertation. Ithaca, New York: Cornell University.

_________ (1991). Mujer, informalidad y pobreza: el caso de Bolivia. Santiago, Chile: Programa Regional del Empleo para América Latina y el Caribe. Mimeographed.

Vlassoff, Michael (1986). Tendencias y diferenciales de la fecundidad en América Latina: un análisis con los datos de la Encuesta Mundial de Fecundidad. *Notas de Población* (Santiago, Chile), vol. XIV, No. 41.

Wainerman, Catalina H. (1992). *Improving the Accounting of Women Workers in Population Censuses: Lessons from Latin America.* World Employment Programme, Research Working Paper, No. 178. Geneva: International Labour Organization.

_________, and Zulma Recchini de Lattes (1981). *El trabajo femenino en el banquillo de los acusados: la medición censal en América Latina.* Colección Economía Sociedad. Mexico, D.F.: The Population Council/Editorial Terra Nova.

West, Kirsten B. (1980). *Sequential Fertility Behavior: A Study of Socioeconomic and Demographic Determinants of Parity Transitions.* Chapel Hill: University of North Carolina.

Whelpton, P. K., A. A. Campbell and J. E. Patterson (1966). *Fertility and Family Planning in the United States.* Princeton, New Jersey: Princeton University Press.

XXV. WOMEN'S ECONOMIC ROLES AND CHILD HEALTH: AN OVERVIEW

Alaka Malwade Basu[*]

Unlike the case of the relation between women's education and the welfare of their children—a relation that appears to be fairly straightforward and universally positive—there has not been enough research interest in the impact on child welfare of that other expected indicator of women's status, female employment. Either the tendency has been to assume that economic independence for women can only be good or the problems encountered in trying to understand the relation are too daunting to have kept more than a few researchers interested in the subject. But with women's employment levels rising all over the world and with child welfare having become a stated concern of Governments and international bodies, as well as myriad voluntary agencies, there is an urgent need to identify some of the ways in which women's economic activity may be good or bad for their children so that the former effects can be accentuated and the latter attenuated through more informed policy.

As already stated, this is not an easy task. This review therefore only presents indicators; it can by no means pass a final judgement on the question whether women's economic roles have a net positive or negative bearing on child health. In the process, it identifies some of the constraints in defining the relation and some of the areas where current knowledge is particularly weak and in need of urgent supplementation. An attempt is also made to elicit some policy implications based on current knowledge, with the acknowledged goal of continuing to encourage rises in female employment while at the same time mitigating any of the possible adverse effects on child health that may accompany such rises.

First, there is a major problem with defining an economic role for women. Who is called an "economically active woman"? One that earns a discernible cash income? Or one whose home-based activities lead to an increase in household income? Or even, as some International Labour Organization (ILO) recommendations suggest (Anker, Khan, and Gupta, 1988), one that does anything at all, including housework and child care, which would cost money if sought from the market? Although the last definition may make meaningless any analysis of the impact of women's economic roles on various indicators of life—with virtually all women being counted as economically active, there will be no yardstick with which to measure the effect of their economic activity—it is nevertheless true that most conventional (that is, usually male-inspired) definitions of economic activity lead to a massive underestimation of women's productivity. As several writers have begun to stress (see, for example, Krishnaraj, 1990), female labour force participation rates, especially in the developing countries, are much higher than those estimated by standard surveys and censuses. Such undercounting is especially acute for work categories in which women are disproportionately represented, such as unpaid farm work, home-based production and activities in the service sector. What gets more easily measured is male-oriented productive work—generally for wages, outside the home and with some regular schedule.

This paper, wherever possible, tries to correct for such measurement biases, especially by disaggregating women's activities according to the type of activity rather than according to their economic worth. Given data limitations, however, it is still often the case that this review of the relations between women's economic roles and child health will slip into a review of relations between conventionally defined economic roles and child health.

This lapse, however, is not as large as it might appear, because several of the postulated effects on child health of women's economic independence (especially several of the positive effects) are indirect and have to do more with changes in the perceptions

[*]Institute of Economic Growth, Delhi University Enclave, Delhi, India.

and values of women than in their actual behaviour. Such differences in perceptions and values are in turn conditioned by women's and society's own perceptions about their economic independence, however back-breaking and gruelling their actual lifestyle may be. The census or survey investigator is therefore often doing no more than reflecting society's bias by recording low female labour force participation rates.

In the context of the changing perceptions, knowledge and values associated with the economic independence of women, the second point to note is that equally important as economic role of the individual woman is the extent of female economic activity in her larger community in general (Basu, 1992a). It is suggested that in a situation of relatively high female activity rates, even non-working women will experience some of the effects of female employment on child health and mortality. This is because as more and more women enter the labour force, the more modern values associated with women's labour force participation percolate down to women that are not yet themselves actually exposed to the economic independence and wider world view which originally encourages such values and attitudes.

To explain this distinction better, the indirect effects of women's economic roles need to be understood not only in comparison to non-working women but separately in comparison to two sets of non-working women—those that are non-working out of choice or out of practical considerations and those that are non-working because their cultural compulsions make it difficult for them to join the labour force. One such cultural compulsion is the practice of female seclusion, or what is called "purdah" in the Indian sub-continent and refers not just to the literal veiling of women but also to the restrictions on their movements in and interactions with the extra-domestic world.

In any case, to return to the main subject of this paper, sections A and B, the potential impact of female economic activity on child health is considered under two broad headings: the expected positive implications of the economic activity of women for the health of children; and the expected negative implications. The net effect will, of course, depend upon the relative strengths of these two sets of factors and will vary from situation to situation. The last section then discusses consider some of the ways in which the balance can be tilted in favour of a preponderance of the positive features of women's economic roles.

One final caveat: the concern in this paper is with the situation of overall economic poverty. Where women are highly educated and/or work primarily for the professional satisfaction that work provides or where their incomes merely add to an already comfortable existence, naturally many of the hypotheses about the positive or negative effects of women's work will be less tenable because they will be swamped by the general advantages of economic prosperity.

A. Women's economic roles and child health: some positive features

The most important positive implication for child health of maternal employment is, of course, the increased income that become theoretically available for child welfare. (Note that this statement referred to women that work for an income and less to those that are productive but have no cash earnings to show for their productivity.) Several detailed analyses in recent times, especially with field data, suggest that it is not the increased money alone that counts; who brings in this additional income is a crucial determinant of how it is used. For example, Mencher (1988) vividly illustrates with village data from the States of Kerala and Tamil Nadu in India that with total household income held constant, a larger proportion of it seems to be spent on child welfare and improvements in the quality of life of household members if the wife is working. Additional income earned by men is more likely to be exhausted on non-essentials, such as tobacco or alcohol or other forms of entertainment. Kumar (1977) also concluded from field data in Kerala that improvements in wage income were translated into improvements in child nutritional status more readily in households where the women were employed. Tucker and Sanjur (1988) concluded similarly, with data from Panama that maternal employment had a positive impact on children's dietary intakes. Popkin and Solon (1976) found in the Philippines that mothers' work had an independent effect on food expenditures.

These findings are consistent with the expectation that working women are likely to have a greater control over household resources, either directly through the physical access to an income or indirectly through the changing power relations within the family brought about by their economic independence. For example, as Sen (1987) points out, economic liberation should increase the "bargaining position" of the wife in the marriage contract because her loss in the case of her lack of subordination being equated with unacceptable insubordination is potentially smaller if she has her own income to fall back upon. Once all parties in the domestic contract are aware of such a strength in the woman, the chances are that she will have a greater say in the disposition of household resources. But the reason that she should want to dispose of such resources for the welfare of her family more often than her husband would, for instance, is not very clear empirically. Perhaps, through inclination or through socialization, women are more altruistic; perhaps, their closer physical bond with their children makes them more aware of children's needs. Whatever the determining factors, the net effect does appear to be a tendency to use income more fruitfully when the woman is in charge.

On the other hand, it is also true that there is not an automatic connection between a woman's wage-earning activities and her control of these wages. Indeed, there is a fair amount of evidence to the contrary as well—how it is not at all uncommon for a woman to hand over her wages to her husband or mother-in-law, how it may even be the case that the wages due to a woman are actually collected from her employer by her husband (see, for example, some of the papers in Dwyer and Bruce, 1988). On the whole, however, it is probably true that the subservience of women is even deeper when they do not have the means to receive an income for their labour.

Secondly, quite apart from the greater control over resources that her access to paid work gives her, the working woman, especially if she works outside the home and in the modern sector of the economy, also has increased access to the information and knowledge needed to make more efficient use of the resources that she now commands. For example, she is likely to learn about better child-bearing and child-rearing practices at her workplace, either through her employers or through the mass media, or through interactions with her colleagues, or even through the daily trip to and from work. Not only is the working woman likely to be more knowledgeable about these things, she is also likely to be more confident about using her knowledge. For example, not only is she likely to be aware of the advantages of a hygienic institutional delivery, she is also more likely not to be put off by the harshness and high-handedness of the health-care system in a typical poor country set-up. As Caldwell (1986) states, it is more likely that such a woman (he was talking about the autonomy that comes with maternal education but his remarks apply just as well to economically active women) "will make her own decision that something must be done when she identifies a child as sick (it also seems to lead her to make that identification at an earlier time), that she will venture outside the home to seek help, that she will struggle for adequate treatment with doctors and nurses, and that she will understand the advice and take responsibility for carrying it out" (1986, p. 202). Similarly, to quote Dyson and Moore, women with lower levels of personal autonomy may be "less prepared and able to innovate, have less access to new information regarding child care, and be more restricted in their ability to utilize health services, either for themselves or for their children" (1983, p. 50).

One very important beneficial effect of female economic activities on child health is, perhaps, specific to the Southern and Western Asian situations. This effect is a lessening of the strong son preference that characterizes much of these regions and a narrowing of the gender differences in child health and mortality that are so adverse to girls, both among working women themselves as well as among all women in regions of high female labour force participation levels (see Basu and Basu, 1991; Basu, 1992b). This is not surprising. One would expect that in a sufficiently pragmatic society and with resources being extremely limited, women's economic roles would have a bearing on the value attached to their survival and, consequently, on the sex differential in health and survival. Such an interpretation explains, for example, why Rosenzweig and Schultz (1982) found a negative correlation between district-level female employment rates and the male-female differential in mortality in India. That at least a part of this outcome is deliberate (even if only subconsciously) is suggested by the strong corresponding relation between female labour force participation rates and the sex ratio of ideal family size (Basu, 1992a).

But women's economic roles and differential health by sex can also be attributed in past to less materialistic calculations, which have to do with the negative association between women's employment levels and their seclusion levels in a society, in both a literal and a metaphorical sense. While psychological seclusion can affect child health through the kind of Knowledge, Attitude and Practice (KAP) variables discussed above, the physical seclusion of women can also have more direct consequences for health. For example, a culture that is conservative to the point of frowning upon economic activity by women is empirically also likely to frown upon the interaction of women with outside males in any context, not just in work-related ones. One implication is then likely to be that women in such a culture will be loathe to visit a hospital for a delivery or to have an adolescent girl examined by a male doctor, the former adversely affecting maternal and infant mortality and the latter accentuating sex differentials in health. The irony is that these same factors of female seclusion and low female economic activity outside the home lead to a shortage of female medical and paramedical staff in the very areas where the need for them is the most desperate. Thus, one has the reported phenomena of sick girls having to make do more frequently with home treatment (Basu, 1989), or females obtaining treatment through symptoms being described to the doctor by a male relative (Khan and others, 1988), or treatment of illness in women and young girls often being delayed until it is too late.

Lastly, there is the possible beneficial relation between women's economic activity and child health and survival through the intermediate variable of fertility. For whatever reason and whatever the direction of causality, there does appear to be some empirical evidence of a negative association between women's labour force participation and their fertility levels. This relation is stronger for women that work outside the home, leading many writers to comment on the determining influence of the incompatibility between a woman's productive and reproductive roles (for example, see Jaffe and Azumi, 1965).

As the review by the National Academy of Sciences (1989) suggests, there is probably a negative relation between fertility and child mortality which persists even after a series of potentially confounding variables are controlled. How much of this is due to higher fertility and how much to the shorter birth intervals associated with high fertility is not clear but needs to be understood, because although it is true that working women tend to have fewer children, there is also some tendency for these children to be more closely spaced. If it is the birth interval that is more important, this proposed advantageous link between maternal employment and child health should be treated as a disadvantage. Moreover, it may also be a disadvantage in the measurement sense that if working women have fewer births, this means that they have a higher proportion of first-order births. Presumably, therefore, this factor increases the proportion of high-risk births as well. Except that once again, not enough is known about the mechanisms behind the higher mortality risks of first births. Is it due to the younger age and experience of the mother? If so, maternal employment may be an advantage because working women tend to typically marry and begin child-bearing at later ages than non-working women.

There is also the complicating consideration that births to young mothers as well as several births are disproportionately high in the lower socio-economic classes. That is, one may be measuring an income impact on child health and mortality and not the impact of young maternal age or several children at all. (For example, see the discussion in National Academy of Sciences, 1989; see also the debate on the relations between fertility and infant mortality (Bongaarts, 1987 and 1988; Trussell, 1988 and Potter, 1988).

These then are some of the ways in which women's economic roles may have a positive impact on child health and survival (although admittedly the last mechanism on the list is somewhat ambiguous). And yet, several data sets do find an overall negative association between women's participation in economic activities and the health of their children (especially as measured by survival; see, for example, United Nations, 1985; Basu and Basu, 1991). To understand why this may be so, the following section discusses some of the mechanisms through which women being economically active may hamper the health and life chances of children.

B. WOMEN'S ECONOMIC ROLES AND CHILD HEALTH: SOME NEGATIVE FEATURES

Perhaps the single most important factor that adversely affects the health and survival of very young children when their mothers work is the reduced amount of breast-feeding that is possible for many categories of women's work. Barring self-employed women, who either work at home or work in a sedentary occupation at a place where they can take their infants with them, employment in other kinds of activities must take its toll on the ability to feed young children frequently and intensely enough.

Having deduced this fact, empirical information is needed on two questions. First, what is the evidence that infants of working mothers do indeed lose out on the goodness of breast milk? Secondly, what is the evidence on a relation between breast-feeding and child health? In particular, are there intervening variables in the relation whose effect can be mimicked even in the absence of breast-feeding?

To examine the first question, that is, the connection between women's economic activities and the extent of breast-feeding of young infants, in a review of the available literature on the subject, Leslie (1989) was able to find remarkably little that pointed to a consistent and significant relationship between these two variables. This result was partially, of course, because both breast-feeding and women's economic activities can be defined in several ways, not all of them mutually consistent. For example, as already stated, a woman that works away from the home is naturally less able to feed her child as often as is one that is economically active but operates from her home. Moreover, even the former woman is able to feed her infant at nights, so that the more affected breast-feeding variable is not whether an infant is breast-fed at all but how often and what kind of substitutes are fed to it when the mother is away. In fact, the more common behaviour may well be for even working women to take time off to allow complete breast-feeding for the first few weeks, or even months in some occupations, and then switch earlier than their non-working counterparts to partial or completely substitute feeding.

Given all these complications and given that many of the studies reviewed by Leslie (1989) were not originally designed to address the specific issue of women's labour activity and infant-feeding practices, it is not surprising that the knowledge on this question is either localized or inconsistent. Moreover, one important question that few research studies seem to have even considered is the role of "modernization" in the possibly shorter durations of breast-feeding among economically active women. The entire problem seems to be posed in the context of an incompatibility between a woman's economic activity and her ability physically to breast-feed her infant. But the working woman's greater interaction with the outside world and especially with the outside world of her social superiors among whom it is unfashionable to breast-feed babies for too long, as well as the generally more aggressive and seductive advertising campaigns of artificial food manufacturers as compared with the more staid breast-feeding lobby, means that a change in values is likely to be an important determinant of the working woman's reduced breast-feeding.

In any case, can any generalizations be made on the subject from existing knowledge? The main one appears to be that there are no significant differentials in the prevalence of breast-feeding among children of employed and unemployed mothers, but that the employed mother's duration of (especially exclusive) breast-feeding is probably shorter. Such shortened breast-feeding can have a clear health impact. For example, Popkin and Doan (1990) report that in their longitudinal study in the Philippines, four-month old urban infants fed breast milk and non-nutritive liquids, such as tea, water and broths, were twice as likely to have diarrhoea as exclusively breast-fed infants, and those given no breast milk were 13 times as likely to have diarrhoea.

This example leads to the question of the value of breast milk for the health of the child, especially the very young infant. In a recent article, VanLandingham, Trussell and Grummer-Strawn (1991) review the extensive literature that seems near unanimous in concluding that breast-feeding is a significant predictor of infant mortality during the first six months of life. This effect is impressive even in sophisticated data analyses which seek to remove the effects of the several possible confounding factors, including the possibility of "reverse causation". Moreover, the relation seems to be stronger in those countries or those subgroups within countries that otherwise face the most unfavourable health conditions. Three intervening mechanisms have been suggested for this virtually universal relation—the nutritive properties of breast milk, its anti-infective properties and its effect on birth-spacing. This second property explains why infants that got no breast milk at all, in the Popkin and Doan study (1990), faced so many times higher risks of infection even compared with infants that were only partially breast-fed and therefore also exposed to the infections in the outside feedings they had.

The nutritional value of breast milk is also, it appears, not easily substitutable by other foods, even if price is not a consideration. In reality, in the segments of populations under discussion here, price is a major consideration and the nutritive properties of human milk are even more difficult to substitute. Overdiluting artificial feeds, mixing them with flour and other less nutritious substitutes which only look like milk and feeding infants tea and broth are all examples of the resort to cheaper methods of feeding a child that cannot be breast-fed; and they explain at least in part why poor countries have such high levels of malnutrition in partially weaned infants, as well as the common occurrence of the "weanling diarrhoea" first described by Wyon and Gordon (1971) in the Khanna study in India. Naturally, the shorter the duration of breast-feeding, the earlier these weaning problems are likely to occur and the more severe they are likely to be.

But the third advantage of breast milk, that it increases birth intervals, is somewhat problematic in the present context. To begin with, as already discussed briefly earlier, the causal mechanisms in a relation between birth intervals and infant health have not been conclusively established, although the case is strong. But more importantly, there is reason to expect that working women will be more capable of substituting breast milk with effective contraception if birth intervals get undesirably short. The main impediment appears to be that economically active women apparently do not want to prolong birth intervals, not that they do not know how to prolong them. One reason is probably convenience—fewer children more closely spaced is one way of narrowing the incompatibility between child-bearing and work.

That is, the relation between women's economic roles and shortened birth intervals as a possible adverse factor in child health should be considered independently of breast-feeding as an intermediate variable. The question then is whether the children of economically active women lose out on health because they come too quickly on each other's heels or whether they gain because there are fewer of them to drain maternal and material resources. Undoubtedly, there is an element of both effects and the net effect will vary with the circumstances.

To return to the role of nutrition as a factor in a negative relation between women's economic activity and child health, once the breast-feeding ages have been passed, it is again not clear if the relation is only negative. This lack of clarity is because women's work can affect child nutrition through two opposite paths—the increased money now available for child nutrition (and, as discussed in the earlier section, this increased money is best used when it is earned by the woman), balanced by the decreased time now available for the mother to see to the child's nutrition. The empirical evidence on the net effect is mixed. For instance, two of the studies cited in Leslie (1989) obtained interesting results by disaggregating children according to age; in both cases, there was a negative association between maternal work and child nutritional status for infants and a positive association for weaning-age children. But Chutikul (1986) concluded from nutritional status data for children in rural Thailand that mother's work in the formal labour market had a significant negative association with child nutritional levels.

Such negative examples should be balanced against the examples indicating a positive relation between child nutrition and maternal work status discussed above. Those examples of a positive relation were an illustration of the income effect of mother's work. The present negative ones are an illustration of the time effect. And this time factor is the last, but perhaps one of the most important, negative repercussions of women's economic activity in the context of child health and survival.

The shortage of time for child care that a working mother experiences can adversely affect child health, not just because of the nutritional effects mentioned above but also because of its impact on various other determinants of child health, including a child's need for shelter, protection, clothing and health care. For example, accidents and injuries are reportedly higher among children left in households with no adult members during the day. The hypothesis here is that a child is best off from the health point of view if cared for by a parent or adult relative from within the family, next best off when left to the care of adult outsiders, worse off when in the care of an older sibling and worst off when left to its own devices for the major part of the day (see, for example, Shah, Walimbe and Dhole, 1979; Bittencourt and DiCicco, 1979; Engle, Pederson and Smidt 1986). Naturally, this ordering is even more important in the poor country setting, where institutional arrangements for child care are virtually non-existent, school enrolments are low and various features of the poor quality of life buttress each other (the synergistic relation between malnutrition and infection, for example).

The impact of maternal work on the quality of child care thus measured will depend upon the circumstances of her work as well as the availability of substitute caregivers. By the circumstances of her work are meant the type of employment she is in, how many hours away from home it entails and the level of concentration required, to name only a few. The quantum of her income is not likely to be relevant because in the contexts discussed here, few women will be earning enough to be able to buy substitute caregivers; indeed, in a typical urban situation, in a developing country, many of these poor working women are likely to be selling their own child-care capabilities to better-off households.

Next, if the working woman is in the situation of not being able to take care of her child(ren) herself, the impact of her inability will depend upon the type of substitutes available. And once again, there should thus in principle be no fixed and universal impact of women's care on child health through this route. At the same time, it is surprising how similar the results are in a range of situations. To consider the worst option first, several studies have found a large proportion of the slightly older children of working mothers being looked after by "no one" when their mothers are at work (see, for example, India, 1981; Basu and Basu, 1991; Overseas Education Fund, 1979).

The second disheartening finding is the number of studies that report young children of working mothers being cared for after by only slightly older siblings. This finding has adverse health and welfare implications for two sets of children, those being looked after by older sisters and brothers and those responsible for the care of younger brothers and sisters. The disadvantage to the latter group should legitimately be counted as a cost of maternal employment; too often, child welfare measures confine themselves to a somewhat arbitrary cut-off age of five years. In particular some more information is needed on one specific effect on older siblings of the child-care responsibilities—this is the drastically reduced convalescence they themselves are entitled to when their mothers work; every extra day in bed is a day's wages lost to the mother if the older sibling is the primary substitute caregivers for the younger children.

This nature of the substitute caregiver is likely to be particularly important in the recognition and treatment of ill health in children. Writers like Caldwell (1986) have, while discussing the advantages of maternal education, stressed the role of the mother (and not necessarily the biological one) in first noticing a child's ill health; if she is also educated (for present purposes, that could read economically independent) and free to take decisions on her own, it is more likely that the sick child will get the appropriate care. But even if the mother is autonomous and confident, she has to be first aware of a child's needs before she can act to meet them.

Similar conclusions have been reached by other studies on infant and child mortality which have looked in some detail at the primary caregiver. For example, Hilderbrand and others (1985) documented the significantly higher risks of death faced by children of the Tamasheq (nobles) in rural Mali than children of the Bella (slaves). The latter children do not have greater economic resources; their main difference from the Tamasheq seems to be that Bella children are rarely separated from their mothers, whereas Tamasheq children are cared for by Bella nursemaids (who are often children themselves) and taken to their mothers only for breast-feeding.

It appears, therefore, that there are almost as many reasons to expect women's economic activity to have an adverse impact on child health as there are reasons for expecting a favourable impact. But since the latter do exist and since women's economic independence does have many other factors in its favour, perhaps the policy question should be not how to reduce women's employment levels but how to reduce the possible negative repercussions of these levels for child health and survival, so that the positive repercussions are paramount; that is, the aim must be not merely to have no relation between women's economic roles and child health but actually to have a positive beneficial relation. The next section addresses some of these policy issues.

C. Some policy implications

The first question that a policy perspective on this whole issue of the negative relation between maternal work and child health should ask is—how substitutable is the working mother? The answer to this question will depend upon the indicator of child welfare being considered. From those indicators considered above, in principle, the working mother should be substitutable on all counts except one—that of her breast-feeding role, that is, if one discounts wet-nursing as a serious option in the present day.

The first point to note is that, strictly speaking, when one talks about maternal work status, what one is actually referring to is joint parental work status. It may well be the case that similar negative effects of paternal employment on child health exist when the mother also works. It is just that this proposition is difficult to establish statistically because the fraction of non-working fathers in any sample is likely to be very small. Except for their impact on breast-feeding, working mothers may therefore be getting an unfair share of the blame for poor child health outcomes.

However, given the reality of the situation, that is, given the fact that rarely is the typical household in a poor country going to face a situation of a mother at work and a father to take care of the children (even unemployed fathers are notoriously unwilling to accept this responsibility, as several anthropological accounts have documented), policy solutions must look elsewhere. First, there is the role of the State in providing good quality and cheap child-care facilities to the children of working mothers. Whatever exists on any large scale today does so mainly on paper; there are scarcely any instances of State-provided social support for the care of young children. Nor have employers been very diligent about implementing the many regulations that exist about concerning responsibility for providing some institutional child-care facilities for the children of their female workers. Even if they had been more compliant, it is doubtful if this would make much of a dent in the problem, given that the vast majority of female workers work outside the formal sector of the economy.

But even where institutional services for child care do exist, there is yet another problem. This is the surprisingly low utilization rates of such facilities reported from diverse regions of the world. One can only conclude that women are irrational or that they are rational but still do not consider the facilities being offered to be worth their while or to be better than what they can arrange for themselves at home. The latter explanation seems to be the more likely possibility and in a review of State-provided child-care facilities around the world, Joekes (1989) points out some of the most frequent problems with such facilities—inconvenient locations, unsuitable timing, little concern for actual child welfare and a chronic shortage of staff and supplies, to name only a few. And when to this list one adds the often haughty impersonality that accompanies most state services in poor countries, it is little wonder that working mothers feel more inclined to leave a child with an older sister or even with no one at all, rather than send him or her to such a state institution.

Child care is one level at which there is much scope for state intervention. Another possible intervention is in the encouragement of female economic activities that are less incompatible with child care. These include more possibilities for home-based employment of young mothers, but for home-based employment of a type that does not increase the physical hazards for a child. All too often, the supposed proximity between a woman working out of her home and her young child is at best notional; if, in addition, the mother is working with dangerous materials, the risks to the child can well be greater than those faced by the child of a mother that leaves the home for a good part of the day with the child in the care of relatively indifferent people.

Lastly, one could stress once again the need for development that pays greater heed to the value of a poor woman's time. Labour-saving devices are so quickly developed for men and for the better-off population as a whole. Poor working women, on the other hand, do an unenviable double shift of work for all practical purposes, so that it is often the home maintenance tasks rather than the demands of her job that take the most time and attention away from the child. Collecting fuel and fetching water are only the most obvious examples; the time, energy and cheer lost on a host of other household activities such as the processing of food, cleaning and actual cooking, are a cost that is difficult to quantify but that can have only an adverse impact on the health and well-being of the child as well as the woman herself, an impact that is multiplied when the woman is also economically active.

The reference in the last paragraph to the adverse impact of productive work and housework on the health of women themselves was deliberate. Unfortunately, even less is known of the nature and extent of this impact than is the case for child health and one cannot overstate the need for more research and planning to take this factor into account, if indeed female employment is to be a worthwhile goal for society as a whole.

References

Anker, Richard, M. E. Khan, and R. B. Gupta (1988). *Women's Participation in the Labour Force: A Methods Test in India for Improving its Measurement.* Women, Work and Employment Series, No. 16. Geneva: International Labour Office.

Basu, Alaka Malwade (1989). Is discrimination in food really necessary for explaining sex differentials in childhood mortality? *Population Studies* (London), vol. 43, No. 2 (June), pp. 192-210.

_________ (1992a). *Culture, the Status of Women and Demographic Behaviour.* Oxford, United Kingdom: Clarendon Press; and New York: Oxford University Press.

_________ (1992b). Women's roles and the gender gap in health and survival. Paper presented at the NCAER and Harvard University Workshop on Health and Development Transition in India, Delhi, January.

_________, and Kavshik Basu (1991). Women's economic roles and child survival: the case of India. *Health Transition Review* (Canberra, Australia), vol. 1, No. 1 (April), pp. 83-103.

Bittencourt, Sonia, and Emily DiCicco (1979). *Child Care Needs of Low Income Women: Urban Brazil.* Washington, D.C.: Overseas Education Fund of the League of Women Voters.

Bongaarts, John (1987). Does family planning reduce infant mortality rates? *Population and Development Review* (New York), vol. 13, No. 2 (June), pp. 323-324.

_________ (1988). Does family planning reduce infant mortality rates?: Reply. *Population and Development Review* (New York), vol. 14, No. 1 (March), pp. 188-190.

Caldwell, John C. (1986). Routes to low mortality in poor countries. *Population and Development Review* (New York), vol. 12, No. 2 (June), pp. 171-220.

Chutikul, Sirilaksana (1986). *Malnourished Children: An Economic Approach to the Causes and Consequences in Rural Thailand.* Papers of the East-West Population Institute, No. 102. Honolulu, Hawaii: East-West Center.

Dwyer, Daisg, and Judith Bruce, eds. (1988). *A Home Divided: Women and Income in the Third World.* Stanford, California: Stanford University Press.

Dyson, Tim, and M. Moore (1983). On kinship structure, female autonomy and demographic behaviour in India. *Population and Development Review* (New York), vol. 9, No. 1 (March), pp. 35-60.

Engle, P. L., M. Pederson and R. K. Smidt (1986). The effects of maternal work for earnings on children's nutritional status and school enrolment in rural and urban Guatemala. Final Project Report to USAID/PPC.

Hilderbrand, K., and others (1985). Child mortality and care of children in rural Mali. In *Population, Health and Nutrition in the Sahel: Issues in the Welfare of Selected West African Communities,* Allan G. Hill, ed. London: Routledge and Kegan Paul.

India, Registrar General (1981). *Survey of Infant and Child Mortality, 1979.* New Delhi.

Jaffe, A. J., and K. Azumi (1960). The birth rate and cottage industries in underdeveloped countries. *Economic Development and Cultural Change* (Chicago, Illinois), vol. 9, No. 1, part I (October), pp. 52-63.

Joekes, Susan (1989). Women's work and social support for child care in the third world. In *Women, Work and Child Welfare in the Third World,* Joanne Leslie and Michael Paolisso, eds. Boulder, Colorado: Westview Press.

Khan, M. E., and others (1988). Inequalities between men and women in nutrition and family welfare services. *Social Action* (New Delhi, India), vol. 38.

Krishnaraj, M. (1990). Women's work in the Indian census: beginnings of change. *Economic and Political Weekly* (Bombay, India), vol. 25.

Kumar, S. (1977). *Role of the Household Economy in Determining Child Nutrition at Low Income Levels: A Case Study of Kerala.* Occasional Paper No. 95. Ithaca, New York: Cornell University, Department of Agricultural Economics.

Leslie, Joanne (1989). Women's work and child nutrition in the Third World. In *Women, Work and Child Welfare in the Third World*, Joanne Leslie and Michael Paolisso, eds. Boulder, Colorado: Westview Press.

_________, and M. Paolisso (eds) (1989). *Women, Work and Child Welfare in the Third World*, Boulder, Colorado: Westview Press.

Mencher, Joan P. (1988). Women's work and poverty: women's contribution to household maintenance in South India. In *A Home Divided: Women and Income in the Third World*, Daisy Dwyer and Judith Bruce, eds. Stanford, California: Stanford University Press.

National Academy of Sciences (1989). *Contraception and Reproduction: Health Consequences for Women and Children in the Developing World*. Washington, D.C.: Academic Press.

Overseas Education Fund (1979). *Child Care Needs of Low Income Mothers in Less Developed Countries*. Washington, D.C.: OEF International.

Popkin, Barry M., and F. S. Solon (1976). Income, time, the working mother and child nutriture. *Journal of Tropical Pediatrics and Environmental Health* (Oxford, United Kingdom), vol. 22.

Popkin, Barry M., and Rebecca Mills Doan (1990). Women's roles, time allocation and health. In *What We Know About Health Transition: The Cultural, Social and Behavioural Determinants of Health*, John Caldwell and others, eds., vol. II. Health Transition Series, No. 2. Canberra: The Australian National University Press.

Potter, Joseph E. (1988). Does family planning reduce infant mortality? An exchange. *Population and Development Review* (New York), vol. 14, No. 1 (March), pp.178-187.

Rosenzweig, M. R., and T. P. Schultz (1982). Market opportunities, genetic endowments and intrafamily resource distribution: child survival in rural India. *American Economic Review* (Nashville, Tennessee), vol. 72, No. 46 (September), pp. 803-815.

Sen, A. (1987). Women, well-being and agency. Paper presented at the Seminar on Women's Issues in Development Policy, Washington, D. C., International Centre for Research on Women.

Shah, P. M., S. R. Walimbe and V. S. Dhole (1979). Wage earning mothers, mother substitutes and care of young children in rural Maharashtra. *Indian Pediatrics* (New Delhi), vol. 16.

Trussell, James (1988). Does family planning reduce infant mortality? An exchange. *Population and Development Review* (New York), vol. 14, No. 1 (March), pp. 171-178.

Tucker, Kathorine, and Div Sanjur (1988). Maternal employment and child nutrition in Panama. *Social Science and Medicine* (Elmsford, New York), vol. 26, No. 6. pp. 605-612.

United Nations (1985). *Socio-economic Differentials in Child Mortality in Developing Countries*. Population Studies, No. 97. Sales No. E.85.XIII.7.

VanLandingham, Mark, James Trussell and Lavrence Grummer-Strawn (1991). Contraceptive and health benefits of breastfeeding: a review of recent evidence. *International Family Planning Perspectives* (New York), vol. 17, No. 4 (December), pp. 131-136.

Wyon, John B., and John E. Gordon (1971). *The Khanna Study: Population Problems in Rural Punjab*. Cambridge, Massachusetts: Harvard University Press.

XXVI. RELATION BETWEEN WOMEN'S ECONOMIC ACTIVITY AND CHILD CARE IN LOW-FERTILITY COUNTRIES

*Shigemi Kono**

The aim of this paper is to review the trends in women's economic activity in the low-fertility countries and to discuss findings, research needs and policy implications concerning the link between economic activity and fertility/child care. References are particularly made to Japan, the country with which the author is most familiar, but at the same time much attention has been paid to Southern European countries and newly industrialized countries or areas in Asia, where fertility has declined precipitously in recent years; and to Sweden, which is currently experiencing an appreciable increase in fertility.

Total fertility rates (TFR) are given in table 47 for 31 industrialized countries in Europe, Northern America and elsewhere. TFR denotes the number of children a woman would have if she lived through the child-bearing years and gave birth at prevailing age-specific fertility rates. With the low mortality prevalent in the developed countries, the replacement level of total fertility is about 2.1 children per woman. A population whose fertility remains indefinitely below this level will eventually decline. Only four of the countries listed in table 47 were above replacement level in 1989: New Zealand; Sweden; Poland; and the former Union of Soviet Socialist Republics. This means that all the other countries (except Romania, where there is uncertainty because of lack of data) have already embarked on what may be called a "long-term declining population trend".

It is particularly interesting to note that recently the lowest fertility has been observed in Southern European countries such as Italy and Spain. This finding is quite surprising for a society whose level of economic development and social welfare still ranks below Northern European standards and that still has a substantial proportion of rural population. Historical ties to a Roman Catholic tradition still influence the normative context and older generations carry the legacy of the former Government that endorsed a pronatalistic ideology. The transition from pre-modern contraceptives to modern means is also quite recent. Even today family planning services are not widespread or promoted in this region (Castro Martin, 1991).

Likewise, table 48 and figure VI show the trends for Japan and for newly industrialized countries or areas in Asia, including Hong Kong, the Republic of Korea, Singapore and Taiwan Province of China. Industrialized Eastern Asian countries or areas currently seem to be following rapidly the trends in Western countries. Needless to say, the experiences of Europe and Northern America are different from those of Japan and the Asian newly industrialized countries and areas, which are now classified as "low-fertility countries". They are very different in political organization, history, religion, philosophy and lifestyle. At the same time, however, even in Europe there are considerable subcultural differences in economic organization, lifestyle and level of living. In spite of such cultural and social diversities, what is really striking is the magnitude and universality of fertility decline that has occurred during the past two or three decades in the industrialized countries of both Asia and the West.

A. SECOND DEMOGRAPHIC TRANSITION

Why have the industrialized societies of Europe and Northern America recently renewed a precipitous

*Director-General, Institute of Population Problems, Ministry of Health and Welfare, Tokyo, Japan. The author wishes to express gratitude to Mary Beth Weinberger, Keiko Ono and Teresa Castro Martin of the Population Division for supplying useful materials on the demography of Europe.

TABLE 47. TRENDS IN TOTAL FERTILITY, DEVELOPED COUNTRIES, 1965-1990

Region and country	1965	1970	1975	1978	1979	1980	1981	1982	1983	1984	1985	1986	1987	1988	1989	1990
Asia																
Japan	2.14	2.13	1.91	1.79	1.77	1.75	1.74	1.77	1.80	1.81	1.76	1.72	1.69	1.66	1.57	1.54
Europe																
Bulgaria	2.03	2.18	2.23	2.15	2.15	2.05	2.01	2.02	2.00	1.99	1.95	1.99	1.96	1.90	1.90	..
Czechoslovakia	2.37	2.07	2.43	2.36	2.33	2.16	2.10	2.10	2.08	2.07	2.06	2.03	2.00	2.02	1.95	..
German Democratic Republic[a]	2.48	2.19	1.54	1.90	1.90	1.94	1.85	1.85	1.79	1.74	1.70	1.74	1.70	1.74	1.67	..
Hungary	1.82	1.96	2.35	2.07	2.01	1.91	1.88	1.79	1.72	1.73	1.83	1.84	1.82	1.81	1.80	..
Poland	2.52	2.20	2.27	2.20	2.25	2.26	2.22	2.31	2.40	2.37	2.33	2.22	2.15	2.20	2.20	..
Romania	1.91	2.89	2.60	2.52	2.48	2.43	2.35	2.19	2.00	2.19	..	..	..	..	..	..
USSR[b]	2.46	2.39	2.41	2.32	2.28	2.26	2.25	2.29	2.37	2.41	2.40	2.46	2.53	2.38	2.40	..
Northern Europe																
Denmark	2.61	1.95	1.92	1.67	1.60	1.55	1.44	1.43	1.38	1.40	1.45	1.48	1.50	1.56	1.62	1.67
Finland	2.47	1.83	1.68	1.64	1.64	1.63	1.64	1.72	1.74	1.70	1.65	1.60	1.59	1.70	1.71	1.79
Iceland	3.71	2.81	2.65	2.35	2.49	1.48	2.33	2.26	2.26	2.08	1.93	1.85	2.05	2.27	2.00	2.31
Ireland	4.03	3.87	3.41	3.24	3.23	3.23	3.08	2.96	2.74	2.58	2.49	2.43	2.32	2.18	2.11	2.17
Norway	2.93	2.50	1.98	1.77	1.75	1.72	1.70	1.71	1.65	1.66	1.68	1.71	1.75	1.84	1.89	1.93
Sweden	2.42	1.94	1.78	1.60	1.66	1.68	1.63	1.62	1.61	1.65	1.73	1.79	1.84	1.96	2.02	2.14
United Kingdom	2.85	2.45	1.81	1.73	1.84	1.89	1.80	1.76	1.76	1.76	1.80	1.78	1.81	1.84	1.81	1.84
Southern Europe																
Greece	2.32	2.43	2.33	2.29	2.29	2.21	2.09	2.02	1.94	1.82	1.68	1.62	1.52	1.52	1.43	..
Italy	2.55	2.46	2.19	1.85	1.74	1.66	1.57	1.57	1.53	1.46	1.41	1.33	1.28	1.34	1.33	1.29
Portugal	3.07	2.62	2.59	2.28	2.17	2.12	2.04	2.02	1.96	1.87	1.70	1.63	1.57	1.53	1.48	..
Spain	2.97	2.87	2.80	2.53	2.31	2.16	1.99	1.87	2.07	1.69	1.61	1.53	1.48	1.38	1.30	..
Yugoslavia	2.71	2.29	2.27	2.15	2.12	2.13	2.06	2.10	2.09	2.10	2.04	1.00	2.00	1.98	2.00	..
Western Europe																
Austria	2.68	2.30	1.83	1.60	1.60	1.65	1.67	1.66	1.56	1.52	1.48	1.45	1.43	1.44	1.45	1.45
Belgium	2.60	2.24	1.73	1.69	1.69	1.68	1.66	1.60	1.56	1.52	1.51	1.53	1.54	1.58	1.59	..
France	2.84	2.47	1.93	1.82	1.86	1.95	1.95	1.91	1.79	1.81	1.82	1.84	1.82	1.82	1.81	1.80
Germany, Federal Rep. of[b]	2.50	2.02	1.45	1.38	1.38	1.45	1.43	1.41	1.33	1.29	1.28	1.35	1.37	1.41	1.44	..
Luxembourg	2.34	1.97	..	1.50	1.48	1.51	1.55	..	1.47	1.43	1.39	1.43	1.39	1.51	1.52	1.62
Netherlands	3.04	2.58	1.66	1.58	1.56	1.60	1.56	1.49	1.51	1.49	1.51	1.55	1.56	1.55	1.55	1.62
Switzerland	2.01	2.10	1.61	1.50	1.52	1.55	1.54	1.55	1.52	1.52	1.52	1.52	1.52	1.57	1.56	1.59
Northern America																
Canada	3.11	2.33	1.90	1.75	1.75	1.73	1.70	1.69	1.67	1.69	1.67	1.67	1.66	1.65	1.68	..
United States of America	2.93	2.48	1.77	1.76	1.81	1.84	1.82	1.83	1.80	1.81	1.84	1.84	1.87	1.93	1.88	..
Oceania																
Australia	2.98	2.86	2.22	1.98	1.94	1.92	1.94	1.94	1.93	1.88	1.89	1.87	1.85	1.84	1.90	..
New Zealand	3.33	3.17	2.36	2.10	2.10	2.03	2.01	1.95	1.92	1.93	1.93	1.96	2.02	2.09	2.10	..

Sources: United Nations, *Demographic Yearbook*, various years; Council of Europe, *Recent Demographic Development in the Member States of the Council of Europe, 1990 Edition* (Strasbourg, 1991); World Bank, *Social Indicators of Development, 1989* (Baltimore, Maryland, The Johns Hopkins University Press, 1990); France, Institut national d'études démographiques; and other country population reports.

[a]Former German Democratic Republic.

[b]Former Union of Soviet Socialist Republics

TABLE 48. TRENDS IN TOTAL FERTILITY RATES, INDUSTRIALIZED COUNTRIES OR AREAS, ASIA, YEARS WITH AVAILABLE DATA, 1947-1989

Year	*Hong Kong*	*Japan*	*Republic of Korea*	*Singapore*	*Taiwan Province of China*
1947	..	4.54	..	6.55	..
1950	..	3.65	..	..	6.03
1951	..	3.26	..	..	7.04
1952	..	2.98	..	6.30	6.62
1953	..	2.69	..	..	6.47
1954	..	2.48	..	..	6.43
1955	..	2.37	5.46	..	6.53
1956	..	2.22	5.33	..	6.51
1957	..	2.04	5.40	6.56	6.00
1958	..	2.11	5.94	6.39	6.06
1959	..	2.04	5.98	6.14	5.99
1960	..	2.00	5.98	5.80	5.75
1961	5.17	1.96	6.02	5.46	5.61
1962	..	1.98	5.85	5.26	5.47
1963	..	2.00	5.89	5.17	5.35
1964	..	2.05	5.23	4.95	5.10
1965	4.93	2.14	4.95	4.62	4.83
1966	4.46	1.58	4.84	4.42	4.82
1967	4.23	2.23	4.50	3.95	4.22
1968	3.98	2.13	4.66	3.50	4.33
1969	3.37	2.13	4.54	3.15	4.12
1970	3.49	2.13	4.47	3.10	4.00
1971	3.42	2.16	4.54	3.06	3.71
1972	3.39	2.14	4.41	3.07	3.37
1973	3.28	2.14	4.01	2.81	3.21
1974	3.20	2.05	3.75	2.37	3.05
1975	2.51	1.91	3.33	2.08	2.83
1976	2.58	1.85	3.00	2.11	3.08
1977	2.42	1.80	2.94	1.82	2.70
1978	2.30	1.79	2.74	1.80	2.71
1979	2.13	1.77	2.83	1.79	2.66
1980	2.06	1.75	2.71	1.74	2.52
1981	1.96	1.74	2.64	1.72	2.46
1982	1.86	1.77	2.37	1.71	2.32
1983	1.71	1.80	2.09	1.59	2.16
1984	1.54	1.81	1.80	1.61	2.05
1985	1.46	1.76	1.71	1.62	1.89
1986	1.34	1.72	1.65	1.42	1.68
1987	1.28	1.69	1.59	1.64	1.70
1988	1.34	1.62	1.61	1.98	1.85
1989	1.25	1.57	1.63	1.79	1.68
1990	1.21	1.54	1.63	1.83	1.81

Sources: Hong Kong, Census and Statistics Department, *Stastical Report, 1991* (Hong Kong, 1992); Japan, Ministry of Health and Welfare, Institute of Population Problems, *Latest Demographic Statistics, 1991* (Tokyo, 1992); Republic of Korea, Economic Planning Board, *Korea Statistical Yearbook, 1991*(Seoul, National Bureau of Statistics, 1992); Singapore, Department of Statistics, *Yearbook of Statistics, Singapore, 1990* (Singapore, 1991); *Taiwan Province of China, Taiwan-Fukien Demographic Fact Book, 1990.*

Figure VI. Total fertility rate, five industrialized countries or areas, Asia, 1947-1990

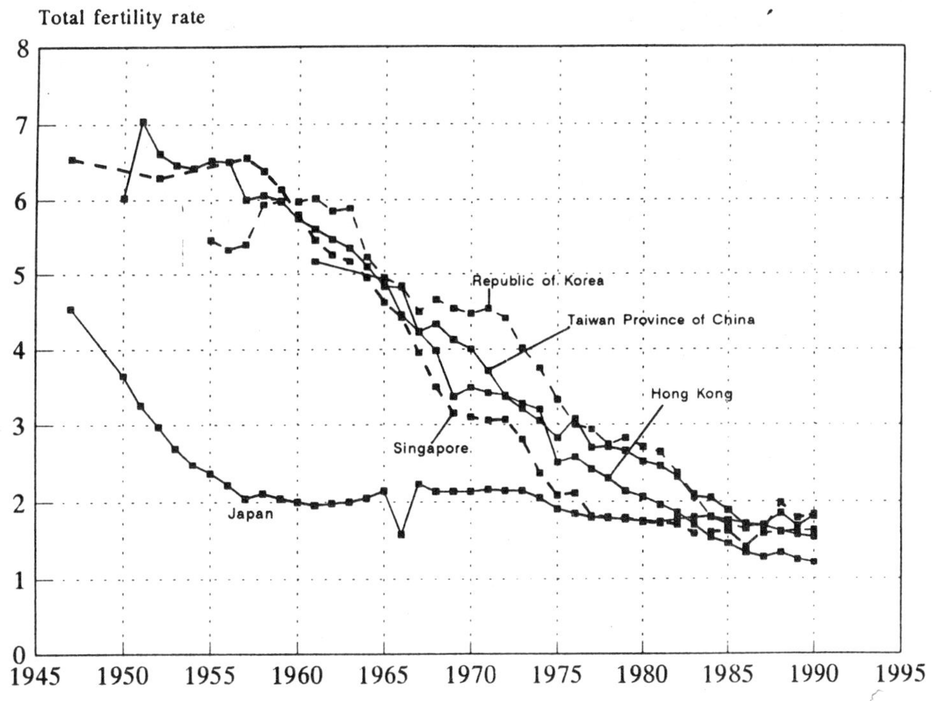

Source: Table 48

fertility decline, the manner of which seems notably different from the previous decline in fertility in the post-war periods? Why have the newly industrialized countries or areas of Asia recently experienced spectacular drops in fertility (figure VI)? It is very interesting to note that although their social and cultural systems are tremendously different from the West, the Asian societies of Hong Kong, Japan, the Republic of Korea, Singapore and Taiwan Province of China, largely share similar econodemographic mechanisms with Europe and Northern America in bringing down their fertility rates. A full account of the causes is beyond the scope of this paper, but the reasons for the historical decline include a wide range of fairly obvious social and economic changes that have accompanied the transformation of society from a rural and agricultural setting to an increasingly urban and metropolitan milieu with a highly industrialized and increasingly service-oriented economy. The transformation encompasses declining infant and child mortality, universal education, decline of religious authority, decline of the patriarchal family system, equality and emancipation of women and pervasive consumer-oriented culture. Such transformations have both decreased the traditional utilities of children and increased the cost of bearing and rearing children. An expansion in female economic participation outside the home has particularly increased the opportunity cost of having children in those industrial settings.

In cognizance of historical continuity, however, the current unprecedentedly low fertility, particularly in Europe, is more appropriately described as reflecting a new social trend and new lifestyle, spreading throughout the market economies of Europe and Northern America in the late 1960s. The emergence of such new social trends and new lifestyles is undoubtedly related to contemporary changes in society and philosophy such that the progressive attitude in all spheres of life has ineluctably increased in Europe in recent years, towards freedom of choice in behaviour and equity of opportunities (Lesthaeghe, 1992; L-esthaeghe and Meekers, 1987). Aspirations for freedom from restrictions and for enjoying the adult-centred life have led parents to cease planning life in terms of the child and his personal future, in contrast to the child-oriented life in nineteenth-century and early twentieth-century Europe, as vividly described by Ariès (see Bernhardt, 1991). Marriage as an institution providing economic security and as an essentially permanent arrangement directed to reproduction and child-rearing is no longer considered indispensable. Indeed, an increasing number of young couples refrain from child-bearing because they do not want to mortgage their future life to children and child-bearing. Van de Kaa (1987) calls the contemporary trends of extremely low fertility the "second demographic transition" (see also Lesthaeghe, 1992).

The more recent continuation of the trend derives from a general shift to a "post-materialist" culture, according to Lesthaeghe (1983). The notion of post-materialism, developed by Inglehart (1977), refers to the effects on people's values of a rising level of affluence that removes worries about satisfying basic material needs, such as food and shelter. With an increase in affluence, the emphasis shifts from survival to satisfaction, from being to having; and an ideology stressing personal fulfilment becomes dominant (Cherlin, 1990). To many social scientists, the heart of the matter in this fertility decline obviously pivots around women's participation in gainful employment outside the home and the enhancement of status of women. It seems to be something to do with what Davis (1984) calls the "sex-role revolution" in the twentieth century and with what Inglehart (1977) calls the "silent revolution", along with changing values and political styles among Western populations.

This sweeping trend of a second demographic transition is fairly well synchronized with the case of Japan where TFR, having remained at a level of about 2.0 for nearly 20 years, suddenly began to decline in 1975 (see table 48 and figure VI). Since then, the decline, though recently slowed, has not stopped. It was once thought that the drop was temporary, due to the postponement of marriage, so that it would eventually halt and the making-up mechanism would soon cause fertility to rise. Unfortunately, Japanese fertility is still declining.

B. Women's participation in economic activity in industrialized societies: general views and issues

It is widely recognized that women's work and fertility are interdependent. Because children absorb a mother's time and also require other resources, a mother's work represents both a constraint on their rearing and a productive resource for their support. Whether women's participation in economic activity increases or decreases with the arrival of additional children will therefore depend upon the particular mix of opportunities available (Lloyd, 1991). There is a huge stock of literature on the linkage between women's increasing role in industrial society and reproductive behaviour. Numerous studies have shown an inverse relation between family size and the extent of female participation in economic activity; that is, gainfully employed married women generally have fewer children than other married women. This relation has been found to be more marked in the industrialized than in the non-industrialized countries, and in urban more than in rural areas. Moreover, it is the women that work for wages, rather than the self-employed or unpaid family workers, that have significantly lower fertility than non-working women (United Nations, 1973; Blake, 1965; Davis, 1984; Fuchs, 1988; Mincer, 1985).

But the relation is not very straightforward. In the long run, fertility changes in accordance with an increase in women's employment underlying economic and social development, but in the short run the association is sometimes not evident. Figure VII indicates the trend of the economic activity rate for females aged 20-39 in comparison with the trend of total fertility in Japan. It is clear from the figure that although TFR declined remarkably between 1950 and 1990, the proportion of employed persons has increased only moderately in the long run and it rather decreased between 1960 and 1975. If one takes instead the proportion of employees, an indicator excluding the self-employed and family workers, then it shows a substantial rise in the secular trend between

Figure VII. Percentage of employed persons and percentage employed among the female population aged 20-39 in comparison with total fertility rate, Japan, 1950-1990

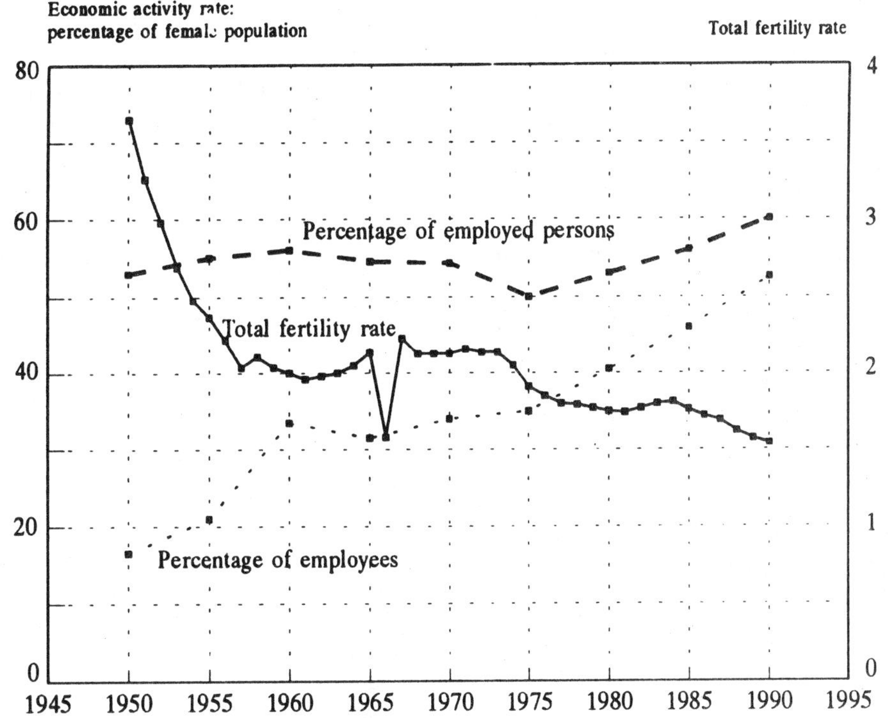

Source: Japan Bureau of Statistics, Management and Coordination Agency, population censuses for quinquennial year beginning in 1950.

1950 and 1990, but with several minor anomalies found in the short run.

At the microlevel of analysis, the interrelation is also complicated and even sophisticated methods do not bring very straightforward findings (Waite and Stolzenberg, 1976; Lloyd, 1991). It seems that a clear inverse relation between women's work and fertility may be modified considerably and may not become manifest, depending upon the availability of a full-fledged child-care system and related child-supporting institutions in some countries.

The study of trends in labour force participation is greatly complicated by the fact that definitions vary between countries and over periods of time. There is a particular need to caution against intercountry and temporal comparisons with regard to female employment, since women's contribution to the total amount of work done in a society is generally underestimated, but to varying degrees. First, housework is not included and other types of unpaid work have frequently been omitted from population censuses and labour force surveys. As women have traditionally had an important function as unpaid family workers, especially in agriculture and small-scale family enterprises, a decline over time in the primary sector, combined with a successive increase in industrial or tertiary employment, would tend to underestimate the growth of female economic activity in the long run.

Traditionally, the pattern of female labour force participation has been termed an "M-shaped age distribution". That is to say, a large proportion of before they deliver their first or second birth. This was a common trend observed in most of the industrialized countries until quite recent years. Now, increasing numbers of women, even after marriage, stay in the labour force. This occurs in part because there are more market opportunities for gainful work with a larger remuneration outside the home, in combination with the development of what might be called "soft industries", which do not require production processes involving heavy, dirty, difficult and dangerous operations; in part because women's work outside has become recognized by the society as rather normal behaviour; and in part because there are increasingly more facilities and institutions available outside for rearing children while women are away from home.

Table 49 presents total fertility rates, female labour force participation rates and proportions of all employed women working part time for selected European countries and Japan in 1975 and 1989. On a very general level, it can be said that during the period 1975-1989 an upward trend in female labour force participation was accompanied by a downward trendin fertility in practically all countries in previous "market-economy Europe". However, the experiences of different countries were so diverse that it is clearly not feasible to distinguish a uniform pattern of a high degree of female labour force participation combined with a relatively low level of fertility or vice versa. The countries with the highest proportion of women in the labour force do not have exceptionally low fertility, and the countries with relatively few women in paid employment do not stand out as having higher fertility levels than the countries with relatively more paid women.

In 1975 the countries of Southern Europe (Greece, Italy, Portugal and Spain) still had above-replacement fertility, but these countries have subsequently experienced notable declines and have joined the below-replacement group. In fact, Italy currently has the lowest fertility rate in Europe, with TFR of only 1.29 in 1990, followed by Spain with of 1.30 in 1989. On the other hand, female labour force participation rates (for age group 25-44) in Italy and Spain were 58.8 and 51.0 per cent, respectively, in 1989, considerably lower than the rate in Sweden 91.3 per cent.

It is clear that this type of very crude intercountry analysis of the relation between fertility and employment in the contemporary Western European context does not give much support to the generally held notion of a negative relation between the two. According to Bernhardt (1991), it is very much an open question whether (women's) employment can be said to exert a strongly fertility-inhibiting effect in contemporary Western Europe, where there is nearly perfect control of reproduction. It depends, among other things, upon the institutional and emotional supports provided for those combining employment and parenthood (Bernhardt, 1991).

C. WORK, MARRIAGE AND CHILD-BEARING IN SOUTHERN EUROPE: AN ENIGMA OF THE LOWEST FERTILITY

As already mentioned, the lowest fertility is observed in Southern European countries, notably in Italy, Portugal and Spain . Southern European countries have been known to lag somewhat behind Northern and Western Europe in socio-economic development and to be more traditional normatively and "totalitarian" politically. The Nordic countries have been known to be most advanced in these respects. Then, why do the Southern European countries have the lowest fertility while Sweden and Norway have now shown considerable upsurges in fertility? In fact, the 1990 figure shows that Swedish fertility currently surpasses the net replacement level. The whole world seems upside-down at first glance.

It is no longer correct to think of Italy in terms of the traditional image of a Southern European Mediterranean country. The current spectacular decline in fertility may mean that Italian people no longer consider children an investment but a burden. In 1987 and 1988, the Population Research Institute in Italy conducted an interesting national sample survey on the opinions and behaviour of the Italians facing the great demographic changes. On the basis of this survey, the Palomba (1990) constructed a table, indicating multiple-choice reasons that contemporary Italian couples do not want another child. Table 50 summarizes the demographic opinions of Italian couples in regard to their rapid fertility decline.

TABLE 49. TOTAL FERTILITY RATES, FEMALE LABOUR FORCE PARTICIPATION AT AGES 25-44 AND PROPORTION OF ALL EMPLOYED WOMEN WORKING PART TIME, SELECTED EUROPEAN COUNTRIES AND JAPAN, 1975 AND 1989

	Total fertility rate		*Female labour force*		*Part time*
Country	*1975*	*1989*	*1975*	*1989*	*1989*
Belgium	1.74	1.58	40.5	69.0	25.0
Denmark	1.92	1.62	59.0	89.1	40.1
France	1.93	1.81	46.8	74.1	23.8
Germany[a]	1.45	1.39	49.8	64.1	30.7
Greece	2.37	1.50	42.7	56.0	8.0
Ireland	3.40	2.11	24.8	47.4	16.5
Italy	2.21	1.29	32.9	58.8	10.9
Luxembourg	..	1.52	..	53.4	16.4
Netherlands	1.66	1.55	24.6	59.7	60.1
Norway	1.99	1.88	31.1	79.0	57.0
Portugal	2.52	1.50	25.9	72.5	10.0
Spain	2.79	1.39	16.6	51.0	11.9
Sweden	1.78	2.02	54.5	91.3	40.0
United Kingdom	1.81	1.81	51.7	72.1	43.6
Japan	1.91	1.57	48.3	60.1[b]	27.5

Sources: For European countries, data adapted from Eva M. Bernhardt, "Working parents in Sweden: an example for Europe?", paper prepared for the Eurostat Conference on Human Resources at the Dawn of the 21st Century, Luxembourg, 27-29 November 1991; for Japan, Bureau of Statistics, *One-percent Census Tabulation of 1990 Census* (Tokyo, 1992).

[a]Data only for the former Federal Republic of Germany.

[b]Figure for 1990.

TABLE 50. REASONS THAT COUPLES DO NOT WANT ANOTHER CHILD, ITALY, 1987-1988

(Percentage)

Reasons	*Important*	*Not important*
Economic costs		
Unsuitable housing	55	44
High cost of raising children	78	22
Psychological costs		
Uncertain future for child	75	23
Difficulty of being a parent	48	50
Difficulty of educating a child	52	47
Lifestyle costs		
Parent's desire for more independence and less responsibility	54	45
Too demanding for the parent	56	42
Mother's work	76	22
General social climate		
Economic and unemployment crisis	88	12
Lack of social services	62	37

Source: Rossella Palomba, "Le opinioni degli italiani su natalità e politiche demografiche", paper prepared for the Conferenza: Popolazione, Società e Politiche Demografiche per l'Europa, Torino, 4-6 April 1990; organized by the Giovanni Agnelli Foundation.

According to table 50, high scores of more than 70 per cent are noted for "high cost of raising children", "uncertain future for child", "mother's work" and "economic and unemployment crisis". "Lack of social services" is also cited with a relatively high score. It is of interest in this connection that the incompatibility between women's work and child-bearing was certainly strongly felt among Italian people, and, by and large, "economic reasons" score very high as reasons for not having another child. In relevance to the present paper, the incompatibility between women's work and family-building was certainly considered as one of the most important reasons that the people were not having an additional child.

In answer to the question why Italy and Spain have such low fertility rates, Castro Martin (1991) adduced the following underlying reasons.

First, economic and social changes occurring in Spain and other Mediterranean countries have been so dramatic in recent years that the families and women have been put in a uncertain state, causing them to delay fertility decisions. There, well-known mechanisms of delayed marriage and childbirth are operating, and the fertility rates for the most recent child-bearing cohort born in the 1960 will probably exceed the current TFR of 1.3. Secondly, the lack of institutional child-care facilities is obvious in the light of the rapid development in service industries and the expansion of women's economic activities. In Spain, child-care facilities are very scarce. Thirdly, long-awaited economic opportunities and affluence have suddenly come to Spain and others since the 1970s. The people feel a temporary sense of euphoria and they do not want to forgo such enjoyment by going through reproduction.

Influences of machismo also prevalent in the Mediterranean region, are taken to work against a reconciliation between women's work and family-building. Although Mediterranean women have changed in a very short period of time from being devoted wives and mothers to being gainfully employed members of the labour force, the family patterns of Mediterranean men have scarcely changed. It is the slight involvement of men in domestic affairs (like men in Eastern Asia) and women's increasing involvement in the public sphere, combined with the lack of social services of child care, that creates an increasing burden for women.

It is argued that there are some similarities between *teishu-kanpaku*(which literally means that husband is the ruler of his home) in Japanese usage and machismo in the Spanish and Mediterranean regions (Gilmore, 1990; Buruma, 1984). Both emphasize a household supremacy attached to adult males and the husband. Historically, however, there are differences in concept between *teishu-kanpaku* and machismo: machismo emphasizes male chauvinism derived from masculine virility; *teishu kampaku* does not include such a sexual connotation. Nevertheless, similarities are also apparent. The present author imagines that, similar to the way that Japanese women have become disenchanted with the male chauvinistic type of marriage and family still prevalent in Japan, Mediterranean women might also have become disenchanted with the traditional husband-wife relationship and child-bearing. Or they may found self-fulfilment through gainful employment. According to Castro Martin (1991), however, one of the primary reasons that fertility has declined to such an unprecedentedly low level in Spain is that women's roles haven changed very rapidly as they made progress in education and work, while the institutional changes needed to reconcile their new roles in the labour force with the demands of child-rearing have been very slow.

Lastly, Perez and Livi-Bacci (1991) maintain that the structural characteristics leading to low fertility in Italy and Spain are essentially the same as in the rest of Western Europe: the decline of nuptiality and the increase of the mean age at marriage; and the increase in women's economic activity rates. Fertility levels achieved by Italy and Spain are currently the lowest, but such levels are not new in Europe. Why then have they appeared in Italy and Spain in spite of an incomplete "contraceptive revolution" and in spite of lagging somewhat behind Northern and Western Europe in terms of economic development? They argue that the societies in Italy and Spain were not ready for the change not only in terms of social services, labour regulations, residential and transportation arrangements etc. but also in terms of social norms, domestic arrangements, division of responsibilities in the family etc. Perez and Livi-Bacci (1991) conclude that, as a result, child-bearing may be costlier for Italian or

Spanish women than in other societies with a longer history of female work in the non-agricultural sector. At the same time, as another type of hindrance they refer to ubiquitous housing shortages for newly-weds in urban areas. The reasons they mentioned seem to be directly applicable to Japan exactly as they are.

D. A Swedish case: harmonized relation between women's work and child-bearing and child-rearing

As mentioned above, Swedish fertility has been increasing steadily since 1986. In 1987, TFR was 1.84: in 1988, 1.96; and in 1989, it surpassed the 2.0 mark. By 1990, it had even risen to 2.14, slightly above net replacement level. It has always been said that whenever Sweden leads the way in the demographic field, the rest of Europe will follow. But it appears enigmatic at first glance that Swedish fertility has undergone this recent upsurge despite having the highest economic activity rate among women of reproductive age, the highest level of cohabitation, one of the highest incomes per capita, the highest age at marriage in Europe etc. Sweden currently shows the highest TFR in Europe, except for Ireland.

It has been argued whether this upswing in TFR is simply a matter of the making-up process of fertility dynamics which has long been overdue. Indeed, the recent upturn of Swedish fertility is, to a large extent, the result of purely demographic factors consistent with a cohort fertility of two children per woman (Gustaffson and Meisaari-Polsa, 1990). Nevertheless, the younger cohorts born in 1956 and afterwards show a stronger propensity to have second- and third-order births, and it looks as though this upward shift is real and is continuing.

In view of the foregoing statement, it is a point well taken that the recent demographic developments in Sweden can in part be attributed to the low-key and largely indirect pronatalism of Swedish social policies (Hoem, 1990). It is well known that the Swedish Government has been trying very hard to provide a State-initiated system of child care that facilitates women's entry into the labour market and continued attachment to child-bearing and child-rearing at minimal cost. Jan Hoem (1990) hence maintains that the record-high and continuously growing labour force participation of Swedish women, combined with comparatively high and increasing fertility, should be seen as a reward for such efforts. The contrast becomes particularly apparent when a comparison is made with the most closely similar country, namely, Denmark. By international standards, Denmark scores high on liberality and modernism, for example, with respect to female labour force participation, cohabitation and non-marital child-bearing, and there is fairly good availability of outside child care. Yet, Denmark has a much lower fertility level (see table 47), a fact that must be connected with the national policies of parental benefits and leave (Hoem and Hoem, 1987).

Jan Hoem is modest in saying that it was tempting to conclude that fertility was responding to the cumulative effects of the determined expansion in public day care, child benefits, parental leave provisions, parents' rights to part-time work and similar measures. But this process underlines the fact that women in Sweden enjoy the highest status of women anywhere.[1] This point may be exemplified by noting that Sweden has the highest proportion of women that are cabinet ministers and executive officers in public office and large industries. The long and arduous efforts of Swedish public and social policies to equalize the status of women with men and to provide parents with a full-fledged child-care system have certainly worked to break through the traditional barriers of incompatibility between female work activities outside the home and child-bearing and child-rearing by mitigating the direct costs and opportunity costs of children.

E. Women's work, marriage and child-bearing and machismo in Eastern Asia

Table 48 and figure VI have already shown the recent spectacular declines in fertility in Japan and the four Asian newly industrialized economies. It is indeed surprising to see that each currently exhibits a below replacement fertility level. Because of the recent convergence of fertility among the countries, it is very tempting to think that there are some common denominators underlying trends in these five countries or areas in Asia.

Although there is still a paucity of systematic models explaining determinants of spectacular falls in fertility in these countries or areas, the common denominators are clear and they may include: *(a)* the remarkable pace of economic development since the 1970s; *(b)* the spread of women's education; *(c)* increases in women's gainful employment outside the home; *(d)* the increase in age at first marriage; *(e)* the fact that children's education has become very costly, not only financially but also psychologically; *(f)* the advent of the mass-consumption society and inundation with high-tech electric and electronic appliances competing with child-bearing; and *(g)* Confucian tradition. At the same time, for the newly industrialized countries or areas in Asia, a word must be mentioned about their Governments' very vigourous campaign of spreading family planning programmes with a well-planned strategy and well-developed bureaucratic organization.

The recent precipitous decline in the fertility of Japan has sent a shock wave through many groups of Japanese people, whether professional or laymen. Some critics have even come to interpret this phenomenon as a result of women's rebellion against the long-standing and nurtured male chauvinism of the society. This reaction by women might even be termed an "anti-machismo movement" in Eastern Asia. Confucianism provides the people in this region with the major moral and ethical code governing their daily conduct. But if there are any gaps in this excellent moral system and philosophy, it is that sufficient attention has not been paid to women. There is no status of women in the ideal society. There is no mention of women in the Analects of Confucius. In the Confucian view, women have long been considered a type of child-bearing machine and domestic servant for men.

Cho, Arnold and Kwon (1982) depict vividly how housewives in the Republic of Korea were ill-treated in their families and communities. In the traditional family there, the suppression and regulation of sex were regarded as virtuous conduct for women. Segregation between husbands and wives was so extensive that their spheres of interest were completely separate: the external world belonged to the husband and the "kitchen" to the wife; each was supposed to be uninterested in the other's world. If a woman lived in an extended family, her behaviour was usually continuously monitored by other members of the family, particularly the mother-in-law, who sometimes even regulated the couple's frequency of union.

Now, in the 1990s, women are quietly or tacitly protesting and rebelling against men, and the long-established Eastern Asian version of machismo is being challenged. Women are understood to be disenchanted with the existing mode of marriage, family and reproduction; and their increasing economic independence permits women to avoid marrying and having a family. The results are the postponement of marriage, non-marriage and fertility decline.

Of course, in Singapore and the Republic of Korea, in particular, family planning programmes have so far been very successful and perhaps too efficiently implemented. At the same time, Japan and the four newly industrialized economies in Asia are either islands or peninsular. Scarcity of resources in relation to population characterizes each country or area. The high population density and psychological resource-scarcity syndrome would certainly have facilitated fertility declines (Kono, 1986; Japan, Ministry of Health and Welfare, 1991).

Table 51 shows a decomposition of the change in TFR in Japan into two elements, one attributable to changes in percentage married and the other attributable to changing age-specific marital fertility rates. In a relatively longer period, the changes in age-specific marital fertility rates account for a greater part of the change in TFR in Japan. But for more recent periods, say, 1975-1990, it is notable that practically all the change in TFR is attributable to changes in the percentage married, which means that the recent reduction in TFR is attributable to late marriage or non-marriage affecting most reproductive ages, rather than to changes in couples' fertility rates.

For the newly industrialized Asian countries or area, that is, the Republic of Korea, Hong Kong, Singapore andTaiwan Province of China, similar decompositions have been performed to show the extent to which changes in marital status structure are important for explaining the change in TFR (Tsuya, 1991). In decomposing these changes, as is shown in table 52, changes in age-specific marital fertility

Table 51. DECOMPASITION OF THE CHANGE IN FERTILITY RATES, JAPAN, VARIOUS PERIODS, 1925-1990

Period of analysis	Level of total fertility rate			Decompositionin into:			
				Difference attributable to changes in percentage married		*Difference attributable to changes in age-specific marital fertility rates*	
	Beginning of period	*End of period*	*Difference in rate*	*Quantity*	*Percentage difference*	*Quantity*	*Percentage difference*
1925-1990	5.1092	1.5426	3.5666	1.7495	49.1	1.8171	50.9
1925-1950	5.1092	3.6524	1.4568	0.9140	62.7	0.5429	37.3
1950-1960	3.6524	2.0039	1.6467	0.2736	16.6	1.3749	83.5
1960-1070	2.0039	2.1349	-0.1310	-0.0513	39.2	-0.0797	60.8
1970-1980	2.1349	1.7465	0.3884	0.2400	61.8	0.1485	38.2
1980-1990	1.7465	1.5426	0.2039	0.3733	183.1	-0.1694	-83.1
1950-1970	3.6524	2.1349	1.5174	0.2222	14.6	1.2952	85.4
1970-1990	2.1349	1.5426	0.5923	0.6132	103.5	-0.0210	-3.5
1950-1975	3.6524	1.9094	1.7429	0.2594	14.9	1.4835	85.1
1975-1990	1.9094	1.5426	0.3668	0.5761	157.1	-0.2093	-57.1

Sources: For rates, calculated by the Institute of Population Problems of the Ministry of Health and Welfare, Tokyo; for method used, Lee-Jay Cho and Robert D. Retherford, "Comparative analysis of recent fertility trends in East Asia", in *International Population Conference, Liège, 1973*, vol. 2 (Liège, International Union for the Scientific Study of Population, 1973).

NOTE: Based on the single year age-specific fertility rates.

rates are in most cases more important than those in marital structure. Yet, for Singapore and for Taiwan Province of China in the most recent period covered by the analysis, changes in marital structure account for more than changes in marital fertility rates themselves. Even for Hong Kong, in the most recent period 1981-1986, shown in table 52, a rather large percentage (35.6) of the change is attributable to that in marital status structure. It can be argued that in these Asian low-fertility countries and areas of Asia, late marriage and non-marriage have increasingly become important explanatory factors for the diminution of fertility in recent years. In the case of Japan and in the newly industrialized economies in Asia to a lesser extent, the people may be encountering incompatibilities between women's work and marriage rather than between women's work and child-bearing (Atoh, 1991).

As was mentioned above, figure VII shows the percentage of employed persons and that of employees among the female population aged 20-39 in comparison with the total fertility rate in Japan. It was noted that the proportion of employed persons has changed only slightly between 1950 and 1990, but the proportion of employees has increased substantially.

Table 53 shows the trends in age-specific labour force participation rates for Japanese females, and table 54 shows the same for the newly industrialized Asian economies. In the five countries or areas together, participation rates have increased moderately to substantially in each age group, except the youngest age group, 15-19. How much these changes are related to fertility declines in those countries or areas is not too clear from this table, of course, but it can be said that there are some significant relation. It may be conjectured that in recent years, at least in Japan, Hong Kong and Singapore, rapid increases in economic activity rates have affected fertility through declines in percentages currently married, particularly for the main reproductive age groups, 20-24, 25-29 and 30-34 years.

F. STATUS OF WOMEN WITHIN THE FAMILY

Tables 55-57 show intercountry comparisons of the status of women within the family. Six countries were surveyed in 1984 and the results indicated how women fared in their daily life and how they felt they were treated within the family (Japan, Prime Minister's Office, 1984). It is regrettable that no Mediterranean

TABLE 52. DECOMPOSITION OF THE CHANGE IN TOTAL FERTILITY RATES, NEWLY INDUSTRIALIZED COUNTRIES OR AREAS, ASIA, PERIODS AROUND 1955-1985

	Level of total fertility rate			*Decomposition into:*	
Period of analysis	*Beginning of period*	*End of period*	*Difference in total fertility rate*	*Differencee attributable to change in percentage married (percentage)*	*Difference attributable to changes in age-specific marital fertility rates (percentage)*
Hong Kong					
1961-1966	5.170	4.455	0.715	24.6	75.4
1966-1971	4.455	3.410	1.045	34.9	65.1
1971-1976	3.410	2.525	0.885	8.5	91.5
1976-1981	2.525	1.975	0.550	28.5	71.5
1981-1986	1.975	1.350	0.625	35.6	64.4
Republic of Korea					
1955-1960	5.460	5.980	-0.520	-92.1	192.1
1960-1965	5.980	4.840	1.140	20.2	79.8
1965-1970	4.840	4.475	0.365	38.5	61.5
1970-1975	4.475	3.330	1.145	11.8	88.2
1975-1980	3.330	2.715	0.615	21.5	78.5
1980-1985	2.715	1.720	0.995	20.9	79.1
Singapore					
1947-1957	6.550	6.470	0.800	-858.2	958.2
1957-1966	6.470	4.505	1.965	53.0	47.0
1966-1970	4.505	3.100	1.405	18.7	81.3
1970-1980	3.100	1.740	1.360	31.1	68.9
1980-1985	1.740	1.625	0.115	183.2	-83.2
Taiwan Province of China					
1956-1960	6.505	5.750	0.755	-74.3	174.3
1960-1966	5.750	4.815	0.935	15.1	84.9
1966-1970	4.815	4.000	0.815	23.3	76.7
1970-1975	4.000	2.825	1.175	36.8	64.4
1975-1980	2.825	2.155	0.310	3.2	96.8
1980-1985	2.515	1.885	0.630	52.2	47.8

Source: Neriko Tsuya, Asia no Shussyoryoku tenkan riron saiko: NIEs no baio chushingto shite (trends and correlates of fertility decline in the NIEs), *Jinkogaku Kenkyu* (Journal of Population Studies) (Tokyo), No. 14 (May 1991), pp. 49-65.

TABLE 53. FEMALE LABOUR FORCE PARTICIPATION RATES, BY FIVE-YEAR AGE GROUP, JAPAN, 1960-1990
(Percentage)

Age group	*1960*	*1965*	*1970*	*1975*	*1980*	*1985*	*1990*
All ages	50.9	49.8	50.9	46.1	46.9	47.7	48.3
15-19	49.6	37.6	35.7	22.6	18.8	17.4	17.5
20-24	69.4	69.7	70.8	66.8	71.1	73.3	75.7
25-29	50.2	46.5	45.1	43.5	49.4	54.1	61.2
30-34	51.4	48.0	47.3	43.2	46.5	49.2	51.0
35-39	55.1	58.3	56.3	52.8	55.5	57.9	59.3
40-44	56.8	62.1	63.6	59.7	61.8	65.8	66.6
45-49	56.8	62.6	64.4	61.9	62.3	65.9	68.3
50-54	51.8	57.8	60.9	58.6	58.7	59.8	62.7
55-59	46.8	50.1	53.7	50.9	50.7	49.8	51.3
60-64	39.2	39.4	43.3	39.2	38.8	37.9	36.9
65 or over	21.0	17.6	19.6	15.8	16.1	15.2	14.9

Source: Japan, Bureau of Statistics, Management and Coordination Agency, *Early Returns of 1990 Population Census: One-Percent Tabulation* (Tokyo, 1992).

countries, such as Italy, Portugal or Spain, were included in the survey, but the survey results show some interesting and meaningful tendencies among different countries. Each of the three tables corresponds well to the others and the patterns are clear. For example, where women felt relatively ill-treated, they believed that the locus of final decision on familial affairs was placed on the husband. Contrasts are great between Japan and the Western countries. The Philippines is somewhere in between. Sweden is the forerunner in enhancing the status of women and gender equality, just as it is in the vanguard in every feature of demographic trends.

As mentioned above, the recent drop in fertility in Japan has been attributed to the sharp reduction in the percentages currently married or the low degree of nuptiality. While a woman's job may induce a male to feel that he could "afford" to marry, it could also encourage a woman to feel that she could "afford" not to marry (Preston and Richards, 1975). It has been pointed out that Japanese or other Asian women are disenchanted, not so much with the possibility of bearing and rearing children but with the traditional male-chauvinistic style of marriage. It is of interest that according to the National Fertility Survey conducted in 1987 by the Institute of Population Problems, nearly 70 per cent of single women answered in the multiple-choice questionnaire that the advantage of not getting married is an assurance of individual freedom in life, not bothered by the family and husband (Japan, Ministry of Health and Welfare, 1989).

To the author's knowledge, there are no comparable surveys among the Asian newly industrialized countries or areas, yet the implication of the above-mentioned survey is clear. In Japan and perhaps in the Republic of Korea, Taiwan Province of China and other areas, women often do not visualize marriage and the family idealistically. In Beckers terms, "the cost of marriage", particularly the opportunity cost, is becoming high in the industrialized societies of Asia, whereas the utility gained from marriage is too small for the women, who work outside the home and earn a substantial amount of money, thus attaining financial autonomy independent of their families (Becker, 1973). It may be argued, therefore, that role incompatibility in Japan does not so much inhibit married women working outside from having children but rather it discourages Japanese women from getting married.

TABLE 54. TRENDS IN FEMALE LABOUR FORCE PARTICIPATION RATES, BY FIVE-YEAR AGE GROUP, FOUR NEWLY INDUSTRIALIZED COUNTRIES OR AREAS, ASIA, VARIOUS YEARS, 1956-1985

Year	*Age group* 15-19	20-24	25-29	30-34	35-39	40-44	45-49
Hong Kong							
1961	47.9	51.1	---------33.9---------		---------38.0---------		42.1[a]
1971	56.4	69.5	39.6		38.7		38.9[a]
1976	47.2	71.8	47.8		42.9		39.6[a]
1981	42.6	79.7	56.8		53.4		46.7[a]
1986	33.6	83.7	64.8		57.9		49.1[a]
Republic of Korea							
1966	38.8	41.3	31.8	35.3	43.3	49.0	46.9
1970	43.7	42.0	30.9	38.6	44.8	49.8	50.2
1975	36.9	44.0	29.2	36.4	48.9	53.6	53.5
1980	30.9	49.2	30.5	41.8	56.0	60.8	64.6
1984	19.1	49.0	31.8	38.7	50.4	59.2	60.4
Singapore							
1957	23.4	22.9	---------18.0---------			---------27.7[b]-------	
1966	25.5	40.9	25.9	21.0	19.2	21.9	20.4
1970	43.0	53.6	30.8	22.7	19.3	17.8	17.5
1975	39.2	64.5	43.3	32.9	28.1	25.4	20.1
1980	48.1	79.0	59.5	45.0	37.7	35.3	27.0
1985	33.8	78.9	66.5	48.8	44.7	39.6	36.3
Taiwan Province of China							
1956	41.1	27.0	16.5	14.9	14.8	13.4	10.7
1966	46.8	33.6	20.6	19.4	20.5	19.9	18.2
1970	45.0	41.4	27.6	28.0	30.6	30.5	27.0
1975	45.6	51.3	34.8	33.7	36.4	37.3	33.7
1980	41.6	55.7	40.3	37.4	43.9	42.2	38.6
1984	34.6	59.3	47.4	47.1	49.0	51.4	44.6

Sources: Hong Kong, Census and Statistics Department, *Hong Kong By-census, 1986* (1987); and *Hong Kong Social and Economic Trends, 1967-1977* (1978); Republic of Korea, *Yearbook of Labour Statistics* (Seoul, Office of Labour Affairs, various years); and *Population and Housing Census Report* (Seoul, National Bureau of Statistics, various years); Singapore, Ministry of Labour, *Yearbook of Labour Statistics*, various years; Singapore, Ministry of National Development and Economic Research Centre, *Singapore Sample Household Survey, 1966* (Singapore, 1967); Taiwan Province of China, *Statistical Yearbook, 1985* (Taipei, Directorate General of Budget, Accounting and Statistics, 1986).

[a] Participation rate for age group 45-54.

[b] Participation rate for age group 40-54.

TABLE 55. INTERNATIONAL COMPARISON OF WOMEN'S PERCEPTION OF HOW WELL THEY ARE TREATED AT HOME, SELECTED COUNTRIES, 1984

(Percentage)

Country	*Number of women surveyed*	*Male much better treated*	*Male somewhat better treated*	*Treated equally*	*Female somewhat better treated*	*Female much better treated*	*Don't know*
Japan	1 294	17.3	49.5	27.1	3.6	0.5	1.9
Philippines	1 200	19.4	10.7	59.1	7.8	2.5	0.05
Germany[a]	1 333	10.1	30.2	47.1	9.4	1.4	1.8
Sweden	1 220	4.4	26.8	62.8	2.4	0.1	3.5
United Kingdom	1 224	11.6	36.9	42.5	6.4	1.1	1.5
United States of America	1 200	19.8	27.8	39.9	7.3	1.5	3.8

Source: Japan, Prime Minister's Office, *Fujin no Seikatsu to Ishiki: Kokusai Hikaku Chosa Kekka Hokoku* (Women's daily life and perception; report of an international comparative study) (Tokyo, 1984).

[a]Data only for the former Federal Republic of Germany.

TABLE 56. INTERNATIONAL COMPARISON OF WOMEN'S PERCEPTION OF LOCUS OF HOUSEHOLD RESPONSIBILITIES WITH RESPECT TO CLEARING THE TABLE AND WASHING DISHES, SELECTED COUNTRIES, 1984

(Percentage)

	Person(s) responsible for tasks						
Country	*Number of women surveyed*	*Husband*	*Wife*	*Children*	*All family members*	*Other persons[a]*	*Not clear*
Japan	1 138	0.8	88.6	3.2	3.5	2.6	1.3
Philippines	976	0.4	57.0	24.5	5.8	10.1	2.2
Germany[b]	983	4.4	72.0	2.8	17.5	2.0	1.2
Sweden	1 000	9.5	52.8	0.7	35.9	0.4	0.7
United Kingdom	1 027	14.9	55.9	3.4	20.2	0.6	5.1
United States of America	888	6.8	64.0	7.3	20.6	0.9	0.5

Source: Japan, Prime Minister's Office, *Fujin no Seikatsu to Ishiki: Kokusai Hikaku Chosa Kekka Hokoku* (Women's daily life and perception; report of an international comparative study) (Tokyo, 1984).

[a]For example, a servant.

[b]Data only for the former Federal Republic of Germany.

TABLE 57. INTERNATIONAL COMPARISON OF LOCUS OF FINAL DECISION IN THE FAMILY WITH RESPECT TO HOUSEHOLD AFFAIRS, SELECTED COUNTRIES, 1984

(Percentage)

Country	*Number of women surveyed*	*Husband*	*Wife*	*Husband and wife together*	*All family members*	*Other persons*	*Not clear*
Japan	1 138	65.5	15.7	13.2	1.1	3.7	0.9
Philippines	976	67.1	7.4	23.8	0.3	1.1	0.3
Germany[a]	983	25.1	6.4	64.5	3.2	-	0.8
Sweden	1 000	11.8	6.3	76.1	5.3	-	0.5
United States of America	888	30.7	10.5	57.3	1.2	-	0.2
United Kingdom	1 027	32.1	19.5	46.1	0.4	0.1	1.9

Source: Japan, Prime Minister's Office, *Fujin no Seikatsu to Ishiki: Kokusai Hikaku Chosa Kekka Hokoku* (Women's daily life and perception; report of an international comparative study) (Tokyo, 1984).

[a]Data only for the former Federal Republic of Germany.

TABLE 58. PROPORTIONAL HAZARD MODEL ANALYSIS OF THE PROBABILITY OF CONCEIVING THE FIRST, SECOND AND THIRD ORDER OF BIRTHS, NATIONAL FERTILITY SURVEY OF JAPAN, 1987

Variables	*Relative degree of birth conception probabilities*		
	First conception	*Second conception*	*Third conception*
Type of marriage			
Match-making	1.00	1.00	1.00
Romantic	0.94	0.97	1.07
Age at first marriage			
Under 23	1.00	1.00	1.00
23-24	0.95	0.94	0.93
25-26	0.95	0.95	0.81[a]
27+	0.78[a]	0.86[a]	0.64[a]
Degree of co-residentiality with parents			
Living together	1.00	1.00	1.00
Living nearby	0.91[b]	0.83[a]	0.72[a]
Living separate	0.86[a]	0.83[a]	0.69[a]
Education of wife			
Junior secondary	1.00	1.00	1.00
Senior secondary	1.02	1.01	0.97
Two-year college	1.04	1.13	1.05
Four-year college and higher education	0.88	1.15	1.50[a]
Occupation of husband at time of marriage			
Agriculture, forestry and fishing	1.00	1.00	1.00
Self-employed but not in agriculture. forestry and fishing	1.00	0.95	0.93
White-collar	0.92	0.94	0.79[a]
Blue collar	0.95	1.00	0.86
Occupation of wife's father			
Agriculture, forestry and fishing	1.00	1.00	1.00
Self-employed but not in agriculture, forestry and fishing	1.04	0.97	1.05
White-collar	0.96	0.90	0.94
Blue-collar	1.02	1.02	1.04
Residence at marriage			
Urban	1.00	1.00	1.00
Rural	1.06	1.09	1.09
Employment status of wife at each pregnancy of birth order			
Permanent work	0.88[a]	0.77[a]	0.60[a]
Part-time work	0.73[a]	0.58[a]	0.32[a]
Family work (2 without pay)	0.81[a]	0.92	0.70[a]
Strictly housewife	1.00	1.00	1.00
Contraceptive experience			
Using contraception	1.00	1.00	1.00
Not using contraception	0.69[a]	0.86[a]	0.62[a]
Waiting time after first conception			
Less than nine months	..	1.00	1.00
More than nine months	..	0.64[a]	0.72[a]
Waiting time after second conception			
Less than 27 months	..	..	1.00
More than 27 months	..	..	0.47[a]
Influence of previous conception			
Feotal death, stillbirth and induced abortion	..	2.50[a]	3.55[a]
Live births	..	1.00	1.00

TABLE 58 *(continued)*

Variables	*Relative degree of birth conception probabilities* *First conception*	*Second conception*	*Third conception*
Notion about education of male children			
Wish to send to college	1.00	1.00	1.00
Dependent upon their will	1.08	1.07	1.10
Do not have to take college education	0.92	1.05	0.91
About fortune			
Life depends upon fortune	1.00	1.00	1.00
Life depends upon hard work	1.03	1.01	1.00
Marriage cohort			
1961-1963	1.00	1.00	1.00
1964-1966	1.07	1.12	1.20
1967-1969	1.16[b]	1.07	1.01
1970-1972	1.18[b]	1.06	0.93
1973-1975	1.24[a]	1.03	1.01
1976-1978	1.19[b]	1.06	1.07
1979-1981	1.29[a]	1.09	0.94
1982-1984	1.20[b]	1.08	0.89
1985-1987	0.99	..	..
	N = 7.587	N = 6.377	N=5.250
	(31) = 483.87[a]	(32) = 832.27[a]	(33) = 1 545.52[a]

Source: Kenji Otani, "Gendai nihonjin josei no ninshin timing ni kansuru proportional hazards model bunseki" (Proportional hazards model analysis of women's reproductive career in present-day Japan), *The Journal of Population Problems* (Tokyo), No. 189 (January 1989), pp. 1-17; English summary.

[a]P<0.001

[b]P<0.001.

G. COMPLEXITIES OF THE RELATION BETWEEN WORK AND FERTILITY

Many studies have been made of the relation between women's economic activity and fertility in the developed countries, but as has been seen, the results are complicated and not straightforward. Some studies have also pointed out the reciprocal nature of the relation, namely, economic activities among women have recently increased since family size has been reduced substantially (Waite and Stolzenberg, 1976; Smith-Lovin and Tickamyer, 1978). The complexities of study results are due in part to the fact that women's economic activity is actually very complex, with repeated entries to and withdrawals from the labour force; and women often work on a part-time or non-permanent basis.

In Sweden, Britta Hoem found no sign of a substantial direct negative influence from labour force participation for progression to the third birth among mothers of two (Hoem, 1991). There is a significant difference in fertility between two-child mothers who are currently employed and the corresponding full-time housewives, but this difference is mainly attributable to the very low fertility among the employed mothers of two children, who have just entered the labour market after a long period of remaining a housewife. Hoem found that current employment status has no significant effect on third births.

The time-series analysis of Japan (figure VII), points out that the percentage of employed persons among women aged 20-39 has changed little since 1950 and even decreased slightly between 1960 and 1975. On the other hand, TFR has been declining very appreciably in a secular trend since 1950, interrupted by a slight temporary upswing from 1960 to 1970. The relative stability of the percentage of employed persons for females is partially due to the definitions used in the Japanese labour statistics, in which unpaid family workers working any number of hours in the week preceding the census, together with the self-employed, are included in the economically active population. On the other hand, however, the percentage of employees, excluding the self-employed and unpaid family workers, among the women aged 20-39 has been increasing continuously since the 1950s. Thus, there seems to be a clear inverse relation in the secular trend between female labour force participation and the total fertility rate. In traditional Japanese agriculture, women used to work on the farm as unpaid family workers, hence in post-war years the mechanization and shrinkage of agriculture in Japan were accompanied by a decline in female economic activity in the primary sector. This tendency operated to offset any increasing trend in female employment in the secondary and tertiary sectors during the 1950s and 1960s.

There is, however, a fundamentally significant inverse relation between women's work and fertility, after controlling various other factors. For example, Otani (1989) worked out an analysis of the 1987 National Fertility Survey of Japan by using a modified proportional hazard model and found that gainful work for women outside the home exerts substantial influences on women's probabilities of first, second and third conceptions, as is shown in table 58. Out of 15 variables included and controlled in the analysis, employment status is found to be among the most important factors affecting pregnancies. In this table, it is puzzling to see that part-time workers tend to have a lesser probability of conceiving than full-time workers. This puzzling pattern may be due in part to the definitional questions; in Japan, "part-time" workers do not necessarily work less than "full-time" working women. Part-time workers may simply not be permanent employees or not be employees on the regular payroll. The part-time worker, however, may not enjoy much leave or fringe benefits. Their inferior working conditions may be much less compatible with child-bearing and child-rearing. The recent national fertility surveys conducted by the Institute of Population Problems indicate a lack of appreciable variation in completed fertility according to labour force status (Japan, Ministry of Health and Welfare, 1988). This means, all in all, that great complexities confront an analysis of women's economic activity and fertility. A strong research agenda should be drawn up to conceptualize the status of women's part-time work in more detailed yet more unambiguous terms.

Cross-sectional studies do not always have the power to disentangle the mechanisms of fertility determination in a meaningful way. Often, as in the case of the Japanese National Fertility Survey, the characteristics of working among women are different in meaning and status at different times throughout their life course. When a woman had been gainfully employed for 15 years but quit work for child-bearing before the survey took place, she was classified as "non-worker" regardless of her past work experience. In a review of World Fertility Survey analyses directed to understanding the relation between women's work and fertility, Lloyd (1991) remarks that a cross-sectional survey cannot be expected to be a useful means of unravelling these causal relation, in the absence of complementary contextual and historical information.

Eiko Nakano has long studied the interrelation between women's employment and fertility in Japan. In a recent study, she demonstrates that a life-course approach to women's economic activity is quite useful and illuminating and substantially contributes to redirect our perspectives on women's labour force participation (Nakano, 1989; Japan, Ministry of Health and Welfare, 1985). That is to say, women's work status is radically different from men's. After they marry, women follow quite unstable and volatile path of economic activity, depending upon their marital status, number of children, economic opportunities and the business cycle.

Figure VIII shows the economic participation of married women by duration of marriage on the basis of a field survey with a sample size of 2,500 married women at Fujisawa City, a middle-sized suburban city of some 350,000 population located on the fringe of the Greater Tokyo Metropolitan area. The survey

Figure VIII. Working experience of married women, by duration of marriage of cohort, Fujisawa City, Japan

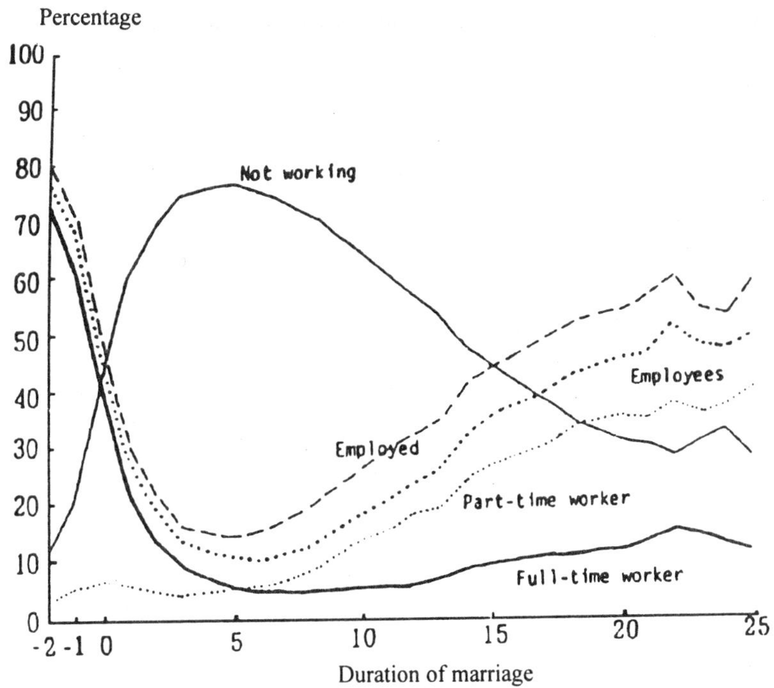

Source: Eiko Nakano, Yuhaigu joshi no life course (Regional differences of the life course pattern among the Japanese married women). *The Journal of Population Problems* (Tokyo), vol. 45, No. 2 (July, 1989), p. 39.

reveals an interesting set of women's patterns of work (Nakano, 1989; Institute of Population Problems, 1985). Among the women gainfully employed, both total employment and "full-time" employment dramatically decrease with the passage of time until 5-10 years after marriage. At that time, the women's full-time employment ratio reaches its nadir at only approximately 5 per cent. After 5-10 years of marriage, full-time employment rises, but not substantially. At the same time, women engaged in part-time work made up a relatively small percentage, but after five years of marriage their relative magnitude starts increasing notably and part-time work soon becomes the predominant pattern of work for married females.

The above-mentioned trends display rather clearly a transitional shift in labour force status from regular and full-time work to a part-time engagement. In this connection, however, a clarification of concepts must be made. Again, as in Otani's study, the terms of "full-time" and "part-time" work, particularly "part-time" work, may be misleading. The part-time workers do not necessarily work fewer hours than the "full-time" workers. In the original questionnaire, the category of "part-time" workers actually was meant to indicate those persons not counted as regular or permanent-status employees. Hence, the "part-time" worker in the survey actually means the "non-permanent" status workers, who do not enjoy seniority-based in-office mobility and many of the company's fringe benefits, including a good number of days of paid leave and vacation.

Figure VIII illustrates some interesting life-course aspects of married women's economic behaviour. At the beginning, before marriage, nearly 80 per cent of women were engaged in the labour force and a large majority of them (nearly 90 per cent) were in full-time jobs. But it is notable that even one or two years before marriage, women began to reduce their full-time employment; and at the time of marriage, almost half of them had quit regular jobs. In the one or two years after marriage, only about 30 per cent or fewer of Fujisawa women were engaged in full-time work. This means that immediately before and after marriage women usually relinquish their full-time work. Hence, there is an anticipation and deep-rooted feeling among the newly-weds and those planning to marry soon that marriage is an obstacle to work and is not compatible with self-fulfilment in working life.

After having one or two children born alive, however, when wives would like to come back to the workforce, they seldom find permanent employment that would give them an equal salary and the same kind of psychological satisfaction that the had previously received. Some women could find permanent jobs somewhere, but the lack of an inexpensive child-care system or one with flexible hours prevents them from resuming permanent employment, perhaps because it would be too hectic physically and mentally to continue to work while rearing children. Thus, a considerable number of married women that were engaged in the labour force dropped out permanently. Part-time or non-regular types of work are considered to be flexible enough to meet the demands of working wives with young children.

It seems a bit too early to draw many general implications out of this case. But women at Fujisawa precisely represent the working patterns of married women in the urban settings of Japan and perhaps, largely exemplify the situation in Japan, which has become substantially urbanized or suburbanized. Even in modern Japan, however, it is surprising that women do not or cannot continue their permanent employment after marriage. Unfortunately, after completing their brief reproductive stint, it is difficult for women to go back to regular or full-time work; hence, they are deprived of their full privileges, seniority and fringe benefits. Do the husbands agree to the idea of their wife's working outside? According to the most recent Mainichi Survey on Family Planning, conducted in 1992, 53.8 per cent of husbands agreed to it and 15.6 per cent flatly disagreed, whereas 22.9 per cent thought that they might have liked to be opposed to it but for practical reasons could not (Mainichi News, 1992). Then, in response to the multiple-choice questions of "why" those husbands agreed to the idea of their spouses' employment, most frequent answers were for "economic reasons", including "helping the household" (40.6 per cent), "for obtaining extra money to help children's education" (17.9 per cent) etc., giving economic reasons a considerable edge over non-economic answers, such as "supporting their wives' self-fulfilment", "because work gives wives goals in life" or "because work expands a social horizon for wives".

According to a survey conducted in the Netherlands in 1985 and 1986, on attitudes regarding marriage, family, sexuality and euthanasia, about 70 per cent of adults found labour force participation of women with school-age children to be acceptable (Van de Kaa, 1987). This is appreciably higher than in the Japanese case.

In Japan and probably in the Asian newly industrialized countries or areas, there remain strong norms that work is for men and the home is for women, and a woman's goal is to be a good wife and a wise mother. In the Republic of Korea, as already cited, the external world belonged to the husband and the "kitchen" to the wife (Cho, Arnold and Kwon, 1982). However, it is very true that the general attitude in these areas of Asia is rapidly changing. The society is becoming ready for change in terms of social services, labour regulations etc., so that role incompatibility might eventually be lessened.

H. A MODEL OF WOMEN'S STATUS AND FERTILITY: SOME IMPLICATIONS

A very speculative and highly simplified model is presented in figure IX to show an approximate relation between the status of women and the level of fertility in various countries. On the X-axis of the figure the degree of status of women is indicated; the Y-axis shows the total fertility rate. "Status of women" here is meant to encompass such a broad area of gender equality and development in the child-care support system.

It is well known that in some Asian countries, particularly in the Indian subcontinent, the status of women is extremely low so that the only means by which women can gain a full-status membership in the family is by having many children, particularly boys, inasmuch as a good number of boys means economic

Figure IX. Speculative relation between status of women and fertility

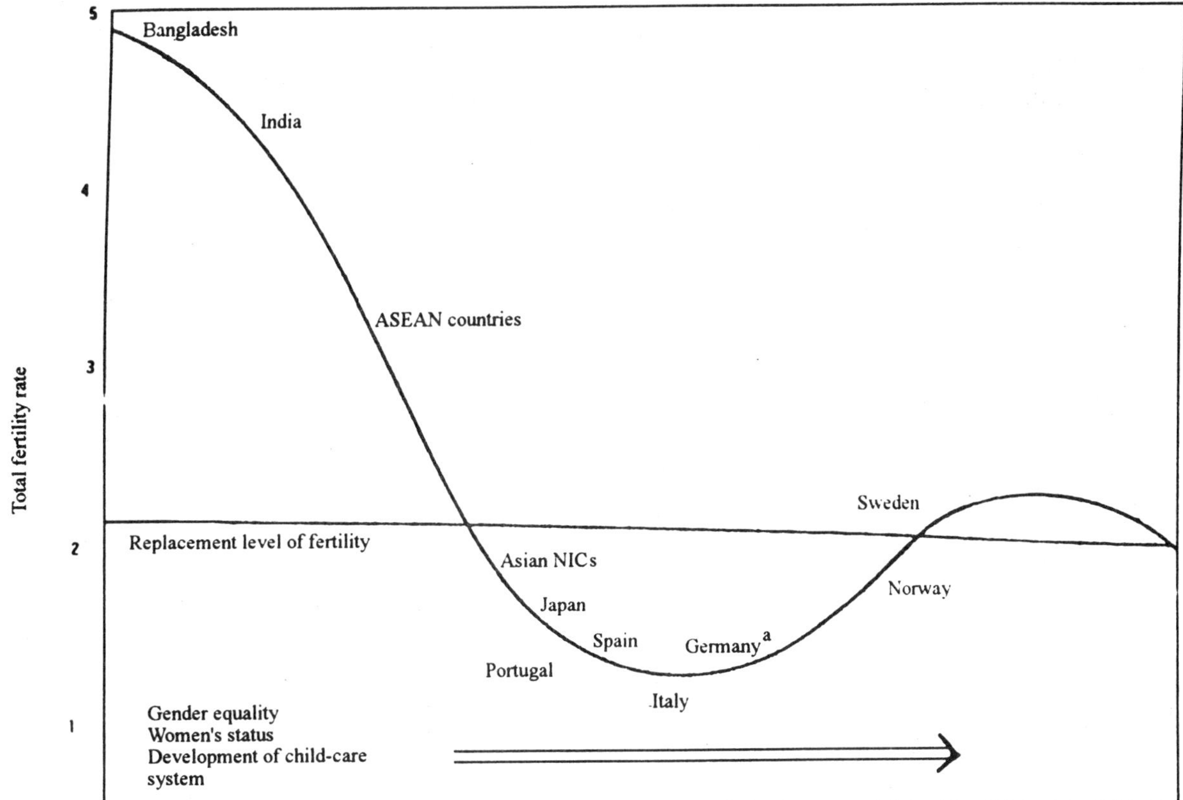

NOTES: ASEAN = Association of South-east Asian Nations; NIC = New industrializing country or area.
[a]Former Federal Republic of Germany.

gains, given labour-intensive agriculture, and future security for the parents, who have nothing but their male heirs to support them after retirement. In addition, families are mostly patriarchal and the existence of a male heir gives the parents an assurance of maintaining their consanguineous and patriarchal lineage. In the traditional families, high fertility is always viewed as good and beneficial for the family and society, but the women are treated as child-producing machines.

If one moves to the right on the X-axis, fertility begins to decline in accordance with the enhancement of the status of women and an increase in women's participation in gainful employment outside the home. This is the case for countries in the Association of South-east Asian Nations where fertility decline is now substantial.

As the fertility rate declines more and more during the course of economic and social development and ideas and methods of family planning spread throughout the population, fertility even sinks below the replacement level. This is the time when a sociopolitical feminist movement takes place and silent struggle for women's status enhancement and self-fulfilment begins. Women begin to rebel against the existing male-chauvinistic norms and the patriarchal family system, requesting widespread reforms in the male-female relationship within the family and in the workplace. This is the stage where such countries as Italy, Spain, Portugal and Japan, together with the Asian newly industrialized economies, are shown in figure IX; and the stage where the former Federal Republic of Germany was several years ago.

When women's struggle for equality becomes widespread, the fertility rate of a country drops to the lowest point. There is then a growing need for reconciliation and terms can be proposed and agreed to by both, men and women. Women would receive privileges and benefits on completely equal terms with men in all the spheres of life, namely, in the family, in husband-wife relations, in offices and other work places, in community and society. Women would be assured of their well-being by securing the compatibility between their work and reproductive activities. Then, fertility will begin to increase (return) to the replacement level. Sweden is now in this stage of development and Norway will soon be.

In Sweden, under the national social welfare system, an attempt is made to lessen the financial burdens of child-bearing and child-rearing. Maternal or paternal leave is available for up to 18 months, during which time 90 per cent of wages are paid. A family allowance scheme pays 485 Swedish kronor (SKr) a month until the child reaches the age of 16 for one child, SKr 970 for two, SKr 1,698 a month for three children etc. (United Nations, 1990). At the same time, among other many useful measures, a number of rules and regulations prohibit sexual discrimination in offices, factories and other workplaces. A working woman should not be penalized in any way when she takes a long paid parental leave. When she returns to work, she can occupy the same post at the same grade without any penalty or demotion due to her long leave of absence. The enactment of rules and regulations maintaining equal status and rights for women and men certainly facilitates the implementation of the world's most generous parental insurance policy in Sweden. This system is an excellent example of "family policy" rather than "population policy" in that it provides the parents with a host of benefits and the ways and means whereby child-bearing and child-rearing can become much less painful and hectic. Although the Swedish family policy is not one every country can copy—it should be remembered that taxpayers have to pay tax based on a high percentage of their income—it would certainly be useful and worth studying if circumstances permit.

According to a Japanese public opinion survey conducted by the Prime Minister's Office (1990), the place where women feel most discriminated against is not in their families but in their workplaces, such as offices, factories and shops. Therefore, it is considered that in Japanese companies, particularly those which are small- or medium-sized, women have difficulty asking their seniors for permission to take parental leave to have babies. These are the places where male chauvinism and gender discrimination are traditionally expressed in a most manifest way. In some cases, it may be most important for the central Government and local governments to introduce stronger equal rights elements into such offices and shops in order to discourage the traditional attitude against female economic activity.

Note

[1]This point is partially bolstered by the international comparisons given in tables 55-57 in section F.

References

Atoh, Makoto (1991). Jinko shosanka no haikei to sono shorai (The decreasing birth rate: backgrounds and prospects). *The Monthly Journal of the Japan Institute of Labor* (Tokyo), vol. 33, No. 8 (August), pp. 2-11.

Becker, Gary S. (1973). A theory of marriage. In *Economics of the Family: Marriage, Children and Human Capital,* Theodore W. Schultz, ed. Chicago, Illinois: The University of Chicago Press.

Bernhardt, Eva M. (1988). Employment and fertility. Paper presented to the Symposium on Population Change and European Society, European University Institute, Florence, Italy, December.

__________ (1991). Working parents in Sweden: an example for Europe? A paper prepared for the Eurostat Conference on Human Resources at the Dawn of the 21st Century, Luxembourg, 27-29 November.

Blake, Judith (1965). Demographic science and the redirection of population policy. In *Public Health and Change: Current Research Issues*, Mindel C. Sheps and Jeanne Clare Ridley, eds. Pittsburgh: University of Pittsburgh Press.

Burvma, Ian (1984). *Japanese Mirror: Behind the Mask: Population on Sexual Demons, Sacred Mothers, Transvestites, Gangsters, Drifters and Other Japanese Cultural Heroes.* New York: Pantheon Books.

Castro Martin, Teresa (1991). Letter to the author, dated 31 September 1991, on the topic of low fertility in Southern Europe.

Cherlin, Andrew (1990). Recent changes in American fertility, marriage, and divorce. In "World population: approaching the year loss", Samuel H. Preston, ed. *The Annals of the American Academy of Political and Social Science* (Newbury Park, California), vol. 510 (July), pp. 145-154.

Cho, Lee-Jay, Fred Arnold and Tai Hwan Kwon (1982). *The Determinants of Fertility in the Republic of Korea.* Committee on Population and Demography Report, No. 14. Washington D.C.: National Academy Press, pp. 98.

Davis, Kingsley (1984). Wives and work: the sex-role revolution and its consequences. *Population and Development Review* (New York), vol. 10, No. 3 (September), pp. 397-417.

Fuchs, Victor R. (1988). *Women's Quest for Economic Equality*. Cambridge, Massachusetts: Harvard University Press.

Gilmore, David D. (1990). *Manhood in the Making: Cultural Concepts of Masculinity*. New Haven, Connecticut: Yale University Press.

Gustafsson, Siv, and Tuija Meisaari-Polsa (1990). Why does fertility in Sweden increase? Draft. Stockholm. Sweden.

Hoem, Britta (1991). The compatibility of employment and childbearing in contemporary Sweden. Paper presented to the European Population Conference, Paris, 21-25 October.

_________, and Jan M. Hoem (1987). *The Swedish Family: Aspects of Contemporary Developments*. Stockholm Research Reports in Demography, No. 43. Stockholm, Sweden: University of Stockholm.

Hoem, Jan M. (1990). Social policy and recent fertility change in Sweden. *Population and Development Review* (New York), vol. 16, No. 4 (December), pp. 735-748.

Inglehart, Ronald (1977). *The Silent Revolution: Changing Values and Political Styles among Western Publics*. Princeton, New Jersey: Princeton University Press.

Japan, Ministry of Health and Welfare, Institute of Population Problems (1985). *Showa 59-nendo Kazoku-Shuki to Toshi no Shugyo Kodo ni Kansuru Jinkogakuteki Chosa*. (Demographic Survey on Married Women's Labor Force Participation). Tokyo.

_________ (1988). *Dai 9-ji Shussanryoku Chosa* (The Ninth Japanese National Fertility in 1987), vol. I, *Marriage and Fertility in Present-Day Japan*. Tokyo.

_________ (1989). *Dai 9-ji Shussanryoku Chosa* (Ninth Japanese National Fertility Survey in 1987), vol. II, *Attitude Toward Marriage and the Family among the Unmarried Japanese Youth*. Tokyo.

_________ (1991). *Heisei 2-nendo Jinko Mondai ni kansuru Ishiki Chosa Hokoku* (Report on the Public Opinion Survey on Population Issues in Japan). Survey Series, No. 4. Tokyo.

_________ Japan, Prime Minister's Office (1984). Fujin no Saikatsu to Ishiki: Kokusai Hikaku Chosa Kekka Hokoku (Women's daily life and perception; report of an international comparative study). Tokyo.

_________ (1990). *Josei ni kansuru Yoron Chosa* (Public Opinion Survey on Women). Report of a public opinion survey that took place in September 1990.

Kono, Shigemi (1986). Perspective on nuptiality and fertility: comment. In "Below-replacement fertility in industrial societies: causes, consequences, policies", Kingsley Davis, Mikhail S. Bernstam and Rita Ricardo-Campbell, eds. *Population and Development Review* (New York), vol. 12, supplement, pp. 171-175.

_________ (1991). Determinants and consequences of the recent subreplacement fertility child welfare. *Quarterly News from Japan* (Tokyo), vol. 12, No. 1 (September), pp. 2-15.

Lesthaeghe, Ron (1983). A century of demographic and cultural change in Western Europe. *Population and Development Review* (New York), vol. 9, No. 3 (September), pp. 411-435.

_________ (1992). The second demographic transition in Western countries: an interpretation. Paper presented to the Seminar on Gender and Family Change in Industrialized Countries, Rome, Italy, 26-30 January 1992. Sponsored by the International Union for the Scientific Study of Population.

_________ Dominique Meekers (1982). Value changes and the dimensions of familism in the European community. *European Journal of Population* (Amsterdam), vol. 2, No. 3/4 (May), pp. 222-268.

Lloyd, Cynthia B. (1991). The contribution of the World Fertility Surveys to an understanding of the relationship between women's work and fertility. *Studies in Family Planning* (New York), vol. 22, No. 3 (May/June), pp. 146-161.

Mainichi News (1992). Dai-21 kai Zenkoku Kazoku Keikaku Yoron Chosa (Summary of the 21st National Survey on Family Planning) (Mainichi News, Tokyo) (11 May).

Mason, Karen Oppenheim (1988). *A Feminist Perspective on Fertility Decline*. Population Studies Center Research Reports, No. 88-119. Ann Arbor: University of Michigan.

Mincer, Jacob (1985). Intercountry comparisons of labor force trends and of related developments: an overview. *Journal of Labor Economics* (Chicago, Illinois), vol. 82, No. 2 (March-April), pp. S1-32.

Nakano, Eiko (1989). Yuhaigu Joshi no life course (Regional differences of the life course patterns among Japanese married women). *The Journal of Population Problems* (Tokyo), vol. 45, No. 2 (July), pp. 209-222. English summary.

Otani, Kenji (1989). Gendai nihonjin josei no ninshin timing ni kansuru proportional hazards model bunseki (Proportional hazards model analysis of women's reproductive career in present-day Japan. *The Journal of Population Problems* (Tokyo), No. 189 (January), pp. 1-17. English summary.

Palomba, Rossella (1990). Le opinioni degli italiani su natalita e politiche demografiche. A paper presented to Conferenza: Popolazione, Societá e Politiche Demografiche per l'Europa, Torino, 4-6 April. Organized by the Giovanni Agnelli Foundation.

Perez, Margarita Delgado, and Massimo Livi-Bacci (1991). Lowest in the world: fertility in Italy and Spain. Unpublished paper.

Preston, Samuel H., and Alan Thomas Richards (1975). The influence of women's work opportunities on marriage rates. *Demography* (Washington, D.C.), vol. 12, No. 2 (May), pp. 209-222.

Smith-Lovin, Lynn, and Ann R. Tickamyer (1978). Nonrecursive models of labor force participation, fertility behavior and sex role attitudes. *American Sociological Review* (Washington, D.C.), vol. 43, No. 4 (August), pp. 541-557.

Tsuya, Noriko (1991). Asia no shussyoryoku tenkan riron saiko: NIEs no baio chushinto shite (Trends and correlates of fertility decline in the NIEs). *Jinkogaku Kenkyu* (Journal of Population Studies) (Tokyo), No. 14 (May), pp. 49-65.

United Nations (1973). *The Determinants and Consequences of Population Trends*, vol. I, *New Summary of Findings on Interaction of Demographic, Economic and Social Factors*. Population Studies, No. 50. Sales No. E.71. XIII.5.

_________ (1990). *World Population Policies*, vol. III, *Oman to Zimbabwe*. Population Studies, No. 102/Add.2. Sales No. E.90. XIII.2.

Van de Kaa, Dirk (1987). *Europe's Second Demographic Transition*. Population Bulletin, vol. 42, No. 1, Washington, D.C.: Population Reference Bureau.

Waite, Linda J., and Ross M. Stolzenberg (1976). Intended childbearing and labor force participation of young woman: insights from non-recursive models. *American Sociological Review* (Washington, D.C.), vol. 41, No. 2 (April), pp. 235-252.

XXVII. INTERNATIONAL LABOUR ORGANIZATION STANDARD-SETTING, POLICY STUDIES AND TECHNICAL COOPERATION IN RELATION TO POPULATION ISSUES AND TO WOMEN

Christine Oppong*

This paper outlines the mandate and a range of activities of the International Labour Organization (ILO) concerning women workers and several labour and population issues. These issues include, on the one hand, promotion of equality and protection in the workplace; and, on the other hand, migration, maternity, fertility, family size, family responsibilities and planning and reproductive health and mortality.

First, relevant aspects of the constitution and mandate are highlighted and then a number of labour issues that are particularly salient for women are discussed. Several matters currently on the ILO agenda are outlined and a number of areas for needed action during the current decade are stressed.

A major emphasis is on the individual and national levels. It will be difficult, even impossible, to promote international labour standards with regard to promotion of equality and protection of vulnerable workers or to meet economic goals if associated demographic concerns and gender issues are ignored. Thus, a number of major points are stressed:

(a) Girls in the teenage years cannot enjoy equal opportunities for vocational training and employment if motherhood and the first pregnancy are not postponed long enough. Girls therefore need adequate protection and resources to help them time these critical transitions to adulthood;

(b) Women workers cannot easily balance and cope simultaneously with occupational and family responsibilities if they are unable to space births adequately. Access to modern means to achieve this goal is required by all workers, as traditional spacing methods fall into disuse or become impracticable. Workplaces, both formal and informal, are after the ideal sites in which relevant information and services can be located;

(c) Women workers need support and facilities of various types in different circumstances to enable them to breast-feed their infants, with sufficient frequency and for sufficient lengths of time to promote child survival and development and maternal health;

(d) Women suffering inequality and precarious labour contracts are not infrequently subject to sexual harassment in their places of work. Realization is growing of the need for sexual protection of weaker workers and of the implications for reproductive morbidity and mortality of failure to promote such protective measures;

(e) Increasing numbers of women are becoming labour migrants, internationally as well as nationally. The potential scope for and actual extent of their sexual as well as economic exploitation is becoming increasingly recognized. The economic, demographic and health implications of these trends are serious and warrant appropriate attention and action of various kinds, including promotion of existing measures to protect migrant workers;

(f) Growing proportions of domestic groups are headed by women alone, who carry out labour-intensive, heavy manual work to maintain dependent families, aided only by their children. The neglect of this vulnerable category of workers in economic and population policies has serious consequences with regard to increasing poverty and continuing high

*International Labour Office, Geneva, Switzerland. Christine Oppong prepared and is responsible for the text, which was drafted mainly on the basis of International Labour Organization documents, with advice and inputs from several colleagues, including Maria Ducci, Eugenia Date-Bah, Azita Berar-Awad, Assefa Bequele, Roger Böhning, Valentina Forastieri, Gretchen Goodale, Beth Goodson, Neleen Haspels, Catherine Hein, J. Krishnamurty, Larry Kohler, Evie Messell, Amerjit Oberai, Pat Pereira, Hélène Pour, Marie Claire Seguret, Constance Thomas, Anne Trebilcock, René Wéry, Patricia Weinert and Linda Wirth. This paper was produced with financial support from the United Nations Population Fund.

levels of infant and maternal mortality and high fertility;

(g) Given the nature of their work, very few women, compared with men, have access to social security benefits and pension schemes, with the result that the majority depend ultimately upon their off-spring for support in their old age or sickness, with corresponding pressures for continuing high fertility;

(h) Greater equality of resources emanating from occupational roles is likely to be linked to greater equality of spouses in the domestic domain. The latter aspect is linked to family size aspirations and outcomes and the capacity of spouses to communicate and plan;

(i) At the national level, before gender issues can be put into the mainstream and full account taken of women's work in policy-making and programme design, the databases available need to reflect more adequately women's productive activities and how they are linked to demographic outcomes. Methods for measuring and evaluating women's work already exist. They need to be adopted and linked to population variables and the resulting data analyses used effectively in the design and execution of more gender-sensitive labour, population and development policies and programmes;

A. Background[1]

This paper outlines the scope and content of past and current ILO standard-setting, policy research and technical support service activities, which focus on women workers, their protection and promotion of equality and have a latent or manifest link with demographic variables.

In the discussion, some of the labour issues currently of most salient concern to women workers are highlighted. These issues include changes occurring in employment opportunities, working conditions and environments and the continual inequalities in access to resources required for economic activities, as well as the growing need for protection in certain areas.

Lastly, the paper calls attention to a number of critical areas in which there is likely to be increasing need and pressure for action of various types on the part of the ILO during the rest of the decade.

The topics highlighted are seen as especially significant, in view of some of the profound impacts of the contemporary economic and demographic changes. The latter changes include:

(a) Growing impoverishment and youthful age structure of populations in the developing world;

(b) Increasing numbers of working mothers shouldering family responsibilities alone or with inadequate support or unequal divisions of domestic labour;

(c) Growing numbers of working mothers for whom employment and family responsibilities are spatially separated, who thus suffer the effects of strains and conflicts between their different sets of responsibilities and tasks, including employment and breast-feeding and child care;

(d) Rapidly growing numbers of vulnerable female workers in precarious, part-time, insecure forms of employment contracts, in sex segregated, male-dominated labour markets; and

(e) Increasing numbers of female migrant workers, who are unprotected economically and sexually because of their separation from spouses and distance from dispersed kin.

Accordingly, the concern of this discussion is with those aspects of the ILO mandate and activities which are, on the one hand, focused on the promotion of equal opportunities and treatment of women workers or their protection in workplaces and, on the other hand, have an explicit or implicit demographic aspect. Thus, they are concerned either with migration, morbidity, mortality, maternity, fertility, family size and planning or with reproductive health of women workers. It does not purport to include and address the total array of ILO activities that concern women workers, even though they may have some tangential bearing on the topic.

B. Constitution and mandates: protection, equality and population issues

Since 1919, when the ILO was created, the principle of equal treatment and opportunities for women workers, including equal pay, has been embodied in the constitution. This principle was restated in the Declaration of Philadelphia (1944), annexed to the Constitution, which proclaims that all human beings, whatever their race, creed or sex, have the right to pursue their material well-being and spiritual development in conditions of freedom and dignity, economic security and equal opportunity.

Since its inception, the ILO has adopted more than 170 conventions and recommendations. These instruments cover a broad range of matters in the field of labour and most of them apply equally to women and men. Thus, women enjoy the same rights as men in various fields covered by the ILO instruments, such as fundamental human rights, employment and training, working conditions and occupational health and safety. In addition to these general instruments, the ILO has also adopted a number of standards directed especially to women workers.

In fact, the ILO, over time, has given continuous attention to the problems of women workers in a variety of ways, through all its means of action, including examination of issues at the International Labour Conference, the regional ILO conferences, industrial committees, meetings of experts and international symposia: in its training and workers' education programmes and materials; in its research and distribution of information, in its technical cooperation activities; and, most specifically, in the setting and promotion of international labour standards.

The ILO Constitution provides for various procedures designed to encourage ratification of the conventions and application of standards generally (article 19), including examination of the application of conventions that have been ratified (article 22).

These procedures involve action by a Committee of Experts on the Application of Conventions and Recommendations and a Tripartite Committee of the Conference on the same subject, which meet annually. In addition, there are representation procedures (article 24) and complaints procedures (article 26) that allow not only Governments but also employers or workers' delegates, or organizations, to call for the examination of cases involving the application of conventions that a country has ratified.

Essentially, the ILO activities focused on women workers are directed to ensuring women's freedom to participate in labour forces on an equal basis with their male peers, and where necessary, protected from occupational hazards and noxious substances in the workplace, especially those to which their female physiology makes them specially vulnerable. These activities are also directed to facilitating a more equitable, harmonious and manageable balance between reproductive and productive activities and responsibilities, that is, parental, occupational and domestic roles—for all workers with family responsibilities, female and male.

With regard to issues of elimination of discrimination against women and promotion of equality of opportunity and treatment for them in employment and connected matters, there are several texts of general scope, comprising several resolutions and plans of action, in addition to conventions and recommendations.

These instruments include a resolution concerning women workers in a changing world, adopted by the International Labour Conference at its 1964 session, which *inter alia,* requested member States to consider the desirability of taking appropriate steps to coordinate research, planning, programming and action on women workers' opportunities, needs and problems and to encourage the dissemination of relevant information.

In 1964, the Conference also adopted a resolution concerning the economic and social advancement of women in developing countries. It requested member States, *inter alia,* to give priority to improving the status of women with respect to training and employment opportunities.

In 1975, the Conference adopted the Declaration on Equality of Opportunity and Treatment for Women Workers, which is very wide-ranging in scope and included a number of specific statements regarding women's reproductive roles (see ILO, 1975). Accordingly, paragraph 5 notes that special measures should be taken to facilitate the continuing education and training of women on the same basis as men and to provide retraining facilities for them, especially during and after periods of absence from the labour force.

Paragraph 6 states that there should be no discrimination against women workers on the grounds of marital status, age or family responsibilities.

Paragraph 8 states that there should be no discrimination against women workers on the grounds of pregnancy and childbirth and that because maternity is a social function, all women workers shall be entitled to full maternity protection in line with the minimum standards set forth in the Maternity Protection Conventions (Nos. 3 and 103), the costs to be borne by social security, public funds or means of collective arrangements. Paragraph 8 also notes that all couples and individuals have the basic right to decide freely and responsibly on the number and spacing of their children and to receive the necessary information, education and means to exercise this right. In addition, paragraph 9 states that studies and research shall be undertaken into processes that might have a harmful effect on women and men from the standpoint of their social function of reproduction.

Furthermore, paragraph 10 states that appropriate measures should be taken to strengthen social infrastructures and to provide the necessary supporting services and equipment in the community, in particular child-care and education services.

In 1975, the Declaration on Equality was also accompanied by a resolution concerning a Plan of Action with a view to promoting equality of opportunity and treatment for women workers. Within the scope of national action, it was urged, *inter alia*, that women with particular difficulties should be given attention, "such as migrant women who are frequently the victim of discrimination and exploitation and who also run social risks".

With regard to girls and young women and their special needs, the Human Resources Development Recommendation of 1975 outlined the measures required, including creating the conditions needed for girls to take up vocational training and employment opportunities in the same ways as their male counterparts.

In the Plan of Action, the need for access to maternity protection and child-spacing methods were again stressed in article 7, as well as in article 8 on the need for strengthening of social infrastructures and for education and measures to encourage more equitable sharing of household tasks and child care.

In 1985, at the end of the United Nations Decade for Women: Equality, Development and Peace, the International Labour Conference produced another resolution on equal opportunities and equal treatment of men and women in employment. This text again underlined the need to ratify and execute the provisions in all the previous relevant conventions and recommendations stressing, *inter alia*, the need for measures designed to encourage such education as would encourage the sharing of family responsibilities between men and women.

In 1987, the ILO Plan of Action on Equality of Opportunity and Treatment of Men and Women in Employment (ILO, 1985a) was intended to implement the conference resolution. Strategies suggested by the Plan include strengthening measures to improve the work environment. This aspect covers occupational safety and health, arrangement of working time, work organization, maternity protection, child-care facilities and harmonization of work and family responsibilities, including population and family welfare programmes.

The Plan notes that attention would focus particularly on measures directed to maternity protection and those relating to arrangement of working time and the development of work-related facilities that are particularly important for promoting equal opportunity, since they can assist workers in coping with family responsibilities that still weigh most heavily on women.

The ILO standard-setting activities directed to women have been guided by two objectives: to protect women against exploitation at work, including the safeguarding of their health, particularly before and after childbirth; and to accord equality of opportunity and treatment for them at work with men.[2]

The principle of equality forms the basis of three major ILO conventions and their accompanying recommendations: the Equal Remuneration Convention of 1951 (No. 100), the Discrimination (Employment and Occupation) Convention of 1958 (No. 111) and the Workers with Family Responsibilities Convention of 1981 (No. 156).

The more recent standards are sufficiently flexible to be adaptable to different national situations and economic conditions. Several are especially relevant to female workers and also to population issues.

Among the latter group are those which concern the protection of migrant workers and the protection of reproductive health and those relevant to the resolution and avoidance of potentially serious role conflicts between productive and reproductive tasks and responsibilities—maternal, occupational and domestic.

These issues have, *inter alia*, implications for child survival and development and birth-spacing, as well as maternal well-being and stress loads suffered. They are relevant to concern for the protection of breast-feeding and more equitable divisions of domestic responsibilities.

Just one decade ago at a United Nations Expert Group Meeting on the Family and Population, a review of international labour standards promoting sexual equality and protection of mothers and the young indicated the potentially profound significance of these labour standards in helping to shape familial roles and relationships, noting their crucial connection with fertility levels and changes.[3]

Maternity protection

There has been a considerable influence on national legislation of the Maternity Protection Conventions of 1919 (No. 3) and 1952 (No. 103, revised). Each has been ratified by 25 countries.[4] Twelve weeks of maternity leave are provided for, including at least six weeks after confinement. During that period, the woman is entitled to receive cash and medical benefits, financed from public funds, the rates of which are to be fixed by national laws or regulations, "so as to ensure benefits sufficient for the full and healthy maintenance of herself and her child in accordance with a suitable standard of living".

During the period of statutory maternity leave there is a prohibition on dismissal. Following maternity leave, mothers should be able to interrupt their working time to breast-feed "at a time or times to be prescribed by national laws or regulations".

The Maternity Protection Recommendation of 1952 (No. 95) advises that whenever necessary or practicable, the maternity leave should be extended to a total period of 14 weeks. In addition, wherever practicable, nursing breaks should be extended to one and a half hours per day and should be capable of adjustment in frequency and length on production of a medical certificate. Furthermore, provision should be made for the establishment of facilities for nursing or day care, preferably outside the undertaking where the women are working, "wherever possible, provision should be made for the financing or at least subsidizing of such facilities, at the expense of the community or by compulsory social insurance".

At the same time, women workers should have the option of avoiding work prejudicial to their own or child's health, work such as heavy weight-lifting or prolonged standing. In view of the workforce coverage of the Maternity Protection Convention and Recommendation—that is, only formal sector employees—only a very small proportion of the world's working mothers and their nursing infants are covered by these legal provisions, vital as they may be for child survival and development and birth-spacing, as well as maternal ability to cope with demands of multiple roles.

Workers with family responsibilities

Other ILO instruments are also relevant to the difficulties arising from simultaneously coping with parental and occupational responsibilities and activities. In 1965, the International Labour Conference adopted the Employment (Women with Family Responsibilities) Recommendation (No. 123). Its goal was to enable women with family responsibilities to exercise their right to work outside the home without being subject to discrimination and to encourage the provision of services and facilities that would enable women to harmonize their work and family responsibilities.

In 1981 the International Labour Conference, recognizing that changes in the traditional roles of men and women in society were necessary to achieve fullequality between the sexes, adopted the Workers with Family Responsibilities Convention (No. 156) and Workers with Family Responsibilities Recommendation (No. 165), which replaced the Women with Family Responsibilities Recommendation. Their aim was to strengthen protection for all workers with family responsibilities and to build workplaces where both men and women would have the choice and opportunity to respond to parental and family duties.

These instruments provide that it should be an aim of national policy for men and women workers to be able to exercise their right to engage in employment, without being subject to discrimination because of their family responsibilities and to the extent possible "without conflict between their employment and family responsibilities".

The Convention calls for account to be taken of the particular needs of workers with family responsibilities in regard to vocational training, terms and conditions of employment and in social security, as well as through the development or promotion of public or private community services such as child care. Appropriate measures should be taken to broaden public understanding of the principle of equality of opportunity and the problems associated with family responsibilities. The latter problems, as such, are not to constitute a valid reason for termination of employment.

These instruments emphasize the importance of providing child care and employment adaptations and note the need for changing traditional attitudes of men and women to their roles at work, in the family and society.

Under article 19 of the Constitution, reports have been requested of all member States on measures taken to give effect to the provisions of these instruments. An analysis of the information submitted will be considered by the Committee of Experts on the Application of Conventions and Recommendations and by the International Labour Conference Committee in 1993. The Committee will accordingly review measures that have been taken worldwide in this area and identify prospects for and obstacles to ratification.

Discrimination in employment and occupations

The most comprehensive standards concerning equality are contained in the Discrimination (Employment and Occupation) Convention (No. 111) and Recommendation (No. 111), adopted in 1958 to deal with the overall problem of discrimination on the grounds of race, colour, sex, religion, political opinion, national extraction or social origin. Both instruments apply to all persons and to all forms of employment, whether in the private or the public sector, salaried or independent. They define the terms "employment" and "occupation" as including " access to vocational training, access to employment and to particular occupations and terms and conditions of employment".

The subsequent instruments relating to particular types of discrimination have referred expressly or by implication to this definition. Certain measures are not deemed to be discrimination. Thus, article 5 of the Convention provides that special measures of protection or assistance provided for in other ILO conventions or recommendations shall not be deemed to be discrimination. These include protection on the grounds of sex.

Member States having ratified the Convention undertake to declare and pursue a national policy directed to eliminating all forms of discrimination in respect of employment and occupation. They are bound to repeal any statutory provisions and modify any administrative instructions or practices that are inconsistent with this policy and to enact legislation and promote educational programmes that favour its acceptance and implementation in cooperation with employers and workers organizations.

In order to promote ratification of Convention No. 111, which has been ratified by 111 countries, it was decided to request those countries which had not yet ratified it to furnish reports every four years under article 19 of the Constitution. Special quadrennial reports have been examined by the Committee of Experts on four occasions, in 1980, 1984, 1988 and 1992. This examination is now a set practice and will continue. This special request is additional to the possibilities of normal use of this procedure, which enabled the Committee of Experts to submit comprehensive studies concerning the instruments on three occasions, in 1963, 1971 and 1988, thus already encouraging ratification of the Convention.[5]

Since their adoption, these instruments have had a significant influence on the promotion of equality of opportunity and treatment. Over time, the Committee of Experts on the Application of Conventions and Recommendations—a key element in the ILO supervisory machinery—has been able to note a great variety of legislative and practical measures taken in a number of countries to eliminate discrimination and promote equality of opportunity and treatment, particularly for women workers.[6]

Since the problem of sex discrimination affects all countries, it was given special attention in the general survey prepared in 1988 by the ILO Committee of Experts on the Application of Conventions and Recommendations. The survey showed that in a number of countries machinery has been established to ensure practical implementation of national policy designed to promote equality of opportunity and treatment in respect of sex.

The problem of indirect discrimination, particularly occupational segregation based on sex, was studied. Outdated attitudes and stereotypes concerning male and female tasks were found to be still pervasive in a great number of countries, even though some progress had been made. The survey also noted that sexual harassment is a potential threat to women workers.

The adoption of affirmative action or corrective programmes derived from the observation that banning discrimination is not sufficient to eliminate de facto discrimination based on sex. The survey stressed that only a combination of legislative and practical measures, such as affirmative action, encouraging the understanding and acceptance of the principle of equality, could lead to the elimination of various forms of discrimination.

The Equal Remuneration Convention (No. 100) and Recommendation (No. 90), both adopted in 1951, relate specifically to the elimination of discrimination between men and women workers in respect of remuneration. The main principle is that men and women should receive equal pay for work of equal value. This Convention therefore acknowledges and addresses the significant problem of the serious undervaluation of women's work and calls upon member States to take measures to remedy that situation.

Other ILO instruments contain provisions proscribing discrimination on the ground of sex in certain areas. These include the Employment Policy Convention (No. 122) and Recommendation (No. 169). These instruments provide that ratifying States shall declare and pursue as a major goal an active policy designed to promote full, productive and freely chosen employment, and mention is made of the need to ensure the fullest possible opportunity for workers to qualify for and use their skills in jobs for which they are suited, irrespective in particular of sex.

In addition, the Termination of Employment Convention of 1982 (No. 158) includes among the causes that do not constitute a valid reason for termination, marital status, family responsibilities, pregnancy and absence from work during statutory maternity leave, in addition to the grounds covered in Convention No. 111.

Protection or equality

While in the early years of ILO activities emphasis was placed on protection, over time there has been a shift of attention towards ensuring application of the principle of equality. This shift in focus led the International Labour Conference in 1985 to call for a tripartite review at the national level of all protective measures to ensure that they shall not infringe on the principle of equality; and where such measures are found to exist, they should either be repealed or, wherever possible, extended to men as well as women.

With regard to protection, in addition to the ILO standards that prohibit the employment of women for tasks or for the handling of substances prejudicial to maternity, there are others relating to such issues as night work and underground work in the mines.

Some countries have denounced the conventions on these subjects on the grounds that they are no longer adapted to changing concepts of equality and changing customs and working conditions. Other countries have remained attached to these instruments and have pointed out that the requirements for elimination of the abuses these conventions were designed to deal with are still far from satisfactory everywhere, particularly in the developing countries.

The question of reconciling protective measures and the standards on the equality of opportunity was discussed by a Meeting of Experts on Special Protective Measures for Women and Equality of Opportunity and Treatment, held in Geneva in October 1989 at the invitation of the ILO. This meeting had a dual function. On one hand, it both re-examined and evaluated the situation in the area of protective measures and equality and, on the other hand, it provided views to the ILO Governing Body on the direction to adopt concerning activities relating to protective measures.

The first preoccupation of the experts was to secure for women workers a safer and healthier working environment and a better quality of life, without creating nor perpetuating discrimination.

Subsequently, at its 77th session (June 1990), the International Labour Conference adopted new international standards on night work. On the one hand, it adopted a convention setting conditions of work applying to night work and to night workers and a recommendation that supplemented it. These instruments covered especially health, safety, remuneration, maternity protection and social services of night workers.

At the same time, the Conference adopted a protocol revising the Night Work (Women) Convention, of 1948 (No. 89, revised). This protocol reconciled the need for the protection of workers engaged in night work and the principle of equality of opportunities and treatment in employment.

The principle of equality between men and women has continued to broaden with the realization that equality in one area, such as pay, can only be achieved through the attainment of equality, dignity and respect in all areas of life. It has thus been recognized in standard-setting that in order to ensure equality for women at work, some attitudes and practices in society have to change, particularly those concerning divisions of family responsibilities.

Moreover, parental responsibilities might commence soon after puberty for girls but not boys and not infrequently do so, immediately making the chances of girls in training systems and labour markets distinctly unequal—an inequality with a marked tendency to continue through life.

The population mandate of the International Labour Office

For a quarter of a century and more, the International Labour Office has been actively concerned with population issues. In 1967, following international debates on the critical linkages between population and development in the mid-1960s, the International Labour Conference invited the Director-General to study the implications of population factors for employment, training, level of living and welfare of workers in developing countries and to formulate proposals for action.

In November 1968, at its 173rd session, the Governing Body endorsed the broad lines of ILO activities in the population field as follows:

(a) Promotion of information and educational activities on population and family welfare questions at various levels, particularly through workers' education, labour welfare and cooperatives and rural institutions programmes;

(b) Policy-oriented research on the links between demographic variables and employment, labour markets and development issues;

(c) Action to stimulate participation of social security and medical services at the level of the enterprise in promoting family planning.

The subsequent establishment of the United Nations Fund for Population Activities (UNFPA) in 1969 assisted in the definition of the scope and nature of the contributions of the ILO and other United Nations agencies to international population activities. Moreover, in the case of the ILO, it also provided substantial and continuing financial support to a range of labour-related activities of several types.

Following the World Population Conference, held at Bucharest in 1974 under the auspices of the United Nations, and the adoption of the World Population Plan of Action, the ILO reviewed the scope of its population programme and commenced a sub-programme, with the goal of assisting member States to strengthen technical and institutional capacity and to incorporate demographic elements systematically into development planning and policies, with emphasis on human resources and employment aspects.

In response to the discussions and outcomes of the International Population Conference held at Mexico City in 1984, the ILO Governing Body instructed the Director-General to continue to give special attention to the further development of population activities within the established framework of standard-setting, technical cooperation activities, advisory services, policy-related studies and dissemination of information. In the same year the Employment Policy (Supplementary Provisions) Recommendation (No. 169), adopted by the International Labour Conference, included a separate section on population policy.

An underlying, still latent premise at the level of the individual worker is that both reproductive and productive choices are required by women (and men) as human rights and that these rights are mutually enhancing and reinforcing.

C. Women and labour issues

Economic activity: occupational and domestic

More women are now recorded as working outside the home than ever before. Many are employed because they want to be, others because they have to be (ILO, 1992h). In developing countries women officially make up a smaller proportion of the recorded labour force (31 per cent) than they do in industrialized countries (40 per cent). But these statistics omit much of the work of the former group in agriculture and their extensive and expanding participation in the informal sector. Indeed, the informal sector is large and growing rapidly and is recognized as the only possible source of employment for increasing numbers of the rapidly growing labour force of both women and men in developing countries (ILO, 1991b). During current recessions and structural adjustments, the numbers of women working in the informal sector is estimated to have risen. Some of the highest participation rates are in Africa.

Efforts are under way to improve the measurement and understanding of economic activities in this sector. An important consideration for the ILO is that informal sector workers are often beyond the protection offered by ILO standards, even those standards which have been ratified by the Governments concerned. Most of the workers in this sector are classified as self-employed or family workers.

The proportion of women recorded as "economically active" varies considerably from region to region and from country to country, and is in part an artefact of the modes of collecting and analysing the data. Many women in the informal sector remain unseen by statistics collectors, a position it is hoped will change in future, as simple and low-cost modes of measurement become more widespread.[7]

There have also been significant rises in wage employment in South-eastern Asia, where female labour has provided the bulk of labour in export-processing zones, and in some countries, the industrialization process has depended upon the low-paid, dexterous, assembly-line work of women.

There is growing evidence from all regions of a hitherto poorly documented phenomenon, the extent to which women, like men, are migrating for work and through their remittances providing important sources of sustenance for dependent family members, who either accompany them or are often left behind, including their children (e.g., Findlay and Williams, 1990).

During the 1980s, profound changes were observed, for example, in the migration streams from Asia. In some countries, the volume of female migrants began to exceed the male and unskilled workers rather than professionals began to predominate. Thus, for example, it has been estimated that in 1987 out of an outflow of 1 million Asian workers, 29 per cent were female; and of these, three quarters went abroad, mainly to the Middle East and Eastern Asian countries with booming economies, as maids and entertainers.[8] More than 1 million of the 6 million workforce in the Middle East were estimated to be foreign female domestic workers, mainly from Sri Lanka and the Philippines (e.g., Gulati, 1992).

In recently compiled estimations, using various sources of time use and activity data, women are estimated to spend more of their time working than men in all the developed regions (United Nations, 1991b). A number of studies have found that women were working for 12-13 hours a week more than men and the prevalent economic crises are noted to be increasing the working hours of many of the poorest women, as they struggle to ensure the survival of their families, with minimal access to resources for basic needs.

This gap between female and male economic activities does not appear in national censuses and surveys, however, for census and survey enumerators and women themselves, or those replying on their behalf, often do not understand that women should be counted as economically active when in fact they are. Traditional measures do not cover much informal sector work, unpaid work on farms and domestic or subsistence activities (Dixon-Mueller and Anker, 1988); nor is the value of women's products generally taken adequately into account, neither in household surveys nor national accounting systems, even though, according to some informed estimates, these products constitute up to one third, or even one half, of all production, particularly in the developing world (Goldschmidt-Clermont, 1982 and 1987).

In the past decade, women throughout the world have been moving in increasing numbers into heavy industrial jobs, construction trades and other new professional fields, as well as the informal sector (ILO, 1992h). Women workers tend to be concentrated in agriculture, micro-electronics, textile industries, small enterprises and home-based piece-work, as well as being in nursing, teaching and clerical positions. In manufacturing, women are concentrated in the same "women's industries" in most countries: clothing, footwear; textiles; leather; and, in some countries, tobacco. They are usually on the lower rungs of the employment ladder. The number of women holding decision-making and managerial posts is substantially lower than their education or experience would warrant.

Women in development and the environment

From the perspective of the ILO, sustainable development cannot be achieved without the equitable sharing of costs and benefits within societies and between countries. Women within this framework are viewed as potential agents of development and change. This includes the protection and rehabilitation of the environment.

It is now increasingly recognized that in many developing countries women are the first to suffer from the degradation of the environment in carrying out their traditional tasks of fetching water and fuel, food production and cooking, and other family responsibilities. Degradation of land, forest and water resources has a direct impact on their daily lives, work, health and even survival (ILO, 1990b). There is evidence that the hours spent on these tasks in many cases are increasing at the expense of other activities.

Daily subsistence tasks, such as fuel and water collection or transport and processing of harvested foodstuffs, may be so onerous that they jeopardize participation in other economic activities as well as the care of infants, including breast-feeding. Hence, there is growing realization that assistance should be directed to innovations that save women's time, including improved transport; infrastructure development related to water, fuel, housing etc.; and labour-saving technologies. Furthermore, as was stressed in the Director-General's address to the International Labour Conference in 1990, women, because of their knowledge and experience of the possibilities and limitations of local natural and living resources, are the first line of defence and protection of the environment in developing countries, for they are frequently the key managers of natural resources of different kinds.

Their vital knowledge and experience is often ignored, however. Thus, effective measures need to be taken to ensure that women shall be able to play a more active role in the design, development, selection and implementation of development policies and projects, particularly those related to the natural and agricultural resources necessary for their livelihood and survival.

As the 1990 International Labour Conference report emphasizes, only recently has attention been given to the health implications of the use of biomass fuels by women cooking and heating, which results in elevated levels of respiratory and eye problems because of their high levels of indoor pollution.

Moreover, women as farmers are often exposed to dangerous chemicals without warning, training or appropriate protective devices. These matters need to be taken into account in all development programmes and policies. It is realized that the ILO constituents could play a more active role at both the national and international levels in this regard.

The lack of equality and need for protection

Girls and women have had—and still have—less access to formal and informal education and training than their male peers. An important factor, recognized as being implicated in this inequality, is the frequently much earlier entry of girls into marriage and motherhood, often in some regions, motherhood alone without marriage or sharing of family responsibilities for children. This situation has serious and continuing effects on their employment opportunities, as well as having far-reaching effects on occupational safety and health.

Moreover, in part because of their unequal opportunities for vocational training, especially in non-traditional subject areas, while women are continuing to enter workforces in unprecedented numbers, they are still mainly visible in a limited number of occupations. The vast majority still continue to be in unpaid or poorly paid activities, requiring limited skills in traditionally female enclaves and offering little or no opportunity for upward mobility or career development.

Furthermore, recent structural changes in the economies of a number of countries have led to increasingly precarious employment for women, jobs lacking access to social security and other benefits. Larger and larger numbers of women are migrating for work, not only in their own countries but internationally. Evidence of discrimination of various types suffered by women workers continues—lower levels of income, greater insecurity and not infrequent sexual harassment.

The existing networks of trade unions and rural workers' organizations, women's organizations and other non-governmental organizations play an important part in providing educational opportunities and training materials adapted to women's needs. Increasingly, these organizations are including information relating to family health, welfare and family planning, in addition to information relevant to technical skills and occupational experiences. The intimate linkages between family welfare and occupational productivity of workers are increasingly recognized by employers; and, at the same time, workers have opportunities to participate in the design of training programmes that meet their own requirements. One of these requirements is to be able to harmonize economic activities and family responsibilities, especially child-bearing and caring for infants and young children.

It has now been realized that there is an appalling gap in the literature on training and drop-out rates for pregnant girls. Often the assumption is that girls drop out to assist their mothers with household work, when the fact is that many of them have conceived. Such conceptions do not always result from voluntary or egalitarian relationships with peers but are often, like the incidence of sexually transmitted diseases, the outcome of harassment and economic seduction by much older men, a phenomenon now evidenced by epidemiological data.

Growing numbers of governmental and non-governmental organizations are becoming very concerned about this issue and some are attempting to stem the flow of drop-outs or to provide programmes of remedial action to cater for the vocational and familial needs of teenage mothers. In some cases, legislation attempts to afford sexual protection of young girls. In other cases, community sanctions are being brought to bear.

The ILO has yet to develop a concerted and systematic programme of action in this regard and at a point in the female's life cycle when future chances for equality of opportunity and treatment in the world of work may be prejudiced for ever.

With regard to continuing sex segregation in labour markets, a special area for concern is that in situations of economic adjustment policies and deregulation of labour markets, women are preponderantly in those occupations and sectors, such as health and education, which are particularly vulnerable to budget cuts and retrenchment. Yet, as household enquiries are increasingly documenting, the economic contributions of women are not only vital to household security, but their incomes, at subsistence levels, often tend to be more directly channelled to the survival and development of their offspring.

Working women everywhere suffer various forms of discrimination. As concerns remuneration, women still earn generally 50-80 per cent of men's wages. Some studies of informal sector incomes have also shown women to gain less than their male counterparts. They continue to bear most of the double burdens of domestic family responsibilities, as well as economic activity, that tends to put them in an inferior marginalized and stressed position.

In industrialized countries, it is recognized that although women now have greater access to employment, a growing number of them are paying for this access through diluted protection and greater vulnerability (ILO, 1990i). They fill most of the part-time, precarious, temporary, occasional and subcontracted jobs, which the restructuring of national and international economies has caused to multiply during the past 10 years. These jobs lack the social protection generally associated with full-time, secure employment. Thus, a growing proportion of women workers are not protected by labour legislation or union membership.

Confined for the most part to women's jobs that are precarious and low skilled, women have few prospects for advancement and are more vulnerable to unemployment than their male counterparts. As a consequence in a number of countries, poverty is increasingly a female phenomenon, that is, for women with children in charge.

Tackling sex discrimination in all its manifold guises is recognized to be a long and difficult task, in which women have taken some of the most important steps—demanding their rights and achieving higher levels of education and training—despite the odds stacked against them. Legislation has also played a part and affirmative action programmes.

Rapid rates of migration of rural women alone into urban areas of the developing and even industrialized world are associated with increasing numbers of women workers in precarious, legally unprotected, ill-paid and illegal forms of employment. Many of them enter unskilled services, such as domestic employment, entertainment and commercial sex work. Recent ILO studies have demonstrated the extent to which foreign female domestic workers may be particularly vulnerable, exploited and therefore in need of protection.[9]

Sexual harassment at work is a further pervasive form of discrimination suffered more frequently by women than men, which is becoming increasingly well documented and gaining more recognition as a problem needing urgent attention and remedial action (ILO, 1990e and 1992d).[10, 11]

At the same time, the increasing numbers of women left behind by migrant husbands are swelling the growing millions of women alone, who are heading and maintaining households and running family farms and businesses without adult male help. This phenomenon is currently under study in a variety of contexts, given that it constitutes the most rapidly growing type of domestic group, with serious implications for the rearing and development of children, as well as for divisions of labour and family responsibilities (e.g., Youssef and Hetler, 1984; Folbre, 1991).

Role conflict and time strain

It is generally recognized that sufficient social support for women's maternal role is an essential element of promotion of equality of opportunity for women workers, as well as a basic form of protection required by women and the family. However, although considerable progress has been achieved in a number of countries, there is evidence that such support often remains inadequate and that maternity is often a cause for discrimination as well as female role conflict and stress.

The ILO review in 1987 of existing facilities for care of children of workers, showed that even in the rich Northern industrialized countries the lack of such facilities constitutes a continuous serious problem for employed parents. Few industrialized countries have social policies and legislation promoting or compelling the setting up of child-care facilities at workplaces or within the community.

Maternity leave, parental leave, child-care facilities, legislative provisions on discrimination and a more equal sharing of domestic workloads are all important parts of the change processes required, as well as workplace-based health, family welfare and planning facilities. However, many industrialized countries have realized that these measures alone are not enough and that a more active stance is needed to redress a persistent bias against women workers and other groups that suffer discrimination in the workplace (ILO, 1992h), for the result is a serious conflict of interests for working parents, especially mothers. Furthermore, there does appear to be a trend in some countries towards developing workplace initiatives responsive to the needs of working parents.

Meanwhile, throughout the world there are multiple signs of evidence from different sources of women's widespread role conflict and strain, as they attempt with varying levels of success to cope with the changing demands of their occupational and domestic as well as maternal roles, in altering social settings. Evidence of continued use of traditional coping mechanisms comes from the data on use of child labour and demographic evidence of fostering of children by non-parental kin. However, these conflicts and strains for women workers between economic and procreative tasks and responsibilities are frequently further aggravated by the diminishing or inadequate levels of support and cooperation from kin, as well as the fathers of their children. Indeed, the numbers of women coping alone with these multiple and conflicting tasks is increasing daily, partially as a result of increasing migration and mobility of labour.

The manifold and serious dimensions of this conflict and strain and their outcomes remain largely undocumented with any system and precision. This situation exists even though in the past the presumed conflict between maternal and occupational tasks was a critical policy tool for population planners seeking to lower fertility levels.

It was, of course, quite an inappropriate tool in contexts in which child care was customarily shared among an available set of substitute caregivers in the same or different households or in which informal sector economic activity, pregnancy, lactation and child care were not incompatible. Similarly, it remains an inappropriate policy response in all those contexts in which women still have no ready access to effective means of lengthening the spacing between births or of postponing or stopping child-bearing.

Compelling women in non-contracepting populations to increase economic activity in sectors incompatible with child care and child-rearing, including lactation, may well lead only to truncated breast-feeding and shorter birth intervals and to higher infant and maternal mortality.

Because women are often overloaded by excessively long hours of work, often combining a variety of economic activities, including market-oriented and non-market work, inside and outside the home, and a greater share of family responsibilities, energy and time constraints leading to pervasive levels of undernourishment, fatigue and stress, are significant for most women. There is evidence that women maintaining families and heading households alone work the hardest of all. Special work-related health problems are likely to result from this role overload and strain, including stress-induced conditions, such as fatigue, premature ageing and other psychosocial and health effects.

Moreover, the unequal distribution of family responsibilities is now recognized to be at the heart of much of the workplace discrimination against women (ILO, 1992h). A variety of policy approaches have been identified, from *laisser-faire* to an attempt at extensive provision of child-care facilities and canteens.

The *World Labour Report* (ILO, 1992h) notes that demographic changes, including increasing numbers of female-headed households, are likely to impel further action on this subject, for with an increasing number of women needing to earn incomes for family maintenance, as larger numbers of fathers, through escalating levels of unemployment, poverty, irresponsibility and labour migration, leave their children to their mothers alone to be maintained; and as more women workers live in isolated areas, far from the traditional kin support for child-rearing, more Governments, employers, workers' organizations and other non-governmental organizations will need to consider the demands from parents, especially mothers, for institutionalized forms of child care.

This consideration is in addition to the need to examine effective means of promoting more responsible fatherhood among male workers and to assist women also to have access to improved means of balancing productive and reproductive responsibilities through birth-spacing and stopping. Recent analyses of available data sets have shown that many millions of working mothers lack the means to exercise conscious control over their child-bearing, even when they do not want another birth (Bongaarts, 1990 and 1991).

Meanwhile, the growing body of evidence on the incidence of abortion among working mothers testifies painfully to the dimensions of the strain experienced and the dilemmas confronted, as family and occupational responsibilities conflict and adequate support and assistance are not forthcoming from husbands, children's fathers, kin or community resources.

D. CURRENT ACTION

Promotion of equality

The resolution concerning ILO action for women workers, adopted by the International Labour Conference in 1991, stressed the need for intensified work to assist member States in putting into practice the principles of equality, to which most of them have subscribed. This resolution provided further impetus for the continuing designation of equality as a priority theme in the biennium 1992-1993.

New organizational arrangements, including the setting-up of an interdepartmental programme of work, seek to ensure the integration of gender concerns in all ILO activities and to enhance the technical content of work relating to women. Particular attention is being paid to the promotion of international labour standards of special importance to women workers. At the same time, advisory services, the dissemination of information, and regional and national tripartite symposia on equality of opportunity and treatment have been addressed to both developed and developing countries, to help them in making legislation more effective and in implementing policies and practices to eliminate continuing barriers to equality. Furthermore, activities related to women have recently been expanded and intensified, particularly in the less developed regions, where appropriate advisory services have been made available.

Moreover, there are moves under way to institutionalize gender analysis and gender sensitization training for officials at the headquarters and for workers, employers and government officials at the Turin Training Centre and in regional and national seminars.

Review of ILO activities for equality of opportunity and treatment for men and women in employment continues to be salient. The Committee on Discrimination of the ILO Governing Body[12] decided in June 1989 that gender equality would be a standing item on their agenda twice a year and equality issues have increasingly featured as an integral part of policies and measures promoted by the Office in all labour matters.

With regard to structural adjustment policies in developing countries and transition to market economies in central and Eastern European countries, there has been a focus, *inter alia*, on: the particularly vulnerable situation of women; personnel policies for public sectors facing retrenchment; industrial relations and conditions of work affecting women in the expanding forms of flexible labour, homework and other atypical forms of employment; issues concerning sexual equality in effective tripartite consultation on adjustment problems; strategies for training and retraining women; the impact of economic and social adjustment on rural women; equality issues in trade union activities in response to changing conditions and other activities to counterbalance the adverse consequences of adjustment for employment and working conditions in which women are a special target group.

The assistance given to Governments and employers and workers' organizations to alleviate poverty has included special provisions to improve the situation of women, mainly in rural areas and in the urban informal sector, as well as that of older, disabled and refugee women.

Women from poor households have been a priority in policy and programme formulation to generate employment and income. The transfer of new and improved appropriate technologies and the creation of opportunities for diversified training and self-employment schemes have been the focuses of action directed to increasing the productivity and earnings of rural women. Some of this work has focused on the crucial issue of dwindling rural sources of biomass and the rural energy crisis and the introduction of energy-saving innovations.

The strengthening of their productive activities and of their impact on regenerating the environment has been supported by the promotion of rural women's organizations and emphasis has been placed on the participation of women in rural workers' organizations. Empowerment of rural women has been an important theme, including a regional project focusing on the needs of female-headed households. The goal was building self-confidence and increasing bargaining power of women's groups in the rural areas, to enable them to analyse their situation, to identify their own priorities, to claim better access to productive resources and to negotiate with local and national authorities their integration into development programmes.

Reduction of drudgery in labour intensive, low-productivity activities has been highlighted as an important prerequisite to releasing time and human energy for the pursuit of income-earning activities by women, as well as adequate time to respond to the needs of infants and growing children. Access to land and assurance of food security, as well as differential impacts of drought, have been important focuses of concern.

Widespread job segregation and women's difficulties in attaining decision-making positions demand continual efforts in the area of training for non-traditional occupations in public and private formal sector enterprises and in improving women's managerial skills (e.g., Phiri, 1990; Sekwao, 1990).

Women's involvement in cooperatives and self-help groups with emphasis on thrift, savings and credit cooperatives is encouraged through multiple strategies. These strategies include the dissemination of information, field research, advisory services, workshops and technical cooperation projects. Women's participation in trade unions and in workers education programmes is also a crucial field of activity at the international, regional and national levels.

The unequal share of family responsibilities shouldered by women workers and the lack of adequate child-care facilities and other measures to alleviate women's time and energy stress in their multiple occupational, domestic and maternal roles, are recognized to affect sex discrimination at work. An effort is being made to deal systematically with gender and family issues affecting the promotion of equality in working conditions for women and men. Such issues as special working-time arrangements for working parents, maternity protection, child- care facilities and the protection of vulnerable groups, including part-time workers and home workers, have been receiving special attention in the ILO. In addition, equality of treatment for women in social security is an area of concern and activity.

Pervasive job segregation and women's difficulties in reaching decision-making positions demand continual efforts in the area of training for non-traditional occupations in public and private formal sector enterprises and in improving women's managerial skills. Thus, in recent years there has been an increasingly concerted effort to examine training policies and institutions and to assist in the promotion of policies and programmes that would serve to increase the numbers of young women in non-traditional forms of training, preparing their entry into technical fields and higher professional and managerial levels. Accordingly, training institutions have been examined and aspects of institutionalized discrimination illumined.[13]

Jobs in technical fields are seen as representing an important avenue for women and a chance to develop skills for which there is a real and growing demand and to have a significant means of increasing their earning power.[14] Attention has thus been focused on measures to expand and diversify women's training, particularly for occupations having higher levels of skill, responsibility and pay.

Technical cooperation strategies

The ILO strategy with regard to the promotion of equality through technical cooperation projects is twofold. It is that, on the one hand, women should be included as decision makers, participants and beneficiaries in all projects and gender issues should be put into the mainstream. On the other hand, where necessary, special projects for women should be designed or should be components of general projects, which means that such matters as those listed below should be consistently taken into account and dealt with:

(a) The inadequate measurement and assessment of and accounting for women's economic activity;

(b) Their unequal access to resources of all kinds;

(c) Their maternal role and responsibilities and their unequal burdens of domestic work and child care;

(d) Their sexual vulnerability.

At the same time, specific projects on women should exist within the ILO technical cooperation programme. Hitherto, the main thrust of these projects included: rural employment creation, vocational training, enterprise and cooperative activities, entrepreneurship development, appropriate technologies and workers' education. Employment creation and income-generating activities with particular emphasis on women have been promoted in a wide range of developing countries with assistance of the ILO.

It is recognized that such activities call for an integrated approach in a framework that is local and participatory and includes, as appropriate, access to land, credit, information, education and training, technology and markets.

Several attempts have been made to assess the impacts of general projects on women as both participants and beneficiaries (e.g., ILO, 1990c) and it is increasingly recognized that special isolated activities directed towards women could lead to ad hoc and marginal impacts and that an integrated and holistic approach is needed which highlights gender issues, explicitly taking into account the needs and capacities of women. Accordingly, it is understood not only that women should take part in the design and implementation of specific projects but that gender issues should be fully taken into account in the design and implementation of all policies and programmes related to employment and sustainable development.

In the past, a wide array of policy relevant studies have helped design technical cooperation projects and to elucidate aspects of women's positions in the area of work.[15] These studies have highlighted aspects of their positions in urban and rural labour markets, in informal and formal sectors and in work-based organizations, including cooperatives and trade unions. They have also examined various aspects of women's roles within the contexts of population and labour issues.[16] This array included syntheses of conceptual, policy-related work, made more readily available to policy makers and planners, as well as methodological work and training manuals.

An important aspect of analytical work is the monitoring of the attempts of countries to put into effect international labour standards ratified and identification of the barriers to their implementation. Currently, the newly established interdepartmental programme for the promotion of equality of women in employment is seeking insights into the types of approaches needed in future activities, in order to achieve this goal. Activities include a programme of data collection and analysis and promotional activities. The emphasis is an integrated approach to examine women workers' issues. Essential objectives include: improved information dissemination on equality for women in employment; strengthening of institutional capacity; organization of women to combat discrimination; promotion of legal rights and measures to promote equality, and statistical and conceptual development, to allow better reflection of the real situation of women at work and put emphasis on some of the specific areas that affect discrimination.

Improved flow of information is recognized as vital to informed decision-making; support for field operations and for highlighting women's concerns in broader developmental issues. A standardized information network on women and work is the goal.

Concerning legal rights and measures, there is a need to inform workers about international labour standards and women workers' rights, as well as procedures to implement the rights set out in law and possible special positive measures that can be taken.

With regard to strengthening institutional capacity and organization of women to combat discrimination,activities are likely to include the promotion and strengthening of tripartite machineries for the promotion of equality, promotional work on the use of collective bargaining for promoting equality and assistance with the organization and strengthening of the unions/associations of women workers in the unorganized sectors, as well as in precarious employment. Tripartite machineries for the promotion of equal opportunities are viewed as a significant institution for the implementation of appropriate legislation on women's rights and other essential elements for the promotion of equality for women in employment.

At the governmental level, women's issues are often represented by national women's machineries; at the trade union level, diverse institutions, which vary from country, to country have also been set up. To date, no formal mechanisms have been set up at the employers' level.

The strengths and weaknesses of the existing institutions have already been the subject of study. Further analytical work is proposed on the possible means to overcome these weaknesses.

Evidence is being amassed and synthesized on the scope and seriousness of sexual harassment of women in workplaces and the need for protective measures. This is an issue of emerging concern both globally and within the ILO. An issue of *Conditions of Work Digest* concerning the situation, due for publication later in 1992, will examine legal remedies and preventive measures being developed at national and workplace levels in industrialized countries, and preventive and remedial action is being promoted in a number of developing countries. Data from many sources, including the discussions and reports of women's organizations, records of trade union meetings, testimony of individual female workers and deliberations of feminist groups, already attest to the widespread and pervasive nature of sexual harassment. Moreover, it is clear that in some regions and contexts it takes the most seriously harmful form, jeopardizing reproductive health, if not threatening morbidity and mortality.

A number of countries have enacted legislation requiring employers to provide a working environment that is free of sexual harassment, and through collective bargaining and enterprise initiatives a number of measures have already been developed. Based on these measures, it is envisaged that it should be possible to draft a code of protective practice in the foreseeable future. This code would provide broadly acceptable guidance on policies, procedures, guidelines and programmes for the prevention of sexual harassment at work.

Meanwhile, an important lesson learned from assessments of selected ILO technical cooperation projects is that benefits of projects may not necessarily accrue to those for whom they are intended; for example, they may not be equally distributed between women and men and activities may not be relevant to the real needs of target groups, if the intended beneficiaries are not identified at the outset and the potential sociocultural barriers to participation identified and addressed (ILO, 1991i).

Investing in girls and young women

The realization that investment in the education and training of young girls is an important human issue in itself and also a necessary key to solve an array of population and development problems has recently grown apace.[17] A pertinent international labour standard in this regard is the Minimum Age Convention, 1973 (No. 138). This Convention requires ratifying States to pursue policies that will lead to the abolition of child labour and to raise progressively the minimum age for admission to employment. The minimum age should be not less than the age of completion of compulsory schooling and in any case not less than 15 years (14 in countries where the economies and educational facilities are insufficiently developed). Ninety per cent of child labourers are estimated to be in Africa and Asia.

The underlying aim of this standard is to ensure that the educational and vocational training of girls and boys shall not be neglected and that their physical and mental well-being shall not be harmed by hard or dangerous work early in life. Unfortunately, only 40 countries have ratified this Convention. Moreover, systems of enforcement and labour inspection services that could uncover abuses are often inadequate. An issue of *Conditions of Work Digest* (ILO, 1991a) provides a review of law and practice on child labour throughout the world.

The ILO currently has a new wide-ranging interdepartmental programme of activities in progress on the elimination of child labour, this including the work of young female domestics and homeworkers. There is clear recognition in this programme of work that the situations and needs of young girls are different from those of their male counterparts and require specially adapted approaches. The strong linkages between a girl's truncated schooling, early economic activity and poverty, teenage child-bearing and high fertility are well documented and will need to be fully taken into account in any planned initiatives.[18]

In 1975, the International Labour Conference adopted the Human Resources Development Convention, which applied to the vocational guidance and vocational training of young persons and adults for all areas of economic, social and cultural life and at all levels of occupational skill and responsibility. This recommendation, *inter alia*, was concerned with the promotion of equality of opportunity of women and men in training and employment.

Among the suggested measures to be taken, as well as equality in vocational training opportunities, were education to bring about changes in traditional attitudes concerning the work of women and men in the home and working life; and provision of day-care facilities, so that girls and women with family responsibilities would have access to normal vocational training, as well as special arrangements (part-time, correspondence, mass media etc.).

This topic has surfaced more than once in the current tripartite debates on vocational training needs, within the context of the impacts of structural adjustment programmes in this year's International Labour Conference.

Migration and population

Currently, a logical merging of work items in the Office has resulted in the integration of a multifaceted programme focusing on a range of population issues, of which the objectives include: helping Governments in the alleviation of poverty; realization of employment-intensive growth and the application of international labour standards by integrating demographic factors in labour policies; and enabling employers and workers' organizations or cooperatives in developing countries to benefit from a range of international assistance.

An important aim is also to support both countries sending out workers and countries receiving them to deal with current priority concerns and to help promote the intercountry cooperation necessary for the recruitment and return of migrant workers, while simultaneously improving the legal and social protection of migrant workers and members of their families.

With regard to the last of those activities, the ILO will accordingly develop its role as a forum for analysis, reflection, exchange of views and policy advice for both emigration and immigration countries, providing a basis for improved and more equitable migration policies and the promotion of a closer and more active partnership between the concerned Governments and social partners.

In pursuance of its mandate and responsibilities regarding migrant workers, the ILO continues to use a variety of means of action, including standard-setting, research, technical cooperation and meetings. Recent examples of standard-setting include close involvement in the new United Nations Convention on the Rights of all Migrant Workers and their Families. Current research topics include discrimination, integration of migrants in Western Europe, future demand for migrant labour in the region of the Persian Gulf, return migration and the possibilities of reducing migration pressure through public international aid.

Due attention is being given to the special vulnerability of migrant women workers. In particular, policy studies have been promoted on the plight of foreign, female domestic servants and entertainers. As already noted, migration for work has increasingly profound impacts upon the situation of women—when left behind, when accompanying husbands and when migrating alone. Given the escalating nature of the phenomenon, it is likely to assume increasingly important proportions within the context of attempts to promote protection of the rights of all migrant workers and to promote equality and sexual protection of vulnerable female workers.

Countries experiencing high urban growth, resulting in slums, unemployment and poverty, are being helped in formulating and implementing cost-effective policies to slow or deflect migration to overpopulated urban centres, in many of which up to half of the population live in slum and squatter settlements with serious environmental problems.[19]

Concern for women workers and gender issues are an integral part of the operational activities of the UNFPA-supported labour and population programme that has in the past provided broadly two types of support, for population and human resources development planning and for family welfare education for workers and trainees. Technical cooperation activities have been designed, *inter alia*, to reduce the excess supply of labour resulting from high fertility and too rapid population growth and to promote family welfare of workers through expansion of workplace facilities and educational programmes. The latter activities are designed both to help workers, female and male, balance and combine more effectively family responsibilities and economic resources and activities, and to promote health and family survival.

Employers' organizations, trade unions and cooperatives concerned with the adverse effects on workers' welfare of large families and the escalation of contagious morbidity and mortality, transmitted through sexual contact, are being assisted to carry out population and workers' welfare education programmes at the workplace. These programmes are designed, *inter alia*, to counteract the effects of large family size on absenteeism, productivity and employment prospects of women, as well as the effects of sickness on family survival and well-being.

Both of these types of programme, of necessity, require the full integration of gender issues and the involvement of women as both beneficiaries and participants. One of the concerns of this types of programme in the past has been to improve its capacity to provide advice related to institutional structures for promoting women's concerns. Many Governments have by now established or strengthened national machineries for the promotion of women's interests and the crucial issue is their effectiveness for integrating gender issues into development planning and for promoting equality of opportunity and treatment for women workers.

In the promotion of the well-being of women workers' nutrition, reproductive health care, family planning and child care are all among the salient issues of concern. The family welfare education component of the population programme has in the past been effective in encouraging the spread of organized-sector population programmes throughout the developing world and particularly in Asia and, more recently, in sub-Saharan Africa.

In recent years, there has been a rise in the number of programmes in informal work settings, where many women increasingly tend to be concentrated. In fact, in many developing countries, as already noted, women are disproportionately represented in the informal sector, given their lack of access to job opportunities in the formal or organized sector. Thus, the majority of women workers in many countries are in self-employment or are family workers, home workers, casual workers and piece-workers. Therefore, expanding the programme to include the informal sector is especially important for reaching women. It is clear that developing communication programmes for workers outside the organized sector presents new challenges linked to the disparate character of the sector.

Experience indicates that programmes and projects that work through and build upon existing structures are more likely to succeed than those which seek to create new structures. In most countries, a variety of governmental and non-governmental organizations that promote income-generating activities for women. Where they are successful, they can provide important channels for family welfare programmes and there is considerable scope for expansion in this area, given the kinds of role conflicts suffered by working mothers, as was indicated above. A recent review highlights the positive aspects of such an approach and the way in which it can answer some of the real and most basic needs of women workers with family responsibilities, as they try, in deprived and straightened circumstances and without the benefits of adequate access to formal maternal health and family planning services, to promote family welfare and child survival through improved birth-spacing, as well as maintaining a frequently precarious balance between their family responsibilities and economic activities (Evans, 1992).

Such approaches are certainly designed to benefit working women, since they bear a major responsibility for the welfare of families, both as workers and as mothers, in all societies and suffer most, together with their children, from the effects of poverty, occupational/maternal role conflicts, unwanted pregnancies and untimely disease and death.

The main goal of ILO/UNFPA-supported projects has been to promote informed and responsible decision-making among workers, concerning the various factors that impinge on the quality of family life. A number of projects specifically designed to benefit women involve the strengthening of the capacity of local women's organizations to implement educational programmes for women. Some projects also include research on women's work roles and fertility. A specially important policy and programme-related research topic is the estimation of the extent to which traditional methods of birth control, geared to enable women to balance occupational and family responsibilities (mainly through strictly sanctioned and closely monitored periods of sexual abstinence) are breaking down and thus in need of replacement by modern methods ("natural family planning" or modern contraception).

Among the salient educational messages to benefit women workers by protecting maternity, promoting equality of opportunity and treatment, and helping women balance occupational, domestic and maternal activities and responsibilities are the following:

(a) The need to postpone the first birth long enough to enable girls to complete their education and training and find suitable jobs;

(b) The need to prolong birth-spacing intervals so as to help working mothers balance potentially conflicting tasks, as well as promoting maternal and child survival, health and development;

(c) The need to raise the awareness of the partners of working women of the potential medical, social and economic benefits of avoiding high-risk pregnancies (too early, too closely spaced and too late).

At the national level, a number of population and human resources development planning projects have been designed to assist member States in building up their technical and institutional capacity to incorporate demographic elements systematically into development processes, planning and policies with special emphasis on human resources and employment aspects. Advisory services and training have been provided mainly to the population and human resources development units of ministries of planning, including the use of computer packages and new methodologies for analysing economic and demographic data required for planning.

With regard to putting gender issues into the mainstream in this programme of work, the lack of adequate information on which to base policy formulation and planning has become an increasingly well-recognized stumbling block. In the past, not only has much of women's economic activity remained undocumented in the databases used in economic planning, as well as being poorly recorded in the very surveys attempting to elucidate economic/demographic processes, especially fertility and work linkages, but women themselves and consideration of their various crucial social roles involved in survival, promotion of family security and welfare and human development have for the most part been systematically marginalized and neglected.

A special problem has been the lack of simultaneous consideration of the interactions between women's several roles involved in production and reproduction and seriously affected by environmental, demographic and economic changes taking place. Progress has been made, as noted above, in developing methods and approaches to better measure and evaluate women's economic activities. However, these new methods still remain to be systematically adopted in national surveys and censuses and are still unused, even on a pilot basis in some regions, such as sub-Saharan Africa. Thus, much yet remains to be done in this regard.

Another major problem to be addressed is the lack of adoption of flexible, sufficiently complex and appropriate models of domestic organization, and family functioning, that can be used to analyse the varied and changing sexual divisions of labour, resources and decision-making, which can occur at the microlevel. Lacking adoption of such models, data collection, policy-making and programming exercises frequently do not attain the goals desired (Oppong, 1991; Palmer, 1991).

Pervasive false assumptions about gender roles and relation affecting planners' perceptions and decisions include ideas about domestic budgets and household property arrangements in which conjugal resources, including labour, money and goods, are imagined to be pooled and jointly administered. They also include models in which women only figure as unpaid family labour, with no leeway for autonomous allocation of labour and decision-making capabilities, as well as mythical male breadwinner figures and managers of households and farms (even when residential criteria and economic evidence indicate the contrary). At the same time, they may underplay the impact of male dominance, aggression and autocracy when it exists either in the domestic or in the occupational domain.

The fact is that models of familial roles and relationships that underlie policy formulation, programme design and data collection in the "informal sector" of economic activity still too often incorporate inappropriate assumptions concerning the degrees of solidarity or jointness in conjugal role relationships and the extent of functional closure of the nuclear family, issues long ago the focus of intensive and detailed concern in comparative cross-cultural analyses of changing family systems (Oppong, 1991). A result is that important roles and relationships of women (and men) that affect their economic and demographic behaviour and outcomes are omitted from population discourse and designs or stereotypes used that are far from the diverse and changing realities.

An excellent example is the sibling and wider kin solidarities and relationships of alternate generations, demonstrated long ago to be crucial in human survival and development strategies in pre-industrial populations. These are still totally omitted from the majority of current analyses, thus demonstrating the need for serious rethinking in any new data-gathering exercises planned for the future. This issue is important not only in developing countries, where there is growing realization of the importance of kinship and customary marriage forms to the organization of family businesses and thus the whole "informal sector" but also in industrialized countries where the ideal norm of the conjugal family is in increasingly stark contrast to the realities of the growing numbers of women and children living alone, often in poverty, without the support needed from husbands and fathers.

In the light of these caveats a necessary planning tool is a conceptual framework of gender roles that does not omit these concerns; and that which is cross-culturally applicable and can be used to model the linkages between different roles, including the conflicts, stresses, supports, constraints, power relations etc. that may act as triggers or breaks to innovation and change. Conceptual models exist but have not yet been fully developed or utilized as planning tools. And existing comparative data sets are as yet deficient in one or more aspects of the required information for holistic, gender-sensitive analyses.

As has been recently stressed, what is needed is not so much the multiplication of projects directed to women but rather improved mechanisms for systematically examining policies and development plans from a gender-sensitive perspective and the identification and eradication of discriminatory practices and barriers to change. This calls for increasing awareness of gender issues and female perspectives at all levels and the building of a national and international consensus that action must be taken and the examination of alternative potential policy instruments and strategies to bring about the desired changes to attain economic and demographic goals.

An important precondition will be that women play an equal part not only in the activities involved but in the decision-making and planning processes.

E. Needed action in the 1990s

Gender, population and development

At last, after the accumulation of the global efforts of many scholars and activists at the local, national and international levels, the significance of gender is being increasingly recognized and taken into account in mainstream population and development discussions and debates and in policy and planning exercises. Although admittedly there is still much lip-service and serious omissions, as key decision makers continue to assume that gender issues are of marginal importance and only of concern to women.

In fact, attention is constantly being called to the relevance to economic and demographic plans, programmes and projects of the fact that divisions of tasks, responsibilities, power etc. between females and males in the reproductive and productive domains, are cross- culturally varied and subject to change and have to be taken into account, if household and national economic and demographic goals are to be met (UNFPA, 1991a). This cross-cultural diversity of gender roles in pre-industrial and industrialized societies had been well documented for decades in the descriptive ethnographies and comparative analyses of anthropologists and others. It has now at last entered the mainstream of population and development discourse and thought.

At the same time, an underlying premise of much current enlightened policy formulation and planning is that economic and demographic policies, plans and goals and environmental issues are inextricably intertwined and mutually reinforcing and need to be gender-sensitive. This is so since these aspects affect and are affected by such matters as labour supply, labour demand, migration for work, individual workers' productivity, stress levels, economic efficiency, the functioning of markets and the levels of welfare of domestic groups and national food security.[20]

There is a mounting body of evidence that past failure to take the varied and changing sexual divisions of labour and production, both inside and outside the home, adequately into account, partially through failure to adopt with alacrity improved modes of measuring and evaluating economic activity of both women and men, has had profoundly deleterious effects. These effects have been marked not only upon labour force statistics and household survey data collection and systems of national accounting, the tools and building blocks for planning purposes, but also upon economic, demographic, social and welfare policies, including attempts to adjust economic structures.[21]

Furthermore, this failure of conceptual tools and measuring devices has also led to an inability to carry out the types of economic/demographic analyses that could in turn promote the improved understanding of the causes and processes of change and innovation. Such analyses are clearly required for the design of more effective gender, population and development programmes and policies, including the identification of hitherto relatively neglected issues. Among the latter issues are those noted above: the greater subordination, vulnerability and precariousness of women workers; the urgent need for promotion and protection of health and safety of workers, including reproductive health; and the too early and unequal shares of parental and domestic responsibilities shouldered by girls and women, leading to their inequality in the workplace.

These are matters of increasing importance to national Governments, to employers and to workers' organizations, as well as women and men, in paid and unpaid, recorded and unrecorded, legal and illegal economic activity. These are problems in which gender, population and development issues are most intimately intertwined. They focus on workplace hazards for the growing numbers of vulnerable, insecure and often exploited female workers.

Some of these hazards in the workplace are clearly linked to male domination, sexual aggression and labour migration and to female insecurity, vulnerability, poverty and heavy burdens of family responsibilities, including economic responsibilities for child survival, maintenance and care. In some countries, these phenomena already show signs of being linked to imminent national health catastrophes, unless solutions that respond simultaneously to the economic and population issues involved are rapidly sought and found in the early part of the decade.

Just as women's economic activities have hitherto remained grossly underreported in official labour statistics and have been poorly documented in demographic and health surveys, so until recently there has been inadequate recording of maternal roles in relation to women's productive activities. This lack includes breast-feeding, weaning and child care, in relation to economic activities of all kinds and the conflicts and stresses experienced by mothers and linked to infant mortality and child development and survival, as well as maternal depletion and stress syndromes. Now the work of women, their death in childbirth, the impacts of abortion (through the Safe Motherhood Initiative) and the effects of prolonged breast-feeding are all being increasingly well documented and addressed in action programmes.

A severe problem remains, however, which hinders a more effective, holistic, policy-related analysis. This problem is the continuing lack of systematic, simultaneous, linked, comparative data sets on women's several roles (occupational, maternal, domestic, kin, conjugal, community) and their interactive effects. This effort would cover economic activities, time use, resource availability and use, and decision-making, together with demographic and health information, including effective access to maternal and child health and family welfare and planning resources. This lack of multifaceted data sets makes it difficult to document and unravel the multiple dimensions of the impacts of occupational, maternal and domestic role conflicts and the intervening effects of changes in conjugal, kin and community statuses, particularly on demographic and contraceptive innovation.[22]

Lastly, in this paper a number of salient issues are identified for needed action this decade.

Vulnerable teenagers: support for role transitions

Teenage pregnancy is the single demographic event that has the most disastrous effects in terms of female inequalities both at home and at work. Pregnancies among girls lacking both conjugal and kin support have deleterious economic and demographic consequences; in terms of truncated schooling, unequal vocational and employment opportunities, consequent poverty, infant and maternal mortality, and child deprivation and neglect.

It is envisaged that programmes of information, education counselling and support on this issue will need to increase rapidly during this decade, as the proportions of populations in the adolescent stage rapidly escalate and as Governments and other organizations become more and more aware and anxious to initiate appropriate action.

It has been estimated that there will be 300 million teenage girls needing training for jobs and at risk of precocious pregnancies by the year 2020. This figure has important implications for provision of all types of services to support the transition of young girls, through adequate training programmes, to motherhood and an occupation.

This is an important area for collaboration between different agencies and governmental and non-governmental organizations, to share information and experiences over the past decade and more and to replicate and give support, as appropriate, to those programmes of action which have already proved efficacious.

Women workers: balancing family responsibilities

As increasing number of women earn their incomes in the rapidly growing informal sector and live in communities lacking easy access to maternal and child health facilities and medically disbursed sources of family planning, the need will grow for community-based support systems to help women combine work and maternity.

Stark evidence exists, both from recent Demographic and Health Surveys and from estimates based on them, as well as from medical reports of abortions and the related heavy tolls of maternal mortality, of the widespread unmet need for access to family planning knowledge and services, among growing millions (100 million according to a recent estimate) of women workers throughout the developing world.

Women for whom traditional methods of birth control, through extended breast-feeding and long periods of post-partum sexual abstinence, are no longer feasible, urgently require access to modern substitutes to enable them to adequately postpone and space births so that they can more easily fulfil the simultaneous, stressful demands being made upon them as workers, mothers, wives, housewives and community members. These modern substitutes include knowledge of natural birth-spacing methods, as well as access to a whole range of modern contraceptives. The ability to plan and space births is vital to wives and mothers in the labour force, if they are to be able to cope with the heavy multiple demands of production and reproduction over the reproductive life cycle.

This situation points to the need, *inter alia*, for the replication by women's informal work-based groups of successful initiatives that have included such assistance to members in their educational and social-support programmes.

Safe working motherhood: reducing role conflicts and strain

On the one hand, there is the accumulating body of comparative demographic and medical evidence, pointing to the importance of six months' uninterrupted and intensive lactation to child survival, development and child-spacing and thus maternal health.

On the other hand, there is growing evidence from comparative surveys of the shortening of breast-feeding duration among women in formal sector employment in urban areas, unable to take their infants with them to workplaces where no crèche facilities exist. This situation often makes it impossible, even for those few, fortunate women covered by protective maternity legislation, to breast-feed their infants.

There is, in addition, the piecemeal evidence documenting the predicaments and survival strategies of working mothers, in all different types of occupations, rural and urban, informal and formal, as they try with limited success to combine heavy demanding schedules of economic activity, frequently at a distance from home, with adequate levels of breast-feeding and child care. Evidence of their stress and strain is witnessed by their attempts to set up crèches and day-care facilities at the community level with often the most rudimentary facilities.

Full consideration of these sets of evidence and their global implications, both for the survival and well-being of children and the stresses endured by working mothers, as well as the implications for equality of opportunity and treatment of working mothers in workplaces, ought to lead to renewed vigour in the design and development of appropriate strategies in the coming decade, strategies to facilitate breast-feeding by working mothers and to support the extended access to adequate forms of child care.

At international level, new forms of inter-agency collaboration would be needed. At the national level, there must be more active commitment to the goals of international labour standards regarding maternity protection and workers with family responsibilities. In the workplace, It would require renewed commitment of workers and employers and their organizations to the promotion of improved levels of survival and well-being of working mothers and their infants, through broader access to and establishment of appropriate facilities.

Women's workplaces and work groups have already proved excellent channels for provision of needed knowledge and services. What is required is a further extension of the now widespread Safe Motherhood Initiatives, adopted with alacrity by a number of international and national organizations in the past few years, a well-working mother and baby initiative.

It is only when adequate public support and protection for maternity become available that mothers will enjoy equality of opportunity and treatment in workplaces, and child-bearing and nursing will be viewed less as occupational hindrances and individual stumbling-blocks for women workers alone to overcome.

Precarious contracts: harassment and reproductive health

There is a set of categories of behaviour in which gender issues, workplace hazards and population outcomes are closely and poignantly linked. Yet, they have hitherto been relatively neglected by researchers, policy makers and programme planners. These are types of behaviour that are becoming increasingly well documented. They include the incidence of the interlinked phenomena of male dominance, power and control of employment opportunities and conditions in workplaces, on the one hand; and, on the other, the precarious work contracts and economic and sexual vulnerability of female workers.

This serious inequality and insecurity of women is known to be widely associated with the incidence of the crudest and most serious forms of sexual harassment in workplaces. These forms of exploitation are potentially ultimately linked to genitally transmitted disease and death, through human immunodeficiency virus (HIV) infection and the acquired immunodeficiency syndrome (AIDS).

The ILO is currently giving increasing attention to the issue of protection against sexual harassment in the workplace and will explore possible modes of promoting successful preventive workplace initiatives in all regions.

Exploited migrant women: protection and support

There is accumulating evidence of the special vulnerability of female international migrant workers, in domestic, entertainment and other forms of employment, to economic, social and sexual exploitation and abuses of the most serious kind.

The special case of the growing numbers of female migrant that are commercial sex workers is a source of increasing anxiety in several countries. It is a matter of concern from several perspectives, including the pressing need for alternative employment and sources of security; the aspect of female workers' degradation and abuse; and, in addition, the population issues of the potentially more rapidly increased spread of morbidity and mortality, through sexually transmitted disease.

The anxiety is particularly acute when such female workers are international migrants, frequenting urban areas with known high levels of mobility and disease incidence. Given the increasing volume of such migration flows from certain countries and the serious problems women workers migrating overseas as maids and entertainers face, it has become urgently necessary to understand more clearly the dimensions and implications of the phenomenon in different countries and regions and to formulate appropriate policies and interventions that are both protective and remedial (Gulati, 1992).

The implications for female workers' rights and protection, family welfare, occupational safety, reproductive health and family planning are potentially enormous.

Female-maintained domestic groups: labour deficits and energy needs

In many regions, increasing labour migration of men has left growing numbers of women alone in rural areas, coping with all the heavy manual tasks and responsibilities of farm and household production, and often almost entirely dependent upon the labour and support of their children, in labour-intensive subsistence economies, lacking mechanical sources of energy and power.

Proportions of female-headed and maintained households are also increasing as the result of war, political upheavals, environmental degradation and the loosening of conjugal bonds and the weakening of community sanctions concerning marital and parental responsibilities of husbands and fathers.

This maternal dependence upon children's labour clearly constitutes a potent reason for continuing high fertility, if child labour is the only source of renewable energy available. At the same time, if mothers and their children are overworked and stressed, other demographic outcomes will include elevated levels of maternal mortality, abortion and infant and child morbidity and mortality, including the serious effects of energy depletion and malnutrition already known to be widespread.

Several dimensions of the impact of labour migration on women and their work and children have become subjects of growing concern. However, the urgency of governmental and workers organizations to provide such women appropriate access to needed resources—including energy, water, transport facilities, credit, cooperative membership, land, employment opportunities, training, agricultural extension assistance and family welfare programmes—has been constrained partially by the lack of dissemination of data and policy analysis, demonstrating to policy makers the obvious roles of such women as maintainers of households, managers of farms and often the sole heads of their households.

Migration and associated development policies to stem labour migration flows and promote employment where the workers are obviously among the needed policy initiatives already began, which require urgent replication and expansion.

No old-age pensions: dependence upon children

Given the informal nature, the insecurity, the subsistence level of much of their arduous work, it is not surprising that far fewer women than men workers have pension rights accruing from their occupations and few have such rights from their community status, which would enable them to be self-supporting in old age. As a result, the majority of the world's women aredependent upon offspring in their declining years, as few can expect in old age to enjoy the support of husbands, who, given age differences at marriage and differential life expectancy levels, are likely to have predeceased or left them by that stage of their life.

The demographic implications are clear. Women workers need modes of investment of savings from their hard work, which would enable them to have some degree of security and autonomy in old age. This need has implications for laws and customs regarding land and property and their ability to save. It also has serious implications for laws and practices regarding social security schemes and their relative equality in the treatment of women and men.

Equality at home and at work

A variety of evidence of different types and from different culture areas and time periods indicates that when men actively enter the domestic domain and share more equally with women in tasks and responsibilities associated with home and children, the status of women in extra domestic roles is likely to be higher and male values and practices concerning family size and planning are likely to be innovative.

A woman's relative equality of resources, such as education, training, employment and income is linked to her relative power and autonomy in the home, as well as to patterns of sharing tasks and responsibilities in the conjugal relationship and the ability to communicate. The implications of such multiple interactive effects for family welfare and demographic change are clearly enormous. Equality of opportunity and treatment for women in the workplace, including equal pay, are obviously key issues affecting these outcomes.

Putting gender issues in plans and policies into the mainstream

Before gender issues can be put into the mainstream, the data required for policy formulation, planning and programme design need to be readily available. During the past decade, the work of women has become more readily recognized but national official statistical records are still very inadequate. The tools to facilitate the improved recording and evaluation of women's work need to be systematically used at the country level in all recording of economic activity and in the design of demographic and health surveys. This use will ensure a more realistic database for planning and will also make it possible for the appropriate links to be documented between different types of economic activity and different health and demographic outcomes, linkages that are vital for the informed design of appropriate population and development programmes and policies.

Another major task for the current decade is to see that other aspects of the varieties and changes in female and male roles, including those occurring in familial institutions, enter fully into the mainstream of economic and demographic planning, policy making and programme design.

To this end, attempts to sensitize, raise the awareness and increase the knowledge of planners and policy makers will need to be expanded and increased rapidly, and training in new techniques of data collection and analysis organized, if this knowledge is to have due impact on population and development plans and programmes. Practical tools will need to be made readily available.

NOTES

[1]It is proposed to update this document at intervals and to use it as a briefing note as appropriate and required. Suggestions for input and amendments are therefore welcome.

[2]International labour standards are legal instruments which provide a model for labour law and practice wherever women and men are at work throughout the world. The adoption of these standards and the supervision of their application are a major means of action of the ILO for the promotion of equality and protection of workers as well as other goals. They are adopted by the International Labour Conference and take two forms: conventions, which create binding legal obligations for the countries that ratify them; and recommendations, which are not subject to ratification and set guidelines for policies, legislation and practice at the national level. The latter instruments often accompany conventions and provide guidelines on how the conventions should be applied. International labour standards encompass a wide field of social and labour issues. They include such matters as basic human rights in occupational domains; for example, freedom of association, the abolition of forced labour and the elimination of discrimination in employment. Standards also deal with such questions as employment policy, minimum wages, working conditions and protection of workers, occupational safety and health.

[3]Various ILO documents and publications over a period of two decades have stressed the potential impact on fertility of employment-oriented development strategies, egalitarian development paths and promotion of labour laws and policies which promote sexual equality and youth protection, affecting familial roles and relationships (Oppong, 1982).

[4]Other standards directed protecting the health of the woman during periods of pregnancy or nursing or the child-bearing capacity of women include article 11 of the Benzene Convention of 1971 (No. 136) and paragraph 19 of the Benzene Recommendation of 1971 (No. 144), which provide that pregnant or nursing women should not be employed in work processes involving exposure to benzene or products containing benzene. Women during pregnancy or within 10 weeks following confinement are not to be assigned to the manual transport of loads if medically determined to be likely to impair their health or that of their child, in accordance with paragraph 18 of the maximum Weight Recommendation of 1967 (No. 128). The Nursing Personnel Recommendation of 1977 (No. 157) generally provides in paragraph 50 that "pregnant women and parents of young children whose normal assignment could be prejudicial to their health or that of their child should be transferred without loss of entitlement, to work appropriate to their situation. Work to which they should not be assigned should include tasks involving exposure to ionizing radiation or anaesthetic substances or those involving contacts with infectious diseases. The Night Work Convention of 1990 (No. 171), which regulates night work for both men and women, provides that for a period of at least 16 weeks before and after childbirth and if necessary for additional periods during pregnancy, women workers that would otherwise be called upon to perform night work shall be offered an alternative to night work. Such alternative may include transfer to day work the provision of social security benefits or an extension of maternity leave. The Lead Poisoning (Women and Children) Recommendation of 1919 (No. 4) prohibits and limits women from work involving exposure to lead poisoning "in view of the danger involved to the functioning of maternity and to the physical development of children, women and young persons". The Radiation Protection Recommendation of 1960 (No. 114) provides that women of child-bearing age should not be exposed to high radiation risks because of the special medical problems involved.

[5]The decision concerning reporting was taken after the adoption by the Conference in 1977 of a resolution on human rights, recalling that non-discrimination is a basic principle of the ILO Constitution, the furtherance of which forms a constitutional obligation for all the Member States. According to this decision, ratification should be a measure giving specific effect to the general obligation which already arises from the constitution. The effectiveness of all these procedures is recognized to be clearly mainly moral pressure, especially that exerted through discussion in the Tripartite Committee of the Conference, but they do eventually produce results, especially in matters connected with non-discrimination (as well as other fundamental rights) where there is particular sensitivity to criticism.

[6]For example, the committee has pointed to measures designed to achieve equality for women through education and vocational training and guidance, including programmes directed to stimulating access of women to jobs traditionally held by men; public advertising and information campaigns; measures to relieve women from assuming the principal responsibility for child care by providing for male and female employees to have equal options to obtain leave for family reasons; the creation of administrative bodies to advise women on their rights, formulate government policies and action and determine cases of alleged discrimination; and measures designed to establish equality of treatment in the areas of social security payments, pensions, family and civil law and income tax.

[7]At the request of the fourteenth international Conference of Labour Statisticians (1987) the Office is currently developing a simple and low-cost system of collecting statistics on employment in the informal sector, based on a common framework for international statistical standards on this topic to be adopted by the Fifteenth International Conference of Labour Statisticians planned to be held in 1993.

[8]The countries included in the regional divisions in this chapter do not in all cases conform to those included in the geographical regions established by the Population Division of the Department of Economic and Social Development of the United Nations Secretariat.

[9]See, for example, Weinert (1991). In the foreword, Böhning remarks: "One of the category of migrant workers whose importance has grown recently in various parts of the world is female domestic staff...in private households. Much anecdotal evidence suggests that foreigners who are domestics, especially where they are women, accumulate disadvantages to an extent that their work and life not infrequently becomes unbearable. The ILO felt that it was time to shed light on this category of migrant workers in a more systematic way than newspaper reports and hearsay can provide. It was decided to focus on foreign domestic workers" (p. ii). There are international labour standard-setting activities that are meant to serve to protect

migrant workers and to prevent discrimination on the basis of sex. Equality of treatment in the application of labour and social security legislation was called for in a special provision of the Migration for Employment Convention (Revised) of 1949 (No. 97) (article 6). Broader provisions were adopted in 1975 with the Migrant Workers (Supplementary Provisions) Convention (No. 143) and the Migrant Workers Recommendation (No. 151). They include provisions specifically designed to take account of the special characteristics and needs of foreign workers and they specify the minimum equality of rights which must be enjoyed even by migrant workers who are in an irregular situation. Convention 143 has not been widely ratified (15 countries) but together with Recommendation No. 151 it has had a major impact on the general trend of thinking, demands and practice in the field.

[10]According to the 1992, *World Labour Report*: "The exclusion of women from certain jobs: A bias towards men for promotion. Unequal pay for work of equal value. Sexual harassment. All are forms of discrimination very firmly established in most countries. Uprooting them has proved a slow and difficult task" (ILO, 1992h, p. 26).

[11]See World Health Organization (1992b) regarding the veil of silence in which "reproductive morbidity, emotional stress and sexual violence" continued to be cloaked.

[12]See I. GB. 253/CD/1/3 May-June 1992.

[13]See ILO, 1991, Training Papers Publications and Documents, Training Policies Branch, ILO, Geneva; " Women's training," pp. 6-8 and 11.

[14]A project entitled "Women in Technical Education, Training and Jobs" has been a particularly important initiative in this regard. The Commonwealth Association of Polytechnics in Africa (APA) has been assisted to conduct a major investigation into factors impeding the entry of women into technical training and employment. The ultimate objective was to identify ways in which vocational and technical training institutions, such as those in the CAPA network, can attract and retain more women in their programmes and as faculty and managers. However, it quickly became clear that the overall situation could not improve without the simultaneous and mutually reinforcing changes in other realms: primary and secondary schools: enterprises; and the overall policy environment. Three regional syntheses of findings were prepared, as well as a research guide (Phiri, 1990; Sekwao, 1990; Odugbesan, 1990).

[15]See, for example, ILO, *Bibliography of Published Research of the World Employment Programme* , 9th ed. International Labour Bibliography, No. 9 (Geneva, 1991); and see, in particular, the monographs in the Women Work and Development Series, many of which were published with the financial support of UNFPA.

[16]See, for example, *Population and Labour Research News*, No. 11 (ILO, 1990f), which outlines the scope of research on women population and development carried out in the late 1980s.

[17]See, *The State of World Population, 1989* (Sadik, 1990).

[18]See the report of the Director-General to the International Labour Conference in 1991: "Whatever form it takes, child labour is an extreme manifestation of poverty, since the poorest families have to rely on their children's labour in order to survive; but it also results in a perpetuation of poverty, since it prevents children from acquiring the education and skills that would equip them for better employment, and better paid jobs, in their adult life" (ILO, 1191i).

[19]This subprogramme is being implemented almost exclusively with the support of UNFPA and includes technical support and regional advisory services and country projects. The operational activities are carried out through national employers' and workers' organizations and through local employers and cooperatives. Workers' welfare courses are being carried out in collaboration with the Turin Centre of the ILO. Technical advisory services are the major focus of this programme, which will also serve to promote the following international labour standards: Equal Remuneration Convention, No. 100, 1951; Maternity Protection Convention (Revised), No. 103, 1952; Discrimination (Employment and Occupation) Convention, No. 111, 1958; Employment Policy Convention, No. 122, 1964; Minimum Age Convention, No. 138, 1973; and Workers with Family Responsibilities Convention, No. 156, 1981.

[20]See the recent work of Palmer (1991) on economic planning, gender, structural adjustment and population issues in sub-Saharan Africa.

[21]See, for example, recent ILO publications on the measurement and recording of women's economic activities (Anker, 1994; and Anker Khan and Gupta, 1988; Pittin, 1984; Wainerman, 1991); the evaluation of women's unpaid work (Goldschmidt-Clermont, 1987) and the importance of these factors for policy making and planning (Dixon-Mueller and Anker, 1988; Goldschmidt-Clermont, 1990).

[22]Small-scale studies have provided a possible framework and model for analysis (Oppong and Abu, 1985 and 1987).

References

Abu, Katherine (1991). *Family Welfare and Work Dynamics in Urban Northern Ghana.* Labour and Population Series for Sub-Saharan Africa, No. 13. Geneva: International Labour Organization.

Akuffo, F. O. (1987). Teenage pregnancies and school drop outs: the relevance of family life education and vocational training to girls' employment opportunities. In *Sex Roles, Population and Development in West Africa*, Christine Oppong, ed. London: James Currey.

Anker, Richard (1983). Female labour force participation in developing countries: a critique of current definitions and data collection methods. *International Labour Review* (Geneva), vol. 122, No. 6 (November-December), pp. 709-723.

_________ (1989). Measuring the female labour force in Egypt. *International Labour Review* (Geneva), vol. 128, No. 4 (July-August), pp. 511-520.

_________ (1994). Measuring women's participation in the African labour force. In *Gender, Work and Population in Sub-Saharan Africa*, Aderanti A. Adepoju and Christine Oppong, eds. London: Currey.

_________, and Catherine Hein, eds. (1986). *Sex Inequalities in Urban Employment in the Third World.* London: Macmillan Press.

Anker, Richard, M. E. Khan and R. B. Gupta (1988). *Women's Participation in the Labour Force: A Methods Test in India for Improving its Measurement.* Women, Work and Development Series, No. 16. Geneva: International Labour Office.

Böhning, W. R. (1988). The protection of migrant workers and international labour standards. *International Migration* (Geneva), vol. 26, No. 22, pp. 133-145.

_________ (1991). Foreword. In *Foreign Female Domestic Workers: Help Wanted*, Patricia Weinert. World Employment Programme, MIG Working Paper, No. 50. Geneva: International Labour Office.

Bongaarts, John (1990). The measurement of wanted fertility. *Population and Development Review* (New York), vol. 16, No. 3 (September), pp. 487-506.

_________ (1991). The KAP-gap and the unmet need for contraception. *Population and Development Review* (New York), vol. 17, No. 2 (June), pp. 263- 313.

Catasus, S., and others (1988). *Cuban Women: Changing Roles and Population Trends.* Women, Work and Development Series, No. 17. Geneva: International Labour Organization.

Cecelski, Elizabeth (1987). Energy and rural women's work: crisis, response and policy alternatives. *International Labour Review* (Geneva), vol. 126, No. 1 (January-February), pp. 41-64.

Dixon-Mueller, Ruth, and Richard Anker (1988). *Assessing Women's Contributions to Development.* Population, Human Resources and Development Planning Training Paper, No. 6. Geneva: International Labour Organization.

Evans, Ann (1992). *Women's Work and Family Welfare: Informal Women's Groups and Family Planning Information and Services.* World Employment Programme Research Working Paper, No. 182. Geneva: International Labour Office.

Evans, M. (1987). Stoves programmes in the framework of improved cooking practices: a change in focus with special reference to Latin America. Technical Cooperation Report. Geneva: International Labour Organization.

Findley, Sally E., and Linda Williams (1990). *Women Who Go and Women Who Stay: Reflections of Family Migration Processes in a Changing World.* Population Policies Pogramme Working Paper, No. 176. Geneva: International Labour Office.

Folbre, Nancy (1991). Mothers on their own: policy issues for developing countries. Working paper prepared for the Population Council/International Center for Research on Women Seminar Series on the Determinants and Consequences of Female-headed Households.

Gavrilescu, N. (1976). *Organization of Family Planning in Occupational Health Services.* Occupational Safety and Health Series, No. 31. Geneva: International Labour Organization.

Goldschmidt-Clermont, Lvisella (1982). *Unpaid Work in the Household: A Review of Economic Evaluation Methods.* Women, Work and Development Series, No. 1. Geneva: International Labour Organization.

__________ (1987). *Economic Evaluations of Unpaid Household Work: Africa, Asia, Latin America and Oceania.* Women, Work and Development Series, No. 14. Geneva: International Labour Organization.

__________ (1990). Economic measurement of non-market household activities: is it useful and feasible? *International Labour Review* (Geneva), vol. 129, No. 3 (May-June), pp. 301-315.

Gulati, L. (1992). Asian women migrant workers: a review. Draft research paper. New Delhi: ILO Regional Programme for International Labour Migration.

Hall, E. K. Eveklien. (1987). Working with refugees in Somalia towards a development perspective. Technical Cooperation Report. Geneva: International Labour Organization.

Harrington, J. (1978). Some micro-economics of female status in Nigeria. Paper presented at a Conference on Women in Poverty: What Do We Know? Washington, D.C.: International Centre for Research on Women.

International Labour Organization (1975). Texts concerning women workers adopted by the 60th Session of the International Labour Conference, 4-25 June. Geneva.

__________ (1980a). *Equal Opportunities and Equal Treatment for Men and Women Workers: Workers with Family Responsibilities.* Report VI(I). International Labour Conference, 66th Session. Geneva.

__________ (1980b). *Standards and Policy Statements of Special Interest to Women Workers.* Geneva.

__________ (1985a). *ILO Plan of Action on Equality of Opportunity and Treatment of Men and Women in Employment.* Geneva.

__________ (1985b). *Resolution on Equal Opportunities and Equal Treatment For Men and Women in Employment.* Adopted by the International Labour Conference at its 71st Session, Geneva.

__________ (1985c). *Rural Development and Women: Lessons from the Field.* Geneva.

__________ (1987a). *Cooking Efficiency Programme in Ethiopia,* Phase 1, *Final Report to the Ethiopian National Energy Committee, Ministry of Mines and Energy.* Geneva.

__________ (1987b). *Linking Energy with Survival: A Guide to Energy, Environment and Rural Women's Work.* Geneva.

__________ (1987c). *Population, Human Resources and Development Planning: The ILO Contribution.* Geneva.

__________ (1987d). Women worker's protection or equality. *Conditions of Work Digest* (Geneva), vol. 6.

__________ (1988a). *Equality in Employment and Occupation.* General Survey by the Committee of Experts on the Application of Conventions and Recommendations. International Labour Conference, 75th session, Geneva.

__________ (1988b). *Women Workers: Selected ILO Documents.* Geneva.

__________ (1988c). Work and family: the child care challenge. *Conditions of Work Digest* (Geneva), vol. 7.

__________ (1989a). *Employment Opportunities for Rural Women through Organization.* Geneva.

__________ (1989b). *Empowering Women: Self-employment Schemes for Female-headed Households.* Geneva.

__________ (1989c). *ILO Activities on Discrimination in Employment and Occupation.* Governing Body, Committee on Discrimination. Geneva.

__________ (1989d). *Women and Land.* Report on the Regional African Workshop on Women's Access to Land, Harare, Zimbabwe, 17-21 October 1988.

__________ (1990a). *A Compendium on Women's Participation in Selected ILO Technical Cooperation Projects.* Geneva.

__________ (1990b). *Environment and the World of Work.* Report of the Director-General of the International Labour Office to the International Labour Conference, Geneva, 1990. Geneva.

__________ (1990c). *ILO Experiences in Making Women Visible in Selected Mainstream Projects in the Southern African Region.* Report from a Workshop held at Lusaka, Zambia, 23-25 January. Geneva.

__________ (1990d). *ILO Standards and Action for the Elimination of Discrimination and the Promotion of Equality of Opportunity in Employment.* International Labour Standards, Department of Equality of Rights Branch. Geneva.

__________ (1990e). National machineries to promote equality of opportunity and treatment for women workers. Background paper prepared for the Asian-Pacific Regional Symposium on the Promotion of Equality for Women Workers, Canberra/Sydney, October. Equality of Rights Programme. Geneva.

__________ (1990f). *Population and Labour Research News,* No. 11. World Employment Programme; report on research and related policy activities in the ILO Population and Labour Policies Programme, mainly with financial support from UNFPA. Geneva.

__________ (1990g). Report on the Asia-Pacific Regional Tripartite Symposium on the Promotion of Equality for Women Workers, Canberra/Sydney, October. Equality of Rights Programme. Geneva.

__________ (1990h). Report on the ILO/PNGTUC Workshop on Labour Standards and Women Workers for Workers' Representatives, October, Papua New Guinea. Papua New Guinea: ILO Office for the South Pacific.

__________ (1990i). Technical background paper. Tripartite Symposium on Equality of Opportunity and Treatment for Men and Women in Employment in Industrialized Countries, Geneva, November. Geneva.

__________ (1991a). Child labour: law and practice. *Conditions of Work Digest* (Geneva).

__________ (1991b). *The Dilemma of the Informal Sector.* Report of the Director-General, International Labour Conference, 78th session, 1991. Geneva.

__________ (1991c). *ILO Standards and Women Workers.* Egalité/1991/D.4.

_________ (1991d). *Lessons Learned.* 1990/1991 Evaluation Highlights, No. 3. Evaluation Unit. Geneva.

_________ (1991e). *Population and Family Welfare Education in the Work Setting: The ILO Contribution.* Geneva.

_________ (1991f). Report of the Tripartite Subregional Seminar on the Promotion of Equality of Opportunity and Treatment in Employment in Central and Eastern Europe, Prague, 14-18 October. Equality of Rights Programme. Geneva.

_________ (1991g). Report of the Tripartite Symposium on the Development of Strategies for the Promotion of Equal Opportunity and Treatment for Women and Men in Employment in Namibia, Windhoek, November 1991. Geneva.

_________ (1991h). Tripartite Symposium on Development of Strategies and Policies for the Promotion of Equal Opportunity and Treatment for Women and Men in Employment in Namibia, Windhoek. Namibia, November. Geneva.

_________ (1991i). *The Window of Opportunity: Strategies for Enhancing Women's Participation in Technical Cooperation Projects.* Geneva.

_________ (1992a). *Adjustment and Human Resources Development.* International Labour Conference, Seventy-ninth Session, Report VI. Geneva.

_________ (1992b). Equality for women in employment: an Interdepartmental Project, No. 1. *Inside News* (Geneva) (16 March).

_________ (1992c). *ILO Activities for Equality of Opportunity and Treatment for Men and Women in Employment.* Committee on Discrimination. GB 253/CD/1/3. Geneva.

_________ (1992d). *International Labour Standards and ILO Population Programmes.* Geneva.

_________ (1992e). International labour standards and technical cooperation. Governing Body, GB 252/15/1.

_________ (1992f). Population, human resources and development planning: priority issues and requirements. In *Population Policies and Programmes.* Proceedings of the United Nations Expert Group Meeting, Cairo, Egypt, 12-16 April 1992. New York: United Nations. Sales No. E.93.XIII.5.

_________ (1992g). Working conditions and environment department. Interdepartmental Project on the Elimination of Child Labour. Geneva.

_________ (1992h). *World Labour Report, 1992: Human Rights at Work, Employment, Labour Relations, Social Protection and Working Conditions. Statistical Appendix.* Geneva.

Islam, M. (1991). *National Machinery for the Integration of Women, Population and Development in Bangladesh.* Labour and Population Team for Asia and the Pacific Working Paper, No. 4. Bangkok: International Labor Organization Regional Office for Asia and the Pacific.

Joekes, Susan (1989). Women's work and social support for child care in the Third World. In *Women Work and Child Welfare in the Third World,* Joanne Leslie and Michael Paolisso, eds. Boulder, Colorado: Westview Press.

Krishnamurty, J. (1992). The incorporation of population concerns into projects for self-employed women: some alternatives. In *Self-employed Women, Population and Human Resource Development,* Pravin Visaria and Unni Jeemol, eds. Ahmedabad: Gujarat Institute of Development Research.

Medel-Anonuevo, C. (1992). *National Machinery for the Integration of Women, Population and Development in the Philippines.* Labour and Population Team for Asia and the Pacific Working Paper, No. 8. Bangkok: International Labour Organization Regional Office for Asia and the Pacific.

Messell, E. (1990). ILO's technical cooperation activities and gender planning. Background paper prepared for the ILO Asian and Pacific Regional Symposium on the Promotion of Equality for Women Workers, Canberra/Sydney, October. Equality of Rights Programme. Geneva: International Labour Organization.

Odugbesan, F. A. (1990). *Women in Technical Education, Training and Jobs.* Africa Western Regional Report. Discussion Paper No. 58. Geneva: International Labour Organization.

Oppong, Christine (1982). *Familial Roles and Fertility: Some Labour Policy Aspects.* World Employment Programme, Research Working Paper, No. 124. Geneva: International Labour Office.

_________ (1991). *Relationships between Women's Work and Demographic Behaviour: Some Research Evidence in West Africa.* World Employment Programme, Research Working Paper, No. 175. Geneva: International Labour Office.

_________, and Katherine Abu (1985). *A Handbook for Data Collection and Analysis of Seven Roles and Statuses of Women.* Geneva: International Labour Office.

_________ (1987). *Seven Roles of Women: Impact of Education, Migration and Employment on Ghanaian Mothers.* Women, Work and Development Series, No. 13. Geneva: International Labour Office.

Page, J. Hilary (1989). Child rearing versus childbearing: co-residence of mother and child in sub-Saharan Africa. In *Reproduction and Social Organization in Sub-Saharan Africa,* Ron Lesthaeghe, ed. Berkeley: University of California Press.

Palmer, Ingrid (1991). *Gender and Population in the Adjustment of African Economies: Planning for Change.* Women, Work and Development Series, No. 19. Geneva: International Labour Office.

Phiri, C. (1990). *Women in Technical Education, Training and Jobs.* Africa: Southern/Central Regional Report. Discussion Paper No. 53. Geneva: International Labour Organization.

Pittin, Renée. 1984. Documentation and analysis of the invisible work of invisible women: a Nigerian case study. *International Labour Review* (Geneva), vol. 123, No. 4 (July-August), pp. 473-490.

Royston, Erica, and Sue Armstrong, eds. *Preventing Maternal Deaths.* Geneva: World Health Organization.

Sadik, Nafis (1990). *The State of World Population, 1989. Investing in Women: Focus of the Nineties.* New York: United Nations Population Fund.

_________, ed. (1991). *Population Policies and Programmes: Lessons Learned from Two Decades of Experience.* New York and London: New York University Press.

Sekwao, C. (1990). *Women in Technical Education, Training and Jobs.* Africa Eastern Regional Report. Discussion Paper No. 54. Geneva: International Labour Office.

Thomas, C. (1990). The role of international standards in reducing discrimination against women. Paper prepared for a Seminar on the Status of Women Working in Large Enterprises, Naberejnye Chelny, USSR, May.

Trebilcock, Anne (1987). Migrant workers: an overview of international labour standards in the legal position of aliens in national and international law. *Beitraege zum Auslandischen Offentlichen Recht und Volkerrecht* (New York), No. 94.

United Nations (1985). *Women's Employment and Fertility: A Comparative Analysis of World Fertility Survey Results for 38 Developing Countries.* Population Studies, No. 96. Sales No. E.85.XIII.5.

_________ (1986). *Review and Appraisal of the World Population Plan of Action: The 1984 Report.* Population Studies, No. 98. Sales No. 86.XIII.2.

_________ (1988). *World Demographic Estimates and Projections, 1950-2025.* ST/ESA/SER.R/79.

_________ (1989). *Adolescent Reproductive Behaviour,* vol. II, *Evidence from the Developing Countries.* Population Studies, No. 109/Add.1. Sales No. E.89.XIII.10.

_________ (1990a). *Handbook for National Statistical Data-Bases on Women and Development.* Sales No. E.89.XVII.9.

_________ (1990b). *Population and Human Rights.* Proceedings of a United Nations Expert Group Meeting, Geneva, 3-6 April 1989. Population Studies, No. 107. Sales No. E.91.XIII.8.

_________ (1991a). *Concise Report on the World Population Situation in 1991, with Special Emphasis on Age Structure.* Sales No. E.91.XIII.17.

_________ (1991b). *The World's Women, 1970-1990: Trends and Statistics.* Series K, No. 8. Sales No. E.90.XVII.3.

United Nations Population Fund (1988). *Integrating Women's Component into Population Programmes.* Report of a Training Workshop for UNFPA Field Staff in the African and Middle Eastern Regions, Mombasa.

_________ (1990). *Report of the International Forum on Population in the Twenty-first Century, Amsterdam, the Netherlands, 6-9 November 1989.* New York.

_________ (1991a). *Incorporating Women into Population and Development: Knowing How and Knowing Why.* New York.

_________ (1991b). *Report: Women, Population and Development.* New York.

Wainerman, Catalina H. (1991). *Improving the Accounting of Women Workers in Population Censuses: Lessons from Latin America.* World Employment Programme, Research Working Paper, No. 178. Geneva: International Labour Office.

Weinert, Patricia (1991). *Foreign Female Domestic Workers: Help Wanted!* World Employment Programme, Working Paper, No. 50. Geneva: International Labour Office.

World Health Organization (1989). Protecting, promoting, supporting breastfeeding: the special role of maternity services. A joint WHO/UNICEF statement. Geneva.

_________ (1991). *Maternal Mortality: A Global Factbook.* Geneva. Compiled by Carla Abou Zahr and Erica Royston.

_________ (1992a). *Report of the Technical Discussions: Women's Health and Development.* Forty-fifth World Health Assembly. A45/Technical Discussion/2, 12 May.

_________ (1992b). *Women's Health: Across Age and Frontier.* Geneva.

Youssef, Nadia H., and Carol B. Hetler (1984). *Rural Households Headed by Women: A Priority Concern for Development.* ILO World Employment Programme, Research Working Paper, No. 31. Geneva: International Labour Office.

Zegers, M. (1992). *Strategies for Women and Development in the Republic of the Congo.* Labour and Population Series for Sub-Saharan Africa, Document No. 14. Geneva: International Labour Organization.

XXVIII. WOMEN'S ACTIVITY AND POPULATION DYNAMICS IN AFRICA

*Economic Commission for Africa**

The demographic transition has, up to now, been recognized as the chief explanatory framework of the dynamics of human populations. Groups of countries have achieved or entered the transition at their own—more or less speedy—pace. In Africa, however, the insufficient data available indicate that the transition is apparently not occurring as expected, or at least is delayed, putting this major area behind the rest of the world.

Mortality has declined significantly, mainly during the second half of the current century. But it remains high in many sub-Saharan African countries, particularly infant, child and maternal mortality (Defence for Children International, 1991). Fertility has not declined significantly and in some countries seems to be on the rise. How can these trends be explained and what is to be expected in the future?

Although findings are not always consistent, research shows that some relation exists between women's activities and population dynamics—particularly fertility, women's morbidity and mortality, and survival of children. The paucity of data, however, leads more to speculation than factual analysis. This situation obviously calls for intensification of research in this field.

Reviews of the proximate determinants of fertility indicate a high correlation with the status of women, which, in turn, is influenced by many factors, including economic activity. How this aspect relates to population dynamics in Africa is the subject of this paper, which attempts also to speculate about future trends.

A. Economic activity of women in Africa

In spite of the limitations of the definitions of employment in censuses and statistical surveys, the reality is that African women engage quite significantly in economic activities (ILO, 1983) in addition to their role as mothers and child-rearers. Their double function in society, as producers and reproducers, has quite often been overlooked and denied, which maker the measurement of their involvement in economic activities more difficult. The best example is in agriculture.

Whereas women spend some 60-80 per cent of their time in productive work and are responsible for three quarters of the food produced, they are usually considered and counted as family help, since they do not receive cash salary for their work. Very little (if anything) is said about the induced morbidity of women resulting from this economic and social burden. Furthermore, their difficulty in sparing enough time to care for their children may explain part of the high infant and child mortality.

For the convenience of this review, a distinction should be made between the traditional and modern sectors:

(a) Traditional sector. Women are heavily involved in this sector, which covers cultivation, land- clearing, trading and some related services, with the use of rudimentary techniques. As a rule, some division of labour prevails. Women take care of the cultivation of subsistence crops, whereas men are engaged in producing cash crops, meant for sale, with the use of, respectively, traditional and modern technology;

(b) Modern sector. In general, access to this sector is restricted to people with some education. Since girls were disadvantaged for access to schools until recently, it is understandable that women active in this sector are usually few in number (United Nations, ECA, 1986). Their proportion declines with the increase in specialization. However, it is

*Population Division, Addis Ababa, Ethiopia.

worth noting that some progress was recorded in the post-independence period, as women have gained entry into all sectors of activity and can be found at almost all levels of the professional hierarchy.

The "slow pace of agricultural modernization" (Boserup, 1985, p. 385) begins first among people close to and around the modern sector. It has been observed that access to modern techniques is made difficult for women engaged in the cultivation of cash crops (Basset, 1991).

How does this involvement of women in economic activities, in either the traditional or modern sector, relate to population dynamics?

African women are, roughly, divided into two groups. The first is composed of the overwhelming majority of women, usually illiterate or with some primary education, residing in the rural areas or in the peripheral urban townships and engaged in the traditional sector or the lowest ranking jobs in the modern sector. For this category, fertility is relatively higher than for the second group.

The second group is composed of educated, urban women engaged in the modern sector, who have had the possibility to attend school, sometimes beyond the primary level, making them relatively privileged. They also live close to some health facilities and have access and are exposed to modern media. As urban centres, particularly the capital city, provide more opportunity for jobs in the modern sector, this group is usually found active in positions traditionally known to be taken by women, although this is not a rule and may vary according to cultural norms. Their fertility tends to be lower than in the rural areas.

Several authors have suggested that in Africa, fertility constitutes an integral part of women's social status. In normal circumstances, it is expected that an improvement in the role and status of women would be at variance with high fertility. This development has been demonstrated, in other areas of the world, by the impressive declines in fertility along with modernization, higher school enrolment of girls, better involvement of women in public affairs and political life etc. In Africa, however, this trend does not appear to be occurring, either because the evolution seems to take a different path or because it unfolds with a different momentum. The explanation of this trend lies, most certainly, in the strong social value attached to high fertility, as a natural function, a source of prestige, economic return and social security for the future.

Hence, if education, employment, income and status are considered together, it is likely that a lower level of one or more of these variables will result in higher fertility, this playing a form of acompensatory role. Boserup, among others, provides one of the best descriptions of the explanatory mechanism governing the relation between women's activities in the traditional sector and fertility. According to her, subsistence agriculture is conducive to large families, because "the father of a large family is likely to become a rich man, while the father of a small family is likely to remain poor. . .in regions of traditional African production and land tenure, polygyny is frequent, family size is large. . ." (Boserup, 1985, p. 395).

To realize the objective of a large family, age at marriage for women is still very low and has changed little with time, for early marriage increases the exposure to risk of pregnancy. Moreover, remarriage takes place quickly, at child-bearing age, after divorce or widowhood; the women concerned wish to remarry in order to avoid social marginalization, as their single status is not well accepted by society (ECA, 1986). The period of sexual union is long to maximize the potential for having children, given the value attached to them for the labour force and social security in old age.

However, according to Boserup and other authors, the situation is changing because of rapid population growth.

B. Future trends

The African pattern of reproductive behaviour could operate as long as production factors, particularly land, were not limited. Rrapid population growth, the increasing population density, and increasing difficulties to catering for the needs of the population and the consequences of the economic crisis will necessarily lead to a reassessment of traditional values, although with some gap in time. The pace of this reassessment depends again upon multiple factors, ranging from climate and availability of production factors to beliefs and cultural values.

For instance, people are coming to realize that it is no longer worthwhile to invest in sending children to attend school in order to permit them to take a remunerative job in town, as a limit has been reached in the supply of jobs and as past opportunities in town no longer exist. Educated children will, sooner or later, question the traditional production methods and social values. It is likely that their economic expectations as parents will differ from those of their ancestors.

Women, for their part, do realize that past practices no longer fulfil their aspirations for a better life. However, the sharp decline in social expenditures because of structural adjustment programmes constitutes a serious constraint to helping them in this endeavour. What little progress achieved in the first years of political independence may not be consolidated. This situation would result in delaying progress for women and hence, their access to family planning, health services etc. Fertility would remain high and its decline would again be postponed.

Assuming, in normal circumstances, that evolution towards modernization takes a normal path, it is expected that the reproductive pattern will probably change from no spacing with prolonged breast-feeding to deliberate birth spacing with shorter breast-feeding and more concentration of births at the beginning of the child-bearing life of women, instead of a more even distribution during the whole span of child-bearing ages. Although shorter breast-feeding is spreading among large segments of women, both rural and urban, without the necessary compensation for the nutrition and protection of the children, the other modalities of change towards a modern model do not seem to occur as obviously as one would expect.

C. Conclusion

African heads of State and Government, in adopting the Lagos Plan of Action (OAU, 1981), called for the integration of women into all spheres of development. They reiterated this call in the Kilimanjaro Programme of Action on Population (United Nations, ECA, 1984), in the form of 12 recommendations, inviting Governments to pursue more aggressively action programmes directed to, among other things, improving and protecting the legal rights and status of women, providing support for equal opportunities to both women and men in the crucial areas of education and employment, and introducing programmes intended to reduce the heavy burden on rural women.

The status of women is likely to change slowly in Africa, unless a breakthrough is made in economic and social development, which appears doubtful at this time. The cultural values boosting high fertility will then adapt to the new perspectives and women will be in a better position to make their own options regarding the number of children and their health and welfare.

References

Basset, T. J. (1991). *Migration et féminisation de l'agriculture dans le nord de la Côte d'Ivoire: les spectres de Malthus*. Paris: Office de la recherche scientifique et technique outre-mer; Centre français sur la population et le développement.

Boserup, Ester (1985). Economic and demographic interrelationships in sub-Saharan Africa. *Population and Development Review* (New York), vol. 11, No. 3 (September), pp. 383-397.

Defence for Children International (1991). *Effects of Maternal Mortality on Children in Africa*. New York.

Gillis, Malcolm, and others (1983). *Economics of Development*. New York and London: W. W. Norton.

Hauser, Philip (1979). *World Population and Development: Challenges and Prospects*. Syracuse, New York: Syracuse University Press.

International Labour Organization (1983). *Women, Work and Demographic Issues*. Report of an ILO/UNITAR seminar, Tashkent, USSR, 11-19 October 1983. Geneva.

Organization of African Unity (1980). *The Lagos Plan of Action for the Implementation of the Monrovia Strategy for the Economic Development of Africa*. Geneva: International Institute for Labour Studies.

Palmer, Ingrid (1991). *Gender and Population in the Adjustment of African Economies: Planning for Change*. Women, Work and Development Series, No. 19. Geneva: International Labour Office.

Sadik, Nafis (1989). *The State of World Population, 1989: Investing in Women: Focus of the Nineties*. New York: United Nations Population Fund.

United Nations, Economic Commission for Africa (1984). Kilimanjaro Programme of Action for African Population and Self-reliant Development. In *Report of the Second African Population Conference, Arusha, United Republic of Tanzania, 9-13 January 1984*. ST/ECA/POP/1. Addis Ababa, Ethiopia.

____ (1986). Impact de l'évolution du role de la femme sur la fécondité. ECA/TP/POP/86/2.3.a. Addis Ababa, Ethiopia.

XXIX. WOMEN IN DEVELOPMENT—AWARENESS-RAISING: LESSONS LEARNED IN TECHNICAL COOPERATION

*United Nations Secretariat**

A. BACKGROUND

Since the 1970s all United Nations agencies have been mandated by their governing bodies to introduce women in development as a priority area in their programmes. As a result, efforts have been directed to incorporate women's issues in most training and awareness-raising activities. The population programme of the Department of Economic and Social Development of the United Nations Secretariat, has prioritized raising awareness with regard to women in development planning and policy formulation. This effort has been implemented through workshops and short focused meetings, especially for middle- and senior-level government officials of developing countries; and through the inclusion of courses on women in development in the curricula of undergraduate and graduate programmes in population and development in universities in developing countries.

Far too often issues and responsibilities related to women in development "fall through the cracks" because of their multidisciplinary and intersectoral nature. Also, general awareness of the issues concerning women in development and their implications is lacking, especially among government planners and policy makers, which diminishes the resolve to include these issues in national agendas. This situation is confirmed by the fact that eight years after the endorsement of the Nairobi Forward-looking Strategy by all the United Nations Member States and the establishment of women's units within government machineries, programmes for raising women's status (where they exist) remain generally weak, imperceptible and lopsided. For example, there is an overemphasis on family planning and little attention to discrimination against female babies, legal and inheritance issues, sexual disparities in salaries/wages, vocational education and agricultural extension services to women. Based on such experience, the population programme of the Department of Economic and Social Development has devoted itself to awareness-raising, training and skill-building as worthy objectives.

B. WOMEN IN DEVELOPMENT CONCERNS IN TECHNICAL COOPERATION

In response to the call to insert women's advancement in all aspects of work at United Nations Headquarters and especially in technical cooperation activities, several guidelines and targets were established. These objectives ranged from raising the proportion of women professionals in the staff composition of departments and divisions, to setting up rosters of qualified women for recruitment at senior-level assignments as advisors and consultants and to making special efforts to include women candidates as participants in training programmes, workshops and conferences. Guidelines were issued on how to integrate women's issues right from the stage of programme/project identification, design, implementation, monitoring and evaluation. Check-lists for ensuring women's participation in each of those phases of programmes or projects were also developed. At the country level, the Department continues to provide guidance and technical assistance for conducting specialized studies for collecting data required for determining women's status, which forms the basis for planning and policy formulation with regard to women in development. Subregional and national seminars are held to discuss specific women's issues using a problem-solving approach. To provide an international forum for exchange of experiences, the Department organized, in collaboration with the Government of Tunisia, a seminar on population, women and development to be held at the end of June 1992. Contemporary issues of concern to Governments of

*Former Population Branch of the former Department of Technical Cooperation for Development.

most developing countries, such as women migrants, women and family and women's employment, will be discussed with the goal of arriving at recommendations for planning and policy formulation. Thus, the objective of the strategy is a plan of action that allocates responsibility and accountability with verifiable objectives regarding women's integration into all aspects of technical cooperation. Although some progress has been made, much is left to be done. This lapse cannot be blamed on lack of effort but may be due to inappropriate approaches.

C. Training and awareness-raising tools

A microcomputer-based simulation model designed for use in awareness-raising events was developed by the Department and has proved to be of immense value. This tool, the United Nations Women in Development Model, is being distributed extensively in the form of computer software with a corresponding manual.

Briefly, the model demonstrates how, by manipulating certain policy variables, women's contribution to economic development can be raised. In its current version, the model focuses on women's productive role in rural agrarian households of developing countries.

The complex two-way relation between women's status and socio-economic development is compounded by the fact that the available concepts and tools define socio-economic development from a policy perspective at the macrolevel. However, women's issues are better defined, and designing of policy becomes more effective, at the microlevel. For official policies effectively to improve the status of women, the female population cannot be aggregated into a single, seemingly homogeneous group. In order to encompass a large majority of women through policy, the female population should be classified into at least three major groups: *(a)* rural primary sector; *(b)* urban informal sector; and *(c)* urban formal sector. Further, in order to reinforce the concept of women's contribution to development, it is necessary for policy makers to better understand women's productive and reproductive roles, including how women regularly allocate the time and resources under their control.

Taking these factors into account, three micromodels are being developed in the population programme (the first of which is ready) of the Department as training tools for policy makers and development planners. The first model, which concerns women in rural agricultural households, has been successfully employed in meetings, seminars and workshops for senior- and middle-level government officials.

This microlevel and essentially static model is based on five assumptions drawn from daily rural life:

(a) Access to productive resources is not equal by gender, that is, such inputs as education, credit, land, technology and agricultural extension services and other factors of production, are complementary to labour, and access to them varies by gender;

(b) There is sex disparity with regard to economic incentives, which adversely affects women's productivity. "Economic incentives" is defined as the ability to retain the returns of one's labour or have control over the use of such returns. A strong positive correlation has been observed between such incentives and productivity;

(c) Women spend a significant amount of their time in unpaid household activities that have a social value but are overlooked in the measurement of macroeconomic indicators, such as gross national product. It is observed that the amount of time women spend on such activities is a function of household size, which in turn is a function of fertility;

(d) Fertility, as established through innumerable country-level data sets, is a function of women's education, labour force participation and access to family planning;

(e) In primary-sector activities, there is sexual division of labour as well as sexual division of productive activities.

The structure of this simulation model reflects the main elements of the role of women in both their productive and reproductive functions. The model is based on the five assumptions given above and incorporates four interrelated components, namely, time allocation, agricultural production, cash income and household size. Twelve exogenous variables, many of which are amenable to policy modifications, have been used in this model: level of education; access to capital; amount of land; access to agricultural extension services; price of agricultural commodities; amount of agricultural production marketed; level of market wage; share of control of women's income; share of men's income going to the home; access to family planning services; and total amount of time available. The endogenous variables are: agricultural production; cash income; household size; time spent on agricultural production; time spent on market employment; time spent on home activities; and household welfare index. For ease of use and understanding, the exogenous variables are implemented in the model as index variables which are greater or less than one in relation to a reference solution. Thus, a value greater than one for education (an important policy variable) represents an increase in education.

The exogenous variables with their corresponding power parameters have been combined in four functional forms. These are: *(a)* time-use function; *(b)* agricultural production function; *(c)* income function; and *(d)* household-size function. The outcome of the model is summarized in a synthetic index termed "household welfare". Household welfare measures and ranks the impact of policies on the main outputs of the model (the dependent variables). The household-welfare index is the outcome of a utility function which uses as inputs, with appropriate weights, parts of the outputs of the four functions specified above:

(a) From the production function (defined separately for women and men), part of agricultural production reserved for home consumption;

(b) From the cash-income function (defined separately for the two sexes), all of women's income and a part of men's income that is under women's control;

(c) From the allocation-of-time function, the amount of time spent on household activities (separately by men and women) averaged by household size.

The household-welfare index is not the outcome of an objective function in the sense that the equation (when solved) does not automatically search for the highest value of the welfare index subject to the other relations in the model; however, it can be optimized in terms of quality and composition. Essentially, this index measures and ranks the impact of policies in areas relevant to women's productive and reproductive activities on the outputs of the model. Thus, the model illustrates the impact of policy variables on women's capacity to contribute to household welfare. In so doing, it represents a microcosm of socio-economic development at the macrolevel.

The model is general enough that it can apply to the situation of women throughout the less developed regions. However, African women are different from Asian women and Asian women are different from Latin American and Caribbean women; but the differences can be accounted for in terms of parameter values, which define the functional relations in the model. Hence, models can eventually be developed for different areas of the world. Ideally, regional model parameters and functions should be established at the regional level through econometric estimation, but it is doubtful that appropriate data exist. Alternatively, a combination of individual country-level data that can be distilled into typical facts for a set of representative countries of a region could be used.

The next step in further developing this model is collecting empirical country-level data to verify the model. Some efforts have been made in this direction, but considerable work remains to be done. Significant progress has been made in building the two urban models, in the formal and informal sectors. It is expected that it will be relatively easy to collect the required data to verify these models.

D. Strategy used in presentation of the model

The strategy used to present the model, especially in short meetings for senior-level administrators, policy planners etc. is: *(a)* to explain briefly the background, assumptions and structure of the model using a "story board"; and *(b)* to present the simple spreadsheet model which contains a "reference solution". This "solution", which forms the first panel of the model, is divided into three parts. The parts contain a different number of variables, some of whose values change in response to changes in the values of the exogenous variables. The last three rows of the top panel of the table are the real outputs of the model: cash income; family size; and household welfare. In the lower panel, below the "reference solution", are the "reference" values of exogenous variables/policy variables indexed for men's values and fractions of these indices corresponding to women's values. One or more of these values is allowed to change in subsequent runs of the model. The remaining factors shown in the lower panel—production, family size and welfare coefficients—are values of parameters that are locked in and are used in the equations corresponding to each of the functions that ultimately determine the level of "household welfare".

When changes are effected in the "reference values" of the policy variables, the values of household welfare change in response, indicating simultaneously percentage changes in the first panel of the model. Thus, an increase in women's education to the same level as men's raises household welfare by 19 per cent, with a corresponding decline in time spent on home activities (7 and 6 per cent for men and women, respectively) and an increase of 34 per cent in women's agricultural production and cash income. Also, the family size declines by 9 per cent. Thus, by changing the values of female exogenous variables/policy variables, one effects dramatic changes in household welfare. Hence, the users of the model are able to prioritize policies to increase women's contribution to development, given specific targets and realistic constraints. Such a simulation has been stimulating to planners and policy makers, who, in response, have reiterated their resolve to accord even higher priority to women's issues.

E. Conclusion

In order to demonstrate even more convincingly applicability of this model at individual country/representative regional or subregional levels, it is necessary to collect the data that the model requires. One of the areas in which data was scarce or non-existent until recently, women's time use, is now increasingly being collected by researchers. It has been proved that such data can be collected reliably. However, more such effort is required.

Data on cash income over which women have control and how it is disbursed, the proportion of men's cash income used for the household over which women have control and input used by women in their productive activities are not available from any of the surveys that have been conducted. Such information is not difficult to gather and can be collected through a special module of continuous household survey programmes that many countries are committed to implementing.

This model has served as an efficient tool for awareness-raising and training in issues related to women in development.

Those interested in the software and the manual of the model may request them from the Population Division of the Department for Economic and Social Development of the United Nations Secretariat.

Part Eight

POPULATION, ENVIRONMENT AND DEVELOPMENT: ISSUES OF SPECIAL CONCERN FOR WOMEN

XXX. WOMEN, POPULATION AND ENVIRONMENT: A GLOBAL CONCERN

*Colette S. Dehlot**

Women throughout the world share a multitude of experiences that transcend the invisible borders of culture, politics and economic status. Despite the vastly different societies in which they live, adult women in Sweden, the United States of America, China and Botswana alike will be expected to assume the double burden of productive and reproductive activities. They will receive inadequate payment, recognition and assistance for the many tasks they perform. Yet, they will establish as their main priority the health and well-being of their family.

Whereas in developed countries women are consumers of natural resources, women of the developing world, "ecologists by tradition", are the persons trying to repair most of the environmental damages caused by overexploitation of natural resources, water pollution, industrial wastes, and unsound development projects to the local indigenous resources. On the other hand, these women till the land, tend the livestock, work in factories, sell in markets and look after their families. Because women's productivity in a developing economy depends so much upon health of natural resources, they have a crucial role to play in limiting the environmental damage that is so often the result of development.

These are probably the reasons that current interest in population, women and environment has become widespread and is growing. However, knowledge of the linkages involved remains poor. Concrete cases and empirical examples that demonstrate causal links between all three variables are scarce. Equally important is the need to identify institutional mechanisms for developing and testing elements of strategic planning in relation to women, population and natural resources. Lastly, guidelines need to be developed to direct the formulation of specific projects involving activities related to population-women-environment where there is no or little sustainability of the natural environment. This is the purpose of the present paper.

A. POPULATION AND RESOURCES: THE INTELLECTUAL BACKGROUND

The World Conservation Strategy defines "conservation" as the management of human use of the biosphere so that it may yield the greatest sustainable benefit to current generations while maintaining the potential to meet the needs and aspirations of future generations (IUCN, 1989). Yet, the current demand for natural resources, coupled with inappropriate technologies and management techniques applied in their use, is diminishing the resource base through overgrazing, overcutting, overcropping, overfishing, overdraining and polluting. The results are soil erosion, desertification, forest depletion, poisoned water and loss of biological diversity.

But concerns about population pressures on resources are more ancient than may be realized. Chinese writers at the time of Confucius inquired into the right balance of population and land to bring the greatest prosperity to the State. Plato estimated the ideal population of a Greek State as one that would be large enough for security and self-sufficiency but small enough to preserve civic cohesion (Keyfitz, 1972).

According to Mostafa K. Tolba, Executive Director of the United Nations Environment Programme (UNEP), for thousands of years, African villagers and townspeople had used local resources prudently so that they had been handed over intact from one generation to the next, often unconsciously as the people observed religious, cultural and other practices finely honed to their environment. In terms of material

*The Population Council, Nairobi.

possessions, these people were poor, but in their respect for is now referred to as "balance between people, resources, environment and development", they were rich indeed (Tolba, 1987). Today, collectively, African countries agree that they must endorse environmentally sound development to restore the balance).

The Stockholm Declaration, which was adopted by the United Nations Conference on Human Environment in June 1972, reads: ". . .man has the fundamental right to freedom, equality and adequate conditions of life in an environment that permits a life of dignity and well-being and bears a solemn responsibility to protect and improve the environment for the present and future generations". Twenty years later, at the Fifteenth World Congress of International Confederation of Free Trade Unions at Caracas, Venezuela, Norwegian Prime Minister Gro Harlem Brundtland emphasized that: "To solve global environmental problems, such as ozone depletion and climate change, we clearly need new and additional resources to enable developing countries to join the global agreements now being negotiated".

The World Population Conference held at Bucharest in 1974 and the International Conference on Population held at Mexico City in 1984 recognized the limitation of population growth as part of the multifaceted approach to furthering socio-economic development and protecting the natural resource base. Both conferences suggested that advances in socio-economic development enhance reduction in population growth. The International Conference in 1984 concluded that family planning activities and socio-economic development policies are mutually reinforcing. Since then, many developing country leaders have repeatedly encouraged the adoption of national population policies, as was proclaimed in the report of the Organization of African Unity.

Human resources can be an important moving force in development. They should not, however, overburden the investment resources. It was the World Conference on the Review and Appraisal of the Achievements of the United Nations Decade for Women, held at Nairobi in 1985, that emphasized the liaison between women's roles and the environment and stipulated that: "Awareness by individual women and all types of women's organizations of environmental issues and the capacity of women and men to manage their environment and sustain productive resources should be enhanced"; and that ". . .all sources of information dissemination should be mobilized to increase the self-help potential of women in conserving and improving their environment" (United Nations, 1986).

In November 1989, the United Nations Population Fund (UNFPA) celebrated its twentieth anniversary by organizing an International Forum on Population in the Twenty-first Century. At the Forum, many Government representatives, including Zimbabwean President Mugabe, spoke on the relationship between population growth and environmental degradation. At the Forum, Nobel Prize winner Willy Brandt stated that about 1 billion people still lived in abject poverty, and the gap between rich and poor countries was getting wider; that the North-South/East-West division of the world was becoming more and more eroded with respect to environmental disaster as the irrational use of natural resources affected both developed and developing countries.

Fortunately, the challenge facing the world is not a stark choice between preserving the natural environment and economic growth. As the World Commission on Environment and Development points out, the ability to make development ecologically sustainable is available. The task is to ensure that the needs of the present shall be met without compromising the ability of future generations to meet their needs (WCED, 1987).

B. Women in ecological engineering: a theoretical framework

If science has provided a better picture of the dynamic workings of the environment, it has also exposed the blanks—areas where there is not sufficient scientific knowledge to permit a consensus on the magnitude of the threat of human engineering to the natural environment, still less on what remedial action is needed. There is an urgent need to fill those gaps to clear up the unknown aspects with regard to the environment. Above all, it is necessary to comprehend women's roles in relation to their use of natural resources and population dynamics in the light of sustainable development. That is, how do women's circumstances and demographic considerations interface with the sustainable use of the natural environment and economic development?

The concept

Resources are the main components of the environment; their utilization is the process of development. Misuse of resources by people leads to deterioration of the environment. In turn, this deterioration represents non-sustainability of the process of development and hence undermines the meeting of people's needs and aspirations. The interactions between people, resources, environment and sustainable development vary according to resource availability, the demands of the people, their cultural, religious, aesthetic and other needs (figure X). These variations are not merely from one region to another, but also from one locality to another.

Hence, the interrelations between population, resources, environment and development are complex: each of the four components affects and is affected by the other three. To be of any use, policies and actions must be relevant to this system as a whole. As a matter of fact, women's productive and reproductive functions are so attuned to the availability of natural resources that any changes in the environment have consequences for their economic productivity, their reproductive health and the health of their family. Figure XI illustrates such interrelationships and highlights their complexities.

The approaches

The earlier approaches to women's roles in development were not helpful in this regard. The first presentation of women as an additional vulnerable category or "target group" for anti-poverty programmes was methodologically suspect. Such special pleading was not well received in an era of budgetary restraint. Next came the tendency to bring the development potential of women to the attention of policy makers on the ground that they represented an underutilized resource. From the beginning this assumption was manifestly erroneous, because women generally work harder and longer than men. Analyses of some development projects have demonstrated that it was rather the failure attributed to the non-utilization of female labour.

The more recent literature makes it clear that women must be regarded more seriously as producers and be given appropriate training and skills to become more productive, so that they can contribute more effectively to alleviate the poverty of rural families in particular. The purpose is not to remove them from the family or to create independent women's power. Rather, it is to enhance their productivity, in ways that add to their capacity and value within the community, giving them more "bargaining" power for fairer treatment by officials, such as politicians and decision-making bodies, and by family members, such as husbands and elders. The status of women will be improved if they have such power for voluntary contribution to the welfare of those whom they value as well as to their own well-being.

It is then argued that the current approach of having women as partners in development with equal access to benefits and resources is targeting the potential input of women's full productivity and reproductivity. However, another approach, which holds the most promising outcome, focuses on women as agents of change (figure XII). This term refers to the entire range of women's domestic and non-domestic, family and non-family activities, including community organization and kinship maintenance, which are not conventionally recognized as having economic value (Dehlot, 1991).

The unit of analysis

According to Russo and her associates (1989), in most natural resource projects, the "household" is taken as the basic unit of analysis; males are assumed to be heads of households and the principal decision makers and sources of information. The roles of other household members are frequently ignored—to the detriment of the project and of those it is meant to serve. Yet, in every society women and men have different roles, have access to different resources and benefits and have different responsibilities (Bledsoe, 1980; Johnson, 1988).

Figure X. Women and ecological engineering

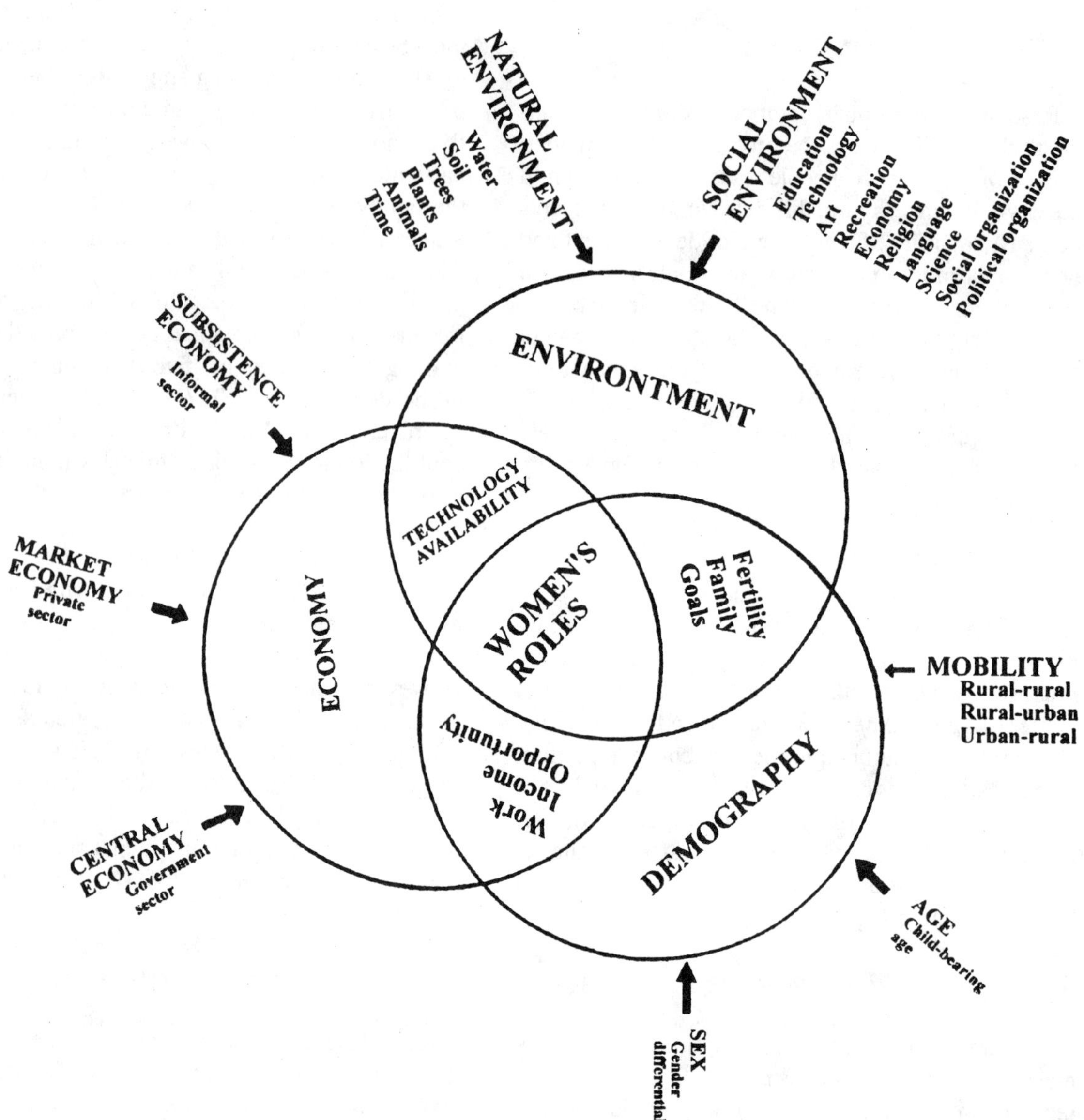

Figure XI. Natural resources: managerial processes

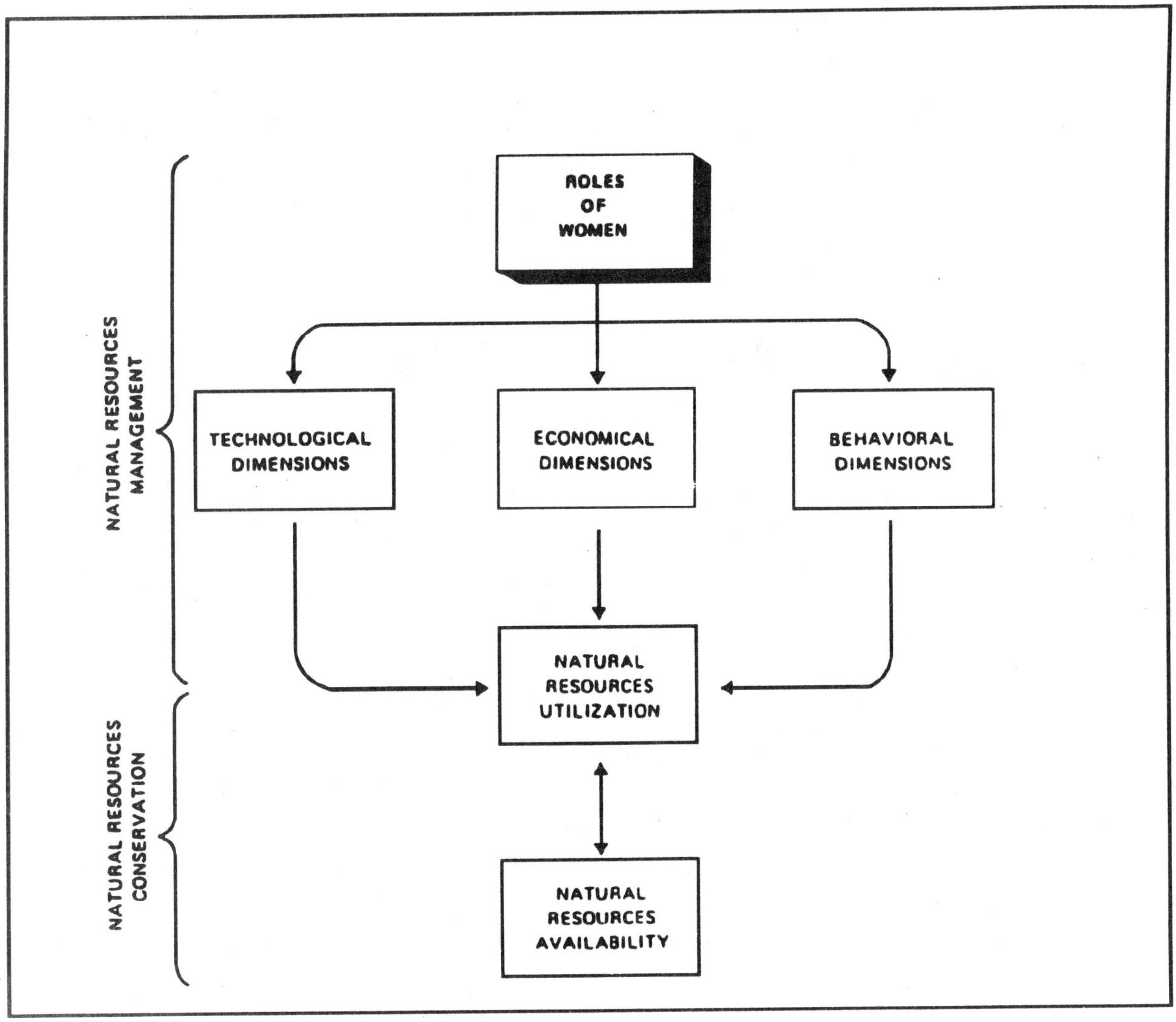

NATURAL RESOURCES MANAGEMENT

ROLES OF WOMEN

TECHNOLOGICAL DIMENSIONS

ECONOMICAL DIMENSIONS

BEHAVIORAL DIMENSIONS

NATURAL RESOURCES UTILIZATION

NATURAL RESOURCES CONSERVATION

NATURAL RESOURCES AVAILABILITY

Source: Annabel Rodda, *Women and the Environment* (London; and Atlantic Highlands, New Jersey, ZED Books, 1991).

Figure XII. Multidisciplinary roles of women

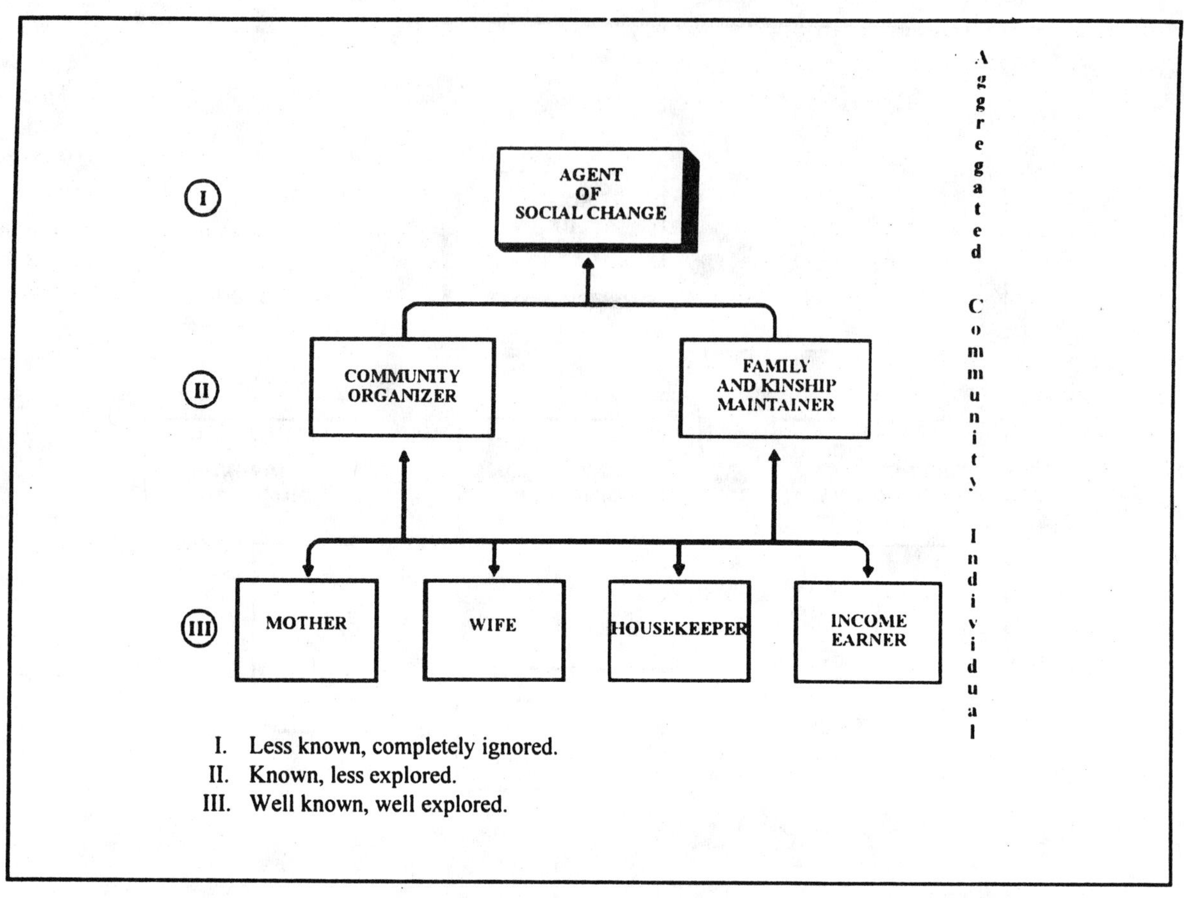

Source: Annabel Rodda, *Women and the Environment* (London; and Atlantic Highlands, New Jersey, ZED Books, 1991).

As Johnson (1988) notes, the emphasis on individual men as the unit of analysis and on women only as wives is an assumption that limits the understanding of what actually happens in many development situations. Assumptions about the appropriateness of individual men as units of analysis, particularly in developing countries, as well as the applicability of the household as a unit of analysis with a tacit assumption that decisions are made by all the members as a unit or that income is distributed equally among household members, have distorted findings.

That is, any consideration of women that concerns only the category "wife" emphasizes only women's reproductive labour. Such simplistic classification often leads to the description of a wife as "an economic dependant" of the husband. At best, it may include married women's contribution to production but it necessarily fails to consider the role played in production by other women in the household who are not married to the head of household, that is, daughters, sisters, mothers, aunts, affines or totally unrelated household members, but whose labour makes major contributions to the economic activities of the household (Johnson, 1988).

Operational research and qualitative studies

Effective environmental programmes need accurate and detailed information about what women do, where and how they work, with whom they cooperate or compete, how they help support their household, what resources they control and how they exert such control and in what ways they make or influence decisions and shape community opinion. Existing ideologies about the sexual divisions of labour, or power, cannot accurately guide the collection of this information. Conventional wisdom about the lack of power or passivity of women, especially in developing countries, seldom reflects the patterns of work and structures of authority that actually prevail.

This information can be collected through focus group discussions, in-depth interviews, observations and individual questionnaires. Also, gender-disaggregated data and gender analysis must be a prerequisite of all environmental programme development and implementation.

C. Women and population

Women as human resources and producers

Due to their charge of caregiving, child-bearing and work, women throughout the world are the primary providers of formal and informal health care. Domestic work represents an invisible contribution of $4 trillion by the women of the world. Women also constitute one third of the world labour force; yet, they work two thirds of the world working hours and own only 1 per cent of world property.

As agriculturalists, women in developing countries produce one half of the food. African women have been called the "invisible farmers" of African agriculture. It has been estimated that African women in sub-Saharan countries produce 60-80 per cent of agricultural output and 90 per cent or more of the food crops, and are 80-100 per cent active in the informal sector. Yet, their poor health results in large part from their low economic status, characterized by widespread illiteracy, lack of income and employment opportunities, and limited access to basic resources, including public-health services, such as safe drinking water and sanitation.

Women as reproducers of human capital

Current fertility rates indicate that majority of women in every country, rich or poor, will bear and nurture at least one child during their lifetime, making pregnancy and childbirth near universal events. But here, the common ties are severed. Few of life's experiences mark so boldly as motherhood the sharply disparate conditions faced by women in the more developed and the less developed regions. Whereas most women in the developed countries will enter into pregnancy as healthy people and safely deliver a healthy infant, women in the developing world cannot hold such expectations. Indeed, women in countries south of the Sahara face higher risks of maternal death and disability than women in any other region of the world.

Women of child-bearing age are also more vulnerable to environmental pollutants than men because of their reproductive function and breast-feeding practice. Many reports have linked reproductive defects to contaminants, such as lead. With the annual increase in the number of chemicals, the impact on women and children is probably rising. The possible effects of exposure to chemicals reportedly include infertility, miscarriage, malformation, neonatal death and growth retardation.

In industrialized countries, birth defects currently cause between 15 and 35 per cent of infant deaths. One fourth of the abnormalities are genetic in origin and between 5 and 10 per cent are consequences of drug and substance abuse, viruses, radiation and chemicals. Contaminants even appear in human milk. Chemicals known to be concentrated in human milk include pesticides and organophosphates. World Health Organization (WHO) experts say that in some countries the daily intake of such substances by breast-fed infants is higher than the acceptable levels.

Each of these conditions exacerbates the health risks women face throughout life; each of them renders pregnancy and child-bearing a life-threatening endeavour. Poor maternal health, therefore, is the result of a lifelong chain of adverse environmental conditions and circumstances, all of which must be addressed to save women from unnecessary suffering and death. It is thus important to create awareness among countries and their people of the dimensions and consequences of maternal mortality and morbidity and to enlist community support in taking action to make pregnancy and motherhood safer for all women.

Women's duality as source of wealth-in-people

Labour and allegiance are critical to people's economic subsistence as well as to their political and economic advancement. Bledsoe (1980) argues that in traditional societies the control of women and children is central to the production of economic surpluses to attract dependants. This system is referred to as the "wealth-in-people system" and can be formalized in the legal notion of rights in people.

For example, in many African societies, patriarchs (men) and matriarchs (older women) have legal rights in women and children. They use rights in women not only to reproduce and to gain labour for supporting their immediate families but also to lure young men into ties of debt and obligation. However, in the view of wealth-in-people institutions the most important female function is child-bearing. Only women that have borne a child or two may assume prestigious roles in society, confirming their dualism as producers and reproducers.

There is, in addition, the high value placed on children whereby children are a source of social security for old age. With infant mortality high and the prospect that surviving children may not be willing to work for their parents, parents prefer to have as many children as possible in order to ensure the survival and future support of at least one or two. Older people also use children to establish important alliances with other families. Whereas boys are sent as wards to unrelated families for economic cooperation or political support, daughters are more valuable for bride service and as potential sexual tokens of powerful men.

Through stratified social institutions, elder men and women maintain power by controlling both access to women and the knowledge of subsistence resources, and they use "secret societies" to ensure their exclusive control of all important information. Hence, information and secrets may better be viewed as ideological dressing on a rigid gerontocratic hierarchy. It does not matter what the secrets are: it is more important that the young believe that the secrets the elders protect are important and that they have no right to know things only elders are entitled to know.

However, women may not always cooperate with the ambitions of elders and men. In their various studies, Sexton (1986) and Strathern (1982) describe the growing tension between men and women generated by the juxtaposition of traditional standards of production and a new economy. In both cases, men have transferred the appropriation and mobilization of women's labour, characteristic of traditional subsistence and ceremonial production, to cash cropping for their own advantage. In doing so, they have created an additional labour burden for women without providing access to the profits of cash cropping commensurate with women's contribution to those profits. Only gender situation analysis can provide accurate information about the political, economic and legal bases of the system in order to understand men's and women's options and constraints.

Demographic variables and population dynamics

Social mechanisms that regulate population growth are found in both traditional and modern societies. Out-migration has always been a response to population pressure. Prolonged breast-feeding and sexual taboos restrict birth rates. In societies subject to high mortality rates, gerontocracy has used wealth-in-people institutions to keep fertility high. Contemporary societies resort to contraception and abortion to keep fertility low and/or to space children. In industrialized democratic societies, population ageing tends to shift political power towards the aged with consequences for fertility levels, which in some developed countries are no longer sufficient to assure the long-term replacement of the population (Davis, Bernstam and Sellers, 1989). However, it is assumed that child-bearing decisions of couples are not made with a view to achieving replacement-level fertility. Low or high birth rates can be viewed as a period of adjustment while society reorganizes around and adjusts to the changing roles of women and as better provision is made for child care.

Population mobility, however, is the most troublesome issue for both the natural environment and population growth. The movement of workers, for instance, modifies the distribution of population as long as there are jobs at the other end. Young adult males, who are mostly rural-urban migrants, feed the growth rates of the cities. In developing countries, urban-urban settlers tend to be impoverished migrants and underemployed young labour force entrants. Whereas older women may be more involved in rural-urban mobility, most women in developing countries are rural-rural migrants, generally changing locality at marriage. Rural-rural female migration contributes to the continuing use of natural resources by rural women. On the other hand, urban-rural migration involves mainly elderly males. As they return to retire in their own rural communities after a period in urban areas, these men may acquire a younger bride and/or invest in farming.

Strategies to address population issues

As a result of worldwide efforts, the global rate of population growth has decreased from 2.2 to 1.7 per cent per annum, although the annual increase in numbers continues to rise. Despite a general decline in birth rates, rapid population growth is continuing in developing countries, due primarily to the sharp decline in mortality rates. Modern public-health measures are largely responsible for these declines, including improvements in water-supply and sanitation, better nutrition, immunization and availability of maternal and child health care and family planning services (Lee, 1985).

Data from areas throughout the world show that improvement of female education and access to better health care, employment and legal rights have contributed to the decline in birth rates (USAID, 1985). Women are also aware that population pressures contribute to environmental degradation, putting heavy strains on natural resources and often depleting them more rapidly than they can be regenerated. For women, therefore, the availability of family planning methods and services is important, as this makes it possible for them to choose the size of their family and to broaden their economic options. Family planning is, furthermore, a necessity for world population stabilization and a sustainable environment.

D. Women and the environment

Our common future

Unlike other species, humans control to a high degree their own demography and their resource base. Diverting most of the resource base for human use, however, leaves less biomass for maintenance of the rest of the biosphere (Woodwell, 1985). Among the consequences of this increasing appropriation are destruction of habitat for other species, leading to impoverished ecosystems and accelerated rates of extinction.

According to resolutions adopted during the United Nations Decade for Women, deprivation of traditional means of livelihood is often the result of environmental degradation resulting from such natural and man-made disasters as droughts, floods, hurricanes, warfare, desertification, deforestation and inappropriate land use. Such conditions have already pushed great numbers of poor women into marginal areas where the critically low output of arable lands and the high population density have deprived them of their livelihood. Yet, the world's soil and water are finite; and biomes, such as forest ecosystems, have a limited capacity to regenerate after damage. After a certain point, regeneration of natural ecosystems is impossible.

Wetlands, for instance, are among the world's most productive ecosystems, along with tropical rain forests and coral reefs. Because their net primary productivity is so high, they provide habitat and breeding grounds for a disproportionate share of fish, crustaceans, amphibians, birds and small mammals. In the humid tropics, forest conversion has imperilled the principal source of the world's biological diversity: millions of plant, animal and insect species whose potential value to agriculture and medicine are yet to be explored. Women living in these biomes have learned through cultural transmission of knowledge to benefit from the biotechnology of nature.

Tropical forests, the richest and least understood ecosystem, are rapidly disappearing not only because of encroachment by rural populations but also because misguided government policies encourage large-scale conversion to ranches and agricultural settlements. Many of these actions, which represent inappropriate land use, could not exist without heavy government subsidies.

As a continent, for example, Africa has the greatest quantity of species, whether animal or plant, on land or in lake basins. About 40-70 per cent of them are indigenous to specific countries, such as Madagascar, South Africa and Zaire. Most of these species are threatened by the invasion of exotic plants, fire, encroaching farms and so forth. Moreover, in logged-over tropical moist forests, the removal of high-grade species has devalued the remaining stands. Timber booms in tropical countries richly endowed with forests (Gabon, the Congo), have depleted the resource rapidly and wastefully. Low taxes and royalties have allowed logging concessionaires to make enormous short-run profits from rich Government-owned tropical hardwood forests. Typically, women in shifting cultivation travel the abandoned logging roads, clear the remaining tree-depleted areas after concessionaires depart and begin food-cropping activities.

Water, consumed mainly in agriculture, is increasingly scarce in many semi-arid areas. There, tree density has fallen as the result of foraging and fuelwood collection. The open savannahs of the Sahel are rapidly being stripped of their remaining trees. The world annual fuelwood consumption alone exceeds annual tree growth by an estimated 30 per cent; in the Niger, about 200 per cent; in Ethiopia, 150 per cent; and in the Sudan and Nigeria, about 70 per cent (Repetto, 1989). In many arid and semi-arid lands, intensive cultivation of marginal lands and overgrazing have led to land degradation. Elsewhere, acute shortages of energy lead to the use of grasses, dung and crop residues as sources of fuel, which deprives the resource base of its nutrients creating a biomass disequilibrium.

Even with "controlled" grazing, the world's grasslands have markedly deteriorated under the growing grazing pressures of domestic livestock that have displaced herds of wild herbivores. Most rangelands are also susceptible to degradation, especially those in dry climates where plant growth is slow. Impoverishment and depletion of vegetative cover as the result of overstocking exposes the organic content of the soil, leads to loss of nutrients and impairs the ability of the soil to hold water, a process known as "desertification".

The overall threat within the life-span of today's children is that significant climate change could raise sealevels, leading to flooding of coastal cities and plains, and make low-lying islands uninhabitable. It could also change the distribution and availability of freshwater resources, alter natural ecosystems and accelerate the extinction of plant and animal species, and change energy usage patterns as well as the productivity and distribution of agricultural lands. It is clear that such an outcome, even if it were to occur gradually, would have major ramifications for human survival and settlement patterns as well as for the environment in general. Such a state of affairs would almost certainly be accompanied by social and economic dislocation.

Women sustaining our common future

Natural resource scarcity affects women's work more than men's, because of the different types of work women do. For women in a subsistence economy, collecting and carrying fuel, tending fires, cooking and washing all take more time as firewood becomes more difficult to find. For urban women in the developing countries, who must buy fuel on limited budgets, structural adjustment and rising prices may mean less money for food. Many women's home industries, such as brewing beer, making pottery and food processing, are fuel-intensive; while other small-scale income-generating activities, such as basket-making and collecting medicinal plants for sale or healing purposes, depend upon forest products.

Although land reform is central to the management of natural resources, it is also one of the most difficult issues to deal with. In developing countries, the relevant decisions are frequently made by small, politically influential groups with interests in commercial logging, ranching and plantation cropping. Having inadequate control over the land they farm and little political weight, women in subsistence economies cannot easily obtain the capital and external information and technology with which they could improve their fortunes.

Yet, the results from the UNEP Commission on Public and Leadership Attitudes to the Environment Surveys (1989) have found that: *(a)* women in general were more aware of various environmental degradation problems than men; *(b)* women were more critical of their Governments' efforts in environmental protection and were more likely to say that various environmental problems become very serious in the next five years; and *(c)* compared with men, women were more likely to choose a lower level of living with fewer health risks over a higher level of living with more health risk. These findings confirm statements at the Caucus on Women, Environment and Sustainable Development, held at Ottawa, Canada, in 1986, that serious consideration should be given to women's roles and their potential contribution to environmental development.

There has so far been a failure to allocate sufficient resources to ensure women potential partnership in environment sustainability and national economic growth. Women are not yet perceived to be part of the environmental conservation scheme, except in a vague way. They are often seen as part of the environmental problems, rarely as part of the solution. As a result, the productive capacity of the majority of women in the developing world is severely weakened as the environment around them is damaged by forces beyond their control. According to UNEP, hundred millions of women throughout the world are struggling to meet basic human needs, many of which depend upon the health and productivity of natural resources. Until consideration of their roles and capacities is fully integrated into both policy and actions, the world community will be increasingly less secure (Tolba, 1987).

E. Women and development: partners for life

The satisfaction of basic human needs draws fundamentally on the earth's natural endowment. The quality of human life, too, depends upon a sound, supporting environment of clean air, safe and plentiful water and adequate food and shelter, as much as upon such factors as health, job satisfaction, education, security and self-fulfilment. While today many people are attaining a higher quality of material life, considerably more join the hundreds of millions living in absolute, desperate poverty. Both trends, in very different ways, impinge on conservation, reducing the long-term capacity of natural resources to provide for human needs.

Environment and economic development

In most cities in developing countries, poverty and rapid urban population growth have resulted in appallingly poor environmental conditions for many inhabitants. In many instances, women are being forced by poverty to plunder the natural resources and/or destroy their heritage to ensure the immediate survival of their family. With population doubling every 20 years or so, it is difficult to marshal the resources for education, health care and other investments needed to escape poverty.

As home economists, women are the prime users of common-property forest resources for multiple purposes. Fuelwood, wild food and fodder and industrial raw material supply are an important part of the essentials for household subsistence, which is generally women's responsibility to provide. They are also important sources of income to poor households. The most significant trend is women's growing awareness of the negative effects of population growth on living conditions and the environment, especially in areas with high population density.

In the developed countries, on the other hand, the greatest threat to the natural environment is their drawing upon the so-called "non-renewable" resources: fossil fuels; metals; and non-metallic minerals. The economic growth of these countries arising from private and short-run gains has little or no regard for longer run environmental implications or broader social costs. According to Repetto (1989), although the industrial market economics have only 774 million of the total world population and a population growth of 0.6 per cent per annum, these people consume a disproportionate share of the world's resources.

In sum, while the high energy consumption of industrialized countries contribute to ozone depletion by global emissions of carbon dioxide from the use of fossil fuels and burning of biomass, rapid urbanization in the developing countries has a dominant influence on the quality of their environment. It is up to Governments to ensure that parameters established by economic policies shall reflect social needs and social costs, so that private interests and environmental quality can coincide. Population and economic growth have also stimulated technological and organizational innovations which show that resources can be supplied and used more efficiently.

Agriculture and technology development

During the early 1960s, when cropland areas were growing slowly, the development of improved high-yielding seed varieties, cheaper chemical fertilizers and new synthetic pesticides, used together on areas with water-supplies assured mostly through irrigation, generated the Green Revolution. This new technological package was a remarkable and critical achievement that supplied needed food and agricultural products at stable and declining real prices during a period of population and economic growth. However, it has also created pressures on the resource base. Both inefficient water use in large irrigation projects due to poor operation and maintenance, and the absence of incentives for water conservation have exacerbated serious water-logging and salinization problems, worsening the problem for women, who must collect water.

The use of synthetic pesticides has had substantial ecological impacts. Unimportant insect species have emerged as major problems when their natural enemies have been reduced by pesticide applications. The implicit analogy to non-human species, which do not approach the human capacity for modifying both his environment and the way of using it, is faulty. Many species have developed partial or complete resistance to a growing number of chemical pesticides. Some crafty arthropods have been able to overcome the toxic effects of every pesticide to which they have been exposed, ultimately forcing farmers to abandon the crops on which they prey. Yet, most Governments heavily subsidize chemical fertilizers, lowering the cost to farmers of compensating for lost soil fertility and discouraging the use of organic nutrients.

Since 1984, the UNEP Ad Hoc Working Group of Legal and Technical Experts has recommended that countries exporting potentially harmful chemicals should provide information, including the type, quantity, physical and chemical characteristics, origin and location within sites, to assist the importing countries in making timely and wise decisions. However, the demand for cash crops has contributed to a vicious cycle. Some of the most fertile land in developing countries is given over to export products, such as beef, peanuts, tea, coffee and cacao, to earn foreign exchange. Developing countries, in an effort to service debt repayment, are turning unsuitable land over to cash crops. Yet, the price paid by developed countries, in relation to the cost of oil and manufactured goods, has fallen.

Results from the Green Revolution have created other environmental effects of great importance. WHO estimates that hundreds of thousands of people die each year from acute pesticide poisoning. Through airborne drift, run-off into aquifers and drinking water supplies, residues of foodstuffs and other routes, chronic pesticide exposure is widespread and the risks uncertain. In the developed countries, most pesticides in use have not been thoroughly screened for health hazards, and developing countries still use those which have been banned elsewhere as excessively risky. Because malnutrition, infectious diseases and other health problems are widely prevalent, the populations of developing countries, particularly women, are susceptible to effects of pesticides on the immune system.

Women in sustainable agriculture

According to the literature on the subject, the most urgent challenge is the need to provide the growing population with an adequate food supply. In some areas, such as in Africa, population growth is outstripping food production. It is important, however, to recognize that inappropriate development patterns fostered by debt pressures, trade imbalances and misguided aid have contributed to this problem. As the World Conservation Strategy emphasizes, one of the most serious current environmental developments is a loss of resources essential for agriculture.

Sustainable agriculture is food production that respects both the natural and the social environment. It is based on wise use of natural and renewable resources with moderate exploitation. Sustainable agriculture is controlled by the community it supports, so that it may flexibly respond to the needs of both people and their environment. A number of methods are now in use to conserve land resources and the diversity of species.

Women's agricultural knowledge has provided security for themselves and for others. As long as women are still engaged in seed selection, the future survival of traditional crops is assured. For example, traditional seeds may survive better when droughts caused the harvest of others to fail. Modern hybrid varieties do not reproduce fertile seeds, so women farmers must buy new seeds every year. They are therefore completely at the mercy of the seed supply system. Modern agricultural engineering has thus contributed to the genetic erosion of crop varieties, and women have become more and more dependent upon the purchase of hybrid seeds.

Innovation, however, has consistently responded to scarcity, whether from population growth or other sources. Biotechnology is now available for livestock as well as for crops and plants. Women have been trained locally in using mulching, multiple cropping and crop rotation, compost and green manure to improve soil fertility along with integrated animal husbandry, natural fertilizers, special varieties and pioneer plants for soils etc. These methods, which produce higher yields over longer periods, have reduced women's dependency upon expensive external input items.

Ultimately, scientists are hoping to develop plant varieties with greater photosynthetic efficiency and resistance to such environmental stresses as drought, flooding, salinity, disease, pests and temperature extremes. Farming operations and technology intensify as farming systems progress from forest fallow to multiple-cropping. These technologies must be strengthened and shared by all women in the subsistence economy. Conversely, agricultural extension services must be reoriented to reach women more efficiently in order to increase their productivity. Some project activities have shown that this is not difficult to achieve when commitment is there (Dunkelman and Davidson, 1988).

Women, partners in life

The importance of women as cultivators is increasingly recognized, especially in sub-Saharan Africa, where they often have the sole charge of operations. In most less developed regions, women usually have control of and responsibility for some subsistence food production from garden plots to small livestock. Their special knowledge of food crop and multi-purpose tree varieties is important for sustainable agriculture, given the objective that sustainable environment involves maintaining biodiversity and promoting integrated cropping systems.

But some institutional and market regulatory constraints have limited women's access to other products–loans, land, technology etc.–which could enhance their labour input and resources for agricultural production. Yet, government actions influence the prices women farmers receive for their holdings, the costs and availability of input and information, and access to markets. All these factors affect women's agricultural adaptation. Moreover, in many developing countries, political instability and policy biases against sustainable development have retarded agricultural improvement. However, household, community institutions and community memberships can mediate responses towards achieving sustainable use of the natural environment.

F. Women's functions and natural resources management

Women's corporate organizations

Studies of women's household economy, although important, have been insufficient for understanding women's social contributions. Neither as a place of work nor as a hub of emotional life is the household or family the sole site of women's activities or culture. Thus, these studies have neglected other forms of extra-domestic and extra-familial relationships which, in a wide variety of settings, consist largely of single-sex associations. Women in all cultures associate with one another as men do, and these gender-specific associations typically animate the life of a community. Anthropologists have described the casual, daily relation among women as the "women's network". They view it as an institution like kinship or marriage that affects people's lives. Hence, through their associations with one another, women not only develop a shared identity but equally broaden their options.

For example, women's networks in almost all countries constitute a natural mechanism for community-based action. Often it is the women's organizations, large or small, that are finding the new solutions women need. Usually, the grass-roots organizations serving poor people in the countryside and city-slum have few links to the formal national development system. Nevertheless, they carry on some development activities on their own initiative. The special characteristics of these organizations make them a key factor in community involvement and ideal for natural resource management.

Women as ecological engineers

Too often excluded from the decision-making levels, women in the community have developed their own informal approaches to problem-solving by means of strategic planning. Strategic planning has been defined in the corporate world as the managerial process of developing and maintaining a strategic fit between the goals and resources of an organization and its changing market opportunities (Kotler and Clarke, 1987). When engaging in strategic planning, women take into account all variables that influence their subsistence as well as that of their family. These variables are political, societal, legal, financial, competitive market and ecological conditions, plus available facilities and women's own goals, resources and technical capacity. All this information is brought to bear on their agro-industrial and entrepreneurial activities (figure X).

Heretofore, the knowledge and experience of generations have permitted women to have great flexibility in cropping practices. But gender-blind development has had several consequences. Among them is an undermining of the ecologically sound traditional agricultural knowledge of women. It should be clear that agriculturist women, as the world's most important food producers, are directly dependent upon the health of the environment. Moreover, rural women themselves are becoming more and more conscious of this dependence. They can contribute to improving their natural environment, soil conditions and crops.

Women as primary environmental caretakers

It is only recently that some development planners and decision-making bodies have come to appreciate women's important role in the economy of development such as agriculture, forestry, small-scale and medium-scale businesses and population programmes. Gradually, some practical efforts to integrate women fully as partners in development programmes and projects are increasing, but at a slow pace. It is thus important to see women as key agents in maintaining and enhancing the quality and stock of natural resources. That is, women's agricultural methods, practised successfully for centuries, are adapted to the environment and are sustainable without long-term damage to the land.

Women are keenly aware of environmental degradation and the need for rehabilitation and conservation. Their close link with the environment helps explain the high number of environmental projects started by women. In many rural areas, women have taken the initiative in ensuring environmental care. In forest areas, seedling nurseries are women's responsibility. Women are also taking care of reforestation. In arid lands, *techniques des murets* are processes to help Sahelian women to grow vegetables and three-tree plants (one for replanting; one for fuelwood; and one for forest planting) using sand and animal wastes. In erosion-prone hills, women are building soil-retaining walls and drawing up village forest plans. In wetlands, women are protecting fragile mangrove ecosystems by farming oysters on metallic holders and so on.

As users of forest resources, women are the most highly motivated to ensure good forestry management if they are in a position to control it. They are also promoting agro-silviculture and encouraging the efficient use of fuelwood. Thus, conferral of use rights in forest land to groups of women and/or creating women-based forestry programmes, such as women's group tree nurseries, village forestry, family woodlot and forest farms, with a combination of exotic and indigenous species, are examples of strategies of great environmental value as well as producers of assets for rural poor women.

But women-centred perspectives lead to the inevitable themes of more consultation with women, more women in decision-making positions enabling them to evaluate their partnership roles and making them more visible in environment programmes, expanding education and training opportunities for them; monitoring the effects of energy projects—hydropower, industrial forestry etc.—on women and the basic needs of their families; and creating demonstration projects to share experience in the design and consultation processes among agricultural, energy and forestry officials and women's local organizations as a starting-point.

G. Women as agents of change: an undeniable force for maneuver

In developing countries, women, as natural resource users, have found that whenever they take less of the depleted resource (fuelwood), others will just take more (timber industry). If they find ways to increase its availability (marginal land turned into cropland), others will garner the fruits of their efforts. Or, if the resource is vast like the atmosphere, their small sacrifices to preserve it would have insignificant effects (karité trees in Mali; the limba-banana tree duet in the Congo).

In industrialized societies, on the other hand, as consumers of natural resources women have greatly contributed to making the environment a central issue. In the former Union of Soviet Socialist Republics, thousands of women were involved in a worldwide movement called Bambi: a children's ecological and ethical movement to create awareness of environmental issues among youth. In the United States of America, the League of Women Voters pioneered in forcing national action against water pollution. In Germany, woman leaders played a key role in the emergence of the Green Party.

As primary users of natural resources or as consumers, women of the world are becoming successful agents of conservation of local and traditional resources. They form a large part of the memberships of environmental organizations. Since the 1970s, women's groups and organizations have been very active in promoting environmental awareness, education, protection and management. Thus, women and their organizations must be identified as a major structural institution with which stronger links ought to be forged.

Women, agents of change for environmental conservation

The role of women as agents of social change is beginning to be recognized in the international forum. Dr. Nafis Sadik, Executive Director of UNFPA, has acknowledged this with reference to the great potentiality of reducing maternal and child mortality and the strengthening of family planning programmes. In fact, the avenues of this overall role are limitless (Dehlot, 1991). Yet, in most development programmes, women are regarded as passive recipients rather than as the active elements in introducing positive change into the community.

Examining women as agents of social change, their roles encompass those of catalysts, solution givers, process helpers and resource links. Their actions range from creating awareness of needs or conditions to considering alternative actions, selecting appropriate courses of action and testing and evaluating those actions. Women's contribution as agents of change can also be seen through their activities as communicators and by their practical involvement at the grass-roots level around the world. This role is crucial for the future of natural environment management in both developed and developing countries (Dehlot, 1991). Because of their capacity as agents of social change, women must be trained as project leaders and extension workers in environmental care activities. This training must include women's knowledge of appropriate resource use as well as the utilization of new and appropriate technologies.

Technical assistance and international collaboration

International population assistance has played a key role in providing support to affect growth rates of developing countries. UNFPA, the largest source of multilateral population assistance, has worked since 1969 with over 150 countries. Its success in overcoming the strong resistance that it met at the outset of its work derives in large measure from respecting national sovereignty and involving the recipient countries as partners in the design and implementation of programmes. The International Planned Parenthood Federation is the largest non-governmental organization in the population field, with affiliates throughout the developing world. The Population Council is a prominent non-governmental organization involved in population studies and biomedical research on contraceptive methods and safety. These organizations, which are funded primarily through donors, can help relieve the inevitable human pressures on the natural environment. These pressures can be further reduced by strengthening the management of the natural resource base.

To cite but a few, World Women Dedicated to the Environment (WorldWIDE) is: *(a)* promoting women's involvement in environmental management; *(b)* working to make political leaders and the public more aware of environmental issues; *(c)* enhancing women's influence in environmental organization; and *(d)* increasing the inclusion of women in development policies. Various United Nations agencies are supporting environmental projects carried out by women. In 1985, UNEP established the Senior Women Advisory Group on Sustainable Development. The Group members are women in leadership positions from 19 developed and developing countries. The Group has increasingly been involved in organizing international regional assemblies on women, environment and sustainable development. Several international non-governmental organizations and donor countries also provide technical assistance and funds for women's environment-related projects around the world.

Room for action

Decisions women make and skills they have materially affect the physical well-being and emotional equanimity of family members. Thus, women at the grass-roots level ought to participate in environmental planning, environmental needs assessment and sustainable development management. Moreover, health-related environment and population issues must be properly incorporated in all formal, informal and non-formal educational programmes. Moreover, research, education and information, demonstration and training, and other forms of technology transfer, must be ongoing activities in environmental management. In addition, sustainable development education and management should be directed to target groups in the community, such as political groups and women's income-generating projects.

Various programmes throughout the world are providing technical assistance to women in need to enhance their capacity to sustain their productivity over the long term. More dialogue is needed, however, to bring these women together for the benefit of global environmental concerns. Government and programme planners should equally increase efforts to ensure that environmentally sound activities, biodiversity conservation and sustainable population shall encompass the roles of women in the ways given below:

(*a*) *At the local level, pertaining to individuals, families and community membership*:

(i) Environmental awareness and conservation and family planning should be an integral part of all urban and rural development projects, with the full participation of community members in the planning, implementation and evaluation of such projects;

(ii) Local mechanisms for assessing and monitoring the environmental impact of development activities should be established, including women's income-generating projects that use natural resources;

(iii) Women must have increased choice about pregnancy and family size, not only as a means of reaching no-growth population levels but also to improve women's status, which is a prerequisite to achieving successful development and attaining resource conservation goals;

(iv) Donor Governments and international funding agencies should respond favourably to requests from local non-governmental organizations for assistance in formulating projects that link population activities and natural resource management;

(v) Research institutions developing biotechnology that may raise yields must interact closely with woman farmers and include research on phytoregeneration, phytogenesis and phytosociology in abandoned logging areas and human settlements;

(*b*) At the national level, pertaining to decision-makers and central governing bodies:

(i) National programmes must integrate a gender-analysis device into all economic development processes and include gender training for men and women to promote full awareness of choices open to them with regard to their role in population management and environmental protection;

(ii) Governments should establish mechanisms to encourage and strengthen national policies directed to stabilizing their population at a level that would permit sustainable resource management and a satisfactory quality of life for all their people;

(iii) Institutionalized structures through which population, environment and development policies are formulated, implemented and/or influenced must be identified in order to permit the creation of national mechanisms to formulate and implement population policies that take into consideration the natural resource base, environmental conditions and human development prospects. Such policies should respect human rights, religious beliefs, cultural values and the right of each individual and couple to determine their family size;

(iv) Government agencies and national non-governmental organizations should take into account the special environmental problems of the urban and rural poor and devise national mechanisms to pursue environmental quality and sustainable rural development. Governments and non-governmental organizations must cooperate to strengthen their capacity to identify, anticipate, assess and resolve issues of environmental rehabilitation, biodiversity conservation and population pressures;

(v) Country-level studies of the interactions between population, environment and development should be undertaken, focusing especially on development programmes serving women and children, in the light of their contribution to women's productivity, and the results should be channelled to and utilized by the international community, national institutions and community organizations as a basis for long-term sustainable development (see annex);

(*c*) At the global level, pertaining to the international community:

(*i*) In making recommendations, UNFPA and its partners should emphasize their convictionthat the provision of contraceptive information and services is essential for humanitarian and health reasons, quite apart from the effect on fertility levels;

(ii) UNFPA, UNEP and the Population Council should jointly support studies on the interrelationships between human population, environmental management, sustainable development and the roles of women in the light of the International Environment Decade;

(iii) International organizations that provide population and research assistance to developing countries should receive more support from donor countries at levels that will permit them to attain the desired slow-down in population growth rates with eventual stabilization of the world population and development that is ecologically sustainable;

(iv) International research programmes for productivity enhancement must undertake a comprehensive review of the totality of women's social functions and not limit economic analysis and policy interventions to their market-related activities alone.

H. Concluding remarks

Governments may inform communities about the nature and extent of environmental problems and enact laws that will provide a framework for responsible behaviour. It is only if each individual appreciates the consequences of his/her actions, reacts to appropriate laws and is confronted with the full cost of his/her decisions that the goal of an ecologically sustainable society is more likely to be attained. Without cooperation at local, national and international levels, and specifically without the support of community members, including women, many of the significant problems will remain unsolved.

The pressing need for global concern about the environment is now virtually unchallenged. The environment is a major item on the agenda of many organizations. Although there is considerable uncertainty about future interactions of population, the environment and resources, there is room to manoeuvre. Humane development and population policies adopted now could help stabilize the world population. However, high rates of population growth constitute but one factor among many that aggravate environment and development problems and the scourge of poverty. Others include overconsumption by developed countries and inappropriate applications of technology, management, trade and aid. The interrelations are mediated by government policies and by such social institutions as family, community and cultural traditions and practices. By adopting wise social and economic policies now, responsible Governments can make the difference.

Literature reviews have demonstrated the importance of women's roles in natural resource management. How one identifies the linkage between women's role, environmental conservation strategy and population control will depend heavily upon one's theoretical framework, interests, policy objectives and mandate. Moreover, although women are central to the issues in environment, population and development, they have been prevented from participating fully by such constraints as social and political recognition, education and the right to land and property, which limit their economic opportunities. Yet, there is a responsibility to future generations as well as to the current one, to preserve the unique biomass and to maintain the earth's biological diversity, because there is only one planet Earth and one human race.

It is obvious that no single approach can provide the solution to preserving the environment. The difficulty in developing a consensus on an approach that could be effective in protecting the environment and to which all countries would be committed remains formidable. In 1992, however, the United Nations Conference on Environment and Development was held at Rio de Janeiro, Brazil; it was the largest meeting ever called to discuss the state of world environment and to try to fine solutions. Participation of heads of States and Governments from virtually all the world areas made it the largest summit ever held. It is hoped that the Earth Summit will provide a major opportunity to support women's vital roles in sustaining the common future of humankind.

ANNEX

Proposed operational research programmes in natural resource management

The following topics are proposed operational research programmes in natural resource management which can be addressed through women's organizations under women's leadership:

(a) Information, communication and education (IEC) on environment issues and the sustainable use of natural resources;

(b) Alternative energy utilization;

(c) Renewable resources management;

(d) Biome resources management (e.g., marine land and forests);

(e) Control of man-made and natural ecological disasters;

(f) Indigenous knowledge, attitudes and practices in natural resources management and self-reliant socio-economic development;

(g) Social marketing in sustainable agriculture and environmental management;

(h) Human ecology and environmental public health;

(i) People-centred environmental rehabilitation.

REFERENCES

Bheenick Rundheersing, and others (1989). *Successful Development in Africa: Case Studies of Projects, Programs, and Policies.* Washington, D.C.: The World Bank.

Bledsoe, Caroline H. (1980). Wealth in people. In *Women and Marriage in Kpelle Society.* Stanford, California: Stanford University Press.

Brown Lester R., and others, eds. (1989). *State of the World, 1989.* A Worldwatch Institute Report on Progress Toward a Sustainable Society. New York and London: W. W. Norton.

Cernea, Michael M. (1985). *Putting People First: Sociological Variables in Rural Development.* Oxford, United Kingdom; and New York: Oxford University Press, for the World Bank.

Dankelman, Irene, and Joan Davidson (1988). *Women and Environment in the Third World: Alliance for the Future.* London: Earthscan Publications.

Davis, Kingsley, Mikhail S. Bernstam and Helen M. Sellers (1989). *Population and Resources in a Changing World: Current Readings.* Stanford, California: Morrison Institute for Population and Resource Studies.

Dehlot, Colette (1991). Women as managers of natural resources. In *Women and the Environment*, Annabel Rodda, ed. London; and Atlantic Highlands, New Jersey: Zed Books, pp. 72-79 and 99-100.

Food and Agriculture Organization of the United Nations (1984). Government consultation on role of women in food production and food security. In *Women in Food Production and Food Security.* Rome.

_________ (1989). *Women in Community Forestry: A Field Guide for Project Design and Implementation.* Rome.

Goliber, Thomas J. (1985). *Sub-Saharan Africa: Population Pressures on Development.* Population Bulletin, vol. 40, No. 1. Washington, D.C.: Population Reference Bureau.

International Union for the Conservation of Nature and Natural Resources (1987). *Population and Sustainable Development: Report of the IUCN Task Force on Population and Conservation for Sustainable Development.* Gland, Switzerland: The World Conservation Centre.

Johnson, Patricia Lyons (1988). Women and development: a highland New Guinea example. *Human Ecology: An Interdisciplinary Journal* (New York and London), vol. 16, No. 2 (June), pp. 105-122.

Keyfitz, Nathan (1972). Population theory and doctrine: a historical survey. In *Readings in Population*, William Peterson, ed. New York: MacMillan Publisher.

Kotler, Philip, and Roberta N. Clarke (1987). *Marketing for Health Care Organizations.* Englewood Cliffs, New Jersey: Prentice-Hall, Inc.

Lee, James A. (1985). *The Environment, Public Health, and Human Ecology: Consideration for Economic Development.* Baltimore, Maryland; and London: The Johns Hopkins University Press.

National Research Council (1986). *Population Growth and Economic Development: Policy Questions.* Commission on Behavioral and Social Sciences and Education, Committee on Population, Working Group on Population Growth and Economic Development. Washington, D.C.: National Academy Press.

Paul, Samuel (1987). *Community Participation in Development Projects: The World Bank Experience.* World Bank Discussion Papers, No. 6. Washington, D.C.: The World Bank.

Repetto, Robert (1989). *Population, Resources, Environment: An Uncertain Future.* Population Bulletin, vol. 42, No. 2. Washington, D.C.: Population Reference Bureau.

Revelle, Roger (1976). The resources available for agriculture. *Scientific American* (New York), pp. 164-178.

Rodda, Annabel, ed. (1991). *Women and the Environment.* London; and Atlantic Highlands, New Jersey: Zed Books.

Russo, S., and others (1989). Gender issues in agriculture and natural resource management. Robert R. Nathan Associates Inc.

Schramm, Gunter, and Jeremy J. Wardford (1989). *Environmental Management and Economic Development.* Baltimore, Maryland; and London: The Johns Hopkins University Press.

Sexton, Lorraine (1986). *Mothers of Money, Daughters of Coffee: The Wok Meri Movement.* Ann Arbor, Michigan: UMI Research Press.

Society for International Development (1984). Women protagonists of change. *Journal of the Society for International Development* (Rome), No. 4.

Strathern, Andrew (1982). The division of labor and processes of social change in Mount Hagen. *American Ethnologist* (Washington, D.C.), vol. 9, No. 2, pp. 307-319.

Tolba, Mostafa Kamal (1987). *Sustainable Development: Constraints and Opportunities.* London; and Boston, Massachusetts: Butterworths Scientific.

Union internationale pour la conservation de la nature et de ses ressources (1980). *Stratégie mondiale de la conservation: la conservation des ressources vivantes au service du développement durable.* Gland, Switzerland.

United Nations (1986). *Report of the World Conference to Review and Appraise the Achievements of the United Nations Decade for Women: Equality, Development and Peace, Nairobi, Kenya, 15-26 July 1985.*

United Nations Development Programme (1989). *Women in Development: Project Achievement Reports.* New York.

United Nations Population Fund (1990). *Report of the International Forum on Population in the Twenty-first Century, Amsterdam, the Netherlands, 6-9 November 1989*. New York.

United States Agency for International Development (1985). *Women of the World: A Chartbook for Developing Regions*. Report of the Office of Women in Development, Bureau for Program and Policy Coordination. Washington, D.C.

Woodwell, George M. (1985). On the limits of nature. In *The Global Possible: Resources, Development and the New Century*, Robert Repetto, ed. New Haven, Connecticut: Yale University Press.

World Bank (1984). *Toward Sustained Development in Sub-Saharan Africa: A Joint Program of Action*. Washington, D.C.

______ (1986). *Population Growth and Policies in Sub-Saharan Africa*. A World Bank Policy Study. Washington, D.C.

World Commission on Environment and Development (1987). *Our Common Future*. Oxford, United Kingdom; and New York: Oxford University Press.

XXXI. WOMEN AND RESOURCE MANAGEMENT: A CRITICAL ISSUE IN DEVELOPING COUNTRIES

*Yulfita Raharjo**

Over the past 20 years, developing countries have had a strong tendency to weaken and marginalize women's role in general under the flag of development and planning, and especially in relation to their economic status and control of the environment.

Because development has been consistently made market-oriented, subsistence economy in many communities in developing countries has tended to be ignored and neglected. More specifically, its importance in providing livelihood for and maintaining the well-being of poor people has often been overlooked. What is meant by subsistence here is community sustenance against the background of local resources in providing daily household needs. This is mainly the responsibility of women in communities throughout the world.

Since in many cases women are directly or indirectly responsible for subsistence economic production, women are usually the most affected. Development plans, laws and government policies have not sufficiently recognized women's need for access to resources. This situation is reflected in the general lack of attention to the conservation of natural resources, upon which subsistence economic production depends.

Faced with this situation, which obviously affects women's strategies for survival and reduces their economic status, women are left with no alternative but more intensive exploitation of natural resources that damages the environment. Thus women, particularly poor women, are indeed part of the environmental problem that faces the planet. However, their caring and nurturing roles and their strong commitment to the survival of their families also make women an important part of the solution.

The objective of this paper is to analyse the role of women in resource management and the impact of this role on the environment. The paper focuses on the situation of women in the developing countries, particularly in Indonesia.

A. Women and sociocultural environment

Cultures throughout the world place women in a subordinate position. Even in a matrilineal society, such as the Minangkabaus (the largest matrilineal society in the world) of West Sumatra, in which land is inherited through women, management of agricultural production is by men. And in the final analysis, it is the men that enjoy most benefits of production surpluses in the form of motor cycles, gathering in coffee-houses, horse-racing, boar-hunting etc. In Minangkabau culture, women must focus their activities at home with family care and domestic chores.

This subordinate position is strengthened by religion. In Islam, the religion that is followed by the Minangkabaus, men are predestined to be leaders, both at home and in the community. In the mosque, men sit and pray in the front, women in the back. In Java, wives are refered to as "men's friends in the back".

As concerns the position of women in the political domain, in Minangkabau and Javanese societies, politics also is an area of men's domination. They control village administration, and the discussions in village councils that decide policies about community affairs are between men.

The term "culture" is used here in its broad, neutral and general sense that includes values, norms knowl-

*Center for Population and Manpower Studies, Indonesian Institute of Sciences, Jakarta.

edge, themes, philosophies and religious beliefs, sentiments, ethical principles, world views, ethos and the like. In other words, culture is a system of ideas that may serve to rationalize, explain, justify, exhort, excuse, assail or account for actions, arrangements, speech, use of objects or feelings. Comparing culture with computer, it is then the software, perhaps the DOS program, that shapes and governs mode of actions and thoughts in social life.

Hence, it is culture that dictates women to be submissive, to consent to become "men's friends in the back" and to allow men to enjoy most benefits of production surpluses.

B. THE CRITICAL ISSUES

Trapped within this kind of unfavourable sociocultural and political environment, women in the community are left with very little room to manoeuvre. In Indonesia, the subordinate position of women is institutionalized in such organizations as Dharma Wanita (literally, the " women's mission", an association of government employees' wives), Dharma Pertiwi (the "motherland's mssion", an association of military men's wives) and Pendidikan Kesejahteraan Keluarga (an organization for educating village women). In those organizations, women are further educated and motivated to support their husbands and to care for their families. They are educated with skills that are relevant to this position, such as sewing, cooking, child care and gardening.

In reality, however, women have to be more active outside domestic boundaries for the survival of their family. In rural areas, women always participate in all aspects of economic life. In the cities, too, women today must earn money as a matter of necessity. In many cases, women register not only equal but also better success in comparison with what men do.

Despite this vast capacity, women's role is still handicapped by old sociocultural and political framework. Consequently, women are willing to be in the shadow of men's domination, allowing decisions that are relevant to their interests to be made by men. Decision-making and policy-making are still the domain of men. Consequently, women have a very small role in the decision-making process that is crucial to their interests.

Because of this small role in the decision-making process, women's position in the economic life and development process is often squeezed between scarce economic resources and inability to compete with men. Currently in Indonesia, women's role in agricultural production is being taken over by men. As a result of the Green Revolution that the Government has pursued during the past two decades, economic activities in the countryside has been further monetized, and traditional labour arrangements that respect women's role are being replaced by commercial labour arrangements to the disadvantage of women.

In the domestic domain, environmental pressure affects natural resources that are crucial to the role of women in caring for their families. In rural areas and cities alike water sources are polluted by overpopulation and inappropriate industrial waste-treatment technologies, and fuelwoods are becoming scarcer.

Women are placed in a difficult situation between rapid changes in the economic environment and slow changes in the sociocultural environment. In the domestic domain, women are squeezed between the demand for natural resources, such as fuelwood and clean water, and scarcer natural resources because of overpopulation and overexploitation.

Throughout the world, women manage family and household needs for sustenance on an everyday basis. They not only manage household services but also take part in management of the local environment.

Women are concerned about local resources and are careful in using these resources because they realize fully their reliance upon them for continued daily sustenance. In dry areas, such as the island of Timor in Indonesia where water is scarce, women treat water very carefully as if it were a commodity that must not be wasted.

C. Development model and deterioration of women's economic status

Development has favoured the use of land for market-oriented production, often by neglecting the rights of those living on the land, such as shifting cultivators, pastoralist and peasants. Agricultural extension has also typically assumed that the cultivators are always men and directed efforts to increase productivity only to men. The development of commercial crops by men as a result of development projects has sometimes directly deprived women of access to land for subsistence crops. Money that goes to women as a reward of their efforts is hardly sufficient to compensate for the lack of subsistence production for feeding their families.

In meeting their various obligations, women must consider both short-term and long-term goals. However, under economic and/or environmental pressure women may find that the fulfilment of their immediate needs contradicts their long-term well-being. This dilemma has been particularly evident in relation to the gathering of fuelwood.

With the erosion of common property right that has resulted from development, women are forced to increase the wood collection from increasingly smaller patches of forest. In urban areas, women have to deal with the problem of monetization. Clean water and fuel are becoming more and more expensive. But very often the level of income among the poor has not risen as much as the ever-increasing demand for commodity. All this is evident in problems of squatting, overcrowding, poor sanitary conditions and illegal settlement on river-banks, which affect not only the environment but often also the rest of the city. Water is polluted with faecal contamination. Repeated flood results from poor drainage systems and population pressure.

On the other hand, women must make an effort to increase their income. Many find they can do this in the informal sector. However, because they must also economize their method of production, the informal sector often becomes another major source of urban pollution. Home industrial production frequently takes place in residential areas.

If the ultimate goal of development is to increase the quality of life and to achieve sustainable development, then efforts must be made to lead policies and strategies towards that direction. However, experience thus far shows that this is not the case. There are reasons to believe that policies that have been adopted do not necessarily operate to the advantage of this environment.

Women can only become part of the solution if they become an integral part of the key development decision-making processes and participate fully in implementing environment-friendly programmes and policies. Many of the current environmental problems have emerged because women were not consulted and their interests were ignored in making decision about development.

However, if women are to be effectively integrated into the decision-making processes, special care is needed. Women have so far been excluded or marginalized because policy makers, most of whom are males, have focused primarily on immediate market-oriented and monetized activities. In contrast, women's activities and interests lie primarily in the domestic sphere and are usually not monetized.

To some extent, the fact that women's activities have not been monetized reflects the low value that society as a whole has given to women's concerns. It is useful to know that when men's activities have moved out of the household, they have usually become monetized and carry a monetary reward, whereas women are typically expected to perform equivalent tasks voluntarily without reward. For example, when community health workers are male they are usually paid, but when they are female they are regarded as health volunteers that work without reward.

If women's potential as environmental managers is to be effectively realized, their role role must not be similarly trivialized and undervalued. There is a risk that in trying to harness women's potential to save the environment, at first the effort will merely add further to women's already heavy burden by giving them yet another unrewarded task. Secondly, if their role is unpaid, the effort will fail because the role will also be unvalued and will fail to prevail against the paid and valued interest of men.

D. Women and resource management

Women, especially the poor, are part of the environmental problem. In their day-to-day strategies they carefully exploit and at the same time often threaten the environment. The real issue is why this has happened. The answer lies in the way development process has often ignored the basic needs of women and poor households, forcing them to adopt short-term strategies that are against their long-term interests.

For the past two decades, the trend in the natural resources management has been moving towards the dispossession of resources care by policy makers away from traditional beneficiaries: local people; and women themselves. Environmental management has been increasingly placed under the control of specialist groups, with a consequence that these groups make decisions that are always not to the benefit of these local people and women. In Indonesia, decisions about industrial arrangements for lumber, areas for plantations and for transmigration settlement areas are made without consulting local people, let alone women. The actions termed "consultations with local communities" are normally negotiations with local élites, who are no longer part of local sociopolitical affairs but more part of the central decision-making process.

The crucial issue, however, is the fact that the sociocultural and political environment has trapped women in subordination. Not only are they squeezed between scarce resources and unfavourable bargaining positions, they are also submissive to their current status. They do not perceive their situation as an unfair arrangement but as a "fact" of their becoming women. What is seen as cultural by observers is perceived by them as natural, as a product of destiny that they simply have to accept.

Women are not without understanding of nature and natural resources. Their close link with nature has given them wisdom. They share these understanding, strategies, fear and frustration, and acceptance among themselves generation after generation. It is that cultural framework that suppresses them from expressing themselves to share those understanding, frustration and acceptance with the wider community. Because of this "communication gap", women are literally forced to accept whatever decisions, restrictions and prohibitions the specialist groups take. Thus, women are left with no alternative but to damage the environment.

Because of women's obvious concern about the sustainability of natural resources, they are the persons that should be most sensitive to resources management. Hence, they should be actively involved in any resource management planning and action. First, however, women should be given the opportunity to shake off that sociocultural and political environment that has placed them into an unfavourable position.

Consciousness-raising programme should be conducted through women organizations and women support groups. However, because like the case in Indonesia in which such organizations have been made part of the unfavourable sociocultural and political environment, the idea of such a programme must first be won. Efforts should be made to transform those well-established women's organizations that support the status quo into organizations for change. These should be done together with efforts directly to involve women in all environmental management planning and implementation programmes.

References

Collier, William L., and Wiradi Gunawan (1973). Recent changes in rice harvesting methods. *Bulletin of Indonesian Economic Studies* (Jakarta), vol. 9 (July), pp. 106-120

Collier, William L., and Makali (1974). Agricultural technology and institutional change in Java. *Food Research Institute Studies* (Rome), vol. 13, pp. 169-194.

Dankelman, Irene, and Joan Davidson (1988). *Women and Environment in the Third World: Alliance for the Future.* London: Earthscan Publications.

Kaplan, David, and Robert A. Manners (1972). *Culture Theory.* Englewood Cliffs, New Jersey: Prentice-Hall Inc.

Lee-Smith, Diana, and Trujillo Hinchey (1992). The struggle to legitimize subsistence: women and sustainable development. *Environment and Urbanization* (London), vol. 4, No. 1 (April).

Levy, Caren (1992). Gender and the environment: the challenge of cross-cutting issues in development policy and planning. *Environment and Urbanization* (London), vol. 4, No. 1 (April).

Putti, Joseph M., and Audrey Chia (1990). *Culture and Management: A Casebook.* Singapore and New York: McGraw-Hill Book Co.

Shiva, Vandana (1988). *Staying Alive: Women, Ecology and Development.* London; and Atlantic Highlands: Zed Books.

XXXII. RURAL WOMEN: THE CLOSING LINK BETWEEN POPULATION AND ENVIRONMENT

*Food and Agriculture Organization of the United Nations**

A. BACKGROUND

It has been widely accepted that women, population and environment are important independent variables in agricultural and rural development. Also, there is substantial evidence and considerable acknowledgement that these three variables are very closely interlinked (FAO, 1990 and 1991a; South Commission, 1990; UNFPA, 1991).

It should be recognized, however, that the variable "women" has become a very strong "closing link" or determinant in complex relations between population and environment. In fact, high population growth, pressure on limited resources and environmental degradation increasingly reflect the gender asymmetries that disfavour women in social, economic and technological conditions for agricultural production and rural life in general (FAO, 1991b, 1991c and 1991d). While it has already been recognized that high fertility sometimes serves as compensation for women's low status and contributes to their economic survival and social prestige (Palmer, 1991; Oppong, 1988; Youssef, 1988), environmental stress may further strengthen rural women's dependence upon large families.

By illustrating the foregoing argument with some typical situations, the present paper attempts to draw attention to the need for gender-responsive population policies and programmes in order to integrate them more effectively with efforts to achieve environmentally sustainable agricultural and rural development.

B. LABOUR DEMANDS, ENVIRONMENTAL STRESS AND THE VALUE OF CHILDREN

Women farmers are the backbone of smallholder agricultural production in many regions. In addition, with increasing out-migration of men in search for wage employment—which has become a major demographic and socio-economic phenomenon in most regions affected by rural poverty—the demands on women's farm labour tend to be intensified. However, women tend not to be targeted by major agricultural programmes and projects. Extension advice and credit for mechanization and input continue to be given, by and large, to men, who often use them for cash cropping. Without having adequate access to these and other productive resources, women thus remain unable to reduce the time demands and level of physical exertion involved in their cultivation practices and other farm operations (FAO, 1990; Rodda, 1991; FAO, 1991d).

Having a sufficient number of children capable of providing labour is often the only "technological solution" available to women farmers: in the absence of time-, labour- and energy-saving technologies, the chances for stable food production and sustenance of family welfare may be enhanced through a large family size. Also, in order to cope with their own and their families' economic insecurity, having a large number of children is a way for women to ensure the availability of a network of people that may assist them economically, both immediately and in the long term (Palmer, 1991; FAO, 1991b and 1991c).

*Rome, Italy.

The high economic and social value placed on children, and on child labour in particular, is reinforced when farm activities are affected not only by labour shortages but also by adverse environmental conditions. The increasing workload in smallholder agricultural production is evident mostly in the poorest and ecologically most fragile regions of the tropics. The most affected are women agricultural producers on overworked, degraded, shrinking and ever more distant cultivable land. While they are denied the use of modern, labour-saving or environmentally sound farming techniques, increasingly hard and time-consuming work is required on their plots, which are often the most susceptible to erosion, desertification and other forms of land degradation. The traditional division of labour by gender and by age for particular farm operations has changed considerably in many regions. In sub-Saharan Africa, for example, women and children's farm work is no longer seasonally specific: high rates of school absenteeism during the peak agricultural season, as well as very high primary-school drop-out rates, are strong evidence of this situation (FAO, 1991b, 1991c and 1991d).

Child labour is highly valuable also in some domestic chores, especially in those most affected by the depletion of natural resources by environmental degradation. For example, collecting and transporting firewood and other forest products may normally take up several hours per day, but with the contraction of forest areas in a growing number of regions, time requirements are increasing drastically. This extra time needed is one of several reasons why children—mainly girls—are taken out of school to help their mothers (FAO, 1987; Rodda, 1991).

Furthermore, to fetch water for domestic use, one of the most time-consuming and physically demanding of all women's daily domestic tasks, often means that several hours a day may be taken away from other productive and reproductive chores, including child care. Girls are introduced to this task at a very young age as a concrete sign and proof of their socialization. Their role increases as mothers' time needed for other home and farm chores is increasing (FAO, 1991d; Rodda, 1991; UNFPA, 1991).

Where soil fertility has been drastically reduced due to overcropping, deforestation, overgrazing, erosion and so forth, or where there is a lack of firewood and potable water, women are often forced to change the dietary practices and standards of their families. Sometimes this change means reducing the number of hot meals per day and substantially lowering family levels of nutrition, as many staple foods cannot be digested without prolonged cooking. The incidence of increasing infant and child mortality due to a poorer quality of diet or undernutrition may serve again as individual and collective "biological justification" for high fertility. The resurgence of environmentally related and poverty-related diseases, such as malaria, Bilharzia or tuberculosis, as well as acquired immunodeficiency syndrome (AIDS), will probably also revive fears of family extinction in some regions (Rodda, 1991; Smyke, 1991; FAO, 1991d; UNFPA, 1991; United Nations Secretariat, 1992).

The general exclusion of women farmers from mainstream agricultural and rural development efforts sometimes has negative consequences not only for their productive performance but also for their reproductive role. For example, while women are striving to increase agricultural production, they lack access to agricultural education on such topics as pesticide management. They are therefore vulnerable to toxic pesticides and heavy metals, putting their own and their families' health at risk. On the other hand, new and growing concern over pollution and contamination from agrochemicals in some countries is forcing Governments to legislate and enforce regulations of which women are unaware (Smyke, 1991; FAO, 1991b).

Women's subordinate socio-economic and legal statuses are often reinforced through structural adjustment policies. For example, policy measures emphasizing the production of export crops contribute to an increase in competition for arable land and in land values. Where the allocation of land held under usufruct rights is controlled by senior males in the lineage, adjustment-induced shifts into more profitable crops often results in men taking over land previously cultivated by women for domestic consumption. In some other cases, women have access only to less productive and more distant plots (South Commission, 1990; Spring and Wilde, 1991). Women's access to land becomes even more difficult as population growth puts pressure on scarce and deteriorating natural resources. Again, children (boys, in particular) often still represent women's most reliable key to land rights and thus to their economic security and social recognition (FAO, 1991d; Palmer, 1991).

C. Conclusions and suggestions

It is likely that in rural areas with high population growth, women's needs for and attitudes in favour of a large family are being reinforced with increasing environmental deterioration, low or worsening health and nutrition conditions (especially for children) and labour shortages due to male out-migration, as well as other social and economic phenomena that contribute to the increasing input of time and human energy required in agricultural production and rural lifestyles. Furthermore, difficult access to land and depletion of natural resources that increasingly affect women's productive and reproductive roles, and thus the sustenance of family food supply and overall welfare, might reaffirm the fears for individual and collective intergenerational economic security and sociocultural identity. In turn, this may undermine many national and international efforts to reduce fertility levels.

As important natural resource users and managers in providing food and securing overall family welfare, rural women actually hold the key to changes in reproductive behaviour and fertility levels. Programmes and projects that reduce time and labour requirements, if executed in conjunction with measures to promote legal incentives and skills for environmentally sound management of natural resources in their farm and domestic tasks, could enable women to become efficient advocates of and contributors to family planning. Ultimately, this development would contribute to a slow-down in population growth and permit a more balanced utilization of scarce natural resources.

An explicit goal in national development policies and programmes, including those related to population and environment, should therefore be to provide rural women with the economic and social conditions, as well as the technical means, to enable them to become more active and self-determined agents of population change. This goal could be achieved, for example, by:

(a) Focusing population policies and programmes and their instruments, such as population education and family planning, on gender differentials in assigning social and economic value to children and in attitudes regarding family size;

(b) Introducing population concerns—that is, trends in sociodemographic structures, patterns of natural increase and migration—into policies, programmes and projects on women and the environment;

(c) Linking environmental protection concerns with policies and programmes on women and population;

(d) Making environmental impact assessment concepts and techniques responsive to gender-related social and economic costs and benefits in agricultural production and rural life generally.

Conceptual and practical region-specific guidelines and manuals could be developed on the integration of rural women's contributions and needs into national and local efforts to reduce population growth and environmental degradation in rural areas. These materials should provide the basis for awareness, and skill creation among policy makers, planners and programme/project formulators that are trying to develop gender-responsive population and environmental policies, programmes and projects in agriculture and rural development.

Although some of the activities suggested above might be implemented by countries themselves, an effective realization of most of the activities would require active collaboration among Governments, non-governmental organizations, international donors and executing agencies at the national, regional or subregional levels.

References

Food and Agriculture Organization of the United Nations (1987). *Restoring the Balance: Women and Forest Resources*. Rome.

_____ (1990). *Women in Agricultural Development: FAO's Plan of Action for Integration of Women in Development*. Rome.

_____ (1991a). *The den Bosch Declaration and Agenda for Action on Sustainable Agriculture and Rural Development.* FAO/Netherlands Conference on Agriculture and the Environment, 'S-Hertogenbosch, the Netherlands, 15-19 April 1991. Rome.

_____ (1991b). *Report of the Expert Consultation on Women in Agricultural Development and Population in Asia, Penang, Malaysia, 5-9 February 1991.* Rome.

_____ (1991c). *Report of the Regional Workshop on Women, Population and Sustainable Agricultural Development, Kariba, Zimbabwe, 3-6 December 1991.* Rome.

_____ (1991d). *Women and Population in Agricultural and Rural Development in Sub-Saharan Africa.* Women in Agricultural Development Series, No. 5. Rome.

Oppong, Christine (1988). The effects of women's position on fertility, family organisation and the labour market: some crisis issues. In *Conference on Women's Position and Demographic Change in the Course of Development (Oslo, 1988): Solicited Papers.* Liège, Belgium: International Union for the Scientific Study of Population.

Palmer, Ingrid (1991). *Gender and Population in the Adjustment of African Economies: Planning for Change.* Women, Work and Development Series, No. 19. Geneva: International Labour Office.

Rodda, Annabel, ed. (1991). *Women and the Environment.* London; and Atlantic Highlands, New Jersey: Zed Books.

Smyke, Patricia (1991). *Women and Health.* London; and Atlantic Highlands, New Jersey: Zed Books.

South Commission (1990). *The Challenge of the South: The Report of the South Commission.* Geneva: South Commission.

Spring, A., and V. Wilde (1991). Women farmers, structural adjustment and FAO's Plan of Action for Integration of Women in Development. In *Structural Adjustment and African Women Farmers,* Christina H. Gladwin, ed. Gainesville: University of Florida Press.

United Nations (1991). *The World's Women, 1970-1990: Trends and Statistics.* Series K, No. 8. Sales No. E.90.XVII.3.

United Nations Secretariat (1994). Population and the environment: an overview. In *Population, Environment and Development.* Proceedings of the United Nations Expert Group Meeting, United Nations Headquarters, 20-24 January 1992. Sales No. E.94.XIII.7.

United Nations Population Fund (1991). *Population, Resources and the Environment: The Critical Challenges.* New York.

Youssef, Nadia. (1988). The interrelationship between the division of labour in the household, women's roles and their impact on fertility. In *Women's Role and Population Trends in the Third World.* Richard Anker, Mayra Buvinic and Nadia H. Youssef, eds. London: Croom Helm.

XXXIII. POPULATION AND NATURE CONSERVATION: ADVOCATING FOR CONSERVATION WITH A HUMAN FACE IN SOUTHERN AFRICA

Tabeth Matiza[*]

The issues of population, the environment and sustainable development, the interactions of population with the environment, population and sustainable development, and economic development and the environment have been widely discussed and debated worldwide. Although these disciplines are complementary, they have often been treated independently of one another. Demographers look at fertility, mortality and population structures without directly relating these structures to the environment that supports and influences these phenomena. The same applies to nature conservationists—for decades nature conservationists have championed and argued for nature conservation/preservation without giving enough attention to human basic needs. Many modern conservationists (especially those from the Western countries) prefer to have ecosystems that exclude mankind. Despite the growing concern for the consideration of human basic needs and community participation in nature conservation, conservationists stand divided on the issues of community participation, incorporation of human basic needs in nature conservation and nature conservation for sustainable development. Economic development, on the other hand, has also progressed without giving due consideration to environmental issues and the subsequent human suffering caused by environmental degradation through economic development.

The scope of this paper is, however, limited to the issues of population and nature conservation in Southern Africa, and how and why nature conservation programmes and projects are affecting the welfare of rural people, especially women. The views expressed here are derived from the field experiences of the author and do not represent the views of the International Union for the Conservation of Nature and Natural Resources (IUCN). The author's thesis is that it is not only population-induced environmental degradation that is causing social, economic and environmental burdens on rural communities, poorly planned nature conservation or environmental protection programmes and projects are also causing much suffering among rural people.

The burdens caused by deforestation, soil erosion, desertification etc. have been extensively documented. Matiza (1985) describes the hardships faced by women in the deforested Seke communal land (Zimbabwe). In this communal land, women spend up to a full day securing firewood and those that cannot travel long distances scavenge for cow dung in the fields every morning. Various studies (Bayliss-Smith, 1980; Blaikie, 1985; Boserup, 1981; Brookfield, 1981) found that population pressure on natural resources causes deforestation, land fragmentation, soil erosion and hardship to rural communities. However, very little has been done about the impacts of nature conservation/environmental protection on rural populations and on women in particular.

A. CONTEMPORARY VIEWS ON POPULATION AND ENVIRONMENT

Population and environmental factors are inextricably linked. Conservationists and demographers have advanced various theories and scenarios to explain the complicated relations between population and the physical environment. It is universally argued that there are ecological limits to population growth and that, if growth is not controlled, it will affect the quantities and quality of the available natural resources. Boserup (1981) argues that as population increases, it gradually exhausts certain types of natural resources, such as forest/woodland products, agricultural land, wildlife and water resources. She further argues that if population growth is not controlled—or

[*]Wetlands Programme Coordinator, Regional Office for Southern Africa, The World Conservation Union, Harare, Zimbabwe.

a change in technology and way of life is encouraged—environmental degradation will ensue.

The concept of ecological limits to population has largely been used to design current nature conservation programmes, which explains why many nature conservation programmes and projects are designed to reduce human interference and/or exclude human beings. In recent years, social scientists have argued that the success of conservation/environmental programmes and the achievement of sustainable development depend significantly upon the inclusion and appreciation of the local population, its social structure, demographic change and its relation to the use and management of natural resources. In-depth research on local people's values, customs, interests and knowledge provides the essential ingredients for sustainable and equitable conservation strategies, thereby promoting nature conservation and enhancing the quality of life of the indigenous inhabitants.

B. Population and nature conservation in Southern Africa

It has been argued that environmental protection, regulations and management as public policy issues are relatively new in Africa (Howard-Clinton, 1984). The environmental problems of Africa are essentially different from those of developed countries. In Africa, environmental problems are predominantly those which reflect poverty. Howard-Clinton (1984) outlines poverty, water-borne and other endemic diseases, inadequate potable water-supply, deforestation, desertification, inadequate trained manpower, inadequate infrastructure development, inadequate sewerage, nutritional deficiency and housing needs as the main environmental problems facing Africa today. It is argued that for Africa, economic development is an essential cure for the major environmental problems of poverty and inadequate infrastructure. Blaikie (1985) argues that the current environmental degradation in Africa is a result, symptom and cause of underdevelopment.

Development of nature conservation culture in Southern Africa

It is often argued that nature conservation is a problem in Africa because the Africans lack a tradition and culture of environmental protection. Howard-Clinton (1984) states: "Environmental protection, regulations and management as public policy issues in Africa are relatively new. Environmental consciousness and need for developing management machineries to protect the African environment first showed among international communities and not within the scientific and academic communities". This perception has influenced nature conservation in Southern Africa.

The foregoing perception is not totally correct, for some evidence and literature suggest that nature conservation is part of the African tradition. The history of traditional societies in Africa suggests the presence of a stable coexistence between traditional societies and nature, as a function of the intrinsic value attached to ecological conservation in the African culture (Hadley, 1985). Oral tradition from Kenya indicates that wetland sites were preserved for traditional rituals, such as circumcision of young boys who were about to become men. In Zimbabwe, spongy areas were avoided and preserved because of the belief that mermaids resided in those areas. Some tree species, such as wild fruit-bearing trees and those important for medicinal purposes, were protected under traditional laws and customs. Thick forest areas, especially those acting as sources of river systems, were also protected. These traditional beliefs and customs conserved very important natural resources from degradation and/or extinction. These unwritten laws and customs were endorsed by traditional leadership, which severely punished lawbreakers. These arrangements were disrupted and undermined by the institutions of colonial centralized Governments, modern religion and national legislation.

The argument that environmental protection, regulation and management are relatively new issues in Africa is thus not true, for nature conservation is a tradition of the African people. The only differences with the type of environmental protection Howard-Clinton (1984) discusses are the reasons for conservation, approaches and values attached to the natural resource concerned.

Current status of nature conservation

Owing to the perception that Africans lack environmental protection awareness, most conservation programmes and projects in Southern Africa are designed to instil environmental consciousness and codes of environmental management in the African people. The institutionalization of colonial centralized Governments and modern religion was used to advance environmental consciousness. The most common approach used to conserve nature has been the application of stringent laws designed to prevent the exploitation of certain resources. In Zimbabwe, for example, a number of restrictive laws are in place to protect the environment, for example, the Water Act, the Natural Resources Act, the Parks and Wildlife Act and the Forest Produce Act. Institutions have been established to enforce those laws. This pattern is common in most, if not all, Southern African countries.

The environmental values and protection of the developed countries were adopted, which is reflected in the current pattern of nature conservation where protected areas have been established and the concept of preservation championed. To date, a considerable proportion of the Southern African landscape (about 62 million hectares) is within protected areas. The size of the protected areas is given below by country.

Country	*Area (hectares)*
Angola	7 386 000
Botswana	9 934 437
Lesotho	6 805
Malawi	1 076 300
Namibia	7 417 353
Mozambique	4 400 000
Swaziland	49 866
Zambia	25 407 000
Zimbabwe	5 626 605

It is clear that protected areas characterize the Southern African landscape, and many more are being gazetted each year. Because of thenature of landownership in many countries, the establishment of protected areas often competes with the basic needs of the communal people, who depend upon common property resources. In Zimbabwe, for example, communal lands, basic needs, national parks, forest reserves and urban developments compete for the 54 per cent of the land area outside private ownership. The situation is similar in Botswana, Botswana and other countries in the region.

The acts that are in place contain various restrictive regulations; for example, in Zimbabwe, the Water Act and the Natural Resources Act prohibit the utilization of land resources that are within 30-100 metres of a stream, and the Parks and Wildlife Act prosecutes trespassers in national parks.

National conservation strategies (fashioned along the lines of the World Conservation Strategy) and national environmental action plans are also becoming fashionable in Southern Africa. To date, Zambia, Zimbabwe and Botswana have launched national conservation strategies and it is the objective of IUCN to encourage other countries in the region to develop such strategies. The United Nations Environment Programme (UNEP) and the World Bank are also encouraging environmental action plans. In recent years, a number of regional and national non-governmental organizations have been established with a mandate to improve nature conservation and management in the region.

Despite these various efforts, environmental protection and management are still problems in Southern Africa. The reasons for these perpetual environmental problems can be found in patterns of current nature conservation programmes and how they affect rural communities. The failure of environmental planners and managers in Southern Africa to include and appreciate the local population, its social structure, demographic change and basic needs explains the current problems in environmental protection and management.

C. Environmental protection and local population

One can argue strongly that the pattern of environmental protection and management in Southern Africa has failed to consider the characteristics of the local population, thereby increasing the burdens people face in securing their basic needs. Conflicts and interdependencies exist between population and the surrounding ecosystems. The issues of population distribution, social structure and demographic changes are often excluded in the design of nature conservation programmes.

Population growth and structure

Population distribution, growth and structure have significant implications for the success and sustainability of nature conservation programmes. Because of the competition between environmental protection and human basic needs, the pattern of nature conservation has adopted a policy of fencing off or exclusion. This policy has largely disrupted the interdependencies between local populations and the surrounding ecosystems, thereby creating the conflicts that exist today. These conflicts can be illustrated by considering the nature and distribution of protected areas in Southern Africa.

Due to the nature of land tenure and natural resource distribution in most countries in Southern Africa, the establishment and gazetting of protected areas have in many cases reduced the land size and range of natural resources available to rural communities. Depending upon the type of protected area, fences may be erected around the natural resources—for example, the electric game fences around some national parks in the region. Very stringent laws designed to protect and prevent exploitation of the resources are enacted and enforced. This system is characteristic in most, if not all, national parks in the region, such as Etosha in Namibia, Moremi-Chobe in Botswana, Hwange and Gonarezhou in Zimbabwe, and Lochnivar and Blue Lagoon in Zambia. Population relocations are also a characteristic of protected area establishment, and this policy has brought much suffering to the households concerned, which are rarely fully compensated.

It is common in Southern Africa to find rural communities squeezed between protected areas or between a protected area and private land. Good examples are the Chobe enclave community between the Chobe-Moremi national parks and the border with Namibia in Botswana and the Dande community between the Chiwore Safari area and the border with Mozambique in Zimbabwe. The population dynamics of the human and animal populations are always in conflict and the rural communities often lose out in these conflicts. It is also the policy of national Governments in Southern African areas to gazette important wetland resources as protected areas (and this policy is advocated by many international nature conservation organizations). Thus, much of the Etosha pan is in a national park; in Botswana, much of the Chobe water frontage and parks of the Okavango delta are under protection; and in Zimbabwe, the water frontages of most large artificial impoundments are gazetted protected areas. Although the author deeply respects the principles of protected areas and conservation, the current pattern has considerably denied the local rural population, especially women, freedom of movement and basic vital natural resources such as water.

Settlement patterns and movements have been disrupted, with very little or no compensation, and population dynamics are not considered in order to accommodate the problems of the rural communities. With the establishment of the Lochnivar National Park-Kafue flats in Zambia, the transhumance movement of indigenous cattle herders was disrupted, forcing them to change slightly their land use. Although the herders are allowed to drive their cattle through the park, they are constantly harassed by the rangers and scouts.

Gender and environmental protection and management

Field observations have indicated that the current environmental programmes and projects in Southern Africa affect rural women more severely than men. This situation is caused by the fact that social and population structure analysis is least understood and considered in nature conservation. There is often talk of people or population and how they will benefit from conservation and development programmes. However, what is not taken into consideration is that the costs and benefits of conservation and development affect people differently by age, sex and social status. Gender roles are rarely considered by nature conservation planners and managers. Many nature conservation programmes and projects in Southern Africa have not accorded the issue of gender the attention it deserves. If one considers the costs and benefits of environmental protection and management in Southern Africa, it is clear that women bear the largest costs and benefit very little.

Women in rural Southern Africa are the producers of food, drawers of water, collectors of firewood and caretakers of family health. The designation of protected areas has reduced the size and quality of land available for food production. Because of the nature of the land rights and the importance given to cash crops, women are bound to be denied land, which will affect household food security and family health in terms of child nutrition. Although the plight of rural women in agriculture has been well documented, little has been done to redress the situation.

Apart from the loss of agricultural land, protected areas have also denied women easy access to water resources. The water resources of large artificial impoundments in Zimbabwe are not easily available to the communities that need them most. The fences erected around some of these resources have increased the distances travelled and the time spent acquiring them, thereby increasing the burden of women. A large proportion of the wetlands of Zambia is in national parks and game management areas where there are specific prescriptions regarding the mode of exploitation. It has been argued that rural communities are not denied access to natural resources in protected areas: what they require are permits/licences. The bureaucracy of acquiring these permits/licences is unconquerable for most illiterate rural people, and the problem is worse for rural women.

Women have also been denied easy access to firewood and other forest products that are important during times of food shortages. Rural communities residing in or adjacent to protected areas are among the poorest in the society, for example, Chiundaponde village in Zambia, Dande community in Zimbabwe and Chobe enclave in Botswana. Due to their low economic base, these communities are often preoccupied with survival, and the advancement of preservation and prohibitive legislation only worsens their situation, especially that of women.

Since food security, water-supply, firewood and other natural resources are the concern of women, any move that will restrict the exploitation of natural resources will affect women more than men. Small crafts, such as pottery, basketwork or brick-making, are dominated by women; and since these activities depend upon the availability of natural resources, prohibitive measures will affect them.

"Community participation" is currently a fashionable phrase. The main question that should be asked is who and which groups are actively participating in conservation and development programmes. In community participation activities, women are usually left out. For example, in the ADMADE and CAMPFIRE programmes in Zambia and Zimbabwe, respectively, women are not actively involved. The males are hired as scouts and to perform other duties while the women sit idle after being denied easy access to what are rightfully their natural resources.

D. Conclusions and recommendations

It is the general trend of environmental and development programmes to neglect the basic needs of rural populations and the issue of gender roles. Often overlooked is the fact that the environment one is trying to protect or manage is inextricably linked to the human population around it or residing in it. If the objective of environmental management is to achieve an acceptable balance between the quality of the human environment and the quality of the natural environment (Petak, 1981), then the exclusionary approaches currently in use will not achieve this acceptable balance but instead will increase human suffering, particularly that of women. To address adequately the environmental problems as described by Howard-Clinton (1984), it is necessary to understand fully and appreciate the population structures and dynamics of the local populations, local people's values, customs, interests and knowledge and their interrelations with resource use and management. This paper has illustrated that ill-planned environmental protection programmes cause the same types of social and economic burdens that are commonly caused by environmental degradation.

Again, looking at the list of environmental problems in Southern Africa, they are issues of special concern for women; yet, women are not fully involved in decision-making and natural resource management at the grass-root and policy-making levels.

Recognizing these problems, the author believes that the following steps should be taken to improve environmental management in Southern Africa:

(a) The issue of poverty and basic needs in environmental programmes should be considered seriously by nature conservation planners and managers;

(b) To ensure the sustainability of environmental programmes, an effort should try to win the support of the rural communities through respect for their values, interests and customs. An acceptable balance between the quality of the human environment and the natural nvironment can only be achieved if the rural communities are participants and partners in environmental management;

(c) An analysis of the impacts of environmental programmes on rural populations and on gender roles should be commissioned in Southern Africa;

(d) Gender analysis should be incorporated in every environmental and development programme.

References

Bayliss-Smith, T. P. (1980). Population pressure, resources and welfare: towards a more realistic measure of carrying capacity. In *Population-Environment Relations in Tropical Islands: The Case of Eastern Fiji*, H. C. Brookfield, ed. Paris: United Nations Educational, Scientific and Cultural Organization.

Blaikie, Piers M. (1985). *Political Economy of Soil Erosion in Developing Countries*. London and New York: Longman.

Boserup, Ester (1981). *Population and Technology*. Oxford: Basil Blackwell.

Brookfield, Harold C. (1981). Man, environment and development in the outer islands of Fiji. *Ambio* (Stockholm), vol. 10, No. 2-3, special issue, pp. 59-67.

Hadley, Malcolm (1985). *Comparative Aspects of Land Use and Resource Management in Savannah Environments*, J. E. Tothil and J. J. Mott, eds. United Kingdom: Commonwealth Agricultural Bureau.

Howard-Clinton, E. G. (1984). The emerging concepts of environmental issues in Africa. *Environmental Management* (New York), vol. 8, No. 3.

International Union for the Conservation of Nature and Natural Resources (World Conservation Union and

United Nations Environment Programme (1987). *A Directory of Protected Areas*. Gland, Switzerland.

Matiza, Tabeth (1985). An analysis of some impacts of population pressure and land use practices on the physical environment of Seke communal land (Zimbabwe). Unpublished doctoral dissertation. Norwich, United Kingdom: University of East Anglia.

Petak, W. J. (1981). Environmental management: a system approach. *Environmental Management* (New York), vol. 5, No. 3.

Ress, P. (1992). Women's success in environmental management. *Our Planet* (Nairobi), vol. 4, No. 1.

XXXIV. ENVIRONMENTAL ISSUES OF SPECIAL CONCERN TO WOMEN AND CHILDREN

United Nations Environment Programme[*]

Women, as managers of much of the world's resources, have special grass-roots knowledge and skills, and it is essential that they be more involved in decision-making with regard to actions and policies concerning environment, development and the distribution of resources. In addition, because of the various roles women play, their understanding of environmental issues and the effects of the environment on people's lives is crucial to motivating protection of the environment.

Sustainable development can be defined as improving the quality of human life while living within the carrying capacity of supporting ecosystems. It is important that women are well informed on the costs and benefits of sustainable use of natural resources. Indeed, where women have been empowered with more decision-making authority and their viewpoints have been taken into consideration, resources have been better managed and environmental degradation reduced.

Women everywhere are influencing the environmental debate in many ways—as managers, consumers, campaigners, educators and communicators. For example, women have shown that uncontrolled dumping of toxic wastes can be stopped.

Environmental issues affect everyone; however, the effects are often first felt by women. Children are more vulnerable to environmental health problems.

Women are finding ways of coping with problems and are playing an increasing role in environmental management.

A. The environment and human well-being

Women

Many people are faced with the major concern of day-to-day survival. Women are primary users of the environment for providing most of the water, fuel, food and other basic needs of families. Environmental degradation resulting from deforestation, overgrazing, pollution etc. is borne first by these women (for example, increased workload and poor-quality water).

Major environmental problems also result from consumption of natural resources, such as, hydrocarbons, and the subsequent production of toxic emissions and solid wastes. High consumption and the irrational use of natural resources contributes to the destruction of ecosystems and environmental deterioration in the region.

Children

Environment and human health are inevitably linked, because people depend upon the environment for air, water and food. Infants and young children are very sensitive to environmental perturbations. Millions of child deaths and debilities throughout the world are caused by environmental degradation, for example, through diseases resulting from lack of safe drinking water, poor sanitation and environmental pollutants.

---

[*]Nairobi, Kenya.

B. Environmental issues of special concern

Serious environmental problems facing the world include: loss of forests and biodiversity; destruction of productive land; presence of dangerous wastes; pollution of air and water; global climate change; ozone depletion; and effects of wars. Central to the daily lives of many women is the provision of food, safe water and fuel for families. The environmental issues that make this task difficult are therefore those which affect the provision of these basic needs; the major issues are briefly outlined below:

Water and sanitation

Water is needed for drinking and for domestic and farm use. Collecting good-quality water can be an arduous task; and in urban shanty town areas, for example, the lack of sanitation and the overcrowded conditions are severe health hazards. Polluted and poisoned by sewage, agricultural run-off and industrial wastes, bad water kills many thousands of people each day.

Women constitute the majority of rural farmers; and because they need water for this activity, they are key players in watershed protection and water quality. When water resources are inadequate, women, as food producers and consumers, must manage this scarce and essential resource to meet community needs.

Environmental contaminants: hazardous wastes and rubbish

Waste is a lost resource, dangerous to ecosystems and to health. Women are increasingly exposed to hazardous wastes from urban and industrial areas and from pesticide residues in water and food.

In the home, people are exposed to different environmental contaminants, the nature of which depends upon the standard of housing and availability of essential services (water, sanitation, electricity etc.).

Some of the results for women of exposure to environmental contaminants differ from those experienced by men because of women's capacity to bear children. Possible effects on women choosing to have children include miscarriage, behavioural changes and cancer in the offspring. The effects produced will depend upon the time and severity of exposure and the type of chemical to which the mother is exposed. Nearly all chemical compounds ingested by a mother will be passed on to breast-fed children. In general, newborns are particularly sensitive to toxic chemicals.

Women that have children are often the first to observe symptoms affecting their families' health. Their awareness of the different hazards involved will undoubtedly reduce the risks involved on them and their children.

Energy and fuel

High energy-consuming industries and large populations in the world exert pressure on the environment and its natural resources and cause more pollution by the use of these resources.

Where the source of most domestic energy is the burning of biomass (derived from vegetable matter), finding and collecting sufficient fuelwood, traditionally the role of women and girls, can involve walking long distances and carrying heavy loads. Where population is dense, there is fuelwood scarcity and women are often forced through their own desperate circumstances to damage the environment, for example, causing deforestation. Deforestation further reduces the availability of fuelwood and contributes to the build-up of greenhouse gases. A shortage of fuelwood also means that more time must be spent searching for and gathering it, with less time for other activities, whether it be agricultural production, other employment, rest or leisure time.

A switch to less efficient fuels than wood, such as agricultural residues and dung, deprives the soil of an important fertilizer and contributes to soil degradation. It also exposes those in the home to more smoke, with its associated respiratory and other health problems.

Land degradation and food production

Land degradation and food production constitute a global problem, which is becoming acute in many areas where population pressures and inappropriate farming practices contribute to soil impoverishment and erosion, deforestation, overgrazing and misuse of agrochemicals. Degradation of the land limits food production, which can lead to undernourishment and malnourishment. Land can be contaminated by pollutants which can be passed on to people through the food supply.

Moreover, when the farmland is worn out for production, it is abandoned. Women as the main farmers and food providers are faced with difficulties growing enough food. In addition, land degradation deprives women of a traditional means of livelihood.

D. CONCLUSION

Consumption and population pressures are depleting natural resources, which undermines development and leads to degradation of the environment, affecting basic human needs, such as food and water.

The global natural resources need to be permanently sustained for current and future generations. Management of consumption and population are critical components of natural resources sustainability, worldwide survival, environmental protection and global well-being.

The awareness of women and the consideration of their views are both vital to environmental protection and sustainable development.

REFERENCES

International Union for the Conservation of Nature and Natural Resources (World Conservation Union) and United Nations Environment Programme and World Food Programme (1991). *Caring for the Earth: A Strategy for Sustainable Living*. Gland, Switzerland.

Rodda, Annabel (1991). *Women and the Environment*. London; and Atlantic Highlands, New Jersey: Zed Books.

United Nations (1985). *Report of the World Conference to Review and Appraise the Achievements of the United Nations Decade for Women: Equality, Development and Peace, Nairobi, 15-26 July 1985*. Sales No. E.85.IV.10.

________ (1991). Advancement of women: implementation of the Nairobi Forward-looking Strategies for the Advancement of Women to the Year 2000. Report of the Secretary-General. A/46/439.

United Nations Children's Fund (1992). *The State of the World's Children, 1992*. New York. Oxford.

United Nations Environment Programme (1988). *State of the World Environment, 1988: The Public and the Environment*. Nairobi.

________ (1990). *The State of the World Environment, 1990: Children and the Environment*. Nairobi.

________ (1991a). *Report of the Asia-Pacific Regional Assembly. Women and Environment: Partners in Life, Bangkok, Thailand, 11-15 March 1991*. Nairobi.

________ (1991b). *Report of the Global Assembly on Women and the Environment: Partners in Life, Miami, Florida, 4-8 November 1991*. Nairobi.

________ (1991c). *Report of the Latin America and the Caribbean Regional Assembly on Women and the Environment, Quito, Ecuador, 19-22 March 1991*. Nairobi.

United Nations Population Fund (1991). *Population and the Environment: The Challenges Ahead*. New York.

________ (1992). *The State of the World Population, 1992: A World in Balance*. New York.

XXXV. RURAL WOMEN AND POVERTY: THE STATUS AND THE IFAD EVOLVING STRATEGIES FOR INTERVENTION*

*Atiqur Rahman***

A. Poor rural women: number and trend

The number of poor rural women, who constitute the majority, the poorest and the most vulnerable of the world poor, was estimated at about 564 million in 1988 (Jazairy, Alamgir and Panuccio, 1992). This total represents an increase of 47 per cent over the number in 1970, as compared with the 30 per cent increase for men during the same period (calculated on the basis of data from 41 countries). Asia, with 374 million poor rural women (153 million, excluding China and India) heads the list of major areas. But sub-Saharan Africa, with a much lower total population than Asia, does not lag far behind, with about 129 million poor rural women. It is in this region that the poverty of rural women remains extremely acute and their disadvantages greatest.

A number of factors work together or in isolation to produce this trend of worsening poverty for rural women. Most important among them are population increase, worsening overall economic situation, weakening of family survival strategies, male migration, separation and desertion under duress, divorce, civil conflicts, natural calamities, degradation of environment, changes and breakdown of traditional values and persistence of overall sociocultural biases against women. Women are doubly disadvantaged compared with poor men: as poor people, they live in the same harsh economic conditions as their male counterparts; and as women, they suffer from social and political biases that undervalue their contribution to economic development and impose extra drudgery on them. They are trebly so because as heads of households they face the same problems while having to carry out the full burden of household management and production, for which they get little support. The last factor is an increasing phenomenon in rural areas of developing countries, due to male migration and the breakdown of traditional bonds and practices.[1]

B. The role of poor rural women

The critical role of women in development manifests itself at three levels:

(a) At the national and community levels, rural women are a source of labour power; they contribute to both market and non-market production and to household savings and accumulation;

(b) At the household level, rural women contribute to food, fuel and water security, off-farm income generation and domestic work; and

(c) At the intergenerational level, women contribute to old-age security, new labour power and the reproduction of households and community-based social and economic values through the care of children and their early education and socialization process.

The burden of this multiple role of women, which is inadequately recognized, reduces the marginal productivity of their income-generating work, the remuneration of which is biased against them. Their lack of access to adequate cash income and the inequality in the distribution of responsibilities are issues of extreme importance for the economic advancement of poor rural women. It needs to be recognized, first, that poor rural women play a critical role in growth and development, albeit almost without institutional support and despite distinct discrimination against them, in such diverse areas as access to nutrition, education, health services, productive resources,

---

*This paper draws heavily on a report published by the International Fund for Agricultural Development (Jazairy, Alamgir and Panuccio, 1992) and on other internal IFAD documents.

**Senior Economist, International Fund for Agricultural Development, Rome.

technology, training and participation in decision-making.

The evidence of women's significant role in developing countries is now overwhelming. Women are the major food producers in developing countries. In Africa today, for example, 85 per cent of rural women are involved in agriculture and produce up to 80 per cent of the food consumed by the family. They also generate a large part of cash income. In both Asia and Latin America and the Caribbean, rural poor women are significantly involved in off-farm household-based activities. It is estimated that 60 million Indian households below the poverty line are dependent upon women's economic contribution (Dhamija, 1991). Women in poorer households put in more work hours, fetch water over longer distances and add more value to other household activity. The African poor rural women, in their roles as mothers, food producers, main income-earners of families and heads of households, face a particularly difficult environment.

Although there is an increasing awareness of women's important role these days, appreciation of the economic and social value of women's roles still falls far short of what is due. The unpaid work of women is a vital contribution to the economy of poor rural households and also to the economy as a whole. The poorer the household and the country, the more hours women work and the greater is their contribution, but the less it is recognized. Women's unpaid work in effect compensates for the lack of adequate services to the community. However, it does not figure in national accounts, nor is it seen to add to the national product. In this light, it becomes apparent that perceiving rural women as primarily consumers of social welfare is a gross misconception. They are in fact unpaid producers of social welfare. Viewed in this way, it makes sense to direct larger shares of social services for women's benefit to lighten their social burden, while allowing their "visible" productive contribution to grow.

In short, the general perception of women's role in the rural economy of developing countries does not reflect the reality. The challenge is to bring about a global awareness of this reality: of the link between rural women's productive and reproductive roles with the growth of the national economy; and at the microlevel, of the link between their non-market domestic work and their income-generating work.

C. Focus on rural poor women: their disadvantages

The key question is how to provide support to women in fulfilling both their productive and reproductive roles. The elements of support are clear enough and have been the subject of numerous discussions, although not always with clarity and based on accurate information. These elements include enhancing women's access to education and literacy, providing access to health services, appreciating the value of women's traditional knowledge, access to resources and opportunities (such as land, credit, income) and most important of all, providing access to the participatory process of development and organizations.

What is less clear, however, is the strategic approach to combine these elements in the most effective way to address specific situations. The form of this approach, its priorities and instrumentalities, should be determined on the basis of a broad assessment of women's status and with specific focus on local conditions pertinent to it. It is in this connection that an accurate assessment of the roles and disadvantages of poor rural women assume critical importance. Such assessments are not readily available, given the apathy and years of neglect of the role of poor rural women in the process of development. Recently, various United Nations agencies, independent bodies and researchers have been trying to collect women-specific information to meet this need.

These attempts at quantitatively measuring the disadvantages have led to the development of a number of indicators, some combined into a composite index (Jazairy, Alamgir and Penuccio, 1992).[2] The indicators generally relate to health (maternal mortality rate etc.), family planning (contraceptive use), education (literacy and school enrolment), labour conditions (participation rate), wages (male-female disparities) etc. Many important dimensions are missing, for data of sufficient quality are not available to reflect women's participation in decision-making, ownership of assets including land, access to skill development and training; and access to financial services and markets.

Education and literacy

Education and literacy are the most easily quantifiable. Overall, there have been great achievements inboth, compared with the period 1965-1970 (table 59). The total percentage of literate women in the 114 countries rose from 33 to 51 per cent. In sub-Saharan Africa, it more than doubled, rising from 14 to 37 per cent. Female primary-school enrolment rates are quite encouraging, with an overall increase from 76 to 91 per cent; and secondary-school enrolment, although still relatively low, has also risen, from 11 to 32 per cent. Despite considerable improvement from the earlier period, enrolment in sub-Saharan Africa lags behind other regions. In the least developed countries, the situation is quite critical, with about 31 per cent literate women in 1988; and primary and secondary enrolment at 48 and 10 per cent, respectively, although substantial improvement is noted here as well.

TABLE 59. INDICATORS OF WOMEN'S EDUCATIONAL STATUS; 114 DEVELOPING COUNTRIES

Region or group	*Female adult literacy rate* (percentage) 1970	1985	*Annual reduction in female illiteracy 1970-1985* (percentage)	*Gross primary female enrolment* (percentage of age group) 1965	1988	*Gross secondary female enrolment* (percentage of age group) 1965	1988
Asia	29	48	1.2	82	95	12	32
Asia (excluding China and India	40	56	2.7	57	81	12	30
Sub-Saharan Africa	14	37	2.4	26	64	2	13
Northern Africa and Near East[a]	22	44	2.8	59	86	11	41
Latin America and the Caribbean	70	82	4.1	97	106	18	52
Least developed countries	16	32	2.0	28	49	3	10
TOTAL (114 countries)	33	51	1.7	76	91	12	33

Source: Idriss Jazairy, Mohiaddin Alamgir and Theresa Panuccio, *The State of World Rural Poverty: An Inquiry into Its Causes and Consequences* (Rome, International Fund for Agricultural Development; and New York, New York University Press, 1992).

[a]The countries included in the regional divisions in this table do not in all cases conform to those included in the geographical regions established by the Population Division of the Department of Economic and Social Development of the United Nations Secretariat.

Wage differentials

Reliable data on wages are difficult to obtain. It appears, however, that women's agricultural wages average 55 per cent of men's in 79 countries, and non-agricultural wages averages 58 per cent in 59 countries (table 60). There is not much variation in women's official labour force participation between the regions, nor between 1965 and 1988 values (table 61). Roughly, women represent 30 per cent of the formal labour force and 22 per cent of women participate in the formal labour force. As mentioned earlier, much of women's work is unpaid or informally contracted, owing to their limited access to formal employment. Therefore, these data should be interpreted rather as a measure of the underrecognition and undervaluation of women's work.

There is, however, considerable regional variation in the breakdown of female labour force between

TABLE 60. WOMEN'S RELATIVE WAGE-EARNING STATUS, 114 DEVELOPING COUNTRIES

Region or group	*Female/male wage ratio* *Agriculture*	*Non-agriculture*
Asia	0.70	0.46
Asia, including China and India	0.54	0.48
Sub-Saharan Africa	0.51	0.70
Northern Africa and Near East[a]	0.57	0.73
Latin America and the Caribbean	0.73	0.61
Least developed countries	0.68	0.53
TOTAL (114 countries)	0.54	0.61

Source: Idriss Jazairy, Mohiaddin Alamgir and Theresa Panuccio, *The State of World Rural Poverty: An Inquiry into Its Causes and Consequences* (Rome, International Fund for Agricultural Development; and New York, New York University Press, 1992).

[a]The countries included in the regional divisions in this table do not in all cases conform to those included in the geographical regions established by the Population Division of the Department of Economic and Social Development of the United Nations Secretariat.

agricultural and non-agricultural occupations. For the 114 countries, this ratio moved from 70:30 in 1970 to 55:45 in 1980. The trend is reflected in all regions, but the most recent ratios range from 81:19 in Northern Africa and the Near East[3] to 12:88 in Latin America and the Caribbean.

Domestic condition has been illustrated by three indicators: the percentage of women-headed households; the hours spent in household work; and the hours spent in collecting water. Although these are the types of data most needed to understand the conditions of rural women's life, unfortunately they are either unavailable or inconsistent in definition. This deficiency raises the important question of a framework for systematic data collection in the field. Data collected by IFAD show that these households average 12 per cent of total rural households and range from 9 per cent in Asia to 31 per cent in sub-Saharan Africa (Jazairy, Alamgir and Penuccio, 1992).

TABLE 61. INDICATORS OF WOMEN'S EMPLOYMENT STATUS, 114 DEVELOPING COUNTRIES

Region	*Women as percentage of total labour force*		*Female labour force participation rate (percentage of female population)*		*Female labour force* *Agricultural (percentage)*		*Non-agricultural (percentage)*	
	1985	*1988*	*1965*	*1988*	*1970*	*1980*	*1970*	*1980*
Asia	35	36	33	33	81	69	19	31
Asia, (excluding China and India)	29	30	22	22	71	51	29	49
Sub-Saharan Africa	41	38	37	29	88	81	12	19
Northern Africa and Near East[a]	21	22	14	13	78	61	22	39
Latin America and the Caribbean	20	27	13	18	21	12	79	88
Least developed countries	34	32	29	23	87	78	13	22
TOTAL (114 countries)	34	35	30	29	79	67	21	33

Source: Idriss Jazairy, Mohiaddin Alamgir and Theresa Panuccio, *The State of World Rural Poverty: An Inquiry into Its Causes and Consequences* (Rome, International Fund for Agricultural Development; and New York, New York University Press, 1992).

[a]The countries included in the regional divisions in this table do not in all cases conform to those included in the geographical regions established by the Population Division of the Department of Economic and Social Development of the United Nations Secretariat.

Access to health services

Rural women's access to health is often seriously compromised by overwork, undernutrition and continuous child-bearing. Perhaps the most common indicator of women's health status is the rate of maternal mortality, which, in the 114 developing countries studied, is more than four maternal deaths per 1,000 live births, 16 times the average in the industrialized countries. However, country averages reach as high as 20 per 1,000 births in Ethiopia (where data are only available for hospital births).

As fiscal constraints have limited Governments' willingness to subsidize health services, rural communities have been forced to pay higher prices for medication and treatment. There is a great need to increase the number of health-care workers, but also important are training and dissemination of information on family planning, birth-spacing, breast-feeding, nutrition, sanitation and hygiene. A general sensitization to issues of women's well-being and their role in society will help to eliminate some harmful cultural practices, such as female circumcision, low age at marriage, frequent pregnancies, unequal intra-family food distribution and taboos against the intake of certain high-protein foods during pregnancy.

Reductions in government spending have also limited the outlay on health-related infrastructure, such as village water-supplies. This is an area where donors have been active, but it is also important that women should be involved in the planning and maintenance of such systems which, although of general benefit, are particularly so for women's workload and well-being.

Formal education and traditional knowledge

During the early 1980s, on average, more than half the men in developing countries were literate, while more than two thirds of women were still illiterate (Seager and Olson, 1986). Rural women's access to formal education is slowly growing but, here again, it is threatened by reductions in fiscal expenditure related to structural adjustment. Lower literacy and education limits women's access to more remunerative types of employment, to decision-making positions in rural organizations and projects, to certain types of modern technology and to institutional resources that require formal procedures. Where these constraints become rigid obstacles to economic opportunities, attempts should be made to provide literacy and relevant educational training to the women that expressly request it.

It should also be recognized, however, that although the lack of formal education has many negative implications, it does not compromise intelligence, enterprise or the ability to innovate. Furthermore, designers of projects for women's education should become aware of the wealth of traditional knowledge rural women have on all aspects of local livestock, crops and wild plants, as well as on methods of soil conservation and enrichment. Participatory methods should be devised to build upon such knowledge through an effective communication between rural women producers and extension/research staff, so that improved technologies can be developed and popularized.

Access to resources and opportunities

Although a majority of developing countries have signed the United Nations Convention for the Elimination of Discrimination against Women (1979), and many have guaranteed a reflection of those principles in their national constitutions, progress in this direction has been slow and uneven. Women's explicit legal rights have improved substantially in Latin America and the Caribbean over the past decade. In Asia and in Northern Africa and the Near East, some progress has been made in legislation but it still fails to be reflected in actual practice. In sub-Saharan Africa, due to the formal recognition of customary law, rural women's marital and land rights remain limited.

Even when women manage important household resources and enterprises, men remain nominally household heads and as such have ultimate control of resources and income in most societies. This situation reflects a long-standing tradition of male dominance and female subordination, which explains women's increased vulnerability, as they have to depend upon men for final decisions in virtually every aspect of their lives.

Land

Women's legal right to own land has been affirmed by many developing countries, but in practice female control of land is virtually nil, due to administrative, economic, religious and cultural constraints. Even in countries where women effectively have rights to landownership and/or control, they may not have control of the income derived thereof. In any case, it is probable that an increased allocation of land to women would result in increased food production for household consumption, as compared with cash-crop production, which is predominantly a male occupation and concern.

Land reforms or resettlement schemes have actually worsened the situation, as land has generally been reallocated to men as heads of households, either explicitly or implicitly, by allocation to the family unit. Thus, although the agrarian reform legislation of the period 1945-1985 did not specifically discriminate against women, its application in the context of existing customs and inheritance laws resulted in the actual loss of women's rights to land. Exceptions are Cuba, where women represented 25 per cent of beneficiaries of the 1985 agrarian reform; and Mexico, where they represented 15 per cent of parcel holders in the *ejido*, or communal-based land system.

Likewise, under customary tenure systems, ultimate male control over land results. However, these systems tend to reaffirm the principle of women's access to such land. In African customary land systems, married women have the right to cultivate certain lots, enabling them to sustain their family's food needs and to earn their own income. This right, however, is contingent on the understanding that they will contribute labour to male-controlled agriculture and will process and prepare food for male kin. Their rights to land use remain insecure, for they can be lost through divorce or widowhood.

Development efforts to increase women's access to land and to enhance their land's productivity must proceed with caution. Male resistance to changing traditional terms and the structure of land allocation will be significant. On the other hand, if land rights are reallocated to family or household units, even women's limited traditional land rights may be lost. Secondly, development may aim at significant improvement in land productivity through technological innovations. If they affect land under the care of women farmers, it should be ensured that they shall be in a position to accommodate possible increases in labour or input requirements. Women's domestic responsibilities and physical limitations in labour-intensive tasks can often represent a major constraint in this sense. Furthermore, the ensuing rise in land values might induce their take-over by men. It is more likely that men's constructive cooperation can be fostered if ways can be found to share development benefits between men and women.

Other resources

Throughout the developing world, women are involved in the care of livestock and generally have their own stock of small ruminants and poultry for household consumption and personal income-earning. However, most livestock-oriented projects are directed to male beneficiaries. Women must be accorded access to improved resources and training in new production methods if they are to gain, rather than lose, from project interventions. Female village vaccinators and paravets should be trained, especially for the type of livestock women traditionally own.

The provision of draught power for women farmers needs to be improved through a more equitable sharing of household-owned draught animals. In addition, ownership of cattle and oxen by small groups of women, for their own use and for renting out to others, should be facilitated. Women's collective ownership of oxen, donkeys or camels can meet transport needs for input delivery or for marketing produce.

Women farmers are constrained by the lack of appropriate modern tools and technologies, partially due to their unavailability in some rural areas and partially because women's incomes are primarily allocated to meeting the household's pressing consumption needs. This overriding priority in turn restricts their income-earning capacity. Access to productivity-enhancing input, in both productive and domestic spheres, could help them break out of this vicious circle.

Due to the general perception that women have a limited production capacity, agricultural research and technology development have paid little attention to women's specific requirements. Development projects have been directed to men implicitly or even explicitly, although many studies have shown that when men receive resources and technological training, these benefits are rarely shared with the female members of the household. Furthermore, high-yielding technology diffused to male farmers can actually result in an increased workload for women, who contribute labour to the same production lots. The development and diffusion of technology appropriate to women's tasks is essential. It is also important to recognize that the best assessment of women's productive requirements and capacity must come from them, whether for agricultural or off-farm income-generating occupations.

Equally important, and equally deficient, are training and extension services to women. Training offered to them is mainly on food and nutrition, health, child care and home management, ignoring their roles as decision-making farmers. Agricultural extension services in nearly all developing countries are overwhelmingly male-dominated, although women farmers often prefer working with female extensionists. There is a need to promote women's entry into the extensionist field and to reorient existing female and male extensionists' skills towards the needs of women farmers.

Credit

Women's access to formal credit is very limited. A worldwide review of credit programmes found that women constituted only 7-11 per cent of beneficiaries in both rural and urban areas (Berger, 1991). This situation is due to numerous constraints basically arising from the belief that their productive capacity is too low to permit loan recovery. Alhough formal collateral requirements can be relaxed or substituted by other forms of guarantee, the fundamental problem remains. It has prevented financial intermediaries from tailoring their services to meet women's requirements in loan size, purpose and terms, and providing information and assistance to them in obtaining loans. Consequently, rural women have become reluctant to seek credit.

Over the past decade, non-governmental organizations and international financial institutions, including IFAD, have demonstrated that such constraints can be eliminated and that women are in fact creditworthy, with repayment and saving records often superior to those of their male counterparts. The key to breaking through the credit barrier for rural women is a better understanding of their dual participation in both subsistence and market-oriented activities. Enhancing the productivity of subsistence activities—through credit provision among other services—means a surplus can be generated for sale. In addition, it would allow women more time for income-generating activities, whether in agriculture or in micro-enterprises.

Income

For women to be viable credit recipients, they must be given assistance to enter the market. This is a major obstacle to increasing their production over the subsistence level. Men are generally facilitated by their orientation towards export crops, whose marketing systems are better developed. Women producers, however, have to make their own marketing arrangements with the limited facilities at their disposal. Their problems are insufficient working capital, lack of storage and transport. Costs are raised and profits limited because of the very small quantities they can offer for sale. Traditions of women's seclusion can make them dependent upon men or children to market their output, resulting in restrictions on their market outreach and on their control of the income derived.

In many poor rural households that depend up wage income, women's wages are essential for survival. Agriculture-based employment offers only limited opportunities for women, while food processing and other agro-industrial enterprises are increasingly introducing capital-intensive labour-reducing technologies. However, rural women engage in a variety of other income-earning activities, including food and beverage processing and catering, producing and selling handicrafts and petty trading. Female rural entrepreneurs are concentrated in those areas which are seldom recorded by surveys and census data.

Past initiatives at developing micro-enterprises have not always been successful, largely due to the weakness of existing infrastructure and services and to the incapacity of the entrepreneurs themselves in the face of the complexities involved. None the less, considerable scope exists for expanding micro-enterprises and this area should be exploited, for they are one of the important linkages between agricultural and non-agricultural spheres and between rural and urban economies, upon which economic growth will depend.

Access to participatory organizations

Participation in rural organizations, such as farmers' associations, labour unions, cooperatives and committees, allows rural men and women increased access to productive resources, training, markets, technology and information. It is also a means for them to articulate and present their requirements to authorities, project managers and employers. Altogether, this can be a powerful instrument for diffusing practical knowledge, promoting changes in attitudes and stimulating motivation.

Rural women have much need of such support but their access to these organizations is severely limited. They are openly excluded if membership is based on landholding or head-of-household status or effectively excluded because membership fees can be quite high. When women do participate, it is often as a minority, who are expected to defer to male leadership.

Development projects need to address seriously the issue of actively involving women in a proportion that reflects their importance in beneficiary populations. Women should be adequately represented throughout planning, management and evaluation functions. As an alternative or a complement to participation in integrated male and female groups, especially where customs of male/female segregation predominate, separate women's groups may be formed. These groups should, however, be given equal authority in decision-making processes.

The participatory approach in development has yet another dimension. It is a forum of interaction with development staff, through which to work together. This is the best means by which development agencies can obtain information and feedback on the conditions operative in the field, the community and the household. A practical way of determining the terms and women's access to resources is to conduct time studies to determine the nature of men's and women's daily tasks and the length and arduousness of their respective labour days. Information required for monitoring and evaluating the impact that projects have had on women can also be collected through this channel.

D. The IFAD approach for economically advancing poor rural women

In pursuit of its mandate of ensuring food security, reducing undernutrition and alleviating rural poverty in developing countries, IFAD has stressed, in particular, the critical role played by rural women in the process of economic development. Over the years, specific women-related components have been made an integral part of IFAD-financed projects, with focus on delivering economic benefits to women. As IFAD learned from field experience, its approach to rural women underwent significant changes. Beginning from an approach in which women were considered to be a part of the rural community and which therefore did not recognize any specific intervention for women, the approach evolved to recognize the need for special efforts for strengthening the position of women. Examples of such processes are ensuring women's part in the land-allocation committees to protect their land rights in the Gambia, women's groups to receive credit in Bangladesh and in Honduras, and specific extension services for women in Kenya.

This approach later evolved to a new approach of targeting specific components and activities for women in home economics, health, nutrition and food processing. The focus of this approach gradually shifted to "women's crops, animals and productive responsibilities". Today, the IFAD approach has gone one step further with the recognition that while specific components and projects are still useful in reaching a great number of disadvantaged women, women should not be looked at as a separate entity. Women should be looked at from the perspective of an overall social and economic framework within which they live and work.

The four Regional Consultations on the Economic Advancement of Rural Women, held in Cyprus, Costa Rica, Senegal and Malaysia during 1991-1992, were attempts by IFAD to strengthen its focus on poor rural women, to begin an international consultative process and to gain from conceptual understanding of the difficult economic and social environment facing women in different parts of the world. The Consultation in Latin America and the Caribbean highlighted the unequal access of women to economic and social power, the inflexible social structure and the non-market contribution of women, which is not economically valued. Access of women to credit, rural financial organizations and production systems was considered essential for economically advancing rural women. The Dakar (Senegal) Consultation highlighted women's role in food production, ownership of land in the context of the communal pattern of land-ownership and the production system that has failed to cater for the particular needs of women producers. The focus on women's economic advancement in this region cannot and should not neglect the question of awareness, participation and empowerment, along with concrete projects for supporting the productive activities of women in their locational specificities. The nexus between women and the environment was highlighted in the context of sub-Saharan Africa in more vivid detail than in any other region. The Asia and the Pacific Consultation highlighted the role of women in various agricultural and non-agricultural activities and the economic and social biases against properly valuing women's work. Women were found to be engaged in family farm and non-farm enterprises to a far larger extent than elsewhere. Given the deep-rooted social biases, women's issues need to be addressed through a comprehensive package of policies and programmes based on both equity and efficiency. The latter basis implies that support for women leads to increases in productivity and growth of the economy. All the consultations highlighted the need for testing and spreading appropriate technologies for rural women and for creating a global awareness about the need to advance rural women economically through concerted actions in the economic, social, political and, above all, legal spheres. The Summit on the Economic Advancement of Poor Rural Women, held in Geneva, 25-26 February 1992, and the Geneva Declaration adopted at the Summit, was a step in that direction.

Some examples highlight the evolving role of IFAD in promoting poor rural women. In protecting and improving women's access to land, the Jahaly and Pacharr Project in the Gambia is a prime example of the special attention and continuous surveillance needed. The settlement scheme of the Integrated Rural Development Project of Dominica achieved the allocation of 20 per cent of land titles to women. However, an IFAD case-study of the project concluded that women may have been allocated poorer quality land. Thus, irrigation and settlement projects need to pay careful attention to women's land rights. In the Development Project in the Zone Lacustre in Mali, the Fund has included in the loan agreement a policy assurance that women farmers will partake in the land distribution of irrigation schemes.

The IFAD experience in providing credit for rural women has underlined two important issues for future activities: the financial viability or profitability of the enterprise financed; and the sustainability of financial services as they relate to costs and institutional arrangements. The Fund has provided loans to women for livestock and crop production, processing and marketing; and for off-farm income-generating activities. Usually, loans for women have been shorter term and smaller than those for men but repayment rates have been better, often close to 100 per cent. The Grameen Bank in Bangladesh remains the most successful IFAD example in providing poor rural women with access to credit, overcoming formidable social constraints in order to focus on poor landless women. Among the borrowers of the Grameen Bank, 75 per cent are women, and loans of as little as $15-20 have transformed their lives from penury to self-reliance. With these loans, women have started their own businesses. In other countries as well, IFAD is helping to ensure that rural women shall have access to financial services, sometimes for the first time. IFAD projects in Burkina Faso, Cameroon, Ghana, Senegal, Seychelles, Somalia and Togo have a special credit window for women, some of them setting a minimum quota (25-40 per cent) for loans under the project to be granted to women. In Honduras, women have been formed into groups and provided with credit for agricultural production. The group approach has also proved successful in Nepal in the Production Credit for Rural Women Project, where disadvantaged rural women have received credit for both individual and group activities. This project is directed exclusively to improving the economic conditions and social status of 16,000 poor rural women by providing credit for income-generating activities, training and community development work.

But access to financial services alone is not enough. Women also need appropriate technology, extension, input and infrastructure to improve the quality of their lives.

The role of women in farming systems is being studied in the development of agricultural technology. About 55 per cent of the IFAD grants awarded to research centres have included at least one parameter that focuses on the role of women in farming systems, and many of these programmes actively involve women in identifying and testing research themes.

The specific gender issues or questions addressed by IFAD technical assistance grants include women's workload or labour availability as a constraint in the selection of technology, women's taste and preferences in food processing or preparation as determinants to whether new varieties of crops are likely to be adopted, women's subsistence food crops and development of new technologies for reducing their workload. More recently, a recognition of the varied input of men and women at all stages of crop or livestock production, processing and marketing has led to an examination of the importance of gender issues for all proposed research programmes.

The on-farm research programme on groundnuts, pigeon-peas and chick-peas, and the transfer of technology to farmers in the semi-arid tropics of India, addressed women farmers as a primary target group and recognized their preferences and constraints during the development of complete packages of production technology for these crops. The research programme on field beans, using participant observation in the villages, found that it was primarily women that decided which bean varieties to grow, based on such factors as seed colour and grain size (which influence cooking time and therefore fuel requirements). This finding led the programme to introduce these characteristics into selection criteria for bean breeding research. The Agro-forestry Development Project in Senegal and the Small Ruminants Project in Togo have also benefited women through the wide spread application of technology developed under research grants financed by IFAD, which reduced the number of hours women previously had to spend in fuelwood and fodder collection.

In China, under the Sichuan Livestock Development Project, experience has shown that women can be reached by support services in numbers proportional to their involvement in livestock production if proper attention is given to gender issues at the design stage. Of trainees in livestock production, 80 per cent are women. In the planning and design stages of this project, surveys were conducted on women's involvement in livestock production. Their interest in the project, possible increases in labour demand, interest in receiving training etc., were all mapped.

IFAD has also integrated women agents into extension services in societies where male-female contact is difficult. The Smallholder Services Rehabilitation Project in Zambia is an example of a project in which more female contact farmers have also been encouraged to target extension messages to women where their crops are concerned. The Southern Regional Agricultural Development Project in Yemen was the first concentrated effort to introduce new technologies to rural women through extension services in which women are hired in larger numbers than before. These will increase their agricultural productivity and income, reduce their workload, improve family health and nutrition and reduce infant and child mortality. The programme is designed to overcome cultural constraints on rural women farmers and to enhance the productivity and profitability of livestock activities that are traditionally their responsibility.

The Fund has recently placed increasing emphasis on mobilizing village women as technical auxiliaries, to be thoroughly trained in technical procedures, such as fertilizer application and row planting. The IFAD Smallholder Support Project in Zanzibar will support an existing two-year training programme for village girls, who will then provide extension to other village women. In addition to home economics, health and nutrition, the curriculum includes farming and livestock tending. Village governments recruit girls that they know will remain in the village, thereby ensuring a sustainable effort.

IFAD remains committed to ensuring the full integration of women in its project and development efforts. This emphasis has grown over the past five years as the IFAD approach to women in development has evolved and innovative strategies have been accordingly developed, but continuous monitoring and surveillance are needed to ensure that gender issues shall not be lost in the design of projects but shall be successfully implemented in the field.

E. POLICY DIRECTIONS FOR ECONOMIC ADVANCEMENT OF POOR RURAL WOMEN IN THE 1990S

IFAD has developed a set of Guidelines for Action on poor rural women, recognizing the vital role the poor rural women play in economic development and taking account of the Nairobi Forward-looking Strategies adopted by consensus in 1985, urging specifically the outlining of strategies for the advancement of poor rural women. The Guidelines for Action, while primarily developed for IFAD, will contribute to complementarity of action between Governments, donor agencies, the United Nations system, regional organizations and non-governmental organizations that believe in and are committed to assisting poor rural women. The main elements of the guidelines are:

(a) Creation of conditions for economic empowerment of rural women through documentation, recognition and valuation of their productive and domestic roles and their contribution to the national product; establishment of a new dialogue with rural women that leads to their freedom from subordination, technology that eases their productive and domestic tasks, representation in decision-making, participation in planning and programmes and access to financial and marketing services;

(b) Elimination of marginalization of women from the development process through strategic action to create conditions for fundamental social and economic transformation by addressing the needs of rural women and ensuring their access and control over resources;

(c) Recognition of the need for broad-based societal support, through sensitization of policy makers;

(d) Assessment of problems, challenges and opportunities in the feminization of smallholder agriculture. Substantive physical, technical and financial support to women involved in smallholder agriculture so that they can face this challenge with ready access to resources;

(e) Addressing of the special needs of female-headed households, rather than viewing them as isolated, deviant and negligible minorities, with special focus on refugee and displaced women and rural women migrating to peri-urban areas;

(f) Recognition of the complexity and multiplicity of the role of poor rural women and alleviating their workload;

(g) Elimination of the financial impediment to the empowerment of poor rural women, by extending financial services to them and helping them to organize self-help financial service groups;

(h) Promotion of private sector initiatives to enhance rural women's employment and entrepreneurial capacity;

(i) Collection and utilization of gender-disaggregated income and agricultural data for formulation of policies and for the implementation of programmes and projects;

(j) Use of an intra-household analysis model and gender-desegregated production subsystems for analysing rural economies;

(k) Support of women's central role in environmentally sustainable development, among others; and

(l) Strengthening of cooperation within the United Nations system.

The Women Summit held in Geneva in February 1992, sponsored by IFAD at the request of a core group of First Ladies, also adopted an action plan based on the foregoing Guidelines for Action in their Declaration for Economic Advancement of Poor Rural Women.

NOTES

[1]This phenomenon also emerges from prolonged war and consequent death of male members and dislocation of families. This is true for many African countries suffering from civil conflict or war, as well as for some Asian countries, such as Cambodia. In some areas of Rwanda, as many as 22 per cent of households are headed by women. War-stricken Cambodia now probably has one of the highest female-headed household ratios (to total rural households) in the world, estimated at about 35 per cent of all households.

[2]The IFAD study on the state of world rural poverty seeks to develop a number of indicators of the status of women in the developing world (see Jazairy, Alamgir and Panuccio, 1992).

[3]The countries included in the regional divisions in this chapter do not in all cases conform to those included in the geographical regions established by the Population Division of the Department of Economic and Social Development of the United Nations Secretariat.

REFERENCES

Berger, Marguerite (1991). *Rural Women and Credit: the Experience of Latin America and the Caribbean.* Rome: International Fund for Agricultural Development.

Davidson, Jean, ed. (1988). *Agriculture, Women and Land: The African Experience.* Boulder, Colorado: Westview Press.

Deere, Carmen Diana, and Magdalena Léon, eds. (1987). *Rural Women and State Policy: Feminist Perspectives on Latin American Agricultural Development.* Boulder, Colorado: Westview Press.

Dhamija, Jasleen (1991). Developing appropriate support systems for women's off-farm income-generating activities. Paper presented at the Regional Consultation on the Economic Advancement of Rural Women in Asia and the Pacific, Kuala Lumpur, Malaysia, 15-21 September 1991. Rome: International Fund for Agricultural Development.

Jazairy, Idriss, Mohiaddin Alamgir and Theresa Panuccio. *The State of World Rural Poverty: An Inquiry into its Causes and Consequences.* Rome: International Fund for Agricultural Development; and New York: New York University Press.

Seager, Joni, and Ann Olson (1986). *Women in the World: An International Atlas,* Michael Kidron, ed. New York: Simon and Schuster.

كيفية الحصول على منشورات الأمم المتحدة

يمكن الحصول على منشورات الأمم المتحدة من المكتبات ودور التوزيع في جميع أنحاء العالم . استعلم عنها من المكتبة التي تتعامل معها أو اكتب إلى : الأمم المتحدة ، قسم البيع في نيويورك أو في جنيف .

如何购取联合国出版物

联合国出版物在全世界各地的书店和经售处均有发售。请向书店询问或写信到纽约或日内瓦的联合国销售组。

HOW TO OBTAIN UNITED NATIONS PUBLICATIONS

United Nations publications may be obtained from bookstores and distributors throughout the world. Consult your bookstore or write to: United Nations, Sales Section, New York or Geneva.

COMMENT SE PROCURER LES PUBLICATIONS DES NATIONS UNIES

Les publications des Nations Unies sont en vente dans les librairies et les agences dépositaires du monde entier. Informez-vous auprès de votre libraire ou adressez-vous à : Nations Unies, Section des ventes, New York ou Genève.

КАК ПОЛУЧИТЬ ИЗДАНИЯ ОРГАНИЗАЦИИ ОБЪЕДИНЕННЫХ НАЦИЙ

Издания Организации Объединенных Наций можно купить в книжных магазинах и агентствах во всех районах мира. Наводите справки об изданиях в вашем книжном магазине или пишите по адресу: Организация Объединенных Наций, Секция по продаже изданий, Нью-Йорк или Женева.

COMO CONSEGUIR PUBLICACIONES DE LAS NACIONES UNIDAS

Las publicaciones de las Naciones Unidas están en venta en librerías y casas distribuidoras en todas partes del mundo. Consulte a su librero o diríjase a: Naciones Unidas, Sección de Ventas, Nueva York o Ginebra.

Litho in United Nations, New York
13423—July 1996—4,840
ISBN 92-1-151306-5

United Nations publication
Sales No. E.96.XIII.10
ST/ESA/SER.R/130